Lecture Notes in Computer Science 8258

Commenced Publication in 1973
Founding and Former Series Editors:
Gerhard Goos, Juris Hartmanis, and Jan van Lee

José Ruiz-Shulcloper
Gabriella Sanniti di Baja (Eds.)

Progress in Pattern Recognition, Image Analysis, Computer Vision, and Applications

18th Iberoamerican Congress, CIARP 2013
Havana, Cuba, November 20-23, 2013
Proceedings, Part I

 Springer

Volume Editors

José Ruiz-Shulcloper
Advanced Technologies Application Center (CENATAV)
7ª A#21406 esq. 214 y 216, Rpto. Siboney, Playa. C.P. 12200 La Habana, Cuba
E-mail: jshulcloper@cenatav.co.cu

Gabriella Sanniti di Baja
Institute of Cybernetics "E. Caianiello", National Research Council (CNR)
Via Campi Flegrei 34, 80078 Pozzuoli (Naples), Italy
E-mail: g.sannitidibaja@cib.na.cnr.it

ISSN 0302-9743   e-ISSN 1611-3349
ISBN 978-3-642-41821-1   e-ISBN 978-3-642-41822-8
DOI 10.1007/978-3-642-41822-8
Springer Heidelberg New York Dordrecht London

Library of Congress Control Number: 2013951329

CR Subject Classification (1998): I.5, I.4, I.2.10, I.2.7, F.2.2, J.3

LNCS Sublibrary: SL 6 – Image Processing, Computer Vision, Pattern Recognition, and Graphics

Typesetting: Camera-ready by author, data conversion by Scientific Publishing Services, Chennai, India

Printed on acid-free paper

Springer is part of Springer Science+Business Media (www.springer.com)

Preface

The 18th Iberoamerican Congress on Pattern Recognition CIARP 2013 (Congreso IberoAmericano de Reconocimiento de Patrones) is the yearly event of a series of pioneer conferences on pattern recognition in the scientific community active in this field in Iberoamerican countries.

As has been the case for previous editions of the conference, CIARP 2013 hosted worldwide participants with the aim to promote and disseminate ongoing research on mathematical methods and computing techniques for pattern recognition, in particular in biometrics, computer vision, image analysis, and speech recognition, as well as their application in a number of diverse areas such as industry, health, robotics, data mining, entertainment, space exploration, telecommunications, document analysis, and natural language processing and recognition. Moreover, CIARP 2013 was a useful forum in which the scientific community could exchange research experience, share new knowledge and increase cooperation among research groups in pattern recognition and related areas.

We like to underline that CIARP conferences have significantly contributed to the birth and growth of national associations for pattern recognition in Iberoamerican countries that are already members of the International Association for Pattern Recognition, IAPR, (Argentina, Brazil, Chile, Cuba, Mexico), or will soon be applying to become IAPR members (Colombia, Peru, Uruguay).

CIARP 2013 received 262 contributions from 37 countries (12 of which are Iberoamerican countries). After a rigorous blind reviewing process, where each submission was reviewed by three highly qualified reviewers, 137 papers by 355 authors from 31 countries were accepted. All the accepted papers have scientific quality above the overall mean rating.

As has been the case for the most recent editions of the conference, CIARP 2013 was a single-track conference in which 22 papers where selected for presentation in oral sessions, while the remaining 115 papers were selected for poster presentation with short poster teasers. Following the tradition of CIARP conferences, the selection of the presentation type does not signify at all a quality grading. CIARP 2013 presentations were grouped into nine sessions: Supervised and Unsupervised Classification; Feature or Instance Selection for Classification; Image Analysis and Retrieval; Signals Analysis and Processing; Biometrics; Applications of Pattern Recognition; Mathematical Theory of Pattern Recognition; Video Analysis; and Data Mining.

We would like to point out that the reputation of CIARP conferences is increasing, especially since the last 11 editions for which the proceedings have been published in the *Lecture Notes in Computer Science* series. Moreover, starting from CIARP 2008, authors of the best papers presented at the conference (orally or as posters) have been invited to submit extended versions of their papers to well-known journals so as to enhance the visibility of their conference submissions and to stimulate deeper insight into the treated topics. For CIARP 2013 two special issues of the *International Journal of Pattern Recognition and Artificial Intelligence IJPRAI* and in *Intelligent Data Analysis IDA* will be published. Moreover, a Special Section of Pattern Recognition Letters has been added to include the two papers of the researchers selected as the winners of the two prizes given at CIARP 2013, namely the IAPR-CIARP Best Paper Prize and the Aurora Pons-Porrata Medal, which is a new CIARP-Award.

The IAPR-CIARP Best Paper Prize has the aim of acknowledging and encouraging excellence, originality and innovativeness of new models, methods and techniques with an outstanding theoretical contribution and practical application to the field of pattern recognition and/or data mining. The Iberoamerican CIARP-Award Aurora Pons-Porrata Medal is given to a living woman in recognition of her outstanding technical contribution to the field of pattern recognition or data mining.

The selection of the winners is based on the wish of the authors to be considered as possible candidates for the prizes, the evaluation and recommendations of members of the Program Committee, for the IAPR-CIARP Best Paper Prize, and the proposal of the national associations on Pattern Recognition, for the Aurora Pons-Porrata Medal, and the evaluation of the respective Award Committees. The task of these committees, whose members are carefully chosen to avoid conflicts of interest, is to evaluate each paper nominated for the IAPR-CIARP Best Paper Prize by performing a second review process including the quality of the (poster or oral) presentation, and the recommendations for the Aurora Pons-Porrata Medal. We express our gratitude to the members of the two Award Committees: Josef Kittler (Surrey University, UK), Jian Pei (Simon Fraser University, Canada), Fabio Roli (University of Cagliari, Italy), Tieniu Tan (National Laboratory on Pattern Recognition of China), Isneri Talavera-Bustamante (Advanced Technologies Applications Center, CENATAV, Cuba), Rita Cucchiara (University of Modena-Reggio, Italy), and Rocio González-Díaz, (University of Seville, Spain).

Besides the 137 accepted submissions, the scientific program of CIARP 2013 also included the contributions of three outstanding invited speakers, namely, Jian Pei (Simon Fraser University of Canada), Fabio Roli (University of Cagliari, Italy) and Tieniu Tan (National Laboratory on Pattern Recognition of China). The papers of these two last keynotes appear in these proceedings. Furthermore, the three invited speakers and Gabriella Sanniti di Baja gave four tutorials on "Mining Uncertain and Probabilistic Data for Big Data Analytics", "Multiple Classifier Systems", "Fundamentals of Iris Recognition", and "Discrete Methods to Analyse and Represent 3D Digital Objects," respectively.

During the conference, the Annual CIARP Steering Committee Meeting was also held.

CIARP 2013 was organized by the Advanced Technologies Applications Center (CENATAV) and the Cuban Association for Pattern Recognition (ACRP) with the endorsement of the International Association for Pattern Recognition (IAPR), and the sponsorship of the Cuban Society for Mathematics and Computer Sciences (SCMC), the Argentine Society for Pattern Recognition (SARP-SADIO), the Special Interest Group of the Brazilian Computer Society (SIGPR-SBC), the Chilean Association for Pattern Recognition (AChiRP), the Mexican Association for Computer Vision, Neural Computing and Robotics (MACVNR), the Spanish Association for Pattern Recognition and Image Analysis (AERFAI), and the Portuguese Association for Pattern Recognition (APRP). We recognize and appreciate their valuable contributions to the success of CIARP 2013.

We gratefully acknowledge the help of all members of the Organizing Committee and of the Program Committee for their support and for the rigorous work in the reviewing process.

We also wish to thank the members of the Local Committee for their unflagging work in the organization of CIARP 2013 that led to an excellent conference and proceedings.

Special thanks are due to all authors who submitted to CIARP 2013, including those of papers that could not be accepted.

Finally, we invite the pattern recognition community to attend CIARP 2014 in Puerto Vallarta, Mexico.

November 2013   José Ruiz-Shulcloper
                                                    Gabriella Sanniti di Baja

Organization

CIARP 2013 was organized by the Cuban Association for Pattern Recognition, endorsed by the International Association for Pattern Recognition (IAPR) and sponsored by the Advanced Technologies Applications Center (CENATAV), DATYS Technologies & Systems, Cuba.

Co-chairs

José Ruiz-Shulcloper   Advanced Technologies Applications Center, (CENATAV), Cuba

Gabriella Sanniti di Baja   National Research Council (CNR) of Italy, Naples, Italy

IAPR-CIARP 2013 Best Paper Prize Committee

Josef Kittler   Surrey University, UK
Jian Pei   Simon Fraser University, Canada
Fabio Roli   University of Cagliari, Italy
Gabriella Sanniti di Baja   CNR, Napoli, Italy
Tieniu Tan   National Laboratory on Pattern Recognition, China

CIARP 2013 Aurora Pons-Porrata Award Committee

Rita Cucchiara   University of Modena-Reggio, Italy
Rocío González-Díaz   University of Seville, Spain
Isneri Talavera-Bustamante   CENATAV, Cuba

Local Committee

Niusvel Acosta-Mendoza   Rainer Larín-Fonseca
José R. Calvo-De Lara   Danis López-Naranjo
Marieli Capote-Rodríguez (DATYS)   José Medina-Pagola
Andrés Gago-Alonso   Heydi Méndez-Vázquez
Edel García-Reyes   Diana Porro-Muñoz
Eduardo Garea-Llano   Maité Romero-Durán
Ricardo González-Gazapo   Isneri Talavera-Bustamante
José Hernández-Palancar

CIARP Steering Committee

Eduardo Bayro-Corrochano, Mexico
Cesar Beltrán Castañón, Perú
Edel García-Reyes, Cuba
Marta Mejail, Argentina
Alvaro Pardo, Uruguay

Roberto Paredes Palacios, Spain
Olga Regina Pereira Bellon, Brazil
João Miguel Sanches, Portugal
Cesar San Martín, Chile

Program Committee

Sergey Ablameyko	Belarusian State University
José Aguilar	Universidad de Los Andes, Venezuela
René Alquézar	Universitat Politécnica de Catalunya, Spain
Akira Asano	Kansai University, Japan
Ali Ismail Awad	Faculty of Engineering, Al Azhar University, Egypt
Ildar Batyrshin	Kazan State Technological University, Russia
Eduardo Bayro-Corrochano	CINVESTAV, Unidad Guadalajara, IPN, México
Rafael Bello	Univ. Central "Marta Abreu" de Las Villas, Cuba
César Beltrán Castañón	Pontificia Universidad Católica del Perú
José Miguel Benedí	Universidad Politécnica de Valencia, Spain
Jón Atli Benediktsson	University of Iceland
Rafael Berlanga-Llavori	Universitat Jaime I Castelló, Spain
Gunilla Borgefors	Uppsala University, Sweden
Dibio Borges	University of Brasilia, Brazil
João Rogério Caldas Pinto	Universidad Técnica de Lisboa, Portugal
José Ramón Calvo de Lara	Advanced Technologies Applications Center, Cuba
Virginio Cantoni	Università di Pavia, Italy
Jesús Ariel Carrasco-Ochoa	Inst. Nac. Astronomía, Óptica Electrónica, México
Mario Castelán	CINVESTAV, Unidad Saltillo, IPN, México
Eduardo Concepción	Universidad de Cienfuegos, Cuba
Mauricio Correa	Universidad de Chile
Marco Cristani	University of Verona, Italy
Isabelle Debled-Rennesson	LORIA, France
Alberto Del Bimbo	Universitá degli Studi di Firenze, Italy
Maria De Marsico	Sapienza University of Rome, Italy
Claudio De Stefano	Università di Cassino e del Lazio Meridionale, Italy
Robert P.W. Duin	Delft University of Technology, The Netherlands

Carlos A. Reyes-García   Inst. Nac. Astronomía, Óptica Electrónica,
                          México
Bernardete Ribeiro   University of Coimbra, Portugal
Daniel Riccio   Università di Napoli Federico II, Italy
Gerhard Ritter   University of Florida, USA
Roberto Rodríguez   Inst. de Cibernética, Mat. y Física, Cuba
Fabio Roli   University of Cagliari, Italy
Edgar Román-Rangel   University of Geneva, Switzerland
Alejandro Rosales-Pérez   Inst. Nac. Astronomía, Óptica Electrónica,
                          México
Arun Ross   Michigan State University, USA
Luis Rueda   University of Windsor, Canada
Javier Ruiz-del-Solar   Universidad de Chile
Hichem Sahli   Vrije Universiteit Brussel, Belgium
João Sanches   Instituto Superior Técnico, Portugal
Dairazalia Sánchez-Cortes Idiap Research Institute, Switzerland
Alberto Sanfeliu   Universitat Politecnica de Catalunya, Spain
César San Martín   Universidad de Concepción, Chile
Carlo Sansone   Universita di Napoli Federico II, Italy
Roberto Santana   University of the Basque Country, Spain
Angel Sappa   Universitat Autónoma de Barcelona, Spain
Basilio Sierra   University of the Basque Country, Spain
Ida-Maria Sintorn   Uppsala University, Sweden
Juan Humberto Sossa Azuela CIC, Instituto Politécnico Nacional, México
Beatriz Sousa Santos   University of Aveiro, Portugal
Concetto Spampinato   University of Catania, Italy
Tania Stathaki   Imperial College London, UK
Robin Strand   Uppsala University, Sweden
Carmen Paz Suárez-Araujo Universidad de las Palmas de Gran Canaria,
                          Spain
Zhenan Sun   National Laboratory on Pattern Recognition,
                          China
Alberto Taboada-Crispi   Univ. Central "Marta Abreu" de Las Villas,
                          Cuba
Isneri Talavera   Advanced Technologies Applications Center,
                          Cuba
Tieniu Tan   National Laboratory on Pattern Recognition,
                          China
Mariano Tepper   Duke University, USA
Massimo Tistarelli   University of Sassari, Italy
Karl Tombre   Université de Lorraine, France
María Inés Torres   Universidad del País Vasco, Spain
Yulia Trusova   Dorodnicyn Computing Center, Russian
                          Academy of Sciences

Ventzeslav Valev	Inst. Math. and Informatics, Bulgarian Academy of Sciences
Sandro Vega-Pons	Neuroinformatics Lab, FBK, Trento, Italy
Cornelio Yáñez-Márquez	CIC, Instituto Politécnico Nacional, México
Vera Yashina	Dorodnicyn Computing Center, Russian Academy of Sciences
Zhi-Hua Zhou	Nanjing University, China

Additional Reviewers

Michael Affenzeller
Danilo Benozzo
Marco Bertini
Battista Bigio
Maria Elena Buemi
Pablo Cancela
Qing Da
Luca Didaci
Fazel Famili
Francesco Fontanella
Luca Ghiani
Luis Gómez
Norberto Goussies
Gabriel Hernández Sierra
Michelle Horta
Svebor Karaman
Gisela Klette
Bruno Leitão
Alexandre Levada
Haiqing Li
Dongwei Liu
Noel Lopes
Itzamá López-Yáñez
Ana Luísa Martins
Pedro Martins

John Mason
Sérgio Matos
Igor Montagner
Antonio Neves
Bao Nguyen
Matias Nitsche
Tomás Oliveira e Silva
Darian Onchis
Caroline Petitjean
Ales Prochazka
Luca Pulina
John Rugis
Denis Salvadeo
Mario Sansone
Riccardo Satta
Alessandra Scotto di Freca
Lorenzo Seidenari
Augusto Silva
Yunlian Sun
César Teixeira
Ana Maria Tomé
Tiberio Uricchio
Susana Vieira
Lihu Xiao

Sponsoring Institutions

Advanced Technologies Applications Center (CENATAV)
International Association for Pattern Recognition (IAPR)
Cuban Association for Pattern Recognition (ACRP)
Cuban Society for Mathematics and Computer Sciences (SCMC)
Argentine Society for Pattern Recognition (SARP-SADIO)
Chilean Association for Pattern Recognition (AChiRP)
Mexican Association for Computer Vision, Neural Computing and Robotics
 (MACVNR)
Special Interest Group of the Brazilian Computer Society (SIGPR-SBC)
Spanish Association for Pattern Recognition and Image Analysis (AERFAI)
Portuguese Association for Pattern Recognition (APRP)

Table of Contents – Part I

Keynote

Mathematical Theory of PR

Supervised and Unsupervised Classification

Feature or Instance Selection for Classification

Image Analysis and Retrieval

Signals Analysis and Processing

Table of Contents – Part II

Keynote

Applications of Pattern Recognition

Biometrics

Video Analysis

Data Mining

Pattern Recognition Systems under Attack

Fabio Roli, Battista Biggio, and Giorgio Fumera

Dept. of Electrical and Electronic Engineering, University of Cagliari,
Piazza d'Armi, 09123 Cagliari, Italy
{roli,battista.biggio,fumera}@diee.unica.it
http://pralab.diee.unica.it/

Abstract. Pattern recognition systems have been increasingly used in
security applications, although it is known that carefully crafted attacks
can compromise their security. We advocate that simulating a proactive
arms race is crucial to identify the most relevant vulnerabilities of pattern recognition systems, and to develop countermeasures in advance,
thus improving system security. We summarize a framework we recently
proposed for designing proactive secure pattern recognition systems and
review its application to assess the security of biometric recognition systems against poisoning attacks.

Keywords: adversarial pattern recognition, biometric authentication,
poisoning attacks.

1 Introduction

Pattern recognition systems have been widely deployed in security-sensitive applications like spam filtering, malware detection, and biometric authentication
[10,6]. Such scenarios exhibit an intrinsic adversarial nature that fully violates
data stationarity usually assumed for design of pattern recognition systems. Accordingly, a different design procedure is required to explicitly deal with the arms
race existing in security settings between system designers and adversaries. We
advocate that design should be based on a what-if analysis simulating a proactive arms race, for improving system security. We further argue that evaluating
security properties through simulations of different, potential attack scenarios is
a crucial step in this arms race for identifying the most relevant vulnerabilities
and for suggesting how to potentially counter them. In Sect. 2 we briefly review
an example of a reactive arms race occurred in spam filtering, and discuss differences with proactive approaches. In Sect. 3 we summarize a framework we
recently proposed for designing proactive secure pattern recognition systems,
and review its application to assess the security of biometric recognition systems
against poisoning attacks. In Sect. 4 we try to be proactive by outlining three
attacks that may emerge in the near future. Conclusions and future research
lines are highlighted in Sect. 5.

J. Ruiz-Shulcloper and G. Sanniti di Baja (Eds.): CIARP 2013, Part I, LNCS 8258, pp. 1–8, 2013.

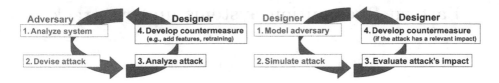

Fig. 1. A schematic representation of the reactive (left) and proactive (right) arms races incurring in security applications involving pattern recognition systems

2   The Arms Race in Pattern Recognition

As a typical example of arms race in pattern recognition we summarize in Sect. 2.1 the story of image-based spam. It also allows us to introduce the concepts of reactive and proactive security, that are explained in Sect. 2.2.

2.1   The Story of Image-Based Spam

Since the 90s, computer viruses and attack threats have evolved towards an increased level of variability and sophistication in response to an increase of the complexity and number of vulnerable attack points of modern security systems. Together with the fact that automatic tools for designing novel variants of attacks can be easily obtained and exploited by not very skilled attackers, and that a flourishing underground economy strongly motivates them, an exponential proliferation of malware and other threats has been recently observed. To cope with such a large amount of malicious data exhibiting both an increasing variability and number of never-before-seen attacks, machine-learning approaches have been increasingly adopted to complement the earlier rule-based systems (*e.g.*, signature-based systems based on string-matching techniques): the latter offer fast and lightweight filtering of most known attacks, while the former can process the remaining (unfiltered) samples and identify novel attacks.

A recent example of arms race in pattern recognition is the so-called *image-based spam* (or image spam, for short) [5,1]. This technique consists of rendering the spam message into attached images to evade the textual-based analysis performed by most of the modern anti-spam filters. Due to the massive volume of image spam sent in 2006 and 2007, researchers and companies developed countermeasures, like generating signatures to filter known spam images, or analyzing suspect images by OCR tools to extract text for standard spam detection. This started an arms race between designers and spammers. Spammers reacted by *randomly* obfuscating images with *adversarial* noise, both to to evade signature-based detection, and to make OCR-based detection ineffective. Researchers responded with (fast) approaches mainly based on machine-learning techniques using visual features extracted from images, aimed at discriminating between images attached to spam and to legitimate e-mails. Image spam volumes have since declined, although the exact cause is debatable: these countermeasures may have played a deterrent role, or image spam became too costly in terms of time to generate and bandwidth to deliver.

2.2   Reactive and Proactive Security

As highlighted by the image spam story, security problems are often cast as a long-lasting *reactive* arms race between the system designer and the adversary, in which each player attempts to achieve his goal by reacting to the changing behavior of his opponent, *i.e.*, basically *learning from the past*. This arms race can be modeled as the following cycle [6]. First, the adversary analyzes the existing pattern recognition system and manipulates data to violate system security (*e.g.*, to evade detection). For instance, a spammer may gather some knowledge of the words used by the targeted anti-spam filter to block spam, and then manipulate the textual content of spam emails accordingly; *e.g.*, words like "cheap" that are indicative of spam can be misspelled as "che4p". Second, the pattern recognition system designer reacts by analyzing the novel attack samples and updating the system consequently; *e.g.*, by retraining the classifier on the newly collected samples, and/or by adding features that can better detect the novel attacks. In the previous spam example, this amounts to retraining the filter on the newly collected spam and, thus, to adding novel words into the filter's dictionary (*e.g.*, "che4p" may be now learned as a spammy word). This *reactive* arms race continues in perpetuity as illustrated in the left plot in Fig. 1.

However, *reactive* approaches to this arms race do not anticipate the next generation of security vulnerabilities, *i.e.*, they do not attempt to *forecast future attacks*, and thus, the system potentially remains vulnerable to new attacks. Computer security guidelines accordingly advocate a *proactive* approach in which the designer should also attempt to *anticipate* the adversary's strategy by (i) identifying the most relevant threats, (ii) designing proper countermeasures for his system, when required, and (iii) repeating this process for his new design *before* deploying the pattern recognition system. This can be accomplished by modeling the adversary (based on knowledge of the adversary's goals and capabilities) and using this model to simulate attacks, to complement the reactive arms race, as shown in Fig. 1 (right). While such an approach does not account for unknown or changing aspects of the adversary, it can improve the level of security by delaying each step of the *reactive* arms race, as it should reasonably force the adversary to exert greater effort (in terms of time, skills, and resources) to find new vulnerabilities. Accordingly, pattern recognition systems that are properly designed according to the reactive and proactive security paradigms should remain useful for a longer time, with less frequent supervision or human intervention and with less severe vulnerabilities.

Although the approach of proactive security has been implicitly followed in most of previous work, it has only recently been formalized within a more general framework for the empirical evaluation of pattern classifier's security [6], which we summarize in the next section.

3   Security Evaluation of Pattern Recognition Systems

We summarize our proactive security evaluation framework [6], and its application to assess the security of adaptive biometric recognition systems.

Fig. 2. Main design steps for deploying a pattern recognition system

3.1   Proactive Security Evaluation Framework

Our framework [6] systematizes and unifies previous work. It aims at empirically evaluating the security of a pattern recognition system under design, through *simulations* of different, potential attack scenarios, *i.e.*, by a systematic *what-if analysis*. Our framework addresses the first three steps of the proactive arms race (Fig. 1, right), overcoming the shortcomings of reactive security: identifying potential attack scenarios, devising the corresponding attacks, and systematically evaluating their impact. This may also suggest countermeasures to the hypothesized attacks, whose implementation is however to be addressed separately in an application-specific manner.

Our framework focuses on attacks consisting of manipulating the data processed by a pattern recognition system to subvert the results. It does not consider attacks to the system's physical infrastructures (*e.g.*, the sensors). It exploits the taxonomy of potential attacks against learning-based pattern classifiers of [2,10], which consists of three main features: (1) the kind of *influence* of attacks on the classifier, either **causative** or **exploratory**, respectively aimed at undermine the learning and the classification phase; (2) the kind of *security violation*: either **integrity** (to gain unauthorized access to the system), **availability** (to generate many classification errors to compromise the normal system operation), or **privacy** (to obtain confidential information from the classifier); (3) the *specificity* of an attack, ranging continuously from **targeted** (focused on a few specific samples) to **indiscriminate** (*e.g.*, affecting all malicious samples).

We describe our framework for the case of supervised pattern classifiers (for different tasks like unsupervised clustering, see [8]). Their classical design steps [9], that do not take adversarial settings into account, are summarized in Fig. 2. In adversarial settings, *each* design step can be subject to attacks. To evaluate their impact, we model the adversary in terms of specific assumptions about (i) her goal, (ii) knowledge of the system, and (iii) capability to modify the data distribution by manipulating samples; this allows one to (iv) develop optimal attack strategies, and to guide the design of resilient classifiers. (i) The **adversary's goal** is based on the kind of anticipated security violation, on the attack's specificity, and of an objective function that the adversary is willing to maximize, which allows for a formal characterization of the *optimal* attack strategy. (ii) The **adversary's knowledge** ranges from no information to complete information, and it is defined for each design step of Fig. 2: the training set, the feature representation, the learning algorithm and its decision function, the learned classifier's parameters, and the feedback from the deployed classifier. Assuming *perfect knowledge* of the targeted classifier is a usual worst-case setting, which provides a lower bound on the classifier performance under attack.

A more realistic *limited knowledge* setting can also be considered; however, it would be contingent on *security through obscurity*, which strongly relies upon *secrets* that must be kept unknown to the adversary. This is complementary to the former setting, that is related to *security by design*, which advocates that systems should be designed from the ground-up to be secure, and secrets, if any, must be well-justified. Accordingly, the knowledge of at least the learning algorithm and feature representation is often assumed. (iii) The **adversary's capability** is defined according to the attack taxonomy, and can incorporate application-specific constraints. Since training and test data may follow different distributions when they are manipulated by the adversary, one should specify: whether the attack manipulates training (TR) and/or testing (TS) data (*i.e.*, the attack influence); whether and to what extent it affects the class priors for TR and TS; which and how many samples can be modified in each class; which features can be modified and how can their values be altered. To perform security evaluation according to the hypothesized attack scenario, the collected data and generated attack samples should be resampled according to the above distributions to produce suitable training and test set pairs [6]. (iv) Assumptions (i)–(iii) allow one to compute the optimal **attack strategy** (*i.e.*, the adversary model), by solving the optimization problem defined by the adversary's goal, under constraints corresponding to her knowledge and capabilities. The attack samples needed to evaluate the classifier's security are produced using the attack strategy.

The above procedure must be repeated for different levels of adversary's knowledge and/or capabilities, if necessary, and for each different hypothesized attack. In the next section we give a specific example of the application of our framework to a biometric identity recognition system.

3.2 Poisoning Attacks to Compromise Biometric Templates

The application of our framework led us to highlight a novel vulnerability of adaptive face recognition systems [7,4]. They aim at dealing with natural temporal variations of the clients' faces, by exploiting biometric data acquired over time during system operation. Template self-update is the simplest approach, inspired by semi-supervised learning techniques. It consists of periodically updating a user's template gallery using samples assigned with high confidence to the corresponding identity during operation. Although adaptation may allow a face recognition system to maintain a good performance over time, an *attacker* may exploit it to compromise the stored templates. This can be achieved by submitting a suitable sequence of fake faces to the camera while claiming the identity of a *victim* user (*poisoning* attack). The fake (or *spoofed*) faces can be obtained by printing a face image on paper [3]. This may eventually compromise the victim's templates by replacing some of them with other desired face images, that may either be sufficiently different from the victim's templates, to deny access to him; or they may include attacker's images, to allow her to impersonate the victim without eventually using any fake trait. In [7,4] we have derived optimal poisoning attacks against adaptive face verification systems, *i.e.*, attacks that *minimize* the number of fake faces to present to the camera, under

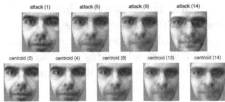

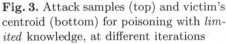

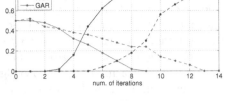

Fig. 3. Attack samples (top) and victim's centroid (bottom) for poisoning with *limited* knowledge, at different iterations

Fig. 4. FAR and GAR for poisoning with *perfect* (solid lines) and *limited* (dashed lines) knowledge, at different iterations

both perfect and limited knowledge of the attacked system. A simple example of attack is detailed in the following, according to our framework of Sect. 3.1.

We consider a face verification system based on Principal Component Analysis (PCA), where each client is authenticated by comparing the submitted face image with the stored template belonging to the claimed identity, in the feature space induced by PCA. If the similarity score exceeds a pre-defined acceptance threshold, then the claimed identity is authenticated as genuine, otherwise it is rejected as an impostor attempt. The *unique* template of each client is obtained by averaging $n = 5$ distinct face images of the same user acquired during enrollment, and it is thus referred to as *centroid*. It is self-updated during operation using face images that satisfy the update condition, *i.e.*, if the similarity score with the stored template is greater than a pre-defined update threshold, which is typically more restrictive (*i.e.*, higher) than the acceptance threshold. The centroid is updated as the average of the latest n images that have satisfied the update condition (moving average update rule with a fixed window size). **Adversary's goal:** we assume she aims to impersonate the victim without eventually using any fake trait, by replacing his template while minimizing the number of submitted fake faces (*queries*). **Adversary's knowledge:** we consider both perfect and limited knowledge. In the former case, the attacker knows the victim's templates, the feature representation, the verification and update algorithm, and their acceptance and update thresholds. In the latter, more realistic case, the attacker does not know the victim's template, but is able to get a similar enough image (*e.g.*, from social networks) such that the update condition is met and the poisoning attack can successfully start. **Adversary's capability:** she can submit a number of fake faces to get access to the victim's template gallery, *i.e.*, to a portion of the *training* data.

We refer the reader to [7,4] for the computation of the optimal attack. Figs. 3 and 4 show some experimental results for a specific attacker-victim pair. Fig. 3 shows how the victim's template is updated by the attack under limited knowledge. Fig. 4 shows the behaviour of the False Acceptance Rate (FAR, the probability of the attacker accessing the system impersonating the victim) and the Genuine Acceptance Rate (GAR, the probability of the victim correctly accessing the system), for both perfect and limited knowledge. In the perfect knowledge case less queries are required to replace the victim's template with the attacker's desired image, which is coherent with theoretical bounds [11]. In both cases, the attacker can violate the victim's account with high probability even when the template is only partially compromised, as shown by the significantly high FAR value after half of the queries. Notably, the GAR also quickly decreases, meaning that the victim can not correctly access the system: this is a side-effect, which can be mitigated by using multiple templates per client [4].

4 Where Do Adversaries Attack Next Time?

Attacks against pattern recognition systems emerged only recently as the application and popularity of these technologies generated sufficient incentives for attackers. Nowadays, we have many reported *spoofing* attacks against biometric recognition systems based on fake biometric traits, *e.g.*, a printed picture is used to fool a facial recognition system.[1] Besides face and fingerprint recognition, the European project TABULA RASA demonstrated successful spoofing attacks against systems using speech and gait.[2] Therefore, additional biometric systems could be the next targets soon. Another little-known type of attack likely to emerge in the near future is an evasion attack against biometric video surveillance systems used to recognize targeted individuals (*e.g.*, individuals on a watch-list). To date this avenue of attack has received little attention because evading a face recognition system is still quite easy (wearing hats or glasses is often sufficient to evade it). However, the arms race to evade these pattern recognition systems has already begun as is evident in the creative CV Dazzle project that proposes new facial makeup and hair styling to evade face recognition systems.[3] Finally, another potential class of attacks that may emerge in the near future involves data clustering, one of the key technologies for the commercial exploitation of massive volumes of both structured and unstructured data (now called *big data*). Clustering algorithms have been increasingly adopted in security applications to spot dangerous or illicit activities. However, they have not been originally devised to deal with deliberate attack attempts that may aim to subvert the clustering process itself. We have recently demonstrated that an attacker may significantly subvert the whole clustering process by adding a relatively small percentage of attack samples to the input data [8]. The market trend of *big data* makes very likely that clustering algorithms used in commercial and security applications will be soon the target of attacks.

5 Conclusions and Future Work

In this work we pointed out some of the issues related to the adoption of pattern recognition systems in security-sensitive settings, and advocated a proactive approach to security evaluation that can be exploited complementarily to the

---

[1] An example of a spoofing attack: http://www.youtube.com/watch?v=2fKGXSgOFYc
[2] http://www.tabularasa-euproject.org
[3] http://cvdazzle.com

well-known reactive paradigm to understand their security guarantees. Thinking proactively, we also discussed some novel potential sources of vulnerabilities, such as data clustering algorithms. For the same reason, one may also think of attackers that combine carefully crafted attacks against specific system components (*e.g.*, data clustering, feature selection, and classifier training) to develop more complex, stealthy attacks. These *multiple* attacks may be indeed more difficult to spot as they may only slightly affect each of the system's components involved, although eventually compromising the overall system security to a large extent. Finally, although the proactive security evaluation of pattern recognition systems advocated in this paper may suggest specific countermeasures, designing general-purpose *secure* classifiers remains an open problem that should be specifically addressed in the future.

Acknowledgments. This work has been partly supported by the project "Security of pattern recognition systems in future internet" (CRP-18293) funded by Regione Autonoma della Sardegna. The opinions expressed in this paper are solely those of the authors and do not necessarily reflect the opinions of any sponsor.

References

1. Attar, A., Rad, R.M., Atani, R.E.: A survey of image spamming and filtering techniques. Artif. Intell. Rev. 40(1), 71–105 (2013)
2. Barreno, M., Nelson, B., Sears, R., Joseph, A.D., Tygar, J.D.: Can machine learning be secure? In: Proc. of the 2006 ACM Symp. on Information, Computer and Comm. Sec., pp. 16–25. ACM, NY (2006)
3. Biggio, B., Akhtar, Z., Fumera, G., Marcialis, G.L., Roli, F.: Security evaluation of biometric authentication systems under real spoofing attacks. IET Biometrics 1(1), 11–24 (2012)
4. Biggio, B., Didaci, L., Fumera, G., Roli, F.: Poisoning attacks to compromise face templates. In: 6th IAPR Int'l Conf. on Biometrics, pp. 1–7 (2013)
5. Biggio, B., Fumera, G., Pillai, I., Roli, F.: A survey and experimental evaluation of image spam filtering techniques. Pattern Rec. Letters 32(10), 1436–1446 (2011)
6. Biggio, B., Fumera, G., Roli, F.: Security evaluation of pattern classifiers under attack. IEEE Trans. on Knowledge and Data Engineering 99(preprints), 1 (2013)
7. Biggio, B., Fumera, G., Roli, F., Didaci, L.: Poisoning adaptive biometric systems. In: Gimel'farb, G., Hancock, E., Imiya, A., Kuijper, A., Kudo, M., Omachi, S., Windeatt, T., Yamada, K. (eds.) SSPR&SPR 2012. LNCS, vol. 7626, pp. 417–425. Springer, Heidelberg (2012)
8. Biggio, B., Pillai, I., Rota Bulò, S., Ariu, D., Pelillo, M., Roli, F.: Is data clustering in adversarial settings secure? In: Proc. of the 2013 Artificial Intelligence and Security Workshop (2013)
9. Duda, R.O., Hart, P.E., Stork, D.G.: Pattern Classification. Wiley-Interscience Publication (2000)
10. Huang, L., Joseph, A.D., Nelson, B., Rubinstein, B., Tygar, J.D.: Adversarial machine learning. In: 4th ACM Workshop on Artificial Intelligence and Security (AISec 2011), Chicago, IL, USA, pp. 43–57 (2011)
11. Kloft, M., Laskov, P.: Online anomaly detection under adversarial impact. In: Proc. of the 13th Int'l Conf. on Artificial Intelligence and Statistics, pp. 405–412 (2010)

Genetic Programming of Heterogeneous Ensembles for Classification

Hugo Jair Escalante[1,*], Niusvel Acosta-Mendoza[1,2,*],
Alicia Morales-Reyes[1], and Andrés Gago-Alonso[2]

[1] Instituto Nacional de Astrofísica, Óptica y Electrónica (INAOE),
Luis Enrique Erro No. 1, Sta. María Tonantzintla, Puebla, CP: 72840, Mexico
[2] Advanced Technologies Application Center (CENATAV),
7a No. 21406 e/ 214 and 216, Siboney, Playa, CP: 12200, Havana, Cuba
hugojair@inaoep.mx, nacosta@cenatav.co.cu

Abstract. The ensemble classification paradigm is an effective way to improve the performance and stability of individual predictors. Many ways to build ensembles have been proposed so far, most notably bagging and boosting based techniques. Evolutionary algorithms (EAs) also have been widely used to generate ensembles. In the context of heterogeneous ensembles EAs have been successfully used to adjust weights of base classifiers or to select ensemble members. Usually, a weighted sum is used for combining classifiers outputs in both classical and evolutionary approaches. This study proposes a novel genetic program that learns a fusion function for combining heterogeneous-classifiers outputs. It evolves a population of fusion functions in order to maximize the classification accuracy. Highly non-linear functions are obtained with the proposed method, subsuming the existing weighted-sum formulations. Experimental results show the effectiveness of the proposed approach, which can be used not only with heterogeneous classifiers but also with homogeneous-classifiers and under bagging/boosting based formulations.

Keywords: Heterogeneous ensembles, Genetic programming.

1 Introduction

Committee-based classifiers have been studied for a considerable time within pattern recognition and machine learning [1]. The effectiveness of ensemble classifiers is widely known, in fact, the combination of experts' outputs has also been adopted in other tasks like feature selection and clustering. The underlying ensembles' principle is that by combining the outputs of (effective-enough) weak-learners that make uncorrelated mistakes, predictive models that outperform any of the individual ones can be obtained [1, 2]. Traditional models for this formulation are boosting (Adaboost [3]), and bagging (random forest [4]).

Heterogeneous ensembles are a type of committee classifiers that combine predictions of weak-learners from different nature (e.g., decision tree, neural

---

* Corresponding authors.

J. Ruiz-Shulcloper and G. Sanniti di Baja (Eds.): CIARP 2013, Part I, LNCS 8258, pp. 9–16, 2013.

networks) [5]. Intuitively, the goal is to build committee classifiers by exploiting the biases of different classifiers. Acceptable performance has been achieved by these ensembles, comparable or even better than by classical techniques [5]. The main problem of these methods is the effective selection of classification models that results in uncorrelated errors. Moreover, output normalization is a problem because different classifiers return predictions in distinct scales, e.g., having a probabilistic method and a support vector machine (SVM).

Independently of its type (homogeneous or heterogeneous), in most ensemble classification models, either a voting strategy or a linear combination of the outputs of individual classifiers is used to fuse decisions of individual classifiers [3–10]. Despite being effective, this is not necessarily the best criterion for outputs combination. For instance, a non-linear function may be preferred for complex decision surfaces. Besides, alternative fusion functions may better exploit classifiers' diversity and accuracy. Thus, regardless of individual models effectiveness/diversity, ensemble methods performance can be improved by learning the appropriate fusion function.

This paper proposes an evolutionary algorithm that aims to learn a function for combining ensemble members outputs in such a way that classification performance is maximized. A genetic program (GP) is proposed such that a population of fusion functions is evolved. Each function combines the outputs of a subset of individual classifiers. The classical linear combination approach is subsumed by this proposal. The proposed GP can automatically deal with variations in the predictions scale and can weight different classifiers outputs. Empirical results are reported using an object recognition data set. The obtained results are encouraging: the proposed method outperforms weighted and unweighted linear combination approaches. Furthermore, to the best of our knowledge, these results are the best so far obtained for the considered data set.

1.1   Problem Statement

Let $\mathcal{D} = (\mathbf{x}_i, y_i)_{\{1,\ldots,N\}}$ be a data set with N pairs of instances $(\mathbf{x}_i)$ and their labels (y_i) associated to a supervised classification problem. Without loss of generality[1] it is assumed $\mathbf{x}_i \in \mathbb{R}^d$ and $y_i \in \{-1, 1\}$, that is a binary classification problem with numeric attributes. We denote by $g_k(\mathbf{x}_i) \in [-1, 1]$ the output of classifier g_k for instance $\mathbf{x}_i$, this value is associated to the confidence that g_k has about the class of $\mathbf{x}_i$. Every g_k term can be thought as a function $g_k : \mathbb{R}^d \to [-1, 1]$, where the predicted class for $\mathbf{x}_i$, denoted by $\hat{y}_i$, is obtained as follows: $\hat{y}_i = sign(g_k(\mathbf{x}_i))$.

Let $f(g_1(\mathbf{x}_i), \ldots, g_L(\mathbf{x}_i))$ be the ensemble fusion function combining L classifiers outputs $g_{\{1,\ldots,L\}}(\mathbf{x}_i)$ for instance $\mathbf{x}_i$. The most used fusion function is:

$$f(g_1(\mathbf{x}_i), \ldots, g_L(\mathbf{x}_i)) = \frac{1}{L} \sum_{k=1}^{L} w_k \cdot g_k(\mathbf{x}_i) \tag{1}$$

---

[1] Multiclass classification problems can be approached with multiple binary classifiers as described in Section 3.

where w_k is the weight associated to classifier k. For Adaboost w_k is iteratively obtained and it is related to the individual performance of weak learner g_k [3]. In random forest and other ensembles w_k is often 1 [4]. In majority vote strategies $w_k = 1$ and $g_k(\mathbf{x}_i) = sign(g_k(\mathbf{x}_i))$. This paper tackles the problem of learning a fusion function $f^*(g_1(\mathbf{x}), \ldots, g_L(\mathbf{x}))$, such that its classification performance (in an unseen data set) is as highest as possible. A GP is proposed to search the functions space that is generated by using a combination of a predefined set of arithmetic operators, constants and classifiers' outputs.

2   Related Work

Evolutionary and bio-inspired algorithms have been widely used to support the construction of ensemble classifiers under both homogeneous and heterogeneous alternatives [6–9, 11]. The most tackled problems from the evolutionary perspective are those of (i) selecting ensemble members and (ii) adjusting weights in a linear combination approach. (i) is a combinatoric problem, where given a set of models it is decided which one include/exclude in the ensemble [6, 7]; thus Equation (1) is reduced to find $w_{1,\ldots,L}$ with $w_k \in \{0, 1\}$. Problem (ii) is a real-function optimization to find optimal weights for base classifiers [8, 9]; thus Equation (1) is reduced to determine $w_{1,\ldots,L}$ with $w_k \in \mathbb{R}$. Methods addressing (ii) subsume those approaching (i). Other evolutionary methods for ensemble learning optimize base learners that compose the ensemble [12]. Although effective models are obtained through previous approaches, the fusion function is always static. The main aim in this paper is to evolve an improved fusion function.

GP has been used for ensemble learning, see [11] for a recent and comprehensive survey. Usually classifiers based on GP are used to build an ensemble [13]. Although satisfactory results have been obtained with those methods, they are limited to work with evolutionary-based classifiers, which are very often outperformed by standard classifiers from pattern recognition (e.g., SVM). A notable exception, closely related to this study proposal, is the work by Langdon et al. c.f. [10] and references therein, where authors use GP to learn ensembles (of ensembles) of binary classifiers. However, that method cannot be applied directly to multiclass problems, it uses a large number of classifiers (up to 90) and only considers two classification methods; more importantly, models structure has huge capacity; thus being highly prone to overfitting.

3   Genetic Programming of Ensembles

This section describes the proposed approach to learn fusion functions to combine heterogeneous classifiers outputs. First, the multiclass problem's version is formulated and second the proposed genetic program (GP) is described.

3.1   Learning a Fusion Function for Ensembles

Using notation introduced in Section 1.1, a general fusion function for multiclass problems is stated as follows:

$$f_m(h_1(\mathbf{x}_i), \ldots, h_L(\mathbf{x}_i)) = \frac{1}{L} \sum_{k=1}^{L} w_k \cdot h_k(\mathbf{x}_i) \tag{2}$$

where $h_k(\mathbf{x}_i)$ is the multiclass classifier output. For a problem with $Q-$classes, $C_1, \ldots, C_Q$, each classifier returns a confidence vector per class, $h_k(\mathbf{x}_i) = \langle h_k^1(\mathbf{x}_i), \ldots, h_k^Q(\mathbf{x}_i) \rangle$. Estimates $h_k^j(\mathbf{x}_i)$ can be obtained in different ways, e.g., the probability (resp. similarity) for the class j given instance $\mathbf{x}_i$ according to a naïve Bayes (resp. KNN) classifier. In this work a general methodology is adopted to be used with any classifier: *one-vs-rest* classifiers. Thus, a binary classifier is trained per class where the $j^{th}-$ classifier uses as positive the training examples from class j and as negative the rest. In this case, $h_k^j(\mathbf{x}_i)$ is the confidence that the jth binary classifier on that label for instance $\mathbf{x}_i$ is C_j.

Hence we seek for the fusion function f_m^* that maximizes the classification performance on unseen data (obtained from the same distribution as the training data set). The aim of the proposed GP is to determine f_m^* among the set of functions that can be built by combining the outputs of multiclass classifiers $(h_1(\mathbf{x}_i), \ldots, h_L(\mathbf{x}_i))$.

3.2   Genetic Programming of Fusion Functions

GP is an evolutionary technique in which the solutions are encoded in data structures more complex than binary or real-valued vectors, as in standard genetic algorithms [14]. A population of individuals (solutions) is randomly generated, and an iterative process begins in which solutions are recombined, mutated and evaluated. Next, a subset of the best solutions are kept for the next generation. The best solution found through the iterative process is returned.

Obtaining a fusion function for heterogeneous ensemble learning via GP requires the codification of a combination function (a solution) as a tree where leaf nodes correspond to classification models outputs augmented with constants (to incorporate a weighting factor). Non-leaf nodes are taken from the following operators: $\{+, -, \times, \div, ^2, \sqrt{}, \log_{10}\}$, these are the ones typically used in GP. An individual is shown in Figure 1.

The GP input is the predictions set obtained by the considered classifiers $(h_1(\mathbf{x}_i), \ldots, h_L(\mathbf{x}_i))$ in a training data set $\mathcal{D}$. Specifically, every instance is classified in $\mathcal{D}$ via 10-fold cross-validation with each classifier, and these are the GP inputs; that is, we have a single value for each instance and classifier obtained when the instance belongs to the test partition in $10-$fold cross-validation. We proceed in this way because we wanted to avoid overfitting as much as possible. The following classifiers are taken from the CLOP toolbox: *random forest, SVM, klogistic, linear-kridge, non-linear kridge, 1NN, 3NN, naïve Bayes, gkridge, and*

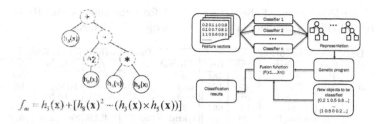

Fig. 1. GP ensemble: Individual sample (left), general scheme (right)

neural network. The GP evolves and returns a fusion function (f_m^*) that is evaluated on (unseen) test data. The general diagram of the proposed approach is shown at the right in Figure 1. During the search process, the fitness value of every function f_m is calculated by evaluating the performance of the tree's induced function: first, the predicted class per instance $\mathbf{x}_i$ is calculated as follows: $\hat{y}_i = \arg\max_Q f_m(h_1(\mathbf{x}_i), \ldots, h_L(\mathbf{x}_i))$, which is simply the index of the class with the maximum confidence; next, f_m predictive performance is assessed with standard measures to determine its fitness.

Two fitness functions are used: (1) accuracy, and (2) f_1-measure. The latter computes the balance between precision and recall per class; f_1-measure's average among classes is herein used. f_1 is more informative when data sets are imbalanced. The GP is implemented on the GPLAP[2] framework. Standard crossover and mutation operators are adopted. The population is initialized with the ramped-half-and-half formulation.

4   Experiments and Results

For experimentation the SCEF data set is used, it is associated to an object recognition problem. This data set is challenging and has been previously used for evaluating heterogeneous ensemble selection methods [12]. The data set comprises 6244 image-regions represented by 737 attributes each (MPEG7/wavelet descriptors) and 10 classes. The data set is divided in two subsets: 3615 images for testing, and 2629 for training. Table 1 (left) shows the distribution of training and testing examples per class.

Empirical results of two GP settings, called EGSP and EGG, are reported. In EGSP only the sum operator is used, whereas in EGG all previously described operators are used. Thus, EGSP resembles the standard approach to learn weights and select ensemble members [7–9]. Results obtained by a standard ensemble (EVP) are also presented, i.e., the fusion function from Equation (2) with $w_k = 1$. For the three ensembles, results obtained by the GP are also reported when using only the top 5 classifiers with better performance in the training data; in order to determine how the accuracy of individual members affects GP-based ensembles performance.

---

[2] http://gplab.sourceforge.net/

Table 1. Left: Description of the data set used for experimentation. Right: Results obtained by individual classifiers in terms of accuracy/$f - 1$ measure.

Data set description					Perf. individual classifiers.					
Class	Train	Test	Class	Train	Test	Model	Acc.	f_1	Model	Acc.	f_1
Building	280	450	Foliage	506	581	RF	**90.7%**	**79.3%**	SVM	55.1%	49.9%
Mountain	203	349	Person	43	129	Klogistic	70.6%	62.8%	Kridge-l	13.64%	2.4%
Road	89	127	Sand	208	273	Kridge-n	74.7%	63.1%	1NN	69.3%	60.1%
Sea	325	338	Sky	461	664	3NN	69.1%	57.4%	N.Bayes	26.5%	21.6%
Snow	43	129	SailingBoat	39	70	Gkridge	20.6%	3.421%	Neural N.	55.8%	37.7%

Table 1 (right) shows the performance obtained by individual classifiers in terms of accuracy and f_1-measure. Random forest significantly outperforms other classifiers. Thus, it is expected that the GP selects the best fusion function from individual classifiers. Table 2 shows the average and standard deviation after 10 runs obtained by the three GP ensemble variants, using 50 individuals and 100 generations per execution. The proposed ensemble variants outperform significantly the raw-fusion function (EVP) in terms of both measures with differences between $40 - 50\%$. GP-ensembles even outperformed EVP when using the top-5 models. This shows the limitations of the raw fusion function for heterogeneous ensembles.

All GP ensembles outperform the best individual classifier. The improvement for both performance metrics is small for all methods but for EGG. Improvements of more than 1.5% and 6% are obtained by EGG with respect to the best individual classifier, in terms of accuracy and f_1 measure, respectively. EGG is able to find very effective fusion functions for heterogeneous classifiers, even when most models performance is low. Moreover, a 6% improvement in f_1-measure is significant when persists across classes, because it focuses on the average performance over classes.

The best results are obtained by the EGG ensemble, i.e., using all operators and classifiers. Using more operators in the GP might allow to obtain better fusion functions. Moreover, the GP has more selection options because it uses all classifiers, which explains the improvement over EGG-Top 5.

The best result in Table 2 improves by more than 10% previously reported accuracy for the same data set (81.49%) [12]. In [12], authors did not optimize the decision threshold thus the ROC curve area (AUC) is also reported. Comparing the best individual AUC (98.44) with the best result reported in [12] (94.05), an improvement of more than 4% is still achieved. These results, to the best of our knowledge, are the best ones so far reported for the SCEF data set.

The EGG performance is evaluated using different population sizes and number of generations. Figure 3 reports the average and standard deviation after 10 runs for different population sizes and 100 generations (left) and different number of generations and 50 individuals (right). Every measure's performance is higher when optimizes itself (e.g., accuracy when optimizing accuracy). Our proposal is somewhat robust to parameters variations, performance differences by distinct settings are very closed to each other. The number of generations seems to have a slightly higher impact in EGG performance than the population

Table 2. Different strategies performance when optimizing accuracy (top) and f_1 (bottom). EVP: raw fusion; EGSP: GP using only sums; EGG: proposed GP.

		Results obtained when optimizing accuracy.				
	EVP	EVP-Top5	EGSP	EGSP-Top5	EGG	EGG-Top5
Acc.	31.5%	81.4%	90.8%(0.001)	91.1% (0.002)	**92.3% (0.002)**	91.2% (0.001)
f_1.	27.2%	71.9%	80.3%(0.007)	80.4% (0.006)	**85.2% (0.004)**	80.7% (0.001)

		Results obtained when optimizing f_1 (macro-average).				
	EVP	EVP-Top5	EGSP	EGSP-Top5	EGG	EGG-Top5
Acc.	31.5%	81.4%	90.8% (0.005)	90.8% (0.005)	**92.0% (0.001)**	91.267% (0.001)
f_1	27.2%	71.9%	80.4% (0.001)	80.4% (0.001)	**85.3% (0.003)**	80.545% (0.003)

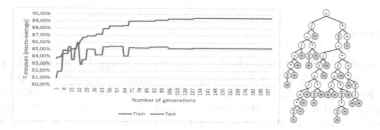

Fig. 2. EGG's best f_1 training and test values per generation (left). Evolved fusion function, shaded nodes represent classifiers' outputs (right).

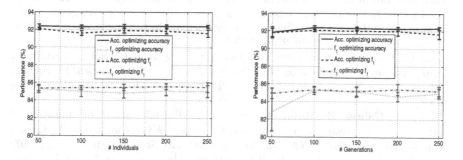

Fig. 3. Parameter selection results varying: the number of individuals (left), the number of generations (right)

size. The best configuration in terms of both performance metrics is 200 individuals and 100 generations (92.385% and 85.57%). A small number of iterations is preferred because a large number would overfit solutions. For example, Figure 2 shows the training and test performance of EGG for the best solution every generation for 200 individuals during 200 generations. After ≈ 30 iterations the GP starts overfitting, and although the fitness performance keeps improving (f_1 in this case), test set performance no longer improves and even degrades. The resultant individual after 200 generations is fairly complex (Figure 2, right). Therefore, special attention must be paid to avoid EGG overfitting.

5   Conclusions

A novel GP approach to learn fusion functions for heterogeneous ensembles was proposed. Its main objective is to search the fusion-functions space generated through an arithmetic operators set. Empirical results on a challenging data set were presented and significant performance improvement over previous work (10%) was achieved. The proposed GP outperformed the best individual model, a raw-ensemble and other variants which optimize models selection and weights. Several research directions were identified: a full experimental study on benchmark data considering parameter selection; adapting the proposed GP to homogeneous ensembles; analytical comparison to other GP-based ensembles.

References

1. Dietterich, T.: Ensemble methods in machine learning. In: Kittler, J., Roli, F. (eds.) MCS 2000. LNCS, vol. 1857, pp. 1–15. Springer, Heidelberg (2000)
2. Kuncheva, L., Whitaker, C.: Measures of diversity in classifier ensembles and their relationship with the ensemble accuracy. Mach. Learn. 51(2), 181–207 (2003)
3. Freund, Y., Schapire, R.E.: A decision-theoretic generalization of on-line learning and an application to boosting. J. Comput. Syst. Sci. 55, 119–139 (1997)
4. Breiman, L.: Random forest. Mach. Learn. 24(2), 123–140 (2001)
5. Bian, S., Wang, W.: On diversity and accuracy of homogeneous and heterogeneous ensembles. International Journal of Hybrid Intelligent Systems 4, 103–128 (2007)
6. de Oliveira, D., Canuto, A., De Souto, M.C.P.: Use of multi-objective genetic algorithms to investigate the diversity/accuracy dilemma in heterogeneous ensembles. In: Proc. of IJCNN, pp. 2339–2346 (2010)
7. Park, C., Cho, S.: Evolutionary computation for optimal ensemble classifier in lymphoma cancer classification. In: Zhong, N., Raś, Z.W., Tsumoto, S., Suzuki, E. (eds.) ISMIS 2003. LNCS (LNAI), vol. 2871, pp. 521–530. Springer, Heidelberg (2003)
8. Macaš, M., Gabrys, B., Ruta, D., Lhotská, L.: Particle swarm optimisation of multiple classifier systems. In: Sandoval, F., Prieto, A.G., Cabestany, J., Graña, M. (eds.) IWANN 2007. LNCS, vol. 4507, pp. 333–340. Springer, Heidelberg (2007)
9. Yang, L., Qin, Z.: Combining classifiers with particle swarms. In: Wang, L., Chen, K., S. Ong, Y. (eds.) ICNC 2005. LNCS, vol. 3611, pp. 756–763. Springer, Heidelberg (2005)
10. Langdon, W.B., Barrett, S.J., Buxton, B.F.: Combining decision trees and neural networks for drug discovery. In: Foster, J.A., Lutton, E., Miller, J., Ryan, C., Tettamanzi, A.G.B. (eds.) EuroGP 2002. LNCS, vol. 2278, pp. 60–70. Springer, Heidelberg (2002)
11. Espejo, P., Ventura, S., Herrera, F.: A survey on the application of genetic programming to classification. IEEE T. Syst. Man. Cyb. C 40(2), 121–144 (2010)
12. Escalante, H.J., Montes, M., Sucar, L.E.: Ensemble particle swarm model selection. In: Proc. of IJCNN, pp. 1–10 (2010)
13. Bhowan, U., Johnston, M., Zhang, M., Yao, X.: Evolving diverse ensembles using genetic programming for classification with unbalanced data. IEEE Transactions on Evolutionary Computation 17(3), 368–386 (2013)
14. Langdon, W.B., Poli, R.: Foundations of Genetic Programming. Springer (2001)

Deletion Rules for Equivalent Sequential and Parallel Reductions

Kálmán Palágyi

Department of Image Processing and Computer Graphics,
University of Szeged, Hungary
palagyi@inf.u-szeged.hu

Abstract. A reduction operator transforms a binary picture only by changing some black points to white ones, which is referred to as deletion. Sequential reductions may delete just one point at a time, while parallel reductions can alter a set of points simultaneously. Two reductions are called equivalent if they produce the same result for each input picture. This work lays a bridge between the parallel and the sequential strategies. A class of deletion rules are proposed that provide 2D parallel reductions being equivalent to sequential reductions. Some new sufficient conditions for topology-preserving parallel reductions are also reported.

Keywords: Discrete Geometry, Digital Topology, Topology-Preserving Reductions.

1 Introduction

A binary picture on the 2-dimensional digital space $\mathbb{Z}^2$ is a mapping that assigns a color of black or white to each point of $\mathbb{Z}^2$ [6]. A reduction (or reductive [3]) operator transforms a binary picture only by changing some black points to white ones, which is referred to as the deletion of 1s. Reductions play important role in various topological algorithms, e.g., thinning [2,7,11] or shrinking [3].

Parallel reductions can alter a set of points simultaneously, while sequential reductions may delete just one black point at a time. Parallel reductions and sequential reductions strategies are illustrated by Algorithm 1 and Algorithm 2, respectively.

By comparing the two approaches, we can state that in the parallel case (see Algorithm 1) the initial set of black points is considered when the deletion rule is evaluated for each elements of the set of interesting points X. On the contrary, the set of black points is dynamically altered during the sequential reduction (see Algorithm 2).

Algorithms 1 and 2 consider a set of interesting points X and its complementary C that is called a constraint set. Constraint sets may contain some types of border points in subiteration-based (or directional) algorithms or points that are not in the activated subfields in the case of subfield-based algorithms [2]. In addition, endpoints (i.e., some points that provide important geometrical information

J. Ruiz-Shulcloper and G. Sanniti di Baja (Eds.): CIARP 2013, Part I, LNCS 8258, pp. 17–24, 2013.

Algorithm 1.   parallel reduction

Input: set of black points B, constraint set $C(\subseteq B)$, and deletion rule R
Output: set of black points P
$X = B \setminus C$
$D = \emptyset$
foreach $p \in X$ **do**
  if $R(p, B) = $ **true** **then**
   | $D = D \cup \{p\}$
$P = B \setminus D$

Algorithm 2.   sequential reduction

Input: set of black points B, constraint set $C(\subseteq B)$, and deletion rule R
Output: set of black points S
$X = B \setminus C$
$S = B$
foreach $p \in X$ **do**
  if $R(p, S) = $ **true** **then**
   | $S = S \setminus \{p\}$

---

relative to the shape of the objects [2]) or isthmuses (i.e., some curve/surface interior points [1] can also be accumulated in C.

Two reductions are said to be *equivalent* if they produce the same result for each input binary picture. A deletion rule is called *equivalent* if it yields a pair of equivalent parallel and sequential reductions.

The rule $R(p, Y)$ says that a point p in question is deletable or not in a set of black points Y. Note that elements in C are omitted when the deletion rule R is evaluated.

The sequential approach suffers from the drawback that different visiting order of interesting points may yield various results. Order-independent sequential reductions can produce the same result for any visiting order of the elements in X [4,9]. It is clear that only order-independent sequential reductions can be equivalent to parallel ones.

In this paper we establish some conditions for deletion rules that provide equivalent parallel and sequential reductions. Some new sufficient conditions for topology-preserving parallel reductions are also proposed.

2   Basic Notions and Results

In this paper, we use the fundamental concepts of digital topology as reviewed by Kong and Rosenfeld [6].

Let p be a point in the 2-dimensional digital space $\mathbb{Z}^2$. Let us denote $N_m(p)$ the set of points that are *m-adjacent* to p and let $N_m^*(p) = N_m(p) \setminus \{p\}$ $(m = 4, 8)$,

	N	
W	p	**E**
	S	

Fig. 1. The considered adjacency relations in $\mathbb{Z}^2$. The set $N_4(p)$ contains point p and the four points marked "**N**", "**E**", "**S**", and "**W**". The set $N_8(p)$ contains $N_4(p)$ and the additional four points marked "•".

see Fig. 1. Note that, throughout this paper, all figures are depicted on the square grid that is dual to $\mathbb{Z}^2$.

The equivalence classes relative to the m-connectivity relation (i.e., the reflexive and transitive closure of the m-adjacency) are the m-components of a set of points $X \subseteq \mathbb{Z}^2$.

A $(8, 4)$ *digital picture* $\mathcal{P}$ is a quadruple $(\mathbb{Z}^2, 8, 4, B)$. Each element of $\mathbb{Z}^2$ is said to be a *point* of $\mathcal{P}$. Each point in $B \subseteq \mathbb{Z}^2$ is called a *black point*. Each point in $\mathbb{Z}^2 \setminus B$ is said to be a *white point*. An *object* is an 8–component of B, while a *white component* is a 4–component of $\mathbb{Z}^2 \setminus B$.

A picture $(\mathbb{Z}^2, 8, 4, B)$ is called *finite* if the set B contains finitely many points. In a finite picture there is a unique infinite white component, which is called the *background*. A finite white component is said to be a *cavity*.

A black point is called a *border point* in a $(8, 4)$ picture if it is 4–adjacent to at least one white point. A border point p is said to be an **N**–*border point* if the point marked "**N**" in Fig. 1 is white. We can define **E**–, **S**–, and **W**–border points in the same way. A black point in a picture is called an *interior point* if it is not a border point.

A 2D reduction is *not* topology-preserving if any object in the input picture is split (into several ones) or is completely deleted, any cavity in the input picture is merged with the background or another cavity, or a cavity is created where there was none in the input picture [5].

A black point is *simple* in a picture if and only if its deletion is a topology-preserving reduction [6]. We state now the following characterization of simple points of $(8, 4)$ pictures:

Theorem 1. [6] *Black point p is simple in a picture $(\mathbb{Z}^2, 8, 4, B)$ if and only if all of the following conditions hold:*

1. *The set $N_4^*(p) \cap B$ contains exactly one 8–component.*
2. $N_4(p) \setminus B \neq \emptyset$.

Condition 2 of Theorem 1 means that only borders points may be simple points. Hence interior points are not simple points.

Reductions generally delete a set of black points and not just a single simple point. Hence we need to consider what is meant by topology preservation when a number of black points are deleted simultaneously. Various authors proposed some sufficient conditions for reductions to preserve topology [5,8,10].

3   Conditions for Equivalent Deletion Rules

Recall that a deletion rule is equivalent if it determines equivalent parallel and (order-independent) sequential reductions (see Algorithms 1 and 2). In this section some sufficient conditions for equivalent deletion rules are introduced.

Definition 1. *Let R be the deletion rule. Let $(\mathbb{Z}^2, 8, 4, B)$ be an arbitrary picture, and let $q \in B$ be any point that is deleted from that picture by R. Deletion rule R is* general *if the following conditions hold:*

1. *If p can be deleted from picture $(\mathbb{Z}^2, 8, 4, B)$ by R, then p can be deleted from picture $(\mathbb{Z}^2, 8, 4, B \setminus \{q\})$ by R.*
2. *If p cannot be deleted from picture $(\mathbb{Z}^2, 8, 4, B)$ by R, then p cannot be deleted from picture $(\mathbb{Z}^2, 8, 4, B \setminus \{q\})$ by R.*

Let us state some useful properties of general deletion rules.

Lemma 1. *Each sequential reduction with a general deletion rule is order-independent.*

Proof. Assume that a sequential reduction with a general deletion rule R produces different results for distinct visiting orders of the set X with k elements. It is obvious that $k \geq 2$ holds. All permutations of the elements of X can be get by swapping a pair of successive points. (Recall the bubble sort algorithm.) Let us consider the following two permutations

$$\Pi_1(X) = \langle\, x_1, \ldots, x_{i-1},\ p,\ q,\ x_{i+2}, \ldots, x_k \,\rangle \quad \text{and}$$
$$\Pi_2(X) = \langle\, x_1, \ldots, x_{i-1},\ q,\ p,\ x_{i+2}, \ldots, x_k \,\rangle\,,$$

such that different results are produced.

Let $(\mathbb{Z}^2, 8, 4, S)$ be the interim picture when point p is visited according to $\Pi_1(X)$ (i.e., when q is investigated by $\Pi_2(X)$). (Note that both p and q are black points in that picture.)

Then we need to take the following two points into consideration:

1. Point p can be deleted from picture $(\mathbb{Z}^2, 8, 4, S)$ by R, but p cannot be deleted from picture $(\mathbb{Z}^2, 8, 4, S \setminus \{q\})$ by R.
2. Point p cannot be deleted from picture $(\mathbb{Z}^2, 8, 4, S)$ by R, but p can be deleted from picture $(\mathbb{Z}^2, 8, 4, S \setminus \{q\})$ by R.

Note that q can be deleted from picture $(\mathbb{Z}^2, 8, 4, S)$ by R.

Since R is general, in both cases we arrived at contradictions. Hence deletion rule R produces the same result for any visiting orders. $\square$

Lemma 2. *Let R be a general deletion rule. Then the parallel and the sequential reductions with R are equivalent.*

Proof. We need to show that both cases produce the same result for any input picture. In other words, $P = S$ when Algorithms 1 and 2 terminate.

Let $p \in X \cap P$ (i.e., $R(p, B) = $ **false**). Since the sequential reduction is order-independent by Lemma 1, we can assume that point p is visited first. Then deletability of p is evaluated in the initial set of black points $S = B$. In this case $p \in X \cap S$ since $R(p, S) = R(p, B) = $ **false**. $p \in S \cap (B \setminus X)$ stands for each $p \in P \cap (B \setminus X)$, thus $P \subseteq S$.

Conversely, $S \subseteq P$ can be seen in the same way. Hence $P = S$.   □

We are ready to state a condition for equivalent deletion rules as an easy consequence of Lemma 2.

Theorem 2. *A deletion rule is equivalent if it is general.*

The following theorem provides some new sufficient conditions for topology-preserving reductions.

Theorem 3. *A (parallel) reduction $\mathcal{R}$ is topology-preserving if the following conditions hold:*

1. *The deletion rule R associated with $\mathcal{R}$ is general.*
2. *R deletes only simple points.*

Proof. If the deletion rule of a sequential reduction may delete a simple point, then the entire sequential reduction with the same rule is topology-preserving. Since R is general, the sequential reduction is equivalent to $\mathcal{R}$ by Theorem 2. Hence $\mathcal{R}$ is topology-preserving.   □

Figure 2 presents an example of a non-general deletion rule.

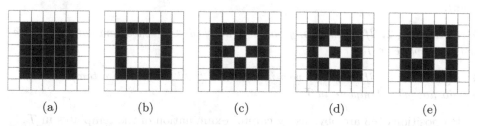

(a)   (b)   (c)   (d)   (e)

Fig. 2. Example of a non-general deletion rule that removes interior points. We can state that the parallel and the sequential reductions with that rule cannot produce the same result for the original object (a). The result produced by the parallel reduction (b). Three of the possible results produced by the sequential reduction with various visiting orders (c)–(e).

4 Example of an Equivalent Deletion Rule

In this section a general and topology-preserving reduction is presented. Hence it is equivalent to a (topology-preserving and order-independent) sequential reduction.

Consider the deletion rule R that is given by the set of 9 matching templates $\mathcal{T}$ depicted in Fig. 3. A black point is deleted by R if at least one template in $\mathcal{T}$ matches it. The constraint set C (see Algorithms 1 and 2) assigned to R is defined as follows:

$$C = \{\, p \mid p \text{ is not an } \mathbf{N}\text{-border point in } B \,\} \,.$$

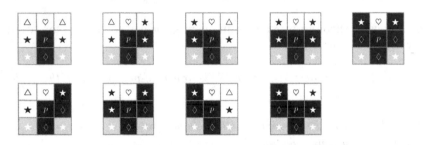

Fig. 3. The set of 9 matching templates $\mathcal{T}$ associated with the deletion rule R. The central point p is matched by a template if each black position matches a black point and each white element matches a white point. The template position depicted in grey matches either a black or a white point.

Let us state some properties of R.

Proposition 1. *Each deletable point is an* **N**-*border point and not an* **S**-*border point.*

Proposition 2. *If we alter any position marked "★" in a template in $\mathcal{T}$, we get a template in $\mathcal{T}$.*

Proposition 3. *If we alter a position marked "♡" or "△" in a template in $\mathcal{T}$, we do not get a template in $\mathcal{T}$.*

Propositions 1–3 are obvious by careful examination of the templates in $\mathcal{T}$.

Proposition 4. *Black points marked "◊" cannot be deleted by R (see Fig. 3).*

It is obvious by Proposition 1 since those points are not **N**-border points. Note that all those points are in the constraint set C.

Proposition 5. *All non-central black and grey positions are marked "◊" or "★" in each template in $\mathcal{T}$.*

Proposition 6. *Simple points are deleted by R.*

It is easy to see that both conditions of Theorem 1 hold for each point that is matched by a template in $\mathcal{T}$.

We are ready to state the following theorem.

Theorem 4. *Deletion rule R with respect to the constraint set C is general.*

Proof. Let $(\mathbb{Z}^2, 8, 4, B)$ be an arbitrary picture. To prove this theorem we must show that the following two conditions are satisfied for any point $q \in B$ that is deleted by R:

1. If p can be deleted from picture $(\mathbb{Z}^2, 8, 4, B)$ by R, then p can be deleted from picture $(\mathbb{Z}^2, 8, 4, B \setminus \{q\})$ by R.
2. If p cannot be deleted from picture $(\mathbb{Z}^2, 8, 4, B)$ by R, then p cannot be deleted from picture $(\mathbb{Z}^2, 8, 4, B \setminus \{q\})$ by R.

Since R is defined by 3×3 templates, there is nothing to prove if $q \notin N_8^*(p)$. Assume that p can be deleted from picture $(\mathbb{Z}^2, 8, 4, B)$ by R. Then at least one template in $\mathcal{T}$ matches it and point $q \in N_8^*(p)$ is an element depicted in black or grey in that template. Since q can be deleted, it cannot be marked "$\Diamond$" by Proposition 4. Then q is marked "$\bigstar$" by Proposition 5. Hence p can be deleted from picture $(\mathbb{Z}^2, 8, 4, B \setminus \{q\})$ by Proposition 2.

To verify the second case, assume that p cannot be deleted from picture $(\mathbb{Z}^2, 8, 4, B)$. Then p is matched by a template $T' \notin \mathcal{T}$. It is easy to see that T' can be derived from a template $T \in \mathcal{T}$ by altering a white position marked "$\heartsuit$" or "$\triangle$" by Proposition 3.

- If a white position marked "$\heartsuit$" is altered in template T, then point p is not an **N**–border point in picture $(\mathbb{Z}^2, 8, 4, B)$. Hence $p \in C$ and it cannot be deleted by R.
- If a white position marked "$\triangle$" is altered in template T, then point q cannot be deleted by Proposition 1. Since q is deleted by R, we arrived at a contradiction. □

Theorems 2 and 4 together imply that the deletion rule R is equivalent. In addition the (parallel) reduction associated with R is topology-preserving by Proposition 6 and Theorem 3.

Note that R may be the base rule of a 4-subiteration 2D parallel thinning algorithm. The deletion rules of the remaining three subiterations are the rotated versions of the rule associated with the deletion direction **N**.

5   Conclusions

This work lays a bridge between the parallel and the sequential reductions. A class of deletion rules are proposed to determine equivalent 2D parallel and order-independent sequential reductions. A new sufficient condition for topology-preserving reductions is also reported. It provides a method of verifying that a parallel algorithm always preserves topology.

We are going to extend this work to the case of 3D $(26, 6)$ pictures, and find 3D deletion rules for equivalent parallel and sequential reductions. We also plan to construct subiteration-based and subfield-based parallel thinning algorithms that produce the same result for any order of deletion directions and subfields.

Acknowledgements. This work was supported by the European Union and co-funded by the European Social Fund. Project title: "Telemedicine-focused research activities on the field of Mathematics, Informatics and Medical sciences." Project number: TÁMOP-4.2.2.A-11/1/KONV-2012-0073.

The author would like to thank the anonymous reviewers for their valuable suggestions and remarks.

References

1. Bertrand, G., Couprie, M.: Transformations topologiques discrètes. In: Coeurjolly, D., Montanvert, A., Chassery, J. (eds.) Géométrie Discrète et Images Numériques, pp. 187–209. Hermès Science Publications (2007)
2. Hall, R.W.: Parallel connectivity-preserving thinning algorithms. In: Kong, T.Y., Rosenfeld, A. (eds.) Topological Algorithms for Digital Image Processing, pp. 145–179. Elsevier Science B.V (1996)
3. Hall, R.W., Kong, T.Y., Rosenfeld, A.: Shrinking binary images. In: Kong, T.Y., Rosenfeld, A. (eds.) Topological Algorithms for Digital Image Processing, pp. 31–98. Elsevier Science B.V (1996)
4. Kardos, P., Palágyi, K.: Order-independent sequential thinning in arbitrary dimensions. In: Proc. Int. Conf. Signal and Image Processing and Applications, SIPA 2011, pp. 129–134 (2011)
5. Kong, T.Y.: On topology preservation in 2-d and 3-d thinning. Int. Journal of Pattern Recognition and Artificial Intelligence 9, 813–844 (1995)
6. Kong, T.Y., Rosenfeld, A.: Digital topology: Introduction and survey. Computer Vision, Graphics, and Image Processing 48, 357–393 (1989)
7. Lam, L., Lee, S.-W., Suen, S.-W.: Thinning methodologies — A comprehensive survey. IEEE Trans. Pattern Analysis and Machine Intelligence 14, 869–885 (1992)
8. Németh, G., Palágyi, K.: Topology preserving parallel thinning algorithms. International Journal of Imaging Systems and Technology 23, 37–44 (2011)
9. Ranwez, V., Soille, P.: Order independent homotopic thinning for binary and grey tone anchored skeletons. Pattern Recognition Letters 23, 687–702 (2002)
10. Ronse, C.: Minimal test patterns for connectivity preservation in parallel thinning algorithms for binary digital images. Discrete Applied Mathematics 21, 67–79 (1988)
11. Suen, C.Y., Wang, P.S.P. (eds.): Thinning methodologies for pattern recognition. Series in Machine Perception and Artificial Intelligence, vol. 8. World Scientific (1994)

Decomposing and Sketching 3D Objects
by Curve Skeleton Processing

Luca Serino, Carlo Arcelli, and Gabriella Sanniti di Baja

Institute of Cybernetics "E. Caianiello", CNR, Naples, Italy
{l.serino,c.arcelli,g.sannitidibaja}@cib.na.cnr.it

Abstract. A 3D object decomposition method is presented, based on the polygonal approximation of the distance labeled curve skeleton. Polygonal approximation is accomplished to divide each skeleton branch into a number of segments along which no significant changes exist as regards curvature or distance label. Each segment is interpreted as the spine of a simple region, which is characterized by i) absence of significant curvature changes along its boundary and ii) thickness that is either constant or evolves linearly along the region. Quantitative information on shape, size, position and orientation of a simple region can be easily derived from spatial coordinates and distance labels of the extremes of the associated spine. Simple regions associated to spines sharing a common extreme partially overlap with each other. Object decomposition into disjoint regions is obtained by suitably dividing each overlapping region among the simple regions including it.

Keywords: Object decomposition, curve skeleton, distance information, polygonal approximation.

1   Introduction

Decomposition is of interest for 3D object recognition, especially when the structural approach is followed. A 3D object having complex shape can be first decomposed into parts characterized by simpler shape. Then, the description of the object, leading to its recognition, can be given in terms of the descriptions of the obtained parts and of the spatial relationships among them.

Different approaches to object decomposition have been suggested in the literature. For example, decomposition can be achieved by identifying in the object a priori defined shape primitives, such as balls, cylinders, cones, prisms and so on. Alternatively, if the object is represented by its boundary surface, the parts can be achieved by using cutting planes passing through curvature minima suitably identified along the boundary surface. Finally, if the object is represented by its skeleton object decomposition can be obtained by decomposing the skeleton in such a way that each part of the decomposed skeleton corresponds to a part of the object.

The skeleton of a 3D digital object consists of the voxels that are placed symmetrically within the object. If objects have tubular shape, symmetry points are mainly aligned along symmetry axes, so that the skeleton is a set of curves.

J. Ruiz-Shulcloper and G. Sanniti di Baja (Eds.): CIARP 2013, Part I, LNCS 8258, pp. 25–32, 2013.
© Springer-Verlag Berlin Heidelberg 2013

For objects with general shape, symmetry points are placed along axes and planes, so that the skeleton is union of surfaces and curves. In this work, we consider objects that can be reasonably represented by curve skeletons, i.e., skeletons exclusively consisting of curves.

Each branch of the skeleton is in correspondence with a part of the object. If the skeleton branch includes an end point, i.e., a voxel having only one neighbor in the skeleton, the branch is a peripheral branch and corresponds to a limb of the object. Otherwise, the branch is an internal branch and is in correspondence with a part of the object, here called core, from which limbs protrude.

The curve skeleton is homotopic to the object and, if its voxels are labeled with their distance from the complement of the object, the object can be recovered by the envelope of the balls centered on the skeleton voxels and having radii equal to the distance values assigned to the skeleton voxels. Actually, a difference exists between an input object and the recovered object. Such a difference is negligible only when the skeleton includes almost all the symmetry points. In all other cases, only a sketched version of the input object can be recovered by the skeleton. As an example, Fig. 1 shows from left to right an object, its curve skeleton and the object recovered by the skeleton. In this case, about 74% of input object voxels are recovered by the skeleton. Thus, the recovered object, which is faithfully represented by the curve skeleton, is a reasonable sketched version of the input object.

Fig. 1. An object, left, its curve skeleton, middle, and the recovered object, right

The curve skeleton can provide a representation of the input object at different levels of detail by using pruning or polygonal approximation. Pruning can be used to trim skeleton branches corresponding to limbs interpreted as object regions having scarce perceptual relevance. If a suitable parameter is introduced to measure perceptual relevance of object regions via the analysis of the skeleton branches mapped into those regions, skeleton pruning can originate different results by using different thresholds for the parameter. In this way, different recovered objects can be obtained, which are sketches at different levels of detail of the input object. In particular, recovered objects differ from each other for the presence/absence of some peripheral regions. Alternatively, each branch of the skeleton can be divided into a number of segments by means of polygonal approximation. In this case, each segment can be seen as the spine of a region of the object, whose boundary is rid of significant curvature changes in the limits of the adopted tolerance. By using different thresholds for the polygonal approximation, different representations of the object are obtained: no object's limbs are lost, while the geometry of each object part is represented in a more or less faithful manner.

In this paper, we continue our work concerning 3D object decomposition via skeleton processing [1]. Here, we decompose 3D objects by decomposing their curve skeletons. We use the 3D skeletonization algorithm described in [2], which is based on the extraction of the curve skeleton from the <3,4,5>-distance transform of the object. We divide the skeleton into its constituting branches, identify only the branches corresponding to meaningful object parts, and perform polygonal approximation on such branches so as to divide them into segments. The regions whose spines are the so obtained segments are sketched versions of the regions into which the object can be interpreted as decomposed.

2   Preliminaries

Let us consider a binary voxel image in a cubic grid, where the object A consists of the voxels with value 1, while the background B consists of the voxels with value 0. The 3×3×3 neighborhood of a voxel p includes the six face- the twelve edge- and the eight vertex-neighbors of p.

The <3,4,5>-distance between two voxels p and q is given by the length of a minimal path from p to q, where the three weights 3, 4 and 5 are respectively used to measure the unit moves from p towards a face-, edge- and vertex-neighbor along the path [3].

The <3,4,5>-distance transform of A is a replica of A, where the voxels are labeled with their <3,4,5>-distance from B.

The curve skeleton S of A is homotopic to A, consists of curves centered in A, and its voxels are labeled with their distance from B. A voxel p of S having in S only one neighbor, exactly two neighbors, and more than two neighbors is respectively termed end point, normal point, and branch point.

Any connected subset of S entirely consisting of normal points, except for the two extremes that are end points or branch points is termed skeleton branch. The skeleton branch is an internal branch if both extremes are branch points, and is a peripheral branch otherwise.

The reverse distance transform of S is the envelope of the balls centered on the voxels of S and having radii equal to the corresponding distance values [4]. We use the <3,4,5>-distance also to compute the reverse distance transform of S.

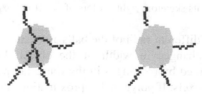

Fig. 2. Left, a skeleton (green) with a zone of influence (gray) including two branch points (red). Right, the centroid (red), common to the four meaningful branches (green).

Let us consider the balls associated with the branch points of *S*. Each connected component of balls is called *zone of influence* of the branch points it includes. Branch points that are neighbors of each other or are closer to each other than the sum of their associated radii are included in the same zone of influence. Actually, these close branch points of *S* can be understood as corresponding to a unique branch point configuration in an ideal skeleton of the object, and the short skeleton branches linking close branch points can be interpreted as non perceptually meaningful. Accordingly, in the following we replace all the voxels of *S* that are included in the same zone of influence by their centroid. The centroid plays the role of an ideal branch point, where skeleton branches of the ideal skeleton meet. We regard as meaningful skeleton branches of *S* the sets consisting only of the skeleton voxels outside the zones of influence plus the corresponding centroids. See Fig. 2.

We use the algorithm [5] to compute the polygonal approximation of skeleton branches. The process is as follows. The extremes of the current digital curve are taken as vertices; the Euclidean distance of all points of the curve from the straight line joining the two extremes is computed; the point with the largest distance is taken as a new vertex, provided that such a distance overcomes an a priori fixed threshold θ (to be set depending on the desired approximation quality). Any detected vertex divides the curve into two subsets, to each of which the above process is applied. The splitting process is repeated as far as new vertices are detected. When recursion is completed, the curve is represented by the ordered sequence of the detected vertices.

3   The Decomposition Method

Generally speaking, *S* includes a number of meaningful branches. For the sake of simplicity, let us describe our method by referring to a simple case where the skeleton consists of a single branch. See Fig. 3. We observe that curvature changes along *S* correspond to bendings of the object. Then, polygonal approximation can divide *S* into straight line segments, each of which can be seen as the spine of a region rid of bendings.

Fig. 3. An object, left, and its skeleton, right. Colors of skeleton voxels denote distance values.

We also note that the different radii of the balls associated with the skeleton voxels take into account the changes in width of the object. Let us consider the 2D representation of *S* obtained by plotting *S* in the Cartesian plane as a function of the radius associated to its voxels. If polygonal approximation is there performed, vertices are detected wherever the radii fail to be aligned in the limits of the adopted tolerance. Thus, the skeleton can be divided in such a way that the radii of the voxels in each segment are either constant, or change in a linear manner. Each segment can be interpreted as the spine of a region characterized by either constant or linearly increasing/decreasing thickness.

By considering at the same time changes along S in geometry and in distance values, the polygonal approximation can divide S into segments characterized by linearity both in geometry and in the distribution of distance values. Each segment of S is the spine of a *simple region* characterized by the following two properties: 1) absence of significant bendings, and 2) thickness that either is constant or is linearly increasing/decreasing. In other words, a simple region is shaped as a cylinder or a cone, delimited by the two balls centered on the extremes of its spine. See Fig. 4.

Fig. 4. Straight line skeleton segments and their corresponding simple regions. Colors of skeletal voxels denote distance values.

To reach the above goal, S is represented in a 4D space, where the four coordinates are the three Cartesian coordinates and the radius of the voxels of S. To compute in such a space the polygonal approximation of S, we need to evaluate the Euclidean distance d of any point c of S from the straight line joining the two extremes v and w of S. This is done by using the following expression:

$$d^2 = \|vc\|^2 - P_{vwc} * P_{vwc} / \|vw\|^2$$

where $\|vw\|$ is the norm of the vector vw, and P_{vwc} is the scalar product between vectors vw and vc. If the point c is the one at maximal distance from the straight line joining v and w, c is taken as a vertex of the polygonal approximation provided that its distance d satisfies the condition $d > \theta$.

The vertices detected in the 4D space are used to identify in the 3D space the corresponding voxels of the skeleton. Accordingly, S can be efficiently represented by orderly giving only the spatial coordinates and radii of these voxels.

When S consists of more than one single branch, polygonal approximation has to be applied to all meaningful skeleton branches, so originating an approximated version of the entire skeleton.

An approximate evaluation of shape, size, position and orientation of the simple regions having the segments of S as spines is readily available without the need of building the regions themselves. In fact, the shape of a simple region depends on whether the extremes of the spine are equally distance labeled (in this case the simple region is shaped as a cylinder, whose bases pass through the two extremes of the spine and are perpendicular to the spine) or have different values (in this case the simple region is shaped as a truncated cone, whose bases pass through the two extremes of the spine and are perpendicular to the spine). Of course, in both cases the shape of the simple region is completed by two semi-spheres placed on the bases of the cylinder or the truncated cone, where the radii are the distance labels of the extremes of the spine. Size can be measured by taking into account the length of the spine and the radii assigned to the extremes. Position and orientation are obviously related to the spatial coordinates of the extremes and to the orientation of the spine. The angle between two spines sharing a common extreme accounts for the bending of the two corresponding simple regions, where these overlap with each other.

To obtain more precise quantitative information on the features of the object's decomposition parts, we do the following two processes: i) construction of the approximated skeleton S^* starting from the available information, i.e., the ordered sequence of spatial coordinates and radii of the vertices, and ii) recovery of the object starting from S^*. To build a given segment of S^*, the absolute values of the differences between homologous Cartesian coordinates of the two corresponding extremes of the segment are computed. These are used for: 1) computing the number of unit moves necessary to link the two extremes by means of a digital straight line segment, 2) establishing how many of these moves are towards face-, edge- and vertex- neighbors and 3) establishing the proper way to alternate different moves. To linearly distribute distance values among the voxels in the obtained digital segment, we use the number of voxels in the segment and the absolute value of the difference between the radii of the two extremes. As an example, see Fig. 5 left, showing the approximated skeleton of the skeleton in Fig. 1 middle. The value θ=8 has been used for polygonal approximation. Different colors are used to denote different segments. Centroids and vertices found during polygonal approximation are shown in black.

Fig. 5. Approximated skeleton (θ = 8), left, and corresponding object decomposition, right

Once S^* has been built, recovery of the simple regions having as spines the segments of S^* can be accomplished by applying the reverse distance transformation to the spines. Actually, any two simple regions whose corresponding spines share a common vertex, called *hinge,* partially overlap. The overlapping region is the ball centered on the hinge. Also simple regions associated to three or more spines sharing the same centroid partially overlap. In this case, the overlapping region is the ball centered on the centroid.

To obtain a decomposition of the object into disjoint components, the overlapping regions (balls centered on the hinges and the centroids) have to be suitably divided among the simple regions sharing them. To reach this goal, we start by applying the reverse distance transformation to S^*. The obtained distance labeled recovered object is used to order the voxels recovered by S^* in decreasing distance order (i.e., from those closer to S^* to those farther from it), so as to decide on their assignment to the proper object's decomposition component. To this aim, each segment of S^* is assigned a different identity label, while all centroids and hinges are assigned a unique common special label. The identity labels of the neighbors of the current recovered object voxel p are checked. If all neighbors of p have the same identity label, also p is assigned that label. Otherwise, p is assigned the special label. Once all recovered voxels have been analyzed, object's components result to labeled with the identity label of their corresponding spines, while surfaces separating adjacent object's components result to be labeled with the special label. Obviously, voxels in the separating surfaces can be assigned to any of the adjacent components. See Fig. 5 right, where voxels with the special label are shown in black.

Depending on whether a meaningful skeleton branch is internal or peripheral, the corresponding region will be a core or a limb. Limbs and cores are elongated regions along which bendings and thickness variations are possible and result to be divided into simple regions.

Differently approximated skeletons can be obtained by using different values for the threshold θ. If the threshold increases, the approximated skeleton represents a rougher version of the object. As an example compare Fig. 5 and Fig. 6. In Fig. 6, the approximated skeleton has been computed by setting $\theta=12$ during polygonal approximation. We may observe that a different number of decomposition components is obtained and that the object in Fig. 6 right is a more schematic representation of the input object.

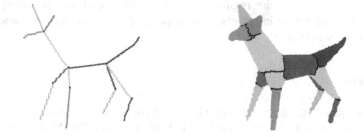

Fig. 6. Approximated skeleton ($\theta=12$), left, and corresponding object decomposition, right

The decomposition method has been implemented on an Intel Core i7 (3.5 GHz, 8 GB RAM) personal computer and tested on a large set of images taken from publicly available shape repositories, e.g., [6], obtaining in general satisfactory results. The method is computationally advantageous, especially if the approximate evaluation of the features of the simple regions is regarded as sufficient for the specific task. In fact, in this case the part of the process dealing with the construction of the digital segments constituting the approximated skeleton and with the recovery process based on reverse distance transformation and identity label assignment is not necessary.

Two more examples to illustrate the performance of the decomposition method are given in Fig. 7, showing the input objects, the skeletons, the approximated skeletons with $\theta=8$, and the corresponding object decompositions.

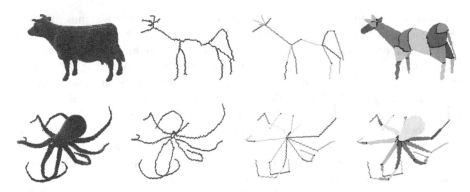

Fig. 7. Each line shows from left to right the input object, the skeleton, the approximated skeleton, and the resulting object decomposition.

4   Conclusion

In this paper, decomposition of the curve skeleton of a 3D object has been used to decompose the object itself. The skeleton is first divided into its constituting branches. Meaningful skeleton branches are detected by using the zones of influence of the branch points. Polygonal approximation in 4D is done so as to divide meaningful skeleton branches into rectilinear segments along which radii change in a linear manner. The regions whose spines are the so obtained segments of the skeleton are sketched versions of the regions into which the object can be interpreted as decomposed. Quantitative information on shape, size, position and orientation of the regions is readily available.

References

1. Serino, L., Arcelli, C., Sanniti di Baja, G.: 4D polygonal approximation of the skeleton for 3D object decomposition. In: De Marsico, M., Fred, A. (eds.) ICPRAM 2013, pp. 467–472. SCITEPRESS, Lisboa (2013)
2. Arcelli, C., Sanniti di Baja, G., Serino, L.: Distance driven skeletonization in voxel images. IEEE Trans. PAMI 33, 709–720 (2011)
3. Borgefors, G.: On digital distance transform in three dimensions. CVIU 64, 368–376 (1996)
4. Nystrom, I., Borgefors, G.: Synthesising objects and scenes using the reverse distance transformation in 2D and 3D. In: Braccini, C., Vernazza, G., DeFloriani, L. (eds.) ICIAP 1995. LNCS, vol. 974, pp. 441–446. Springer, Heidelberg (1995)
5. Ramer, U.: An iterative procedure for the polygonal approximation of plane curves. CGIP 1, 244–256 (1972)
6. Shilane, P., Min, P., Kazhdan, M., Funkhouser, T.: The Princeton Shape Benchmark. In: Proc. Shape Modeling International SMI 2004, Genova, Italy, pp. 1–12 (2004)

Analysis of Dynamic Processes
by Statistical Moments of High Orders

Stanislava Šimberová[1] and Tomáš Suk[2],*

[1] Astronomical Institute, Academy of Sciences of the Czech Republic,
Ondřejov, Czech Republic
[2] Institute of Information Theory and Automation, Academy of Sciences
of the Czech Republic, Prague 8, Czech Republic
ssimbero@asu.cas.cz, suk@utia.cas.cz
http://asu.cas.cz, http://utia.cas.cz

Abstract. We present a new approach to image analysis in temporal
sequence of images (data cube). Our method is based on high-order statistical moments (skewness and kurtosis) giving interesting information
about a dynamic event in the temporal sequence. The moments enable
precise determination of the "turning points" in the temporal sequence of
images. The moment's curves are analyzed by continuous complex Morlet wavelet that leads to the description of quasi-periodic processes in the
investigated event as a time sequence of local spectra. These local spectra are compared with Fourier spectrum. We experimentally illustrate
the performance on the real data from astronomical observations.

Keywords: Statistical moments, Frequency analysis, Fourier and wavelet
transformations, Dynamic processes.

1 Introduction

Random variables can be characterized for application purposes by consideration of quantities called "moments". Since simple and widely known statistical
moments about the origin - EX (mean value μ, the first order moment) via the
central moments of second order $E(X - EX)^2$ (variance σ^2) and its square root
$S = \sqrt{E(X - EX)^2}$ (standard deviation σ), we ascend to the third and higher
orders. In pattern recognition these moments are used as the regional descriptors
for structural shape of regions, boundary determination, texture analysis, etc.
The practical use of moments in statistics is e.g. in [1].

The third order moment m_3 is called the "skewness" of the distribution of
random variable X. It is defined: $m_3 = E(X - EX)^3/S^3$. The skewness is a
measure of reflection symmetry, i.e. if the distribution of X is symmetric, then
$m_3 = 0$. If the distribution is steeped in left (right) of μ, it is denoted skewed
to the right (left), respectively. The fourth moment called "kurtosis" is defined

* This research was supported by Czech Science Foundation GAČR P103/11/1552
and GAČR 205/09/0170.

J. Ruiz-Shulcloper and G. Sanniti di Baja (Eds.): CIARP 2013, Part I, LNCS 8258, pp. 33–40, 2013.

similarly: $m_4 = E(X - EX)^4/S^4$. It expresses the peakedness, in other words it is a measure of how "heavy" the tails of distribution are. The distribution is said to be leptokurtic (narrower than Gaussian), platykurtic (broader than Gaussian), or mesokurtic (as Gaussian). The Gaussian distribution has $m_4 = 3$, therefore the value $\hat{m}_4 = m_4 - 3$ is sometimes used.

Each plane of data cube in the temporal sequence of images consists of pixels of different brightnesses. It can be statistically described by their distribution as well as by the high-order statistical moments. These moments have applications in signal and image processing. A detailed study of the statistical moments in pattern recognition is in [2]. In astronomical applications they are used for example in the investigation of statistical system behavior, mass-density field distribution, statistical studies of the interstellar medium [3], [4]. Pattern analysis of cosmic structure formation is in [5], statistical modeling of lines in atomic spectra [6], detection of non-Gaussianity deviations [7], etc. The generalized spectral-kurtosis estimator and its statistics is in [8] and [9]. Another type of statistical moments applied in the UV spectral range was described in [10].

Our contribution deals with an analysis of the dynamical temporal sequences obtained by the ground-based astronomical observations in optical range. By our methodology we reliably identify the "turning point" where the dynamic event starts. Determination of this point leads to the specification of temporal intervals for further analysis. In these selected sections the periodicity of signals has been searched and results by Fourier and wavelet analysis have been compared. The next section introduces the typical behavior of moments during an observed temporal sequence where a dynamical event appears. The following sections present results of frequency analysis and conclusions.

2   Dynamical Event Diagnostic by Statistical Moments

An example of the observed temporal sequence is in Fig. 1. It is monospectral observation of the Sun surface - solar chromosphere ($\lambda = 656.3$ nm).

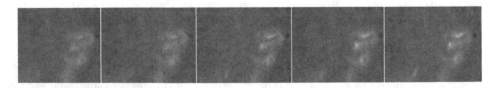

Fig. 1. Patterns of the data cube planes: the light parts in the image represent an active region with arising flare. From left to the right: the beginning of the sequence, the second pattern is from the "trigger area" and gradually up to the fully developed flare.

The dimensionless third and fourth moments are computed from the image histogram. In this sense the skewness of one image is estimated as the third moment normalized to scaling by the standard deviation

$$s = \frac{1}{\sigma^3} \frac{1}{N} \sum_{i=0}^{N-1} (x_i - \mu)^3 \tag{1}$$

and similarly the normalized fourth moment - kurtosis

$$k = \frac{1}{\sigma^4} \frac{1}{N} \sum_{i=0}^{N-1} (x_i - \mu)^4, \tag{2}$$

where x_i is the ith realization of the random variable X. In our case x_i is the brightness of the ith pixel of a region of interest, where N is the total number of pixels in the area. The simplified flowchart of this part of processing follows:

1. Observational sequence (data cube) of active-region images covering the time of a dynamical event (e.g. solar flares).
2. Computation of the high-order moments $[s_i, k_i]$ of each image in the whole data sequence to obtain their temporal evolution.
3. Determination of the starting point of the flare (time or corresponding plane number) and selection of the time interval for consecutive frequency analysis.

The typical evolution of m_3 and m_4 during the flare development is in Fig. 2. It is very interesting to see a fast increase of moments, the temporal curves of m_3 bears resemblance to the m_4 and both unambiguously enable determination of the starting point. As a matter of interest the temporal curve of μ (called the light curve) of the same sequence does not provide any relevant information about the position of "trigger area", see Fig. 2b. The dynamic phenomenon causes both lighter and darker regions with respect to the quiet state, the densities are averaged and the light curve cannot intercept any change of trend.

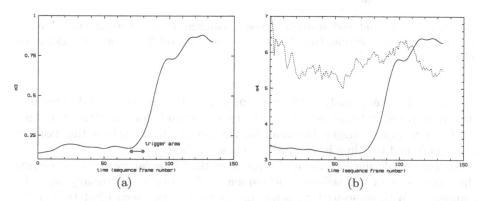

(a)   (b)

Fig. 2. Temporal characteristic of (a) skewness and (b) kurtosis during solar flare development. Temporal evolution of mean μ has been drawn for comparison (b, dotted).

3   Frequency Analysis

For an automatic searching of significant points (times) in the temporal moment's curves we decided for filtering by the Laplacian, the significant points
= maxima of the Laplacian. Since the observation is often distorted by high-
frequency noise, a combination of appropriate filters would be suitable. The
Gaussian and Laplacian can be combined into one filter, proposed in 2D by [11].
The 1D version is

$$gl_i = \left(\frac{i^2}{\sigma_g^2} - 1\right) \frac{1}{\sigma_g^3\sqrt{2\pi}} e^{-\frac{i^2}{2\sigma_g^2}}, \quad i = -n_g, -n_g + 1, \dots n_g. \tag{3}$$

Application of convolution filter (3) enables an automatic identification of
changes in the noisy moment curve. The absolute maximum of the Marr-filtered
curve then determines the precise position of the main "fault" assigned as the
flare starting time (ST). Likewise the subsidiary maxima also give useful information, especially the period of maxima. See Fig. 3a.

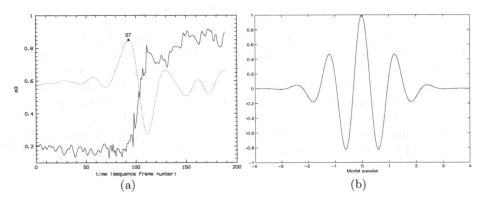

Fig. 3. (a) Significant and start (ST) point searching in the moment curve (black)
and Marr filter convolution, (red dotted, mask size 59), (b) The Morlet wavelet in its
effective support [-4,4].

For the frequency analysis the moment's curve can be basically divided into
two parts: pre-flare time interval, i.e. the time interval before the flare start time
ST (located in the trigger area and determined by an analysis of the moment
evolution), and the time interval after this start time.

To get an information about the pre-flare time interval we need to analyze
the frequencies of a quasi-periodic sequence. The analysis is usually done by
comparison with some pattern wave that is used as the kernel function of the
integral transformation. We can use either a global wave passing through the
whole sequence, typically the sinusoidal signal $\exp(-2\pi i x)$ of Fourier transformation, or some local wave, typically wavelet. There are several wavelet families,
some continuous wavelet is suitable for this type of frequency analysis. In our

experiments we used the real part of Morlet wavelet $\cos(\sigma x)\exp(-x^2/2)$ with the most usual parameter $\sigma = 5$ that yields good compromise between time and frequency resolution, see Fig. 3b and e.g. [12].

The real data experiments consist of seven various events from the two different ground-based telescopes. We introduce two cases illustrative for each type of data, see Fig. 4a (the sampling period is 5 s) and Fig. 5a (the sampling period is 6 s). The left part of the second signal was interpolated from the sampling period 60 s to 6 s. The results of the frequency analysis by Morlet wavelets are in Figs. 4b and 5b. They show absolute value of its real part: in a row, there is the significance of a specific frequency; in a column, there is the local spectrum.

The period of the oscillation is related to the length of the sequence. If there are 210 samples in the first sequence, then the part from -0.5 to 0.5 of the wavelet with length 1 from Fig. 3b was mapped onto the whole sequence in the first row of Fig. 4b. If we are interested in the response of the whole wavelet from Fig. 3b with the length 8, we have to look at the row $210/8 \approx 26$ of Fig. 4b and $225/8 \approx 28$ of Fig. 5b.

The Fourier spectra are in Figs. 4c and 5c. To be comparable as most as possible, we use the real parts of the spectra and the same frequencies as in the case of the wavelets. The most significant maxima (i.e. those with the highest absolute value) are summarized in Tab. 1. Both times and periods are expressed in sample numbers, i.e. if the first sequence has 5 s per sample, then 140 samples represent $140 \times 5 = 700$ s. The Fourier transformation yields frequencies prevailing in the whole sequence, while the wavelet transformation yields an idea about the significant frequencies in the individual samples.

Table 1. Wavelet and Fourier analysis – sample numbers, periods (in the samples) and sizes of the most significant maxima

Sequence from Fig. 4a					Sequence from Fig. 5a				
Wavelets			Fourier		Wavelets			Fourier	
Sample	Period	Size	Period	Size	Sample	Period	Size	Period	Size
140	210	1.76	169	12.56	119	225	7.62	186	79.6
1	210	1.28	94	7.88	116	124	7.55	130	58.1
174	117	1.05	121	7.01	193	124	7.51	101	44.2
101	117	0.77	58	6.76	38	127	7.11	82	40.2
202	37	0.73	50	5.16	202	78	5.06	60	27.9
178	38	0.61	45	4.44	26	75	4.13	69	27.6
58	61	0.59	37	4.07	158	73	3.67	53	20.8
22	60	0.57	76	3.92	70	72	3.08	43	19.86

The comparison of the lowest frequencies is difficult, because the difference of the wave form over whole sequence is too significant. So, the wavelet periods 210 and 225 samples does not correspond to the Fourier maxima 169 and 186 samples. The precise wave form is less important in the higher frequencies, we can see the oscillations with period 117 samples detected by wavelets have good counterpart in the 121 samples of the Fourier spectrum in the case of the first

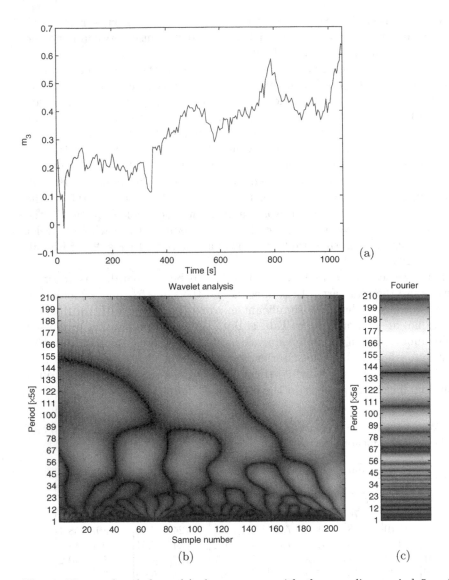

Fig. 4. The analyzed data, (a) the sequence with the sampling period 5 s, (b) the wavelet analysis and (c) Fourier amplitude spectrum

sequence. Similarly 37-38 correspond to 37 samples and 60-61 correspond to 58 samples. In the case of the second sequence, 124-127 samples correspond to 130 samples and 72-78 correspond to 69-82 samples. In both Fourier spectra, there are local maxima without direct counterpart in the wavelet analysis (94, 76, 50 and 45 samples in the first case and 101 and 60 samples in the second case, 53 and 43 samples have weak counterparts). They are not significant in any local time, while their sum over the whole sequence is significant.

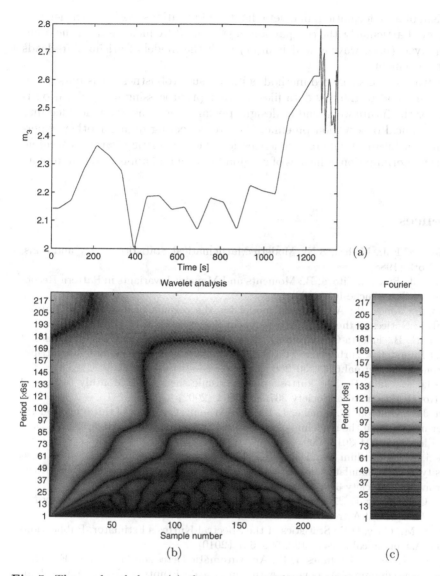

Fig. 5. The analyzed data, (a) the sequence with the sampling period 6 s, (b) the wavelet analysis and (c) Fourier amplitude spectrum

4   Conclusion

The moment curves express evolution of a dynamic process in a new way. Our experiments proved the moments of high orders are sensitive to changes in the image brightness during the initial phase. Determination of the starting point is of great importance for astrophysical interpretation as well as the oscillation analysis in the pre-flare times. It can give more information about the mechanism of flare formation, magnetic field configurations, cosmic weather prediction, etc. Particularly, the comparison of the found frequencies from the oscillation analysis (both wavelet and Fourier) with the model of arising flare leads to its improvement.

The advantage of suggested method is its unusual robustness, it is possible to apply the method to the raw data files, neither preprocessing nor calibration is needed. For the future we intend to design special algorithms to be included into the astronomical observation pipeline. We are collecting data for other experiments in the future: temporal sequences for the meteoritic swarms searching, automatic determination of flashes of gamma lighting and applications in remote sensing.

References

1. Dudewicz, E.J., Mishra, S.N.: Modern Mathematical Statistics. Wiley and Sons, New York (1988)
2. Flusser, J., Suk, T., Zitová, B.: Moments and Moment Invariants in Pattern Recognition. Wiley, Chichester (2009)
3. Coles, P., Jones, B.: A lognormal model for the cosmological mass distribution. Monthly Notices of the Royal Astronomical Society 248, 1–13 (1991)
4. Burkhart, B., Falceta-Gonçalves, D., Kowal, G., Lazarian, A.: Density Studies of MHD Interstellar Turbulence: Statistical Moments, Correlations and Bispectrum. Astronomical Journal 693, 250–266 (2009)
5. Takada, M., Jain, B.: The kurtosis of the cosmic shear field. Monthly Notices of the Royal Astronomical Society 337, 875–894 (2002)
6. Pain, J.C., Gilleron, F., Bauche, J., Bauche-Arnoult, C.: Effect of third- and fourth-order moments on the modeling of unresolved transition arrays. High Energy Density Physics 5, 294–301 (2009)
7. Grossi, M., Branchini, E., Dolag, K., Matarrese, S., Moscardini, L.: The mass density field in simulated non-Gaussian scenarios. Monthly Notices of the Royal Astronomical Society 390, 438–446 (2008)
8. Nita, G.M., Gary, D.E.: The generalized spectral kurtosis estimator. Monthly Notices of the Royal Astronomical Society 406, L60–L64 (2010)
9. Nita, G.M., Gary, D.E.: Statistics of the Spectral Kurtosis Estimator. Publications of the Astronomical Society 122, 595–607 (2010)
10. Alipour, N., Safari, H., Innes, D.E.: An Automatic Detection Method for Extreme-ultraviolet Dimmings Associated with Small-scale Eruption. Astronomical Journal 746, 12 (2012)
11. Marr, D., Hildreth, E.: Theory of edge detection. Proceedings of the Royal Society of London. Series B, Biological Sciences 207(1167), 187–217 (1980)
12. Li, H.: Complex Morlet wavelet amplitude and phase map based bearing fault diagnosis. In: Proceedings of the 8th World Congress on Intelligent Control and Automation, pp. 6923–6926. IEEE (July 2010)

Distance Transform Separable
by Mathematical Morphology in GPU

Francisco de Assis Zampirolli* and Leonardo Filipe

Universidade Federal do ABC, São Paulo, Brazil
{fzampirolli,leonardo.filipe}@ufabc.edu.br
http://www.ufabc.edu.br

Abstract. The Distance Transform (DT) is one of the classical operators
in image processing, and can be used in Pattern Recognition and Data
Mining, and there is currently a great demand for efficient parallel implementations on graphics cards, known as GPU. This paper presents simple
and effective ways to implement the DT using decompositions of erosions
with structuring functions implemented on GPU. The DT is equivalent
to a morphological erosion of the binary image by a specific structuring
function. However, this erosion can be decomposed by a sequence of erosions using small structuring functions. Classical and efficient algorithms
of the DT are implemented on CPU. New 1D and 2D algorithms are implemented on GPU, using decomposition of structuring functions, inspired by
implementations of convolution filters. All the GPU implementations used
in this paper are known as *brute-force*, and even then present excellent results, comparable to the best CPU algorithms, which might contribute to
future applications in image processing.

Keywords: Distance Transform, Mathematical Morphology, GPU.

1 Introduction

The Distance Transform (DT) [12,2] is an important algorithm in image processing because it can be used in many other transformations, such as dilation,
erosion, the shortest path between two pixels, skeleton, SKIZ (Skeleton of Influence Zone), Voronoi diagram, Delaunay triangulation, Grabriel Graph, pattern
matching, image compression, etc. [4,18,11,14,5]. Besides being a basic operator
in image processing, it helps in the study of other similar algorithms, such as
watershed [17] and IFT (Image Floresting Transform) [6]. Thus, improving the
efficiency of DT makes it possible to improve the efficiency of similar operators.
The DT can also be computed by a sequence of local operations, using 3×3 or
one-dimensional neighborhoods, making the algorithms simpler and faster.

DT implementations can be classified by the method it employs to raster of the
pixels in the image. *Sequential algorithms* perform very well, but it is not possible
to calculate the Euclidean DT (EDT) using only this type of algorithm [12,2,16].
Parallel algorithms for the DT can be implemented using parallel architectures,

* This research is sponsored by FAPESP (Process: 2009/14430–1) and CAPES.

J. Ruiz-Shulcloper and G. Sanniti di Baja (Eds.): CIARP 2013, Part I, LNCS 8258, pp. 41–48, 2013.

and are the most intuitive form of implementation. Such parallel algorithms are also able to compute the EDT [12,2,16,8,15], but usually perform poorly on single processor architectures. It is also possible to calculate the EDT using *propagation algorithms*, which use *queue* structures to store the pixels that might have their values changed in a given iteration. Such pixels are called *boundary* pixels [16,20,9].

Mathematical Morphology is an area based on set theory. This theory is heavily applied in image processing, with the basic operators of dilation and erosion, in which the neighborhood can be defined by structuring functions [1].

There is a relationship between EDT and Mathematical Morphology, and the goal of this paper is to study this relationship using parallel programming on GPU (*Graphics Processing Unit*), exploring several implementations of EDT. Furthermore, comparisons are made with the most efficient CPU algorithms with a parallel version of the algorithm defined in Lotufo and Zampirolli [9].

Previous works have focused in accelerating the computation of EDT using GPUs, achieving good results, as in Schneider et al. [13]. However, their work still uses *DirectX*, a computer graphics API, to implement the algorithm, instead of a proper GPU computing framework. Also, their approach does not use Mathematical Morphology to define the EDT.

2 Methods

A two-dimensional *binary image* is a function f that maps the *elements* (or *pixels*) of a space E in $\{0, k\}$, where E is usually a matrix. The position of a pixel is given by their position in the array. Thus, the line x and column y of the pixel is associated with point (x, y) of the Cartesian plane. Then, any distance function defined on the Cartesian plane induces a distance function in the field of the image [3]. For a given distance function, the *Distance Transform* (DT) assigns to each pixel of an object from a binary image the smallest distance between these pixels and background pixels. Consider any two finite and non-empty sets E and K. A ψ *operator* of E and K is defined as a mapping of E in K and denoted $\psi : E \to K$ or $\psi \in K^E$. A *digital image*, or simply *image*, is defined as a function of the K^E lattice. Thus, if f is an image then $f \in K^E$. Consider E the *domain* of the image, which is *one-dimensional* if $E \subset Z$, where Z is the set of the integers, and *two-dimensional* if $E \subset Z^2$.

2.1 Decomposition of the Structuring Function

Some properties of Minkowski operators produce a method for the *decomposition of a structuring element* [19]. For example, one dilation by a 3×3 structuring element is equivalent to perform two uni-dimensional dilations, one 1×3 and one 3×1. The result of a decomposition is a *generalized Minkowski sum*, defined as $B_G = B_1 \oplus \cdots \oplus B_k$, where $\{B_1, \cdots, B_k\}$ are the elements in which B_G can be decomposed. Thus,

$$\varepsilon_{B_G}(f) = \varepsilon_{B_k}(\cdots(\varepsilon_{B_1}(f))\cdots). \tag{1}$$

These procedures of decomposition are useful for implementations of erosion and dilation [7] and will be addressed in this paper. To illustrate the following equation of erosion, an erosion algorithm is defined by $\forall x \in E$,

$$\varepsilon_b(f)(x) = \min\{f(y) \overset{.}{-} b(y - x) : y \in B_x \cap E\}, \qquad (2)$$

where b is a *structuring function* defined on B with $b : B \to Z$. If the elements of b are nonzero, b is called a *non-flat structuring function* or *non-planar structuring function*. Let $v \in Z$, we define $t \to t \overset{.}{-} v$ in K [7]. For the Equation 2, with an input image with a domain E of dimensions $h \times w$, the algorithm performs the erosion in $\Theta(hw)$ time. By Huang and Mitchell [8], considering Equations 1 and 2, applying the erosion several times using varying structuring functions, as the one shown in Equation 3, the EDT is computed. This process is defined in Algorithm 1.

$$b_i = \begin{bmatrix} -4i + 2 & -2i + 1 & -4i + 2 \\ -2i + 1 & \mathbf{0} & -2i + 1 \\ -4i + 2 & -2i + 1 & -4i + 2 \end{bmatrix}, \qquad (3)$$

where the origin, at the center, is bold and $i \in \{1, 2, \ldots\}$.

ALGORITHM 1: Euclidean DT: $g = EDT(f)$

1: Calculates the EDT of f
2: $i = 1$;
3: **while** $f \neq g$ **do**
4:     b_i is defined by Equation 3;
5:     $g = f$;
6:     $f = ero(g, b_i\}$; by Equation 2.
7:     $i + +$;
8: **end while**

The convergence of Algorithm 1 occurs due to the idempotent property of the erosion when considering these particular structuring functions. In this algorithm, the structuring function changes with each iteration, at line 4. If no pixel has its value changed, then the algorithm has converged. Depending on the image, the amount of necessary erosions to achieve convergence may vary. In the worst case, an image with a single 0 value at one end of one of its diagonals, $\sqrt{h^2 + w^2}$ erosions are necessary, where h the image height and w the width. Knowing that the erosion runs in $\Theta(hw)$ time, once again considering a small neighborhood of b size, the EDT has $O(hw\sqrt{h^2 + w^2})$ complexity. Assuming $h = w$, we can simplify and say that the complexity is $O(h^3)$.

2.2 Separable Convolution Using Shared Memory Using the GPU

Graphics Processing Units (GPUs) are coprocessors specialized in generating computer graphics. For several years, their graphics pipelines only allowed the use of fixed functions to render a set of primitives, such as lines and triangles, to create computer graphics. More recently, however, to allow for more realistic graphics, several parts of that pipeline have become programmable. With such programmable pipelines, it became possible, with small changes to GPU architectures, to use the rapidly increasing processing power within them to solve general computing problems. To allow for that *General Purpose GPU computing (GPGPU Computing)*, technologies such as the *CUDA architecture* and the *OpenCL API* were created. This work focuses in the use of the CUDA architecture, through the *CUDA C* library for *ANSI C*, on nVidia GPUs to create new implementations for the EDT.

In a GPU, consider a 16×16 block that can be stored on a block of shared memory, a much faster kind of memory. A (x, y) pixel within an image can be accessed through the following conversion of the thread and block indexes, provided as built-in variables by the CUDA API: $x = threadIdx.x + blockIdx.x * blockDim.x$ and $y = threadIdx.y + blockIdx.y * blockDim.y$, where $(threadIdx.x, threadIdx.y)$ represents a pixel within the block, indexed by the values $blockIdx.x * blockDim.x$ and $blockIdx.y * blockDim.y$. Thus, if an image processing problem can be solved by analyzing a neighborhood stored on a portion of shared memory, the (x, y) pixels are transferred from the global memory to this efficient memory. In this example, the image must be subdivided in subimages of 16×16 size. These divisions increase the complexity of implementing algorithms that rely on access to neighbor pixels. The problem becomes even worse when dealing with global problems, such as the EDT or *labeling*.

Most of that extra difficulty introduced when using the shared memory comes from the fact that, for each block of threads, there is a separate portion of this memory. Pixels on the border of a shared memory block will have neighbors stored on another block, which are inaccessible to the thread assigned to the current pixel. There might even be missing neighbors if the pixel is not only on the border of a block, but also on the border of the image. Convolution filters and morphological operators share several similarities. For example, the decomposition of strucutirng functions based on the presented Minkowski sum is similar to the problem of convolution separability. Taking these similarities into account, it is interesting to analyze existing GPU implementations for the convolution filter, in order to learn from their shared memory management and try to improve the performance of the EDT implementations.

An algorithm for the separable bi-dimensional convolution will be presented as a two-step uni-dimensional algorithm. The code for this algorithm can be found in the CUDA SDK library. The convolution filter is an image processing technique that is mostly used for pre-processing, in order to remove noise and obtain a smoother image. In addition, it can be used for edge detection in objects. As the convolution and morphological operators work with neighborhoods, the border processing on blocks need special treatment. To minimize these border operations, this border must be as small as possible. Thus, it is more efficient to have a border with a thickness of one pixel. For a convolution, the border is initialized with the 0 (zero) value. For an erosion, as the operation is performed using the neighboring minimum, this border must be initialized with the maximum value supported by the used image type. The separable convolution implemented in [10] has two steps: In the first, the load phase, data from the global memory is transferred to shared memory. The second step performs filtering and writes the results back to the global memory. The filtering step also occurs in two stages, filtering the lines first, and then filtering the columns.

3   Results

3.1   EDT on the GPU Using Erosions and Shared Memory

In the same way as the Algorithm 1 for EDT, and the Equation 2, the EDT is implemented using successive erosions by varying structuring functions using shared memory on GPU. In this first algorithm, each thread copies a pixel and its neighbors from the global memory to their corresponding places in the space of shared memory of the thread's block. This way, each 16×16 image block is stored in a 18×18 block of shared memory (in the case of a 3×3 structuring function). The calculation of the minimum value in this pixel is done in Algorithm 2, making this algorithm inefficient. One solution would be to calculate the erosion for all pixels in a block. We have also found that an erosion in 16×16 blocks can be implemented using two 16×1 and 1×16 erosions, requiring less operations.

ALGORITHM 2: Erosion using shared memory: $g(x) = \varepsilon_b(f)(x)$, where $x = [x0][y0]$ and $[tx][ty]$ is the offset in a block

---

```
 1: tx = threadIdx.x; ty = threadIdx.y; // offset in block
 2: x0 = blockIdx.x*blockDim.x+ tx;
 3: y0 = blockIdx.y*blockDim.y+ ty; // offset in image
 4: data[18][18]; // allocates shared memory define data[x][y] of f[x0][y0]
 5: if border block[tx][ty] then
 6:     if border f[x0][y0] then
 7:         data[x][y] = MAX;
 8:     else
 9:         data[x][y] = f[x0][y0];
10:     end if
11: end if
12: data[tx+1][ty+1] = f[x0][y0];
13: g[x0][y0] = erosion in data[tx+1][ty+1];
14: ...
```

3.2   EDT on the GPU Using 1D Erosions on Shared Memory

The algorithm presented in this section computes the EDT in two steps. In the first one, the EDT is calculated for the columns using a sequential algorithm, on the CPU. On the second step, the EDT is computed for the lines, using a brute force algorithm on the GPU until convergence.

In the second part, the GPU's shared memory is used, in a similar fashion to the 1D convolution found in the SDK, `convolutionSeparable` [1]. This algorithm

---
[1] Source: `http://developer.nvidia.com/cuda-toolkit-sdk`

was inspired by the LZ algorithm [9]. By Equation 3, b_i can be decomposed into four structuring functions of one dimension, two vertical *North* (b_{Ni}) and *South* (b_{Si}), and two horizontal *East* (b_{Ei}) and *West* (b_{Wi}):

$$b_{Ni} = \begin{bmatrix} -2i+1 \\ \mathbf{0} \end{bmatrix}, b_{Ei} = \begin{bmatrix} \mathbf{0} & -2i+1 \end{bmatrix}, b_{Si} = \begin{bmatrix} \mathbf{0} \\ -2i+1 \end{bmatrix}, b_{Wi} = \begin{bmatrix} -2i+1 & \mathbf{0} \end{bmatrix}.$$
(4)

This part of the algorithm is calculated through successive erosions by the structuring functions $b_{E1}, b_{E2}, \ldots$, and $b_{W1}, b_{W2}, \ldots$ until stabilization, due to the idempotence property. The LZ implementation uses queue structures to store the pixels that could be altered in an erosion, minimizing the necessary operations. In order to efficiently use the shared memory, the algorithm to compute the successive erosions for the lines uses structuring functions that have the same dimension as the *thread* blocks. Thus, using blocks with a 16×16 dimension and considering erosions in a single dimension, the structuring function to be used will have a 1×16 dimension. Consider $b_{l_i} = [-2i+1 \quad \mathbf{0} \quad -2i+1]$ where the origin, at the center, is bold and $i \in \{1, 2, \ldots\}$. It is possible to define b_{G_1} of 1×16 dimension, as $b_{G_1} = b_{l_1} \oplus \cdots \oplus b_{l_8}$. To generalize this equation, consider $b_{G_k} = b_{l_{8(k-1)+1}} \oplus \cdots \oplus b_{l_{8(k-1)+8}}$, where $k \in \{1, 2, \ldots\}$. The b_{G_1} structuring function will be used on the first iteration of the 1D erosion on the columns. On the second iteration, the b_{G_2} structuring function, also of 1×16 dimension, will be used, and so on. Refer to Figure 1.

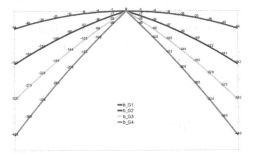

Fig. 1. Illustration of the structuring functions $b_{G_1}, b_{G_2}, b_{G_3}$ e b_{G_4}

The second algorithm (as in Algorithm 1) computes successive erosions on the GPU, with varying structuring functions $b_{G_1}, b_{G_2}, \ldots$, using the sequential erosion as its input image f. With this 1×16 structuring function, each thread performs erosion on eight pixels, instead of a single one, as in Algorithm 2, improving the efficiency of the algorithm.

4   Conclusions

The algorithms presented in this paper were compiled and executed on the following computer: *MacBook OS X - v.10.6.5 - 1.26GHz Intel Core 2 Duo*, with *2GB RAM*, and a *NVIDIA GeForce 9400M* GPU.

The table 1 shows the performance of the algorithms presented in this paper when applied to three images, as shown in Figure 2. The classic and efficient `Eggers-CPU` algorithm runs on the CPU [5]. The `1D-LZ-CPU` algorithm runs on the CPU and was described in [9]. The `2D-GPU`, `1D-GPU` and `1D-LZ-GPU` algorithms presented in this paper compute the EDT using the GPU and its shared memory. The `2D-GPU` algorithm considers a 3×3 neighborhood. The `1D-GPU` algorithm decomposes the structuring function in 1×16 and 16×1 dimensions. The `1D-LZ-GPU` version computes the EDT for the image lines using a sequential algorithm running on the CPU, while its second part uses the GPU to compute the EDT for the columns.

Table 1. Execution times of several algorithms applied to different images (time in seconds)

	512×512			1024×1024		
	$img1$	$img2$	$img3$	$img1$	$img2$	$img3$
$Eggers - CPU$	0.051	0.018	0.022	0.201	0.095	0.095
$1D - LZ - CPU$	0.014	0.012	0.303	0.138	0.077	2.494
$2D - GPU$	0.012	0.625	0.626	0.048	4.903	4.905
$1D - GPU$	0.018	0.152	0.224	0.063	1.148	1.717
$1D - LZ - GPU$	0.013	0.083	0.088	0.057	0.614	0.654

Analyzing this table we observe good performance on the GPU implementations for the image `img1`, Figure 2. This is due to the low number of iterations (erosions) since the objects for computation of the EDT are small. As for the images `img2` and `img3`, the number of required erosions to compute the EDT is high, and these GPU implementations need improvement and/or the use of machines with increased processing power, such as the TESLA GPUs. Even so, the `1D-LZ-GPU` implementation already performs comparatively well against `Eggers-CPU`. It should also be noted that all the GPU implementations used in this paper are known as *brute-force*, and even then have results comparable to the best CPU algorithms for some kinds of images.

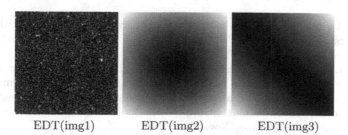

EDT(img1)   EDT(img2)   EDT(img3)

Fig. 2. EDT obtained from input images: img1, img2 and img3 (refer to the text)

References

1. Banon, G.J.F., Barrera, J.: Decomposition of mappings between complete lattices by mathematical morphology, Part I: general lattices. Signal Processing 30, 299–327 (1993)
2. Borgefors, G.: Distance transformations in digital images. Computer Vision, Graphics and Image Processing 34, 344–371 (1986)
3. Breu, H., Gil, J., Kirkpatrick, D., Werman, M.: Linear time euclidean distance transform algorithms. IEEE - TPAMI 17(5), 529–533 (1995)
4. Danielsson, P.E.: Euclidean distance mapping. Computer Graphics and Image Processing 14, 227–248 (1980)
5. Eggers, H.: Two fast euclidean distance transformations in z^2 based on sufficient propagation. In: Computer Vision and Image Understanding (1998)
6. Falcao, A.X., Stolfi, J., Lotufo, R.A.: The image foresting transform: theory, algorithms, and applications. IEEE Transactions Pattern Analysis and Machine Intelligence 26(1), 19–29 (2004)
7. Heijmans, H.J.A.M.: Morphological Image Operators. Acad. Press, Boston (1994)
8. Huang, C.T., Mitchell, O.R.: A euclidean distance transform using grayscale morphology decomposition. IEEE Transactions on Pattern Analysis and Machine Intelligence 16, 443–448 (1994)
9. Lotufo, R.A., Zampirolli, F.A.: Fast multidimensional parallel euclidean distance transform based on mathematical morphology. In: Proceedings of SIBGRAPI, pp. 100–105 (2001)
10. Podlozhnyuk, V.: Image convolution with cuda. In: nVidia (2007)
11. Ragnemalm, I.: Neighborhoods for distance transformations using ordered propagation. In: CVGIP: Image Understanding (1992)
12. Rosenfeld, A., Pfalz, J.L.: Distance functions on digital pictures. Pattern Recognition 1, 33–61 (1968)
13. Schneider, J., Kraus, M., Westermann, R.: GPU-based real-time discrete euclidean distance transforms with precise error bounds. In: International Conference on Computer Vision Theory and Applications, pp. 435–442 (2009)
14. Sharaiha, Y., Christofides, N.: Graph-theoretic approach to distance transformations. Pattern Recognition Letters (1994)
15. Shih, F.Y.C., Mitchell, O.R.: A mathematical morphology approach to euclidean distance transformation. IEEE Trans. on Image Processing 1, 197–204 (1992)
16. Vincent, L.: Morphological algorithms. Mathematical Morphology in Image Processing Edition. vol. Marcel-Dekker, ch. 8, pp. 255–288. E. Dougherty (September 1992)
17. Vincent, L., Soille, P.: Watersheds in digital spaces: an efficient algorithm based on immersion simulations. IEEE Transactions on Pattern Analysis and Machine Intelligence 13(6), 583–598 (1991)
18. Vincent, L.: Exact euclidean distance function by chain propagations. In: IEEE Int. Computer Vision and Pattern Recog. Conf., Maui, HI, pp. 520–525 (June 1991)
19. Wang, X., Bertrand, G.: An algorithm for a generalized distance transformation based on minkowski operations. In: 9th International Conference on Pattern Recognition, vol. 2, pp. 1164–1168 (November 1988)
20. Zampirolli, F.A., Lotufo, R.A.: Classification of the distance transformation algorithms under the mathematical morphology approach. In: Proceedings of SIBGRAPI, pp. 292–299 (2000)

Estimation of Single-Gaussian and Gaussian Mixture Models for Pattern Recognition

Jan Vaněk, Lukáš Machlica, and Josef Psutka

University of West Bohemia in Pilsen, Univerzitní 22, 306 14 Pilsen
Faculty of Applied Sciences, Department of Cybernetics
{vanekyj,machlica,psutka}@kky.zcu.cz

Abstract. Single-Gaussian and Gaussian-Mixture Models are utilized in various pattern recognition tasks. The model parameters are estimated usually via Maximum Likelihood Estimation (MLE) with respect to available training data. However, if only small amount of training data is available, the resulting model will not generalize well. Loosely speaking, classification performance given an unseen test set may be poor. In this paper, we propose a novel estimation technique of the model variances. Once the variances were estimated using MLE, they are multiplied by a scaling factor, which reflects the amount of uncertainty present in the limited sample set. The optimal value of the scaling factor is based on the Kullback-Leibler criterion and on the assumption that the training and test sets are sampled from the same source distribution. In addition, in the case of GMM, the proper number of components can be determined.

Keywords: Maximum Likelihood Estimation, Gaussian Mixture Model, Kullback-Leibler Divergence, Variance, Scaling.

1 Introduction

In this article the estimation of parameters of a single Gaussian and Gaussian Mixture Models (GMMs) is investigated. Gaussian models are often used in pattern recognition in order to classify or represent the data. An input training set is given and the task is to extract relevant information in a form of a statistical model. The training set is often limited, thus it is difficult, sometimes even impossible, to capture the true/source data distribution with high accuracy. Moreover, in extreme cases the estimation can produce numerically unstable estimates of unknown model parameters. In order to estimate the model parameters often Maximum Likelihood Estimation (MLE) is used. MLE focuses just on the training set [1], not respecting the representativeness of the true/source distribution from which the given data were sampled. However, in the pattern recognition, the performance of a system on unseen data is crucial.

Methods proposed in this article are based on a reasonable assumption that the source distribution of the training and test set are the same. Therefore, the proposed criterion focuses on the similarity of the true data distribution and estimated model parameters. For this purpose we use the Kullback-Leibler Divergence (KLD) [2] and we integrate over the entire parameter space. We investigate the case where at first the model parameters are estimated via MLE, and subsequently only the variance parameters are modified. Indeed, the variance does reflect the uncertainty of the model.

J. Ruiz-Shulcloper and G. Sanniti di Baja (Eds.): CIARP 2013, Part I, LNCS 8258, pp. 49–56, 2013.

At first, the situation with single Gaussian models is examined. Further, the conclusions are extended to the case of Gaussian mixture models. The proposed method is able to determine a proper number of GMM components, which is often set empirically (several data-driven approaches were already studied, see [3–5]).

We demonstrate on a sequence of experiments that the log-likelihood of the modified model given an unseen test set increases, mainly in situations when the number of training data is low.

2   Estimation of Parameters of a Single-Gaussian Model

Assume a random data set $X = \{x_1, x_2, \ldots, x_n\}$, which is iid (independent and identically distributed), and sampled from univariate normal distribution $\mathcal{N}(0, 1)$. The sample mean $\hat{\mu}$ and sample variance $\hat{\sigma}^2$ are given by the formulas:

$$\hat{\mu} = \frac{1}{n} \sum_{i=1}^{n} x_i, \quad \hat{\sigma}^2 = \frac{1}{n-1} \sum_{i=1}^{n} (x_i - \hat{\mu})^2. \tag{1}$$

From Central Limit Theorem, it can be derived that the estimate of the sample mean $\hat{\mu}$ has normal distribution $\mathcal{N}(0, \frac{1}{n})$, and the estimate of the sample variance $(n-1)\hat{\sigma}^2$ has a Chi-square distribution $\chi^2(n-1)$ with $n-1$ degrees of freedom and variance equal to $2n - 2$ [6]. Note that both the distributions of sample mean and sample variance depend only on the number of samples n. Estimates (1) give the best log-likelihood on the training set, but since MLE does not involve any relation to the source distribution of the data, these estimates do not achieve the highest value of the log-likelihood for unseen data generated from the source distribution $\mathcal{N}(0, 1)$.

Since maximization of the log-likelihood of the model given data sampled from the source distribution is strongly related to the minimization of a KLD [7], we propose a new criterion based on KLD:

$$J(\alpha, n) = E_{\hat{\mu}, \hat{\sigma}^2} \left\{ D_{\mathrm{KL}}(\mathcal{N}(0, 1) \| \mathcal{N}(\hat{\mu}, \alpha\hat{\sigma}^2)) \right\}, \tag{2}$$

$$\hat{\mu} \sim \mathcal{N}(0, 1/n), \quad (n-1)\hat{\sigma}^2 \sim \chi^2(n-1)$$

$$J(\alpha, n) = \iint D_{\mathrm{KL}}(\mathcal{N}(0, 1) \| \mathcal{N}(\hat{\mu}, \alpha\hat{\sigma}^2)) p_{\hat{\mu}} p_{\hat{\sigma}^2} \mathrm{d}\hat{\mu} \mathrm{d}\hat{\sigma}^2, \tag{3}$$

where $E_{\hat{\mu}, \hat{\sigma}^2}\{\}$ denotes the expectation computed over parameters $\hat{\mu}$, $\hat{\sigma}^2$; α is the unknown scaling factor of the sample variance, and $p_{\hat{\mu}}$, $p_{\hat{\sigma}^2}$ are the prior distributions (normal and scaled χ^2) of sample mean and sample variance, respectively. Thus, we measure how much information is lost when the source distribution $\mathcal{N}(0, 1)$ is approximated by the estimated model $\mathcal{N}(\hat{\mu}, \alpha\hat{\sigma}^2)$. The task is to find an optimal scaling factor α, which depends on the number of samples n and provides the best match of the sample model and the source distribution.

Given the assumptions above the KLD is equal to:

$$D_{\mathrm{KL}}(\mathcal{N}(0, 1) \| \mathcal{N}(\hat{\mu}, \alpha\hat{\sigma}^2)) = \frac{1}{2} \left(\frac{\hat{\mu}^2}{\alpha\hat{\sigma}^2} + \frac{1}{\alpha\hat{\sigma}^2} + \ln \alpha + \ln \hat{\sigma}^2 - 1 \right) \tag{4}$$

Before the derivation of the solution of (3), let us define:

$$Q(n) = \int_0^\infty \frac{1}{\hat{\sigma}^2} p_{\hat{\sigma}^2} d\hat{\sigma}^2 = G(n) \int_0^\infty \frac{1}{\hat{\sigma}^2} (\hat{\sigma}^2)^{n/2-1} \exp\left(-\frac{1}{2}\hat{\sigma}^2\right) d\hat{\sigma}^2, \quad (5)$$

$$G(n) = (2^{n/2} \Gamma(n/2))^{-1}, \quad (6)$$

where $G(n)$ is the normalization term guaranteeing that the χ^2 probability distribution function integrates to one. In order to get an analytical solution for $Q(n)$ let us use the integration by substitution, where the substitution $\delta = 1/\hat{\sigma}^2$ is used. Then, it is easy to show that [6]:

$$Q(n) = G(n) \int_0^\infty \delta \left[\delta^{-n/2-1} \exp\left(-\frac{1}{2\delta}\right) \right] d\delta$$

$$= \int_0^\infty \delta \, p_\delta \, d\delta = \frac{1}{n-2}, \quad n > 2, \quad (7)$$

where p_δ is the Inv-$\chi^2(n)$ distribution with n degrees of freedom, therefore (7) is in fact the mean of this distribution.

Now, substituting for KLD in (3) from (4) and utilizing (7) we get:

$$J(\alpha, n) = const + \frac{1}{2}\left(\frac{1}{\alpha}\int_{-\infty}^\infty \hat{\mu}^2 p_{\hat{\mu}} d\hat{\mu} \int_0^\infty \frac{1}{\hat{\sigma}^2} p_{\hat{\sigma}^2} d\hat{\sigma}^2 + \frac{1}{\alpha}\int_0^\infty \frac{1}{\hat{\sigma}^2} p_{\hat{\sigma}^2} d\hat{\sigma}^2 + \ln \alpha\right)$$

$$= const + \frac{1}{2}\left(\frac{n-1}{n\alpha}Q(n-1) + \frac{n-1}{\alpha}Q(n-1) + \ln \alpha\right)$$

$$= const + \frac{(n+1)(n-1)}{2n\alpha}Q(n-1) + \frac{1}{2}\ln \alpha, \quad (8)$$

where $const$ represents the part of the criterion independent of α. To find the minimum of (8), the partial derivative is taken with respect to the unknown parameter α. Setting the derivative to zero yields:

$$\frac{\partial J}{\partial \alpha} = 0 \implies \frac{1}{2\alpha} - \frac{(n^2-1)}{2n\alpha^2}Q(n-1) = 0, \quad (9)$$

$$\alpha_n = \frac{n^2-1}{n}Q(n-1) = \frac{n^2-1}{n(n-3)}. \quad (10)$$

It should be stated that $Q(n-1)$ given in (7) has no solution for $n < 4$. However, sometimes also models for a low amount of samples may be requested (such situation may occur quite often when estimating GMM parameters, see Section 3). Therefore, we extrapolated the α values in order to get the solution for $n > 1$. The function used for extrapolation was a rational one, what is in agreement with the solution given in (10). Moreover, we request that the first derivative and the value at the point $n = 3.5$ (this point was taken to match the experimental values for $n < 4$ reported below) of the extrapolation function and function given by equation (10) are equal. The form of the extrapolation function is:

$$\alpha_n = \frac{66.83}{n-1} - 20.31, \quad (11)$$

which goes to infinity at the point $n = 1$.

To support the analytically derived values we performed several experiments. At first we draw a large amount of n-tuples for a specific value of n, and computed sample mean and sample variance of samples in each tuple. Next, we took each sample mean and sample variance computed in the previous step, multiplied the sample variance by one specific value of α, evaluated the KLD (4) for each sample mean and scaled sample variance, and computed the mean $m_{\alpha,n}^{\mathrm{KLD}}$ across all the obtained KLDs. This was repeated for various values of α. Finally, the optimal value α^* was the one which gave minimal $m_{\alpha,n}^{\mathrm{KLD}}$, thus $\alpha^* = \arg\min_\alpha m_{\alpha,n}^{\mathrm{KLD}}$. The process was repeated several times, hence the optimal value of α was a random variable. The graph of optimal variance scaling factors α^* obtained analytically and experimentally is depicted in Figure 1, note that for increasing n the value of α^* converges to 1.

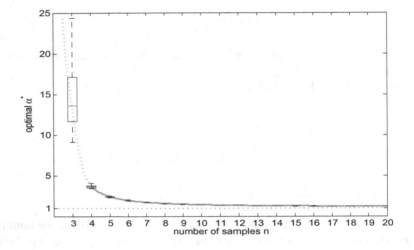

Fig. 1. Dependence of the optimal value of variance scaling factor α on the number of samples. The solid line represents the optimal values given by the analytical solution (10), the dotted line represents the extrapolation (11). The edges of the boxes represent the 25th and 75th percentile of the optimal α^* computed using the Monte Carlo simulations described in the text, and the line inside the box is the median value.

2.1   Additional Notes

- When deriving the multiplication factor α, for simplicity the source distribution was assumed standard normal $\mathcal{N}(0,1)$. Without any loss of generality the solution is valid also for the more general case of the source distribution $\mathcal{N}(\mu, \sigma^2)$, but the derivations would involve additional shifting and scaling.
- The solutions (10) and (11) can be used also for non-integer values, e.g. in the estimation process of GMM discussed below.
- As illustrated in Figure 1 and from the fact that for $n < 4$ analytical solution for α is not defined, models estimated from such a low amount of samples are unreliable. Hence, a careful consideration should precede before they are used.

- By now, only a univariate case was assumed. In the multivariate case with a diagonal covariance matrix, individual dimensions are mutually independent. Therefore, the scaling factor α can be applied on each diagonal element of the covariance matrix separately (recall that α depends only on the number of training data).
- Dealing with multivariate normal distributions with full covariance matrices is considerably more difficult. A method based on two multiplicative constants, one for diagonal and one for non-diagonal elements of the covariance matrix, was proposed in [8].

3 Robust Estimation of Parameters of a GMM

In the case of a Gaussian mixture model with diagonal covariance matrix, the conclusions made in the previous section may be used. Thus, variance of individual Gaussians is multiplied by the scaling factor α_n in dependence on the number of samples accounted for this Gaussian. However, rather than an exact number of samples accounted for each Gaussian, a soft count n_m^s is given for each Gaussian $m = 1, \ldots, M$:

$$n_m^s = \sum_{t=1}^{n} \gamma_{mt}, \quad \gamma_{mt} = \frac{\omega_m \mathcal{N}(\boldsymbol{x}_t; \boldsymbol{\mu}_m, \boldsymbol{C}_m)}{\sum_{i=1}^{M} \omega_i \mathcal{N}(\boldsymbol{x}_t; \boldsymbol{\mu}_i, \boldsymbol{C}_i)} \tag{12}$$

where γ_{mt} is the a-posterior probability of feature vector $\boldsymbol{x}_t$ occupying m-th Gaussian in the GMM, n is the overall number of samples, ω_m is the weight of the m-th Gaussian. Now, new ML estimates of mean vectors $\hat{\boldsymbol{\mu}}_m$ and diagonal covariance matrices $\hat{\boldsymbol{C}}_m$ of a GMM are computed as:

$$\hat{\boldsymbol{\mu}}_m = \frac{1}{n_m^s} \sum_{t=1}^{n} \gamma_{mt} \boldsymbol{x}_t, \tag{13}$$

$$\hat{\boldsymbol{C}}_m = \operatorname{diag}\left(\frac{1}{n_m^s} \sum_{t=1}^{n} \gamma_{mt} (\boldsymbol{x}_t - \hat{\boldsymbol{\mu}}_m)(\boldsymbol{x}_t - \hat{\boldsymbol{\mu}}_m)^{\mathrm{T}} \right), \tag{14}$$

where the function diag() zeros the non-diagonal elements.

As discussed in Section 2, the distribution of diagonal elements of sample covariance matrix $\hat{\boldsymbol{C}}_m$ is the scaled $\chi^2(n_m^e - 1)$ distribution with variance $n_m^e - 1$, but note that n_m^e does not equal n_m^s. The value of n_m^e will depend on a-posteriors γ_{mt}, and in order to derive the correct value we will proceed as follows.

Given two sample sets X_a of size n_a and X_b of size n_b drawn from $\mathcal{N}(0, 1)$, the variance of the sample mean of each set will be $1/n_a$ and $1/n_b$. Note that the variance of the total sum of sample sets X_a, X_b is:

$$\operatorname{var}\left(\sum_{x \in X_a} x \right) = n_a, \quad \operatorname{var}\left(\sum_{x \in X_b} x \right) = n_b. \tag{15}$$

Now, let all the samples in the set X_a be weighted by a scalar a and the samples in X_b by a scalar b. The variance of the total sum of sample sets X_a, X_b changes to:

$$\operatorname{var}\left(\sum_{x \in X_a} ax \right) = a^2 n_a, \quad \operatorname{var}\left(\sum_{x \in X_b} bx \right) = b^2 n_b. \tag{16}$$

Let X_c be the set constructed from all of the weighted samples from both X_a and X_b. The weighted sample mean and the variance of the total sum of samples in X_c are given by formulas:

$$\hat{\mu}_c = \frac{\sum_{x \in X_a} ax + \sum_{x \in X_b} bx}{an_a + bn_b},$$ (17)

$$\text{var}\left(\sum_{x \in X_a} ax + \sum_{x \in X_b} bx\right) = a^2 n_a + b^2 n_b,$$ (18)

respectively, and therefore for the variance of the weighted sample mean $\hat{\mu}_c$ we get:

$$\text{var}(\hat{\mu}_c) = \frac{a^2 n_a + b^2 n_b}{(an_a + bn_b)^2}.$$ (19)

In the case, where each sample in the set X_c is weighted by a different weight c_i, equation (19) changes to:

$$\text{var}(\hat{\mu}_c) = \frac{\sum_{i=1}^{n_c} c_i^2}{\left(\sum_{i=1}^{n_c} c_i\right)^2}.$$ (20)

Comparing the variance of weighted and unweighted sample mean, the equivalent number of unweighted samples n^e can be derived:

$$\frac{1}{n^e} = \frac{\sum_{i=1}^{n_c} c_i^2}{\left(\sum_{i=1}^{n_c} c_i\right)^2}, \quad n^e = \frac{\left(\sum_{i=1}^{n_c} c_i\right)^2}{\sum_{i=1}^{n_c} c_i^2}.$$ (21)

Hence, in the case of mth Gaussian in the GMM the value of n_m^e is given as:

$$n_m^e = \frac{\left(\sum_{t=1}^{n} \gamma_{mt}\right)^2}{\sum_{t=1}^{n} \gamma_{mt}^2}.$$ (22)

Note that the value of n_m^e is a real number, but this is not a problem since both (10) and (11) are defined also for non-integer values.

3.1 Robust Update of GMM Variances

According to equations derived above, the robust estimation of GMM consists of steps:

1. Compute new maximum likelihood estimate of means (13) and covariances (14) of the GMM.
2. Evaluate the value of n_m^e given in (22) for each $m = 1, \ldots, M$.
3. Compute the scaling factor α_{m,n_m^e} for each Gaussian $m = 1, \ldots, M$ given the respective n_m^e.
4. Multiply diagonal elements of each covariance matrix $\hat{C}_m$ by α_{m,n_m^e}.

We performed simple experiments, which demonstrate the effect of the proposed procedure. Results are given in Figure 2. Note that when the GMM components with $n_m^e < 4$ are discarded during the estimation process, the log-likelihood of the test (unseen) samples is higher. Since the training of a GMM is an iterative procedure, the number of equivalent samples n_m^e is determined in each iteration for each GMM component m. Thus, the number of GMM components is controlled through the entire estimation. Hence, a GMM with a proper number of components is obtained at the end of the estimation.

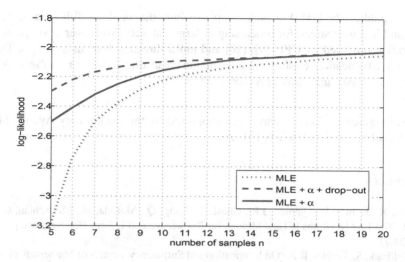

Fig. 2. Dependence of the log-likelihood of a GMM given a large number of samples generated from the source distrubtion on the number of samples used to train the GMM. The source distribution of samples is represented by a GMM with 2 components, from which limited amount of data is sampled. In common, 3 GMMs with 2 components were trained, but only from the limited number of samples (x-axis) generated from the source distribution. Dotted line represents the baseline (GMM trained via MLE, no variance adjustments); in the case of the solid line MLE estimates of the GMM's variance were multiplied by the optimal scaling factor α; in the case of the dashed line the scaling factor α was used and GMM components with $n_m^e < 4$ were discarded during the estimation process (only a single Gaussian model was used). The experiment was run a large number of times, and for each number of training samples (x-axis) the mean value of log-likelihood, obtained in each run of the experiment, was computed.

4   Conclusions

The paper investigated the estimation of parameters of Gaussian models in cases with low amount of training data. It was shown that the model trained via MLE does not generalize well to unseen data. We have demonstrated how to adjust the parameters if the source distribution of test and training data is identical. The method is based on the Kullback-Leibler divergence, we adjust the variance of the model multiplying it by a scaling factor α, which depends only on the number of samples.

Through the paper a crucial assumption was made that the samples are mutually independent. However, this is often not the case in real applications (e.g. time series of a measurement), where instead of number of given samples one should estimate the number of independent samples. I.e. the information content present in a set of mutually dependent samples is lower than the information content in a sample set of the same size containing independent samples. Therefore, the estimated number of independent samples should be lower. Technique aimed to estimate the independent number of samples was investigated in [8].

The proposed estimation updates were incorporated into the GMM estimation software implemented at the Faculty of Applied Sciences, University of West Bohemia,

Czech Republic. The GMM estimator supports both diagonal and full covariance matrices, and it is well suited for processing of large datasets. Moreover, it supports also acceleration provided by GPU [9], [10] and multi-threaded SSE instructions. The license is free for academic use. More information are available at http://www.kky. zcu.cz/en/sw/gmm-estimator.

Acknowledgments. This research was supported by the Technology Agency of the Czech Republic, project No. TA01011264.

References

[1] Wu, X., Kumar, V., Quinlan, J.R., Ghosh, J., Yang, Q., Motoda, H., McLachlan, G.J., et al.: Top 10 Algorithms in Data Mining. In: Knowledge and Information Systems, pp. 1–37 (2007)

[2] Kullback, S., Leibler, R.A.: On Information and Sufficiency. Annals of Mathematical Statistics 22, 79–86 (1951)

[3] Bell, P.: Full Covariance Modelling for Speech Recognition. Ph.D. Thesis, The University of Edinburgh (2010)

[4] Figueiredo, M., Leitão, J., Jain, A.: On Fitting Mixture Models. In: Hancock, E.R., Pelillo, M. (eds.) EMMCVPR 1999. LNCS, vol. 1654, pp. 54–69. Springer, Heidelberg (1999)

[5] Paclík, P., Novovičová, J.: Number of Components and Initialization in Gaussian Mixture Model for Pattern Recognition. In: Proc. Artificial Neural Nets and Genetic Algorithms, pp. 406–409. Springer, Wien (2001)

[6] Taboga, M.: Lectures on Probability Theory and Mathematical Statistics. CreateSpace Independent Publishing Platform (2008) ISBN: 978-1480215238

[7] Bishop, C.M.: Pattern Recognition and Machine Learning, 1st edn. Springer (2007) ISBN: 978-0387310732

[8] Vanek, J., Machlica, L., Psutka, J.V., Psutka, J.: Covariance Matrix Enhancement Approach to Train Robust Gaussian Mixture Models of Speech Data. In: SPECOM (2013)

[9] Machlica, L., Vanek, J., Zajic, Z.: Fast Estimation of Gaussian Mixture Model Parameters on GPU using CUDA. In: Proc. PDCAT, Gwangju, South Korea (2011)

[10] Vanek, J., Trmal, J., Psutka, J.V., Psutka, J.: Optimized Acoustic Likelihoods Computation for NVIDIA and ATI/AMD Graphics Processors. IEEE Transactions on Audio, Speech and Language Processing 20(6), 1818–1828 (2012)

Set Distance Functions
for 3D Object Recognition*

Luís A. Alexandre

Instituto de Telecomunicações, Univ. Beira Interior, Covilhã, Portugal

Abstract. One of the key steps in 3D object recognition is the matching between an input cloud and a cloud in a database of known objects. This is usually done using a distance function between sets of descriptors. In this paper we propose to study how several distance functions (some already available and other new proposals) behave experimentally using a large freely available household object database containing 1421 point clouds from 48 objects and 10 categories. We present experiments illustrating the accuracy of the distances both for object and category recognition and find that simple distances give competitive results both in terms of accuracy and speed.

1 Introduction

There is a growing interest in the use of 3D point cloud images for many tasks, since the recent introduction of cheap sensors that produce RGB plus depth images, such as the Microsoft Kinect or the Asus Xtion.

One of the most challenging tasks to be achieved with such data is to recognize objects in a scene. An important part of the process of recognition is to be able to compare the representations of the input (test or probe) data against stored (train or gallery) data. The objects are usually represented by sets of descriptors. Several distances exist that are able to work with sets of descriptors, notably the Pyramid Match Kernel [1], for object recognition from images.

It is important to obtain a quantitative notion of the performance of such distance functions. In this paper we present a comparison between 8 distance functions for 3D object recognition from point clouds. Two types of descriptors are used and the relative distance performance is similar in both cases. We show both the object and category accuracies that can be obtained from these distances and also the computational cost in terms of the time it takes to process the test set used. From the experiments we conclude that good performance can be obtained using quite simple distance functions, both in terms of accuracy and speed.

The rest of the paper is organized as follows: the next section presents an overview of the 3D object recognition pipeline used in this paper, the following section explains the descriptors used; section 4 presents the distances that are evaluated; section 5 contains the experiments and the paper ends with the conclusions in section 6.

---

* We acknowledge the financial support of project PEst-OE/EEI/LA0008/2013.

J. Ruiz-Shulcloper and G. Sanniti di Baja (Eds.): CIARP 2013, Part I, LNCS 8258, pp. 57–64, 2013.

2   The 3D Object Recognition Pipeline

The input cloud goes through a keypoint extraction algorithm, the Harris3D keypoint detector implemented in PCL [2]. The covariance matrix of the surface normals on a point neighborhood is used to find the point's response to the detector. Then descriptors are obtained on the extracted keypoints and these form a set that is used to represent the input cloud. This set is matched against sets already present in the object database and the one with largest similarity (smallest distance) is considered the match for the input cloud.

3   Descriptors

In this paper we use the two descriptors that produced the best results in the comparative evaluation performed in [3]. They both use color information.

The first one is the Point Feature Histograms (PFH) [4]. This descriptor's goal is to generalize both the surface normals and the curvature estimates.

Given two points, p and q, a fixed reference frame, consisting of the three unit vectors (u, v, w), is built centered on p using the following procedure: 1) the vector u is the surface normal at p; 2) $v = u \times \frac{p-q}{d}$ 3) $w = u \times v$; where $d = \|p-q\|_2$. Using this reference frame, the difference between the normals at p (n_p) and q (n_q), can be represented by : 1) $\alpha = \arccos(v \cdot n_q)$; 2) $\phi = \arccos(u \cdot (p-q)/d)$; 3) $\theta = \arctan(w \cdot n_p, u \cdot n_p)$.

The angles α, ϕ, θ and the distance d are computed for all pairs in the k-neighborhood of point p. In fact, usually the distance d is dropped as it changes with the viewpoint, keeping only the 3 angles. These are binned into an 125-bin histogram by considering that each of them can fall into 5 distinct bins, and the final histogram encodes in each bin a unique combination of the distinct values for each of the angles. One of these 125-bin histograms is produced for each input point.

The version of PFH used in this paper includes color information and is called PFHRGB. This variant includes three additional histograms, one for the ratio between each color channel of p and the same channel of q. These histograms are binned as the 3 angles of PFH and hence produce another 125 float values, giving the total size of 250 values for the PFHRGB descriptor.

The second descriptor used is the SHOTCOLOR [5]. This descriptor is based on the SHOT descriptor [6], that obtains a repeatable local reference frame using the eigenvalue decomposition around an input point. Given this reference frame, a spherical grid centered on the point divides the neighborhood so that in each grid bin a weighted histogram of normals is obtained. The descriptor concatenates all such histograms into the final signature. It uses 9 values to encode the reference frame and the authors propose the use of 11 shape bins and 32 divisions of the spherical grid, which gives an additional 352 values. The descriptor is normalized to sum 1. The SHOTCOLOR adds color information (based on the CIELab color space) to the SHOT descriptor. It uses 31 bins each with 32 divisions yielding 992 values, plus the 352 from the SHOT which gives the total of 1344 values (plus 9 values to describe the local reference frame). The histograms in this case store the L_1 distance between the CIELab color of a point and the color of its neighbors.

4   Set Distances

The focus of this paper is on the distance function that should be used when comparing two point clouds that are represented by sets of descriptors. Note that the word "distance" should be interpreted loosely since some of the functions presented below do not verify all the conditions of a norm (for instance, D_4 and D_5 can produce a value of zero even if the two input clouds are not the same).

A descriptor can be seen as a point in $X \subset \mathbb{R}^n$. We investigate the performance of functions that receive two sets of descriptors, $A \subseteq X$ and $B \subseteq X$, with a possible different number of elements, $|A| \neq |B|$, and return a (distance) value in $\mathbb{R}$.

We will use below the following distances between descriptors (not sets) $x, y \in X$:

$$L_p(x, y) = \left(\sum_{i=1}^{n} | x(i) - y(i) |^p \right)^{1/p}, \; p = 1, 2$$

$$d_{\chi^2}(x, y) = \frac{1}{2} \sum_{i=1}^{n} \frac{(x(i) - y(i))^2}{x(i) + y(i)}.$$

We will assign a code to each set distance in the form D_z, where z is an integer to make it easier to refer to the several distances throughout the paper.

4.1   Hausdorff Distance

Consider $S(X)$ to be the set of subsets of X that are closed, bounded and non-empty. Let $A, B \in S(X)$. The Hausdorff distance, D_1, between sets A and B is defined as

$$D_1(A, B) = \max\{\sup\{d(a, B) \mid a \in A\}, \sup\{d(b, A) \mid b \in B\}\}$$

where $d(a, B)$ is a distance between a point a and a set B, defined by

$$d(a, B) = \min\{d(a, b_i), \; i = 1, \ldots, |B|\}$$

and $d(a, b_i)$ is the distance between two points a and b_i in $\mathbb{R}^n$. In our case we use the L_1 distance between two points.

4.2   Pyramid Match Kernel

The pyramid match kernel (D_2) [1] uses a hierarchical approach to matching the sets. It finds the similarity between two sets as the weighted sum of the number of feature matchings found at each level of a pyramid.

Consider the input space X of sets of n-dimensional vectors bounded by a sphere of diameter D. The feature extraction function is

$$\Psi(x) = [H_{-1}(x), H_0(x), \ldots, H_L(x)]$$

where $L = \lceil \log_2 D \rceil + 1$, $x \in X$, $H_i(x)$ is a histogram vector formed over data x using n-dimensional bins of side length 2^i. Then, the pyramid referred above is given by:

$$K_\Delta(\Psi(y), \Psi(z)) = \sum_{i=0}^{L} N_i/2^i$$

where N_i is the number of newly matched pairs at level i. A new match at level i is defined as a pair of features that were not in correspondence at an finer level $(j < i)$ became in correspondence at level i. To become in correspondence means that both fall in the same histogram bin.

4.3   Other Set Distances

We propose to evaluate also the following set distances, that are all variations around the same theme: use statistical measures like the mean, standard variation, maximum and minimum of the points in each set to develop simple representations for the set. The goal is to search for a simple set distance that produces accurate results and at the same time is fast, such that, other things permitting (the time the keypoints take to be detected plus the time the descriptor takes to extract) would allow for real time cloud processing.

Below we use $a_j(i)$ to refer to the coordinate i of the descriptor j.

The distance D_3 is obtained by finding the minimum and maximum values for each coordinate in each set and sum the L_1 distances between them

$$D_3 = L_1(\min{}_A, \min{}_B) + L_1(\max{}_A, \max{}_B)$$

where

$$\min{}_A(i) = \min_{j=1,\ldots,|A|} \{a_j(i)\}, \ i = 1, \ldots, n$$

and

$$\max{}_A(i) = \max_{j=1,\ldots,|A|} \{a_j(i)\}, \ i = 1, \ldots, n$$

and likewise for $\min_B(i)$ and $\max_B(i)$.

The next two distances are simply the distance between the centroids of each set, c_A and c_B respectively, using the descriptor distances L_1 and L_2:

$$D_4 = L_1(c_A, c_B) \ \text{ and } \ D_5 = L_2(c_A, c_B) \ .$$

Distance D_6 is the sum of D_4 with the L_1 distance between the standard deviation for each dimension (coordinate) of each set:

$$D_6 = D_4 + L_1(std_A, std_B)$$

where

$$std_A(i) = \sqrt{\frac{1}{|A|-1} \sum_{j=1}^{|A|} (a_j(i) - c_A(i))^2}, \ i = 1, \ldots, n$$

and likewise for std_B.

Distance D_7 is similar to D_6 but instead of using the L_1 distance uses the d_{χ^2} distance between two vectors:

$$D_7 = d_{\chi^2}(c_A, c_B) + d_{\chi^2}(std_A, std_B) \ .$$

The final distance to be evaluated consists on the average L_1 distance between all points in one set to all the points in the other (the normalized average linkage set distance):

$$D_8 = \frac{1}{|A||B|} \sum_{i=1}^{|A|} \sum_{j=1}^{|B|} L_1(a_i, b_j) \ .$$

5   Experiments

5.1   Dataset

We used a subset of the large dataset of 3D point clouds from [7]. The original dataset contains 300 objects from 51 different categories captured on a turntable from 3 different camera poses. We used 48 objects representing 10 categories. The training data contain clouds captured from two different camera views, and the test data contains clouds captured using a third different view. The training set has a total of 946 clouds while the test set contains 475 clouds. Since for each test cloud we do an exhaustive search through the complete training set to find the best match, this amounts to a total of 449.350 cloud comparisons for each of the evaluated descriptors and each of the distance functions used.

5.2   Setup

The code used in the experiments was developed in C++ using the PCL library [2] on a linux machine. The code used for D_2 was from [8]. We used the UniformPyramidMaker with the following parameters obtained from experiments with a 10% subset of the one used in the final evaluation: finest_side_length $= (1/250, 10^{-4})$, discretize_order$=(3, 3)$ and side_length_factor$=(2, 2)$ for (PFHRGB, SHOTCOLOR), respectively. To make a fair comparison between the distances, all steps in the pipeline are equal.

The descriptors are found on the keypoints obtained using the Harris3D keypoint detector with the following parameters: the radius for normal estimation and non-maxima supression (Radius) was set to 0.01 and the sphere radius that is to be used for determining the nearest neighbors used for the keypoint detection (RadiusSearch) was also set to 0.01.

The only parameter needed for the descriptor calculation is the sphere radius that is to be used for determining the nearest neighbors used in its calculation. It was set at 0.05 for both descriptors.

Table 1. Category and object recognition accuracy and the time used for evaluating the test set in seconds, for the different distances and descriptors

	PFHRGB Accuracy[%]			SHOTCOLOR Accuracy[%]		
Distance	Category	Object	Time[s]	Category	Object	Time[s]
D_1	91.14	70.04	1914	67.72	44.09	175
D_2	63.92	42.19	2197	26.58	17.93	1510
D_3	88.82	67.93	1889	88.82	67.72	132
D_4	90.93	75.95	1876	87.97	69.20	137
D_5	82.70	67.72	1886	79.75	55.49	134
D_6	93.88	78.06	1891	87.76	65.82	134
D_7	94.73	79.96	1894	88.19	65.82	127
D_8	77.64	60.13	1914	71.73	41.35	174

5.3   Results

Table 1 and figure 1 contain the results of the experiments done.

An object is considered to be recognized when an input cloud is matched by one of the views of the same object in the database, whereas a category is considered to be recognized when the input cloud is matched to a view of any of the objects that are in the same category as the input object. So, category recognition is an easier task than that of object recognition, since in the latter case the system needs to distinguish between the (similar) objects within a given category. That category recognition is easier than object recognition can be seen in table 1. For all distance functions, category accuracy is always higher than object recognition.

Regarding the accuracies obtained, these results show the importance of choosing a good distance function. For a given descriptor there are considerable variations in terms of accuracy: in terms of object recognition the results for the PFHRGB vary from around 42% to almost 80% whereas for the SHOTCOLOR descriptor the results vary from around 18% to over 69%.

The best results are obtained for the PFHRGB with distance D_7 and for the SHOTCOLOR with distance D_3 for category recognition and D_4 for object recognition.

From the recall × (1-precision) curves in figure 1, we note that the results can be grouped into three sets: the best results for both descriptors, and with similar curves, are obtained with distances D_4, D_6 and D_7 (for SHOTCOLOR, D_3 is also on this first group). The second group contains the distances D_1, D_5 and D_8 (D_3 is in this second group for PFHRGB) that show a decrease in performance when compared with the first group. The difference in performance from group 1 to group 2 is larger with SHOTCOLOR than with PFHRGB. This might have to do with the fact that SHOTCOLOR works on a much higher dimensional space (1344) than PFHRGB (250). Distance D_2 is the sole member of the third group with a poor performance. We believe this might have to do with a poor choice of parameters. But having to choose 3 parameters for a distance that is very heavy

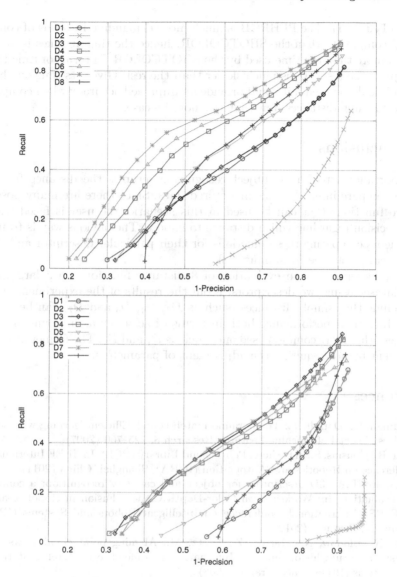

Fig. 1. Recall × (1-Precision) curves for the object recognition experiments using the PFHRGB (top) and SHOTCOLOR (bottom) descriptors (best viewed in color)

from a computational point of view is not an easy task and we might needed to spent more time searching for the optimal parameters to obtain a better result.

Distance D_4 is better than D_5 (these are simply the L_1 and L_2 distances between cloud centroids) for both descriptors, confirming the fact that the Euclidian distance is not appropriate for these high dimensional spaces.

The fifth and seventh columns of table 1 contain the time in seconds that took to run the evaluation (test set) on a 12 thread version using a i7-3930K@3.2GHz

CPU on Fedora 17. The PFHRGB is much more demanding in terms of computational complexity than the SHOTCOLOR, hence the time it takes is around
10 times more than the time used by the SHOTCOLOR. In terms of time taken
to complete the tests, D_2 is much slower than the rest. Given its time overhead,
D_2 should only be used if it could provide an improved accuracy when compared
to the remaining distances, but that was not the case.

6   Conclusions

An important part of a 3D object recognition setup is the distance function
used to compare input data against stored data. Since there are many possible
distance functions that can be used in this scenario, the user is faced with a
tough decision regarding which distance to choose. The obvious way is to make
experiments comparing these functions for their particular descriptor and data,
but this can be a time consuming task.

This paper presents an evaluation of 8 distance functions on a large point
cloud dataset using two descriptors. From the results of the experiments made
we conclude that simple distances (such as D_3, D_4, D_6 and D_7) can be a good
choice since their performance both in terms of accuracy as in terms of speed
surpasses other more common used ones such as D_1 and D_2. The former distances
also benefit by not requiring the adjustment of parameters.

References

1. Grauman, K., Darrell, T.: The pyramid match kernel: Efficient learning with sets of
   features. Journal of Machine Learning Research 8, 725–760 (2007)
2. Rusu, R., Cousins, S.: 3D is here: Point Cloud Library (PCL). In: IEEE International
   Conference on Robotics and Automation (ICRA), Shanghai, China (2011)
3. Alexandre, L.A.: 3D descriptors for object and category recognition: a comparative evaluation. In: Workshop on Color-Depth Camera Fusion in Robotics at the
   IEEE/RSJ International Conference on Intelligent Robots and Systems (IROS),
   Vilamoura, Portugal (2012)
4. Rusu, R., Blodow, N., Marton, Z., Beetz, M.: Aligning point cloud views using
   persistent feature histograms. In: International Conference on Intelligent Robots
   and Systems (IROS), Nice, France (2008)
5. Tombari, F., Salti, S., Di Stefano, L.: A combined texture-shape descriptor for enhanced 3D feature matching. In: IEEE International Conference on Image Processing
   (2011)
6. Tombari, F., Salti, S., Di Stefano, L.: Unique signatures of histograms for local
   surface description. In: Daniilidis, K., Maragos, P., Paragios, N. (eds.) ECCV 2010,
   Part III. LNCS, vol. 6313, pp. 356–369. Springer, Heidelberg (2010)
7. Lai, K., Bo, L., Ren, X., Fox, D.: A Large-Scale hierarchical Multi-View RGB-
   D object dataset. In: Proc. of the IEEE International Conference on Robotics &
   Automation, ICRA (2011)
8. Lee, J.J.: Libpmk: A pyramid match toolkit. Technical Report MIT-CSAIL-TR-
   2008-17, MIT Computer Science and Artificial Intelligence Laboratory (2008)

Single-Step-Ahead and Multi-Step-Ahead Prediction with Evolutionary Artificial Neural Networks

Víctor Manuel Landassuri-Moreno[1], Carmen L. Bustillo-Hernández[2], José Juan Carbajal-Hernández[2], and Luis P. Sánchez Fernández[2]

[1] Mexico Valley University Center (CUUAEM-VM) – Autonomous University of the State of Mexico, Boulevard Universitario, Predio San Javier, Atizapán de Zaragoza, Estado de México, C.P. 54500, México
[2] Center of Computer Research – National Polytechnic Institute. Av. Juan de Dios Bátiz s/n, Nueva Industrial Vallejo, Gustavo A. Madero, México D.F., C.P. 07738, México
vmlandassurim@uaemex.mx,
{chbustillo004,jcarbajalh,lsanchez}@cic.ipn.mx

Abstract. In recent years, Evolutionary Algorithms (EAs) have been remarkably useful to improve the robustness of Artificial Neural Networks (ANNs). This study introduces an experimental analysis using an EAs aimed to evolve ANNs architectures (the FS-EPNet algorithm) to understand how neural networks are evolved with a steady-state algorithm and compare the Single-step-ahead (SSP) and Multiple-step-ahead (MSP) methods for prediction tasks over two test sets. It was decided to test an inside-set during evolution and an outside-set after the whole evolutionary process has been completed to validate the generalization performance with the same method (SSP or MSP). Thus, the networks may not be correctly evaluated (misleading fitness) if the single SSP is used during evolution (inside-set) and then the MSP at the end of it (outside-set). The results show that the same prediction method should be used in both evaluation sets providing smaller errors on average.

Keywords: evolutionary algorithms, artificial neural networks, EANNs, single-step-ahead prediction, multi-step-ahead prediction.

1 Introduction

Artificial Neural Networks (ANNs) are mathematical models inspired by the structural and functional organization of biological neural networks. They are characterized by having input, hidden and output units with interconnection between them, where each connection has an associated weight which is updated during the training phase to allow the network to learn a given task. Since their origin, they have been used to solve control [1], classification [2, 3] and prediction [4] tasks, showing a performance and adaptability superior to those of conventional mathematical models. Even though neural networks have proved to be a robust method for solving different kinds of problem, they involve several different parameters that need to be chosen appropriately to obtain a functional network. Early studies used to select many of those parameters by trial and error [5]. Another difficulty is that some of these

J. Ruiz-Shulcloper and G. Sanniti di Baja (Eds.): CIARP 2013, Part I, LNCS 8258, pp. 65–72, 2013.
© Springer-Verlag Berlin Heidelberg 2013

parameters may change over time, and thus more elaborate methods are needed to adjust them. On the other hand, ANNs and Evolutionary Algorithms (EAs) have been widely inspired by biological organisms, usually giving them superior performance when both are applied together to solve a problem than when they are applied in separate stages. Thus, Evolutionary Artificial Neural Networks (EANN), have been remarkably useful at adapting the ANNs' parameters during evolution [2, 6, 7]. This work uses the FS-EPNet algorithm [8], which is based on the EPNet algorithm [3], with the difference that the input Feature Selection is performed, i.e. the FS-EPNet algorithm evolves the inputs of ANNs.

The usage of EAs over ANNs requires an extra error-evaluation (inside-set to test), because during evolution several ANNs are evaluated (fitness assignment). Note that hand design ANNs (HDANNs), usually require one test set to measure the generalization performance. Therefore, there may be different evaluation sets within an EANN: validation set to discover overtraining; inside-set to obtain the fitness of an individual during evolution, and a final test set called outside-set to evaluate the generalization performance after the evolution has finished. In this way, inside and outside terms are used to make reference to performance evaluation, during and after the evolutionary process has been completed. Besides test sets, a prediction method is needed; e.g. the Single-step-ahead (SSP) and Multiple-step-ahead (MSP) prediction methods. It may be worth to remark that those methods have been previously used in econometrics [17]; nevertheless, they have not been used before with EANNs, as in this work.

Thus, this paper is aimed to compare SSP and MSP procedures over both test sets (inside and outside) to forecast two chaotic time series (TS): Lorenz and Mackey-Glass, usually tested in prediction tasks. Thus, the networks (evolved with the FS-EPNet algorithm) may not be correctly evaluated (misleading fitness) if the single SSP is used during evolution (inside-set) and then the MSP at the end of it (outside-set), i.e. both evaluations may be performed in the same terms. Moreover, no previous studies have been found explaining such scenario, which should be tested empirically.

2   FS-EPNet Algorithm

The FS-EPNet algorithm [8] is based upon the standard Evolutionary Programming (EP) approach, aimed at evolving ANN architectures and weights at the same time as obtaining smaller network topologies. The original algorithm (EPNet) [3] does not tackle the feature evolution; i.e. input adaptation in the same evolutionary process. However, further improvements consider their evolution [8]; i.e. Feature Selection EPNet algorithm (FS-EPNet), being the algorithm used during this empirical study. The FS-EPNet algorithm emphasizes the evolution of ANN behaviors by EP, like node-splitting, which maintains the behavioral (i.e. functional) link between the parent and its offspring. It does not have a crossover operator, nor a genotype to represent the individuals. Instead it carries out the evolutionary process by performing only nine different mutation operations directly on the phenotype as shown in Fig. 1: (1) hybrid training composed of training with the Modified Back Propagation (MBP) algorithm and Simulated Annealing (SA); (2) node deletion; (3) connection deletion; (4) input deletion; (5) delay deletion; (6) connection addition; (7) node addition; (8)

input addition; and (9) delay addition. The algorithm performs only one such mutation on the selected individual in each generation. The training in the EPNet algorithm is only a partial training; i.e. the networks are not trained until they converge. This is motivated by computational efficiency, which lets the evolution advance faster, with the individuals improving their fitness through the generations. For a more detailed description of the EPNet algorithm see [3, 8].

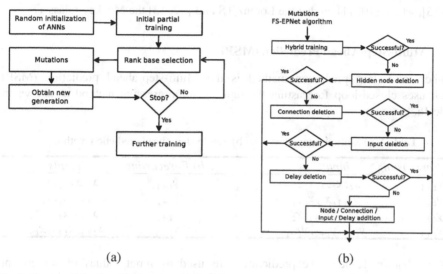

(a)   (b)

Fig. 1. Feature Selection EPNet algorithm (FS-EPNet); a) general procedure and b) FS-EPNet mutations

3   Time Series Prediction

For the Time Series (TS) prediction problem with ANNs, it is common to try to use a small subset of recent TS information to perform the prediction. Therefore, we are aiming to obtain accurate predictions using only a finite segment of previous values up to the point to be predicted. Thus we have:

$$x_{t+1} = f\left[x_t, x_{t-k}, x_{t-2k}, \dots, x_{t-(d-1)k}\right] \qquad (1)$$

where d is the number of inputs, k is the time delay and f is the method or algorithm that performs the prediction (the network for this work). There is one condition that needs to be satisfied: given an attractor of dimension D, we must have $d \geq 2D + 1$ [9]. There are two general ways to perform the prediction of TS in terms of the desired number of values to be forecast. Thus, assume the TS X is $[x_1, x_2, \dots, x_t]$, the number of points ahead to predict is n, the test set is $[x_{t+1}, x_{t+2}, \dots, x_{t+n}]$, and the forecast in the same interval is $[y_{t+1}, y_{t+2}, \dots, y_{t+n}]$. In the following examples (Table 1), we are assuming that the number of inputs (past information) is 3, delays are set at 1 and the prediction step is $\Delta t = 1$.

3.1   Single-Step-Ahead Prediction (SSP)

The simplest method is just to predict a value in the future, and we may call this method One-step or Open-loop or Single-step-ahead prediction (SSP). It is called Open-loop forecasting because a pattern is used to predict a value and no feedback is used to continue the predictions as in an autoregressive method. Table 1b shows the single-step prediction method. A sample of previous works that have used (SSP) are [10–13], where [10, 11] predict the Lorenz TS and [12, 13] the Mackey-Glass TS.

3.2   Multi-Step-Ahead Prediction (MSP)

Another interesting prediction method is the Multi-step-ahead prediction (MSP) which uses closed-loop forecasting through an autoregressive method as shown in Table 1a.

Table 1. a) Multiple-step-ahead and b) Single step-ahead prediction methods

a) Forecasting	inputs	b) Forecasting	inputs
y_{t+1}	x_t, x_{t-1}, x_{t-2}	y_{t+1}	x_t, x_{t-1}, x_{t-2}
y_{t+2}	y_{t+1}, x_t, x_{t-1}	y_{t+2}	x_{t+1}, x_t, x_{t-1}
y_{t+3}	y_{t+2}, y_{t+1}, x_t	y_{t+3}	x_{t+2}, x_{t+1}, x_t
y_{t+4}	$y_{t+3}, y_{t+2}, y_{t+1}$	y_{t+4}	$x_{t+3}, x_{t+2}, x_{t+1}$

Note that in Table 1 the predictions are used as input values in subsequent predictions; i.e. it is repeated one-step prediction several times, using the actual prediction to predict the next value. The input vector from the SSP (Table 1b) and MSP (Table 1a) methods may be seen as a window of d values with k delays that is moved one position ahead every time a value is predicted, to be ready to predict the next value. The real difference between both methods is that the SSP moves the window input vector over the original data available, meanwhile the MSP starts with the original data, overlap original and predicted data, and finish with predicted values in the window input vector. Previous publications that used the MSP method are [3, 14, 15], where [14, 15] are focused on the Lorenz TS and [3] predicting the Mackey-Glass TS.

3.3   MSP and SSP Comparison

For the previous section, it can be said that prediction tasks with SSP are similar to classification tasks as one input vector produce one output vector and there is no feedback in the output as in MSP. Having said that, a standard procedure in the literature is to evaluate an inside-set with the SSP method for classification and prediction tasks to obtain the itness of individuals. Moreover, any publication has been found so far that uses MSP over the inside-set, that kind of evaluation is never said and it may be assumed to be SSP as it is the standard.

4   Experimental Set-Up and Data Sets

As previously remarked, it was decided to use an extra test set during evolution as tasks solved with MSP require to test the fitness of individuals with the same method (MSP) when the evolution finish. Thus, the networks may not be correctly evaluated (misleading fitness) if the single SSP is used during evolution and then the MSP at the end of it. For example, it can be assumed that SSP method is easier than MSP by the feedback in the later, therefore, if a prediction task requiring MSP is evaluated with SSP during evolution (inside-set), it will probably produce a different fitness than if the MSP is used in the same inside-set, which could produce a bias in the selection process with networks not so fit. For that reason it was needed to use an extra test set in prediction tasks, so the validation set is used mainly to evolve the learning rate and the inside-set to measure the fitness as it were a real prediction. However, it may be expected to obtain a smaller fitness error during evolution with SSP than MSP. Besides these two sets, the training set was subdivided again (30 patterns) to have a validation set to avoid overtraining (Early Stopping) and provides the maximum generalization performance for the selected architecture. In this way the training may be stopped if over fitting is occurring. As validation set is independent of the task at hand, or the prediction method, it was used the SSP approach to introduce it after each epoch of the training process, as the standard in the literature.

There are some common parameters that were fixed for the experiments throughout this study: population size 30, generations of evolution 3000, initial connection density 30%, initial learning rate 0.15, minimum learning rate 0.01, epochs for learning rate adaptation 5, number of mutated hidden nodes 1, number of mutated connections 1-3, temperatures in SA 5, iterations per temperature in SA 100, 1500 epochs of training inside the FS-EPNet, and 2000 of further training at the end of the algorithm. The only stopping criterion was the number of generations. For all the experiments, 30 independent runs were performed to ensure statistical validity of the results. The inside-set was setup with 30 patterns to perform the prediction and the MSP is performed on the outside-set in all TS tested. Thus, from al data available, the last 100 patterns were taken for the final test set (outside-set) and the next 30 patterns for the inside-set to obtain the fitness of individuals, the rest of the data (from the beginning) was taken for the training set. All these parameters were set at convenient traditional values and are not intended to be optimal. Therefore, it is worth to say that those parameters were set up after some preliminary experiments and they have not been studied thoroughly to say they are the best. Further studies may optimize them.

Two chaotic TS were used to test the insights presented in this study: a) the first one is the Lorenz TS [16] generated with the fourth order Runge-Kutta method as done in [14], i.e. the following values are used to generate the TS: $\Delta t = 1$, $\sigma = 10$, $r = 28$, $\beta = 8/3$ and time step $= 0.05$ using 1000 values to train and 100 to test (outside-test); and b) the Mackey– Glass TS usually generated with fourth order Runge-Kutta method as Lorenz TS, where the parameters used here to generate it are: $x(0) = 1.2$, $\tau = 17$, $\alpha = 0.2$ and $\beta = -0.1$ as done in [3] using 500 values to train and 500 to test (outside-set). Therefore, the outside-set for Lorenz TS was set to 100 and for Mackey– Glass to 500 patterns, where the last part of the training set was subdivided into the inside-set as commented above. Note that in this work, the same parameters as the literature were replicated to have a fair comparison in the experimental results. Moreover, the FS-EPNet algorithm uses less patterns that in the literature to train the networks (as the inside-set is used), thus a drawback is induced, instead of giving an advantage. The Normalized Root Mean Squared Error (NRMSE) is used to measure the error in the inside and outside sets.

5   Experimental Results

This section presents the results from a set of experiments developed to determine if the usage of SSP in the inside-set may degrade the performance of task requiring MSP on the outside-set. To illustrate this, consider Fig. 2 for the best predictions found for the Lorenz with MSP (Fig. 2a and 2b) and SSP (Fig. 2c and 2d) on the inside-set during evolution and using MSP on the outside-set. Interestingly to note (and as previously expected), the average fitness of the networks evaluated with SSP on the inside-set have a lower error during all the evolutionary process than the fitness obtained from the MSP as can be seen in Fig. 3. The best prediction error on the inside-set at the end of the 3000 generations of evolution were smaller with the SSP than with the MSP as expected too (Table 2, NRMSE Inside-set row). It was also obtained a smaller error with the SSP on the average fitness over all independent trials as shown at the end of generations in Fig. 3. At the end of the evolution, even the network that uses MSP have a bigger fitness error in the inside-set, it obtained the smallest generalization error, with statistical significant having a $p\text{-}value < 0.01$ (Fig. 2a), because the selection mechanism during evolution was in the same terms as the generalization measurement.

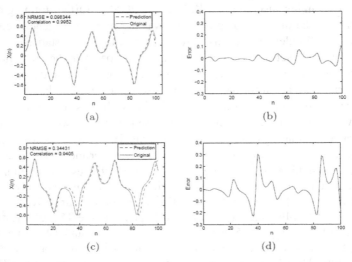

(a)

(b)

(c)

(d)

Fig. 2. Best predictions for Lorenz TS after 3000 generations, inside-set with MSP (Fig. 2a and 2b) and inside-set with SSP (Fig. 2c and 2d). Figs. 2b and 2d present the error in terms of $Y_i(t)-Z_i(t)$, where $Y_i(t)$ is the prediction at time t and $Z_i(t)$ is the original data to be predicted (outside-set)

Table 2 presents the individual parameters evolved for the Lorenz TS, showing how the NRMSE over the inside-set is smaller when the SSP is used during evolution than MSP, but the generalization performance is smaller when the MSP is used in both test sets. Also note that using SSP produces the convergence of delays as it is easier to predict with SSP than MSP for the feedback in the latter as previously remarked.

Table 2. Lorenz time series individual results

Parameter	MSP – MSP				SSP – MSP			
	Mean	Std Dev	Min	Max	Mean	Std Dev	Min	Max
Number of Inputs	6.70000	1.91455	3	10	6.13333	1.79526	3	9
Number of Delays	2.46666	0.93710	1	4	1	0	1	1
Number of Hidden Nodes	13.3333	4.25346	5	26	12.8	3.28423	6	18
Number of Connections	108.466	56.1989	39	351	92.9333	35.5614	43	172
NRMSE Validation Error	0.02475	0.02848	0.00062	0.12563	0.00145	0.00104	0.00035	0.00447
NRMSE Inside-set	0.01657	0.00775	0.00676	0.03480	0.00189	0.00084	0.00123	0.00477
NRMSE Outside-set	0.52301	0.26162	0.09834	0.92639	0.73256	0.23340	0.34431	1.20320

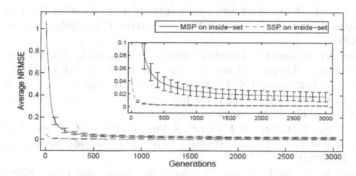

Fig. 3. Average fitness value of Lorenz TS with MSP and SSP over the inside-set

Comparing these results against results found in the literature, Dudul [14] obtain a NRMSE for the best individual with a State-space 8th order of NRMSE = 0.1822 and a NRMSE = 0.7325 with a Regularized ANN-ARMA, while the FS-EPNet obtain a NRMSE = 0.09834 (Table3) for the best individual found. To finalize the results of this work for the Mackey-Glass TS are similar for those presented for the previous case, nevertheless there was no statistically significance in the results. They are no presented here for space reasons.

6   Discussion and Conclusions

This work compares two prediction methods: Single step-ahead (SSP) and Multi-step-ahead, during the evolution of Artificial Neural Networks (ANNs) for time series (TS) prediction. The experiments were carried out using the FS-EPNet algorithm designed to evolve ANNs architectures and weights simultaneously through a steady-state procedure. From two chaotic TS tested (Lorenz and Mackey-Glass), it was determined that tasks that use SSP will use SSP for the fitness during evolution and to evaluate the generalization performance. Contrary, tasks that use MSP will use the same MSP method in both parts of the process. Further research is required to test a broad range of TS to generalize these results.

References

1. Stanley, K., Miikkulainen, R.: Evolving neural networks through augmenting topologies. Evolutionary Computation 10(2), 99–127 (2002)
2. Bullinaria, J.: Understanding the emergence of modularity in neural systems. Cognitive Science 31(4), 673–695 (2007)
3. Yao, X., Liu, Y.: A new evolutionary system for evolving artificial neural networks. IEEE Transactions on Neural Networks 8(3), 694–713 (1997)
4. Cholewo, T., Zurada, J.: Sequential network construction for time series pre¬diction. International Conference on Neural Networks 4, 2034–2038 (1997)
5. Bishop, M.: Neural Networks for Pattern Recognition. Oxford University Press (1995)
6. Yao, X.: Evolving artificial neural networks. Proceedings of the IEEE 87(9), 1423–1447 (1999)
7. Bullinaria, A.: Evolving neural networks: Is it really worth the effort? In: Proceedings of the European Symposium on Artificial Neural Networks, Evere, Belgium: d-side, pp. 267–272 (2005)
8. Landassuri, V., Bullinaria, J.: Feature selection in evolved artificial neural networks using the evolutionary algorithm EPNet. In: Proceedings of the 2009 UK Workshop on Computational Intelligence, UKCI '2009. University of Nottingham, Nottingham (2009)
9. Belaire, J., Contreras, D.: Recurrence plots in non-linear time series analysis: Free software. Journal of Statistical Software 7(9) (2002)
10. Rojas, I., Pomares, H., Bernier, J., Ortega, J., Pino, B., Pelayo, F., Prieto, A.: Time series analysis using normalized pg-rbf network with regression weights. Neurocomputing 42(1-4), 267–285 (2002)
11. Gholipour, A., Araabi, B., Lucas, C.: Predicting chaotic time series using neural and neurofuzzy models: A comparative study. Neural Processing Letters 24(3), 217–239 (2006)
12. Müller, K., Smola, A., Rätsch, G., Schökopf, B., Kohlmorgen, J., Vapnik, V.: Using support vector machines for time series prediction, pp. 243–253 (1999)
13. Müller, K.R., Smola, A., Rätsch, G., Schölkopf, B., Kohlmorgen, J., Vapnik, V.: Predicting time series with support vector machines. In: Gerstner, W., Hasler, M., Germond, A., Nicoud, J.-D. (eds.) ICANN 1997. LNCS, vol. 1327, pp. 999–1004. Springer, Heidelberg (1997)
14. Dudul, S.: Prediction of a Lorenz chaotic attractor using two-layer perceptron neural network. Applied Soft Computing 5(4), 333–355 (2005)
15. Guerra, F., Dos, S.: Multi-step ahead nonlinear identification of Lorenz's chaotic system using radial basis neural network with learning by clus¬tering and particle swarm optimization. Chaos, Solitons & Fractals 35(5), 967–979 (2008)
16. Lorenz, E.: Deterministic non periodic flow. Journal of Atmospheric Science 20, 130–141 (1963)
17. Hansen, L.P., Hodrick, R.J.: Forward Exchange Rates as Optimal Predictors of Future Spot Rates: An Econometric Analysis. Journal of Political Economy 88(5), 829–853 (1980)

Conformal Hough Transform
for 2D and 3D Cloud Points

Gehová López-González[1], Nancy Arana-Daniel[2],
and Eduardo Bayro-Corrochano[1]

[1] Department of Electrical Engineering and Computer Science, CINVESTAV,
Guadalajara, Jalisco, México
[2] CUCEI, University of Guadalajara, Guadalajara, Jalisco, México

Abstract. This work presents a new method to apply the Hough Transform to 2D and 3D cloud points using the conformal geometric algebra framework. The objective is to detect geometric entities, with the use of simple parametric equations and the properties of the geometric algebra. We show with real images and RGB-D data that this new method is very useful to detect lines and circles in 2D and planes and spheres in 3D.

1 Introduction

The Hough transform is an algorithm for feature extraction used in image analysis, computer vision, and digital image processing [4]. This technique collects imperfect instances of objects within a certain class of shapes by a voting procedure in accumulators or cells. This voting scheme is carried out in a parameter space, where candidate objects are obtained as local maximas in the accumulator space. The selection of the maxima of possible clusters are identified by a type of K-means algorithm. The Hough transform was developed for the identification of lines in the image [1], but later works extended the Hough transform to identifying positions of different shapes, for example circles or ellipses[2][3].

In this work, using the conformal geometric framework, we extend the randomized Hough transform to detect lines and circles in 2D cloud points of images and lines, planes, circles and spheres in 3D cloud points, obtained by 3D scanners and RGB-D sensors. We show the efficiency of our algorithm using real images and data of a RGB-D sensor.

This paper is organized as follows: Section II explains the Randomized Hough Transform. Section III presents a short introduction to geometric algebra and the operations that will be used in this work. Section IV outlines the conformal geometric algebra and the concepts used in the algorithm. Section V includes a description of the algorithm, and section VI discusses some algorithmic details. Section VII presents some experimental results. Finally section VIII is devoted to the conclusions.

2 Randomized Hough Transform

This work is an extension of the Randomized Hough Transform, RHT, [9]. The RHT is an algorithm proposed to solve the problems of the Hough Transform,

J. Ruiz-Shulcloper and G. Sanniti di Baja (Eds.): CIARP 2013, Part I, LNCS 8258, pp. 73–83, 2013.

HT. In the HT algorithm for each image pixel not only the cells of the possible entities are increased, but also of many other. This creates a problem to find the local maxima. Also the accumulator array is predefined by windowing and sampling the parameter space. For the correct detection of the entities we need a good parameter resolution. For this we need a big array that takes too much storage and computing time. Without some previous knownledge of the image is very hard to determine the size of the accumulator array. A bad accumulator array can lead to the next problems: a failure to detect some specific entities, difficulties in finding local maxima, low accuarcy, large storage and low speed.

The RHT solves these problems using parametric equations to only compute the posible entities and a dynamic accumulator array to solve the problems with the storage. By doing this the storage space is greatly reduced. Other concept added is a scalar δ used as tolerance for similitude. When the difference between two computed entities is smaller than δ, then we consider that the two are the same. This scalar is used to set the resolution of the accumulator array. If we increase δ the resolution and storage space will be lower.

The steps of the algorithm are:

1) Randomly take n points from the set, being n the number of points needed to define the entity.

2) Solve the parametric equations to get a candidate.

3) Search for the candidate in the dinamyc accumulator array. If the candidate is found increase the accumulator by one. Otherwise add a new cell for the candidate and set its accumulator to one.

4) If an accumulator surpasses a threshold, we check if the entity exists in the image. If it exists, we add it to a list of detected entities and delete from the set all the points that belong to it.

Finally, we must note that the RHT is a stochastic method which its performace depends on the selection of δ and the randomized selection of the points.

3   Geometric Algebra

Geometric algebra is a coordinate-free approach to geometry based on the algebras of Grassmann and Clifford [5][6][7].

Let $\mathbb{V}$ be a vector space of dimension n. We will define an algebra $\mathbb{G}_n$, called a geometric algebra. Let $e_1, e_2, ...e_n$ be a set of basis vectors of $\mathbb{V}^n$.

The product, called the geometric product, of 2 basis vectors is anticommutative, $e_j e_k = -e_k e_j, \forall j \neq k$. These basis vectors must square to 1 or -1; this means that there are positive integers, p and q, such that $n = p + q$ and $e_i^2 = 1$, $i = 1...p$, $e_i^2 = -1$, $i = p + 1, ...n$.

The product of elements of the basis of $\mathbb{G}_n$ will simply be denoted by juxtaposition. In this way, from any two basis vectors, e_j and e_k, a new element of the algebra is obtained, and denoted as $e_j e_k = e_{jk}$. This introduces the concep of grade. The product of n non-equal basis vectors will result in a new generator of grade n. An algebra with n basis vectors will have 2^n generators $\{1, e_1, ...e_n, e_{12}, ...e_{(n-1)n}, ...e_{1...n}\}$. The generator of grade n is called the unit pseudoscalar of the algebra, and is generally denoted by the letter I. The $\mathbb{G}_n$ is a direct sum of the linear subspaces of grades $0,1,2,...n$.

$$\mathbb{G}_n = \overset{0}{\bigwedge} \mathbb{V}_n \oplus \overset{1}{\bigwedge} \mathbb{V}_n \oplus \overset{2}{\bigwedge} \mathbb{V}_n \oplus ... \overset{n}{\bigwedge} \mathbb{V}_n \qquad (1)$$

A multivector $A \subset \mathbb{G}_n$ is separated in its blade elements of grade r as:

$$A = \langle A \rangle_0 + \langle A \rangle_1 + \langle A \rangle_2 + ... + \langle A \rangle_n = \sum_{r=0}^{n} \langle A \rangle_r \qquad (2)$$

The most commons operations in geometric algebra are

– Geometric product
$$C = AB \qquad (3)$$

It is associative, and distributive with respect to addition
For each $A \in G_n$ it may exist an element A^{-1} which is called the multiplicative inverse of A and it is defined as follows:

$$AA^{-1} = 1 \qquad (4)$$

$$A^{-1} = \frac{A}{A^2} \qquad (5)$$

– Inner product, also known as dot product

$$\langle A \rangle_r \cdot \langle B \rangle_s = \langle AB \rangle_{|r-s|} \qquad (6)$$

$$A \cdot B = \sum_r \sum_s \langle A \rangle_r \cdot \langle B \rangle_s \qquad (7)$$

If r or s are 0, the result is 0. This is a grade decreasing operation.
– Outer product, also known as wedge product

$$\langle A \rangle_r \wedge \langle B \rangle_s = \langle AB \rangle_{r+s} \qquad (8)$$

$$A \wedge B = \sum_r \sum_s \langle A \rangle_r \wedge \langle B \rangle_s \qquad (9)$$

This is a grade increasing operation. If a and b are blades of grade 1 then $a \wedge b = -b \wedge a$. This means that the wedge product of two vectors is anti-commutative.
– Reverse and Norm

The reverse operation is denoted by $\dagger$. As its name suggests, it reverse the order of the elements of a k-blade, e.g. the reverse of e_{123} is e_{321}, also $e_{321} = -e_{123}$, so to compute the reverse of a k-blade, we must count the number of signs caused by the interchange of elements. This can be computed whit the next formula

$$\langle A \rangle_r^\dagger = (-1)^{(r(r-1)/2)} \langle A \rangle_r \tag{10}$$

The norm of a multivector is computed as follows

$$|A| = \sqrt{A^\dagger A} \tag{11}$$

This operation is defined to be applied in euclidean spaces, where all the basis square to 1. In this work, all the equations that involve the norm in conformal space are written as $|A| = \sqrt{AA}$.

4   Conformal Geometric Algebra

Conformal geometric albebra is a representation of the vector space as presented in [8]. The objective is to expand the vector space $\mathbb{R}^n$ with the Minkowski space $\mathbb{R}^{1,1}$. The algebra of the Minkowski space has an orthonormal basis $\{e_+, e_-\}$ with the properties:

$$e_+^2 = 1, e_-^2 = -1 \tag{12}$$

$$e_+ \cdot e_- = 0 \tag{13}$$

A null basis, formed by $\{e_\infty, e_0\}$, is used to represent the point at infinity and the origin of a projective space and they can be defined as:

$$e_\infty = e_- - e_+ \quad e_0 = \frac{e_- + e_+}{2} \tag{14}$$

The vectors of the null basis have the properties:

$$e_\infty^2 = e_0^2 = 0 \quad e_\infty \cdot e_0 = -1 \tag{15}$$

The Minkowski Plane E is the unit pseudoscalar of this space and is defined as:

$$E = e_+ \wedge e_- = e_\infty \wedge e_0 \tag{16}$$

$\mathbb{G}_3$ is the algebra of the 3D space. The orthonormal basis of this algebra is defined as $\{e_1, e_2, e_3\}$. A point in this algebra is called an euclidean point, and is denoted by x_E.

$$x_E = Xe_1 + Ye_2 + Ze_3 \tag{17}$$

The unit pseudoscalar of this algebra is denoted by I_E and is defined as

$$I_E = e_1 \wedge e_2 \wedge e_3 \tag{18}$$

Conformal geometric algebra can be defined as:

$$\mathbb{G}_{4,1} = \mathbb{G}_3 \oplus \mathbb{G}_{1,1} \tag{19}$$

The unit pseudoscalar of this algebra is I_c and is defined as

$$I_c = e_1 \wedge e_2 \wedge e_3 \wedge e_\infty \wedge e_0 = I_E \wedge E \tag{20}$$

The sphere is the basic unit of calculus in $\mathbb{G}_{4,1}$. The sphere is defined as a set of points that are at the same distance (radius) from one point called center. If this definition is applied to $\mathbb{R}^n$ the entity that fulfills it changex in each vector space, i.e. in $\mathbb{R}^0$ this entity is the point, in $\mathbb{R}^1$ it is the point pair, in $\mathbb{R}^2$ it is the circle, in $\mathbb{R}^3$ it is the sphere and in $\mathbb{R}^4$ and higher dimensions is called a hypersphere.

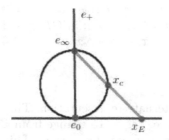

Fig. 1. Projection of the point $x_E \in \mathbb{G}_1$ into the conformal space $\mathbb{G}_{2,1}$ (which is a circle)

In CGA the Euclidean space is embedded in a higher dimension. Because $\mathbb{G}_{2,1}$ is posible to visualize, we use it to exemplify this process, see figure 1. First the basis e_+ expand the space by one dimension. In this dimension we can draw a unitary sphere centered in the origin. The basis e_- allows us to lift the bottom of the sphere to the origin of the space. Now we make a line from the top of the sphere to the euclidean point x_E. The intersection of this line with the sphere is the conformal point x_c. The conformal point x_c can be obtained with:

$$x_c = x_E + \frac{x_E \cdot x_E}{2} + e_0 = Xe_1 + Ye_2 + Ze_3 + \frac{X^2 + Y^2 + Z^2}{2}e_\infty + e_0 \tag{21}$$

Now a sphere in $\mathbb{R}^0$, a point, is a blade of grade 1. As defined before, the wedge product is a grade increasing operation. If we take 2 spheres of grade 1, points, the result is a sphere of grade 2, a point pair. Therefore the wedge product of 3 points is the circle and with 4 points we get a sphere.

There exist 2 special cases to consider: the first one occurs when the points are not in general position (GP), this means that there are 3 collinear points or 4 coplanar points. In this case the result will be a line with 3 points and a plane with 4 points. The line and plane are a circle and a sphere respectively with infinite radius. The other is known as the dual property of the conformal space: The result of the wedge product between an entity and a point will be 0 if the point lies on the entity.

The combination of the wedge product results and the dual property give us the Outer Product Null Space, OPNS, representation. A visualization of this is presented in the figure 2.

Entity	Notation	OPNS representation	Grade
Point	x_c	$x_E + \frac{x_E^2}{2}e_\infty + e_0$	1
Point Pair	ON(PP)	$x_{c1} \wedge x_{c2}$	2
Circle	ON(Z)	$x_{c1} \wedge x_{c2} \wedge x_{c3}$; in GP	3
Line	ON(L)	$x_{c1} \wedge x_{c2} \wedge x_{c3}$	3
Sphere	ON(S)	$x_{c1} \wedge x_{c2} \wedge x_{c3} \wedge x_{c4}$; in GP	4
Plane	ON(P)	$x_{c1} \wedge x_{c2} \wedge x_{c3} \wedge x_{c4}$	4

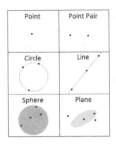

Fig. 2. OPNS representation

In $\mathbb{G}_{4,1}$ there exist an alternate representation. This representation is called the Inner Product Null Space, IPNS. To change from OPNS to IPNS representations one multiply by the unit pseudoscalar I_c. This multiplication is called the dual operation. Because $I_c^2 = -1$ its inverse is $-I_c$, so to return to OPNS we multiply by $-I_c$. This is done to avoid a change of sign between both representations.

$$ON(X)(I_c) = IN(X) \quad IN(X)(-I_c) = ON(X) \tag{22}$$

A special case is the point representation x_c. The OPNS representation of the conformal point is also valid in IPNS.

The combinations of these two representations allow us to obtain the information of the blades that define the geometric entities, as it is shown next along with the equations to obtain the parameters.

– Sphere

$$IN(S) = \pm\alpha(C_c - \frac{r^2}{2}e_\infty) \tag{23}$$

Where C_c is the conformal point of the center C_E, r is its radius and α is some scale. Because of the fact that the blade e_0 can only be equal to 1 in the sphere case, the scale can be obtained as:

$$\pm\alpha = -IN(S) \cdot e_\infty \tag{24}$$

The equations to compute the parameters of the normalized sphere are

$$C_E = (IN(S) \cdot (-I_E))I_E \tag{25}$$

$$r^2 = IN(S)^2 \tag{26}$$

– Plane

$$\mathbb{IN}(P) = \pm\alpha(n_E + de_\infty) \tag{27}$$

Where n_E is the normal of the plane, d is the distance to the origin and α is a scale factor equal to $|n_E|$. The equations to compute the parameters of the normalized plane are:

$$n_E = (\mathbb{IN}(P) \cdot (-I_E))I_E \tag{28}$$

$$d = -\mathbb{IN}(P) \cdot e_0 \tag{29}$$

– Circle

To obtain the plane in which the circle lies we use:

$$\mathbb{ON}(P) = e_\infty \wedge \mathbb{ON}(Z) \tag{30}$$

The norm of $\mathbb{ON}(Z)$ is the same of $\mathbb{ON}(P)$. The sphere with the same center and radius as the circle is obtained by:

$$\mathbb{IN}(S) = \mathbb{ON}(Z) \cdot \mathbb{ON}(P)^{-1} \tag{31}$$

– Line

$$\alpha = \sqrt{\mathbb{ON}(L) \cdot \mathbb{ON}(L)} \tag{32}$$

where α is the scale of factor used to normalize the line. Once we have normalized the line we can get its direction d_E, momentum m and closes point to the origin O_E.

$$d_E = \mathbb{ON}(L) \cdot E \tag{33}$$

$$m = (0.5e_\infty - e_0) \cdot \mathbb{IN}(L) \tag{34}$$

$$O_E = -d_E \cdot mI_E \tag{35}$$

5 Conformal Geometric Hough Transform

The steps for the algorithm are the same as the RHT. These steps can be described as follows:

1) Transform the euclidean points in the cloud to conformal points. Then randomly take sets of 4 points, x_{ci}.

2) Do the wedge product between the first 3 points to get a circle $\mathbb{ON}(Z)$. Do $\mathbb{ON}(S) = \mathbb{ON}(Z) \wedge x_{c4}$.

2.1) If $\mathbb{ON}(S)$ is 0 then x_{c4} lies on $\mathbb{ON}(Z)$. Do the wedge product between $\mathbb{ON}(Z)$ and e_∞. If the result is 0, $\mathbb{ON}(Z)$ is a line, otherwise a circle.

2.2) If $\mathbb{ON}(S)$ is not 0 then do the wedge product between $\mathbb{ON}(S)$ and e_∞. If the result is 0, $\mathbb{ON}(S)$ is a plane, otherwise a sphere.

3) After we detect the entity that the points x_{ci} form, we must eliminate two ambiguities. The first one is the scale factor and the second is a variant sign caused by the anticommutative behavior of the wedge product between 2 vectors. To eliminate these ambiguities we work in $\mathbb{IPNS}$ for the sphere and plane. A division by the $\pm\alpha$ obtained in equation 24, solves both ambiguities for the sphere. For the plane we can get $\alpha = |n_E|$ to solve the scale factor. For the variant sign we use the function atan2 with n_E, because it can distinguish between diametrically opposite directions. The function atan2 has the interval $[-\pi, \pi]$, so the sign of the angle obtained is used to eliminate the variant sign. In the only exception to this method, where $X = Y = 0$, we use the sign of Z. To eliminate these ambiguities we work in $\mathbb{OPNS}$ for the line and circle. For the line we get α with equation 32. We also solve the varaint sign with the function atan2 and its direction d_E. The circle can be converted to a plane and use the same steps.

Once we have discarded the ambiguities we search for the candidate in its correspodig dinamyc accumulator array. If the candidate is found increase the accumulator by one. Otherwise add a new cell for the candidate and set its accumulator to one.

4)If an accumulator surpasses a threshold k we check if it exists in the cloud. If it exist we added it to a list of detected entities and delete all the points that belong to it from the set. To eliminate those points we comput their distance to the entity to see if they are close enough with the next formulas:

$$D = ||C_E - x_E| - r| \quad (36)$$
$$D = |x_C \cdot \mathbb{IN}(P)| \quad (37)$$

Equation 37 is also valid for the line. With the circle we use both.

There are some minimal changes to apply this algorithm in the planar case. The first one is that we only detect lines and circles, so we take sets of 3 points instead of 4. We only have 2 coordinates, X and Y, so Z is set to 0 by default. The elimination of the ambiguities of the circle will be diferent, because all the circles lie on the image plane $\mathbb{IN}(Pimg) = 0e_1 + 0e_2 + e_3 + 0e_\infty$. If we obtain the plane of the circle this will be like $\mathbb{IN}(P) = \pm\alpha e_3$, then both ambiguities can be discarded with a division by $\pm\alpha$.

6 Analysis

One good reason to use CGA to attack this problem is the parametric equations. They are more simple than the regular equations. For example the equations used for circles in 2D with center (a, b) and radius r with 3 given points are:

$$m_a = \frac{y_2 - y_1}{x_2 - x_1} \quad (38) \qquad m_b = \frac{y_3 - y_2}{x_3 - x_2} \quad (39)$$

$$a = (m_a(m_b(y_1 - y_3)) + m_b(x_1 + x_2) - \frac{m_a(x_2 + x_3)}{2(m_b - m_a)} \qquad b = \frac{-a}{m_a} + \frac{x_1 + x_2}{2m_a} + \frac{y_1 + y_2}{2}$$
$$(40) \qquad\qquad\qquad\qquad\qquad (41)$$

$$r = \sqrt{(x - a)^2 + (y - b)^2} \qquad (42)$$

These equations are more complicated than the equation used to represent a circle in OPNS. Other advantage is that the OPNS representations are related between them. For instance, the equations of the circle and line are the same, the result only depends of the position of the points, this also occurs with the sphere and plane. Also the result of the equation with tree points partially solves the one with four. As has been stated in other works [10], to maintain this advantage we need an optimal way to implement the equations in CGA. For this purpose we use GAALOP [11]. GAALOP is a precompiler for C/C++ and OpenCL. This tool allows to make an efficient implemention. It reduces the storage space by using only the space needed to store the nonzero coefficients of the multivectors, and also ignores all the unnecessary operations.

In the worst case scenario this algorithm has a computational complexity of $\mathcal{O}(\binom{n}{s})$, where n is the numbers of points in the cloud, and s is the number of points in each set, 4 for 3D cloud points and 3 in the planar case. For comparison this is similar to $\mathcal{O}(n^s)$ but discarding permutations and repetitions. This is reduced by only taking a sample of the points from the cloud and eliminate those that already has been detected. In the 3D case other viable option will be to use a deep segmentation and then apply the algorithm to each zone.

7 Experimental Results

For the first experiments we used 2D images. In the first we take the picture of a candy, see figure 3a, to detect the circle shaped candy and its stick. We first apply a gaussian filter to reduce noise and then the Canny [12] algorithm to detect borders and then our algorithm. In the figure 3b, we observe the detected circle in color green and the stick lines in color red.

For the next image we use the picture of a bycicle, see figure 3c. The original image shows a bicicle in a white background. The algorithm was able to detect the 2 weels and 3 lines that form the frame.

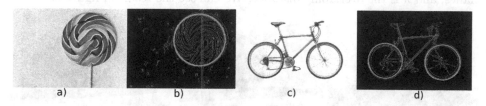

Fig. 3. Experiments with the candy and bicicle images. Detected lines are in red and circles in green.

In the last experiment, we used a RGB-D sensor, see figure 4.

As proposed in the analysis section, we use depth segmentation to reduce the computational cost, see figure 5. We also use the Canny algorithm in the RGB image to reduce the number of points, see figure 5. By doing this we have been able to detect a sphere, the ball, and two planes, the table and the wall.

Fig. 4. (left) The RGB image obtained with the sensor. (right) the depth image.

To delimite the table, the quality of the points were not enough to detect a circle, but by using the parameters of the detected plane and the points that are close to it as constrains, we can get an aproximation. The final result is visualized using the sofware Webots [13], see figure 5.

Fig. 5. Depth segmentation and edge image used for the detection process

Although the aproximation of the table is good, we observe that it overlaps with the wall and ball. We can correct this with the use of conformal transformations. In order to do this we construct a translator

$$T = 1 + \frac{\lambda}{2} n_E e_\infty \tag{43}$$

Where n_E is the direction of the translation, in this case the norm of the planes, and λ is the overlaping distance. We can see the result in figure 6.

Fig. 6. (Left)Detection of the gemetric entities. (Middle)Angle used to show the error in the aproximation of the table. (Right)Rectification of the table.

8   Conclusion

In this work we have presented the advantages of use CGA to implement the Hough Transform. This mathematical framework let us detect different kind of shapes with very simple equations even in 3D. We must remark the representations of the entities are vectors an also have an algebraic and geometric interpretations that can be used for detection algorithms at higher levels of complexity.

Future development of the algorithm will be focused in solving the high computational cost. Other extension to be developed is to work in higher dimension algebras to detect more complex entities, e.g. $\mathbb{G}_{6,3}$ to detect ellipses.

References

1. Hough, P.V.C.: Machine Analysis of Bubble Chamber Pictures. In: Proc. Int. Conf. High Energy Accelerators and Instrumentation (1959)
2. Duda, R.O., Hart, P.E.: Use of the Hough Transformation to Detect Lines and Curves in Pictures. Comm. ACM 15, 11–15 (1972)
3. Ballard, D.H.: Generalizing the Hough transform to detect arbitrary shapes. Pattern Recognition 13(2), 111–122 (1981)
4. Shapiro, L., Stockman, G.: Computer Vision. Prentice-Hall, Inc. (2001)
5. Hestenes, D., Sobczyk, G.: Clifford Algebra to Geometric Calculus: A Unified Language for Mathematics and Physics. D. Reidel, Dordrecht (1984)
6. Bayro-Corrochano, E.: Geometric Computing: For Wavelet Transforms, Robot Vision, Learning, Control and Action. Springer, London (2010)
7. Perwass, C.: Geometric Algebra with Applications in Engineering. Springer, Heidelberg (2009)
8. Li, H., Hestenes, D., Rockwood, A.: Generalized homogeneous coordinates for computational geometry. In: Sommer, G. (ed.) Geometric Computing with Clifford Algebra, pp. 27–52. Springer (2001)
9. Kultanen, P., Xu, L., Oja, E.: Randomized Hough transform (RHT). In: Proceedings of the 10th International Conference on Pattern Recognition, ICPR 1990, Atlantic City, USA, June 16-21, vol. 1, pp. 631–635 (1990)
10. Li, Z., Hong, X., Liu, Y.: Detection Geometric Object in the Conformal Geometric Algebra Framework. In: Proceedings of the 2011 12th International Conference on Computer-Aided Design and Computer Graphics, CADGRAPHICS 2011, pp. 198–201. IEEE Computer Society, Washington, DC (2011)
11. Hildenbrand, D., Pitt, J., Koch, A.: Gaalop High Performance Parallel Computing based on Conformal Geometric Algebra. In: Bayro-Corrochano, E., Sheuermann, G. (eds.) Geometric Algebra Computing for Engineering and Computer Science, ch. 22, pp. 477–494 (2010)
12. Canny, J.: A Computational Approach to Edge Detection. IEEE Transactions on Pattern Analysis and Machine Intelligence PAMI-8(6), 679–698 (1986)
13. Michel, O.: Webots: Professional Mobile Robot Simulation. International Journal of Advanced Robotic Systems 1(1), 39–42 (2004)

Sieve Bootstrap Prediction Intervals for Contaminated Non-linear Processes

Gustavo Ulloa[1], Héctor Allende-Cid[1], and Héctor Allende[1,2]

[1] Universidad Técnica Federico Santa María,
Dept. de Informática, Casilla 110-V, Valparaíso, Chile
gulloa@alumnos.inf.utfsm.cl, {vector,hallende}@inf.utfsm.cl
[2] Universidad Adolfo Ibañez, Facultad de Ingeniería y Ciencias,
Avenida Padre Hurtado 750, Viña del Mar, Chile
hallende@uai.cl

Abstract. Recently, the sieve bootstrap method has been successfully used in prediction of nonlinear time series. In this work we study the performance of the prediction intervals based on the sieve bootstrap technique, which does not require the distributional assumption of normality as most techniques that are found in the literature. The construction of prediction intervals in the presence of patchy outliers are not robust from a distributional point of view, leading to an undesirable increase in the length of the prediction intervals.

In the analysis of financial time series it is common to have irregular observations that have different types of outliers, isolated and in groups. For this reason we propose the construction of prediction intervals for returns based in the winsorized residual and bootstrap techniques for financial time series. We propose a novel, simple, efficient and distribution free resampling technique for developing robust prediction intervals for returns and volatilities for TGARCH models. The proposed procedure is illustrated by an application to known synthetic time series.

Keywords: Sieve bootstrap, Time series, Financial prediction intervals, Forecasting in time series, Winsorized filter, GARCH, TGARCH models, Volatility.

1 Introduction

The construction of prediction intervals in time series models with a finite number of parameters and with known innovative processes, have been widely discussed in the literature and it is known that these intervals are extremely sensitive to the presence of innovation outliers [16].

Moreover, in the last two decades several free distribution models have been proposed as an alternative for the construction of prediction intervals [15]. This alternative consists in using a resampling technique commonly known as bootstrap. Given that the realization of a time series does not satisfy the assumption of being a succession of independent and identically distributed random variables, and given the highly dependent structure which characterizes the data,

J. Ruiz-Shulcloper and G. Sanniti di Baja (Eds.): CIARP 2013, Part I, LNCS 8258, pp. 84–91, 2013.

the authors [4,13,8] propose a bootstrap procedure based on the resampling of the residuals, which provides good results in the context of time series in comparison with other alternatives. The first proposals based on bootstrap were applied to linear $ARMA(p, q)$ models, and then extended to other nonlinear models, like $GARCH(p, q)$, were the prediction intervals, were not only focused in future observations of the series, in this case returns, but also in the volatility.

For linear models, the sieve bootstrap approach proposed by [1] is widely used in non-parametric time series models, because of its effectiveness, computational efficiency and for being constraint-free [13,8,9,3,11]. The idea of the Sieve bootstrap method is to approximate the observed process by a high-order autorregresive linear model, $AR(\infty)$, and generate new realizations from the resampling of the residuals [3]. The first application of bootstrap to nonlinear ARCH/GARCH models was proposed by Miguel and Olave [10]. The proposal consisted in the construction of prediction intervals of returns and volatilities by directly adding resampled residuals from an ARCH model to the respective point forecasts. In 2005 an extension of this proposal was presented, by taking into account the variability of the estimation of the parameters of the ARCH model, by adding an additional step, that consisted in re-estimating the ARCH parameters for each bootstrap realization of the returns [14]. Pascual et al. (2006) [12] combined and extended these procedures by developing prediction intervals for both returns and volatilities from GARCH models, and the obtained prediction intervals were found to be well-calibrated, i.e., the number of observed data falling within a prediction interval coincides with the declared coverage. In 2011 Chen et. al. proposed an alternative bootstrap method that was less demanding in terms of computational cost [5]. The proposal was based in a Sieve bootstrap procedure used in linear models, because ARCH/GARCH models can handle the AR/ARMA Box-Jenkins family of linear models representation. The linear representation is possible because the square of the ARCH/GARCH returns is a linear process represented by AR/ARMA models [17,7]. However, if the original data has innovative outliers, the classic and free distribution approaches that include the Sieve bootstrap procedure are affected by them, producing inflations in the length of the prediction interval, which is unwanted. In the present work we propose a methodology based on a winsorized filter for the residuals to mitigate the inflation in the length of the prediction interval of Sieve bootstrap algorithms proposed in 2011 [5] for ARCH/GARCH non-linear models. We show a comparative study between the prediction interval length and its coverage with respect to other proposals in the literature. The study was performed over the prediction intervals of future values of returns and volatility. The paper is presented as follows: In the next section we present the methodology used in this work. In section 3 we show some simulation results. In the last section we present some concluding remarks.

2   Methodology

The proposed method is an extension of the Sieve bootstrap method for ARCH/GARCH models proposed in 2011 [5]. It consists in adding a stage in the algorithm, specifically step 4, which consists in computing the winsorized filter for the estimated residuals. The algorithm is described below.

2.1   Winsorized Sieve Bootstrap Procedure of $ARCH/GARCH$ Process

The $ARCH$ processes (Autoregressive Conditional Heteroskedastic) introduced by Engle in 1982 [6], allow to model the variance or volatility dynamic as a function of past observations of a return series. In 1986 [2] Bollerslev proposed an extension of the ARCH models, incorporating available information on previous volatilities in the Generalized ARCH or GARCH models.

GARCH(p,q) model [2]:

$$y_t = \sigma_t \epsilon_t \tag{1}$$

$$\sigma_t^2 = \alpha_0 + \sum_{i=1}^{p} \alpha_i y_{t-i}^2 + \sum_{j=1}^{q} \beta_j \sigma_{t-j}^2 \tag{2}$$

where there is a restriction over its parameters $\alpha_0 \geq 0$, $\alpha_i \geq 0$ and $\beta_j \geq 0$, for $i = 1, \ldots, p$ and $j = 1, \ldots q$, with a gaussian white noise process $\epsilon_t \sim i.i.d.(0,1)$. For this process to be weakly stationary $\sum_{i=1}^{\max(p,q)} (\alpha_i + \beta_j) < 1$ must hold, implying that $Var[y_t] \geq 0$ is satisfied.

As mentioned in section 1 the use of Sieve bootstrap in ARCH/GARCH models is possible, because the square of the returns can be represented as linear AR/ARMA models

$$y_t^2 = \alpha_0 + \sum_{i=1}^{m} (\alpha_i + \beta_i) y_{t-i}^2 + \nu_t - \sum_{j=1}^{q} \beta_j \nu_{t-j} \tag{3}$$

where $\{\nu_t\}_{t=1}^{T}$ is the innovation process of y_t^2 and $m = \max(p,q)$.

The algorithm with the winsorized step is described below

Winsorized Sieve Bootstrap Prediction Intervals for ARCH/GARCH (WSB)

1. Estimate the ARMA coefficients $\hat{\alpha}_0, \widehat{(\alpha_1 + \beta_1)}, \ldots, \widehat{(\alpha_m + \beta_m)}, \hat{\beta}_1, \ldots, \hat{\beta}_q$, by means of Least Squares. Then estimate $\hat{\alpha}_i = \widehat{(\alpha_1 + \beta_1)} - \hat{\beta}_i$ for $i = 1, \ldots, p$.

2. Estimate the residuals $\{\hat{\nu}_t\}_{t=m+1}^{T}$ by means of

$$\hat{\nu}_t = y_t^2 - \hat{\alpha}_0 - \sum_{i=1}^{m} \widehat{(\alpha_i + \beta_i)} y_{t-i}^2 + \sum_{j=1}^{q} \hat{\beta}_j \nu_{t-j} \text{ for } t = m+1, \cdots, T \tag{4}$$

3. Center the estimated residuals by means of

$$\tilde{\nu}_t = \left(\hat{\nu}_t - \frac{1}{T-m}\sum_{t=m+1}^{T}\hat{\nu}_t\right) \tag{5}$$

where the empirical distribution is

$$\hat{F}_{\nu,T}(y) = \sum_{m+1}^{T}1_{\{\tilde{\nu}_t \le y\}} \tag{6}$$

4. Apply the winsorized filters of order k to the residuals

$$\tilde{\nu}_{(t)} = \begin{cases} \tilde{\nu}_{(p+k+1)} & \text{if } t < p+k+1 \\ \tilde{\nu}_{(t)} & \text{if } p+k+1 \le t \le T-k \\ \tilde{\nu}_{(T-k)} & \text{if } t > T-k \end{cases} \tag{7}$$

5. Generate a resample $\{\nu_t^*\}_{t=1}^{T}$ from $\hat{F}_{\nu,T}(y)$.
6. Generate a Bootstrap sample of the squared returns $\{y_t^{2*}\}_{t=1}^{T}$ with

$$y_t^{2*} = \hat{\alpha}_0 + \sum_{i=1}^{m}\widehat{(\alpha_i + \beta_i)}y_{t-i}^{2*} + \nu_t^* - \sum_{j=1}^{q}\hat{\beta}_j\nu_{t-j}^* \tag{8}$$

where $y_k^{2*} = \frac{\hat{\alpha}_0}{1-\sum_{i=1}^{m}(\hat{\alpha}_i+\hat{\beta}_i)}$ and $\nu_k^* = 0$ for $k \le 0$

7. Given $\{y_t^{2*}\}_{t=1}^{T}$ from step 6, estimate the coefficients $\hat{\alpha}_0^*$, $\widehat{(\alpha_1 + \beta_1)}^*, \ldots$, $\widehat{(\alpha_m + \beta_m)}^*$, $\hat{\beta}_1^*, \ldots, \hat{\beta}_q^*$, $\hat{\alpha}_i^* = \widehat{(\alpha_i + \beta_1)}^* - \hat{\beta}_i^*$ for $i = 1, \ldots, p$. The Bootstrap sample of the volatility $\{\sigma_t^{2*}\}_{t=1}^{T}$ is obtained with

$$\sigma_t^{2*} = \hat{\alpha}_0^* + \sum_{i=1}^{p}\hat{\alpha}_i^*y_{t-i}^{2*} + \sum_{j=1}^{q}\hat{\beta}_j^*\sigma_{t-j}^{2*} \quad \text{for } t = m+1, \cdots, T \tag{9}$$

with $\sigma_t^{2*} = \frac{\hat{\alpha}_0}{1-\sum_{i=1}^{m}(\hat{\alpha}_i+\hat{\beta}_i)}$, for $t = 1, \cdots, m$.

8. Sample with replacement from $\hat{F}_{\nu,T}(y)$ to obtain the Bootstrap prediction error process $\{\nu_{t+h}^*\}_{h=1}^{s}$ where $s \ge 1$.
9. Be $y_{T+h}^* = y_{T+h}$, $\nu_{T+h}^* = \tilde{\nu}_{T+h}$ y $\sigma_{T+h}^{2*} = \sigma_{T+h}^{2*}$ for $h \le 0$

$$y_{T+h}^{2*} = \hat{\alpha}_0^* + \sum_{i=1}^{m}\widehat{(\alpha_i + \beta_i)}^*y_{T+h-i}^{2*} + \nu_{T+h}^* - \sum_{j=1}^{q}\hat{\beta}_j^*\nu_{T+h-j}^* \tag{10}$$

$$\sigma_{T+h}^{2*} = \hat{\alpha}_0^* + \sum_{i=1}^{p}\hat{\alpha}_i^*y_{T+h-i}^{2*} + \sum_{j=1}^{q}\hat{\beta}_j^*\sigma_{T+h-j}^{2*} \quad \text{for } h = 1, \ldots, s \tag{11}$$

10. Repeat steps 4 to 8, B times.

11. Finally, prediction intervals are obtained $(1 - \alpha)\%$ for y_{T+h} y σ^2_{T+h} using $\hat{F}^*_{y^{2*}_{T+h}}$ and $\hat{F}^*_{\sigma^{2*}_{T+h}}$.

– For y_{T+h}:

$$\left[-\sqrt{H^*_{(1-\alpha)}}, \sqrt{H^*_{(1-\alpha)}} \right], h = 1, \cdots, s \qquad (12)$$

where $H^*_{(1-\alpha)}$ is the quantile $1 - \alpha$ of $\hat{F}^*_{y^{2*}_{T+h}}$

– For σ^2_{T+h}:

$$\left[0, K^*_{(1-\alpha)} \right], h = 1, \cdots, s \qquad (13)$$

where $K^*_{(1-\alpha)}$ is the quantile $1 - \alpha$ of $\hat{F}^*_{\sigma^{2*}_{T+h}}$

3   Simulation Results

In this section we compared our proposal (WSB) with state of the art models applied to nonlinear time series models (GARCH).

The following tables show the results of the comparison of the models regarding coverage and length of the intervals, in addition of the combined metric CQM proposed in [1], which depends of the theoretical coverage and length, and the empirical values obtained with the bootstrap prediction intervals. This metric is a discrepancy metric between the theorical aim and the empirical performance, for that, a smaller value obtained in this metric indicates a better performance of the prediction interval.

3.1   Simulation for Nonlinear ARCH/GARCH Models

We compared the proposed method (WSB) with the proposal [5] for prediction intervals of future values and volatility.

The parameters of the simulation were: $B = 1000$ resamples of X^*_{T+h} and σ^{2*}_{T+h}, $R = 1000$ future values X_{T+h} and σ^2_{T+h} were simulated for each $h = 1, 5$ and 10 step-ahead. $S = 1000$ simulated the $ARCH(2)$ process

$$y_t = \sigma_t \cdot \varepsilon_t \qquad (14)$$

$$\sigma^2_t = 0.1 + 0.2y^2_{t-1} + 0.15y^2_{t-2} \qquad (15)$$

with the two different distributions for the innovation process $\{\varepsilon_t\}_{t \in \mathbb{Z}}$ given by

$$F_{\varepsilon_t} = N(0, 1) \qquad (16)$$

and

$$F_{\varepsilon_t} = (1 - \zeta)N(0, 1) + \zeta N(0, 100) \qquad (17)$$

where (17) is the contaminated innovations process generated with the convex linear distribution

$$F_{\varepsilon_t} = (1 - \zeta)N(0, 1) + \zeta N(0, \sigma^2) \qquad (18)$$

where $\sigma^2 = 100$ with a $\zeta = 0.05$ level of contamination.

For each simulated series the same procedure described in subsection 2.1 was performed.

In tables 1 and 2 we present the results of the comparison of the prediction interval for $h = 1$, 5 and 10 steps-ahead of the two methods with respect to their average coverage, length of the intervals and the combined measure CQM.

In Table 1 we observe the results of the simulation of the innovative process without contamination (16). We observe that algorithm (SB) and the proposed (WSB) with different orders k, have similar results in terms of coverage and empirical length, and that taking the residuals out of the extremes, decreases a bit the performance, because the CQM value increases its magnitude. The 1-step ahead predictions of volatility given by (11) are constant, so the CQM value can not be calculated.

It is observed that under the presence of contamination in the innovative process the prediction intervals of the algorithm (SB) are clearly affected by the coverture of the returns and volatility, and also the increment in the length of them. This can be seen in Table 2 by comparing the coverture and length of the prediction intervals of the proposed method (SB) with the empirical coverture and length. Also it is observed that the method (WSB) has a positive impact in the performance of the prediction intervals of the returns and volatility. As the order k of the proposed method is increased, the magnitude of the measure CQM decreases for the returns and the volatility, thus diminishing the inflation of the prediction intervals and average covertures. It seems that if the filter order of algorithm WSB increases, the covertures and lengths of the prediction intervals converge to the theoretical covertures and lengths.

Table 1. Results of the simulation of model ARCH(2) with an innovation process $N(0, 1)$

h	k	Method	Coverture return (d.e.)	Length return (d.e.)	CQM return	Coverture volatility (d.e.)	Length volatility (d.e.)	CQM volatility
h=1	-	EMP	95%	1.52	-	95%	0.00	-
	-	SB	94.71 (3.23)	1.52 (0.12)	0.005	88.9 (31.41)	0.17 (0.08)	–
	1	WSB	94.70 (3.23)	1.52 (0.12)	0.005	88.00 (32.50)	0.17 (0.08)	–
	2	WSB	94.69 (3.24)	1.52 (0.12)	0.006	87.90 (32.61)	0.17 (0.08)	–
	3	WSB	94.69 (3.24)	1.52 (0.12)	0.006	86.90 (33.74)	0.17 (0.08)	–
h=5	-	EMP	95%	1.55	-	95%	0.23	-
	-	SB	94.77 (1.37)	1.54 (0.08)	0.008	93.77 (3.72)	0.27 (0.05)	0.211
	1	WSB	94.72 (1.37)	1.54 (0.08)	0.008	93.70 (3.73)	0.27 (0.05)	0.207
	2	WSB	94.70 (1.37)	1.53 (0.08)	0.012	93.63 (3.79)	0.27 (0.05)	0.204
	3	WSB	94.67 (1.37)	1.53 (0.08)	0.014	93.53 (3.81)	0.27 (0.05)	0.200
h=10	-	EMP	95%	1.55	-	95%	0.23	-
	-	SB	94.74 (1.33)	1.54 (0.08)	0.009	93.74 (3.72)	0.27 (0.05)	0.214
	1	WSB	94.71 (1.34)	1.53 (0.08)	0.011	93.67 (3.75)	0.27 (0.05)	0.210
	2	WSB	94.67 (1.33)	1.53 (0.08)	0.013	93.60 (3.78)	0.27 (0.05)	0.206
	3	WSB	94.67 (1.33)	1.53 (0.08)	0.015	93.53 (3.80)	0.27 (0.05)	0.202

Table 2. Results of the simulation of model ARCH(2) with an innovation process $F_{\varepsilon_t} = (1 - \zeta)N(0, 1) + \zeta N(0, 100)$

h	k	Method	Coverture return (d.e.)	Length return (d.e.)	CQM return	Coverture volatility (d.e.)	Length volatility (d.e.)	CQM volatility
h=1	-	EMP	95%	2.44	-	95%	–	-
	-	SB	98.34 (6.11)	7.86 (15.71)	2.248	98.40 (12.55)	112.43 (1236.36)	–
	1	WSB	97.33 (8.24)	4.57 (3.59)	0.898	97.90 (14.34)	14.85 (81.14)	–
	2	WSB	96.52 (9.76)	2.94 (2.59)	0.647	97.80 (14.67)	7.74 (34.23)	–
	3	WSB	96.26 (9.78)	3.71 (2.04)	0.544	97.70 (14.99)	4.99 (15.92)	–
h=5	-	EMP	95%	1.78	-	95%	0.94	-
	-	SB	99.73 (0.84)	10.55 (18.51)	4.969	99.74 (1.31)	144.36 (1537.29)	152.633
	1	WSB	99.51 (2.51)	6.99 (4.95)	2.970	99.62 (1.97)	20.85 (107.61)	21.186
	2	WSB	99.52 (1.83)	6.35 (3.71)	2.616	99.57 (2.16)	11.44 (56.02)	11.292
	3	WSB	99.48 (2.10)	5.97 (2.65)	2.397	99.52 (2.34)	7.28 (16.23)	6.792
h=10	-	EMP	95%	1.61	-	95%	0.29	-
	-	SB	99.83 (0.18)	10.89 (18.87)	5.803	99.89 (0.17)	149.95 (1579.38)	507.893
	1	WSB	99.77 (0.34)	7.38 (5.49)	3.627	99.84 (0.21)	23.06 (113.41)	77.270
	2	WSB	99.55 (3.24)	6.67 (4.36)	3.187	99.82 (0.23)	13.56 (67.12)	45.054
	3	WSB	99.51 (3.03)	6.25 (3.35)	2.92	99.79 (0.25)	8.79 (19.69)	28.800

4   Conclusion

In [1] and [5] the authors show that the Sieve bootstrap procedures obtains better results than state of the art models for coverage and length of prediction intervals and combined metric CQM.

In this work we show the effects of the presence of innovation outliers in prediction intervals, which extend their length and coverage. We also show how to mitigate these effects by applying a winsorized filter to the residual estimates.

The proposed method generates prediction intervals that are more accurate in coverage terms and with shorter length. These improvements are reflected in a lower value of the CQM metric.

As future work we propose the search for a method to identify the optimal order k of the filter and we plan to test our proposal with real nonlinear time series with outliers in order to perform a comparative study.

Acknowledgment. This work was supported by the following Research Grants: Fondecyt 1110854 and FB0821 Centro Científico Tecnológico de Valparaíso. Partial support was also received from Mecesup FSM 0707.

References

1. Alonso, A., Peña, D., Romo, J.: Forecasting time series with sieve bootstrap. Journal of Statistical Planning and Inference 100, 1–11 (2002)
2. Bollerslev, T.: Generalized autorregressive conditional heteroskedasticity. Journal of Econometrics 31, 307–327 (1986)
3. Bühlmann, P.: Sieve bootstrap for time series. Bernoulli 2(3), 123–148 (1997)

4. Bühlmann, P.: Bootstrap for time series. Statistical Science 17(1), 52–72 (2002)
5. Chen, B., Gel, Y., Balakrishna, N., Abraham, B.: Computationally efficient bootstrap prediction intervals for returns and volatilities in arch and garch processes. Journal of Forecasting 30, 51–71 (2011)
6. Engle, R.F.: Autorregressive conditional heteroskedasticity with estimates of the variance of united kindom inflation. Econometrica 50, 987–1007 (1982)
7. Francq, C., Zakoian, J.: GARCH Models: Structure, statistical inference and financial applications. Wiley (2010)
8. Härdle, W.: Bootstrap methods for time series. International Statistical Review 71, 435–459 (2003)
9. Kreiss, J.P.: Asymptotic statistical inference for a class of stochastic processes. Habilitationsschrift, Universität Hamburg (1998)
10. Miguel, J., Olave, P.: Bootstrapping forecast intervals in arch models. Sociedad de Estadıstica e Investigación Operativa 8(2), 345–364 (1999)
11. Pascual, L., Romo, J., Ruiz, E.: Bootstrap predictive inference for arima processes. Journal of Time Series Analysis 25, 449–465 (2004)
12. Pascual, L., Romo, J., Ruiz, E.: Bootstrap prediction for returns and volatilities in garch models. Computational Statistics and Data Analysis 50, 2293–2312 (2006)
13. Politis, D.N.: The impact of bootstrap methods on time series analysis. Statistical Science 28, 219–230 (2003)
14. Reeves, J.J.: Bootstrap prediction intervals for arch models. Internal Journal of Forecasting 21, 237–248 (2005)
15. Thombs, L.A., Schucany, W.R.: Bootstrap prediction intervals for autoregression. Journal of the American Statistical Association 85, 486–492 (1990)
16. Tsay, R.S.: Outliers, level shifts, and variance changes in time series. J. Forecast 7, 1–20 (1988)
17. Tsay, R.S.: Analysis of Financial Time Series, 2nd edn. Wiley Interscience (2005)

A Genetic Algorithm-Evolved
3D Point Cloud Descriptor*

Dominik Węgrzyn and Luís A. Alexandre

IT - Instituto de Telecomunicações
Dept. of Computer Science, Univ. Beira Interior, 6200-001 Covilhã, Portugal

Abstract. In this paper we propose a new descriptor for 3D point clouds that is fast when compared to others with similar performance and its parameters are set using a genetic algorithm. The idea is to obtain a descriptor that can be used in simple computational devices, that have no GPUs or high computational capabilities and also avoid the usual time-consuming task of determining the optimal parameters for the descriptor. Our proposal is compared with other similar algorithms in a public available point cloud library (PCL [1]). We perform a comparative evaluation on 3D point clouds using both the object and category recognition performance. Our proposal presents a comparable performance with other similar algorithms but is much faster and requires less disk space.

1 Introduction

The current cheap depth+RGB cameras like the Kinect and the Xtion have increased the interest in 3D point cloud acquisition and processing. One of the key steps when processing this type of data are the descriptors, that enable a compact representation of a region of a point cloud. Although there are already several available descriptors [1,2], the motivation for this work was two-fold: first, many of the available descriptors are computationally demanding, and make it difficult to use them in computationally restricted devices; second, all the descriptors require the adjustment of one or more parameters, which is usually done using a grid search or other similar process, which can be a lengthy process.

The aim of this work is to design a descriptor that is computationally simple and hence fast and that has its parameters obtained using a genetic algorithm (GA), so as to address the two points raised above.

Section 2 presents the pipeline used in this work, from the input clouds to the matching stage. Section 3 explains the ideas behind the proposed descriptor. The following section describes the use of the GA with our descriptor. Section 5 illustrates the results of the new descriptor and compares it to similar available descriptors. The final section contains the conclusion and possible future work.

2 3D Object Recognition Pipeline

In this work the proposed descriptor uses both shape and color information. In order to represent this information histograms were used.

* We acknowledge the financial support of project PEst-OE/EEI/LA0008/2013.

J. Ruiz-Shulcloper and G. Sanniti di Baja (Eds.): CIARP 2013, Part I, LNCS 8258, pp. 92–99, 2013.

First keypoints are extracted from the input clouds in order to reduce the cost of computing the histograms. The keypoint cloud represents the input cloud by containing only a subset of the original cloud such that an increased processing speed can be achieved.

After computing the keypoints we find the normals of both, the input and the keypoint clouds. The normals are used in the calculation of the shape histograms that will be part of the final descriptor, as described below. The keypoint cloud is obtained from the input cloud using a VoxelGrid [1] with leaf size of 2 cm.

The second part of the descriptor consists in adding color information. For this purpose the RGB colors are transformed into HSV. This model is used because with the HSV color space we can use only the H and S channels and obtain illumination invariance in terms of color representation. We create another histogram for the color component using the hue and saturation channels. For the matching process the input cloud descriptor is compared against the stored descriptors of known objects, using a set distance function. The object recognition pipeline used is presented in figure 1.

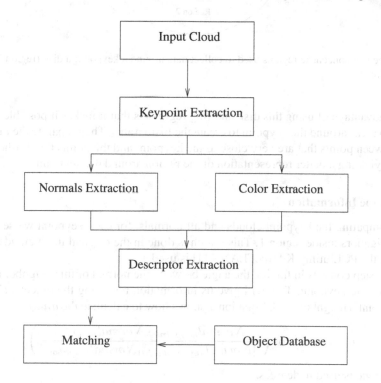

Fig. 1. Object recognition pipeline

3   Descriptor

3.1   Regions around the Keypoints

The descriptor contains two parts: one to represent the shape and another to represent the color. The data used are collected from two regions around the keypoints, the first is a disk with radius R_1 and the second is a ring obtained by removing the first disk from the one obtained using radius R_2. This approach was proposed in [3]. These regions are illustrated in figure 2.

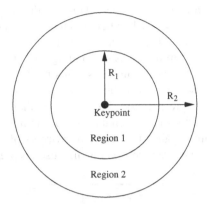

Fig. 2. The two concentric regions used to collect data around a keypoint: a disk (region 1) and a ring (region 2)

The advantage of using this disk and ring regions is that it makes it possible to analyze two areas around the keypoint to create the histograms. They separate the information between points that are very close to the keypoint and the points that further away from it, yielding a better representation of the region around the keypoints.

3.2 Shape Information

After computing the keypoint clouds and all normals, for each keypoint we search all of its neighbors inside region 1. This search is done in the original input cloud and for this task the PCL utility KdTreeFLANN [1] is used.

The next step consists in finding the angle between the normal of this neighbor and the normal of the keypoint. This will give us information regarding the object's shape in the keypoint's neighborhood. Equation 1 shows how to calculate the $angle$.

$$angle = \arccos \left(\frac{Normal_{keypoint} \cdot Normal_{neighbor}}{||Normal_{keypoint}|| \cdot ||Normal_{neighbor}||} \right) \qquad (1)$$

The angle is used in degrees.

We use an histogram to count the occurrences of the angles in the keypoint's neighborhood. The incremented bin is found using equation 2, where $shape_{bins}$ is the total number of histogram bins.

$$bin = \frac{angle \cdot (shape_{bins} - 1)}{360} \qquad (2)$$

After we have found all $angle$ for the points in a keypoint's neighborhood, the histogram is normalized to sum 1.

The process just described is done also for the region 2 and a second shape histogram is obtained, at the same keypoint.

3.3 Color Information

The color histogram contains the saturation and hue information.

Again we look at the neighbors of a keypoint for their hue, H, and saturation, S, values and select a bin_h and a bin_s, using the equations (3 and 4), where the total number of bins is m^2.

$$bin_h = \frac{H \cdot m}{360} \tag{3}$$

$$bin_s = \frac{S \cdot m}{100} \tag{4}$$

Now to find the correct $color_{bin}$ to be incremented in the color histogram, we use the coordinates (bin_h, bin_s) in the equation 5.

$$color_{bin} = m \cdot bin_h + bin_s \tag{5}$$

The color histogram is normalized to sum 1.

As we did in the case of the shape information, the process is repeated for region 2, yielding a second normalized color histogram.

The two histograms for regions 1 and 2 are concatenated yielding a single color histogram with a total number of bins equal to $2m^2$.

3.4 Cloud Distance

To find the matching objects we need to compute the distances between two clouds.

In order to get the distances between shape histograms from two clouds first we compute the centroid of the shape histograms of each cloud (c_1 and c_2), then using the chi-squared distance [4] (equation 6) we get the distance between the two centroids.

$$d_{cent} = \sum_i \frac{(c_1[i] - c_2[i])^2}{2(c_1[i] + c_2[i])} \tag{6}$$

Then we do a similar step but instead of using the centroids we use the standard deviation of the histograms of each cloud. Equation 7, shows how to find this value for cloud 1, and a similar calculation should be done for the second cloud to be compared. h_1 is the shape histogram, while c_1 is the centroid and N_1 is the number of keypoints in this cloud. We use the same process (equation 6) to get the distance, d_{std}, between these standard deviations histograms (std_1 and std_2) as we used for the centroid histograms (c_1 and c_2).

$$std_1 = \sqrt{\frac{\sum_i (h_1[i] - c_1[i])^2}{N_1 - 1}} \tag{7}$$

Finally we sum the centroid distance, d_{cent}, with the standard deviation distance d_{std}, [2] for the final shape distance: $d_{sh} = d_{cent} + d_{std}$. The same process is used to compute the color histogram distance, d_{cl}.

Equation 8 shows how we compute the final distance (d_{final}) between two clouds, where d_{sh} is the shape distance between two histograms and d_{cl} is the color distance between the same histograms. We use the weight w to represent the relative importance of the shape and color information regarding the final distance.

$$d_{final} = d_{sh} \cdot w + d_{cl} \cdot (1 - w) \tag{8}$$

The next step is to find which test cloud fits best to each training cloud, this means the one with the smallest distance. The results of the matching of all test point clouds are used to produce the final result of the dataset.

4   Genetic Algorithm

In this work a genetic algorithm [5], tries to find the optimal parameters for the 3D cloud descriptor. The chromosomes encode the following 5 descriptor parameters: $Shape_{bins}$, m, R_1, R_2 and w (which is in fact used in the distance between the descriptors, and not in the descriptors themselves).

The role of each of these parameters in the creation of the descriptor was explained in the previous section.

The GA has some restrictions, which are the intervals in which the parameters lie. The parameter $Shape_{bins}$ is set between 8 and 64. The parameter m is set between 3 and 8. The parameter R_1 is set between 0.5 and 2.0 cm and R_2 is set between 2.1 and 5.0 cm. The R_2 has the maximal value possible set to 5.0 cm as the other descriptors used to compare with our descriptor also use this value. The last parameter optimized by the GA is the weight w, that is allowed to vary between 0 and 1.

The chromosomes are binary encoded. The initial population is set randomly. The population used consisted of 10 chromosomes. This small value was chosen in order to avoid the generations taking too much time to compute. The object error represents the percentage of correctly matched point clouds from the training set 1 among the point clouds from training set 2 and is used as the fitness of the chromosome (training set 1 and training set 2 that are explained in the experiments section). The elitism selection [6] and the roulette-wheel selection [6] were used in order to make the selection. The used crossover technique is the uniform crossover [6]. Mutation makes it possible to search a wide area of solutions in order to find the optimal solution. The mutation used is the in-order mutation [6]. The mutation probability is set to 40% in the first generation and decreases exponentially after each successive generation.

The GA needs to be able to stop the evolution when the goal is achieved. The stopping criterion is set to either the number of generations reaching 200 generations, or if no better solution in 40 consecutive generations is found, or if a solution with 100% of correct object matches is found.

After each generation we measure the validation error of the best chromosome. This way we avoid the overfitting of the descriptor that could lead to the loss of the ability that the descriptor has to recognize point clouds. For this purpose we check in a validation subset of point clouds (apart from the clouds used by GA to determine the best parameters for the descriptor) for the validation error of the best chromosome. When this error begins to rise, we stop the AG and consider that we have found the best descriptor.

5   Experiments

5.1   Dataset

A subset of the large dataset[1] of 3D point clouds [7] was used to perform experiments. The clouds were divided into four subsets, constituted by two training subsets, one validation subset and one test set. The $test_{clouds}$ subset is composed by 475 different views of 10 objects and is used to calculate the final performance of the descriptor using 943 training clouds as possible match. The $validation_{clouds}$ subset has 239 clouds and is used to avoid the overfitting of the descriptor. We calculate the validation error of the best chromosome of each generation when making use of the GA. For this purpose we check how many clouds from the $validation_{clouds}$ are correctly matched, using 704 training clouds as the matching clouds. On the other hand these 704 training clouds are divided into $training_1$ and $training_2$ subsets. Those two training subsets were used by the GA to get the object error of the chromosomes (both $training_1$ and $training_2$ subsets contain 352 clouds).

5.2   Results

The code used to implement our descriptor can be downloaded online[2].

The best chromosome optimized by the GA has 60 shape bins, $m = 8$, $R_1 = 1.3$ cm, $R_2 = 3.6$ cm and $w = 0.67$. After the matches are done, we check how many of the 475 test clouds were correctly matched to the 943 training clouds. The best descriptor uses 248 bins to represent the point cloud. This descriptor has an accuracy of 72.47% in matching the cloud to the correct object (from the 474 test clouds 344 were correctly matched – one of the test clouds was not used since it had less than 10 points) and 89.66% in matching the cloud to the correct category.

In the paper [2] some available descriptors were tested to get their performance and computational time. Table 1 shows the performance of those descriptors, that were extracted using the same point clouds as the ones used to evaluate the descriptor proposed in this paper. The column time refers to the necessary time to match the 475 test clouds using 943 point clouds as the training set. The column size refers to the number of real values required to store one descriptor.

As we can see the SHOTCOLOR takes 178 s to compute, while our descriptor takes only 72 s using the same machine. Although we have a slightly lower accuracy, the temporal advantage can be important in real time applications. The PFHRGB has the best accuracy, however it takes 2992 s to compute. In terms of size, we can see that our

---

[1] http://www.cs.washington.edu/node/4229/
[2] http://www.di.ubi.pt/~lfbaa

Table 1. Descriptors performance: test errors for the object and category recognition tasks along with time and size requirements

Descriptor	Object (%)	Category (%)	Time (s)	Size
PFHRGB	20.25	5.27	2992	250
SHOTCOLOR	26.58	9.28	178	1353
Our	27.43	10.34	72	248

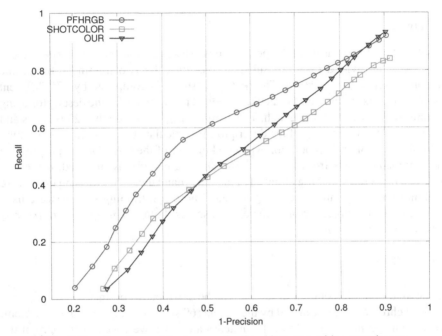

Fig. 3. Recall × (1-precision) curves for the object recognition experiments

descriptor uses only 248 real values that is significantly less than the SHOTCOLOR's 1353 and still less than the 250 values per descriptor that PFHRGB uses. Figure 3 contains the recall × (1-precision) curves for the object recognition experiments.

Although the PFHRGB curve is better than ours, we can see that our curve is close to the SHOTCOLOR curve and when we have a recall larger than 0.35 our curve is better than the SHOTCOLOR's.

6   Conclusion

In this paper we presented a new descriptor for 3D point clouds that takes advantage of a genetic algorithm to find good parameters. It presents a performance similar to other existing descriptors, but is faster to compute and uses less space to store the extracted descriptors.

Our descriptor when compared to the SHOTCOLOR presents a slightly higher error (27.43% versus 26.58% object recognition error) but it is much faster (uses 40% of the time needed by the SHOTCOLOR) and occupies less space. When compared to the PFHRGB, it is substantially faster (uses only 2.5% of the time needed by PFHRGB), uses the same space but has higher error (27.43% error versus 20.25%). So our proposal can be used to replace these descriptors, when extraction speed is important.

A possible way to improve the quality of the descriptor is to let the GA optimize not only the values of the parameters, but also the entire structure of the descriptor (types of angles used, their number, types of regions to consider and their shapes).

References

1. Rusu, R.B., Cousins, S.: 3d is here: Point cloud library (pcl). In: IEEE International Conference on Robotics and Automation, ICRA (2011)
2. Alexandre, L.A.: 3D descriptors for object and category recognition: a comparative evaluation. In: Workshop on Color-Depth Camera Fusion in Robotics at the IEEE/RSJ International Conference on Intelligent Robots and Systems (IROS), Vilamoura, Portugal (October 2012)
3. Fiolka, T., Stuckler, J., Klein, D.A., Schulz, D., Behnke, S.: Place recognition using surface entropy features. In: Proc. of IEEE ICRA Workshop on Semantic Perception, Mapping, and Exploration, Saint Paul, MN, USA (2012)
4. Puzicha, J., Hofmann, T., Buhmann, J.M.: Non-parametric similarity measures for unsupervised texture segmentation and image retrieval. In: 2012 IEEE Conference on Computer Vision and Pattern Recognition, pp. 267–272 (1997)
5. Holland, J.H.: Adaptation in Natural and Artificial Systems. A Bradford Book (1975)
6. Engelbrecht, A.P.: Computational Intelligence, An Introduction. John Wiley & Sons (2002)
7. Lai, K., Bo, L., Ren, X., Fox, D.: A large-scale hierarchical multi-view rgb-d object dataset. In: Proc. of the IEEE International Conference on Robotics and Automation, ICRA (2011)

Reconstruction and Enumeration of hv-Convex Polyominoes with Given Horizontal Projection*

Norbert Hantos and Péter Balázs

Department of Image Processing and Computer Graphics
University of Szeged
Árpád tér 2., 6720, Szeged, Hungary
{nhantos,pbalazs}@inf.u-szeged.hu

Abstract. Enumeration and reconstruction of certain types of polyominoes, according to several parameters, are frequently studied problems in combinatorial image processing. Polyominoes with fixed projections play an important role in discrete tomography. In this paper, we provide a linear-time algorithm for reconstructing hv-convex polyominoes with minimal number of columns satisfying a given horizontal projection. The method can be easily modified to get solutions with any given number of columns. We also describe a direct formula for calculating the number of solutions with any number of columns, and a recursive formula for fixed number of columns.

Keywords: discrete tomography, reconstruction, enumeration, polyomino, hv-convexity.

1 Introduction

Projections of binary images are fundamental shape descriptors that are widely used in tasks of pattern recognition and image processing (see, e.g., [1, 10, 11], and the references given there). In binary tomography [8, 9], projections are used to reconstruct binary images from them. Several theoretical results are known, regarding the efficient reconstruction and the number of solutions, using just the horizontal and vertical projections. From theoretical point of view, hv-convex polyominoes form an extensively studied class of binary images. Although, we know quite a lot about the reconstruction complexity and the number of solutions in this class when the horizontal and vertical projections are available [2, 3, 5], surprisingly, those problems have not yet been investigated if only one projection is given. In this paper, we fill this gap by describing a linear-time reconstruction

* This work was supported by the OTKA PD100950 grant of the National Scientific Research Fund. The research was also supported by the European Union and the State of Hungary, co-financed by the European Social Fund in the framework of TÁMOP 4.2.4. A/2-11-1-2012-0001 'National Excellence Program', and under the grant agreement TÁMOP-4.2.2.A-11/1/KONV-2012-0073 'Telemedicine-focused research activities on the field of Mathematics, Informatics and Medical sciences'.

J. Ruiz-Shulcloper and G. Sanniti di Baja (Eds.): CIARP 2013, Part I, LNCS 8258, pp. 100–107, 2013.

algorithm and providing formulas for the number of solutions with minimal and with any given number of columns.

The paper is structured as follows. In Section 2 we give some preliminaries. In Section 3, we provide a linear-time algorithm for reconstructing hv-convex polyominoes from the horizontal projection. Section 4 describes formulas for enumerating hv-convex polyominoes with given horizontal projection, for arbitrary, and also for fixed number of columns. The conclusions are given in Section 5.

2 Preliminaries

A *binary image* is a digital image where each pixel is either black or white. Binary images having m rows and n columns can be represented by binary matrices of size $m \times n$, where the value in the position of the matrix is 1 (respectively, 0) if the corresponding pixel in the image is black (respectively, white).

The *horizontal projection* of a binary image F is a vector representing the number of black pixels in each row of F. Using the matrix representation, it is the vector $\mathcal{H}(F) = (h_1, \ldots, h_m)$, where

$$h_i = \sum_{j=1}^{n} f_{ij} \quad (i = 1, \ldots, m) .$$

The vertical projection of the image can be defined analogously. Throughout the paper, without loss of generality, we assume that each projection component of the binary image is positive.

Two positions $P = (p_1, p_2)$ and $Q = (q_1, q_2)$ in a binary image are said to be *4-adjacent* if $|p_1 - q_1| + |p_2 - q_2| = 1$. The positions P and Q are *4-connected* if there is a sequence of distinct black pixels $P_0 = P, \ldots, P_k = Q$ in the binary image such that P_l is 4-adjacent to P_{l-1}, respectively, for each $l = 1, \ldots, k$. A binary image F is *4-connected* if any two points in F are 4-connected. The 4-connected binary images are also called *polyominoes* [7]. The binary image F is horizontally and vertically convex, or shortly *hv-convex* if the black pixels are consecutive in each row and column of the image (see the polyomino T in Fig. 1). *Upper stack polyominoes* are special hv-convex polyominoes which contain the two bottom corners of their minimal bounding rectangles. Similarly, *lower stack polyominoes* are hv-convex polyominoes that contain the two top corners of their minimal bounding rectangles. Finally, *parallelogram polyominoes* are hv-convex polyominoes that contain both their top left and bottom right, or both their top right and bottom left corners of their minimal bounding rectangles. Any hv-convex polyomino can be constructed (not necessarily uniquely) from an upper stack, a parallelogram and a lower stack polyomino. Figure 1 shows examples for the special types of polyominoes, and such a construction.

3 Reconstruction from the Horizontal Projection

Let $H = (h_1, \ldots, h_m) \in \mathbb{N}^m$ be a vector of size m. We first give an algorithm, called *GreedyRec* which constructs an F binary image with m rows and the

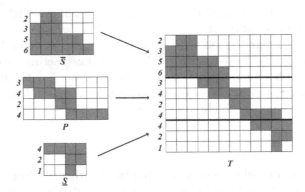

Fig. 1. An hv-convex polyomino T composed of an upper stack $\overline{S}$, a parallelogram P, and a lower stack $\underline{S}$ polyomino

minimal possible number of columns. Due to h-convexity, the 1s are consecutive in each row of the binary image to reconstruct. We will refer to them as the i-th *strip* of the image ($i = 1, \ldots, m$). The sketch of the algorithm is the following (Fig. 3a shows an example result of the algorithm).

1. The first strip must be aligned to the left.
2. The position of the i-th strip of F depends on the position of the $(i - 1)$-th strip ($i = 2, \ldots, m$):
   (a) if $h_i = h_{i-1}$, then the i-th strip is just below the $(i - 1)$-th strip (see Fig. 2a),
   (b) if $h_i < h_{i-1}$, then the i-th strip is aligned to the right of the $(i - 1)$-th strip (see Fig. 2b),
   (c) if $h_i > h_{i-1}$, then the i-th strip is aligned to the left of the $(i - 1)$-th strip (see Fig. 2c).

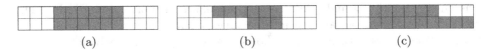

| (a) | (b) | (c) |

Fig. 2. Steps of *GreedyRec* with the $(i - 1)$-th and the i-th rows. Cases: (a) $h_i = h_{i-1}$, (b) $h_i < h_{i-1}$, and (c) $h_i > h_{i-1}$

Theorem 1. *GreedyRec constructs an hv-convex polyomino satisfying the horizontal projection with minimal number of columns, in $O(m)$ time.*

Proof. It is clear that the resulted image is an hv-convex polyomino with the required horizontal projection. We prove by induction that no solution exists with less number of columns.

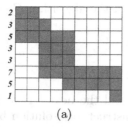   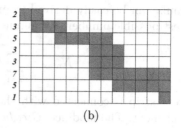

(a)   (b)

Fig. 3. (a) The minimum-size output of *GreedyRec* for $H = (2,3,5,3,3,7,5,1)$ with 9 columns, and (b) another solution with 13 columns

Let $n_o^{(k)}$ be the number of columns in a minimal-column solution of the problem (i.e., an hv-convex polyomino satisfying the projections with minimal number of columns), considering only the first k components of the input $(h_1, \ldots, h_k)$ ($k \le m$). Similarly, let $n_g^{(k)}$ be the number of columns in the result of *GreedyRec* for the first k components of the input. For $k = 1$, $n_g^{(1)} = n_o^{(1)} = h_1$, so *GreedyRec* is optimal. For $k > 1$ assume that $n_g^{(k-1)} = n_o^{(k-1)}$.

If $h_k \le h_{k-1}$, then $n_g^{(k)} = n_g^{(k-1)}$ (Cases 2(a) and 2(b) of *GreedyRec*), therefore the number of columns does not change. Since $n_o^{(k)} \ge n_o^{(k-1)}$, therefore $n_g^{(k)} = n_o^{(k)}$, and *GreedyRec* is still optimal.

If $h_k > h_{k-1}$, then $n_g^{(k)} = n_g^{(k-1)} + h_k - h_{k-1}$ (Case 2(c) of *GreedyRec*). Assume to the contrary that an arbitrary optimal algorithm provides a better result, hence $n_o^{(k)} < n_o^{(k-1)} + h_k - h_{k-1}$.

For a further analysis, let us call a column k-*simple* if its $(k-1)$-th element is 0 and its k-th element is 1. The number of k-simple columns is at least $h_k - h_{k-1}$, and due to vertical convexity, in a k-simple column there can be no 1s above the k-th row. Therefore, the first $k-1$ number of strips must fit into $n_o^{(k)} - (h_k - h_{k-1})$ number of non-k-simple columns at most. Due to h-convexity and connectivity, non-k-simple-columns must be successive. Therefore, the first $k-1$ number of strips fit into a matrix with a column number of $n_o^{(k)} - (h_k - h_{k-1}) < n_o^{(k-1)} + h_k - h_{k-1} - (h_k - h_{k-1}) = n_o^{(k-1)}$, which is a contradiction to the minimality of $n_o^{(k-1)}$. Hence, *GreedyRec* is still optimal.

The complexity of the algorithm is straightforward, if the polyomino is represented by the first positions of its strips.   □

One can easily modify the output of *GreedyRec* to expand it to have a predefined number of columns (if possible) by moving the k-th, $(k+1)$-st, $\ldots$, m-th strips further to the right, if the previous strip allows it (i.e., when the image remains hv-convex and 4-connected). The smallest possible number of columns (provided by *GreedyRec*) is $N_{\min} = N_m$, where

$$
N_i = \begin{cases} h_i & \text{if } i = 1\,, \\ N_{i-1} & \text{if } h_i \le h_{i-1}\,, \\ N_{i-1} + h_i - h_{i-1} & \text{if } h_i > h_{i-1}\,. \end{cases} \tag{1}
$$

This formula can be easily derived from the steps of the algorithm *GreedyRec*. The biggest possible number of columns is

$$N_{\max} = \sum_{i=1}^{m} h_i - m + 1 \,, \tag{2}$$

where every strip is connected with the previous and the next strips through only one element. The modified *GreedyRec* can construct any solution between $N_{\min}$ and $N_{\max}$ in linear time. An example result of the modified algorithm is given in Fig. 3b.

4   Enumerating *hv*-Convex Polyominoes with Fixed Horizontal Projection

Enumeration of polyominoes according to several parameters (e.g., area, perimeter, size of the bounding rectangle, etc.) is an extensively studied field of combinatorial geometry. Regarding the number of *hv*-convex polyominoes satisfying two projections, in [2–5] several results have been published. In [6] a method was proposed to determine the number of *hv*-convex polyominoes that fit into discrete rectangle of given size. In this section, we provide formulas to enumerate *hv*-convex polyominoes satisfying the given horizontal projection.

4.1   Arbitrary Number of Columns

We first give a formula to calculate the number of *hv*-convex polyominoes with a given horizontal projection $H = (h_1, \ldots, h_m)$, if there is no restriction on the number of colums of the resulted image.

Given an *hv*-convex polyomino, the smallest integer k for which $f_{k1} = 1$ is called the *smallest left anchor position*. Similarly, the *greatest right anchor position* is the greatest integer l for which $f_{ln} = 1$. Furthermore, let K denote the greatest integer for which $h_1 \le h_2 \le \cdots \le h_K$. Similarly, let L be the smallest integer for which $h_L \ge h_{L+1} \ge \cdots \ge h_m$. Figure 4 illustrates these definitions.

First, assume that $K < L$. Then, $K < k, l < L$ cannot hold, due to *v*-convexity. Also note that for every $k < l$ solution, a vertically mirrored image is also a solution with $l < k$, and vice versa. For this reason, we only count the cases with $k < l$ (i.e., $1 \le k \le K$ and $L \le l \le m$), and multiply the result by 2.

Let $\overline{S}_k(H)$ denote the number of upper stack polyominoes having the horizontal projection $(h_1, \ldots, h_k)$. Similarly, let $\underline{S}_l(H)$ denote the number of lower stack polyominoes having the horizontal projection $(h_l, \ldots, h_m)$. Furthermore, let $P_{k,l}(H)$ denote the number of parallelogram polyominoes with the horizontal projection $(h_k, \ldots, h_l)$, having the smallest left anchor position k and the greatest right anchor position l.

Lemma 1. $\overline{S}_1(H) = 1$, and $\overline{S}_k(H) = \prod_{i=2}^{k}(h_i - h_{i-1} + 1)$ $(k \ge 2)$. $\underline{S}_m(H) = 1$, and $\underline{S}_l(H) = \prod_{i=l}^{m-1}(h_i - h_{i+1} + 1)$ $(l < m)$.

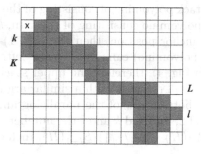

Fig. 4. An hv-convex polyomino with $H = (1, 2, 4, 6, 6, 2, 5, 4, 4, 3, 2)$, where $K = 5$, and $L = 7$. The smallest left anchor position is $k = 3$, the greatest right anchor position is $l = 9$. The $(k-1)$-th strip can be placed on the top of the k-th strip in 2 different ways, and cannot occupy the position marked by $\times$, since the k-th strip must be the leftmost strip

Proof. The formula $\overline{S}_1(H) = 1$ is trivial. If $k \geq 2$, then the $(k-1)$-th strip can be placed on the top of the k-th strip in $h_k - h_{k-1} + 1$ different ways. Similarly, the $(k-2)$-th strip can be placed on the top of the $(k-1)$-th strip, in $h_{k-1} - h_{k-2} + 1$ different ways. And so on. Finally, the first strip can be placed in $h_2 - h_1 + 1$ ways on the top of the second strip. The formula for the lower stack polyominoes can be proven analogously. □

Lemma 2. $P_{k,l}(H) = \prod_{i=k}^{l-1} \min\{h_i, h_{i+1}\}$.

Proof. The k-th strip is fixed (it is in the leftmost position), and we can place the $(k+1)$-th strip under the k-th strip in $\min\{h_k, h_{k+1}\}$ ways. The $(k+2)$-th strip can be placed under the $(k+1)$-th strip in $\min\{h_{k+1}, h_{k+2}\}$ ways. And so on. Finally the l-th strip can be placed under the $(l-1)$-th strip in $\min\{h_{l-1}, h_l\}$ ways. □

In the rest of the paper, we will use the convention that empty (non-defined) factors of a product will be always 1.

Theorem 2. *Let $H \in \mathbb{N}^m$. If $K < L$ then the number of hv-convex polyominoes with the horizontal projection H is*

$$P_{K<L}(H) = 2 \cdot \sum_{k=1}^{K} \sum_{l=L}^{m} \left(\overline{S}_{k-1}(H) \cdot (h_k - h_{k-1}) \cdot P_{k,l}(H) \cdot (h_l - h_{l+1}) \cdot \underline{S}_{l+1}(H) \right).$$

(3)

If $K \geq L$, then the number of solutions is

$$P_{K \geq L}(H) = P_{K<L}(H) - \overline{S}_L(H) \cdot \underline{S}_K(H).$$

(4)

Proof. We observe that an hv-convex polyomino with the smallest left anchor position k and the greatest right anchor position l can be uniquely decomposed into a (possibly empty) upper stack polyomino consisting of the first $k-1$ rows, a (possibly empty) lower stack polyomino of consisting of the last rows from $l+1$ to m, and a parallelogram polyomino consisiting of the k-th, $k+1$-th, ..., l-th rows. If k is the smallest left anchor position, then the $(k-1)$-th strip (the bottom strip of the upper stack polyomino) cannot reach the leftmost position (see the position marked by $\times$, in Fig. 4), therefore the upper stack can be connected to the parallelogram in $(h_k - h_{k-1})$ ways. With a similar argument, the lower stack can be connected to the bottom row of the parallelogram in $(h_l - h_{l+1})$ ways. Thus, using lemmas 1 and 2, for fixed k and l the number of possible solutions is $\overline{S}_{k-1}(H) \cdot (h_k - h_{k-1}) \cdot P_{k,l}(H) \cdot (h_l - h_{l+1}) \cdot \underline{S}_{l+1}(H)$. Including also the mirrored cases we get (3).

If $K \geq L$, then the same formula as in (3) can be applied. However, in this case, it counts some of the solutions twice through symmetry (where the parallelogram poliominoes are rectangular). Note that the longest strips in H are $h_L = h_{L+1} = \cdots = h_K$, and (3) counts all the cases twice when these strips are right under each other. Regarding that the L-th strip is the bottom of the upper stack polyomino, and the K-th strip is the uppermost row of the lower stack polyomino, the number of cases counted twice is $\overline{S}_L(H) \cdot \underline{S}_K(H)$, using Lemma 1.   □

4.2   Fixed Number of Columns

Now, we give a recursive formula to calculate the number $P_n(H)$ of hv-convex polyominoes having the horizontal projection $H = (h_1, \ldots, h_m)$, when the number of columns is fixed to n. First, assume again that $K < L$. Let $r \geq 1$ and $P(p_1, \ldots, p_r, n)$ denote the number of parallelogram polyominoes with n columns, having the horizontal projection $(p_1, \ldots, p_r)$.

Lemma 3. $P(p_1, n) = 1$ if $p_1 = n$. $P(p_1, n) = 0$ if $p_1 \neq n$. Furthermore, for $r > 1$ we have the following recursion

$$P(p_1, \ldots, p_r, n) = \begin{cases} \sum_{i=1}^{p_1} P(p_2, \ldots, p_r, n-i+1) & \text{if } p_1 \leq p_2, \\ \sum_{i=1}^{p_2} P(p_2, \ldots, p_r, n-(p_1-p_2)-i+1) & \text{if } p_1 > p_2. \end{cases}$$

Proof. If $r = 1$, then either the strip itself of length p_1 occupies n number of columns (and should be counted as a solution) or not. If $r > 1$ and $p_1 \leq p_2$, then we count recursively every possible solution where the second strip is shifted to the right under the first strip, and the number of remaining columns decreases proportionately. If $r > 1$ and $p_1 > p_2$, then additionally, we have to substract the difference from the number of required columns, since the second strip must be shifted with at least $p_1 - p_2$ positions to the right, relatively to the first position of the first strip.   □

Therefore, including the possible stack polyominoes and the mirrored cases, the number of solutions for a fixed n is

$$P_n(H) = 2 \cdot \sum_{k=1}^{K} \sum_{l=L}^{m} \left(\overline{S}_{k-1}(H) \cdot (h_k - h_{k-1}) \cdot P(h_k, \ldots, h_l, n) \cdot (h_l - h_{l+1}) \cdot \underline{S}_{l+1}(H) \right),$$

where $P(h_k, \ldots, h_l, n) = 0$ if $k > l$.

If $K \geq L$ then we have to substract some of the solutions in the same way as in (4). Note that this concerns only $P_{N_{\min}}(H)$ (where n is minimal), since for every other case a mirrored solution is truly a different solution.

$P_n(H)$ also provides a different formula for calculating the number of solutions, if the size of the polyomino can be arbitrary, namely

$$\sum_{n=N_{\min}}^{N_{\max}} P_n(H),$$

where $N_{\min}$ and $N_{\max}$ is given by (1) and (2), respectively.

5 Conclusion

In this paper, we showed how to reconstruct hv-convex polyominoes from a given horizontal projection with minimal number of columns in linear time. This algorithm can easily be extended to give a solution with any required number of columns, if such a solution exists. We also gave formulas for counting all possible solutions, one for any number of columns, and another one for fixed number of columns. The results can be used in various fields of pattern recognition, image processing, and especially, in binary tomography.

References

1. Anagnostopoulos, C.-N.E., Anagnostopoulos, I.E., Psoroulas, I.D., Loumos, V., Kayafas, E.: License plate recognition from still images and video sequences: A survey. IEEE Trans. on Intelligent Transportation Systems 9(3), 377–391 (2008)
2. Barcucci, E., Del Lungo, A., Nivat, M., Pinzani, R.: Medians of polyominoes: A property for the reconstruction. Int. J. Imaging Syst. and Techn. 9, 69–77 (1998)
3. Del Lungo, A.: Polyominoes defined by two vectors. Theor. Comput. Sci. 127, 187–198 (1994)
4. Del Lungo, A., Duchi, E., Frosini, A., Rinaldi, S.: Enumeration of convex polyominoes using the ECO method. In: Discrete Mathematics and Theoretical Computer Science, Proceedings, pp. 103–116 (2003)
5. Del Lungo, A., Nivat, M., Pinzani, R.: The number of convex polyominoes recostructible from their orthogonal projections. Discrete Math. 157, 65–78 (1996)
6. Gessel, I.: On the number of convex polyominoes. Ann. Sci. Math. Québec 24, 63–66 (2000)
7. Golomb, S.W.: Polyominoes. Charles Scriber's Sons, New York (1965)
8. Herman, G.T., Kuba, A. (eds.): Discrete Tomography: Foundations, Algorithms and Applications. Birkhäuser, Boston (1999)
9. Herman, G.T., Kuba, A. (eds.): Advances in Discrete Tomography and its Applications. Birkhäuser, Boston (2007)
10. dos Santos, R.P., Clemente, G.S., Ren, T.I., Calvalcanti, G.D.C.: Text line segmentation based on morphology and histogram projection. In: Proceedings of the 10th International Conference on Document Analysis and Recognition, pp. 651–655 (2009)
11. Vezzani, R., Baltieri, D., Cucchiara, R.: HMM based action recognition with projection histogram features. In: Ünay, D., Çataltepe, Z., Aksoy, S. (eds.) ICPR 2010. LNCS, vol. 6388, pp. 286–293. Springer, Heidelberg (2010)

A Constraint Acquisition Method for Data Clustering

João M.M. Duarte[1,2], Ana L.N. Fred[1], and Fernando Jorge F. Duarte[2]

[1] Instituto de Telecomunicações, Instituto Superior Técnico, Lisboa, Portugal
{jduarte,afred}@lx.it.pt
[2] GECAD - Knowledge Engineering and Decision-Support Research Center,
Institute of Engineering Polytechnic of Porto, Portugal
{jmmd,fjd}@isep.ipp.pt

Abstract. A new constraint acquisition method for parwise-constrained data clustering based on user-feedback is proposed. The method searches for non-redundant intra-cluster and inter-cluster query-candidates, ranks the candidates by decreasing order of interest and, finally, prompts the user the most relevant query-candidates. A comparison between using the original data representation and using a learned representation (obtained from the combination of the pairwise constraints and the original data representation) is also performed. Experimental results shown that the proposed constraint acquisition method and the data representation learning methodology lead to clustering performance improvements.

Keywords: Constraint Acquisition, Constrained Data Clustering.

1 Introduction

Data clustering is an unsupervised learning technique which aims to find structure in data. Domain objects are grouped into clusters such that objects that are alike are placed in the same cluster while dissimilar objects are assigned to different clusters [1]. Due to its unsupervised nature, a data clustering algorithm only has access to features that describe the objects or to (dis)similarities between pairs of objects, and the clustering solution is obtained by optimizing the same objective-function, irrespectively the application.

In many situations, the data analyst may have extra information for a particular application, or may want to express his preferences or conditions to guide data clustering. To accomplish it, the data representation can be manipulated (e.g.: by adding, removing or modifying data features) although it can be very difficult or impractical. A simpler and more intuitive way of doing it consists of using constraints in data clustering. Constrained data clustering algorithms [2–4] use *a priori* knowledge about the data, mapped in form of constraints, to produce more useful clustering solutions. The constraints can be set at a general level by defining rules which are applied to the entire data set, such as data clustering with obstacles [5]; at an intermediate level, where clustering is guided by rules involving the data features [6] or the groups' characteristics, such as, the minimum and maximum capacity [7]; or at a more particular level, where

J. Ruiz-Shulcloper and G. Sanniti di Baja (Eds.): CIARP 2013, Part I, LNCS 8258, pp. 108–116, 2013.

the constraints are applied to the domain objects, by using some labeled data
[3] or defining relations between pairs of objects [2]. Relations between pairs of
objects, usually represented as must-link and cannot-link constraints, have been
the most studied due to their versatility. Many constraints on more general levels
can be transformed into must-link and cannot-link constraints.

It would be expected that the use of constraints should always improve, or at
least not to worsen, the quality of data clustering. However, it was demonstrated
that the use of constraints may in fact harm clustering performance, even when
the set of constraints is not noisy [8]. Therefore, the acquisition of constraint
sets that effectively improve clustering performance is a very important topic in
constrained clustering. Some active learning algorithms for constraint acquisition
have already been proposed regarding the search of labels for some data [9, 10]
and the identification of relations between pairs of objects [2, 11].

It is known that learning distance metrics can improve the performance of
classification and clustering. Typically, distance learning algorithms can be categorized into the supervised and unsupervised categories, depending on the existence of class labels for the objects. Nonetheless, some methods [12–14] can use
the pairwise constraints to learn a new distance function or data representation.

In this work, we propose a new method for acquiring useful pairwise constraints. Our method tries to identify relevant query candidates for a given clustering algorithm, ranks the candidates according to their importance, and then
selects the top candidates to query the user. We compare the proposed method
with the random acquisition of constraints and the Explore-Consolidate [11]
approach. We also evaluate the effectiveness of using distance metric learning
in constrained clustering, the effect of the constraint acquisition methods in the
distance learning, and the corresponding impact in the quality of data clustering.

The rest of the paper is organized as follows. In section 2 we briefly present
some related work on constrained clustering and distance metric learning with
constraints. A new approach for selecting pairwise constraints is presented in
section 3. The performance of the proposed method is evaluated in section 4.
The conclusions and future work is presented in section 5.

2   Related Work

Let $\mathcal{X} = \{\mathbf{x}_1, \cdots, \mathbf{x}_n\}$ be a data set composed of n domain objects $\mathbf{x}_i$, $\mathcal{R}_=$
the set of must-link constraints which contains pairs of objects $(\mathbf{x}_i, \mathbf{x}_j)$ that
should belong to the same cluster, and $\mathcal{R}_{\neq}$ the set of cannot-link constraints
containing pairs of objects that should belong to different clusters. The goal of a
constrained clustering algorithm consists of dividing $\mathcal{X}$ into K clusters regarding
both the data representation (e.g. vectorial and (dis)similarity representations)
and the constraints expressed in $\mathcal{R}_=$ and $\mathcal{R}_{\neq}$, resulting in a data partition $P = \{C_1, \cdots, C_K\}$ where C_k represents an individual cluster.

The Constrained Average-Link (CAL) [15] is based on the agglomerative
hierarchical clustering algorithm Average-Link [16]. The algorithm works as
follows. It starts with n clusters, one for each domain object $\mathbf{x}_i$. Then, at

each step, the two closest clusters, according to a distance measure between clusters, are merged. The process iterates until some stopping criteria is met (e.g. a predefined number of clusters K is reached) or all objects belong to same cluster. The distance between clusters measures the average distance between all pairs of objects belonging to different clusters plus a penalization for each constraint that is not satisfied. This distance is defined as $d(C_k, C_l) = \frac{1}{|C_k||C_l|}(\sum_{i=1}^{|C_k|}\sum_{j=1}^{|C_l|} \text{dist}(\mathbf{x}_i, \mathbf{x}_j) - I_=(\mathbf{x}_i, \mathbf{x}_j) + I_{\neq}(\mathbf{x}_i, \mathbf{x}_j))$, where $I_a(\mathbf{x}_i, \mathbf{x}_j) = p$ if $(\mathbf{x}_i, \mathbf{x}_j) \in \mathcal{R}_a$ and 0 otherwise. $p \geq 0$ is a user parameter that influences the "softness" of the constraints. In our experiments we defined p as the maximum distance between objects in a data set.

An easy but naive way to generate pairwise constraints is the Random Acquisition of Constraints (RAC) and consists of randomly selecting, iteratively, two objects $(\mathbf{x}_i, \mathbf{x}_j) \in \mathcal{X}$ that were not previously tested and ask the user (or some oracle) if both objects should be assigned to the same group. If the answer is "Yes", a must-link constraint is added to the set of must-link constraints, $\mathcal{R}_= = \mathcal{R}_= \cup \{(\mathbf{x}_i, \mathbf{x}_j)\}$. If the answer is "No" a cannot-link constraint is added to the set of cannot-link constraints $\mathcal{R}_{\neq} = \mathcal{R}_{\neq} \cup \{(\mathbf{x}_i, \mathbf{x}_j)\}$. If the user cannot decide, simply skip to the next iteration. The process repeats until a predefined number of constraints is achieved.

The Explore-Consolidate [11] is another method for constraint acquisition and consists of two phases: the Explore phase, where the algorithm identifies a neighborhood $\mathcal{N}_k$ for each cluster in the data set which defines a skeleton of the clusters' structure; and the Consolidate phase, where objects not attributed to any neighborhood are assigned to one of them. The Explore algorithm starts by selecting a random object which forms the first neighborhood. Then, while the maximum number of queries is not reached and until K disjoint neighborhoods are not found, the farthest object $\mathbf{x}$ from all the existing neighborhoods is selected. Queries between $\mathbf{x}$ and a random object belonging to each neighborhood are posed. If $\mathbf{x}$ does not belong to any neighborhood, a new one is formed with $\mathbf{x}$. The Consolidate algorithm first computes the centroids $\bar{\mathbf{x}}_k$ of each neighborhood $\mathcal{N}_k$. Then, while the maximum number of queries is not reached, an object $\mathbf{x}$ that does not belong to any neighborhood is randomly selected. Queries are posed between $\mathbf{x}$ and each neighborhood by increasing order of its distance to the centroids $\bar{\mathbf{x}}_k$ until a must-link is obtained. After the Explore and Consolidate phases, the pairwise constraint sets are formed by adding a must-link constraint for each pair of objects that belong to the same neighborhood, and a cannot link constraint for each pair of objects belonging to different neighborhoods.

There may be contradictions between the relations of objects in the original representation of the data and sets of constraints. We are interested to find out how learning a new data space representation, which simultaneously represents both the original data and the clustering preferences, influences the performance of data clustering. The Discriminant Component Analysis (DCA) [14] is a distance metric learning algorithm capable of learning a new data representation from the original data and a set of constraints. The DCA builds a set of chunklets $\mathcal{Q} = \{Q_1, \cdots, Q_q\}$, i.e. groups of domain objects connected by must-link constraints, and a set of discriminative chunklets $\mathcal{S} = \{S_1, \cdots, S_q\}$, one for each chunklet Q_i. Each element of the discriminative chunklet S_i indicates the chunklets that have at least one cannot-link constraint connecting a object in Q_i. Then DCA learns a data transformation which minimizes the variance between domain objects in the same chunklet Q_i and maximizes the variance between discriminative data chunklets S_i. The covariance matrices, $\mathbf{C}_b$ and $\mathbf{C}_w$, store the total variance between domain objects in each $S_i \in \mathcal{S}$ and the total variance within domain objects in the same chunklets $\forall Q_i \in \mathcal{Q}$. These matrices are computed as $\mathbf{C}_b = \frac{1}{\sum_{i=1}^{q} |S_i|} \sum_{i=1}^{q} \sum_{i \in S_j} (\mathbf{m}_j - \mathbf{m}_i)(\mathbf{m}_j - \mathbf{m}_i)^\top$ and $\mathbf{C}_w = \frac{1}{q} \sum_{j=1}^{q} \frac{1}{|Q_j|} \sum_{\mathbf{x}_i \in Q_j} (\mathbf{x}_i - \mathbf{m}_j)(\mathbf{x}_i - \mathbf{m}_j)^\top$, respectively, where $\mathbf{m}_j$ is the mean vector of Q_j. The optimal transformation matrix $\mathbf{A}$ is obtained by optimizing $J(\mathbf{A}) = \arg\max_{\mathbf{A}} \frac{|\mathbf{A}^\top \mathbf{C}_b \mathbf{A}|}{|\mathbf{A}^\top \mathbf{C}_w \mathbf{A}|}$.

3   A New Method for Acquiring Pairwise Constraints

The idea of our method is to identify good intra- and inter-cluster query-candidates given a data partition, and select the q most relevant candidates to prompt the user. The motivation for using a data partition as input relates to the importance of finding constraints sets with high informativeness, i.e., with high level of information that the clustering algorithm cannot determine on its own [8]. We also want to avoid performing redundant queries, i.e., queries involving similar pairs of objects. The details of the methods are given below. The proposed (dis)similarity-based constraint acquisition method consists of four phases:

1. Identify intra-cluster candidates. Pairs of objects which are far from each other have higher probability of having different labels than pairs of objects which are close. Therefore, the proposed method selects as candidates intra-cluster pairs of objects which are far apart. Given a distance matrix $\mathbf{D}$, c candidates Q_l are selected for each cluster $C_k \in P$ (more detail on defining c will be given later). Iteratively, the most distant pair of objects $(\mathbf{x}_i, \mathbf{x}_j)$ in C_k according to $\mathbf{D}$ is selected as candidate, i.e., $(\mathbf{x}_i, \mathbf{x}_j) = \arg\max_{\mathbf{x}_i \in C_k, \mathbf{x}_j \in C_k} \mathbf{D}(i,j)$, and is added to the set of query-candidates $Q = Q \cup Q_l$, $Q_l = \{(\mathbf{x}_i, \mathbf{x}_j)\}$. Then, $\mathbf{D}$ is updated such the distance between the objects belonging to the neighborhoods of $\mathbf{x}_i$ and $\mathbf{x}_j$ become 0, i.e., $\mathbf{D}(q, r) = 0$, $\mathbf{D}(r, q) = 0$, $\forall \mathbf{x}_q \in \mathcal{N}_i$, $\forall \mathbf{x}_r \in \mathcal{N}_j$ where $\mathcal{N}_l$ corresponds to the set of the mth closest objects to $\mathbf{x}_l$ in C_k (including itself). The neighborhood size $1 \leq m \leq |C_k|$ is a parameter that should be defined as a compromise between selecting redundant (values close to 1) and non-interesting (values close to $|C_k|$) query-candidates. Note the $\mathcal{N}_i$ and $\mathcal{N}_j$ are computed using the original distance matrix. The process repeats until c candidates are found.

2. Identify inter-cluster candidates. Two objects in different clusters which are nearby have higher probability of belonging to the same *natural* cluster than objects which are distant. Hence, the algorithm selects as query-candidates pairs of objects in different clusters which are close. For each pair of clusters (C_l, C_o), $C_l \in P$, $C_o \in P$, $l < o$, c query-candidates are selected the following way. First, the closest pair of objects $(\mathbf{x}_i, \mathbf{x}_j)$ in different clusters are selected, i.e., $(\mathbf{x}_i, \mathbf{x}_j) = \arg\min_{\mathbf{x}_i \in C_l, \mathbf{x}_j \in C_o} \mathbf{D}(i,j)$, and is added to Q. Next, the neighborhoods $\mathcal{N}_i$ and $\mathcal{N}_j$ are computed as the sets of the m_i^{th} and m_j^{th} closest objects to $\mathbf{x}_i$ in C_1 and $\mathbf{x}_j$ in C_l, and the distances between objects in distinct neighborhoods are set to ∞, i.e., $\mathbf{D}(q,r) = \infty$, $\mathbf{D}(r,q) = \infty$, $\forall \mathbf{x}_q \in \mathcal{N}_i$, $\forall \mathbf{x}_r \in \mathcal{N}_j$. Again, this will restrict the algorithm from choosing identical query-candidates. The procedure goes on until the desired number of candidates c is reached.

3. Rank candidates. This phase consists in ranking the candidates in descending order of interest. For this purpose a score is calculated for each candidate taking into account two situations: if the candidate has been obtained during the intra-cluster phase, the shorter the distance between one of its objects with any object from another cluster the more interesting the candidate is considered; if the candidate has been selected during the inter-cluster phase, the smaller the distance between the two objects of the query-candidate the higher the interest. Thus, the score S_l for each candidate $Q_l \in Q$, $(\mathbf{x}_i, \mathbf{x}_j) = Q_l$ is computed as $S_l = \min_{m:\mathbf{x}_m \in X \setminus C_{P_i}} \min\left[\mathbf{D}(i,m), \mathbf{D}(j,m)\right]$ if Q_l is an intra-candidate and $S_l = \mathbf{D}(i,j)$ otherwise. The sorted set of candidates Q^{sorted} is obtained by sorting the candidates according to their scores $\{S_i\}_{i=1}^{|Q|}$ in ascending order.

4. Query the user. Finally, the set of must-link and cannot-link constraints are obtained by querying the user if a pair of objects in a sorted query-candidate should belong to the same cluster, starting from the first query-candidate Q_1^{sorted} and stopping when the predefined number of queries q is obtained.

In this work, the number of candidates c for each intra- and inter-cluster search is the same (but it is not required). To ensure that at least q candidates are obtained (the number of candidates must be equal or higher than the number of desired queries) the following inequality must hold: $q \leq ck + c\frac{k(k-1)}{2}$, where k is the number of clusters. Thereby, $c \geq \lceil \frac{2q}{k^2+k} \rceil$. It is usually helpful to generate more candidates that the strictly required because some clusters are more interesting than others (e.g. touching clusters). By doing so, candidates from non-interesting regions will naturally be ruled out in the ranking phase.

The obtained constraint set can be used by a constrained clustering algorithm using the original data representation to partition the data. However, we hypothesize that using a learned space which represents both the original data and the constraints (e.g. DCA) can further enhance clustering quality.

4   Experimental Results

In our experiments, 5 synthetic data sets (shown in figure 1) and 5 real data sets taken from the UCI ML repository (http://archive.ics.uci.edu/ml/) were used to assess the performance of the constraint acquisition approach. A brief description for each real data set is given next. The Iris data set consists of 50 objects from each of three species of Iris flowers (setosa, virginica and versicolor) characterized by four features. The Breast Cancer data set is composed of 683 domain objects characterized by nine features and divided into two clusters: benign and malignant. The Optdigits is a subset of Handwritten Digits data set

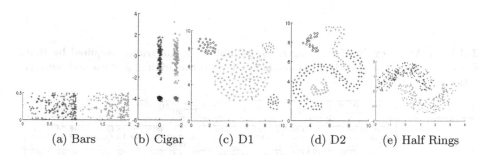

(a) Bars   (b) Cigar   (c) D1   (d) D2   (e) Half Rings

Fig. 1. Synthetic data sets

containing only the first 100 objects of each digit, from a total of 3823 domain objects characterized by 64 attributes. The House Votes data set is composed of two clusters of votes for each of the U.S. House of Representatives Congressmen on the 16 key votes identified by the Congressional Quarterly Almanac (125 democrats and 107 republicans). The Wine data set consists of the results of a chemical analysis of wines divided into three clusters with 59, 71 and 48 objects, described by 13 features.

Table 1 shows the average accuracy and standard deviation of the partitions obtained using CAL algorithm (K was set as the real number of clusters) using no constraints, constraints acquired using RAC, Explore-Consolidate and the proposed method, with the original data representation and a learned data representation obtained using DCA (identified with "+L"). The average values were computed over 50 repetitions using data resampling with replacement (the size of the samples corresponds to the original size of the data sets). Constraints sets were obtained by performing 10, 20, 30, 40 and 50 queries. Answers were given using ground-truth information. The number of clusters was defined as the "natural" number of cluster for each data set. The number of candidates for each intra-cluster and inter-cluster searches was defined as $c = \lceil 2 \times \frac{2q}{k^2+k} \rceil$, and the size of the neighborhood of an object $\mathbf{x}_i \in C_k$ was set to $m = \lceil 0.35|C_k| \rceil$. The partitions obtained using the original data representation with constraints were usually (not always) better than the ones produced without constraints. Also, the average accuracy (percent of correctly clustered objects) of the proposed method and the Explore-Consolidate were generally superior than the accuracy achieved by the RAC method. However, by comparing our method with the Explore-Consolidate no method was clearly a winner. The results achieved by using a learned data representation representing both the constraint sets and the original data representation were usually superior than the results obtained using the original representation. The distance learning algorithm obtained better data representations with the proposed and Explore-consolidate approaches than the random acquisition of constraints, since the corresponding partitions are more accurate.

Table 1. Accuracy for CAL using no constraints, the constraints acquired by RAC, Explore-Consolidate and the proposed method, with the original and learned representations

Data set	Acquisition Method	Number of queries				
		10	20	30	40	50
Bars	No const	97.48 (2.98)				
	Random	97.64 (2.76)	97.78 (2.70)	97.94 (2.28)	98.03 (2.36)	**98.76** (1.25)
	Expl.Consol.	97.28 (3.07)	**97.83** (2.70)	**98.07** (2.25)	**98.10** (2.28)	98.52 (1.59)
	Proposed	**97.66** (2.79)	**97.83** (2.81)	98.03 (2.76)	98.09 (2.70)	98.23 (2.53)
	Random+L	95.10 (8.38)	97.28 (2.40)	97.59 (2.30)	98.02 (1.87)	97.99 (1.98)
	Expl.Consol.+L	96.36 (3.58)	97.45 (3.17)	**98.06** (2.44)	98.09 (2.54)	**98.56** (1.74)
	Proposed+L	**97.52** (2.96)	**98.01** (2.34)	98.04 (2.48)	**98.11** (2.60)	98.17 (2.37)
Half Rings	No const	83.08 (5.78)				
	Random	82.26 (6.32)	82.23 (5.60)	82.62 (5.76)	81.65 (6.24)	81.79 (5.86)
	Expl.Consol.	**82.86** (6.34)	81.98 (5.16)	**82.93** (6.60)	**86.13** (6.58)	**86.39** (7.53)
	Proposed	82.59 (6.23)	**83.47** (6.03)	82.05 (5.65)	82.29 (5.52)	83.53 (5.90)
	Random+L	84.15 (7.08)	86.84 (6.05)	**89.67** (5.32)	89.07 (4.50)	88.93 (5.10)
	Expl.Consol.+L	81.21 (4.27)	82.14 (3.17)	83.01 (3.41)	83.44 (3.15)	84.61 (2.70)
	Proposed+L	**85.96** (6.90)	**89.01** (3.69)	89.45 (3.44)	**89.58** (3.90)	**89.87** (2.77)
Cigar	No const	75.06 (14.09)				
	Random	75.48 (14.13)	75.87 (14.56)	78.32 (14.14)	77.30 (14.10)	78.90 (13.46)
	Expl.Consol.	74.77 (15.12)	**79.52** (12.59)	79.68 (13.25)	**83.96** (10.21)	**87.18** (10.07)
	Proposed	**75.63** (13.31)	78.23 (12.67)	**81.51** (11.77)	82.11 (10.79)	84.96 (8.70)
	Random+L	**91.67** (11.00)	94.90 (6.04)	94.79 (5.89)	94.79 (5.89)	97.05 (4.88)
	Expl.Consol.+L	86.11 (7.66)	94.02 (7.25)	96.69 (4.83)	98.11 (3.92)	98.22 (2.99)
	Proposed+L	91.58 (9.46)	**96.02** (5.72)	**98.02** (3.82)	**98.67** (3.10)	**99.17** (1.93)
D1	No const	68.78 (13.56)				
	Random	68.99 (14.45)	73.60 (14.27)	77.47 (15.15)	79.48 (14.34)	**85.21** (13.41)
	Expl.Consol.	**72.94** (14.36)	**75.72** (13.60)	**82.46** (11.96)	**80.34** (12.22)	82.74 (12.46)
	Proposed	71.42 (14.37)	70.81 (14.50)	72.79 (14.51)	76.60 (13.90)	76.70 (13.09)
	Random+L	67.82 (8.58)	71.82 (10.93)	74.79 (12.10)	78.65 (15.57)	81.11 (14.38)
	Expl.Consol.+L	**69.55** (11.13)	**76.53** (10.39)	**78.58** (11.14)	**81.98** (10.44)	**82.73** (10.22)
	Proposed+L	63.13 (12.83)	70.29 (10.40)	72.45 (14.33)	74.52 (12.43)	77.33 (12.94)
D2	No const	55.12 (6.84)				
	Random	53.45 (6.19)	53.67 (6.02)	53.60 (4.73)	54.04 (4.70)	53.90 (4.43)
	Expl.Consol.	53.64 (5.14)	52.00 (5.13)	54.96 (8.15)	52.77 (7.17)	55.15 (8.10)
	Proposed	**55.50** (7.14)	**55.63** (7.14)	**56.09** (7.69)	**56.71** (8.26)	**57.18** (7.97)
	Random+L	52.83 (6.38)	53.47 (5.85)	50.88 (5.53)	53.08 (4.63)	53.29 (5.11)
	Expl.Consol.+L	53.11 (4.74)	52.91 (5.32)	53.54 (5.90)	53.82 (6.07)	**58.19** (8.46)
	Proposed+L	**55.16** (7.29)	**55.43** (7.05)	**56.48** (7.99)	**57.60** (7.96)	58.02 (7.60)
Crabs	No const	53.08 (2.31)				
	Random	52.85 (2.20)	53.57 (2.89)	53.43 (2.45)	53.12 (2.11)	53.47 (2.88)
	Expl.Consol.	53.53 (2.74)	**54.03** (2.71)	**54.59** (3.15)	**56.17** (3.56)	**59.04** (3.94)
	Proposed	**53.70** (2.50)	53.91 (2.98)	53.26 (2.14)	54.00 (2.84)	54.14 (3.26)
	Random+L	**65.74** (14.95)	65.69 (16.10)	**72.01** (17.14)	68.74 (18.14)	**72.62** (18.83)
	Expl.Consol.+L	54.20 (3.22)	54.78 (4.13)	57.59 (7.72)	59.46 (5.71)	60.98 (5.62)
	Proposed+L	62.24 (12.98)	**70.12** (14.51)	70.14 (16.45)	**72.64** (17.06)	66.75 (17.36)
House Votes	No const	89.22 (2.49)				
	Random	89.41 (2.92)	89.16 (2.84)	90.07 (2.98)	89.55 (3.34)	90.32 (3.26)
	Expl.Consol.	89.32 (2.64)	89.73 (2.41)	**90.51** (2.35)	90.47 (2.35)	**90.92** (2.06)
	Proposed	**89.62** (2.55)	**90.03** (2.45)	90.38 (2.73)	**90.48** (2.84)	90.78 (2.56)
	Random+L	67.36 (15.42)	67.71 (16.53)	66.97 (18.10)	65.34 (18.37)	63.58 (18.67)
	Expl.Consol.+L	**89.02** (2.42)	**89.47** (2.53)	**90.09** (2.25)	**90.45** (2.38)	**90.51** (1.91)
	Proposed+L	69.14 (17.32)	75.77 (18.10)	74.78 (20.03)	80.68 (18.84)	82.22 (19.95)
Wine	No const	60.98 (5.87)				
	Random	**60.96** (5.94)	62.04 (5.94)	62.37 (6.41)	62.36 (5.23)	63.63 (5.44)
	Expl.Consol.	59.94 (5.80)	60.99 (5.58)	61.51 (5.57)	63.34 (5.75)	**65.11** (6.12)
	Proposed	60.82 (5.67)	**62.54** (6.05)	**63.76** (5.60)	**64.47** (5.12)	64.47 (4.73)
	Random+L	51.17 (11.51)	47.09 (8.54)	49.28 (10.92)	54.97 (14.03)	58.47 (12.91)
	Expl.Consol.+L	59.30 (12.05)	**63.54** (7.75)	58.42 (7.27)	**69.06** (6.39)	**72.13** (8.90)
	Proposed+L	**60.53** (11.75)	57.24 (11.55)	58.22 (11.66)	59.74 (9.68)	58.78 (11.66)
Iris	No const	78.40 (10.18)				
	Random	78.16 (9.92)	78.15 (9.94)	79.60 (10.42)	79.04 (10.89)	82.11 (10.78)
	Expl.Consol.	80.73 (10.05)	**87.12** (8.48)	**90.15** (7.44)	**92.03** (5.27)	**93.24** (3.21)
	Proposed	**81.99** (9.72)	83.61 (9.82)	85.27 (8.44)	87.56 (8.27)	87.87 (7.70)
	Random+L	61.69 (22.48)	77.41 (18.44)	82.65 (12.52)	85.67 (13.60)	85.97 (13.33)
	Expl.Consol.+L	81.01 (13.43)	82.53 (12.41)	90.45 (9.45)	93.65 (5.15)	94.64 (3.21)
	Proposed+L	**85.43** (13.58)	**89.45** (11.51)	**93.23** (8.60)	**94.39** (8.37)	**96.49** (4.75)
Breast Cancer	No const	95.36 (1.48)				
	Random	95.07 (1.61)	95.41 (1.48)	95.43 (1.56)	95.45 (1.48)	95.58 (1.53)
	Expl.Consol.	95.17 (1.57)	95.53 (1.57)	95.32 (1.62)	95.54 (1.26)	95.75 (1.47)
	Proposed	**95.53** (1.53)	**95.70** (1.44)	**95.80** (1.44)	**95.75** (1.42)	**95.76** (1.56)
	Random+L	80.52 (12.61)	74.54 (9.27)	72.98 (8.57)	71.23 (8.21)	69.09 (5.94)
	Expl.Consol.+L	**95.80** (4.84)	**96.24** (1.66)	**95.84** (1.94)	**96.37** (1.48)	**96.18** (1.50)
	Proposed+L	76.40 (11.91)	74.87 (12.18)	76.03 (12.74)	76.13 (13.28)	76.50 (13.81)

5 Conclusions

We proposed a new constraint acquisition method for constrained data clustering which identifies intra- and inter-cluster query-candidates, ranks them by decreasing order of relevance and uses the most interesting candidates to query the user. We assessed the proposed method against not using constraints at all, using random constraints, and using the Explore-Consolidate approach. Results shown the use of constraints obtained using the proposed and the Explore-Consolidate methods both results in better partitions than using random constraints or not using constraints at all. The use of data representations obtained from the set of constraints and the original data usually increases the clustering performance.

Acknowledgements. This work is supported by FCT "Fundação para a Ciência e a Tecnologia" under the project "LearningS" - PTDC/EEI-SII/2312/2012.

References

1. Jain, A.K.: Data clustering: 50 years beyond k-means. Pattern Recogn. Lett. **31**(8) (June 2010) 651–666
2. Wagstaff, K.L.: Intelligent clustering with instance-level constraints. PhD thesis, Ithaca, NY, USA (2002) Chair-Claire Cardie.
3. Basu, S.: Semi-supervised clustering: probabilistic models, algorithms and experiments. PhD thesis, Austin, TX, USA (2005) Supervisor-Mooney, Raymond J.
4. Davidson, I., Ravi, S.: Clustering with constraints feasibility issues and the k-means algorithm. In: 2005 SIAM International Conference on Data Mining (SDM'05), Newport Beach,CA (2005) 138–149
5. Tung, A.K.H., Hou, J., Han, J.: Coe: Clustering with obstacles entities. a preliminary study. In: PADKK '00: Proceedings of the 4th Pacific-Asia Conference on Knowledge Discovery and Data Mining, Current Issues and New Applications, London, UK, Springer-Verlag (2000) 165–168
6. Béjar, J., Cortés, U.: Experiments with domain knowledge in unsupervised learning: Using and revising theories. Revista Iberoamericana de Computación. Computación y Sistemas **1**(3) (1998) 136–144
7. Ge, R., Ester, M., Jin, W., Davidson, I.: Constraint-driven clustering. In: KDD '07: Proceedings of the 13th ACM SIGKDD international conference on Knowledge discovery and data mining, New York, NY, USA, ACM (2007) 320–329
8. Davidson, I., Wagstaff, K.L., Basu, S.: Measuring constraint-set utility for partitional clustering algorithms. In: Proc. 10th European Conference on Principles and Practice of Knowledge Discovery in Databases. (2006)
9. Huang, S.J., Jin, R., Zhou, Z.H.: Active learning by querying informative and representative examples. Advances in neural information processing systems **23** (2010) 892–900
10. Jain, P., Kapoor, A.: Active learning for large multi-class problems. In: IEEE Conference on Computer Vision and Pattern Recognition. (2009) 762–769

11. Basu, S., Banjeree, A., Mooney, E., Banerjee, A., Mooney, R.J.: Active semi-supervision for pairwise constrained clustering. In: In Proceedings of the 2004 SIAM International Conference on Data Mining (SDM-04. (2004) 333–344
12. Xing, E.P., Ng, A.Y., Jordan, M.I., Russell, S.J.: Distance metric learning with application to clustering with side-information. In Becker, S., Thrun, S., Obermayer, K., eds.: NIPS, MIT Press (2002) 505–512
13. Bar-Hillel, A., Hertz, T., Shental, N., Weinshall, D.: Learning a mahalanobis metric from equivalence constraints. J. Machine Learning Research $6(1)$ (2006) 937
14. Hoi, S., Liu, W., Lyu, M., Ma, W.Y.: Learning distance metrics with contextual constraints for image retrieval. In: Computer Vision and Pattern Recognition, 2006 IEEE Computer Society Conference on. Volume 2. (2006) 2072–2078
15. Duarte, J.M.M., Fred, A.L.N., Duarte, F.J.F.: Evidence accumulation clustering using pairwise constraints. In: Proceedings of the International Conference on Knowledge Discovery and Information Retrieval. (2012) 293–299
16. Sokal, R.R., Michener, C.D.: A statistical method for evaluating systematic relationships. University of Kansas Scientific Bulletin **28** (1958) 1409–1438

Auto-encoder Based Data Clustering

Chunfeng Song[1], Feng Liu[2], Yongzhen Huang[1], Liang Wang[1], and Tieniu Tan[1]

[1] National Laboratory of Pattern Recognition (NLPR),
Institute of Automation, Chinese Academy of Sciences, Beijing, 100190, China
[2] School of Automation, Southeast University, Nanjing, 210096, China

Abstract. Linear or non-linear data transformations are widely used processing techniques in clustering. Usually, they are beneficial to enhancing data representation. However, if data have a complex structure, these techniques would be unsatisfying for clustering. In this paper, based on the auto-encoder network, which can learn a highly non-linear mapping function, we propose a new clustering method. Via simultaneously considering data reconstruction and compactness, our method can obtain stable and effective clustering. Experiments on three databases show that the proposed clustering model achieves excellent performance in terms of both accuracy and normalized mutual information.

Keywords: Clustering, Auto-encoder, Non-linear transformation.

1 Introduction

Data clustering [4] is a basic problem in pattern recognition, whose goal is grouping similar data into the same cluster. It attracts much attention and various clustering methods have been presented, most of which either deal with the original data, e.g., K-means [10], its linear transformation, e.g., spectral clustering [7], or its simple non-linear transformation, e.g., kernel K-means [2]. However, if original data are not well distributed due to large intra-variance as shown in the left part of Figure 1, it would be difficult for traditional clustering algorithms to achieve satisfying performance.

To address the above problem, we attempt to map original data space to a new space which is more suitable for clustering. The auto-encoder network [1] is a good candidate to handle this problem. It provides a non-linear mapping function by iteratively learning the encoder and the decoder. The encoder is actually the non-linear mapping function, and the decoder demands accurate data reconstruction from the representation generated by the encoder. This process is iterative, which guarantees that the mapping function is stable and effective to represent the original data. Different from kernel K-means [2], which also introduces non-linear transformations with fixed kernel functions, the non-linear function in auto-encoder is learned by optimizing an objective function.

The auto-encoder network is originally designed for data representation, and it aims to minimize the reconstruction error. However, to the best of our knowledge, though widely used, the auto-encoder network has not been utilized for

J. Ruiz-Shulcloper and G. Sanniti di Baja (Eds.): CIARP 2013, Part I, LNCS 8258, pp. 117–124, 2013.

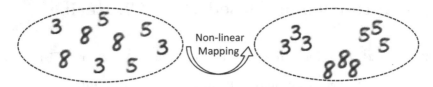

Fig. 1. Left: Original distribution of data. Due to large intra-variance, it is difficult to classify them correctly. Right: By applying a non-linear transformation, the data become compact with respect to their corresponding cluster centers in the new space.

clustering tasks. To make it suitable for clustering, we propose a new objective function embedded into the auto-encoder model. It contains two parts: the reconstruction error and the distance between data and their corresponding cluster centers in the new space. During optimization, data representation and clustering centers are updated iteratively, from which a stable performance of clustering is achieved and the new representation is more compact with respect to the cluster centers. The right part of Figure 1 illustrates such an example. To evaluate the effectiveness of this model, we conduct a series of experiments in three widely used databases for clustering. The experimental results show that our method performs much better than traditional clustering algorithms.

The rest of the paper is organized as follows: firstly we propose our method in Section 2, then experimental settings and results are provided in Section 3. Finally, Section 4 concludes the paper and discusses future work.

2   Proposed Model

In this section, we explain the proposed clustering model in details. As shown in Figure 2, the data layer (e.g., the pixel representation) of an image is firstly mapped to the code layer, which is then used to reconstruct the data layer. The objective is minimizing the reconstruction error as well as the distance between data points and corresponding clusters in the code layer. This process is implemented via a four-layer auto-encoder network, in which a non-linear mapping is resolved to enhance data representation in the data layer. For clarity, in the next subsections, we firstly introduce the auto-encoder network, and then explain how to use it for clustering.

2.1   Auto-encoders

Without loss of generality, we take an one-layer auto-encoder network as an example. It consists of an encoder and a decoder. The encoder maps an input x_i to its hidden representation h_i. The mapping function is usually non-linear and the following is a common form:

$$h_i = f(x_i) = \frac{1}{1 + \exp(-(W_1 x_i + b_1))}, \tag{1}$$

where W_1 is the encoding weight, b_1 is the corresponding bias vector.

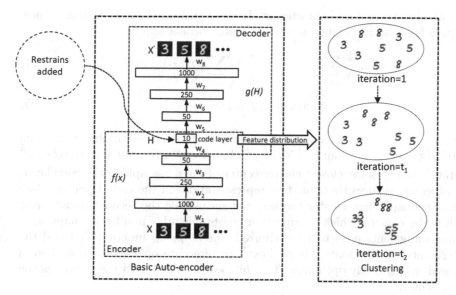

Fig. 2. Framework of the proposed method

The decoder seeks to reconstruct the input x_i from its hidden representation h_i. The transformation function has a similar formulation:

$$x_i' = g(h_i) = \frac{1}{1 + \exp(-(W_2 h_i + b_2))}, \tag{2}$$

where W_2, b_2 are the decoding weight and the decoding bias vector respectively. The auto-encoder model aims to learn a useful hidden representation by minimizing the reconstruction error. Thus, given N training samples, the parameters W_1, W_2, b_1 and b_2 can be resolved by the following optimization problem:

$$\min \frac{1}{N} \sum_{i=1}^{N} \|x_i - x_i'\|^2. \tag{3}$$

Generally, an auto-encoder network is constructed by stacking multiple one-layer auto-encoders. That is, the hidden representation of the previous one-layer auto-encoder is fed as the input of the next one. For more details of the auto-encoder network and its optimization, readers are referred to [1].

2.2 Clustering Based on Auto-encoder

Auto-encoder is a powerful model to train a mapping function, which ensures the minimum reconstruction error from the code layer to the data layer. Usually, the code layer has less dimensionality than the data layer. Therefore, auto-encoder can learn an effective representation in a low dimensional space, and it can be considered as a non-linear mapping model, performing much better than PCA [3]. However, auto-encoder contributes little to clustering because it does not pursue that similar input data obtain the same representations in the code layer, which is the nature of clustering. To solve this problem, we propose a new objective function and embed it into the auto-encoder model:

$$\min_{W,b} \frac{1}{N} \sum_{i=1}^{N} \|x_i - x_i'\|^2 - \lambda \cdot \sum_{i=1}^{N} \|f^t(x_i) - c_i^*\|^2 \qquad (4)$$

$$c_i^* = \arg\min_{c_j^{t-1}} \|f^t(x_i) - c_j^{t-1}\|^2, \qquad (5)$$

where N is the number of samples in the dataset; $f^t(\cdot)$ is the non-linear mapping function at the tth iteration; c_j^{t-1} is the jth cluster center computed at the $(t-1)^{th}$ iteration[1]; and c_i^* is the closest cluster center of the ith sample in the code layer. This objective ensures that the data representations in the code layer are close to their corresponding cluster centers, and meanwhile the reconstruction error is still under control, which is important to obtain stable non-linear mapping.

Two components need to be optimized: the mapping function $f(\cdot)$ and the cluster centers c. To solve this problem, an alternate optimization method is proposed, which firstly optimizes $f(\cdot)$ while keeps c fixed, and then updates the cluster center:

$$c_j^t = \frac{\sum_{x_i \in C_j^{t-1}} f^t(x_i)}{|C_j^{t-1}|}, \qquad (6)$$

where C_j^{t-1} is the set of samples belonging to the jth cluster at the $(t-1)^{th}$ iteration and $|C_j|$ is the number of samples in this cluster. The sample assignment computed in the last iteration is used to update the cluster centers of the current iteration. Note that sample assignment at the first iteration C^0 is initialized randomly. For clarity, we conclude our method in Algorithm 1.

Algorithm 1. Auto-encoder based data clustering algorithm

1: **Input:** Dataset X, the number of clusters K, hyper-parameter λ, the maximum number of iterations T.
2: **Initialize** sample assignment C^0 randomly.
3: **Set** t to 1.
4: **repeat**
5:    Update the mapping network by minimizing Eqn. (4) with stochastic gradient descent for one epoch.
6:    Update cluster center c^t via Eqn. (6).
7:    Partition X into K clusters and update the sample assignment C^t via Eqn. (5).
8:    $t = t + 1$.
9: **until** $t > T$
10: **Output:** Final sample assignment C.

---

[1] We use stochastic gradient descent (SGD) [5] to optimize the parameters of auto-encoder.

3   Experiments

3.1   Experimental Setups

Database. All algorithms are tested on 3 databases: MNIST[2], USPS[3] and YaleB[4]. They are widely used for evaluating clustering algorithms.

1. **MNIST** contains 60,000 handwritten digits images (0~9) with the resolution of 28 × 28.
2. **USPS** consists of 4,649 handwritten digits images (0~9) with the resolution of 16 × 16.
3. **YaleB** is composed of 5,850 faces image over ten categories, and each image has 1200 pixels.

Parameters. Our clustering model is based on a four-layers auto-encoder network with the structure of 1000-250-50-10. The parameter λ in Eqn. (4) is set by cross validation. That is 0.1 on MNIST, 0.6 on USPS and YaleB. The weights W in the auto-encoder network are initialized via a standard restricted Boltzmann machine (RBM) pre-training [3].

Baseline Algorithms. To demonstrate the effectiveness of our method, we compare our method with three classic and widely used clustering algorithms: K-means [10], spectral clustering [7] and N-cut [9].

Evaluation Criterion. Two metrics are used to evaluate experimental results explained as follows.

1. **Accuracy (ACC)** [11]. Given an image x_i, let c_i be the resolved cluster label and r_i be the ground truth label. ACC is defined as $\sum_{i=1}^{N} \delta(r_i, map(c_i))/N$, where N is the number of instances in the dataset and $\delta(x, y)$ is the delta function that equals one if $x = y$ and zero otherwise. $Map(c_i)$ is the function that maps each cluster label c_i to the equivalent label from the datasets. The best mapping can be found by using the Kuhn-Munkres algorithm [8].
2. **Normalized mutual information (NMI)** [6]. Let R denote the label obtained from the ground truth and C be the label obtained by clustering. The NMI is defined as $\mathrm{MI}(R,C)/\max(\mathrm{H}(R), \mathrm{H}(C))$, where $\mathrm{H}(X)$ is the entropies of X, and $\mathrm{MI}(X,Y)$ is the mutual information of X and Y.

3.2   Quantitative Results

In this subsection, we firstly evaluate the influence of the iteration number in our algorithm. Figure 3 shows the change of NMI and ACC as the iteration number increases on three databases.

It can be found that the performance is enhanced fast in the first ten iterations, which demonstrates that our method is effective and efficient. After dozens of

---

[2] http://yann.lecun.com/exdb/mnist/

[3] http://www.gaussianprocess.org/gpml/data/

[4] http://vision.ucsd.edu/~leekc/ExtYaleDatabase/ExtYaleB.html

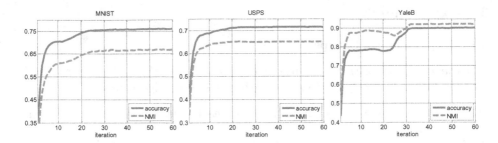

Fig. 3. Influence of the iteration number on three databases

Table 1. Performance comparison of clustering algorithms on three databases

Datasets	MNIST		USPS		YaleB	
Criterion	NMI	ACC	NMI	ACC	NMI	ACC
K-means	0.494	0.535	0.615	0.674	0.866	0.793
Spectral	0.482	0.556	**0.662**	0.693	0.881	0.851
N-cut	0.507	0.543	0.657	0.696	0.883	0.821
Proposed	**0.669**	**0.760**	0.651	**0.715**	**0.923**	**0.902**

iteration, e.g., 40~60, both NMI and ACC become very stable. Thus, in the rest of experiments, we report the results after 50 iterations. The performances of the different methods on three datasets are shown in Table 1. Apparently that our method is better than or at least comparable to their best cases.

3.3   Visualization

In this subsection, the visualized results on MNIST are shown to provide an in-depth analysis. We draw in Figure 4 the distribution of ten categories of digits obtained by our method. Most of histograms in Figure 4 are single-peak distributions, demonstrating the compactness of data representation. Admittedly, the cases of digits 4 and 9 are not so good. We will discuss possible solutions to this problem in Section 4. The small digital images in subfigures are the reconstructed results of cluster centers in the code layer.

For comparison, we also show the average data representations over all clusters by K-means in Figure 5. The result is much worse, and can be easily understood with the motivation of our method. Generally, K-means uses a similar iteration procedure as ours in Algorithm 1 except that it is performed in the original pixel space. That is, the iteration of K-means is performed in the data layer, whereas ours in the code layer, which is mapped from the data layer with a highly non-linear function, learned by exploiting the hidden structure of data with the auto-encoder network.

3.4   Difference of Spaces

In this subsection, we analyze the difference of three spaces, i.e., the original data space, the space learned via non-linear mapping with original auto-encoder, and

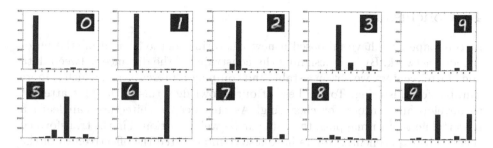

Fig. 4. Distribution of data over ten clusters and the visualized images of cluster centers after reconstruction with the learned decoder

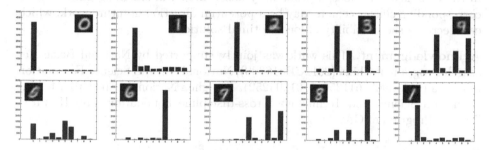

Fig. 5. Distribution of digits over 10 classes and the visualized images of 10 cluster centers generated by K-means

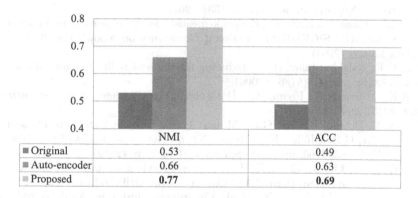

	NMI	ACC
■ Original	0.53	0.49
■ Auto-encoder	0.66	0.63
■ Proposed	**0.77**	**0.69**

Fig. 6. Performance comparison in three different spaces

the one learned by our method. Correspondingly, we apply K-means clustering in these spaces. Their clustering results are shown in Figure 6. Obviously, the clustering performance in the space of auto-encoder is much better than the one in the original space, and much worse than the one proposed by us. This result justifies two viewpoints: 1) Non-linear mapping by auto-encoder can greatly improve the representation of data for clustering; 2) Our proposed objective function, defined in Eqn. (4)~(6), is effective to further enhance clustering due to the design of increasing data compactness as analyzed in Section 2.2.

4 Conclusions

In this paper, we have proposed a new clustering method based on the auto-encoder network. By well designing the constraint of the distance between data and cluster centers, we obtain a stable and compact representation, which is more suitable for clustering. To the best of our knowledge, this is the first attempt to develop auto-encode for clustering. As this deep architecture can learn a powerful non-linear mapping, the data can be well partitioned in the transformed space. The experimental results have also demonstrated the effectiveness of the proposed model. However, as is shown in Figure 4, some data are still mixed. This problem might be resolved by maximizing the difference among cluster centers in the code layer. Besides, a probability-based model in assigning data to their corresponding cluster centers may be a potential direction in future work, which can decrease the possibility of local optimal solution.

Acknowledgement. This work was jointly supported by National Basic Research Program of China (2012CB316300), National Natural Science Foundation of China (61175003, 61135002, 61203252), Tsinghua National Laboratory for Information Science and Technology Cross-discipline Foundation, and Hundred Talents Program of CAS.

References

1. Bengio, Y., Courville, A., Vincent, P.: Representation learning: A review and new perspectives. arXiv preprint arXiv:1206.5538 (2012)
2. Dhillon, I.S., Guan, Y., Kulis, B.: Kernel k-means: spectral clustering and normalized cuts. In: ACM SIGKDD International Conference on Knowledge Discovery and Data Mining (2004)
3. Hinton, G.E., Salakhutdinov, R.R.: Reducing the dimensionality of data with neural networks. Science 313(5786) (2006)
4. Jain, A.K., Murty, M.N., Flynn, P.J.: Data clustering: a review. ACM Computing Surveys 31(3), 264–323 (1999)
5. LeCun, Y.A., Bottou, L., Orr, G.B., Müller, K.-R.: Efficient backProp. In: Montavon, G., Orr, G.B., Müller, K.-R. (eds.) Neural Networks: Tricks of the Trade, 2nd edn. LNCS, vol. 7700, pp. 9–48. Springer, Heidelberg (2012)
6. Li, Z., Yang, Y., Liu, J., Zhou, X., Lu, H.: Unsupervised feature selection using nonnegative spectral analysis. In: AAAI Conference on Artificial Intelligence (2012)
7. Ng, A.Y., Jordan, M.I., Weiss, Y., et al.: On spectral clustering: Analysis and an algorithm. Advances in Neural Information Processing Systems 2, 849–856 (2002)
8. Plummer, M., Lovász, L.: Matching theory, vol. 121. North Holland (1986)
9. Shi, J., Malik, J.: Normalized cuts and image segmentation. IEEE Transactions on Pattern Analysis and Machine Intelligence 22(8) (2000)
10. Wagstaff, K., Cardie, C., Rogers, S., Schroedl, S.: Constrained k-means clustering with background knowledge. In: International Conference on Machine Learning, pp. 577–584 (2001)
11. Xu, W., Liu, X., Gong, Y.: Document clustering based on non-negative matrix factorization. In: ACM SIGIR Conference on Research and Development in Informaion Retrieval (2003)

On the Generalization
of the Mahalanobis Distance

Gabriel Martos[1], Alberto Muñoz[1], and Javier González[2]

[1] University Carlos III, Department of Statistics, Madrid, Spain
[2] J. Bernoulli Institute for Mathematics and Computer Science,
University of Groningen, The Netherlands
{gabrielalejandro.martos,alberto.munoz}@uc3m.es,
j.gonzalez.hernandez@rug.nl

Abstract. The Mahalanobis distance (MD) is a widely used measure in
Statistics and Pattern Recognition. Interestingly, assuming that the data
are generated from a Gaussian distribution, it considers the covariance
matrix to evaluate the distance between a data point and the distribution
mean. In this work, we generalize MD for distributions in the exponential
family, providing both, a definition in terms of the data density function
and a computable version. We show its performance on several artificial
and real data scenarios.

1 Introduction

The Mahalanobis distance (MD) [5], widely used in Statistics and Machine
Learning for classification and outlier detection tasks, is a scale-invariant metric
that provides a measure of distance between two points taking into account the
correlation between the variables. It can be seen as the composition of the linear
transformation $T_M : \mathbf{x} \xrightarrow{T_M} \mathbf{x}' = \Sigma^{-\frac{1}{2}}\mathbf{x}$, where Σ is the covariance matrix of a
vector of random variables $\mathbf{x}$, plus the computation of the ordinary Euclidean
distance (ED) between the transformed data. This is illustrated in Fig. 1 for two
data points from a bivariate Gaussian distribution. The distance in probability
(d_M) from B to the mean μ is larger than the distance from A to μ, which is
correctly detected by the MD, but not by the ED (d_E).

The Mahalanobis distance is a particular case of the Bregman Divergence
(see Def. 1), a generalization of the concept of distance. We will show that
this connection allows us to generalize the concept of distance from a point
to the center of a distribution (the densest point) for density functions in the
exponential family, a quite general case. The rest of this paper is organized as
follows. In Section 2 we introduce the new distance, in terms of the data density
function and then we provide a computable version of the distance. In Section
3 we show the performance of the generalized MD for outlier detection and
classification problems.

J. Ruiz-Shulcloper and G. Sanniti di Baja (Eds.): CIARP 2013, Part I, LNCS 8258, pp. 125–132, 2013.

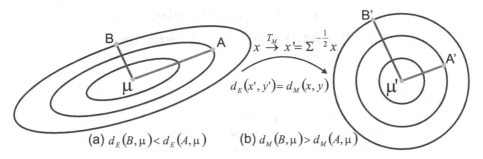

Fig. 1. The effect of the Mahalanobis transformation T_M

2   A Generalized Mahalanobis Bregman Divergence

Our goal in this section is to define a Generalized Mahalanobis distance to the center of a general Probability Measure (distribution), that is, a distance for distributions non necessarily Gaussian.

Consider a measure space $(\mathcal{X}, \mathcal{F}, \mu)$, where $\mathcal{X}$ is a sample space (here a compact set of a real vector space), $\mathcal{F}$ a σ-algebra of measurable subsets of $\mathcal{X}$ and $\mu : \mathcal{F} \to \mathbb{R}^+$ the ambient σ-additive measure, the Lebesgue measure. A probability measure $\mathbb{P}$ is a σ-additive finite measure absolutely continuous w.r.t. μ that satisfies the three Kolmogorov axioms. By Radon-Nikodym theorem, there exists a measurable function $f : \mathcal{X} \to \mathbb{R}^+$ (the density function) such that $P(A) = \int_A f d\mu$, and $f = \frac{d\mathbb{P}}{d\mu}$ is the Radon-Nikodym derivative.

In the Multivariate Gaussian case, say $f = \mathbf{N}_d(\mu, \Sigma)$ where $\mu \in \mathbb{R}^d$ and $\Sigma \in \mathbb{R}^{d \times d}$ are respectively the mean vector and the covariance matrix, it holds that for $\mathbf{x} \in \mathbb{R}^d$, $f(\mathbf{x}|\mu, \Sigma) \propto e^{-\frac{1}{2}d_M^2(\mathbf{x},\mu)}$ and MD is defined by:

$$d_M(\mathbf{x}, \mu) = \sqrt{(\mathbf{x} - \mu)^T \Sigma^{-1}(\mathbf{x} - \mu)}.$$

Next we show that MD is as a particular case of the Bregman Divergence:

Definition 1. *(**Bregman Divergence**): Let $\mathcal{X} \subset \mathbb{R}^d$ be a compact domain and ξ a strictly convex and differentiable function $\xi : \mathcal{X} \to \mathbb{R}$. Define the* Bregman Divergence *(BD) for a pair of points $(\mathbf{x}, \mathbf{y}) \in \mathcal{X}$ as follows*

$$BD_\xi(\mathbf{x}, \mathbf{y}) = \xi(\mathbf{x}) - \xi(\mathbf{y}) - \langle \mathbf{x} - \mathbf{y}, \nabla\xi(\mathbf{y}) \rangle, \tag{1}$$

where $\nabla\xi(\mathbf{y})$ is the gradient vector evaluated at the point $\mathbf{y}$. Taking $\xi(\mathbf{x}) = \mathbf{x}^T \Sigma^{-1} \mathbf{x}$, it is immediate to verify that BD is the square of MD.

In general, there exists a bijective correspondence between Bregman divergences and the class of (regular) exponential distributions [1,3]. An example is the mentioned Normal distribution whose corresponding BD is the square of the MD. However, the square of the MD can be expressed in an alternative and interesting way as follows:

$$f(\mathbf{x}) \propto e^{-\frac{1}{2}d_M^2(\mathbf{x},\mu)} \implies d_M^2(\mathbf{x}, \mu) \propto \log\left(\frac{1}{f(\mathbf{x})}\right), \tag{2}$$

Now, if f belongs to the regular exponential family, f can be expressed by $f(\mathbf{x}) \propto e^{-\frac{1}{2} BD_\xi(\mathbf{x}, \mu)}$ for appropriate ξ [1,3] and, thus:

$$f(\mathbf{x}) \propto e^{-\frac{1}{2} BD_\xi(\mathbf{x}, \mu)} \implies BD_\xi(\mathbf{x}, \mu) \propto \log\left(\frac{1}{f(\mathbf{x})}\right), \tag{3}$$

which gives us the hint to generalize the MD to any distribution in the exponential family.

Definition 2. *(Generalized Mahalanobis Distance): Given a (d-dimensional) distribution f in the exponential family and denote by $\mathbf{m}_o$ the mode of f, that is, $f(\mathbf{m}_o) = \max_\mathbf{x} f(\mathbf{x})$, we define the Generalized Mahalanobis distance (GM) between $\mathbf{x} \in \mathcal{X}$ and the mode $(\mathbf{m}_o)$ of f by*

$$d_{GM}^2(\mathbf{x}, \mathbf{m}_o) = \log\left(\frac{f(\mathbf{m}_o)}{f(\mathbf{x})}\right). \tag{4}$$

When $\mathbf{x} = \mathbf{m}_o$, $d_{GM}^2(\mathbf{x}, \mathbf{m}_o) = \log(1) = 0$, and $d_{GM}^2(\mathbf{x}, \mathbf{m}_o)$ increases when $\mathbf{x}$ moves off from the mode $\mathbf{m}_o$. What is the connection between BD and GM? As already told, BD is only defined for distributions on the exponential family. In the important case of the normal distribution[1], $BD_\xi(\mathbf{x}, \mathbf{m}_o) = 2d_{GM}^2(\mathbf{x}, \mathbf{m}_o)$. In the case of the gamma distribution[1] with shape parameter α, $BD_\xi(\mathbf{x}, \mathbf{m}_o) = \frac{\alpha}{\alpha-1} d_{GM}^2(\mathbf{x}, \mathbf{m}_o)$ (provided that there exist a mode: $\alpha > 1$). Thus, BD and GM are "formally" equivalent for distributions in the exponential family. The advantage of the GM are two: First, it is always defined for any continuous regular distribution, but BD is not out of the exponential family. Second, it is possible to derive a sample version of the GM by just providing an estimator of $f(\mathbf{x})$.

From a practical point of view, we are interested in the GM to solve classification and outlier detection problems. Thus the relevant information here is not the exact value of the distance, but the relative order among the distances from data points to the center of the distribution (the densest point). Therefore, we do not need to know $f(\mathbf{x})$, but given $\mathbf{x}$ and $\mathbf{y}$, it is enough to know if $f(\mathbf{x}) < f(\mathbf{y})$ or $f(\mathbf{x}) > f(\mathbf{y})$. To this aim, we just need to estimate the α-level sets of f: Given a probability measure $\mathbb{P}$ with density function $f_\mathbb{P}$, the minimum volume sets (or α-level sets) are defined by $S_\alpha(f_\mathbb{P}) = \{\mathbf{x} \in \mathcal{X} | f_\mathbb{P}(\mathbf{x}) \geq \alpha\}$, such that $P(S_\alpha(f_\mathbb{P})) = 1 - \nu$, where $0 < \nu < 1$. If we consider an ordered sequence $\alpha_1 < \dots < \alpha_m$, then $S_{\alpha_{i+1}}(f_\mathbb{P}) \subseteq S_{\alpha_i}(f_\mathbb{P})$. Let us define $A_i(\mathbb{P}) = S_{\alpha_i}(f_\mathbb{P}) - S_{\alpha_{i+1}}(f_\mathbb{P})$, $i \in \{1, \dots, m-1\}$. We can choose $\alpha_1 \simeq 0$ and $\alpha_m \geq \max_{\mathbf{x} \in \mathcal{X}} f_\mathbb{P}(\mathbf{x})$ (which exists, given that $\mathcal{X}$ is compact and $f_\mathbb{P}$ continuous). If the $\{\alpha_i\}_{i=1}^m$ sequence is long enough, we can assume constant density for the points contained in $A_i(\mathbb{P})$, that is, they have the same value $f(\mathbf{x})$.

If $\mathbf{x} \in A_i(\mathbb{P})$, and because of the definition of $A_i(\mathbb{P})$, then $f(\mathbf{x}) \approx \alpha_i$ and thus:

$$d_{GM}^2(\mathbf{x}, \mathbf{m}_o) = \log\left(\frac{f(\mathbf{m}_o)}{f(\mathbf{x})}\right) \approx \log\left(\frac{f(\mathbf{m}_o)}{\alpha_i}\right). \tag{5}$$

Next we introduce the algorithm to estimate the $A_i(\mathbb{P})$ sets.

---

[1] Proof is omitted for lack of space.

Table 1. Algorithmic formulation of Theorem 1

Obtention of $R_n = \hat{S}_\alpha(f)$:
1 Choose a constant $\nu \in [0, 1]$.
2 Consider the order induced in the sample s_n by the sparsity measure $g_n(\mathbf{x})$, that is, $g_n(\mathbf{x}_{(1)}) \leq \cdots \leq g_n(\mathbf{x}_{(n)})$, where $\mathbf{x}_{(i)}$ denotes the ith sample, ordered after g.
3 Consider the value $\rho_n^* = g(\mathbf{x}_{(\nu n)})$ if $\nu n \in \mathbb{N}$, $\rho_n^* = g_n(\mathbf{x}_{([\nu n]+1)})$ otherwise, where $[\mathbf{x}]$ stands for the largest integer not greater than $\mathbf{x}$.
4 Define $h_n(\mathbf{x}) = \text{sign}(\rho_n^* - g_n(\mathbf{x}))$.

2.1 Level Set Estimation

Usually the available data are given as a finite sample. We will consider an *iid* sample $s_n(\mathbb{P}) = \{\mathbf{x}_i\}_{i=1}^n$ drawn from the density function $f_\mathbb{P}$. To estimate level sets from a data sample (useful to obtain $\hat{S}_\alpha(f_\mathbb{P})$) we present the following definitions and theorems, concerning the One-Class Neighbor Machine [7,8].

Definition 3 (Neighbourhood Measures). *Consider a random variable X with density function $f(\mathbf{x})$ defined on $\mathbb{R}^d$. Let S_n denote the set of random independent identically distributed (iid) samples of size n (drawn from f). The elements of S_n take the form $s_n = (\mathbf{x}_1, \cdots, \mathbf{x}_n)$, where $\mathbf{x}_i \in \mathbb{R}^d$. Let $M :$ $\mathbb{R}^d \times S_n \longrightarrow \mathbb{R}$ be a real-valued function defined for all $n \in \mathbb{N}$. (a) If $f(\mathbf{x}) < f(\mathbf{y})$ implies $\lim_{n\to\infty} P(M(\mathbf{x}, s_n) > M(\mathbf{y}, s_n)) = 1$, then M is a **sparsity measure**. (b) If $f(\mathbf{x}) < f(\mathbf{y})$ implies $\lim_{n\to\infty} P(M(\mathbf{x}, s_n) < M(\mathbf{y}, s_n)) = 1$, then M is a concentration measure.*

The Support Neighbour Machine [7,8] solves the following optimization problem:

$$\max_{\rho,\xi} \nu n\rho - \sum_{i=1}^n \xi_i$$
$$\text{s.t.}\quad g(\mathbf{x}_i) \geq \rho - \xi_i,$$
$$\xi_i \geq 0, \qquad i = 1, \ldots, n, \tag{6}$$

where $g(\mathbf{x}) = M(\mathbf{x}, s_n)$ is a sparsity measure, $\nu \in [0, 1]$, ξ_i with $i = 1, \ldots, n$ are slack variables and ρ is a threshold induced by the sparsity measure.

Theorem 1. *The set $R_n = \{\mathbf{x} : h_n(\mathbf{x}) = \text{sign}(\rho_n^* - g_n(\mathbf{x})) \geq 0\}$ converges to a region of the form $S_\alpha(f) = \{\mathbf{x}|f(\mathbf{x}) \geq \alpha\}$, such that $P(S_\alpha(f)) = 1 - \nu$.*

Therefore, the Support Neighbour Machine estimates a density contour cluster $S_\alpha(f)$ (around the mode). Theorem 1 [7,8] can be expressed in algorithmic form as in Table 1: Hence, we take $\hat{A}_i(\mathbb{P}) = \hat{S}_{\alpha_i}(f_\mathbb{P}) - \hat{S}_{\alpha_{i+1}}(f_\mathbb{P})$, where $\hat{S}_{\alpha_i}(f_\mathbb{P})$ is estimated by R_n defined above (for further details on the estimation refers to [7,8]). Whit the estimation of level sets and the relation presented in Equation 2, we will test with some experiment the performance of the proposed distance.

3   Experimental Section

To demonstrate the capability of the proposed distance, we test it in one artificial and two real data experiments.

Artificial Experiments

The goal of the first experiment is to demonstrate that the GM adequately captures a significant amount of outliers in non-Gaussian scenarios. We keep the distribution simple and visually tractable in this example. We simulate 1000 points from a bimodal and asymmetric bi-logistic distribution [9], with parameters $BL(\alpha = 0.5, \beta = 0.9)$. The values of the parameters $\alpha = 0.5$ and $\beta = 0.9$ where selected in order to obtain a bi-modal distribution in the sampled data. We replace some of these observations with contaminated observations (noise) normally distributed with parameters $N_d(\mu = (3,3), \Sigma = 5I_{2\times2})$. The simulation process was: first we generate a vector u of size 1000, uniformly distributed in $[0,1]$. Then for each value of $u \leq .95$ we generate a data point from the $BL(\alpha = .5, \beta = .9)$ distribution, in the other case we generate a data from a $N_d(\mu = (3,3), \Sigma = 5I_{2\times2})$.

Table 2. Outlier detection performance

Metric/Technique	% of: Outliers captured	False-positives (Type I error)	False-negatives (Type II error)
pc-Outlier[2]	36.5%	23.2%	65.8%
sign-Outlier[2]	23.1%	7.4%	76.9%
locoutPercent[2]	13.4%	**7.3%**	86.4%
Percentile 5% Euclidean Distance	3.8%	10.7%	96.1%
Percentile 5% Mah. Distance	23.1%	10.4%	76.9%
Percentile 5% Gen. Mah. Distance	**38.5%**	10.3%	**65.4%**

We use a battery of different algorithms [2,10] to identify contaminated points (outliers) for the simulated data. The results are summarized in Table 2. Our metric outperforms the other metrics in the detection of the contaminated points. We also get the lowest rate of unidentified outliers (false-negatives rate) and a very competitive rate of false identification of outliers (false-positives rate) compared to other more sophisticated techniques. In Figure 2, we present the points revealed as contaminated points in all the considered cases. The GM adequately capture those points that are far apart from the "center" of the bimodal and asymmetric sampled distribution.

Real Data Experiments

For the first real example, we consider a collection of 1774 documents (corresponding to 13 topics) extracted from three bibliographic data bases (LISA,

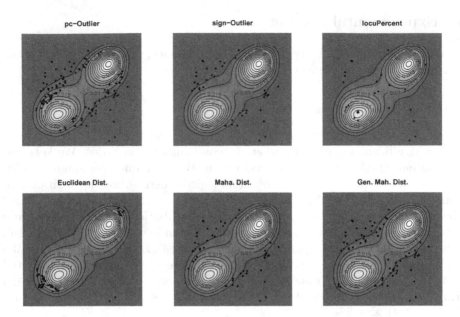

Fig. 2. Contaminated points detected for each of the method/metric

Table 3. Classification percentage errors for a three-class text database and four classification procedures. In parenthesis the St. Error on test samples are shown.

Method — - % of:	Train Error	Test Error
SVM	0.000%	0.005% (0.000)
LDA	6.100%	7.035% (0.007)
QDA (Mahalanobis)	6.426%	6.960% (0.001)
Generalized Mahalanobis	2.553%	2.761% (0.002)

INSPEC and Sociological Abstracts). Each document is converted into a vector into the Latent Semantic Space using the Singular Value Decomposition. We considers 3 classes of similar topics: "dimensionality reduction" and "feature selection" (311 documents), "optical cables" and "power semiconductor devices" (384 documents) and "rural areas" and "retirement communities" (165 documents). In order to implement the classification we divide the 860 documents into a training sample (516 documents, 60% of the data) and a test sample (the remaining 344 documents). In order to give a robust classification result we repeat the experiment 100 times. We report in Table 3 the average error rate on the test sample and the standard error for each classifier. We can see that our metric clearly outperforms Mahalanobis distance. This is explained because we are dealing with highly dimensional data and few observations, therefore it is difficult to estimate an appropriate covariance matrix in order to adequately compute the Mahalanobis distance to the centers. Our distance does not suffer this inconvenience and is capable to approximate the classification performance of a variety of very sophisticated classification methods.

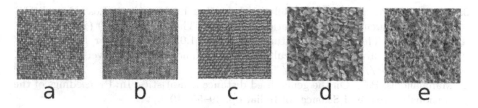

Fig. 3. Textures images: a) blanket, b) canvas, c) seat, d) linseeds and e) stone

Table 4. Outlier detection performance

Metric/Technique	% of: Outliers captured	False-positives (Type I error)	False-negatives (Type II error)
pc-Outlier[2]	60%	13.23%	28.65%
sign-Outlier[2]	40%	5.13%	37.75%
locoutPercent[2]	35%	2.80%	39.39%
Percentile 5% Euclidean Distance	25%	4.00%	42.85%
Percentile 5% Mah. Distance	35%	3.60%	39.39%
Percentile 5% Gen. Mah. Distance	**100%**	5.10%	**0.00%**

The second real data example considers the detection of outliers in sample of texture images. We consider the texture images from the Kylberg texture database [4]. We use 500 texture images with a resolution of 576×576 pixels. The first 480 texture images are very similar textures (Fig. 3 a) to c)). We also consider 20 "outliers" images with different textures (Fig. 3 d) and e)). We represent each image using the 32 parameters of the wavelet coefficient histogram proposed in [6]. We report the results in Table 4. Only the proposed distance is able to capture all the outliers in the sample. We also get an acceptable performance regarding the Type I Error rate (with 5.1%).

Future Work: The list of tasks for next future include an exhaustive simulation study of the performance of the proposed metric (some of this work is not included because the lack of space), the generalization of the proposed metric to define a Generalized "inter-point" Mahalanobis distance, and the study of properties of the proposed metric and its relations with the strictly convex and differentiable function ξ that originates the definition of the Bregman Divergences.

Acknowledgments. This work was partially supported by projects **MIC 2012/ 00084/00**, **ECO2012-38442**, **DGUCM 2008/00058/002** and **MEC 2007/ 04438/001**.

References

1. Banerjee, A., Merugu, S., Dhillon, I., Ghosh, J.: Clustering with Bregman Divergences. Journal of Machine Learning Research, 1705–1749 (2005)
2. Filzmoser, P., Maronna, R.A., Werner, M.: Outlier identification in high dimensions. Computational Statistics & Data Analysis 52(3), 1694–1711 (2008)

3. Forster, J., Warmuth, M.K.: Relative Expected Instantaneous Loss Bounds. In: Annual Conference on Computational Learning Theory, pp. 90–99 (2000)
4. Kylberg, G.: The Kylberg Texture Dataset v. 1.0. In: Centre for Image Analysis. Swedish University of Agricultural Sciences and Uppsala University, Uppsala, Sweden, http://www.cb.uu.se/
5. Mahalanobis, P.C.: On the generalised distance in statistics. In: Proceedings of the National Institute of Sciences of India, pp. 49–55 (1936)
6. Mallat, S.: A Theory for Multiresolution Signal Decomposition: The Wavelet Representation. IEEE Trans. on Pattern Analysis and Machine Intelligence 11(7), 674–693
7. Muñoz, A., Moguerza, J.M.: Estimation of High-Density Regions using One-Class Neighbor Machines. IEEE Trans. on Pattern Analysis and Machine Intelligence 28(3), 476–480
8. Muñoz, A., Moguerza, J.M.: A Naive Solution to the One-Class Problem and Its Extension to Kernel Methods. In: Sanfeliu, A., Cortés, M.L. (eds.) CIARP 2005. LNCS, vol. 3773, pp. 193–204. Springer, Heidelberg (2005)
9. Smith, R.L.: Extreme value theory. In: Ledermann, W. (ed.) Handbook of Applied Mathematics, vol. 7, pp. 437–471 (1990)
10. Zimek, A., Schubert, E., Kriegel, H.P.: A survey on unsupervised outlier detection in high-dimensional numerical data. Statistical Analysis and Data Mining 5(5), 363–387 (2012)

Encoding Classes of Unaligned Objects Using Structural Similarity Cross-Covariance Tensors

Marco San Biagio[1], Samuele Martelli[1], Marco Crocco[1],
Marco Cristani[1,2], and Vittorio Murino[1,2]

[1] Istituto Italiano di Tecnologia - Pattern Analysis & Computer Vision
Via Morego 30, 16163, Genova, Italy
[2] Università degli Studi di Verona - Dipartimento di Informatica
Strada le Grazie 15, 37134, Verona, Italy
{marco.sanbiagio,samuele.martelli,marco.crocco,
marco.cristani,vittorio.murino}@iit.it

Abstract. Encoding an object essence in terms of self-similarities between its parts is becoming a popular strategy in Computer Vision. In this paper, a new similarity-based descriptor, dubbed Structural Similarity Cross-Covariance Tensor is proposed, aimed to encode relations among different regions of an image in terms of cross-covariance matrices. The latter are calculated between low-level feature vectors extracted from pairs of regions. The new descriptor retains the advantages of the widely used covariance matrix descriptors [1], extending their expressiveness from local similarities inside a region to structural similarities across multiple regions. The new descriptor, applied on top of HOG, is tested on object and scene classification tasks with three datasets. The proposed method always outclasses baseline HOG and yields significant improvement over a recently proposed self-similarity descriptor in the two most challenging datasets.

Keywords: object recognition, scene classification, covariance.

1 Introduction

In pattern recognition, the representation of an entity can be addressed following two complementary paradigms: feature-based and similarity-based. In the first case the characteristics of the entity, or of parts of it, are encoded by descriptors concerning for example shape and color. Most descriptors (e.g. SIFT [4], LBP histograms [5], HOG [6]) are enclosed in this class. In the latter case the focus is on a similarity measure allowing to relate new entity to a set reference ones.

Whenever an entity can be structurally represented by its parts, the similarity philosophy can be applied to the internal relationship among parts, each one represented in terms of features. In other words, a self-similarity descriptor can be constructed on top of feature descriptors related to different entity parts, joining the advantages of the two approaches. An example of this strategy, applied to the pedestrian detection task, can be found in [7]: each image is subdivided in

J. Ruiz-Shulcloper and G. Sanniti di Baja (Eds.): CIARP 2013, Part I, LNCS 8258, pp. 133–140, 2013.

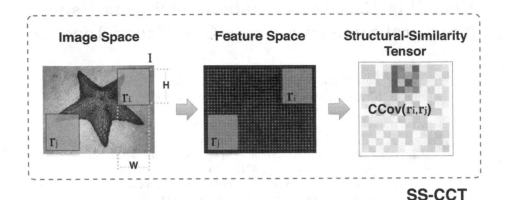

Fig. 1. Building process of the SS-CCT: each region is described by a set of local feature descriptors; the pairwise similarity among two regions is encoded by a cross-covariance matrix of the feature descriptors.

regions from which HOG are extracted; similarity among these regions are then encoded by Euclidean pairwise distances among HOG descriptors. This approach is effective and computationally efficient but has some drawbacks, which are shared by all the similarity-based approaches relying on point-wise distances. In particular, if entities to be detected are not aligned, i.e. the entity's parts do not occupy the same image regions across the images, point-wise distance approaches are not statistically robust, as the single distance may undergo too much variability in the same entity class. Moreover, all the information on the similarity among two descriptors (i.e. two vectors) collapses in a single scalar value, potentially obscuring discriminative relations between single elements of the descriptor (e.g. the single bins of an HOG).

In order to overcome these limitations a different self-similarity approach is here proposed: the key idea is to provide a rich and, at the same time, statistically robust notion of similarity among different regions of an image, exploiting covariance measures among couples of low-level features across different regions.

Covariances of low-level features, in the form of covariance matrices, bear several advantages when used as single region descriptors, as pointed out in [1,2,3]. The representation provides a natural way of fusing multiple features that might be correlated. The single pixel noise is largely filtered out with the average operation intrinsic to the covariance calculation. In comparison to other statistical descriptors, such as multi-dimensional histograms, covariances are intrinsically low-dimensional as their size is only $O(N^2)$, with N being the number of features. Since covariance matrix is invariant with respect to pixels position inside the region, the descriptor has also some degree of robustness against pose change and object rotation.

Till now covariances of low-level features have been employed essentially as a *single region* descriptors [1,2,3]. What we propose here is to employ covariances as a measure of similarity *across different regions*. Thus, covariance matrices have to be generalized with the *Cross-Covariance matrices*, which capture the covariance among two generally different feature vectors, in our case related to two different regions. In particular, a *Structural Similarity Cross-Covariance Tensor (SS-CCT)* is here proposed, which encodes all the pairwise similarities among regions by means of Cross-Covariance matrices, each one encoding all the pairwise relationships between the single features extracted in a given couple of regions. Any region descriptor can be ideally adopted (e.g. *HOG* [6], *SIFT* [4], *LBP* [5]).

As a proof of concept and for computational reasons, the proposed method is applied to the well-known *HOG* feature descriptor, implemented according to [6], and tested on two different classification tasks: objects and scenes. The classification results show significant performance improvements with respect to both the simple feature-based descriptors and the point-wise similarity based approach in [7].

The remaining of the paper is organized as follows: in Section 2 the SS-CCT descriptor is introduced; in Section 3 some information on the object model is provided; in Section 4 the SS-CCT performance on Caltech 101 [8], Caltech-256 [9] and SenseCam ([10]) datasets is displayed and compared with two literature methods; finally, in Section 4 some conclusions are drawn.

2   Proposed Method

Given an image I, we define R regions each one of size $W \times H$ pixels (see Fig. 1). Each region is divided into M patches and, for each patch, a given feature descriptor is applied, obtaining M feature vectors of size N.

The global *Feature Level* descriptor (FL) of the image I is obtained stacking together the feature vectors for all the regions and all the patches as follows:

$$FL = [\mathbf{z}_{1,1}^T \ldots \mathbf{z}_{r,m}^T \ldots \mathbf{z}_{R,M}^T] \tag{1}$$

where $\mathbf{z}_{r,m}$ is the feature vector obtained applying the descriptor to the patch m in the region r.

The proposed *Similarity Level* structural descriptor is built on top of FL, encoding the similarity among each couple of regions. In order to achieve a statistically robust and highly invariant description of this similarity, we calculate the covariance among each couple of features, using the patches of the two regions as spatial samples (Fig. 1).

In detail, given two regions r_1 and r_2, we calculate the $N \times N$ cross-covariance matrix $\mathbf{Ccov}_{r_1,r_2}$ among the feature vectors $\mathbf{z}_{r,m}$ in the following way:

$$\mathbf{Ccov}_{r_1,r_2} = \frac{1}{M-1} \sum_{m=1}^{M} (\mathbf{z}_{r_1,m} - \bar{\mathbf{z}}_{r_1})(\mathbf{z}_{r_2,m} - \bar{\mathbf{z}}_{r_2})^T, \tag{2}$$

where $\bar{\mathbf{z}}_{r_1}$ and $\bar{\mathbf{z}}_{r_2}$ are the mean of the feature vectors inside regions r_1 and r_2, respectively. In practice the i,j-th element of $\mathbf{Ccov}_{r_1,r_2}$ is the spatial covariance of feature i in region r_1 and feature j in region r_2. Notice that Cross-Covariance matrices do not share the same properties of covariance matrices. In particular, $\mathbf{Ccov}_{r_1, r_2}$ are *not* symmetric and, consequently, *not* semi-definite positive. Therefore cross-covariance matrices do not live on the Riemannian manifold defined by the set of semi-definite positive matrices [1], and the only known modality to use these descriptors in a machine learning framework is to vectorize them.

Calculating Eq. (2) across all the possible region pairs, we define a block matrix $\mathbf{CcovBlock}$ of size $NR \times NR$ as follows:

$$\mathbf{CcovBlock}(I) = \begin{bmatrix} \mathbf{Ccov}_{1,1} & \cdots & \mathbf{Ccov}_{1,R} \\ \vdots & \ddots & \vdots \\ \mathbf{Ccov}_{R,1} & \cdots & \mathbf{Ccov}_{R,R} \end{bmatrix}. \tag{3}$$

It can be noticed from Eq. (3) that this matrix is block-symmetric, i.e. $\mathbf{Ccov}_{r_1, r_2} = \mathbf{Ccov}_{r_2, r_1}$. Therefore the final structural descriptor, named *Structural-Similarity Cross Covariance Tensor (SS-CCT)*, is built vectorizing $\mathbf{CcovBlock}(I)$ in the following manner:

$$SS\text{-}CCT = [\text{Vec}(\mathbf{Ccov}_{1,1}) \ \text{Vec}(\mathbf{Ccov}_{1,2}) \ \cdots \tag{4}$$
$$\text{Vec}(\mathbf{Ccov}_{1,R}) \ \text{Vec}(\mathbf{Ccov}_{2,2}) \ \cdots \ \text{Vec}(\mathbf{Ccov}_{R,R})].$$

where Vec is the standard vectorization operator.

The length of the *SS-CCT* descriptor is therefore $(R+1)(R/2)N^2$. The final descriptor is obtained joining together the *Feature Level* (Eq. 1) and the *Similarity Level* (Eq. 4) descriptors, with a final length equal to $(R+1)(R/2)N^2 + RMN$.

3   Object Model

The adopted object model is dependent on the size of the images considered and on the general characteristics of the dataset. In general, given an image I, containing the object of interest, we calculate the low-level descriptor on a uniformly sampled set of MR patches, of size $w \times w$, whose overlap is $w/2$ in both x and y dimensions. For every patch, we encoded the appearance of an object through the use of *Histograms of Oriented Gradients* descriptor, as defined in [6]. We adopted this descriptor since it is relatively fast to compute and still considered one of the most expressive one.

After that, we defined a set of R regions, subdividing the MR patches in R corresponding subsets of size M. The region size is defined considering the following criteria: 1) each region should contain a number of patches sufficient to yield a significant statistics in the cross-covariance matrix calculus; 2) the patch size should be sufficiently large so as to retain the descriptor expressiveness; 3) finally, the region size should match the size of significant parts of the objects to be detected or classified.

In this way, we calculate the SS-CCT descriptor evaluating the cross-covariance between all the couples of regions as formalized in Eq. 3 and Eq. 4. The final descriptor, here dubbed *SS-CCT(HOG)*, is given by the concatenation of SS-CCT and the HOG descriptors.

4 Experiments

In this section, we report experimental results obtained on two different tasks, using three datasets: object classification (Caltech-101 [8] and Caltech-256 [9]), and scene classification (SenseCam Dataset [10]). In all the experiments, we employ a multiclass one-vs-all linear Support Vector Machine classifier [11].

The comparisons are carried out with the HOG baseline descriptor [6] and the *Self-Similarity Tensor* described in [7]. The latter, named SST(HOG), is built joining together the HOG descriptor and the pairwise Euclidean distances between all the patches, sharing the mixed feature-based and similarity-based philosophy of SS-CCT.

4.1 Object Classification

In the object classification community, Caltech-101 [8] dataset represents an important benchmark. It consists of 102 classes (101 object categories plus background) with a number of images per class ranging from 31 to 800. Despite its importance, Caltech-101 has some cues, notably the presence of strongly aligned object classes, which significantly ease the classification process. To overcome such limitation, the larger Caltech-256 dataset was subsequently introduced. It consists of 256 classes (256 + Clutter class) with a minimum of 80 images per class and a total number of images equal to 30607. In Caltech-256 objects position inside the image is significantly varying for a lot of classes, as can be seen observing the average images for the 256 classes in Fig. 2, so making the classification task more challenging with respect to Caltech-101.

To test our descriptor, the object model introduced in Sec. 3 is adopted. The HOG descriptor is calculated on dense patches of size 32×32 with an overlap of 16 pixels. The number of regions R is set to 9, 3 along both the horizontal and vertical image direction. For Caltech-101 we considered 15 images per class for training and 15 images per class for testing, repeating the experiments with five different splits according to a standard procedure [12]. The same was done for Caltech-256 except for the number of training images which ranged from 5 to 30 with a step of 5.

Experimental results on the Caltech-101 are displayed in Tab. 1. As can be seen both SS-CCT(HOG) and SST(HOG) outperform the baseline HOG with a 6% increment in the overall accuracy. On the other hand, SS-CCT(HOG) and SST(HOG) yield roughly the same performance: this is easily explainable considering that in Caltech-101 images are strongly aligned, reducing the need for robustness against position variation.

Results on the Caltech-256 in terms of accuracy vs the number of training images per class, are displayed in Fig. 3. As figure shows, our method outperforms both HOG and SST(HOG) in all the cases and the gap between our method and the others increases with the increase of the training set size. Differently from the Caltech-101 case, the higher complexity of the dataset highlights the superiority of our method with respect to SST(HOG).

Table 1. Classification results on the Caltech-101 dataset

	HOG	SST(HOG)	SS-CCT(HOG)
Accuracy %	41.3	47.6	**47.77**

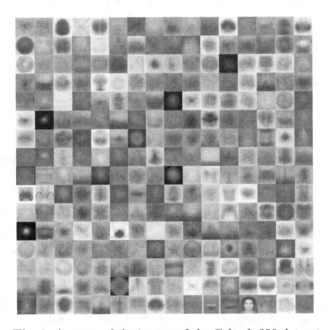

Fig. 2. Average of the images of the Caltech-256 dataset

4.2   Scene Classification

In the second experiment, the proposed framework is tested on the SenseCam Dataset [10]. This dataset consists of images acquired with a SenseCam, a wearable camera which automatically shoots a photo every 20 secs. It consists of 912 images labeled according to 32 classes (e.g. Bathroom Home, Car, Garage Home, Biking...). The images are divided into 479 images for training and 433 for testing. The dataset is challenging because most images present dramatic viewing angle, translational camera motions and large variations in illumination and scale: Fig. 4 shows four images belonging to two classes extracted from the dataset.

The HOG descriptor has been calculated on dense patches of size 32×32 with an overlap of 16 pixels. The number of regions was set to 15 : 5 along the x axis and 3 along the y axis. Experimental results are displayed in Tab. 2.

Our method outperforms both HOG and SST(HOG) with a difference in accuracy of about 8% and 3% respectively, so confirming its effectiveness in classifying images containing objects with an high degree of position variability.

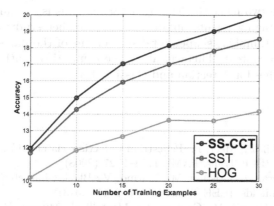

Fig. 3. Results obtained on the Caltech-256 dataset

Table 2. Classification results for the SenseCam dataset

	HOG	SST(HOG)	SS-CCT(HOG)
Accuracy %	36.72	41.10	**44.12**

Fig. 4. Four images extracted from the SenseCam Dataset: (a) Bathroom Home and (b) Kitchen

5   Conclusions and Future Works

This paper proposes a novel similarity-based descriptor for image classification purposes. The idea is to encode similarities among different image regions by means of cross-covariance matrices calculated on low level feature vectors, obtaining a robust and compact representation of structural (dis)similarities of a given entity. The final descriptor, obtained joining together the low-level features (HOG in our case) and their structural similarities, has proven to outperform baseline HOG, on all the datasets tested, and a recent literature similarity-based method [7], on the two most challenging datasets. This is a seminal work, and, despite the encouraging results obtained, needs further study for setting the best object model (number, shape and displacement of the parts) and the best features in a given context. This will allow the comparison with popular state-of-the-art approaches for detection and classification.

References

1. Tuzel, O., Porikli, F., Meer, P.: Pedestrian detection via classification on riemannian manifolds. IEEE Trans. PAMI, 1713–1727 (2008)
2. Tosato, D., Spera, M., Cristani, M., Murino, V.: Block Characterizing humans on riemannian manifolds. IEEE Trans. PAMI, 2–15 (2013)
3. San Biagio, M., Crocco, M., Cristani, M., Martelli, S., Murino, V.: Heterogeneous Auto-Similarities of Characteristics (HASC): Exploiting relational information for classification. In: Proc. ICCV (2013)
4. Lowe, D.G.: Object recognition from local scale-invariant features. In: Proc. ICCV, vol. 2, pp. 1150–1157 (1999)
5. Wang, X., Han, T.X., Yan, S.: An hog-lbp human detector with partial occlusion handling. In: Proc. ICCV, pp. 32–39 (2009)
6. Dalal, N., Triggs, B.: Histograms of oriented gradients for human detection. In: Proc. CVPR, vol. 1, pp. 886–893 (2005)
7. Martelli, S., Cristani, M., Bazzani, L., Tosato, D., Murino, V.: Joining feature-based and similarity-based pattern description paradigms for object detection. In: Proc. ICPR (2012)
8. Fei-Fei, L., Fergus, R., Perona, P.: Learning generative visual models from few training examples: An incremental bayesian approach tested on 101 object categories. CVIU 106(1), 59–70 (2007)
9. Griffin, G., Holub, A., Perona, P.: Caltech-256 object category dataset. Tech. Rep. 7694, California Institute of Technology (2007)
10. Perina, A., Jojic, N.: Spring lattice counting grids: Scene recognition using deformable positional constraints. In: Fitzgibbon, A., Lazebnik, S., Perona, P., Sato, Y., Schmid, C. (eds.) ECCV 2012, Part VI. LNCS, vol. 7577, pp. 837–851. Springer, Heidelberg (2012)
11. Chang, C.-C., Lin, C.-J.: LIBSVM: A library for support vector machines. ACM Transactions on Intelligent Systems and Technology 2, 27 (2011), http://www.csie.ntu.edu.tw/cjlin/libsvm
12. Vedaldi, A., Gulshan, V., Varma, M., Zisserman, A.: Multiple kernels for object detection. In: Proc. ICCV, pp. 606–613 (2009)

Dynamic K: A Novel Satisfaction Mechanism for CAR-Based Classifiers

Raudel Hernández-León

Centro de Aplicaciones de Tecnologías de Avanzada (CENATAV),
7a ♯ 21406 e/ 214 and 216, Rpto. Siboney, Playa, C.P. 12200, La Habana, Cuba
rhernandez@cenatav.co.cu

Abstract. In this paper, we propose a novel satisfaction mechanism, named "Dynamic K", which could be introduced in any Class Association Rules (CAR) based classifier, to determine the class of unseen transactions. Experiments over several datasets show that the new satisfaction mechanism has better performance than the main satisfaction mechanism reported ("Best Rule", "Best K Rules" and "All Rules"). Additionally, the experiments show that "Dynamic K" obtains the best results independent of the CAR-based classifier used.

Keywords: Supervised classification, Satisfaction mechanisms, Class association rules.

1 Introduction

The Classification Association Rule Mining (CARM) or associative classification, introduced in [2], integrates Classification Rule Mining (CRM) and Association Rule Mining (ARM). This integration involves mining a special subset of association rules, called Class Association Rules (CARs), using some quality measure (QM) to evaluate them. A classifier based on this approach usually consists of an ordered CAR list l, and a satisfaction mechanism for classifying unseen transactions using l [2,3,5]. Associative classification has been applied to many tasks including automatic error detection [19], detection of breast cancer [15], prediction of consumer behavior [17] and prediction of protein-protein interaction types [16], among others.

In associative classification, similar to ARM, a set of items $I = \{i_1, \ldots, i_n\}$, a set of classes C, and a set of labeled transactions D, are given. Each transaction in D is represented by a set of items $X \subseteq I$ and a class $c \in C$. A lexicographic order among the items of I is assumed. The Support of an itemset $X \subseteq I$ is the fraction of transactions in D containing X. A CAR is an implication of the form $X \Rightarrow c$ where $X \subseteq I$ and $c \in C$. The most commonly used QM to evaluate CARs is the Confidence. The rule $X \Rightarrow c$ is held in D with certain Support s and Confidence α, where s is the fraction of transactions in D that contains $X \cup \{c\}$, and α is the probability of finding c in transactions that also contain X. A CAR $X \Rightarrow c$ covers a transaction t if $X \subseteq t$.

J. Ruiz-Shulcloper and G. Sanniti di Baja (Eds.): CIARP 2013, Part I, LNCS 8258, pp. 141–148, 2013.

In general, CAR-based classifiers could be divided in two groups according to the strategy used for computing the set of CARs: (1) Two Stage classifiers - in a first stage, all CARs satisfying the Support and Confidence are mined and later, in a second stage, a classifier is built by selecting a small subset of CARs that fully covers the training set [2,3] and (2) Integrated classifiers - in these classifiers a small subset of CARs is directly generated [5,7,13].

Regardless of the strategy used for computing the set of CARs, in order to build the classifier we need to sort the CARs. In the literature, there are six main strategies for ordering CARs:

a) CSA (Confidence - Support - Antecedent size): First, the rules are sorted in a descending order according to their Confidence. In case of ties, the tied CARs are sorted in a descending order according to their Support, and if the tie persist, CSA sorts the rules in ascending order according to the size of their rule antecedent [2].

b) ACS (Antecedent size - Confidence - Support): This strategy is a variation of CSA, but it takes into account the size of the rule antecedent as first ordering criterion followed by Confidence and Support [7].

c) SrQM (Specific rules - QM): First, the rules are sorted in a descending order according to the size of the CARs and in case of tie, the tied CARs are sorted in a descending order according to their quality measure [18].

d) WRA (Weighted Relative Accuracy): The WRA rule ordering strategy assigns to each CAR a weight and then sorts the set of CARs in a descending order according to the assigned weights [12,14].

e) LAP (Laplace Expected Error Estimate): LAP was introduced by Clark and Boswell [1] and it has been used to order CARs in CPAR classifier [5].

f) χ^2 (Chi-Square): The χ^2 rule ordering strategy is a well known technique in statistics, which is used to determine whether two variables are independent or related. After computing an additive χ^2 value for each CAR, this value is used to sort the CARs in a descending order in the CMAR classifier [3].

Once the classifier has been built, we need to select a satisfaction mechanism for classifying unseen transactions. Three main satisfaction mechanisms have been reported in previous works [2,3,14]:

1. **Best Rule:** This mechanism selects the first ("best") rule in the order that satisfies the transaction to be classified, and then the class associated to the selected rule is assigned to this transaction [2].

2. **Best K Rules:** This mechanism selects the best K rules (per each class) that satisfy the transaction to be classified and then the class is determined using these K rules, according to different criteria [14].

3. **All Rules:** This mechanism selects all rules that satisfy the transaction to be classified and use them to determine the class of the new transaction [3].

Classifiers following the "Best Rule" mechanism could suffer biased classification or overfitting since the classification is based on only one rule. On the other hand, the "All Rules" mechanism includes rules with low ranking for classification and this could affect the accuracy of the classifier. The "Best K Rules" mechanism has been the most used satisfaction mechanism for CAR-based classifiers, reporting the best results. However, the classification accuracy could be affected when most of the best K rules were obtained extending the same item, or when there is an imbalance among the numbers of CARs with high Confidence (or another QM) values, per each class, that cover the new transaction.

In this paper, we propose a novel satisfaction mechanism, named "Dynamic K", to determine the class of unseen transactions. "Dynamic K" obtains better performance than the main satisfaction mechanism mentioned above and it could be introduced in any CAR-based classifier. This paper is organized as follows: The next section describes our proposal. In the third section the experimental results are shown. Finally, the conclusions are given in section four.

2   Our Proposal

As we mentioned above, the three satisfaction mechanisms reported have limitations that can affect the classification accuracy. In general, the "Best K Rules" mechanism has been the most widely used for CAR-based classifiers, reporting the best results [11]. However, using this mechanism could affect the classification accuracy. Ever more when most of the best K rules were obtained extending the same item, or when there is an imbalance among the numbers of CARs with high QM values, per each class, that cover the new transaction (see examples 1 and 2, respectively).

Example 1. Given the set of CARs shown in Tables 1(a) and 1(b). Suppose that you would like to classifier the transaction $\{i_1, i_2, i_3, i_4, i_5, i_6\}$ using the "Best K Rules" mechanism with $K = 5$, value commonly used in previous works. First, the CARs are sorted with SrQM rule ordering strategy (see Tables 1(c) and 1(d)). Then, for each class, the top five rules covering the transaction $\{i_1, i_2, i_3, i_4, i_5, i_6\}$ are selected. The average of those top five rules QM values (delimited by a line in Tables 1(c) and 1(d)), are 0.93 and 0.91, respectively; which means that c_1 would be assigned. Note that all antecedents of the selected CARs, belonging to class c_1, are subsets of $\{i_1, i_2, i_3, i_4\}$ (almost all rules were obtained from extensions of $\{i_1\} \Rightarrow c_1$). On the other hand, the antecedents of the top five rules in class c_2 (see Table 1(d)) involve a higher number of different items, resulting more intuitive to assign the class c_2.

Example 2. Given the set of CARs shown in the Tables 2(a) and 2(b). Suppose that you would like to classifier the transaction $\{i_1, i_2, i_3, i_4\}$ using the "Best K Rules" mechanism with $K = 5$. First, the CARs are sorted with SrQM rule ordering strategy (see Tables 2(c) and 2(d)). Then, for each class, the top five rules covering the transaction $\{i_1, i_2, i_3, i_4\}$ are selected. The average of those top five rules QM values, delimited by a line in Tables 2(c) and 2(d), are 0.90 and 0.92 respectively; which means that c_2 would be assigned. However, note if you only consider the top three CARs of each class, you would obtain the averages 0.95 and 0.92, respectively; which means that c_1 would be assigned. That happens because the class c_2 has more rules with QM greater than 0.90

than class c_1; and the "Best K Rules" mechanism does not take into account the imbalance among the number of CARs with high QM values, for each class, covering the new transaction.

Table 1. Example of two set of rules ((a) and (b)) and the result of sort them using the SrQM rule ordering strategy ((c) and (d))

	(a)			(b)	
#	CAR	QM	#	CAR	QM
1	$\{i_1\} \Rightarrow c_1$	0.91	1	$\{i_2\} \Rightarrow c_2$	0.86
2	$\{i_1, i_2\} \Rightarrow c_1$	0.96	2	$\{i_2, i_3\} \Rightarrow c_2$	0.87
3	$\{i_1, i_2, i_3\} \Rightarrow c_1$	0.96	3	$\{i_2, i_3, i_4\} \Rightarrow c_2$	0.93
4	$\{i_1, i_2, i_3, i_4\} \Rightarrow c_1$	0.96	4	$\{i_2, i_4\} \Rightarrow c_2$	0.85
5	$\{i_1, i_3\} \Rightarrow c_1$	0.92	5	$\{i_2, i_4, i_5\} \Rightarrow c_2$	0.96
6	$\{i_2\} \Rightarrow c_1$	0.84	6	$\{i_3\} \Rightarrow c_2$	0.88
7	$\{i_2, i_3\} \Rightarrow c_1$	0.84	7	$\{i_3, i_5\} \Rightarrow c_2$	0.88
8	$\{i_2, i_3, i_4\} \Rightarrow c_1$	0.85	8	$\{i_3, i_5, i_6\} \Rightarrow c_2$	0.90
9	$\{i_3\} \Rightarrow c_1$	0.81	9	$\{i_4\} \Rightarrow c_2$	0.87
10	$\{i_3, i_4\} \Rightarrow c_1$	0.83	10	$\{i_4, i_5\} \Rightarrow c_2$	0.89

	(c)			(d)	
#	CAR	QM	#	CAR	QM
1	$\{i_1, i_2, i_3, i_4\} \Rightarrow c_1$	0.96	1	$\{i_2, i_4, i_5\} \Rightarrow c_2$	0.96
2	$\{i_1, i_2, i_3\} \Rightarrow c_1$	0.96	2	$\{i_2, i_3, i_4\} \Rightarrow c_2$	0.93
3	$\{i_2, i_3, i_4\} \Rightarrow c_1$	0.85	3	$\{i_3, i_5, i_6\} \Rightarrow c_2$	0.90
4	$\{i_1, i_2\} \Rightarrow c_1$	0.96	4	$\{i_4, i_5\} \Rightarrow c_2$	0.89
5	$\{i_1, i_3\} \Rightarrow c_1$	0.92	5	$\{i_3, i_5\} \Rightarrow c_2$	0.88
6	$\{i_2, i_3\} \Rightarrow c_1$	0.84	6	$\{i_2, i_3\} \Rightarrow c_2$	0.87
7	$\{i_3, i_4\} \Rightarrow c_1$	0.83	7	$\{i_2, i_4\} \Rightarrow c_2$	0.85
8	$\{i_1\} \Rightarrow c_1$	0.91	8	$\{i_3\} \Rightarrow c_2$	0.88
9	$\{i_2\} \Rightarrow c_1$	0.84	9	$\{i_4\} \Rightarrow c_2$	0.87
10	$\{i_3\} \Rightarrow c_1$	0.81	10	$\{i_2\} \Rightarrow c_2$	0.86

Table 2. Example of two set of rules ((a) and (b)) and the result of sort them using the SrQM rule ordering strategy ((c) and (d))

	(a)			(b)	
#	CAR	QM	#	CAR	QM
1	$\{i_1\} \Rightarrow c_1$	0.80	1	$\{i_1\} \Rightarrow c_2$	0.80
2	$\{i_1, i_2\} \Rightarrow c_1$	0.82	2	$\{i_2\} \Rightarrow c_2$	0.83
3	$\{i_1, i_2, i_3\} \Rightarrow c_1$	0.95	3	$\{i_2, i_3\} \Rightarrow c_2$	0.92
4	$\{i_2\} \Rightarrow c_1$	0.83	4	$\{i_2, i_3, i_4\} \Rightarrow c_2$	0.92
5	$\{i_2, i_3\} \Rightarrow c_1$	0.94	5	$\{i_3\} \Rightarrow c_2$	0.91
6	$\{i_3\} \Rightarrow c_1$	0.84	6	$\{i_3, i_4\} \Rightarrow c_2$	0.92
7	$\{i_3, i_4\} \Rightarrow c_1$	0.96	7	$\{i_4\} \Rightarrow c_2$	0.91

	(c)			(d)	
#	CAR	QM	#	CAR	QM
1	$\{i_1, i_2, i_3\} \Rightarrow c_1$	0.95	1	$\{i_2, i_3, i_4\} \Rightarrow c_2$	0.92
2	$\{i_3, i_4\} \Rightarrow c_1$	0.96	2	$\{i_2, i_3\} \Rightarrow c_2$	0.92
3	$\{i_2, i_3\} \Rightarrow c_1$	0.94	3	$\{i_3, i_4\} \Rightarrow c_2$	0.92
4	$\{i_1, i_2\} \Rightarrow c_1$	0.82	4	$\{i_3\} \Rightarrow c_2$	0.91
5	$\{i_3\} \Rightarrow c_1$	0.84	5	$\{i_4\} \Rightarrow c_2$	0.91
6	$\{i_2\} \Rightarrow c_1$	0.83	6	$\{i_2\} \Rightarrow c_2$	0.83
7	$\{i_1\} \Rightarrow c_1$	0.80	7	$\{i_1\} \Rightarrow c_2$	0.80

In this paper, in order to overcome the drawbacks of the existing satisfaction mechanisms, we propose the "Dynamic K" mechanism. First, "Dynamic K" sorts the CARs using the SrQM rule ordering strategy. Later, "Dynamic K"

selects, for each class $c \in C$, the set of rules $X \Rightarrow c$ covering the new transaction t and satisfying the following conditions:

- $X \Rightarrow c$ is a maximal rule.
- for all $i \in I$, with i lexicographically greater than all items of X,
  $QM(X \cup \{i\} \Rightarrow c) < QM(X \Rightarrow c)$ holds.

Thereby we included more large rules with high QM values in the classification, avoiding redundancies and including more different items in the antecedents of the selected CARs. For example, Tables 3 and 4 show the rules of examples 1 and 2 that were selected for "Dynamic K" and cover transactions $\{i_1, i_2, i_3, i_4, i_5, i_6\}$ and $\{i_1, i_2, i_3, i_4\}$, respectively;

Table 3. Rules of Example 1 that were selected by "Dynamic K" and cover transaction $\{i_1, i_2, i_3, i_4, i_5, i_6\}$

	(a)			(b)	
#	CAR	QM	#	CAR	QM
1	$\{i_1, i_2, i_3, i_4\} \Rightarrow c_1$	0.96	1	$\{i_2, i_4, i_5\} \Rightarrow c_2$	0.96
2	$\{i_2, i_3, i_4\} \Rightarrow c_1$	0.85	2	$\{i_2, i_3, i_4\} \Rightarrow c_2$	0.93
3	$\{i_1, i_3\} \Rightarrow c_1$	0.92	3	$\{i_3, i_5, i_6\} \Rightarrow c_2$	0.90
4	$\{i_3, i_4\} \Rightarrow c_1$	0.83	4	$\{i_4, i_5\} \Rightarrow c_2$	0.89
	Average	0.89		Average	0.92

Table 4. Rules of Example 2 that were selected by "Dynamic K" and cover transaction $\{i_1, i_2, i_3, i_4\}$

	(a)			(b)	
#	CAR	QM	#	CAR	QM
1	$\{i_1, i_2, i_3\} \Rightarrow c_1$	0.95	1	$\{i_2, i_3, i_4\} \Rightarrow c_2$	0.92
2	$\{i_3, i_4\} \Rightarrow c_1$	0.96	2	$\{i_3, i_4\} \Rightarrow c_2$	0.92
3	$\{i_2, i_3\} \Rightarrow c_1$	0.94	3	$\{i_4\} \Rightarrow c_2$	0.91
			4	$\{i_1\} \Rightarrow c_2$	0.80
	Average	0.95		Average	0.92

Let N_i be the set of maximal CARs of class c_i that were selected for "Dynamic K" mechanism. After selecting all N_i (for $i = 1$ to $|C|$), "Dynamic K" assigns the class c_j such that the QM average of all rules of N_j is greater than the QM average of the top $|N_j|$ rules of each N_i, with $i \neq j$ and $|N_i| \geq |N_j|$. In case of tie among classes with different number of CARs, the class with less number of CARs is preferred because the CARs are sorted in descendent order according to their sizes (SrQM rule ordering strategy); in case of tie among classes with equals number of CARs, the class with greater Support is selected, if the tie persist the class is selected randomly.

If in examples 1 and 2, we applied the "Dynamic K" mechanism to classify the transactions $\{i_1, i_2, i_3, i_4, i_5, i_6\}$ and $\{i_1, i_2, i_3, i_4\}$, respectively, we will obtain the class c_2 in the first example (see Table 3) and the class c_1 in the second one (see Table 4).

The "Dynamic K" mechanism does not have the drawbacks of the other existent mechanisms since:

- It selects the maximal rules with high QM values, avoiding redundancies and allowing the inclusion of more different items in the antecedents of the selected CARs, thereby CARs of low quality are not included for classifying.
- The result is not affected when there is an imbalance among the numbers of CARs with high QM values, for each class, that cover the new transaction, this happens because to classify a new transaction, "Dynamic K" considers the average of the same amount of CARs.
- It considers all good quality CARs that cover the new transaction and not only the best one. Thereby, "Dynamic K" does not fall on the mistake of assuming that the best rule is going to classify correctly all transactions that it covers.

3   Experimental Results

In this section, we present the results of our experimental comparison among "Dynamic K" and the main satisfaction mechanisms reported in the literature: "Best rule" [2], "Best K rules" [14] and "All rules" [3].

For the experiment showed in Table 5, the four satisfaction mechanisms were implemented inside the CAR-IC classifier [18], using the Confidence threshold set to 0.5 and the Support threshold set to 0.01, as it was reported in other works [3,5,7,14,20]. All our experiments were done using ten-fold cross-validation reporting the average over the ten folds. All the tests were performed on a PC with an Intel Core 2 Duo at 1.86 GHz CPU with 1 GB DDR2 RAM. Similar to other works [2,3,6,13,20], we used several datasets, specifically 20. The chosen datasets were originally taken from the UCI Machine Learning Repository [10], and their numerical attributes were discretized by Frans Coenen using the LUCS-KDD [4] discretized/normalized CARM Data Library.

For the experiment showed in Table 6, the codes of CBA, CMAR, CPAR and TFPC were downloaded from the Frans Coenen's homepage (http://www.csc.liv.ac.uk/~frans) and the codes of DDPMine and CAR-IC was provided by their authors. For CBA, CMAR, CPAR, TFPC and CAR-IC classifiers we used the Confidence threshold set to 0.5 and the Support threshold set to 0.01, as their authors suggested.

In Table 5, the results show that "Dynamic K" yields an average accuracy higher than all other evaluated mechanisms, having a difference of 0.92% with respect to the mechanism in the second place ("Best K rules" with K set to 5, the same value used in other works [5,11,12,14]). Additionally, "Dynamic K" wins in 16 of the 20 datasets and ties in the other four. In Table 6, we show that "Dynamic K" obtains the best results independent of the CAR-based classifier used, being CAR-IC the most benefited with the new mechanism (see rows 3 and 4 of Table 6).

Finally, in order to determine if the results shown in Table 5 are statistically significant, we performed a pairwise comparison between "Dynamic K" and the other satisfaction mechanisms. Each cell in Table 7 contains the number of

Table 5. Classification accuracy of CAR-IC using the different satisfaction mechanisms

Dataset	Best rule	All rules	Best K rules	Dynamic K
adult	82.14	81.09	82.61	**82.85**
anneal	91.77	90.95	92.73	**93.26**
breast	84.45	83.52	90.03	**90.46**
connect4	55.98	55.01	56.02	**57.24**
dermatology	78.45	77.22	80.16	**83.93**
ecoli	82.04	80.46	82.06	**82.16**
flare	86.00	85.38	85.98	**86.45**
glass	68.10	67.29	68.95	**71.12**
heart	53.23	52.14	54.35	**56.48**
hepatitis	84.54	83.66	**84.62**	**84.62**
horseColic	82.48	81.75	82.47	**84.54**
ionosphere	84.06	83.02	86.10	**86.24**
iris	96.07	95.98	96.67	**97.91**
led7	72.70	71.43	**73.02**	**73.02**
letRecog	73.17	72.50	73.14	**75.23**
mushroom	98.51	97.86	**98.54**	**98.54**
pageBlocks	91.85	91.13	92.26	**92.59**
penDigits	77.83	76.42	81.93	**82.78**
pima	75.35	74.59	**76.01**	**76.01**
waveform	73.14	72.24	74.39	**75.06**
Average	79.59	78.68	80.60	**81.52**

Table 6. Average accuracy of other classifiers over the tested datasets, for different satisfaction mechanisms

Dataset	CBA	CMAR	CPAR	TFPC	DDPMine	CAR-IC
All rules	70.03	75.28	74.39	73.08	77.81	78.68
Best rule	71.81	76.49	75.64	74.21	78.88	79.59
Best K rules	72.71	77.99	76.86	75.76	79.72	80.60
Dynamic K	**73.28**	**78.53**	**77.32**	**76.21**	**80.16**	**81.52**

Table 7. Pairwise comparison between "Dynamic K" and the other satisfaction mechanism, using CAR-IC classifier. Each cell shows the number of times "Dynamic K" Win/Lose with respect to the corresponding mechanism over the 20 selected datasets.

	All rules	Best rule	Best K rules	Dynamic K
All rules		0/6	0/14	0/19
Best rule	6/0		0/5	0/10
Best K rules	14/0	5/0		0/7
Dynamic K	19/0	10/0	7/0	

datasets where "Dynamic K" significantly Win/Lose to each other mechanism. We detected ties using a one-tailed T-Test [8] with significance level of 0.05. The results in the pairwise comparison reveal that the "Dynamic K" mechanism beats all other evaluated mechanisms over most of the tested datasets.

4   Conclusions

In this paper, a new satisfaction mechanism, called "Dynamic K", was presented. "Dynamic K" overcomes the drawbacks of the existing satisfaction mechanisms and it could be introduced in any CAR-based classifier. Experimental results show that "Dynamic K" obtains a classification accuracy higher than all other evaluated mechanisms, independent of the CAR-based classifier used.

References

1. Clark, P., Boswell, R.: Rule Induction with CN2: Some Recent Improvments. In: Proc. of European Working Session on Learning, pp. 151–163 (1991)
2. Liu, B., Hsu, W., Ma, Y.: Integrating classification and association rule mining. In: Proc. of the KDD, pp. 80–86 (1998)
3. Li, W., Han, J., Pei, J.: CMAR: Accurate and efficient classification based on multiple class-association rules. In: Proc. of the ICDM, pp. 369–376 (2001)
4. Coenen, F.: The LUCS-KDD discretised/normalised ARM and CARM Data Library (2003), http://www.csc.liv.ac.uk/~frans/KDD/Software/LUCS-KDD-DN
5. Yin, X., Han, J.: CPAR: Classification based on Predictive Association Rules. In: Proc. of the SIAM International Conference on Data Mining, pp. 331–335 (2003)
6. Wang, J., Karypis, G.: HARMONY: Efficiently mining the best rules for classification. In: Proc. of SDM, pp. 205–216 (2005)
7. Coenen, F., Leng, P., Zhang, L.: Threshold Tuning for Improved Classification Association Rule Mining. In: Ho, T.-B., Cheung, D., Liu, H. (eds.) PAKDD 2005. LNCS (LNAI), vol. 3518, pp. 216–225. Springer, Heidelberg (2005)
8. Demšar, J.: Statistical Comparisons of Classifiers over Multiple Data Sets. J. Mach. Learn. Res. 7, 1–30 (2006)
9. Steinbach, M., Kumar, V.: Generalizing the notion of confidence. Knowl. Inf. Syst. 12(3), 279–299 (2007)
10. Asuncion, A., Newman, D.J.: UCI Machine Learning Repository (2007), http://www.ics.uci.edu/~mlearn/{MLR}epository.html
11. Wang, Y.J., Xin, Q., Coenen, F.: A Novel Rule Weighting Approach in Classification Association Rule Mining. In: International Conference on Data Mining Workshops, pp. 271–276 (2007)
12. Wang, Y.J., Xin, Q., Coenen, F.: A Novel Rule Ordering Approach in Classification Association Rule Mining. In: Perner, P. (ed.) MLDM 2007. LNCS (LNAI), vol. 4571, pp. 339–348. Springer, Heidelberg (2007)
13. Cheng, H., Yan, X., Han, J., Philip, S.Y.: Direct Discriminative Pattern Mining for Effective Classification. In: Proc. of the ICDE, pp. 169–178 (2008)
14. Wang, Y.J., Xin, Q., Coenen, F.: Hybrid Rule Ordering in Classification Association Rule Mining. Trans. MLDM 1(1), 1–15 (2008)
15. Karabatak, M., Ince, M.C.: An expert system for detection of breast cancer based on association rules and neural network. Expert Syst. Appl. 36, 3465–3469 (2009)
16. Park, S.H., Reyes, J.A., Gilbert, D.R., Kim, J.W., Kim, S.: Prediction of protein-protein interaction types using association rule based classification. BMC Bioinformatics 10(1) (2009)
17. Bae, J.K., Kim, J.: Integration of heterogeneous models to predict consumer behavior. Expert Syst. Appl. 37, 1821–1826 (2010)
18. Hernández, R., Carrasco, J.A., Martínez, F.J., Hernández, J.: Classifying using Specific Rules with High Confidence. In: Proc. of the MICAI, pp. 75–80 (2010)
19. Malik, W.A., Unwin, A.: Automated error detection using association rules. Intelligent Data Analysis 15(5), 749–761 (2011)
20. Hernández, R., Carrasco, J.A., Martínez, F.J., Hernández, J.: CAR-NF: A Classifier based on Specific Rules with High Netconf. Intelligent Data Analysis 16(1), 49–68 (2012)

Weighted Naïve Bayes Classifiers by Renyi Entropy

Tomomi Endo and Mineichi Kudo

Division of Computer Science
Graduate School of Information Science and Technology
Hokkaido University, Sapporo, Japan
{tomomi,mine}@main.ist.hokudai.ac.jp

Abstract. A weighted naïve Bayes classifier using Renyi entropy is proposed. Such a weighted naïve Bayes classifier has been studied so far,
aiming at improving the prediction performance or at reducing the number of features. Among those studies, weighting with Shannon entropy
has succeeded in improving the performance. However, the reasons of the
success was not well revealed. In this paper, the original classifier is extended using Renyi entropy with parameter α. The classifier includes the
regular naïve Bayes classifier in one end ($\alpha = 0.0$) and naïve Bayes classifier weighted by the marginal Bayes errors in the other end ($\alpha = \infty$). The
optimal setting of α has been discussed analytically and experimentally.

1 Introduction and Related Studies

In the field of pattern recognition, there are various kinds of large-scale datasets.
The features expressing an object may be continuous, discrete or categorical, and
sometimes all these kinds of features appear at the same time. Such a feature
set containing more than one kind of features is called a *mixed feature set*. In
a large-scale dataset with mixed features, we have to solve two problems: 1)
how we deal with mixed features consistently and effectively and 2) how we
suppress the bad effect due to many features useless for classification (feature
selection). Especially, feature selection for large-scale datasets is desired to have
a low computational complexity, e.g., linear or less in the number of features.

The authors had proposed a weighted naïve Bayes classifiers in which every
continuous/ordered feature was converted into categorical one, coping with the
first issue, and feature weights were introduced to reduce the effective number of
features, coping with the second issue. In the weighting, the degree of importance
of each feature was measured by a Shannon entropy of data and the computation cost was linear in the number of features. The proposed classifier, indeed,
succeeded to reduce a large number of features without a large degradation of
performance [1]. However, in the viewpoint of performance improvement, it was
not satisfactory. It was better in only a few cases compared with the naïve Bayes
classifiers. This is probably because the way of using Shannon entropy was not
optimal. Therefore, we examine the validity to use a more general Renyi entropy
and analyze the property in the same framework.

J. Ruiz-Shulcloper and G. Sanniti di Baja (Eds.): CIARP 2013, Part I, LNCS 8258, pp. 149–156, 2013.

The studies related to weighted naïve Bayes classifiers are mainly divided into two groups. One group aims at choosing a small number of features or at shrinking weights of useless features [2,3]. Another group aims at improving the performance by controlling the weights appropriately [4,5]. For example, by regarding each term as a new feature and the weight as a coefficient, we can control these coefficients as in the same way of linear classifiers or of linear support vector machines.

Some of these studies, however, suffer from the large computation cost [3,4]. The others could not improved the performance as expected or could not deal with mixed features appropriately. Therefore, we proposed another way [1] in which all features were converted into categorical features and the weights were derived from the Shannon entropy or mutual information of each feature.

After we proposed the method, we noticed a very similar study by Chang-Hwan Lee et $al.$ [6]. In their method, the weights are derived from a different formulation via Kullback-Leibler divergence, but the resultant weights coincide with ours. They showed the effectiveness of their approach as well as ours. The difference is that they normalized the weights within a finite range while we left them as they were, preferring two extreme values of zero and infinity.

2   Weighted Naïve Bayes and Proposed Methods

The naïve Bayes classifier is a Bayes classifier simplified by the assumption of independence between features in each class. It assigns a class label $c^* \in \{1, 2, \ldots, K\}$ for a class-unknown sample $x = (x_1, x_2, \ldots, x_D)$ by the rule:

$$
\begin{aligned}
c^* &= \arg\max_c P(c \mid x) \quad \text{(maximum posterior method)} \\
&= \arg\max_c P(x \mid c)P(c) \quad \text{(Bayes rule)} \\
&= \arg\max_c P(c) \prod_{d=1}^{D} P(x_d \mid c) \quad \text{(Independence assumption)} \\
&= \arg\max_c \left\{ \log P(c) + \sum_{d=1}^{D} \log P(x_d \mid c) \right\} \\
&= \arg\max_c \left\{ \log P(c) + \sum_{d=1}^{D} \log \frac{P(c \mid x_d)P(x_d)}{P(c)} \right\} \\
&= \arg\max_c \left\{ \log P(c) + \sum_{d=1}^{D} \log \frac{P(c \mid x_d)}{P(c)} \right\}.
\end{aligned}
$$

We have derived the last two formulae because it is more natural to use $P(c \mid x_d)$ than $P(x_d \mid c)$ when x_d is one value of a categorical feature. Indeed, we can estimate the probability by counting the number of samples taking the value x_d class-wisely without a special assumption of distribution necessary for estimation of $P(x_d \mid c)$. Here, we use the base 2 for log through the paper.

Referring to this assignment rule, we consider the following discriminant functions to be maximized by c^*:

$$\delta^c(x) = w_0 \log \frac{P(c)}{P_0(c)} + \sum_{d=1}^{D} w_d \log \frac{P(c|x_d)}{P(c)}, \quad P_0(c) = 1/K. \quad (1)$$

This is different from many studies including our previous study in the point that is includes w_0 and $P_0(c)$. These modifications are made for two reasons: 1) to control the degree of affection by the prior probability by w_0, e.g., make $w_0 = 0$ if $P(c) = 1/K$ and 2) to bring consistency and interpretability to every term as pieces of evidence to support class c, e.g., a positive log-odds $\log \frac{P(c|x_d)}{P(c)}$, i.e., $P(c|x_d) > P(c)$, gives a positive piece of evidence to support class c by knowing the value of x_d and a negative odds gives a negative piece of evidence.

In this study, we convert continuous and discrete features into categorical ones to enable a unified treatment of mixed features. This is because it is hard to give a reasonable metric between categorical values, e.g. people's names. Conversely, discretizing a continuous value does not always mean a loss of significant information. Discretization sometimes even improves the performance of classifiers [7]. In this paper, we simply use, equally-spaced bins within the minimum and maximum values of training samples because our objective is to investigate the effect of the proposed weighting method. The number of bins is in common set to $\log N$ where N is the number of samples.

3   Extension by Renyi Entropies

When we introduce a weight on each term in the discrimination function, we have to determine two things: 1) how we measure the importance of each feature and 2) how we connect the degree of importance to the corresponding weight.

For the second issue, we use a monotonically decreasing function $w(h)$ of entropy h such that $w(h) \to 0$ as $h \to \log K$ and $w(h) \to \infty$ as $h \to 0$. This property is required to achive 1) features having no or less information for classification should be given zero or a smaller value of weight and 2) a feature having a "perfect" information for classification, if any, should govern the other features by taking a very large value of weight. In this study, we use a class of functions:

$$w(h) = \frac{e^{-ah} - e^{-ac_0}}{1 - e^{-ah}}, \quad \text{where } h = H(\mathsf{C}|\mathsf{X}), \ c_0 = H(\mathsf{C}), \ a \geq 0, \quad (2)$$

where $H(\mathsf{C}|\mathsf{X})$ is the conditioned entropy given a feature X. Since $w(h) \to (c_0 - h)/h$ as $a \to 0$, this weight function includes our previous one [1]. For avoiding many parameters included, we use $a = 1$ in this paper.

As a measure of importance on the first issue, we use Renyi entropy that is a general entropy taking a value in $[0, \log K]$, where K is the number of possible events. The formal definition with a random variable C is given by

$$H_\alpha(\mathsf{C}) = \frac{1}{1-\alpha} \log \sum_{i=1}^{K} p_i^\alpha \quad \alpha \geq 0, \ \alpha \neq 1. \quad (3)$$

This includes Shannon entropy as a special case of when $\alpha \to 0$. The other two special cases are $H_0(\mathsf{C}) = \log \#\{p_i > 0\}$ ($= \log K$ in most cases), and $H_\infty(\mathsf{C}) = -\log \max_i p_i$ $= -\max_i \log p_i$. The following monotonicity holds: $\log K = H_0 \geq H_1 = H \geq H_2 \geq \cdots \geq H_\infty$.

3.1   Bounds by the Prediction Error

Next, let us make clear the relationship between a conditional Renyi entropy and a Bayes error. In the following, we will first show lower and upper bounds of Renyi entropy $H_\alpha(\mathsf{C}|\mathsf{X} = x)$ by a prediction error $\epsilon(x) = 1 - \max_c P(\mathsf{C} = c|\mathsf{X} = x)$ at a point x. Here C is a random variable for class and X is a random variable for one feature.

For $H_\alpha = \frac{1}{1-\alpha} \log \sum_{i=1}^K p_i^\alpha$ and $\epsilon = 1 - \max_i p_i$ on a probability distribution $\mathbf{p} = (p_1, p_2, \ldots, p_K)$, we have derived lower bounds $\phi_\alpha(\epsilon)$ and upper bounds $\Phi_\alpha(\epsilon)$ of H_α defined by $\phi_\alpha(\epsilon) = \frac{1}{1-\alpha} \log \{i(1-\epsilon)^\alpha - (K-1)(i\epsilon - i + 1)^\alpha\}, \frac{i-1}{i} \leq \epsilon <$ $\frac{i}{i+1}, i = 1, 2, \ldots, K$ and $\Phi_\alpha(\epsilon) = \frac{1}{1-\alpha} \log \left\{ (1-\epsilon)^\alpha - (K-1)\left(\frac{\epsilon}{K-1}\right)^\alpha \right\}$, In particular, $\phi_\infty(\epsilon) = \Phi_\infty(\epsilon) = -\log(1-\epsilon)$. These bounds are shown in Fig. 1. These bounds are extensions of a known result for Shannon entropy [8]. The derivation is easily understood by considering two extreme distributions attaining the minimum and maximum. Since both $\phi_\alpha(\epsilon)$ and $\Phi_\alpha(\epsilon)$ are monotonically increasing in ϵ, we may regard Renyi entropy as a measure of importance of knowing the value x.

Now let us show the relationship between the Bayes error $\epsilon_{\text{Bayes}} = \sum_x P(x)\epsilon(x)$ and the *conditional* Renyi entropy $H_\alpha(\mathsf{C}|\mathsf{X}) = \sum_x P(x)H_\alpha(\mathsf{C}|\mathsf{X} = x)$. Since the point $(\epsilon_{\text{Bayes}}, H_\alpha(\mathsf{C}|\mathsf{X}))$ is given by averaging similar points at $\mathsf{X} = x$ as $\sum_x P(x)(\epsilon(x), H_\alpha(\mathsf{C}|\mathsf{X} = x))$, the point is included in the convex region bounded by $\phi_\alpha(\epsilon)$, $\Phi_\alpha(\epsilon)$ and two special functions: $\phi^*(\epsilon) = $ lines connecting $(0,0)$, $(1/2, \log 2)$, $\ldots$, $((K-1)/K, \log K)$ and $\Phi_*(\epsilon) = \frac{K \log K}{K-1}\epsilon$ (Fig. 1). Then we have the lower and upperbound as:

$$\{\phi^*(\epsilon_{\text{Bayes}}), \phi_\infty(\epsilon_{\text{Bayes}}), \phi_\infty(\epsilon_{\text{Bayes}})\} \leq H_\alpha(\mathsf{C}|\mathsf{X}) \leq \{\Phi_\alpha(\epsilon_{\text{Bayes}}), \Phi_1(\epsilon_{\text{Bayes}}), \Phi_*(\epsilon_{\text{Bayes}})\},$$

where $\{A, B, C\}$ corresponds to three cases $\{\alpha \leq 1, 1 < \alpha < \infty, \alpha = \infty\}$. We inverted relationships with Φ_α^{-1} or ϕ_α^{-1} from their strict monotonicity. Note in Fig. 1 that $H_\infty(\mathsf{C}|\mathsf{X})$ is close to $-\log(1 - \epsilon_{\text{Bayes}})$ for small values of ϵ_{Bayes}.

3.2   Weights with H_0, H_∞ and H_α

We will show that 1) a weighted naïve Bayes classifier with H_0 simulates the original naïve Bayes classifier without weights and 2) weights with H_∞ reflect the marginal Bayes errors.

When we concentrate on a feature represented by X, for example, dth feature, our weight w_d with Renyi entropy becomes

$$w_d = w_\alpha(h) = \frac{e^{-h} - e^{-c_0}}{1 - e^{-h}}, \quad \text{where } h = H_\alpha(\mathsf{C}|\mathsf{X}), \ c_0 = H_\alpha(\mathsf{C}). \tag{4}$$

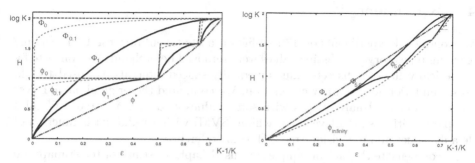

Fig. 1. Lower bound ϕ_α and upper bound Φ_α of Renyi entropy H_α by the prediction error ϵ for $K = 4$. Left: those for $\alpha = 1.0, 0.1, 0.0$; Right: those for $\alpha = 1.0, 5.0, +\infty$. The definition of ϕ^*, Φ_* and ϕ_∞ are given in the text.

Hereafter, we will not mention to w_0 for simplicity, but a similar process is applied to w_0, e.g., above values are replaced with $h = H_\alpha(\mathsf{C})$ and $c_0 = H_\alpha(\mathsf{C}_0)$.

When $\alpha \to 0$, e^{-h} and e^{-c_0} approach to $e^{-\log K}$ in most cases, but $w_\alpha(h)/w_\alpha(h')$ (h' is for a different feature) converges to a different value other than one depending on the underlying distributions. Thus, we introduce a small value δ in the weight function so as to converge into a common value:

$$w_\alpha(h) = \frac{e^{-h} - e^{-c_0} + \delta}{1 - e^{-h}} \to \frac{\delta}{1 + \log K} \quad \text{as} \quad \alpha \to 0. \qquad (5)$$

With this modification, we can guarantee that $\alpha = 0$ achieves the original naïve Bayes classifier, because a constant multiplication does not change the ranking of discriminant functions.

When $\alpha = \infty$, our weighted naïve Bayes classifier is connected to the marginal Bayes errors. Here, we call the error of Bayes classifier constructed on a subset of features a *marginal Bayes error*. From the monotonicity of Bayes error on feature subsets, the Bayes error is less than or equal to marginal Bayes errors. When we denote by $\epsilon_{\text{Bayes}}^d$ the marginal Bayes error on dth feature only, it holds that $\epsilon_{\text{Bayes}} \leq \epsilon_{\text{Bayes}}^d, \forall d \in \{1, 2, \ldots, D\}$. Since, as described, for $\alpha = \infty$ and small values of ϵ_{Bayes}, we may assume that $\epsilon_{\text{Bayes}}^d = 1 - \exp(-H_\infty(\mathsf{C}|\mathsf{X}_d))$. Therefore we have

$$w_d = w_\infty(h) \simeq \frac{1 - \epsilon_{\text{Bayes}}^d - e^{-c_0} + \delta}{\epsilon_{\text{Bayes}}^d} \simeq \frac{\epsilon_{\text{Bayes}}^{\text{prior}} - \epsilon_{\text{Bayes}}^d}{\epsilon_{\text{Bayes}}^d} \leq \frac{\epsilon_{\text{Bayes}}^{\text{prior}} - \epsilon_{\text{Bayes}}}{\epsilon_{\text{Bayes}}},$$

where $\epsilon^{\text{prior}} = 1 - \max_c P(c)$, that is, the error on the basis of prior probabilities. The second approximation holds because $c_0 = H_\infty(\mathsf{C}) = -\log \max_c P(c)$. This relationship means that weight w_d is inversely proportional to the marginal Bayes error $\epsilon_{\text{Bayes}}^d$ and upper-bounded by Bayes error ϵ_{Bayes} in the same function.

When a middle value of α is taken, the corresponding weights and classifier have a neutral nature between two extreme cases.

4   Experiment

We conducted experiments on 17 real-life datasets taken from the UCI machine learning repository [9]. Missing values were removed beforehand. We converted a numerical value to a discrete value by equally-spaced intervals. We used 10-fold cross validation for accuracy calculation. We compared the original naïve Bayes with our weighted naïve Bayes with some values of α and $\delta = 0.01$. We also compared with a support vector machine (SVM) with a radial basis function of default values and a decision tree (C4.5) for reference.

To compensate the lack of samples, we used Laplace estimator to estimate the probability $P(c|x)$: $\hat{P}(c|x) = \frac{n_{x,c}+1}{n_x+K}$, where n_x is the number of samples taking value x and $n_{x,c}$ is the number of samples belonging to class c among them. This works especially for when $n_{x,c}$ is close to zero. We used this Laplace modification for the other probabilities as well.

4.1   Result

The result is shown in Table 1. It includes also the number of selected features whose weights are more than 10% of the maximum weight.

The optimal value of α varies over datasets. In summary, 1) a larger value of α accelerates feature selection at the expense of a small amount of performance degradation (about a half of features is removed at $\alpha = 10.0$) , 2) a smaller value of α is useful for improving the performance while keeping almost all features (in 8 cases of 17 cases, $\alpha = 0.1$ achieved the best performance), and 3) a small value of α is effective for problems with many classes (e.g., dermatology). In these senses, changing the value of α from the Shannon settling ($\alpha = 1$) is worth considering. It is also noted that the weighted naïve Bayes outperforms C4.5 and SVM in datasets whose features are almost all categorical (e.g., splice and dermatology have only categorical features).

A better performance seems to be obtained for a smaller value of α. Indeed, we confirmed that a better rate of 99.20% can be obtained for $\alpha = 0.01$ in mushroom. However, it does not mean that the smaller value of α, the better. This is obvious from the recognition rate of 97.39% attained by the original naïve Bayes classifier for which $\alpha = 0.0$. The weights in mushroom are shown in Fig. 2 at $\alpha = 0.01$ and $\alpha = 10$. Although no feature selection was made at $\alpha = 0.01$, the difference of weights contributed to the increase of performance.

5   Discussion

We have analyzed the weighted naïve Bayes classifier using Renyi entropy H_α. It inherits the merit and demerit from the original naïve Bayes classifier without weights. It cannot show a satisfactory performance if the classification problem needs combinations of features in essence. However, it can often beat the curse of dimensionality by the virtue of the simplicity. Weighting on features suppresses useless features and improves the performance.

Table 1. Recognition rate estimated by 10-fold CV on 17 datasets taken from UCI. Here, D is the number of features, N is the number of samples and K is the number of classes. The proposed method (Weighted NB :$\alpha = 0.1, 1.0, 10.0$) are compared with Naïve Bayes (NB), C4.5 and linear SVM. A recognition rate is represented at percent and a number in parentheses is the number of selected features. In the last two rows, #wins is the number of victories in the naïve Bayes family and "Reduction" is the average of reduction rate of features. The best classifier is underlined.

Dataset	D	N	K	NB $\alpha = 0.1$	Weighted NB $\alpha = 1$	$\alpha = 10$	C4.5	SVM
haberman	3	306	2	<u>74.83</u> 72.89(3)	73.22(3)	73.22(1)	72.22	71.90
breast-c	9	277	2	74.39 73.94(9)	**74.83**(9)	71.87(8)	<u>75.09</u>	71.84
tic	9	958	2	69.93 **70.42**(9)	68.98(9)	65.62(1)	84.55	<u>98.33</u>
heart-c	13	296	2	83.46 83.34(13)	84.71(13)	**84.72**(11)	77.70	84.12
credit-a	15	653	2	85.60 **86.85**(15)	86.39(4)	86.39(5)	85.14	85.60
hepatitis	19	80	2	82.50 82.50(19)	**87.50**(9)	83.75(1)	86.25	82.50
credit-g	20	1000	2	74.80 **74.90**(20)	74.20(20)	70.00(2)	71.10	74.40
mushroom	22	5644	2	97.39 **98.47**(15)	98.44(4)	98.44(2)	<u>100.0</u>	<u>100.0</u>
leukemia	7129	72	2	73.49 80.31(7129)	82.85(2240)	84.28(1210)	83.33	<u>98.61</u>
iris	4	150	3	93.33 **94.66**(4)	**94.66**(4)	**94.66**(3)	95.33	<u>96.00</u>
tae	5	151	3	55.54 **56.25**(5)	54.29(5)	53.00(5)	51.65	52.32
cmc	9	1473	3	49.29 48.95(9)	49.83(9)	**52.47**(9)	51.53	47.72
splice	60	3190	3	<u>95.36</u> 95.23(60)	94.54(30)	94.20(7)	94.26	92.98
car	6	1728	4	<u>85.64</u> 85.02(6)	70.02(4)	70.02(1)	92.47	<u>93.23</u>
lymph	18	148	4	56.62 **80.06**(18)	78.89(10)	79.35(11)	77.70	<u>84.46</u>
glass	9	214	6	49.39 49.39(9)	**52.25**(9)	47.01(9)	<u>66.35</u>	57.47
dermatology	34	366	6	97.62 **97.62**(34)	**97.62**(34)	95.95(32)	93.71	96.72
#wins				4 8	5	4		
Reduction(%)				(0%) (1.87%)	(23.77%)	(49.93%)		

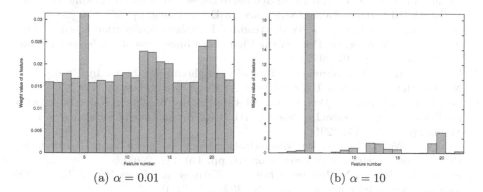

(a) $\alpha = 0.01$ (b) $\alpha = 10$

Fig. 2. The weights of features in `mushroom` for two extreme values of α. Here, feature #5 is "odor", #20 is "spore-print-color." The task is to predict the edibility.

It is not easy to find an optimal value of parameter α in the proposed method, because it depends on the problems, e.g., the number of features and the number of classes. Our analysis gave just a simple guideline: choose a smaller value, say $\alpha = 0.1$, if you put a priority on improving the performance; choose a larger value, say $\alpha = 10.0$, if you need to reduce the feature set size; otherwise $\alpha = 1$ as an acceptable compromise.

As predicted from our analysis, a very small value of α made the classifier be close to the the the original Bayes classifier. A large value of α emphasizes on the marginal Bayes errors. Note that Bayes error does not tell anything about classes except for the class with the largest probability. This may explain why larger values of α did not bring better results for problems with many classes.

6   Conclusion

We have extended a weighted naïve Bayes classifier using Renyi entropy H_α from the Shannon entropy version and analyzed its property. It becomes the regular naïve Bayes classify in one end with $\alpha = 0$ and a naïve Bayes classifier of which wights are inversely proportional to the marginal Bayes errors using individual features in the other end with $\alpha = \infty$. It is not so easy to find the optimal value of α depending on dataset at hand, but we gave a rough guideline for selection.

References

1. Omura, K., Kudo, M., Endo, T., Murai, T.: Weighted naïve Bayes classifier on categorical features. In: Proc. of 12th International Conference on Intelligent Systems Design and Applications, pp. 865–870 (2012)
2. Chen, L., Wang, S.: Automated feature weighting in naive bayes for high-dimensional data classification. In: Proc. of the 21st ACM International Conference on Information and Knowledge Management, pp. 1243–1252 (2012)
3. Zhang, H., Sheng, S.: Learning weighted naive Bayes with accurate ranking. In: Proc. of Fourth IEEE International Conference on Data Mining, pp. 567–570 (2004)
4. Grtner, T., Flach, P.A.: WBCSVM: Weighted Bayesian Classification based on Support Vector Machines. In: Proc. of the Eighteenth International Conference on Machine Learning, pp. 207–209 (2001)
5. Frank, E., Hall, M., Pfahringer, B.: Locally weighted naive bayes. In: Proc. of the Nineteenth Conference on Uncertainty in Artificial Intelligence, pp. 249–256 (2002)
6. Lee, C.H., Gutierrez, F., Dou, D.: Calculating Feature Weights in Naive Bayes with Kullback-Leibler Measure. In: Proc. of 11th IEEE International Conference on Data Mining, pp. 1146–1151 (2011)
7. Yang, Y., Webb, G.I.: On why discretization works for naive-bayes classifiers. In: Proc. of 16th Australian Conference on AI, pp. 440–452 (2003)
8. Feder, M., Merhav, N.: Relations Between Entropy and Error Probability. IEEE Transactions on Information Theory 40, 259–266 (1994)
9. Newman, D.J., Hettich, S., Blake, C.L., Merz, C.J.: UCI Repository of machine learning databases. University of California, Department of Infromation and Computer Science, Irvine, http://www.ics.uci.edu/~mlearn/MLRepository.html

CICE-BCubed: A New Evaluation Measure for Overlapping Clustering Algorithms

Henry Rosales-Méndez[1] and Yunior Ramírez-Cruz[2]

[1] Computer Science Department
Universidad de Oriente, Santiago de Cuba, Cuba
henry.rosales@csd.uo.edu.cu
[2] Center for Pattern Recognition and Data Mining
Universidad de Oriente, Santiago de Cuba, Cuba
yunior@cerpamid.co.cu

Abstract. The evaluation of clustering algorithms is a field of Pattern Recognition still open to extensive debate. Most quality measures found in the literature have been conceived to evaluate non-overlapping clusterings, even when most real-life problems are better modeled using overlapping clustering algorithms. A number of desirable conditions to be satisfied by quality measures used to evaluate clustering algorithms have been proposed, but measures fulfilling all conditions still fail to adequately handle several phenomena arising in overlapping clustering. In this paper, we focus on a particular case of such desirable conditions, which existing measures that fulfill previously enunciated conditions fail to satisfy. We propose a new evaluation measure that correctly handles the studied phenomenon for the case of overlapping clusterings, while still satisfying the previously existing conditions.

1 Introduction

Clustering is one of the most widely investigated problems in Pattern Recognition. It consists on separating an object collection into a set of clusters, generally attempting to place similar objects in a common cluster and dissimilar objects in distinct clusters. Partitional clustering algorithms split the collection into a set of disjoint clusters, in such a way that an object may belong to only one cluster. On the other hand, overlapping clustering algorithms allow objects to belong to multiple clusters.

Evaluating the quality of the outcomes of clustering algorithms is a necessary, yet challenging task, for which a large number of evaluation measures have been proposed. In the literature, evaluation measures are divided into external, relative or internal. Some authors refer to external measures as extrinsic and to internal measures as intrinsic, respectively. Internal measures asses the quality of a clustering by analyzing intra- and inter-cluster properties, without considering any external knowledge. Relative measures compare the results of multiple runs of a clustering algorithm, such runs differing in the parameter combinations used. On the other hand, external measures compare candidate clusterings to a

J. Ruiz-Shulcloper and G. Sanniti di Baja (Eds.): CIARP 2013, Part I, LNCS 8258, pp. 157–164, 2013.

gold standard, i.e. a handcrafted set of known clusters built by human experts taking into account the characteristics of the collection. In this work, we focus on external evaluation measures.

Due to the abundance of evaluation measures, some authors have devoted a considerable effort to enunciate desirable conditions that evaluation measures are expected to satisfy. While these conditions are inherently intuitive, and no universal consensus is likely to be obtained regarding their validity, extensive argumentation has been offered regarding their usefulness for providing criteria to consider when choosing an evaluation measure to assess the quality of clustering algorithms under different real-life and laboratory conditions.

Generally, most existing conditions have been enunciated for the particular case of partitional clustering, hinting to their extensibility to overlapping clustering. However, situations arrive when evaluation measures that have been proved to fulfill a wide range of conditions for partitional clusterings behave in an undesired manner when applied to overlapping clusterings. In this work, we take as starting point the work by Amigó et al. [1], who enunciate four conditions, prove them to cover all previously enunciated conditions, and show that BCubed F_α [2] is the sole to fulfill all four conditions. Amigó et al. propose Extended BCubed as an extension to BCubed for the case of overlapping clusterings. Here, we target a specific problem that is inadequately handled by Extended BCubed, namely that of assigning the optimum score to clusterings that are not identical to the gold standard. We formalize this desired behavior as a condition and propose CICE BCubed, a new extension to Extended BCubed, that satisfies the new condition while maintaining the established good characteristics of its predecessor.

The remainder of this paper is organized as follows. In Section 2 we briefly review existing work, focusing on the sets of conditions that have been previously enunciated, as well as the Extended BCubed family of evaluation measures. We describe our proposals in Section 3, and, finally, present our conclusions in Section 4.

2 Previous Work

Several authors have enunciated sets of conditions aiming to assess the convenience of using specific evaluation measures. Meila [3] enunciated twelve properties that were satisfied by the evaluation measure Variation Information. Later on, other authors used these properties as a set of conditions to be satisfied by other quality measures. Dom [4] proposed a distinct set of five conditions, which were later extended to seven by Rosenberg [5].

Amigó et al. [1], after conducting an extensive survey of existing conditions, summarized them into a set of four conditions and proved that all previous conditions were covered by these.

All of the four conditions proposed by Amigó et al. are expressed as situations under which a clustering D_1, which is considered to be worse than a clustering D_2, is expected to be given a worse score. An evaluation measure is considered to satisfy the condition if it behaves in this expected manner for all cases where such a situation arises. The conditions proposed by Amigó et al. are enunciated as follows:

- *Homogeneity*: Let D_1 be a clustering where one cluster G_k contains objects belonging to two classes[1]: C_i and C_j. Let D_2 be a clustering identical to D_1, except for the fact that instead of the cluster G_k, it contains two clusters G'_{k_1} and G'_{k_2}, one of them containing only objects belonging to C_i and the other containing only objects belonging to C_j. An evaluation measure satisfying the homogeneity condition should score D_1 worse than D_2.

- *Completeness*: Let D_1 be a clustering where two clusters G_1 and G_2 contain only objects belonging to one class C_k. Let D_2 be a clustering identical to D_1, except for the fact that instead of the clusters G_1 and G_2, it contains one cluster $G_{1,2}$, which is the union of G_1 and G_2. An evaluation measure satisfying the completeness condition should score D_1 worse than D_2.

- *Rag Bag*: Let D_1 be a clustering where one cluster G_{clean} contains n objects belonging to one class C_i plus one object belonging to a different class C_j and one cluster G_{noise} contains n objects belonging to n distinct classes. Let D_2 be a clustering identical to D_1, except for the fact that the object in G_{clean} that does not belong to the same class as all other objects is placed instead in G_{noise}. An evaluation measure satisfying the rag bag condition should score D_1 worse than D_2.

- *Clusters size versus quantity*: Let D be a clustering where one cluster G_{large} contains $n + 1$ objects belonging to one class C_1 and n clusters G_1, G_2, ..., G_n, contain each on two objects belonging to the same class. Let D_1 be a clustering identical to D, except for the fact that instead of the two-object clusters G_1, G_2, ..., G_n, it contains $2n$ unary clusters containing the corresponding objects. Let D_2 be a clustering identical to D, except for the fact that instead of the cluster G_{large}, it contains one cluster of size n and one cluster of size 1. An evaluation measure satisfying the clusters size versus quantity condition should score D_1 worse than D_2.

Upon the presentation of their four conditions, Amigó et al. conducted an extensive study on a large number of existing evaluation measures to determine the extent to which they satisfy the proposed conditions. They concluded that the BCubed F_α measure [2] is the sole evaluation measure that satisfies all four conditions. Since BCubed is defined for non-overlapping clustering, Amigó et al. propose Extended BCubed, an extension of BCubed suited for evaluating overlapping clusterings, which contains BCubed as an special case when zero overlapping is present.

---

[1] Amigó et al. and other authors refer to the clusters of the gold standard clustering as *classes* or *categories*. Here, we will follow this terminology convention for simplicity.

The Extended BCubed family builds on the traditional Information Retrieval triad of evaluation measures Precision, Recall, F-measure [6]. Unlike these, the Extended BCubed measures do not rely on directly calculating the amount of set-matching between classes and candidate clusters. Instead, they analyze the set of object pairs and consider the decisions of placing pairs together or not, with respect to the gold standard. Extended BCubed precision evaluates the amount to which the decisions made by the evaluated algorithm of placing pairs of objects together in one or several clusters are correct, whereas Extended BCubed Recall evaluates the amount to which the evaluated algorithm is capable of putting together the pairs of objects that co-occur in classes of the gold standard. As in the case of the traditional IR measures, the Extended BCubed F-measure provides a trade-off between Extended BCubed precision and Extended BCubed recall.

The Extended BCubed precision is defined as

$$P = \frac{1}{|U|} \sum_{o \in U} \frac{1}{|\bigcup_{g \in G(o)} g|} \sum_{o' \in E(o,G)} \frac{min(|G(o) \cap G(o')|, |C(o) \cap C(o')|)}{|G(o) \cap G(o')|} \quad (1)$$

where U represents the collection, G stands for the candidate clustering, C for the gold standard, $G(o)$ represents the set of candidate clusters containing object o, $C(o)$ is the set of classes of the gold standard containing o, $E(o,G)$ is the set of objects co-occurring with o in at least one candidate cluster, and $E(o,C)$ is the set of objects co-occurring with o in at least one class of the gold standard. The sets of objects yielded by $E(o,G)$ and $E(o,C)$ contain object o itself.

In a similar manner, Extended BCubed recall is defined as

$$R = \frac{1}{|U|} \sum_{o \in U} \frac{1}{|\bigcup_{g \in C(o)} g|} \sum_{o' \in E(o,C)} \frac{min(|G(o) \cap G(o')|, |C(o) \cap C(o')|)}{|C(o) \cap C(o')|} \quad (2)$$

whereas the Extended BCubed F-measure is defined as

$$F_\alpha(P, R) = \frac{1}{\alpha(\frac{1}{P}) + (1-\alpha)(\frac{1}{R})} \quad (3)$$

The authors propose to use $\alpha = 0.5$ so F_α behaves as the harmonic mean between precision and recall. The original BCubed measures analyze the fact that pairs of objects are placed together or not in clusters and/or classes. To adjust to the overlapping clustering case, the Extended BCubed measures additionally analyze the number of clusters and/or classes in which pairs of documents are placed together.

3   Our Proposal

Starting from the premise that the four conditions proposed by Amigó et al. are the most complete set of conditions, and the fact that the Extended BCubed family is the overlapping clustering-oriented extension of the BCubed family, out of which BCubed F_α was proved to be the sole that satisfies all three conditions, we take Extended BCubed as the basis for further amelioration.

Here, we focus on a problem pointed out by Amigó et al., namely the fact that the maximum Extended BCubed F_α score may be obtained when evaluating a candidate clustering that is not identical to the gold standard, as shown in the following example:

Candidate	*Gold*
$C_1 : 1, 2, 4$	$G_1 : 1, 3, 4$
$C_2 : 1, 3$	$G_2 : 1, 2$
$C_3 : 4, 3$	$G_3 : 4, 2$
$C_4 : 2, 5$	$G_4 : 3, 5$
$C_5 : 3, 5, 6$	$G_5 : 2, 5, 6$
$C_6 : 2, 6$	$G_6 : 3, 6$

The reason why Extended BCubed F_α yields the maximum score for these cases is that it only checks for the number of clusters and/or classes where object pairs co-occur, but at no point attempt to establish a mapping between the set of candidate clusters and the set of classes. Such mapping would allow to determine whether the set of clusters where an object pair co-occurr in the candidate clustering is equivalent to the set of classes where they co-occurr in the gold standard.

We will treat this desired behavior as a supplementary condition, which we will refer to as the *Perfect match condition*, and is formally enunciated as follows:

Perfect match condition: an evaluation measure must yield the maximum score for a candidate clustering if and only if it is identical to the gold standard.

When evaluating non-overlapping clusterings, most of the existing evaluation measures satisfy the perfect match condition. However, when overlapping clusterings are involved, it is a challenge for a measure to fulfill that condition. Being Extended BCubed F_α the sole measure that satisfies the initial four conditions, we take it as a starting point to propose a new extension that, while maintaining the desirable characteristics of Extended BCubed, also satisfies the perfect match condition.

We propose a new family of evaluation measures: *Cluster-Identity-Checking Extended BCubed* (*CICE-BCubed* for short). Analogous to the BCubed and the Extended BCubed families, CICE-BCubed consists in a new way to calculate precision, recall and the F-measure.

Being an extension of Extended BCubed, CICE-BCubed works by analyzing the object pairs that co-occur in clusters and/or classes. Unlike its predecessor, the measures of the CICE-BCubed family establish a mapping between the set of candidate clusters and the classes of the gold standard, in such a way that the candidate clustering's respect of that matching is evaluated along with the number of co-occurrences of object pairs. To do so, we introduce the *Cluster*

Identity Index (*CII* for short), a factor $\Phi(o_1, o_2, A, B)$ that yields values in the interval $[0, 1]$. For a pair of objects, the CII estimates the degree of similarity of all the clusters in A to their most similar class in B containing the pair. To define the CII, we use the auxiliary function $\psi_B(A_i)$ that determines the cluster $B_j \in B$ that best matches A_i, as follows:

$$\psi_B(A_i) = B_j \in B \ such \ that \ \left[sim(A_i, B_j) = \max_k sim(A_i, B_k) \right] \qquad (4)$$

where *sim* represents some function that calculates how similar two clusters are. Here, we calculate cluster similarity using Jaccard's index [7], which is defined as:

$$Jaccard(A_i, B_j) = \frac{|A_i \cap B_j|}{|A_i \cup B_j|} \qquad (5)$$

We chose Jaccard's index because it only yields the maximum score for two identical clusters. Other functions displaying the same behavior may as well be used, e.g. Rand's coefficient or the traditional IR F-measure.

When comparing a candidate clustering A to the gold standard B, for a pair of objects belonging to A, the CII averages the similarity values of clusters $A_i \in A$ that contain the pair to their best matching classes $B_j \in B$. Considering $A(o, o')$ as the set of all the clusters in A that contain the pair of objects (o, o'), the CII is defined as

$$\Phi(o, o', A, B) = \frac{1}{|A(o, o')|} \sum_{A_i \in A(o, o')} sim(A_i, \psi_B(A_i)) \qquad (6)$$

The CII will yield the maximal value only if the best matching classes for every cluster in $A_i \in A$ are identical to their corresponding clusters. The aforementioned auxiliary functions are used for defining the measures of the CICE-BCubed family. CICE-BCubed precision is defined as

$$\hat{P} = \frac{1}{|U|} \sum_{o \in U} \frac{1}{|\bigcup_{g \in G(o)} g|} \sum_{o' \in E(o, G)} \frac{min(|G(o) \cap G(o')|, |C(o) \cap C(o')|) \cdot \Phi(o, o', G, C)}{|G(o) \cap G(o')|} \qquad (7)$$

whereas CICE-BCubed recall is defined as

$$\hat{R} = \frac{1}{|U|} \sum_{o \in U} \frac{1}{|\bigcup_{g \in C(o)} g|} \sum_{o' \in E(o, C)} \frac{min(|G(o) \cap G(o')|, |C(o) \cap C(o')|) \cdot \Phi(o, o', C, G)}{|C(o) \cap C(o')|} \qquad (8)$$

and the CICE-BCubed F-measure is defined as

$$\hat{F}_\alpha(\hat{P}, \hat{R}) = \frac{1}{\alpha(\frac{1}{\hat{P}}) + (1 - \alpha)(\frac{1}{\hat{R}})} \qquad (9)$$

In order to keep the desirable characteristics of Extended BCubed F_α, both CICE-BCubed precision and recall maintain the terms from their Extended

BCubed homologous, but in both cases the terms in the numerators are multiplied by the factor CII, which prevents them from yielding optimal values for candidate clusterings that are not identical to the gold standard.

We will now analyze the behavior of the CICE-BCubed family of evaluation measures. Firstly, it is straightforward that CICE-BCubed precision and recall always obtain a maximum score for a candidate clustering which is identical to the gold standard. In this case, when calculating the CII, every cluster is always mapped to the class of the gold standard that is identical to it, thus always yielding the maximum value. Since the portions of Equations 7 and 8 inherited from Extended BCubed also contribute a maximum score, both CICE-BCubed precision and recall yield the maximum score and, consequently, so does the CICE-BCubed F-measure.

Secondly, we will demonstrate, using proof by contrapositive, that the fact of obtaining a maximal score of CICE-BCubed precision and recall implies that the candidate clustering is identical to the gold standard. Let A be a candidate clustering, which is not identical to the gold standard B. Under this condition, there must be at least one cluster $A_i \in A$ whose best matching class is not identical to it. For object pairs occurring in such cluster A_i, the CII will not yield the maximum score, thus preventing CICE-BCubed precision and CICE-BCubed recall, as defined in Equations 7 and 8, from yielding the maximum score. If CICE-BCubed precision and recall do not yield the maximum score, neither does the CICE-BCubed F-measure. Thus, we have proven that evaluating a candidate clustering which is not identical to the gold standard yields non-maximal CICE-BCubed precision, recall and F-measure, which, in turn, demonstrates that obtaining maximal CICE-BCubed precision, recall and F-measure implies that the evaluated candidate clustering is identical to the gold standard.

As a consequence of the previous proofs, we may conclude that CICE-BCubed F_α satisfies the perfect match condition. Additionally, it inherits from Extended BCubed F_α the behavior that satisfies the original four conditions enunciated by Amigó et al., which is not modified by the CII factor. This factor, while always causing the measure to yield values that are at most equal to the equivalent Extended BCubed F_α, does not alter the orientation of the inequalities that prove that Extended BCubed F_α satisfies the four conditions [1].

The measures of the CICE-BCubed family have a considerably high worst-case time complexity, $O(n^3 \log n)$, where n is the number of objects in the collection, for the case where the candidate clustering has n clusters, each containing $n-1$ objects. However, taking into account that evaluation is generally performed as an offline task during the process of tuning an algorithm for practical application, we consider that this time complexity is affordable given the benefits of relying on more robust evaluation measures.

4   Conclusions

We have proposed CICE-BCubed, a new family of evaluation measures for clustering algorithms, which correctly handle phenomena arising in the evaluation of overlapping clusterings that are inconveniently handled by previously existing measures.

We took as a starting point the four conditions enunciated by Amigó et al., as well as the Extended BCubed F_α measure, which is reported to be the sole measure that satisfies the initial four conditions, and attacked one of the known problems that it faces when used for overlapping clusterings, namely that of assigning the maximum score to candidate clusterings that are not identical to the gold standard. We prove that our proposed counterpart, CICE-BCubed F_α, does handle this situation adequately, while continuing to satisfy the previous four conditions.

It should be noted nonetheless that the four conditions proposed by Amigó et al., as well as any other set of conditions, do not necessarily enjoy universal acceptance. Because of that, absolute statements regarding whether a particular evaluation measure should be considered better than others may not be appropriate. However, we consider that the existing conditions, as well as the new condition we treated in this paper, do reflect desirable characteristics of clustering evaluation measures, thus supporting the strength of the proposed measures and the convenience of their use.

References

1. Amigó, E., Gonzalo, J., Artiles, J., Verdejo, F.: A comparison of extrinsic clustering evaluation metrics based on formal constraints. Information Retrieval 12(4), 461–486 (2009)
2. Bagga, A., Baldwin, B.: Entity-based cross-document coreferencing using the vector space model. In: Proceedings of the 36th Annual Meeting of the Association for Computational Linguistics and the 17th International Conference on Computational Linguistics, pp. 79–85 (1998)
3. Meilă, M.: Comparing Clusterings by the Variation of Information. In: Schölkopf, B., Warmuth, M.K. (eds.) COLT/Kernel 2003. LNCS (LNAI), vol. 2777, pp. 173–187. Springer, Heidelberg (2003)
4. Dom, B.: An information-theoretic external cluster-validity measure. In: Proceedings of the Eighteenth Conference on Uncertainty in Artificial Intelligence, pp. 137–145 (2002)
5. Rosenberg, A., Hirschberg, J.: V-measure: A conditional entropy-based external cluster evaluation measure. In: Proceedings of the 2007 Joint Conference on Empirical Methods in Natural Language Processing and Computational Natural Language Learning, pp. 410–420 (2007)
6. van Rijsbergen, C.: Foundation of evaluation. Journal of Documentation 30(4), 365–373 (1974)
7. Halkidi, M., Batistakis, Y., Vazirgiannis, M.: On Clustering Validation Techniques. Journal of Intelligent Information Systems 17(2-3), 107–145 (2001)

Supervised Classification
Using Homogeneous Logical Proportions
for Binary and Nominal Features

Ronei M. Moraes[1,2], Liliane S. Machado[1,2], Henri Prade[2], and Gilles Richard[2]

[1] LabTEVE Federal University of Paraiba,
Cidade Universitaria s/n, Joao Pessoa, Brazil
[2] IRIT University of Toulouse, 118 route de Narbonne,
31062 Toulouse Cedex 09, France
ronei@de.ufpb.br, liliane@di.ufpb.br, {prade,richard}@irit.fr

Abstract. The notion of homogeneous logical proportions has been recently introduced in close relation with the idea of analogical proportion. The four homogeneous proportions have intuitive meanings, which can be related with classification tasks. In this paper, we proposed a supervised classification algorithm using homogeneous logical proportions and provide results for all. A final comparison with previous works using similar methodologies and with other classifiers is provided.

Keywords: supervised classification, analogical proportion, analogical dissimilarity.

1 Introduction

Numerical as well as analogical proportions are used since the ancient Greeks. However, this is only recently that logical models for analogical proportions were laid bare [14]. *Analogical proportion* was proposed first and *reverse analogical proportion* and *paralogical proportion* came after (proposed for Boolean [10] and multiple-valued [12] features). The last logical proportion we consider here, named *inverse paralogical proportion*, and the characterization of those four proportions as homogeneous logical proportions were presented recently [14] for the Boolean case.

A particular instance of analogical reasoning is based on the notion of analogical proportion (or analogy, or for short A) linking four situations or items a, b, c, d. It focuses on the differences between a and b and between c and d that are the same. The reverse analogical proportion (or reverse analogy, or for short R) does the same, but reverses the directions of changes, i.e. differences between a and b, are the same as between d and c. The paralogical proportion (or paralogy, or for short P) focuses on similarities, unlike previous proportions. It points out that similarities between a and b and between c and d are the same. The inverse paralogical proportion (or inverse paralogy, or for short I) focuses on similarities also, and expresses that what a and b have in common, c and

J. Ruiz-Shulcloper and G. Sanniti di Baja (Eds.): CIARP 2013, Part I, LNCS 8258, pp. 165–173, 2013.

d do not have it, and vice versa. Those proportions have intuitive meanings, which can be related with classification tasks. However, in the recent literature, only one (analogical proportion) was studied for classification tasks and has been shown as a competitive supervised classifier [7], which, from descriptions of known objects (their features and classes), classifies another object, whose class is unknown. This reasoning is similar to the one used by k-NN classifiers [3] or in case-based reasoning [5]. For instance, in general pattern recognition terms, and using analogical proportions, from three objects (obj1, obj2, obj3), whose descriptions are made of a finite number of features (desc1, desc2, desc3), we want to classify a fourth object (obj4), with description desc4. Then, if an analogical proportion A(desc1, desc2, desc3, desc4) holds, it may be possible to suggest a class for obj4. Besides, an analogical dissimilarity (AD) measure was proposed by [2], which can be used on Boolean and also multi-valued features. This measure is able to assess the truthfulness of an analogical proportion [7].

In this paper, using a modified version of analogical dissimilarity, we provide some relations among analogy, reverse analogy, paralogy and inverse paralogy. It is shown that, using those relations, all those proportions can be computed in a simplified way and an algorithm for supervised classification is provided. Moreover, we present some results for binary and/or nominal classification tasks, using databases from UCI repository and also a comparison with other methodologies.

2   Characterization of Homogeneous Proportions

Analogy, reverse analogy, paralogy and inverse paralogy are formal relations T involving 4 items a, b, c and d. In this study, T is a Boolean proportion. This means that a, b, c, d are Boolean variables and can be pointwisely generalized by vectors of Boolean variables. A detailed investigation with respect to the basic semantics has been done in [10] [11] [14]. They obey different characteristic postulated [12]. For $a, b, c, d \in \{0, 1\}$ the considered properties are: a) *Reflexivity*, which validates the proportion $T(a, b, a, b)$; b) *Reverse reflexivity*, which validates the proportion $T(a, b, b, a)$; c) *Identity*, which validates the proportion $T(a, a, b, b)$; d) *Full identity*, which validates the proportion $T(a, a, a, a)$; e) *Symmetry*, which requires the equivalence between $T(a, b, c, d) \Leftrightarrow T(c, d, a, b)$; f) *Central permutation*, which requires the equivalence between $T(a, b, c, d) \Leftrightarrow T(a, c, b, d)$; g) *Code independency*, which requires the equivalence between $T(a, b, c, d) \Leftrightarrow T(\neg a, \neg b, \neg c, \neg d)$. It should be noted that all homogeneous proportions satisfy the symmetry and code independency properties [14]. However, some of the other properties are not satisfied by all four proportions (see Table 1). As shown in [13], there is close relation among three of those proportions:

Proposition 1: $R(a, b, c, d)$ is a reverse analogy if and only if $A(a, b, d, c)$ is an analogy, i. e. $R(a, b, c, d) \Leftrightarrow A(a, b, d, c)$; $P(a, b, c, d)$ is a paralogy if and only if A(a, d, c, b) is an analogy, i. e. $P(a, b, c, d) \Leftrightarrow A(a, d, c, b)$.

Prade and Richard [14] established further relations among those four proportions, with respect to analogy, through permutations and negation:

Proposition 2: $R(a, b, c, d)$ is a reverse analogy if and only if $A(a, b, \neg c, \neg d)$
is an analogy, i. e. $R(a, b, c, d) \Leftrightarrow A(a, b, \neg c, \neg d)$; $P(a, b, c, d)$ is a paralogy if and
only if $A(a, \neg b, c, \neg d)$ is an analogy, i. e. $P(a, b, c, d) \Leftrightarrow A(a, \neg b, c, \neg d)$; $I(a, b, c, d)$
is an inverse paralogy if and only if $A(a, \neg b, \neg c, d)$ is an analogy, i. e. $I(a, b, c, d) \Leftrightarrow$
$A(a, \neg b, \neg c, d)$.

Table 1. Homogeneous proportions and their properties

Properties	A	R	P	I
Reflexivity	✓	–	✓	–
Reverse reflexivity	–	✓	✓	–
Identity	✓	✓	–	–
Full identity	✓	✓	✓	–
Symmetry	✓	✓	✓	✓
Central permutation	✓	–	–	✓
Code independency	✓	✓	✓	✓

To introduce formally the four proportions, let us consider the items a, b, c, d
as described by sets of binary features, which belong to the universe X, i. e. each
item is viewed as a subset of X. An analogical proportion, denoted by $A(a, b, c, d)$
focuses on the differences and should hold when the differences between a and
b, and c and d are the same [8]:

$$a \wedge \neg b = c \wedge \neg d \text{ and } \neg a \wedge b = \neg c \wedge d \qquad (1)$$

Reverse analogy, denoted by $R(a, b, c, d)$ exchanges c and d, with respect to
analogy and expresses that the changes from a to b in relation to c to d (if any)
are now in opposite directions:

$$a \wedge \neg b = \neg c \wedge d \text{ and } \neg a \wedge b = c \wedge \neg d \qquad (2)$$

If instead of differences, we focus on similarities, we have a different proportion, denoted by $P(a, b, c, d)$ and named paralogy, which expresses that a and b
have in common, c and d have it too:

$$a \wedge b = c \wedge d \text{ and } \neg a \wedge \neg b = \neg c \wedge \neg d \qquad (3)$$

The inverse paralogy [14], denoted by $I(a, b, c, d)$ focuses on similarities also
and expresses a and b have in common, c and d do not have it, and vice versa:

$$a \wedge b = \neg c \wedge \neg d \text{ and } \neg a \wedge \neg b = c \wedge d \qquad (4)$$

Table 2 presents the Boolean truth table for each logical proportion presented
above. We can note that there are only 6 situations in which the logical value
is true for each proportion. Observing this Table, it is easy to see that there is
no situation where analogy, reverse analogy, paralogy and inverse paralogy hold
true together. However, there are some cases in which all proportions hold false.
These relations will be discussed in details in Section 4, after we provide some
relevant details about the measure of analogical dissimilarity.

Table 2. Boolean truth tables for Proportions: A, R, P and I:

A	R	P	I
0 0 0 0	0 0 0 0	0 0 0 0	0 0 1 1
1 1 1 1	1 1 1 1	1 1 1 1	1 1 0 0
0 0 1 1	0 0 1 1	0 1 1 0	0 1 1 0
1 1 0 0	1 1 0 0	1 0 0 1	1 0 0 1
0 1 0 1	0 1 1 0	0 1 0 1	0 1 0 1
1 0 1 0	1 0 0 1	1 0 1 0	1 0 1 0

These four logical proportions are called homogeneous proportions because they are true only for patterns having an even number of 1 (and thus an even number of 0), due to the fact they are strongly linked together by the relations:

$$A(a,b,c,d) \equiv R(a,b,d,c) \equiv P(a,d,c,b) \equiv I(a,\bar{b},\bar{c},d), \qquad (5)$$

Their semantical properties have been extensively investigated in [14].

3   Analogical Dissimilarity Measure and an Approximation Function

An analogical dissimilarity (AD) measure was proposed by [6] for binary and by [2][7] for nominal data, using a binary encoding. So, for both cases the binary definition is appropriate and for this reason we present the definition for AD only for this case.

Definition 1. The analogical dissimilarity among four binary values $(u, v, w, x \in \{0, 1\})$ is given by the following truth table [7]:

u	0 0 0 0 0 0 0 0 1 1 1 1 1 1 1 1
v	0 0 0 0 1 1 1 1 0 0 0 0 1 1 1 1
w	0 0 1 1 0 0 1 1 0 0 1 1 0 0 1 1
x	0 1 0 1 0 1 0 1 0 1 0 1 0 1 0 1
$AD(u,v,w,x)$	0 1 1 0 1 0 2 1 1 2 0 1 0 1 1 0

As can be seen, AD is a function whose domain is $\{0,1\}^4$, but its range is $\{0,1,2\}$. This is not completely in agreement with the homogeneous logical proportions, whose domains and ranges are Boolean. However, AD is consistent with the analogical proportion when we have $AD(u, v, w, x) = 0$ [6].

Definition 2. The AD measure among four objects $(u, v, w, t \in \{0,1\}^n)$ of a finite set X defined by binary features is the sum of the values of analogical dissimilarities for each feature [7].

Using the Definition 2 and encoding nominal variables as binary ones, it is possible to use AD for nominal variables as well. In [6][7] procedures to compute binary analogical proportions on $\mathbb{R}^n$ and on sequences, are presented. However, in order to obtain an efficient algorithm for AD computing that fits with all the homogeneous proportions mentioned in Section 2, it is necessary to use a mathematical function which approximates and replaces the AD definition.

The algorithm should also use the relationships given above in order to provide the values of all proportions from the values given by computing an approximation function for AD for each one. Thus, let the function $AD^* : \{0,1\}^4 \Rightarrow \{0,1\}$:

$$AD^*(a,b,c,d) = \left[(a-b-c+d)^2\right]^{1/2}, \text{ for } a,b,c,d \in \{0,1\} \qquad (6)$$

be an approximation for computing the function AD, according to Definition 1. Obviously, AD^* can also be written: $AD^*(a,b,c,d) = |a-b-c+d|$. That function has interesting properties: The codomain for AD^* is $\{0,1\}$. Using the binary values $\{0,1\}$ as truth values, the function AD^* given by (6) is able to provide exact estimation for 14 values among 16 values of the AD table for the binary case. The exceptions are the cases in which $AD = 2$. Moreover, even if AD^* is less discriminating, it is closely related to the value of the proportions.

4   Relations

As mentioned before, each logical proportion holds true in only 6 situations, which can be seen in the Table 2. However, they are not true in the same situations. As pointed out by [13], in the Boolean interpretation and according to their intuitive meaning, the pattern $T(a,b,b,a)$ is false for analogy; $T(a,b,a,b)$ is false for reverse analogy, T(a,a,b,b) is false for paralogy and $T(a,a,a,a)$ is false for inverse paralogy. For any of these proportions in the binary case, it is possible to find a relationship between the values provided by the proportions and the value provided by AD measure. In the case of Analogy and AD, it was announced as a property of AD [6]. More precisely, we have $AD = 0 \Leftrightarrow AD^* = 0$ and $AD \in \{1,2\} \Leftrightarrow AD^* = 1$, and besides, we have the relationship with respect to analogical proportion:

$$A(a,b,c,d) = 1 - AD^*(a,b,c,d) \qquad (7)$$

For the Reverse Analogy and Paralogy we use Proposition 1 for finding the following relations:

$$R(a,b,c,d) = 1 - AD^*(a,b,d,c) \qquad (8)$$
$$P(a,b,c,d) = 1 - AD^*(a,d,c,b) \qquad (9)$$

The same can be done for Inverse Paralogy, using Proposition 2:

$$I(a,b,c,d) = 1 - AD^*(a,\neg b,\neg c,d) \qquad (10)$$

These relations allow us to implement an algorithm using AD^* for computing to what extent the four proportions hold, in a new and simpler way than in [2].

5   Algorithm for Supervised Classification Using AD^*

The algorithm presented in this paper partly relies on a previous work [2]. The first difference of what is proposed here is the possibility to use any of the four proportions mentioned above. The second one is a change the ordering of execution of the steps of the previous algorithm, in order to take advantage of AD^* and to avoid the step of sorting the partial results. It improves the computational performance of the proposed classifier, with respect to [2]. It is important to remark that the algorithm proposed by [2] uses AD to implement analogical proportion only. The task is to classify m objects (obj_i), whose descriptions are made in terms of a finite number N_f of binary features $(desc_i)$, where $i = 1, ..., m$, using AD^*, into a finite and known number of classes in set C. A collection S of such objects is available, with their descriptions and respective classes in C, for the training of the classifier. Let x be a new object, not belonging to set S, and for which we desire to assign a class. The algorithm depends on a parameter p, with $0 \leq p \leq N_f$, which means that for each 4-tuple of description vectors analyzed, we accept that the proportion is false for at most p features. In other words, among the total number of features N_f, it is intended that for each 4-tuple (triple in S^3 and x) analyzed, at least $(N_f - p)$ features yield perfect proportions. We call this rule "*Rule of maximum p dissimilar 4-tuples*". The algorithm consists in the following steps:

Step 1: Given a vector x, find all triples in S^3 which satisfies the sum of $AD^* \leq p$ and $0 \leq p \leq N_f$. Store those n triplets (a_j, b_j, c_j), with $j = 1, ..., n < m)$.

Step 2: Solve the proportion equations (for A, R, P or I) on the label of the class of x and the n triples. Compute the solution as a vote for a class $c \in C$, obtained by solving the logical proportion on the classes (when there is solution, which means that the objects corresponding to a triple should belong to 1 or 2 classes only in order to have a useful triple for predicting the class).

Step 3: Assign the winner of votes among the n results, as the class for x.

It is worth noting when using AD^* and changing one step in the algorithm of [2], that it is no longer necessary to sort partial results anymore. So, the parameter k used in the algorithm in [2] does not have any role here. A new parameter p was added in the Step 1 to control the maximum number of dissimilar 4-tuples which the user can accept in each processing.

6   Results

In order to analyze the behaviour of the proposed algorithm, we applied it to some databases from UCI Repository [1]. These databases were used also by [7] and for this reason are used here to provide a comparison with the results obtained in this paper: The SPECT (SP.) database is related to heart data, with 22 binary features and contained with 80 samples for training and 187 for test. The databases MONK 1,2 and 3 (MO.1, MO.2 and MO.3) are related to classification problems with six nominal features. The databases contains 124, 169 and 122 samples for training, respectively and all of them 432 samples for test. The MO.3 database is corrupted with noise. All three MONK databases were binarized using standard techniques, i. e., replacing a nominal feature with n different values with n binary features. The results are summarized in Table 3. The first five lines give some characteristics of the databases used. In the following we indicate the best percentage of correct classification obtained for each proportion and for which value of p this is obtained. The last line shows the best results presented by [7] for comparison. It is worth noting in Table 3, all results for A, R and P are the same for all databases and all of them using the same value for p. In fact this is due to a property of three of the homogeneous proportions (A, P and R) which can be seen in equation (5). The difference among them is just a permutation of the elements in the 4-tuple. So, any of these three proportions proportions can be used for classification and it provides the same final results. However, this is not valid for proportion I, because beyond the permutation of elements, it is necessary also to perform negation for two of them [9].

Table 3. Results

	SP.	MO.1	MO.2	MO.3
number of nominal attributes	22	7	7	7
number of binary attributes	22	15	15	15
number of training instances	80	169	122	124
number of test instances	172	432	432	432
number. of class	2	2	2	2
Best results (%)				
Analogy (A):	$58(p=5)$	$98(p=2)$	$100(p=1)$	$98(p=3)$
Reverse Analogy (R):	$58(p=5)$	$98(p=2)$	$100(p=1)$	$98(p=3)$
Paralogy (P):	$58(p=5)$	$98(p=2)$	$100(p=1)$	$98(p=3)$
Inverse Paralogy (I):	$11(p=8)$	$79(p=8)$	$62(p=6)$	$83(p=6)$
Comparisons (%)				
Miclet *et al.* [7]	$58(k=100)$	$98(k=100)$	$100(k=100)$	$96(k=100)$
Decision Table	72	98	67	98
PART	82	93	75	99
Multilayer Perceptron	73	100	100	94
IBk (k=1)	59	91	69	89
Naive Bayes	75	72	61	98
J48 (C4.5)	76	100	71	100

It is possible to see in Table 3, that proportion I achieved results of lower quality than the other proportions and with values of p higher. In comparison with results provided by [7], for three among the four databases, the results obtained by the new algorithm were the same. However, the new algorithm provided better results for the MO.3 database, which is corrupted by noise. We made some comparisons with classifiers found in the literature and we used the Weka package [4] with default values. It is possible to note the Multilayer Perceptron provides best classification for MO.1 and MO.2. J48 Decesion Tree achieved the complete accuracy for MO.1 and MO.3. PART provides best classification for SP. However, our algorithm provides competitive results for three of those databases.

7   Conclusion and Future Works

This paper proposes a new algorithm for supervised classification using homogeneous logical proportions. The algorithm was presented and we provided a short discussion in relation to the previous one proposed by [2], which implemented only one of those proportions. Implementation results are presented for all homogeneous proportions, as well as a final comparison with a previous paper using similar methodologies and other classifiers too. The results achieved showed that proportions A, R and P provide the same results when it is used with the same value for p. This way, they yielded the same best results in comparison with results reported in [7] (which used AD and analogical proportion). The new algorithm provides results as good as the previous one or better, as it was the case of MO.3 (which is a database corrupted with noise).

As future works, we intent to improve comparisons using other classifiers and by considering more databases in order to extend our study about the relative performance of our approach with respect to other classifiers. Another issue is to determine how value p influences classification results.

Acknowledgement. This work is supported by CNPq, processes 246939/2012-5, 246938/2012-9, 310561/2012-4, 310470/2012-9 and INCT-MACC (process 181813/2010-6).

References

1. Bache, K., Lichman, M.: UCI machine learning repository, http://archive.ics.uci.edu/ml (2013)
2. Bayoudh, S., Miclet, L., Delhay, A.: Learning by analogy: A classification rule for binary and nominal data. In: Proc. Inter. Conf. on Artificial Intelligence, IJCAI 2007, pp. 678–683 (2007)
3. Duda, R.O., Hart, P.E., Stork, D.G.: Pattern Classification, 2nd edn. Wiley-Interscience (2001)
4. Hall, M., et al.: The Weka data mining software: An update. SIGKDD Explorations 11, 10–18 (2009)
5. Hüllermeier, E.: Case-Based Approximate Reasoning. Theory and Decision Library. Springer, New York (2007)
6. Miclet, L., Delhay, A.: Analogical Dissimilarity: definition, algorithms and first experiments in machine learning. Technical Report 5694, IRISA (September 2005)
7. Miclet, L., Bayoudh, S., Delhay, A.: Analogical dissimilarity: definition, algorithms and two experiments in machine learning. JAIR 32, 793–824 (2008)
8. Miclet, L., Prade, H.: Handling analogical proportions in classical logic and fuzzy logics settings. In: Sossai, C., Chemello, G. (eds.) ECSQARU 2009. LNCS, vol. 5590, pp. 638–650. Springer, Heidelberg (2009)
9. Moraes, R.M., Machado, L.S., Prade, H., Richard, G.: Classification based on homogeneous logical proportions. Proc. 33th Int. Conf. on Artificial Intelligence (AI 2013), Cambridge (to appear, 2013)
10. Prade, H., Richard, G.: Analogy, paralogy and reverse analogy: Postulates and inferences. In: Mertsching, B., Hund, M., Aziz, Z. (eds.) KI 2009. LNCS, vol. 5803, pp. 306–314. Springer, Heidelberg (2009)

11. Prade, H., Richard, G.: Analogical proportions: another logical view. In: Proc. 29th Int. Conf. Artif. Intellig (AI 2009), Cambridge, pp. 121–134. Springer (2009)
12. Prade, H., Richard, G.: Multiple-valued logic interpretations of analogical, reverse analogical, and paralogical proportions. In: Proc. 40th IEEE International Symp. on Multiple-Valued Logic (ISMVL 2010), Barcelona, pp. 258–263 (2010)
13. Prade, H., Richard, G., Yao, B.: Enforcing regularity by means of analogy-related proportions - A new approach to classification. Int. Jour. Computer Information Systems and Industrial Management Applications 4, 648–658 (2012)
14. Prade, H., Richard, G.: Homogeneous Logical Proportions: Their Uniqueness and Their Role in Similarity-Based Prediction. In: Proc. XIII International Conference on Principles of Knowledge Representation and Reasoning, pp. 402–412 (2012)

Multimodal Bone Cancer Detection Using Fuzzy Classification and Variational Model

Sami Bourouis[1,3], Ines Chennoufi[2], and Kamel Hamrouni[1]

[1] Universit de Tunis El Manar, Ecole Nationale dingnieurs de Tunis
[2] ESPRIT : School of Engineering, Tunis, Tunisia
[3] Taif University, KSA
sami.bourouis@ensi.rnu.tn, ines.channoufi@esprit.tn,
kamel.hamrouni@enit.rnu.tn

Abstract. Precise segmentation of bone cancer is an important step for several applications. However, the achievement of this task has proven problematic due to lack of contrast and the non homogeneous intensities in many modalities such as MRI and CT-scans. In this paper we investigate this line of research by introducing a new method for segmenting bone cancer. Our segmentation process involves different steps: a registration step of different image modalities, a fuzzy-possibilistic classification (FPCM) step and a final segmentation step based on a variational model. The registration and the FPCM algorithms are used to locate and to initialize accurately the deformable model that will evolve smoothly to delineate the expected tumor boundaries. Preliminary results show accurate and promising detection of the cancer region.

Keywords: Multimodality image fusion, non-rigid registration, fuzzy classification variational model.

1 Introduction

Accurate segmentation of bone cancer is an important task for several medical applications. For example, it can be helpful for therapy evaluation, treatment planning, modeling of pathological bones, etc. However, this task is a challenging problem because there is a large class of tumor types which vary greatly in size and position, have a variety of shape and appearance properties, have intensities overlapping with normal bone areas, and may deform and defect the surrounding structures. Moreover, the majority of images modalities may contain various amounts of noise and artifacts. Traditionally, bone cancers segmentation is performed manually by marking the tumor regions by a human expert. This process is time-consuming, impractical and non- reproducible. So, a semi or a fully automatic and robust segmentation is highly required in order to generate quickly satisfactory segmentation results. In general, a single medical image modality cannot provide comprehensive and accurate information, so considering more than one acquisition protocols can provide much more useful information about the bone tumor and this can be achieved through image fusion process. Such process is used to derive useful information in order to enhance and taking account

J. Ruiz-Shulcloper and G. Sanniti di Baja (Eds.): CIARP 2013, Part I, LNCS 8258, pp. 174–181, 2013.

the image content by fusing for example computer tomography (CT) image and magnetic resonance imaging (MRI).

Recently, various promising works have studied medical image segmentation, offering a diversity of methods and evaluation criteria [1–5]. However, to the best of our knowledge, only few approaches were proposed in the literature for bone tumor segmentation. Indeed, Frangi et al. in [6] proposed to segment a bone tumor in MR images using a neural network-based classifier approach. Authors used a pharmacokinetic model of the tissue perfusion which can reduce the MR image sequence into three parametric images. A neural network classifier is used to combine temporal and spatial information to determine the tumor region. In [1], a semi-automatic method for gross cancer volume delineation was proposed. It is based on the fusion of pixel intensity from both X-ray, CT and MRI scans. The segmentation process was initialized manually by a physician expert. Statistical shape model has been used also in [3]. In their paper, author proposed an automatic process to segment the Human pelvic bones from CT datasets. Another recently work was proposed in [4] for bone and cartilage segmentation in MRI images of the knee. Their procedure is based mainly on the using of active appearance models (AAM) which is a statistical model of the target shape constructed from manually segmented examples of the Osteoarthritis. Schmid et al. [5] developed a method based on deformable models approach with shape priors to address the segmentation issue of bone structure in MRI. They exploit both prior knowledge and image information for better efficiency. In addition, global shape variation was defined by PCA analysis and local deformation was defined though Markov Random Field (MRF) method.

According to this study, we think that statistical classification, image fusion and active contours are often complementary segmentation strategies. For example, statistical classification can be often successfully applied for a global classification of major anatomical structures, and active contours have been successfully applied to delineate locally the boundary of a particular region. Based on this assumption, we suggest in this paper a new method for bone cancer detection in 2D digitized MRI and CT-scans. This paper is organized as follows. In section 2, we describe the different steps involved in the building of our proposed method for bone cancer segmentation. In section 3, we present and discuss obtained results on different images. Finally, we conclude our paper and point out future research directions.

2   Bone Cancer Segmentation Procedure

We propose a method which operates on MRI and CT scans to segment bone cancer. First, input images are co-registered with a non-rigid deformation algorithm into the same coordinate system, so that we can fuse them properly in the next step. Then, a step of determining a coarse region of the cancer is performed using a fuzzy possibilistic classification method. Finally, a variational model is performed to delineate accurately the bone cancer region. The overall computational steps are illustrated in figure 1.

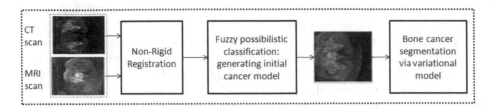

Fig. 1. Proposed method for bone cancer detection

2.1   Non-rigid Multimodal Image Registration

Image registration is the process of aligning two images by computing a geometrical transformation that can match the first image to the second one. Such transformation can be affine, rigid or non-rigid. In this paper, we investigate this line of research by exploiting information of different modalities through a non rigid registration step which is more suitable in our case to match both MRI and CT scans. Over recent years, a number of non-rigid registration techniques have been proposed. Looking at non-linear multi-modal image registration, we choose to apply the registration algorithm proposed in [7, 8] which is based on free-form deformations and cubic B-spline. It has shown to be very robust for multi-modal images even on low quality. More details can be found in their publication.

2.2   Initial Segmentation Using FPCM

Fuzzy classification algorithms have been widely used in medical image analysis due to its ability to model the uncertainty. It is a process of grouping pixels into a fuzzy set [9]. One of the widely used fuzzy algorithms is Fuzzy C-Means (FCM). Indeed, unlike hard clustering algorithms which force pixels to belong to only one class, FCM allows pixels to belong to multiple classes. However, FCM fails to deal with main properties in images given that neighbor pixels are strongly correlated, which results in poor segmentation. To address this problem and to improve the performance of the FCM algorithm in noisy environment, the possibilistic c-means (PCM) clustering [10], has been shown to be more robust as compared with FCM. Nevertheless, PCM also has the disadvantages in its sensitivity to initialization and easily leading to coincident clustering. To overcome this problem, a new mixed Fuzzy Possibilistic C-Means Algorithm (FPCM) was proposed [11]. By combining FCM and PCM, PFCM can simultaneously produce membership, possibilities and the cluster centers for each cluster. It can provide a better insight into how regions are distributed. Moreover, it can solve the noise sensitivity defect of Fuzzy C-Means algorithm and overcomes the problem of coincident clusters of possibilistic C-means algorithm. These desirable properties of FPCM make it suitable to be a basic model of our entire procedure. So, we adopt in our study FPCM in order to classify the target image into appropriate classes. According to Pal et al. [11] that he proposed to use membership values, as well as typicality values, looking for a better clustering algorithm, this problem is equivalent to an optimization objective function given as follows:

$$F_{PCM} = \sum_{i=1}^{C} \sum_{k=1}^{N} (a\mu_{ik}^{m} + bt_{ik}^{n}) * \|z_k - v_i\|^2 + \sum_{i=1}^{c} r_i \sum_{k=1}^{N} (1 - t_{ik})^n$$

Subject to the constraints $\sum_{i=1}^{C} \mu_{ik} = 1 \quad \forall\, k; \quad \mu_{ik} \geq 0, \quad t_{ik} \leq 1$ and the constants a, b>0 and n>1.

The parameters a and b define the relative importance between the membership values and the typicality values. μ_{ik} defines the absolutes importance of the membership values and t_{ik} defines the absolutes importance of the typicality values. While detailed proofs are not included, the interested reader can refer to citations and detailed descriptions in the publication [11].

Based on the possibility theory, input images (MRI and CT) are fused in three steps. First, information are modeled in order to manage ambiguous and imperfection information. Second, these information are combined and aggregated though a fusion operator. Such operator must avoid the redundancies and exploit the complementarities between the MR and CT images. Third, a decision step in which the resulted image is classified by taken into account a decision rule such as the maximum of possibility. In other word, each pixel is assigned to an appropriate tissue/structure according to its greatest membership (maximum of possibility). The fusion procedure can be summarized as follows:

1. Information modeling:
   For each pixel in {MRI, CT}:
   We compute the FPCM (for this pixel), i.e the membership degree for both images (MRI and CT).
2. Possibilistic fusion:
   Through FOP operator, we aggregate each class of MRI with the same one of CT.
3. Decision :
   Image is finally classified based on the maximum of possibility rule.

2.3   Variational Model for Cancer Region Detection

Although the FPCM algorithm has been proposed as robust when estimating the cluster center of the image and yields good results when we have high contrast between soft tissues, it fails to segment complex medical images and results in "poor" segmentation when more noise are involved. For these reasons, we propose to perform our developed variational level-set model which is applied successfully in our previous works for 3D brain segmentation [2, 12]. We present in the following briefly this model.

Unlike the traditional parametric active contours-based methods, geometric level set-based methods are considered an appropriate framework for merging heterogeneous information that provide a consistent geometrical representation suitable for image analysis. Moreover, level-sets do not depend on the parameterizations of the contour/surface and have become popular thanks to its ability to handle complex geometries and topological changes. These advantages make level-set very attractive and flexible in shape modeling and image segmentation. According to Sethian [13], the implicit level set function can be evolved by solving the following PDE (partial differential equations):

$$\frac{\partial \phi}{\partial t} = F.|\nabla \phi|$$ (1)

Where F is a scalar velocity (speed) function depending on the local geometric properties (i.e. curvature) and on the external parameters related to the input data (i.e. image gradient). The construction of a speed function is crucial in applying the level set method. Our intention in this work is to exploit the advantage of the cooperation of different information in the same evolution equation. So, we propose basically to constrain our variational model by both boundary and regional information. Recently, we have proposed a new formulation [2, 12] for the evolution of the variational model which is expressed as:

$$\frac{\partial \psi}{\partial t} = [\alpha_r F_{region}(I) + \alpha_b F_{boundary}(I)]|\nabla \psi|$$ (2)

$F_{boundary}$ causes the evolving of the front to be more strongly attracted to image edges. It is expressed as :

$$F_{boundary}(I) = sign(F_{boundary}).\frac{c+k}{1+|\nabla I|}$$ (3)

$$sign(F_{boundary}) = \begin{cases} +1 \; if & F_{region} < 0 \\ -1 \; otherwise \end{cases}$$ (4)

F_{region} controls the evolution of the model and segments the cancer region based on the following equation:

$$F_{region}(I) = \begin{cases} I - (m_T - \epsilon_T) \; \text{if} \; I < m_T \\ (m_T + \epsilon_T) - I \; \text{otherwise} \end{cases}$$ (5)

Where ϵ_T is a constant parameter, and m_T is the mean value of the bone cancer region. This value is calculated on the estimated region after the classification step. ϵ_T controls the brightness of the region to be segmented and define a range of greyscale values that could be considered inside the expected region of interest. More technical details are found in the papers [2, 12].

3   Experimental Results

We focus in this work only on the detection of the bon tumor boundaries from 2D images (CT and MRI). We have validated qualitatively the performance of the proposed method on several couple of MRI and CT scan images. Figures 2 c, 3 c, 4 c, and 5 c show the result of the non-rigid registration. In this study, images

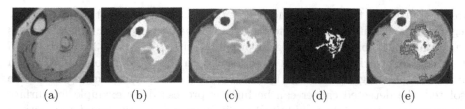

(a)   (b)   (c)   (d)   (e)

Fig. 2. (a) T2 weighted MR image of lower leg , (b) CT image of lower leg, (c) registered image (d) initial region of the tumor region (PFCM classification result), (e) Final segmented tumor region

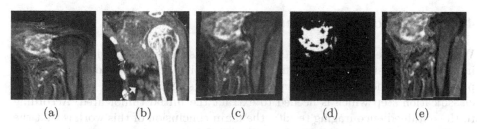

(a)   (b)   (c)   (d)   (e)

Fig. 3. (a) T1 weighted MR image of the left shoulder, (b) CT image for lower leg, (c) registered image (d) initial region of the tumor region (PFCM classification result), (e) Final segmented tumor region

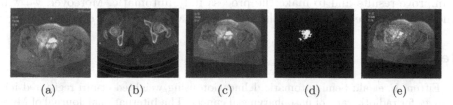

(a)   (b)   (c)   (d)   (e)

Fig. 4. (a) T1 weighted MR image of pelvic, (b) CT image of pelvic, (c) registered image (d) initial region of the tumor region (PFCM classification result), (e) Final segmented tumor region

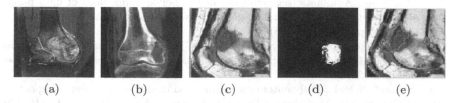

(a)   (b)   (c)   (d)   (e)

Fig. 5. (a) T1 weighted MR image of osteosarcoma-femur, (b) CT image of osteosarcoma-femur, (c) registered image (d) initial region of the tumor region (PFCM classification result), (e) Final segmented tumor region

are classified into four classes and one of them is assigned for the bone cancer region. This classification is performed using PFCM algorithm which provides an initial coarse pathological region presented in figures 2 d, 3 d, 4 d, and 5 d. Finally, our variational model is performed on the previous output to give a final segmented region shown in the last result for each row in same figures. Once isolated, the detected cancer can be further processed for example for surface measurement. According to obtained preliminary results, we found our method is able to give acceptable results. This is due principally to the potential use of both FPCM-based clustering, data fusion process and variational model for segmentation of multimodal images.

4   Conclusion and Future Work

We have presented a method for 2D bone cancer segmentation using multimodal images possibilistic fuzzy classification and active contour model. The entire process of our method is automatic except the selection of one pixel after the classification step which is needed to extract the initial tumor area. According to the obtained encouraging results, the main conclusion of this work is that the combination of the possibilistic fuzzy classification and the variational model in a sequential manner is suitable for such problem. Our future research in bone cancer segmentation consists in the quantitative evaluation of our results against a ground truth. It would be also very interesting to investigate a prior knowledge to improve results and to make the process fully automatic. Moreover, we will concentrate on the detection of three-dimensionally (3D) bone cancer.

References

1. Fitton, I., et al.: Semi-automatic delineation using weighted ct-mri registered images for radiotherapy of nasopharyngeal cancer. The International Journal of Medical Physics Research and Practice 38, 4662–4666 (2011)
2. Bourouis, S., Hamrouni, K.: 3d segmentation of mri brain using level set and unsupervised classification. International Journal in Image and Graphics (IJIG) 10(1), 135–154 (2010)
3. Seim, H., et al.: Automatic segmentation of the pelvic bones from ct data based on a statistical shape model. In: Eurographics Workshop on Visual Computing for Biomedicine, pp. 224–230 (2008)
4. Vincent, G., Wolstenholme, C., Scott, I., Bowes, M.: Fully automatic segmentation of the knee joint using active appearance models. In: Proc. Medical Image Analysis for the Clinic (2010)
5. Jrme Schmid, N.M.T.: Fully automatic segmentation of the knee joint using active appearance models. Med. Image Comput. Comput. Assist. Interv. 11, 119–126 (2008)
6. Frangi, A., et al.: Bone tumor segmentation from mr perfusion images with neural networks using multi-scale pharmacokinetic features. In: Image and Vision Computing, pp. 679–690 (2001)
7. Myronenko, A., Song, X.: Intensity-based image registration by minimizing residual complexity. IEEE Trans. on Medical Imaging 29, 1882–1891 (2010)

8. Myronenko, A., Song, X., Carreira-perpinán, M.A.: Free-form nonrigid image registration using generalized elastic nets. In: IEEE Conf. of Computer Vision and Pattern Recognition, pp. 1–8 (2007)
9. Zadeh, L.A.: Fuzzy sets. Information and Control 8, 338–353 (1965)
10. Krishnapuram, R., Keller, J.: A possibilistic approach to clustering. IEEE Trans. Fuzzy Syst. 1(2), 98–110 (1993)
11. Pal, N.R., Pal, S.K., Keller, J.M., Bezdek, J.C.: A possibilistic fuzzy c-means clustering algorithm. IEEE Transactions on Fuzzy Systems 13(4), 517–530 (2005)
12. Bourouis, S., Hamrouni, K.: Fully automatic brain tumor segmentation based on multi-modality mri and level-set. Journal of Ubiquitous Systems and Pervasive Networks 3(2), 47–54 (2011)
13. Sethian, J.: Level Set Methods and Fast Marching Methods: Evolving Interfaces in Geometry, Fluid Mechanics, Computer Vision, and Materials Science, 2nd edn. Cambridge University Press (1999)

Extreme Learning Classifier with Deep Concepts

Bernardete Ribeiro[1] and Noel Lopes[1,2]

[1] CISUC - Department of Informatics Engineering, University of Coimbra, Portugal
[2] UDI/IPG - Research Unit, Polytechnic Institute of Guarda, Portugal
bribeiro@dei.uc.pt, noel@ipg.pt

Abstract. The text below describes a short introduction to extreme learning machines (ELM) enlightened by new developed applications. It also includes an introduction to deep belief networks (DBN), noticeably tuned into the pattern recognition problems. Essentially, the deep belief networks learn to extract invariant characteristics of an object or, in other words, an DBN shows the ability to simulate how the brain recognizes patterns by the contrastive divergence algorithm. Moreover, it contains a strategy based on both the kernel (and neural) extreme learning of the deep features. Finally, it shows that the DBN-ELM recognition rate is competitive (and often better) than other successful approaches in well-known benchmarks. The results also show that the method is extremely fast when the neural based ELM is used.

Keywords: Extreme Learning Machines, Deep learning, Neural Networks.

1 Introduction

Since the ability of pattern recognition systems to correctly recognize objects in real time with high accuracy is of primary concern, in this paper, we will consider the performance of machine learning-based systems with respect to classification accuracy. In particular we will focus on neural networks approaches. First, on Extreme Learning Machines (ELM) which are shallow architectures with high potential in regression and classification problems [6]; second, on deep neural networks more precisely on Deep Belief Networks (DBNs) which seek to learn concepts instead of recognizing objects. In fact, motivated by the extreme efficiency of the visual recognition system recent studies in brain science show that this is largely due to the expressive deep architecture employed by human visual cortex systems [14]. Deep architectures transform inputs through multiple layers of nonlinear processing. This nonlinearity is in parametric form such that they can learn deep concepts and be adapted through training. Both methodologies have gained popularity in recent years and many successful applications have been reported [13,11,12,9]. Finally, we empirically show that by designing an extreme learning classifier over deep concepts learned in pattern recognition benchmark problems will enhance the performance as compared to the baseline approaches. More concisely, in both cases of kernel (and neural) based ELM over

J. Ruiz-Shulcloper and G. Sanniti di Baja (Eds.): CIARP 2013, Part I, LNCS 8258, pp. 182–189, 2013.

extracted learned features from deep belief networks, respectively, on Convex, Rectangles and HHreco image datasets the approach is shown to be competitive and extremely fast for the neural based ELM. The paper is organised as follows. Section 2 presents the basic principles of extreme learning machine. Section 3 illustrates the rationale behind deep belief networks. In section 4 we describe the proposal of the extreme learning classifier of deep concepts. In section 5 the experimental set up and the benchmarks are described, and the results discussed. Finally, in section 6 conclusions and future work are presented.

2 Extreme Learning Machines

There has been a raising interest in Extreme Learning Machines (ELM) since the original work of Huang et al. [5]. The ELM randomly chooses the hidden-unit weights and analytically determines the output weights of single hidden-layer feedforward network (SLFN). Since then many applications have spread in various fields of pattern recognition. Extreme learning machine is a simple learning algorithm for (SLFN) with attractive properties such as fast learning speed, no need for tuning of parameters, universal function approximation and good generalization [6].

2.1 Basic Form of Extreme Learning Network

Suppose we are given N instances of training data. Each instance consists of a $(\mathbf{x}_i, t_i)$ pair where $\mathbf{x}_i \in \mathbb{R}^d$ is a vector containing d attributes of the instance i, and $t_i \in \{+1, -1\}$ is the correspondent class label. The method uses input-output training pairs from $\mathcal{D} = \left\{(\mathbf{x}_i, t_i) \in \mathcal{X} \subseteq \mathbb{R}^d \times \mathcal{T} : 1 \leq i \leq N\right\}$ such that the ELM classifies correctly unobserved data $(\mathbf{x}, t)$. In its basic form ELM with L hidden nodes are mathematically modeled as:

$$f_L = \sum_{i=1}^{L} \beta_i h_i(\mathbf{x}) = \mathbf{h}(\mathbf{x})\boldsymbol{\beta} \tag{1}$$

where $\boldsymbol{\beta} = [\beta_1, \cdots, \beta_L]^T$ is the output weight vector connecting the hidden nodes and the output node, and $\mathbf{h}(\mathbf{x}) = [h_1, \cdots, h_L]$ is the vector with the outputs of the L hidden nodes with respect to the vector $\mathbf{x}$. The model above $\mathbf{h}(\mathbf{x})$ with L hidden nodes maps the N data samples from the d-dimensional input space to the feature hidden space H. The ELM minimizes the training errors as well as the norm of the output weights to achieve better generalization [5,6] according to:

$$\text{Minimize:} \sum_{i=1}^{N} ||\mathbf{h}(\mathbf{x}_i)\boldsymbol{\beta} - t_i|| \tag{2}$$

The solution is given by:

$$\boldsymbol{\beta} = \mathbf{H}^\dagger \mathbf{T}, \tag{3}$$

where $\mathbf{H}^\dagger$ is the Moore-Penrose generalized inverse of matrix $\mathbf{H}$. The singular value decomposition (SVD) method can be used to calculate the generalized Moore-Penrose generalized inverse of matrix $\mathbf{H}$:

$$\mathbf{H} = \begin{bmatrix} \mathbf{h}(\mathbf{x}_1) \\ \vdots \\ \mathbf{h}(\mathbf{x}_N) \end{bmatrix}.$$

2.2   Kernel Based Extreme Learning Machine

The equality constrained optimization method is proposed in [4] to solve the optimization problem in eq. (2). With the universal approximation capability as shown in [6] this classification problem can be formulated as:

$$\text{Minimize: } L_{PELM} = \frac{1}{2}||\boldsymbol{\beta}||^2 + \lambda\frac{1}{2}\sum_{i=1}^{N}\xi^2$$

$$\text{Subject to: } \mathbf{h}(\mathbf{x}_i)\boldsymbol{\beta} = t_i - \xi_i \tag{4}$$

where λ is the regularization constant and ξ are the slack variables. By solving the above equations the output of the ELM classifier is (5); if the feature mapping $\mathbf{h}(\mathbf{x})$ is unknown, Mercer's conditions apply [4] and the kernel matrix $\boldsymbol{\Omega}_{ELM}$ can be constructed; the final form is shown in (6):

$$f_L(\mathbf{x}) = \mathbf{h}(\mathbf{x})\boldsymbol{\beta} = \mathbf{h}(\mathbf{x})\mathbf{H}^T \left(\frac{\mathbf{I}}{\lambda} + \mathbf{H}\mathbf{H}^T\right)^{-1} \mathbf{T} \tag{5}$$

$$= \begin{bmatrix} K(\mathbf{x}, \mathbf{x}_1) \\ \vdots \\ K(\mathbf{x}, \mathbf{x}_N) \end{bmatrix} \left(\frac{I}{\lambda} + \boldsymbol{\Omega}_{ELM}\right)^{-1} \mathbf{T} \tag{6}$$

3   Deep Belief Networks

DBNs were proposed by Hinton who showed how to carry out unsupervised greedy learning with Contrastive Divergence (CD) [3]. This algorithm learns a generative model from the data distribution. With the proviso that by combining Restricted Boltzmann Machines (RBMs) learning in DBNs is sequentially achieved [3], the approach represents an efficient way of accomplishing tasks that would otherwise be out of reach. Figure 1 illustrates this process.

Each RBM has a layer of visible units $\mathbf{v}$ that represent the data and a layer of hidden units $\mathbf{h}$ that learn to represent features that capture higher-order correlations in the data. Given an energy function $E(\mathbf{v}, \mathbf{h})$ on the whole set of visible and hidden units, the joint probability is $p(\mathbf{v}, \mathbf{h}) = \frac{e^{-E(\mathbf{v}, \mathbf{h})}}{Z}$ where Z is a normalizing partition function.

The two layers are connected by a matrix of symmetrically weighted connections, $\mathbf{W}$, and there are no connections within a layer. Given conditionally

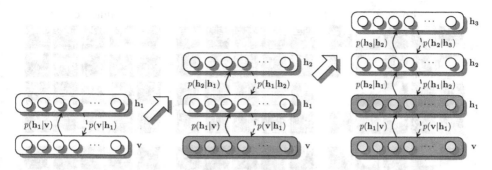

Fig. 1. Training process of a Deep Belief Network (DBN) with one input layer, $\mathbf{v}$, and three hidden layers $\mathbf{h_1}$, $\mathbf{h_2}$, $\mathbf{h_3}$. From left to right, trained layers are drawn with lighter color, otherwise layers are with darker color.

independence it is easy to sample from the factorial posterior distribution over hidden vectors $p(\mathbf{h}|\mathbf{v}, \mathbf{W})$ and from the factorial posterior distribution over visible units $p(\mathbf{v}|\mathbf{h}, \mathbf{W})$. By starting with the data vector on the visible units and alternating several times between sampling from $p(\mathbf{h}|\mathbf{v}, \mathbf{W})$ and $p(\mathbf{v}|\mathbf{h}, \mathbf{W})$, it is easy to get the learning weights $\mathbf{W}$.

4   Proposed Approach

Most of the problems in pattern recognition fall in the category of classification where objects are represented by a set of features (or attributes) usually extracted manually. Very often the challenging nature of many problems lie on the difficulty of extracting features such as behavioral characteristics like mood, fatigue, energy, etc.. This is a very hard task for manual extraction of features. The unsupervised training of the DBNs allows to learn complex functions by mapping the input to the output directly from data, without depending on human-crafted features [1]. The process works as follows. The first layers are expected to extract low-level features from the input data while the upper layers are expected to gradually refine previously learnt concepts, therefore producing more abstract ones [7]. Now the output of the higher DBN layer can easily be functioning as the input to a supervised classifier [2,10]. The idea is to use an extreme learning machine (ELM) as the classifier of the deep concepts. Notwithstanding the training cost of DBNs, however, our recent work with an adaptive learning rate technique and Graphics Processing Units (GPU)[1] implementation of DBNs [8] has highlighted the way to circumvent these pitfalls which appear to favor (deep) architectures. The inputs to the (shallow) ELM are thus the extracted features from the top DBN layer and its output are the classes of the target pattern problem.

---

[1] http://gpumlib.sourceforge.net/

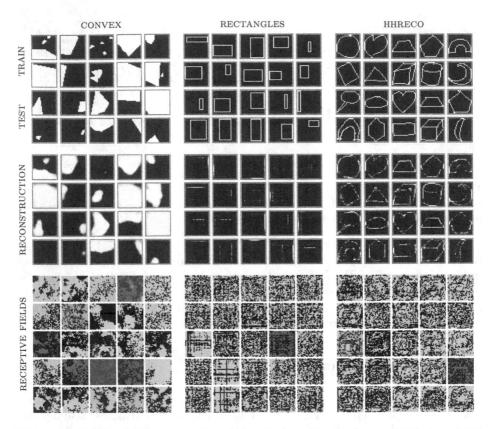

Fig. 2. From left to right examples of the Convex, Rectangles and HHreco multi-stroke images datasets. Each square figure contains a symbol while each row contains images of each data set. The first two top rows correspond to training samples of the three data sets w.r.t. the order above (e.g. the upper right first two rows correspond to Convex images); the second two rows correspond to the test samples. The corresponding reconstruction for train and test data is in the middle row-range. The DBNs were trained with two and three layers and the best configuration chosen. The local receptive fields (weights of the hidden neurons) which play an important role in visual tasks are illustrated in the last row-range.

Table 1. DBN-ELM and DBN-SVM F1-measure versus the baseline (DBN-MLP)

Datasets	Sampling			Methods		
Images	Training	Testing	Classes	**DBN-SVM**	**DBN-ELM**	**DBN-MLP**
Data	samples	samples	Nr.	$C = 1, \gamma$	$\lambda = 1 \; \gamma = 0.1$	F1 $n_H = 100$
Convex	8000	50000	2	**98.32** $(\gamma = 10)$	77.58	73.85 $(10 - 1)$
Rectangles	1200	50000	2	89.90 $(\gamma = 0.5)$	**92.55**	91.01 $(10 - 1)$
HHreco	650	7141	13	88.93 $(\gamma = 0.05)$	**91.33**	80.37 $(10 - 13)$

5   Results and Discussion

5.1   Experimental Setup and Dataset Benchmarks

In our testbed experiments we have used HHreco images, Convex and Rectangles datasets. Figure 2 presents examples of the three datasets. The first two benchmarks are purely synthetic data sets[2]. The task in Convex is to classify a single white region that appears in each image as convex or non-convex. The task in Rectangles is to classify a single rectangle that appears in each image as tall or wide. Finally, the HHreco database[3], contains a total of $7,791$ samples generated by 19 different persons, and contains a total of 13 different symbol classes. Each user created at least 30 multi-stroke images per class, which means that for each symbol there are at least $19 \times 30 = 570$ samples. We converted the original HHreco vector strokes into a $28 \times 28 = 784$ raster pixel image, maintaining the aspect ratio of the images. Moreover, the resulting images have been binarized and no further pre-processing was done. Since we are interested in evaluating the capacity of the DBNs for extracting information from the original (images) raw data, we discarded both the number of strokes and time span information.

5.2   Experiments and Results

The performance of kernel (and neural) based ELM, SVM and MLP classifiers were tested on the output of the DBN which learned well the features for image representation as demonstrated through the reconstruction obtained in the previous step (see Figure 2). For all the datasets the input data have been normalized into $\{-1, +1\}$. Note that the patterns in Rectangles and Convex datasets involve abstract, shape-based features that cannot be computed directly from raw pixel inputs, but rather seem to require many layers of processing. The positive and negative examples also exhibit tremendous variability, making these problems difficult for template-based approaches (e.g., SVMs with RBF kernels). For the kernel based ELM, SVM and MLP classifiers the generalization performance depends on the setting of parameters. Specifically, for SVM classifiers the combination of C cost parameter and γ kernel parameter have to be carefully chosen to get the best results. In our simulations, we have carried the parameter selection based on the F1 measure. Its computation for binary class is given by $F\text{-}measure = 2 \times \frac{precision \times recall}{precision + recall}$ where precision and recall are determined from the confusion matrix as the rate of true positives (tp) from all retrieved positives given by the algorithm while the recall gives the rate of tp from all the positives in the dataset. For multi-class, let tp_c be the number of samples belonging to class c that were correctly classified. Let fp_c be the number of samples that were incorrectly classified as being of class c when in fact they belong to a different class ($i \neq c$). Let fn_c be the number of samples that were

---

[2] http://www.iro.umontreal.ca/~lisa/twiki/bin/view.cgi/
   Public/PublicDatasets
[3] http://embedded.eecs.berkeley.edu/research/hhreco/

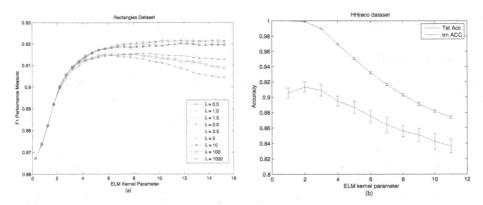

Fig. 3. DBN-ELM performance for datasets (a) Rectangles and (b) HHreco. In (a) the various plots for several values of the kernel parameter γ and regularization constant λ are shown. Notice in (b) the standard deviation for train and test data.

incorrectly classified as belonging to class $i \neq c$ when in fact they belong to class c. Assuming that there are C different classes the macro-average precision and macro-average recall can be computed as follows: $precision = \frac{1}{C} \sum_{c=1}^{C} \frac{tp_c}{tp_c + fp_c}$ and $recall = \frac{1}{C} \sum_{c=1}^{C} \frac{tp_c}{tp_c + fn_c}$. The macro-average F-measure can be now computed as indicated above.

For each specific training set we search the optimal cost parameter from the following settings: Parameters $\gamma = \{0.01, 0.05, 0.1, 0.5, 1, 10, 100\}$ e $\lambda, C = \{0.001, 1, 10, 100, 1000, 10000\}$. The kernels chosen for both SVM and kernel-based ELM were RBF and Linear. The results are presented in Table 1[4]. The kernel based ELM can achieve better results than both the SVM and the baseline MLP as highlighted in the Table 1 for the Rectangles and HHreco datasets. However, for the Convex data set the SVM is better while ELM still outperforms MLP. This might be due to an DBN not properly tuned into this difficult dataset and as such it deserves further study. Figure 3 plots the parameters sensitivity for the rectangles and HHreco datasets. For the sake of comparison we also tested neural-based ELM with neurons in the range $\{10, 100, 1000, 5000\}$ and activation functions *sigmoid*, *hardlim* and *radbas* and *sin*. We observed that F1 obtains the best value for *sigmoid* activation function on the convex dataset and decreases, respectively, by 12.6%, 5.19% and 1.98% for *hardlim*, *radbas* and *sin*. Regarding the training and testing times the neural-based ELM network is extremely fast compared to kernel-based ELM (with similar parameters settings) by a factor ca. 270. This is expected since in the former an $L \times L$ matrix must be inverted while in the second the matrix is $N \times N$ where L (number of hidden units) $< N$ (number of data points).

---

[4] Due to paper space restrictions, larger tables with more results are not presented.

6   Conclusions and Future Work

We explored extreme learning machines (ELM) in the classification stage of features constructed by nonlinear processing in deep architectures (DBN) on leading benchmarks. Comparison of the DBN-ELM with previous approaches show that they uphold competitive accuracies. When it comes to training times they are extremely fast when the shallow neural ELM is used. This might be due to the fact that there is no need to tune weights and bias in the final classification step which allows us to harness the advantages of extreme learning of deep concepts in visual tasks. While the paper focus on extreme learning classifier with deep concepts for model construction, future work envisaging hybrid methods will be pursued to deal with unbalanced data and their geometric distribution in the feature space.

References

1. Bengio, Y.: Learning deep architectures for AI. Foundations and Trends in Machine Learning 2(1), 1–127 (2009)
2. Hinton, G.: A practical guide to training Restricted Boltzmann Machines. Tech. rep., Dep. of Computer Science, University of Toronto (2010)
3. Hinton, G.E., Osindero, S., Teh, Y.-W.: A fast learning algorithm for deep belief nets. Neural Comput. 18, 1527–1554 (2006)
4. Huang, G.-B., Zhou, H., Ding, X., Zhang, R.: Extreme learning machine for regression and multiclass classification. IEEE Transactions on Systems, Man, and Cybernetics, Part B 42(2), 513–529 (2012)
5. Huang, G.-B., Zhu, Q.-Y., Siew, C.-K.: Extreme learning machine: A new learning scheme of feedforward neural networks. In: IEEE International Joint Conference on Neural Networks, pp. 985–990 (2004)
6. Huang, G.-B., Zhu, Q.-Y., Siew, C.-K.: Extreme learning machine: Theory and applications. Neurocomputing 70, 489–501 (2006)
7. Le Roux, N., Bengio, Y.: Representational power of restricted boltzmann machines and deep belief networks. Neural Comput. 20, 1631–1649 (2008)
8. Lopes, N., Ribeiro, B.: GPUMLib: An efficient open-source GPU machine learning library. International Journal of Computer Information Systems and Industrial Management Applications 3, 355–362 (2011)
9. Lu, B., Wang, G., Yuan, Y., Han, D.: Semantic concept detection for video based on extreme learning machine. Neurocomputing 102, 176–183 (2013)
10. Ranzato, M., Boureau, Y., LeCun, Y.: Sparse feature learning for deep belief networks. In: Advances in Neural Information Processing Systems, vol. 20 (2007)
11. Shi, L.C., Lu, B.L.: EEG-based vigilance estimation using extreme learning machines. Neurocomputing 102, 135–143 (2013)
12. Wu, S., Wang, Y., Cheng, S.: Extreme learning machine based wind speed estimation and sensorless control for wind turbine power generation system. Neurocomputing 102, 163–175 (2013)
13. Yeu, C.W., Lim, M.H., Huang, G.B., Agarwal, A., Ong, Y.S.: A new machine learning paradigm for terrain reconstruction. IEEE Geoscience and Remote Sensing Letters 3(3), 382–386 (2006)
14. Yu, K., Xu, W., Gong, Y.: Deep learning with kernel regularization for visual recognition. In: Neural Information Processing Systems, NIPS (2009)

Automatic Graph Building Approach
for Spectral Clustering

Andrés Eduardo Castro-Ospina, Andrés Marino Álvarez-Meza,
and César Germán Castellanos-Domínguez

Signal Processing and Recognition Group, Universidad Nacional de Colombia,
Manizales, Colombia
{aecastroo,amalvarezme,cgcastellanosd}@unal.edu.co

Abstract. Spectral clustering techniques have shown their capability
to identify the data relationships using graph analysis, achieving better
accuracy than traditional algorithms as k-means. Here, we propose a
methodology to build automatically a graph representation over the input data for spectral clustering based approaches by taking into account
the local and global sample structure. Regarding this, both the Euclidean
and the geodesic distances are used to identify the main relationships between a given point and neighboring samples around it. Then, given the
information about the local data structure, we estimate an affinity matrix by means of Gaussian kernel. Synthetic and real-world datasets are
tested. Attained results show how our approach outperforms, in most of
the cases, benchmark methods.

Keywords: Graph analysis, kernel function, spectral clustering.

1 Introduction

Clustering techniques are widely used to explore data patterns and they provide the advantage to work with unlabeled data. These techniques have been
addressed in many disciplines as data mining, image segmentation, and pattern classification [1, 2]. Although, well-known algorithms, such as k-means, are
employed in clustering applications, however, they only consider similarity values from instances to a fixed number of centers. Moreover, they require extra
information about cluster shape, which is not always available.

Therefore, two approaches have emerged as an alternative to analyze clusters
that are non-linearly separable, namely, kernel k-means and spectral clustering.
Spectral techniques seek data representation as a graph, with a set of nodes
and an affinity matrix capturing relationships among samples [1]. In addition,
using an affinity matrix allows to employ powerful operators such as kernel
functions, in order to reveal the main data structures. Regarding this, fixing
kernel operators is crucial for the clustering performance. In [3], a local scaling
parameter is introduced to identify a suitable kernel function considering the
neighborhood relationships. Nonetheless, it requires to fix a free parameter that

J. Ruiz-Shulcloper and G. Sanniti di Baja (Eds.): CIARP 2013, Part I, LNCS 8258, pp. 190–197, 2013.

is not always a straightforward task. Moreover, due to the fact that the method
considers a different local scaling for a given sample, the obtained representation
does not correspond to conventional kernel function class satisfying the Mercer
conditions [4]. Though some applications are discussed on this matter [5–7],
this method can not longer be framed as a suitable kernel based representation.
Moreover, as shown in our experiments, it is not always a good alternative to
build the graph for spectral clustering.

We propose a new alternative to construct automatically the graph representation in spectral clustering approaches. Particularly, inspired by a previous
method that allows to identify the local and global data structures for manifold learning tasks [8], two different operators (namely, the Euclidean and the
geodesic distances) are used to highlight the main relationships between a given
point and the neighboring samples. To this end, a neighborhood size is calculated
for each sample, looking for the largest patch that allows to model each neighborhood as locally linear. Provided that local data structure information is encoded
into neighborhood sizes, we estimate an affinity matrix by means of a Gaussian
kernel fixing the band-width parameter as a function of the found neighborhoods. For the sake of assessing the proposed methodology performance, some
experiments are done over synthetic and real-world datasets. Obtained results
are compare against state of the art approaches [3, 5, 6].

2 Methods

2.1 Spectral Clustering Main Concepts

Let $X \in \mathbb{R}^{n \times p}$ be an input data matrix holding n samples and p features. To discover the input data structure, relationships among samples can be highlighted
by means of a complete, weighted, undirected graph representation $G(V, \Omega)$,
which contains a set of nodes $V = \{v_1, \ldots, v_n\}$ corresponding to the n samples. Edge weights for connecting nodes i and j ($i \neq j$) are defined through an
affinity matrix $\Omega \in \mathbb{R}^{n \times n}$, with $\Omega_{ij} = \kappa(x_i, x_j)$, being $\kappa(\cdot, \cdot)$ a kernel function,
mostly, the Gaussian kernel [1]. Using a kernel function ensures an stable spectral
decomposition, due to it must satisfy the Mercer conditions. The goal of clustering approaches is to decompose V into C disjoint subsets as $V = \cup_{c=1}^{C} V_c$,
with $V_l \cap V_c = \emptyset \ \forall l \neq c$. To this end, spectral information and orthogonal
mappings from Ω are employed to represent suitably inputs [2]. Thus, using
spectral concepts of graph analysis, the so-called Laplacian matrix is estimated
as $L = D^{-\frac{1}{2}} \Omega D^{-\frac{1}{2}}$, where $D \in \mathbb{R}^{n \times n}$ is a diagonal matrix whose elements
$d_{ii} = \sum_{i=1}^{n} \Omega_{ij}$ are the degree of the nodes in G. Spectral decomposition of L
gives useful information about graph properties, being able to cluster together
similar patterns [1]. Therefore, spectral clustering methods find a new representation of patterns from the first C eigenvectors of graph Laplacian L. Then,
given a matrix $Z \in \mathbb{R}^{n \times C}$ whose column vectors stack the found eigenvectors,
each of them with unit length, a clustering algorithm, such as K-means, is employed to minimize distortion. Note that the Z matrix can be viewed as a data
mapping into a unit hypersphere, where a traditional clustering approach is used

to estimate the disjoint subsets V_c and the label vector $y \in \mathbb{R}^{n \times 1}$ containing the subset membership $y_i \in \{1, \ldots, C\}$ for each x_i.

2.2 Local Data Analysis for Automatic Graph Building - AGB

Computation of affinity matrix Ω is a crucial step in spectral clustering, since it models both local and global data properties. Commonly, the relationships among samples are identified by means of a Gaussian kernel, defined as $\Omega_{ij} = \exp\left(-||x_i - x_j||_2^2/2\sigma^2\right)$. However, the question arises as how to select the kernel band-width $\sigma \in \mathbb{R}^+$ for revealing the real data structure. In [3], as an alternative solution, a local scaling is introduced that finds a different band-width for each pair of points, namely, $\Omega_{ij} = \exp\left(-||x_i - x_j||_2^2/2\sigma_i\sigma_j\right)$, where $\sigma_i = ||x_i - x_h||_2^2$, being x_h the h-th neighbor of x_i according to the Euclidean distance. Nonetheless, selection of h is not a straightforward task. In [3,5], h is empirically fixed as 7, but as shown in our experiments, it is not always a suitable value. Moreover, taking into account that a kernel representation induces a nonlinear mapping $\varphi : \mathbb{R}^{n \times p} \to \mathcal{H}$, where $\mathcal{H}$ is a Reproducing Kernel Hilbert Space - RKHS, choosing a different kernel generates a different RKHS for each pair of nodes (i, j). Therefore, variation of Gaussian kernel band-width, as the product $\sigma_i\sigma_j$, generates a different RKHS for each input sample. Hence, matrix Ω should not correspond to a kernel representation satisfying Mercer conditions [4]. Certainly, the above mentioned procedure is often carried out in practice, but it can no longer be framed as a suitable kernel based representation.

In this work, we propose an alternative solution to build the graph G in spectral clustering based approaches, considering both the density and the linearity of each sample neighborhood. Inspired by a previous approach for fixing the neighborhood size of each sample x_i in manifold learning related tasks [8], the local data structure is studied using two main distance operators: the Euclidean and the geodesic distances. The main idea is to construct patches, i.e., neighborhoods, as large as possible, in order to conserve the global data properties, but ensuring that any data point and its nearest neighbors can be modeled as locally linear, preserving the local data structure. For each point, the nonlinear properties of its neighboring region are highlighted comparing the neighborhood found by the Euclidean distance against the neighborhood found by the geodesic distance. If the region around a point is linear and dense, the Euclidean and geodesic distances should obtain a similar set of nearest neighbors for each x_i. Otherwise, the neighborhood computed using Euclidean distance should contain short circuits, while geodesic distance will be able to correctly identify the neighbors of each sample avoiding such short circuits, because it is able to model nonlinear data structures. Mainly, the algorithm to find each neighborhood size can be summarized as follow.

Firstly, to conserve the global data properties, a set of possible neighborhood size values k are calculated, where a lower bound is computed as the minimum k that allows to construct a connected graph G over X. Second, varying the patch size two kind of neighbor sets are obtained according to each distance operator. Then, the vector $k \in \mathbb{R}^{n \times 1}$ that holds the size of each computed neighborhood is calculated, where k_i is fixed as the largest neighborhood size that shares the maximum percentage of neighbors between the two kind of sets. Finally, vector k is refined by an outlier detection stage to avoid the influence of noisy samples. For a complete description about the algorithm, see [8].

Given a vector k holding information about the local data structure, our goal is to estimate an affinity matrix by means of a kernel function that allows to model properly the data. In this regard, to fix the Gaussian kernel band-width parameter, a $\sigma_i^\dagger$ value is computed for each sample as $\sigma_i^\dagger = \|x_i - x_{k_i}\|_2$, where x_{k_i} is the k_i-th nearest neighbor of x_i. Note that $\sigma_i^\dagger$ provides information about the data dispersion into the largest local linear patch around each node in the graph. Afterwards, the kernel band-width value is computed as $\hat{\sigma} = E\{\sigma_i^\dagger\}$, where $\mathcal{E}\{\cdot\}$ stands for expectation operator. Finally, the graph G is built over X using the $\hat{\sigma}$ value to estimate Ω. Fig. 1 presents the general scheme of the proposed approach, termed *Automatic Graph Building* - AGB.

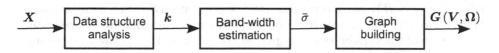

Fig. 1. Automatic graph building general scheme

3   Experimental Set-Up and Results

To test the capability of the proposed approach AGB for finding a suitable graph representation in spectral clustering based methods, some synthetic and real-world dataset are used. AGB is employed to compute the affinity matrix Ω building a graph G over the input data. Then, a spectral clustering method is employed to estimate the label vector y. Firstly, three well-known synthetic datasets are studied: four Gaussians, elongated groups, and happy face [3]. All datasets encode complex structures and are commonly used to test the capability of clustering algorithms. For concrete testing, the number of groups C is manually fixed as 4, 4, and 3, respectively, as detailed in [3]. Synthetic data clustering results are depicted in Fig. 2, which can be visually evaluated.

Regarding to real-world datasets experiments, some well-known images for segmentation tasks are employed. More precisely, several samples of the free access Berkeley Segmentation dataset are studied [1]. It is important noting that the dataset also provides hand-labeled segmentations. In our experiments, randomly selected images identified as *100075-bears, 113044-horses, 12003-starfish, 388016-woman, 56028-wall,* and *124084-flowers* are studied. Again, AGB is employed to represent properly relationships among samples, taking into account the RGB color space and the 2D position of each pixel as an input sample. However, due to limitations in memory usage, images are resized at 15%. Furthermore, a closed approach, termed

---

[1] http://www.eecs.berkeley.edu/Research/Projects/CS/vision/bsds/

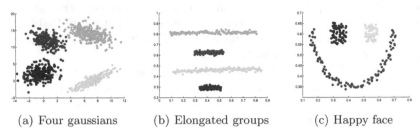

(a) Four gaussians   (b) Elongated groups   (c) Happy face

Fig. 2. AGB clustering results over synthetic data

7-Nearest Neighbor Spectral Clustering - 7-NNSC, is tested. 7-NNSC is based on a local scaling analysis to build G, as discussed in section 2.2 (for details see [3,5]). Besides, an index, called Normalized Probabilistic Rand - NPR, is computed to quantify the image segmentation performance, since it allows to compare a test segmentation with multiple hand-labeled ground-truth images [9]. NPR can be seen as a function $\phi(S, H)$, which compares a test segmentation S with a multiple hand-labeled ground truth images H, through soft nonuniform weighting of pixel pairs as function of the variability in the ground-truth set [9]. Fig. 3 shows images segmentation results.

Finally, some classification experiments are developed to verify the advantages of our AGB approach for highlighting the main data structures. Thus, the UCR time-series dataset is used [2]. This repository contains contributed labeled time-series datasets from different fields, such as: shape identification on images, time-series extracted from physical process, or even synthetic data. All datasets contain different number of classes, observations, and lengths. Moreover, it is assumed to be used on both classification and clustering tasks. As recommended in UCR, we test the 1-Nearest Neighbor - 1-NN classifier using the Euclidean distance as benchmark. UCR databases are divided into training and testing sets. In this case, AGB is employed to compute the affinity matrix Ω over the training set, which is employed as features in the 1-NN classifier. So, given a new sample x_{new} (testing set), the similarity among x_{new} and the training set is calculated using the AGB kernel band-width. Then, the 1-NN estimated testing set labels are used to compute the system performance. Also, 7-NNSC approach is used to compare the performance of the proposed algorithm. The attained time-series classification results are presented in Table 1.

4   Discussion

Taking into account the synthetic clustering results, from Fig. 2 it can be seen how the proposed AGB methodology is able to find a suitable kernel function, i.e. Gaussian kernel band-width, which allows to build the graph G over the input data, identifying the complex synthetic dataset structures. Note that, even when some dataset are composed by disjoints data structures, with different properties, our algorithm allows to find a complete graph that encodes the main

---

[2] http://www.cs.ucr.edu/~eamonn/time_series_data/

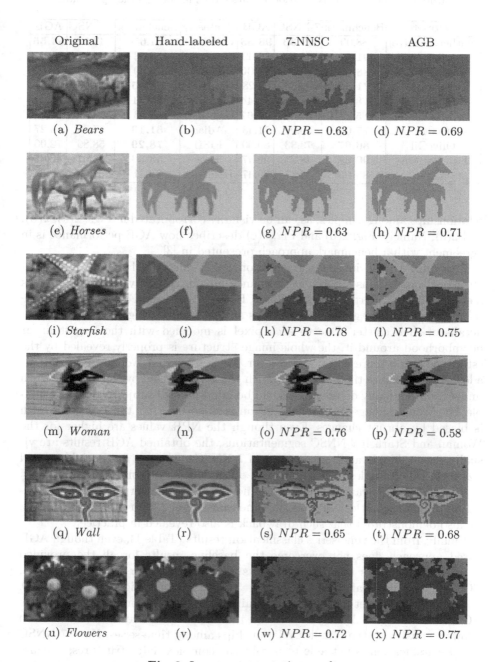

Original   Hand-labeled   7-NNSC   AGB

(a) *Bears*   (b)   (c) $NPR = 0.63$ (d) $NPR = 0.69$

(e) *Horses*   (f)   (g) $NPR = 0.63$ (h) $NPR = 0.71$

(i) *Starfish*   (j)   (k) $NPR = 0.78$ (l) $NPR = 0.75$

(m) *Woman*   (n)   (o) $NPR = 0.76$ (p) $NPR = 0.58$

(q) *Wall*   (r)   (s) $NPR = 0.65$ (t) $NPR = 0.68$

(u) *Flowers*   (v)   (w) $NPR = 0.72$ (x) $NPR = 0.77$

Fig. 3. Images segmentation results

Table 1. Time-series classification results - testing set accuracy percentage

Dataset	Benchmark	7-NNSC	AGB	Dataset	Benchmark	7-NNSC	AGB
synthetic control	88.00	**99.33**	**98.33**	OSULeaf	51.65	47.52	**54.55**
Gun Point	**91.33**	66.67	86.00	50words	63.08	51.87	**63.52**
ECG200	**88.00**	79.00	**88.00**	Trace	76.00	53.00	**77.00**
FaceAll	**71.36**	35.50	67.28	wafer	**99.55**	32.17	99.43
SwedishLeaf	78.88	71.04	**81.44**	Lighting2	**75.41**	67.21	**75.41**
CBF	85.22	57.00	**91.67**	Lighting7	57.53	42.47	**63.01**
Coffee	**75.00**	50.00	71.43	Adiac	**61.13**	37.85	56.27
OliveOil	**86.67**	73.33	80.00	FISH	**78.29**	58.86	72.00
Two Patterns	**90.67**	48.25	90.47	Beef	**53.33**	36.67	46.67
yoga	**83.03**	52.37	79.47	FaceFour	78.41	37.50	**80.68**

relationships among samples, as can be visually corroborated in Figs. 2(a), 2(b), and 2(c). Namely, Fig. 2(b) and Fig. 2(c) describes how AGB performance is in agreement with a benchmark approach presented in [3].

Regarding to the images segmentation results described in Fig. 3, overall, our algorithm obtains a better performance in comparison with the benchmark method 7-NNSC. Particularly, for Bears, Horses, Wall, and Flowers AGB is able to find the local and global relationships among samples, highlighting the main details of each cluster. Due to each pixel is modeled with the largest linear neighborhood around it, the whole image structure is properly revealed by the estimated graph representation. However, for Starfish and Woman AGB obtains a lower performance than 7-NNSC, which can be explained by the fact that such images contain many details, that could be hand-labeled subjectively. For example, the Woman image AGB segmentation is smoother than the 7-NNSC, which is biased by abrupt changes. Even though the NPR values are higher for the Woman and Starfish 7-NNSC segmentations, the obtained AGB results are visually acceptable. In addition, because of 7-NNSC employs a fixed neighborhood size for all the samples, it is sensitive to outliers, thus is, noisy data structures. Moreover, 7-NNSC can no longer be framed as a suitable kernel based representation from a theoretical view, as explained in section 2.2. In these experiments, we also demonstrated that such drawback is also revealed in practice.

Finally, from the time-series classification results (Table 1), even though AGB based approach does not overcome the baseline results for all the provided datasets, it achieves competitive results. For example, for synthetic control, ECG200, SwedishLeaf, CBG, OSULeaf, 50words, Trace, Lighting2, Lighting7, and FaceFour dataset our approach attained the best performance. Again, the AGB local and global analysis encoded into the neighborhood size estimation allows to deal with the complex relationships among time-series. Now, 7-NNSC based classification is not able to unfold the complex data structures, because such technique assumes an unique neighborhood size. It is important to note that some of the time-series datasets are composed for many classes, which can not be suitable modeled by one kernel function, being necessary to extend the data structure analysis considering different affinity matrices.

5   Conclusions

A methodology to build automatically a graph representation over the input data for spectral clustering based approaches was proposed. For such purpose, a data structure analysis is performed using the Euclidean and geodesic distances to identify the linear and density properties of each sample neighborhood. Thus, the local and global properties of the data are revealed to estimate a suitable kernel function, which is used to construct a data graph representation. Our approach, AGB, was tested over synthetic and real-world data. Attained results showed how our approach achieved good results for clustering, image segmentation, and even classification tasks. A benchmark approach 7-NNSC, which aims to make a local scaling analysis to build the graph, was also tested. However, 7-NNSC is not able to unfold complex data structures in many cases. Such issues were demonstrated from both theoretic and experiments. As future work, it would be interesting to deal with multi-kernel methods for finding a suitable graph representation that allows to deal with non-stationary signals. Furthermore, it would be interesting to test different data model for building the graph and other association measures could be tested to highlight different data properties, e.g., entropy and rank based correlations.

Acknowledgements. Under grants provided by *Jóvenes Investigadores e Innovadores - 2012*, and a Ph.D. scholarship funded by Colciencias.

References

1. Filippone, M., Camastra, F., Masulli, F., Rovetta, S.: A survey of kernel and spectral methods for clustering. Pattern Recognition 41(1), 176–190 (2008)
2. Ng, A.Y., Jordan, M.I., Weiss, Y., et al.: On spectral clustering: Analysis and an algorithm. Advances in Neural Information Processing Systems 2, 849–856 (2002)
3. Perona, P., Zelnik-Manor, L.: Self-tuning spectral clustering. Advances in Neural Information Processing Systems 17, 1601–1608 (2004)
4. Pokharel, R., Seth, S., Príncipe, J.: Additive kernel least mean square. In: IJCNN (2013)
5. Liping, C., Xuchuan, Z., Jiancheng, S.: The approach of adaptive spectral clustering analyze on high dimensional data. In: ICCIS, pp. 160–162 (2010)
6. Garcia, C., Flenner, A., Percus, A.: Multiclass semi-supervised learning on graphs using ginzburg-landau functional minimization. In: Pattern Recognition Applications and Methods (2013)
7. Kontschieder, P., Donoser, M., Bischof, H.: Beyond pairwise shape similarity analysis. In: Zha, H., Taniguchi, R.-i., Maybank, S. (eds.) ACCV 2009, Part III. LNCS, vol. 5996, pp. 655–666. Springer, Heidelberg (2010)
8. Álvarez, A., Valencia, J., Daza, G., Castellanos, G.: Global and local choice of the number of nearest neighbors in locally linear embedding. Pattern Recognition Letters 32(16), 2171–2177 (2011)
9. Unnikrishnan, R., Pantofaru, C., Hebert, M.: Toward objective evaluation of image segmentation algorithms. IEEE Transactions on Pattern Analysis and Machine Intelligence 29(6), 929–944 (2007)

Qualitative Transfer for Reinforcement Learning with Continuous State and Action Spaces

Esteban O. Garcia, Enrique Munoz de Cote, and Eduardo F. Morales

Instituto Nacional de Astrófisica, Óptica y Electrónica,
Luis Enrique Erro # 1. Tonantzintla, Puebla, México
{eomargr,jemc,emorales}@inaoep.mx
http://ccc.inaoep.mx

Abstract. In this work we present a novel approach to transfer knowledge between reinforcement learning tasks with continuous states and actions, where the transition and policy functions are approximated by Gaussian Processes (GPs). The novelty in the proposed approach lies in the idea of transferring qualitative knowledge between tasks, we do so by using the GPs' hyper-parameters used to represent the state transition function in the source task, which represents qualitative knowledge about the type of transition function that the target task might have. We show that the proposed technique constrains the search space, which accelerates the learning process. We performed experiments varying the relevance of transferring the hyper-parameters from the source task into the target task and show, in general, a clear improvement in the overall performance of the system when compared to a state of the art reinforcement learning algorithm for continuous state and action spaces without transfer.

Keywords: Transfer learning, Reinforcement learning, Gaussian Processes, Hyper-parameters.

1 Introduction

The objective in reinforcement learning (RL) is to find a sequence of actions that maximizes a long-term cumulative reward. An RL algorithm achieves such an objective by exploring the world and collecting information about it in order to determine such sequence of actions [16]. RL algorithms provide mechanisms to learn solutions without the need of human experience. However, when these are applied to real world problems, two major problems arise: (i) a large number of samples or interaction time with the environment is needed to learn an optimal solution, and (ii) after an agent has learned to solve a task, if it is required to solve a different (although similar) task, the learning process must be restarted.

Typically, RL is used on discrete state-action spaces, despite the fact that, most real-world problems involve continuous domains and discretizations of the domain variables may lead to very large discrete state-action spaces or imprecise policy functions that may harm the learning process [7,3]. Several approaches

J. Ruiz-Shulcloper and G. Sanniti di Baja (Eds.): CIARP 2013, Part I, LNCS 8258, pp. 198–205, 2013.
© Springer-Verlag Berlin Heidelberg 2013

have been proposed to deal with continuous domains, (e.g., [9,8,11,7,2]), most of them use function approximators. In particular, Gaussian Processes (GPs) have been used to represent value functions [6,5,14,1], and more recently, to represent transition function models with very promising results [12,13,4,3,2]. In this paper, we use GPs to represent policy and state transition functions.

A common approach to lessen the problem of learning a new, although similar task is use transfer learning (TL). Several approaches have been proposed where the source and target tasks may have different transition functions, state spaces, start or goal states, reward functions or action sets [18]. In this paper, we assume that there is only one source task and that the source and target tasks have the same variables.

Most of the TL methods for RL that use the same assumptions as us, focus on discrete tasks and model-free learning methods. In [10] and [17] model-based learning methods are proposed to transfer samples (tuples or instances of the form $< s, a, r, s' >$) from the source task to the target task. Contrary to previous approaches, in this paper, we are interested in transferring information about the transition function. In particular, we propose a *batch learning* method which transfers information from the GP hyper-parameters of the state transition function to represent prior distributions of functions over the state transition function of the target task. We will show that by providing a family of functions as prior information about the underlying state transition function, significant reductions can be obtained in the convergence of the algorithm. Our proposal gradually incorporates the information from the target task producing a more stable process and faster convergence times. The proposed methodology also uses the source task policy function to initialize the policy in the target task. This creates more informative initial traces in the target task and a further boost to the convergence of the algorithm. The main contribution of this paper is a relatively simple, yet very effective approach for transfer learning in continuous state and action spaces, based on two intuitive ideas: (i) Within similar domains, you can expect similar properties on the state transition functions. This is implemented with a gradual transit between the hyper-parameters of the source task to those of the target task. (ii) Without any prior knowledge, your best initial trial is obtained using the policy learned in the source task. We performed experiments on the inverted pendulum under different conditions and show a significant improvement in the learning process.

2   Background

RL problems are typically formalized as MDPs, defined by $\langle S, A, P, R \rangle$, where S is the set of states, A is the set of possible actions that the agent may execute, $P : S \times A \times S \to [0, 1]$ is the state transition probability function, describing the task dynamics, $R : S \times A \to \mathbb{R}$ is the reward function measuring the performance of the agent. A policy $\pi : S \to A$ is defined as a probability distribution over state action pairs. In the case of continuous tasks, S and A are continuous spaces and functions approximators have to be used to represent the functions P and π, in this work we use GPs.

A Gaussian Process is a generalization of the Gaussian probability distribution. Given a set of input vectors x_i arranged as a matrix $\mathbf{X} = [\mathbf{x_1}, \ldots, \mathbf{x_n}]$ and a vector of training observations $\mathbf{y} = [y_1, \ldots, y_n]^\top$, Gaussian Process methods for regression problems assume that the observations are generated as $y_i = h(\mathbf{x_i}) + \epsilon$, $\epsilon \sim \mathcal{N}(0, \sigma_\epsilon^2)$. Thus the objective is to infer a model of the function h that generates the data. Similar to a Gaussian distribution, which is fully specified by a mean vector and a covariance matrix, a GP is specified by a mean function $m(\cdot)$ and a covariance function $k(\cdot, \cdot)$, also called a *kernel*.

Given a GP model of the *latent function* $h \sim \mathcal{GP}(m, k)$, it is possible to predict function values for an arbitrary input $\mathbf{x_*}$.

The covariance function k commonly used is the squared exponential kernel:

$$k(\tilde{\mathbf{x}}, \tilde{\mathbf{x}}') = \alpha^2 \exp(-\frac{1}{2}(\tilde{\mathbf{x}} - \tilde{\mathbf{x}}')^\top \mathbf{\Lambda}^{-1}(\tilde{\mathbf{x}} - \tilde{\mathbf{x}}')) + \delta_{\tilde{x}\tilde{x}'}\sigma_\epsilon^2 \tag{1}$$

where $\tilde{\mathbf{x}} = [\mathbf{x}^\top \mathbf{u}^\top]^\top$, α^2 is the variance of the transition function f, $\Lambda = \mathrm{diag}([\ell_1^2, \ldots, \ell_D^2])$, which depends on length-scales ℓ_i, and $\delta_{\tilde{x}\tilde{x}'}$ denotes the Kronecker delta.

The hyper-parameters α^2, ℓ, σ_ϵ^2 describe the shape of the functions in the prior distribution (e.g., smoothness, noise tolerance).

These hyper-parameters are often optimized by evidence maximization (see [15] for further details).

The unknown transition function P can be described as $\mathbf{x}_t = f(\mathbf{x}_{t-1}, \mathbf{a}_{t-1})$, $f \sim \mathcal{GP}(m, k)$, where $\mathbf{x}_t \in S$ is the state of the agent at time t, with continuous-valued states $\mathbf{x} \in \mathbb{R}^D$ and actions $\mathbf{a} \in A$, $A = \mathbb{R}^F$. Following [2], the transition model f is distributed as a Gaussian Process with mean function m and covariance function k, with sample tuples of the form $(\mathbf{x}_{t-1}, \mathbf{a}_{t-1}) \in \mathbb{R}^{D+F}$ as inputs and corresponding $\Delta_t = \mathbf{x}_t - \mathbf{x}_{t-1} + \epsilon \in \mathbb{R}^D$, $\epsilon \sim \mathcal{N}(0, \Sigma_\epsilon)$, as training targets.

The objective in RL is to find a policy $\pi \colon \mathbb{R}^D \mapsto \mathbb{R}^F$ that minimizes the expected accumulative cost given as:

$$V^\pi(\mathbf{x}_0) = \sum_{t=0}^{T} \mathbb{E}[c(\mathbf{x}_t)], \mathbf{x}_0 \sim \mathcal{N}(\mu_0, \Sigma_0) \tag{2}$$

which is the sum of expected cost $c(\mathbf{x}_t)$ of a trace $(\mathbf{x}_0, \ldots, \mathbf{x}_T)$, T steps ahead, where π is a continuous function approximated by $\tilde{\pi}$, using some set of parameters ψ.

The state transition function can be learned as a GP, using available data, going from a prior distribution of transition functions to a posterior one [15]. The learned transition model can then be used to simulate the system and speculate about the long-term behavior without the need of interaction (batch learning). The policy is then optimized according to these simulations and then used to get more tuples (state, action, successor state).

3 Qualitative Transfer Learning

The problem that we study is one where the source and target tasks have the same state variables and are variants of the same task. For instance, the source task could be to learn how to drive a car while the target task could be to learn how to drive a small truck. We expect, that at least "qualitatively", the behavior of both task should be the same. Following these ideas, we transfer information from the hyper-parameters of the transition function of the source task to the target task. With the samples from the source task, we learn the state transition function using GPs with a squared exponential kernel k as defined in the previous section.

In GP learning however, when no expert knowledge is available about the function properties, kernel hyper-parameters are often adjusted taking data into account and optimizing the log *marginal likelihood* (see [15] for more detail). That is the case of PILCO [2], where hyper-parameters are adjusted each time new data is added. Hyper-parameters are learned given the tuples $\tilde{\mathbf{X}} = [\tilde{\mathbf{x}}_1, \ldots, \tilde{\mathbf{x}}_n]$ and their corresponding $\mathbf{y} = [\Delta_1, \ldots, \Delta_n]$ acquired during the interaction with the environment.

In our approach, we do not let the evidence maximization process to take control of the hyper-parameters values in the target task, instead, we adjust the hyper-parameters using a forgetting factor. Let $\theta = [\alpha^2, \ell, \sigma_\epsilon^2]^\top$ denote the vector of hyper-parameters. Let $\theta^{(s)}$ denote the hyper-parameters transferred from the source task, θ_i the hyper-parameters used in the kernel for the target task at episode i, $\theta_i^{(p)}$ the hyper-parameters learned by evidence maximization in target task at episode i. We calculate the values of the hyper-parameters in the target task as follows:

$$\theta_0 = \theta^{(s)} \tag{3}$$

$$\theta_i = \gamma\theta_{i-1} + (1-\gamma)\theta_i^{(p)}, i > 0 \tag{4}$$

where $\gamma \in [0,1]$ is the ratio in which previous episode hyper-parameters are being incorporated into the kernel function.

Interaction with the environment when it is completely unknown requires an exploration phase where actions are chosen randomly. However, it is reasonable to believe that more accurate action heuristics exist when one has already learned a policy in a related task. For this reason, we also transfer the learned policy function from the source task and use it only in the first interaction with the environment for the target task.

4 Experiments

In this section we show experimental results in the well known inverted-pendulum task, commonly used as benchmark to compare reinforcement learning algorithms. We compare the performance of the proposed learning approach, QTL-PILCO, against PILCO [2] under different conditions.

Algorithm 1. Qualitative Transfer Learning

Require: $\theta^{(s)}$, $\psi^{(s)}$
 1: $\tilde{\pi} \leftarrow \pi(\psi^{(s)})$
 2: $\theta \leftarrow \theta^{(s)}$
 3: Interact with environment, apply $\tilde{\pi}$ to obtain tuples.
 4: **repeat**
 5:    Infer transition function distribution f from tuples and hyper-parameters θ.
 6:    **repeat**
 7:       Evaluate policy $\tilde{\pi}$ over f. Get $V^{\tilde{\pi}}$
 8:       Improve $\tilde{\pi}$ ▷ Updating parameters ψ
 9:    **until** convergence
10:    $\tilde{\pi} \leftarrow \pi(\psi)$
11:    Interact with environment, apply $\tilde{\pi}$ to obtain more tuples.
12:    Learn $\theta^{(p)}$ from all tuples.
13:    $\theta \leftarrow \gamma\theta + (1 - \gamma)\theta^{(p)}$
14: **until** task learned

In the experiments, an inverted pendulum has to be swung up and then balanced. The pendulum is attached to a cart that moves along one axis when an external force is applied (action). The inverted pendulum problem involves applying actions that temporarily move the pendulum away from the target state, and the agent has to apply two different control criteria, one to swing the pendulum up and the other to balance it, thus it is non trivial to solve.

In the continuous scenario, a state $\mathbf{x}$ is represented by the position x of the cart, its velocity $\dot{x}$, the angle θ of the pendulum, and its angular velocity $\dot{\theta}$. The cost function is expressed as $c(\mathbf{x}) = 1 - \exp(-\frac{1}{2}a \times d^2)$, where a is a scale constant of the cost function (set to 0.25 in the experiments) and d is the Euclidean distance between the current and desired states, expressed as $d(\mathbf{x}, \mathbf{x}_{target})^2 = x^2 + 2xl\sin\theta + 2l^2 + 2l^2\cos\theta$. In the current setup, the reward remains close to zero if the distance of the pendulum tip to the target is greater than $l = 0.6m$.

The source task consists of swinging a pendulum of mass 0.5 Kg. while in the target tasks the pendulums weights are changed to 0.8, 1.0, 1.5, and 2.0 Kg., respectively. Even when tasks have the same state and action spaces, their dynamics vary significantly and transferring the learned policy from the source task does not improve over learning from scratch and may even lead to negative transfer.

In our experiments, the source task was learned using PILCO. From that learning process, we transferred the hyper-parameters of the transition function and used the policy function for the first trial of the target task.

We repeated the procedure 5 times, randomly drawing the initial state $\mathbf{x} \sim \mathcal{N}(\mu_{s0}, \Sigma_0)$, the learning curves were averaged and plotted with their corresponding standard deviation. For PILCO, the Kernel hyper-parameters in the source task were initialized with heuristic values, as proposed in [2]. The initial training set for the transition function was generated by applying actions drawn uniformly from $[-\mathbf{a}_{max}, \mathbf{a}_{max}]$. For policy transfer, the whole policy learned in the source task was used as initial policy in the target task instead of a random policy to obtain initial samples, followed by QTL-PILCO (see Algorithm 1) to refine the policy.

In our proposed methodology, 8 hyper-parameters for each of the kernels $\mathbf{K}_i$, are taken from the source task, so 32 free variables are considered (considering the four variables for this domain). Those hyper-parameters are used as initial ones in the target tasks, and after the first episode, they are updated via evidence maximization from the samples and a weighted history of the original values, as described in Eq. 4. We performed experiments with different values for γ, from $\gamma = 0$, which is equivalent to learning with PILCO, to $\gamma = 0.9$ which provides more "inertia" to the hyper-parameters found in the source task.

A comparison of the learning curves for target tasks is showed in Figure 1, where we plot PILCO and QTL-PILCO with different values of γ. The horizontal axis shows the number of episodes (interactions with the environment) while the vertical axis shows the total reward, which is computed as the cumulative count of $1 - c(\mathbf{x})$ at every step.

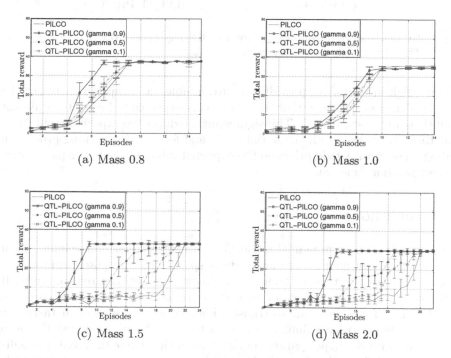

(a) Mass 0.8

(b) Mass 1.0

(c) Mass 1.5

(d) Mass 2.0

Fig. 1. Learning curves for target tasks 0.8Kg, 1.0Kg, 1.5Kg and 2.0Kg learned from 0.5Kg source task. Error bars represent ±1 standard deviation.

As can be appreciated from the figures, the proposed transfer learning approach can significantly reduce the learning process. When the target task is quite similar to the source task (in this case, with a similar mass), QTL-PILCO shows a clear improvement over learning without transfer. When the target task is less similar (larger mass) the improvement is much more noticeable.

The values of the hyper-parameters learned by evidence maximization can change drastically during the first iterations of the learning process due to poor samples. This is illustrated in the top graph of Figure 2(a). On the other hand, it can be seen in the lower graph of this figure, that with QTL-PILCO the values of the hyper-parameters are more stable and help to learn faster an adequate policy.

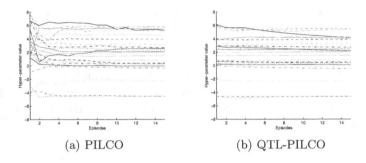

(a) PILCO   (b) QTL-PILCO

Fig. 2. Hyper-parameters convergence for the 0.8 Kg. task. PILCO oscillates more while QTL-PILCO leads to steadier values.

Our weighting technique provides a more suitable way to approximate target's hyper-parameters, provided that their values are expected to be not too different from those of the source task. This significantly reduces the expected oscillations that their values take with the initial trials and focuses the learning process in finding a policy with good priors on the expected values of the hyper-parameters of the transition function.

5   Conclusions

In this paper we have presented a transfer learning approach for reinforcement learning with continuous state and action spaces. The proposed approach is simple, yet very effective for transferring knowledge between related tasks. It is based on two general ideas for transfer learning. The first one is based on the idea that if you are going to transfer knowledge between similar tasks you can expect them to have similar general behaviors. We implemented this idea by starting with the hyper-parameters learned in the source task and gradually incorporating information from the learned hyper-parameters of the target task. The second idea is based on starting the new task with your "best guess". In this case, we used as starting policy the policy learned in the source task.

As future work, we would like to know the limits of our approach as the source and target tasks become less similar. We would also like to explore how to transfer knowledge from several source tasks. Finally, we would like to perform experiments in other more challenging domains.

Acknowledgements. Work supported by CONACyT grant No. 51415.

References

1. Deisenroth, M.P., Peters, J., Rasmussen, C.E.: Approximate dynamic programming with Gaussian processes. In: American Control Conference, pp. 4480–4485 (2008)
2. Deisenroth, M.P., Rasmussen, C.E.: PILCO: A Model-Based and Data-Efficient Approach to Policy Search. In: ICML 2011, pp. 465–472 (2011)
3. Deisenroth, M.P., Rasmussen, C.E., Fox, D.: Learning to control a low-cost manipulator using data-efficient reinforcement learning. In: Proceedings of Robotics: Science and Systems, Los Angeles, CA, USA (2011)
4. Deisenroth, M.P., Rasmussen, C.E., Peters, J.: Model-based reinforcement learning with continuous states and actions. In: 16th European Symposium on Artificial Neural Networks, pp. 19–24 (April 2008)
5. Engel, Y., Mannor, S., Meir, R.: Bayes meets Bellman: The Gaussian process approach to temporal difference learning. ICML 20(1), 154 (2003)
6. Engel, Y., Mannor, S., Meir, R.: Reinforcement learning with Gaussian processes. In: ICML 2005, pp. 201–208 (2005)
7. Hasselt, H.V.: Insights in Reinforcement Learning Formal analysis and empirical evaluation of temporal-difference learning algorithms (2011)
8. Hasselt, H.V.: Reinforcement Learning in Continuous State and Action Spaces. In: Reinforcement Learning: State of the Art (2011)
9. Lazaric, A., Restelli, M., Bonarini, A.: Reinforcement learning in continuous action spaces through sequential monte carlo methods. In: Advances in Neural Information Processing Systems (2007)
10. Lazaric, A., Restelli, M., Bonarini, A.: Transfer of samples in batch reinforcement learning. In: Proceedings of the 25th International Conference on Machine Learning, ICML 2008, pp. 544–551 (2008)
11. Martín, J.A., de Lope, H.J., Maravall, D.: Robust high performance reinforcement learning through weighted k-nearest neighbors. Neurocomputing 74(8), 1251–1259 (2011)
12. Murray-Smith, R., Sbarbaro, D.: Nonlinear adaptive control using non-parametric Gaussian process prior models. In: 15TH IFAC, pp. 21–26 (July 2002)
13. Rasmussen, C.E., Deisenroth, M.P.: Probabilistic inference for fast learning in control. In: Girgin, S., Loth, M., Munos, R., Preux, P., Ryabko, D. (eds.) EWRL 2008. LNCS (LNAI), vol. 5323, pp. 229–242. Springer, Heidelberg (2008)
14. Rasmussen, C.E., Kuss, M.: Gaussian Processes in Reinforcement Learning. Advances in Neural Information Processing Systems 16, 16 (2004)
15. Rasmussen, C.E., Williams, C.: Gaussian Processes for Machine Learning. International Journal of Neural Systems 14(2), 69–106 (2006)
16. Sutton, R., Barto, A.G.: Introduction to Reinforcement Learning. MIT Press (1998)
17. Taylor, M.E., Jong, N.K., Stone, P.: Transferring Instances for Model-Based Reinforcement Learning. Machine Learning (September 2008)
18. Taylor, M.E., Stone, P.: Transfer Learning for Reinforcement Learning Domains: A Survey. Journal of Machine Learning Research 10, 1633–1685 (2009)

New Penalty Scheme for Optimal Subsequence Bijection

Laura Alejandra Pinilla-Buitrago, José Francisco Martínez-Trinidad,
and Jesús Ariel Carrasco-Ochoa

Instituto Nacional de Astrofísica, Óptica y Electrónica
Departamento de Ciencias Computacionales
Luis Enrique Erro # 1, Puebla, México
{laurapin,fmartine,ariel}@inaoep.mx

Abstract. Optimal Subsequence Bijection (OSB) is a method that allows comparing two sequences of endnodes of two skeleton graphs which represent articulated shapes of 2D images. The OSB dissimilarity function uses a constant penalty cost for all endnodes not matching between two skeleton graphs; this can be a problem, especially in those cases where there is a big amount of not matching endnodes. In this paper, a new penalty scheme for OSB, assigning variable penalties on endnodes not matching between two skeleton graphs, is proposed. The experimental results show that the new penalty scheme improves the results on supervised classification, compared with the original OSB.

Keywords: skeleton graph, classification, matching.

1   Introduction

In object recognition, the use of shape similarity based on skeleton matching usually performs better for articulated shape recognition than contour or other shape descriptors in the presence of partial occlusion and articulation of parts [1-4]. The skeleton integrates geometrical and topological features of an object, which makes it a good descriptor. Moreover, skeleton-based recognition methods compared with contour matching or other methods have lower sensitivity to articulation or rearrangement of parts [5].

In this work, we develop a method based on the work proposed in [5], which computes a dissimilarity value between skeleton graphs that represent articulated shapes. The dissimilarity value is computed from the distances between the shortest paths for each pair of endnodes in the skeleton graph, calculated by applying the OSB method, but unlike [6] where the same penalty cost is assigned for those not matching endnodes; in our proposal we include a variable penalty cost for all not matching endnodes.

Maintaining a fixed penalty, as proposed in the original OSB method, could have a negative effect in those cases where the penalty is a small value and the number of not matching nodes is big.

This paper is organized as follow: In the section 2 we review the related work. In the section 3 we explain the proposed modification to the OSB method. The section 4

J. Ruiz-Shulcloper and G. Sanniti di Baja (Eds.): CIARP 2013, Part I, LNCS 8258, pp. 206–213, 2013.

shows experimental results of the proposed method compared against the original OSB. Finally, conclusions and future work are shown in section 5.

2   Related Work

In the literature, there are many approaches for computing skeleton similarity [7-12]. However one recent approach for computing shape similarity, which has shown good results, was proposed in [5]. This approach unlike other approaches, does not explicitly consider the topological structure of skeleton graphs. Instead, it is focused on the similarity of skeletons by comparing paths between skeleton endpoints. In this paper, we propose an extension to [5]. For this reason in this section we describe the original approach:

Definition 1. *A skeleton point having only one adjacent point is called endpoint (skeleton endpoint); a skeleton point having three or more adjacent points is called a skeleton junction point. If a skeleton point is not an endpoint or a junction point, it is called a connection point.*

Definition 2. *The sequence of connection points between two directly connected skeleton points is called a skeleton branch.*

Definition 3. *In a skeleton graph the endpoints and junction points are chosen as the nodes for the graph, and all the skeleton branches between the nodes are the edges. An endpoint in a skeleton graph is called an endnode; a junction point is called a junction node.*

Definition 4. *The shortest path between a pair of nodes in a skeleton graph is called an skeleton path.*

Suppose that we have a skeleton graph G with N endnodes, and $v_i(i = 1,2, ... , N)$ denotes the i th endnode along the shape contour labeled in clockwise direction, from the first contour pixel found in the y axis from top to bottom. $p(v_m, v_n)$ denotes the skeleton path from v_m to v_n nodes.

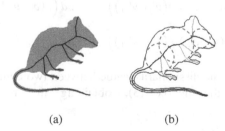

(a)   (b)

Fig. 1. (a) Skeleton of a shape (mouse) and (b) sequence of maximal disks between two endnodes on the skeleton path in (a). (Source: [13])

Given a set of M equidistant points on the path $p(v_m, v_n)$, $R_{m,n}(t)$ denotes the radius of the maximal disk (Fig. 1.) inside of the shape in the point t in $p(v_m, v_n)$.

The vector containing the radius of the maximal disk centered in the M equidistant points in $p(v_m, v_n)$ is denoted as:

$$R_{m,n} = (R_{m,n}(t))_{t=1,2,\ldots,M} = (r_1, r_2, \ldots, r_M) \tag{1}$$

Definition 5. *The shape dissimilarity between two skeleton paths is called a path distance. If R and R' denote the vectors of radii of two shape paths $p(u,v)$ and $p(u',v')$, respectively, the path distance is defined as:*

$$pd\big(p(u,v), p(u',v')\big) = \sum_{i=1}^{M} \frac{(r_i - r_i')^2}{r_i + r_{i'}} + \alpha \frac{(l-l')^2}{l+l'} \tag{2}$$

Where l y l' are the lengths of $p(u,v)$ and $p(u',v')$ and α is a weight factor. The OSB method is scale invariant since both the path length and radii are normalized.

The *Optimal Subsequence Bijection* (OSB) method works over two sequences of different lengths m and n. The OSB method uses two finite sequences of endnodes of two skeletons $a = (a_1, \ldots, a_m)$ and $b = (b_1, \ldots b_n)$ respectively. The aim is to find subsequences a' of a and b' of b such that a' best matches b'.

2.1 Dissimilarity between Two Endnodes

Let G and G' be two skeleton graphs to be matched, with endnodes $v_i (i = 0,1,\ldots,K)$ and $v'_j (j = 0,1,\ldots,N)$ respectively and $K \leq N$. The dissimilarity between the two endnodes v_i and v'_j is estimated by computing all path distances that emerge from nodes v_i in G and v'_j in G', obtaining in this way a matrix of size $K \times N$.

The matrix in (3) contains the path distances (computed using (2)) that emerge from $v_i = v_{i0}$ in G and $v'_j = v'_{j0}$ in G':

$$pd(v_{i0}, v'_{j0}) = \begin{pmatrix} pd\big(p(v_{i0},v_{i1}), p(v'_{j0},v'_{j1})\big) & \cdots & pd\big(p(v_{i0},v_{i1}), p(v'_{j0},v'_{jN})\big) \\ pd\big(p(v_{i0},v_{i2}), p(v'_{j0},v'_{j1})\big) & \cdots & pd\big(p(v_{i0},v_{i2}), p(v'_{j0},v'_{jN})\big) \\ \cdots & \ddots & \cdots \\ pd\big(p(v_{i0},v_{iK}), p(v'_{j0},v'_{j1})\big) & \cdots & pd\big(p(v_{i0},v_{iK}), p(v'_{j0},v'_{jN})\big) \end{pmatrix} \tag{3}$$

In the order to obtain the dissimilarity value between two endnodes, the OSB method is applied to the matrix (3), obtaining the matrix (4) of size $(K+1) \times (N+1)$.

$$C(G,G') = \begin{pmatrix} OSB(pd(v_0, v'_0)) & \cdots & OSB(pd(v_0, v'_N)) \\ OSB(pd(v_1, v'_0)) & \cdots & OSB(pd(v_1, v'_N)) \\ \vdots & \ddots & \vdots \\ OSB(pd(v_K, v'_0)) & \cdots & OSB(pd(v_K, v'_N)) \end{pmatrix} \tag{4}$$

For ensuring consistence in the matching between pairs of endnodes and to obtain the dissimilarity value between two shapes, which are represented by graphs, we applied OSB to the matrix $C(G, G')$ (4), as in [6].

In [6], at applying OSB in $C(G, G')$ the penalty for not matching endnodes is constant as proposed in the original method. In this case, we maintain the conditions that allow the link between the endnodes of skeletons, but, unlike the original OSB we apply a variable penalty cost on those not matching endnodes.

2.2   Optimal Subsequence Bijection

OSB works over two finite sequences of skeleton endnodes $a = (a_1, ..., a_m)$ and $b = (b_1, b_2, ..., b_n)$ for $|a| \leq |b|$. The main property of OSB is that some endnodes that form part of the sequences a and b can be jumped if it is necessary. However, excluding too many endnodes could influence in the dissimilarity value obtained. Each time that one endnode is jumped, a penalty is added. The cost of jumping some elements is called *jumpcost*. In [6] the jumpcost is constant when two specific sequences are compared and it is computed as:

$$ jumpcost = mean_i \left(min_j \left(d(a_i, b_j) \right) \right) + std_i \left(min_j \left(d(a_i, b_j) \right) \right) \tag{5} $$

Where $d(a_i, b_j)$ is the dissimilarity value computed between two elements of a and b. In this paper, the distance d is the path distance pd defined in equation (2).

For computing the optimal correspondence between the sequences a and b we must enforce the following conditions:

$d(a_i, b_j)$ is matched to $d(a_k, a_l)$ if and only if: $k - i = 1$ and $j < l$

Respecting the matching conditions and applying the penalty over not matching endnodes, we can define the matching cost as:

$$ w\big((i,j),(k,l)\big) = \begin{cases} d(a_i, b_j) & if\ j+1 = l\ y\ i+1 \leq k \\ (k+i-l).jumpcost & if\ j+1 < l\ y\ i+1 \leq k \\ \infty & Otherwise \end{cases} \tag{6} $$

3   Variable Penalty

Unlike [5], we propose to use variable penalty for all not matching endnodes, in dependence of each element jumped in the sequence b.

Applying a variable penalty over not matching endnodes, allows that the penalty depends on the currently jumped endnode. If the distance computed from the jumped endnode to all the endnodes in the other skeleton graph is big, the penalty cost will be big and vice versa. The above, allow us to obtain a dissimilarity value smaller or bigger, depending on the amount and the kind of jumped endnodes between two sub-sequences.

Maintaining matching conditions of the original method and applying variable penalty cost over not matching endnodes, we can define the matching cost as:

$$w\big((i,j),(k,l)\big) = \begin{cases} d(a_i,b_j) & if\ j+1=l\ y\ i+1\le k \\ \sum_{j=j+1}^{l-1} min_j\ C(i,j) & if\ j+1 < l\ y\ i+1 \le k \\ \infty & Otherwise \end{cases} \qquad (7)$$

In this way, the total dissimilarity between skeleton paths or skeleton endnodes is given by the sum of the matching cost $w\big((i,j),(k,l)\big)$.

4   Experiments

We built two databases for our experiments. The first database contains 36 shapes and 9 classes (4 shapes by class): *elephant, fork, heart, horse, human, L-star, star, tortoise* and *whale* (Fig. 2.). In this case we try to build a similar dataset to that one used in [6] which unfortunately is not available online.

The second database contains 32 shapes and 4 classes (8 shapes by class): *butterfly, cat, dolphin* and *fish* (Fig. 3.).

The shapes were obtained from different sources and the skeletons were semi-automatically constructed. First we compute an approximation to the skeleton of each figure, we used the source code by Bai[1] which uses *Discrete Skeleton Evolution* [14]. The skeleton achieved by this method allows us obtain an approximation to axis medial (or skeleton) of shapes, by means of the radii of maximal disk inside the shapes. Later, some branches were manually pruned, connected and/or added in order to ensure that the skeleton is simple and connected. Notice that this does not affect the modification proposed to the OSB method, since our method, in the same way as the original one, computes the dissimilarity between skeleton graphs once they have been built.

For our experiments on classification the *KNN* with $k = 1$, the proposed OSB with variable penalty and *leave-one-out cross validation* were used.

Fig. 2. Database containing 36 shapes and 9 classes

---

[1] https://sites.google.com/site/xiangbai/

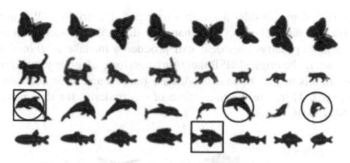

Fig. 3. Database containing 32 shapes and 4 classes

In Fig. 2 and Fig. 3, the errors obtained by applying OSB with constant penalty cost correspond to shapes labeled whit a circle and shapes marked with squares are errors with variable penalty, which is proposed in this paper. In the table 1 we can observe the obtained accuracy.

Table 1. Accuracy obtained for two databases with the original OSB and the proposed modification

	Database Fig. 2	Database Fig.3
OSB with constant penalty cost	77.7%	90.62%
OSB with variable penalty cost	88.8%	93.7%

In both databases, the new penalty scheme for OSB obtains better results than the original OSB.

In order to explain why we get better results with the new penalty scheme, let us consider the shapes in Fig. 4.

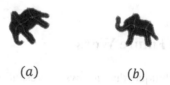

(a) (b)

Fig. 4. The shape (a) is correctly classified with the proposed penalty scheme for OSB obtaining the smallest dissimilarity value with the shape (b)

The matrix (8) contains the dissimilarity values between endnodes for this shapes. In this matrix a complete correspondence is obtained (values marked) and therefore the total dissimilarity value between shapes (a) and (b) from Fig. 3. is 9,04 no matter if the original or the proposed OSB is applied.

$$
\begin{pmatrix}
1.82 & 14.93 & 12.90 & 24.98 & 37.67 & 14.95 \\
12.36 & 3.16 & 3.49 & 13.52 & 22.30 & 16.08 \\
9.73 & 1.40 & 0.90 & 5.41 & 12.70 & 11.01 \\
13.48 & 3.76 & 3.56 & 1.30 & 4.40 & 7.89 \\
27.67 & 8.37 & 8.89 & 7.66 & 1.98 & 20.52 \\
4.27 & 12.83 & 10.38 & 12.14 & 19.54 & 2.34
\end{pmatrix} \qquad (8)
$$

Nevertheless, if we consider the shapes in Fig. 5, the original OSB method would obtain a smaller dissimilarity value than the dissimilarity value obtained by the proposed variable penalty scheme, it will produce a mistake at classification stage. This is because, in the original OSB the *jumpcost* for each node jumped in the matrix (9) is 1,40. In this matrix, three endnodes are jumped and three endnodes are linked (values marked). Therefore the total value of dissimilarity for this matrix using the original OSB is 9.04.

(a) (b)

Fig. 5. The shape (a) is erroneously classified into class of star with the original OSB method, obtaining the smallest dissimilarity value with the shape (b).

$$\begin{pmatrix} 10.04 & 3.66 & 3.82 & \boxed{1.35} & 3.66 & 6.38 \\ 10.71 & 2.78 & 2.91 & 1.77 & \boxed{2.20} & 7.11 \\ 3.42 & 7.19 & 5.67 & 4.99 & 11.41 & \boxed{1.29} \\ 16.15 & 4.49 & 5.09 & 3.19 & 1.08 & 11.21 \\ 17.20 & 4.79 & 5.38 & 3.96 & 1.09 & 12.03 \end{pmatrix} \quad (9)$$

However, using the proposed variable penalty scheme the three nodes jumped in the matrix (9) have a total jump cost of 9,11 and the total dissimilarity between shapes (a) and (b) from Fig. 5. is 13,95. Since the last value is bigger than the value obtained with the original OSB, the new scheme allows to correctly classify the shape (a) from Fig. 5.

5   Conclusions and Future Work

Building skeletons is a technique that allows representing and catching structural information of shapes. In this work, we proposed a variable penalty scheme for the OSB comparison method. The experimental results show that using the proposed penalty scheme allows to get better classification results that those results obtained by the original OSB.

As future work, we propose, to include in the description of the skeletons other characteristics, in order to distinguish important segments inside the figures, which would allow to get better classification results.

Acknowledgment. This work was partly supported by the National Council of Science and Technology of Mexico (CONACyT) through the project grants CB2008-106443 and CB2008-106366; and the scholarship grant 283120.

References

1. Sebastian, T.B., Kimia, B.B.: Curves vs Skeleton in Object Recognition. Signal Processing 85(2), 247–263 (2005)
2. Basri, R., Costa, L., Geiger, D., Jacobs, D.: Determinig the Similarity of Deformable Shapes. Vision Research 38, 2365–2385 (1998)
3. Huttenlocher, D.P., Klandeman, G.A., Rucklidge, W.J.: Comparing Images Using the Hausdorff Distance. IEEE Transaction Pattern Analysis and Machine Intelligence 15(9), 850–863 (1993)
4. Belongie, S., Puzhicha, J., Malik, J.: Shape Matching and Object Recognition Using Shape Contexts. IEEE Transaction Pattern Analysis and Machine Intelligence 24(4), 509–522 (2002)
5. Bai, X., Latecki, L.: Path Similarity Skeleton Graph Matching. IEEE Transactions on Pattern Analysis and Machine Intelligence 30, 1282–1292 (2008)
6. Shen, W., Wang, Y., Bai, X., Wang, L., Latecki, L.: Shape Clustering Common Structure Discovery. Pattern Recognition 64, 539–550 (2013)
7. Zhu, S.C., Yuille, A.L.: FORMS: A Flexible Object Recognition and Modeling Sys-tem. Proceedings of International Journal of Computer Vision 20(3), 187–212 (1996)
8. Liu, T., Geiger, D.: Approximate Tree Matching and Shape Similarity. In: Proceedings of IEEE 7th International Conference on Computer Vision, pp. 456–462 (1999)
9. Siddiqi, K., Shkoufandeh, A., Zucker, S.: Shock Graphs and Shape Matching. Proceedings of International Journal of Computer Vision 35, 13–32 (1998)
10. Shokoufandeh, A., Macrini, D., Dickinson, S., Siddiqi, K., Zucker, S.W.: Indexing Hierarchical Structures Using Graphs Spectra. IEEE Trans. Pattern Analysis and Machine Intelligence 27, 1125–1140 (2005)
11. Sebastian, T.B., Klein, P., Kimia, B.B.: Recognition of Shapes by Editing Shocks Graphs. In: Proceedings of International Conference in Computer Vision, pp. 755–762 (2001)
12. Torsello, A., Hancock, E.R.: A Skeletal Measure of 2D Shape Similarity. Computer Vision and Image Understanding 95, 1–29 (2004)
13. Bai, X., Liu, W., Tu, Z.: Integrating contour and skeleton for shape classification. In: IEEE 12th International Conference on Computer Vision Workshops (2009)
14. Bai, X., Latecki, L.J.: Discrete Skeleton Evolution. In: Yuille, A.L., Zhu, S.-C., Cremers, D., Wang, Y. (eds.) EMMCVPR 2007. LNCS, vol. 4679, pp. 362–374. Springer, Heidelberg (2007)

Missing Values in Dissimilarity-Based Classification of Multi-way Data

Diana Porro-Muñoz[2], Robert P.W. Duin[2], and Isneri Talavera[1]

[1] Advanced Technologies Application Center (CENATAV), Cuba
[2] Pattern Recognition Lab, TU Delft, The Netherlands
dporro@gmail.com, r.duin@ieee.org, italavera@cenatav.co.cu

Abstract. Missing values can occur frequently in many real world situations. Such is the case of multi-way data applications, where objects are usually represented by arrays of 2 or more dimensions e.g. biomedical signals that can be represented as time-frequency matrices. This lack of attributes tends to influence the analysis of the data. In classification tasks for example, the performance of classifiers is usually deteriorated. Therefore, it is necessary to address this problem before classifiers are built. Although the absence of values is common in these types of data sets, there are just a few studies to tackle this problem for classification purposes. In this paper, we study two approaches to overcome the missing values problem in dissimilarity-based classification of multi-way data. Namely, imputation by factorization, and a modification of the previously proposed Continuous Multi-way Shape measure for comparing multi-way objects.

Keywords: missing values, multi-way data, dissimilarity representation.

1 Introduction

Classification problems are very common in most research areas, and a suitable representation of objects plays an important role in this task. However, even when this representation is found, problems like the absence of values for some of the measured features can affect the accuracy of classifiers. There can be several reasons for data to be missing. Namely, equipments malfunctioning, data were not entered correctly or data just do not exist for some objects, etc. In other cases, missing values are not actually present in the obtained data. Nonetheless, they are inserted as a postprocessing in order to make the data more appropriate to be described for some specific models [1, 2].

For many applications e.g. neuroinformatics, chemometrics, data sets can have a multi-dimensional structure e.g. *objects × frequencies × time*, instead of the simple vector representation. These structures are often richer in information, thus advantageous for many purposes as classification. Therefore, it is important to employ proper tools in order to analyze them. As in the two-dimensional case, these types of data may be affected by the presence of missing values. For multi-way data, different behaviors for missing data can be observed [3, 4]. The simplest

J. Ruiz-Shulcloper and G. Sanniti di Baja (Eds.): CIARP 2013, Part I, LNCS 8258, pp. 214–221, 2013.
© Springer-Verlag Berlin Heidelberg 2013

case is when missing values are random without any pattern, denoted as RMV in [3]. Another common pattern is when complete fibers i.e. rows or tubes are missing at random (RMF). A third pattern is when missing values are systematic for all objects (SMV) i.e. the same values are missing for all objects. In contrast with the two-way case, there is just a limited research addressing the problem of missing values in multi-way data. Most of the related studies are dedicated to the robustness of factorization methods. Examples of the most common methods are PARAFAC algorithms based on Expectation Maximization - Alternating Least Squares [3] and based on the Levenberg - Marquadt method known as INDAFAC [3]. A more recent development is the CP-WOPT algorithm [5]. Other extensions of the multi-way methods, like TUCKER3, for dealing with missing values can be found in [6, 7, 4]. However, these methods are based on seeking accuracy in the obtained factor.

In this paper, we make a study on how to deal with missing values with the aim of minimizing the error function in the classification of multi-way data. We will use the Dissimilarity Representation (DR) [8] approach recently extended for the classification of multi-way data [9]. Roughly speaking, in this approach, (dis) similarities between objects are used as new features to describe them in a new space. Classifiers can be used in this space as in the traditional feature space. One of the approaches to deal with missing data in this case could be to reconstruct the data by a factorization method before the computation of the dissimilarity matrix. Another variant for dealing with missing data, particularly for the DR approach, consists in modifying the dissimilarity measure. With this purpose, we introduce a modification of the dissimilarity measure that will be used here such that it can deal with missing values.

The paper is organized as follows. The DR approach is briefly explained in Section 2. A description and comparative analysis of the studied approaches is presented in Section 3. Section 4 is dedicated to the experiments and discussion. Conclusions are presented in Section 5.

2   Dissimilarity Representation

The Dissimilarity Representation (DR) [8] approach has been introduced for classification purposes. It consists in a representation of objects by their (dis) similarities to a set of prototypes of each class identified in the problem at hand. One of the advantages of this approach is that it can be obtained from any representation of objects e.g. graphs, multi-dimensional objects, as long as a suitable measure is used. Moreover, this approach allows introducing discriminative context information that helps for a better discrimination of objects.

Let us define the Dissimilarity Space (DS) approach, given a t-way array $\underline{Y} \in \mathbb{R}^{I_1 \times I_2 \times \ldots \times I_t}$ where each object is represented by a $(t-1)$-dimensional array, a representation set $\underline{R}(\underline{R_1}, ..., \underline{R_h})$ where h is the number of prototypes, and a dissimilarity measure d [8, 9]. A mapping $\phi(\cdot, \underline{R}) : \mathbb{R}^{I_1 \times I_2 \times \ldots \times I_{t-1}} \to \mathbb{R}^h$ is done, such that every object $\phi(\underline{Y_i}, \underline{R}) = [d(\underline{Y_i}, \underline{R_1}), d(\underline{Y_i}, \underline{R_2}), ..., d(\underline{Y_i}, \underline{R_h})]$ is associated by its dissimilarities to all objects in $\underline{R}$. Hence, a dissimilarity matrix $\mathbf{D}(\underline{Y}, \underline{R})$

is obtained, which is used to build a classifier in the correspondent dissimilarity space of dimension h. The prototypes are usually the most representative objects of each class, $\underline{R} \subseteq \underline{Y}$ or $\underline{Y}$ itself. Any traditional classifier can be built in the dissimilarity space as in the feature space. Few work has been done to treat missing data in the DR approach. In [10], two alternatives for dealing with missing values in the dissimilarity representation-based classification are proposed. However, this work is only based on 2D data, where objects are represented by vectors in the feature space. It does not fit multi-way data. In this paper, we study two alternatives for classifying incomplete multi-way data by using the DR. The first approach is based on completing the multi-way data with a factorization method before computing the dissimilarity matrix (See Section 3). The second alternative consists in adapting the dissimilarity measure, such that dissimilarities between objects are obtained from the available information only.

The data sets to be studied here have a continuous nature. The characteristic shape of the surfaces for each class of objects is an important discriminative property of these type of data. Moreover, the information from the multi-way structure should be taken into account. Recently, the Continuous Multi-way Shape (CMS) [11] was introduced with this purpose. It consists in the comparison of multi-way objects based on the differences of their multi-way shape, considering the connectivity that exists between the neighboring points in the different directions. Differences between the gradients of the surfaces of these objects are computed, based on the application of linear filters by convolution. Thus, given $\underline{Y_a}$, $\underline{Y_b}$ two multi-way objects from a multi-way data set $\underline{Y}$, the dissimilarity measure CMS can be defined as:

$$d_G(\underline{Y_a}, \underline{Y_b}) = \left\| \sum_{i=1}^{f} \underline{Y_a} * \underline{G_\sigma} * \underline{H_i} - \underline{Y_b} * \underline{G_\sigma} * \underline{H_i} \right\|_F \tag{1}$$

where $\| \cdot \|_F$ is the Frobenius norm for tensors [12], $*$ is the convolution operator [13], $\underline{G_\sigma} \in \mathbb{R}^{I_1 \times I_2 \times \cdots \times I_{t-1}}$ a Gaussian convolution kernel to smooth the data, $\underline{H_i} \in \mathbb{R}^{I_1 \times I_2 \times \cdots \times I_{t-1}}$ is a partial derivative kernel and f is the number of partial derivatives in the different directions to obtain the gradient. The modification of the CMS measure for missing values will be given in the next Section.

3   Dealing with Missing Values in Multi-way Data

3.1   Factorization-Based Estimation

Factorization methods are very common for the analysis of multi-way data. They are used to extract and model their underlying structure. These methods are affected by the missing values, as data can be improperly analyzed. Therefore, creating robust methods to missing data has been one of the main tasks in the development of factorization methods [4]. Such is the case of the PARAFAC [3, 4], which is one of the most used methods for multi-way data analysis.

Given the three-way array $\underline{Y}$ of dimensions $I \times J \times K$, the PARAFAC model (decomposition) [14, 7] can be expressed by the factor matrices $A(I \times F)$, $B(J \times F)$ and

$C(K \times F)$, such that $\underline{y}_{ijk} = \sum_{f=1}^{F} a_{if} b_{jf} c_{kf}$, where $i = 1, 2, \ldots, I$, $j = 1, 2, \ldots, J$, $k = 1, 2, \ldots, K$ and F is the number of selected factors. In principle, factorization methods handle missing data with the aim of obtaining the most accurate data model. However, once the factorization has been computed, the resulting factor matrices can be used to reconstruct the original data and missing values are then estimated. Thus, a multi-way without missing values $\hat{\underline{Y}} \approx \underline{Y}$ can be obtained, using the information from the whole multi-way structure.

PARAFAC-Alternating Least Squares (ALS) [3] and CANDECOMP/ PARAFAC Weighted OPTimization (CP-WOPT) [5] are two of the main algorithms for fitting the PARAFAC model with missing data. PARAFAC-ALS works well for small amounts of missing data and it is very simple and fast. However, it may suffer of slow/no convergence as the amount of missing values increases [3]. It also depends on the patterns of the missing values. CP-WOPT is a scalable algorithm, which is based on direct non-linear optimization to solve the least squares problem. This algorithm has shown to work well even with 70% of missing data and it is fast. Both algorithms will be used here as means of estimation of missing values for the classification of incomplete multi-way data sets.

3.2   Ignoring Missing Values in DR: Adjustment of CMS Measure

An alternative for dealing with missing values in the DR approach is to compute proximities on available data only. However, this approach depends on the measure to be used i.e. the definition of each measure has to be adapted for this purpose, which is not always straightforward. In this paper, the adaptation of the CMS measure will be explained. Although the CMS measure was proposed for multi-way data in general, in this paper we will focus on three-way data only.

In this measure, missing values will be treated in the first step i.e. Gaussian filter. The idea is to use a filter that will only process the non-missing values in the analyzed window. In practice, if we have a matrix $\mathbf{Y}$ and a 2D filter kernel $\mathbf{G}$, the result of applying the filter $\mathbf{G}$ (or any other filter) at each position of matrix $\mathbf{Y}$ is defined as:

$$\mathbf{Y}'(u, v) = \sum_{k=-P}^{P} \sum_{l=-P}^{P} \mathbf{Y}(u - k, v - l) \cdot \mathbf{G}(k, l)$$

where $2P+1$ is the size of the filter in both the horizontal and vertical directions of the convolution kernel $\mathbf{G}$. So, suppose we are analyzing a part of the data with q missing values. The filter is only applied to the $(2P + 1)^2 - q$ non-missing values. In such case, as the number of summed values are less, the filtering result S for the analyzed position will not correspond to that if the data was complete. Therefore, a normalization like $S' = \frac{S}{(2P+1)^2 - q} \cdot (2P + 1)^2$ should be applied. If S' is used as the filtering result, instead of S, we are doing an implicit estimation of the missing values. That is, we are assuming that each missing value contributes in the filtering result S' with a value of $\frac{S}{(2P+1)^2 - q}$. However, this can be considered a drawback, since the implicit estimation of the missing value can change according to the position of the filter on the 2D matrix. When the amount of missing values is large, it could happen that all values in the window of the analyzed point are missing. In such situation, the previous adaptation does not work, it assigns NaN to the analyzed point. In this case, the idea is then to omit these points when objects are compared.

4   Experimental Setup and Discussion

The main goal of the experiments is to evaluate how the factorization methods and the adaptation of the CMS measure contribute to the DR-based classification of incomplete multi-way data. With this purpose, 2 three-way continuous data sets are used. The first data set is private and it comes from 1200 patches of 1024×1024 pixels of 36 colon tissue slides from Atrium hospital in Heerlen, The Netherlands. Patches were filtered with Laplace filters in 90 different scales using $\sigma = 2.\hat{}[0.1 : 0.1 : 9]$. The log-squares of the results are summarized in 60 bin normalized histograms with bin centers $[-50 : 1 : 9]$. Thus, a 90×60 array is obtained for every patch, leading to a three-way array of $1200 \times 90 \times 60$. The patches are labeled in two classes: Normal and Tumor. The second data set consists in metabolite data containing HPLC measurements of commercial extract of St. John's wort [15]. HPLC-PDA (HPLC with photo-diodo array detection) profiles were obtained from 24 different examples of St. Johns' wort from several continents: Africa (8 objects), Asia (6 objects), Europe (45 objects) and North America (30 objects). The final three-way data has a size of $89 \times 97 \times 549$.

In the two data sets there are no missing values originally, but these were generated artificially to test the methods. For each of them, 10 new data sets were first created by inserting various amounts $(1 - 5, 10, 20, 30, 50, 70\%)$ of missing values in the whole data set. Thus, all objects have the same probability of having missing values and the amount per object is completely random. This procedure was done for RMV and RMF patterns. Hence, we have generated in total 30 new data sets from the original ones. To avoid that results are influenced by a specific random pattern, we repeated the previous configurations 5 times for each of the two data sets.

The imputation by factorization and the modified CMS measure explained in Section 3 are evaluated on all data sets. There are different methods for the selection of the number of components in the factorization-based methods [7]. However, as in our case the interest is to reconstruct the original data as good as possible, we will use the residuals evaluation criteria. This consists on trying to find a minimum sum of squares of errors in the approximation of the non-missing values. In all cases, classifiers performed better for those models that fulfilled the previous criteria. Results are given in terms of classification error. The Regularized linear discriminant classifier was used on the dissimilarity space [8]. To find the regularization parameters of RLDC, an automatic regularization (optimization over training set by cross-validation) process was done. For the different data sets, experiments were carried out differently. For small data sets (St John's), classification errors were obtained in a 10 times k-fold cross-validation (CV). In the case of Colon data, 10 different training (90%) and test (10%) sets were randomly chosen and the error values were averaged. Experiments for the 5 repetitions of each of the configurations were averaged.

In the DR approach, for the small data set, the representation set has the same size of the training set obtained in each fold of the cross-validation procedure. For the Colon data set, a representation set of 550 prototypes was randomly chosen for each generated training set.

Table 1. Classification errors of Colon Cancer and St John's data sets after treatment of missing values. Results for different percents and patterns of missing data are shown. The baseline errors with the complete data are 0.095 and 0.02 respectively.

	Colon Cancer data set									
	Random missing values (%)									
Methods	1	2	3	4	5	10	20	30	50	70
PARAFAC	0.27	0.3	0.32	0.32	0.32	0.33	0.34	0.32	0.36	0.39
CP-WOPT	0.18	0.2	0.22	0.22	0.26	0.26	0.28	0.28	0.36	0.36
Adapted CMS	0.12	0.13	0.14	0.14	0.14	0.17	0.19	0.21	0.28	0.30
	Complete tubes missing(%)									
PARAFAC	0.30	0.30	0.31	0.31	0.31	0.31	0.31	0.32	0.33	0.40
CP-WOPT	0.2	0.2	0.2	0.26	0.22	0.24	0.24	0.26	0.28	0.36
Adapted CMS	0.14	0.14	0.14	0.14	0.13	0.16	0.17	0.19	0.24	0.29
	Complete rows missing(%)									
PARAFAC	0.31	0.31	0.31	0.32	0.32	0.32	0.32	0.34	0.38	0.4
CP-WOPT	0.19	0.24	0.2	0.22	0.24	0.22	0.22	0.28	0.28	0.34
Adapted CMS	0.14	0.15	0.15	0.15	0.15	0.14	0.15	0.18	0.19	0.25
	St John's data set									
	Random missing values (%)									
Methods	1	2	3	4	5	10	20	30	50	70
PARAFAC	0.05	0.05	0.05	0.05	0.05	0.05	0.05	0.05	0.05	0.05
CP-WOPT	0.03	0.03	0.03	0.03	0.04	0.04	0.10	0.10	0.10	0.12
Adapted CMS	0.02	0.02	0.02	0.03	0.03	0.04	0.05	0.07	0.17	0.26
	Complete tubes missing (%)									
PARAFAC	0.05	0.05	0.05	0.05	0.05	0.06	0.05	0.05	0.05	0.06
CP-WOPT	0.04	0.04	0.04	0.04	0.04	0.04	0.04	0.04	0.04	0.05
Adapted CMS	0.03	0.03	0.03	0.04	0.03	0.03	0.04	0.08	0.24	0.41
	Complete rows missing (%)									
PARAFAC	0.05	0.05	0.05	0.04	0.05	0.06	0.07	0.11	0.13	0.23
CP-WOPT	0.04	0.04	0.04	0.04	0.05	0.07	0.07	0.09	0.12	0.19
Adapted CMS	0.02	0.03	0.03	0.03	0.03	0.06	0.13	0.22	0.32	0.46

Table 1 summarizes the classification errors of the two data sets after reconstructing the data. The classification errors on the complete data sets are used as a baseline for the comparison. Factorization-based methods work well in general when they converge, like in the case of St John's. However, this is not the case when convergence is not reached. It can be observed in Colon data set that performance of the classifier is bad for all patterns of missing values. It is actually the worst result. In this case, both algorithms took long to converge and for large amounts of missing data convergence was never reached. There is a slight improvement of CP-WOPT based results over those of PARAFAC-ALS, specially for large amounts of missing data, as expected. It has to be noticed that for large amounts of missing values these methods are stable. Nonetheless, even when the stability of these methods (when they converge) for different amounts of missing data is very attractive, their slow/no convergence problem is a strong drawback when comparing methods to reconstruct the missing data.

Let us analyze the adapted CMS measure directly applied on the incomplete data. It has to be remarked that for small amounts of missing data $(1 - 5\%)$, classifiers performance is comparable with the baseline classification error. In fact, for St John's data set, the baseline classification error is reached. A very attractive characteristic of the modified measure is that without a preprocessing step i.e. imputation, approximation, it has shown to work well with small amounts of missing data. Therefore, it can be a good option for these types of problems. Good performances can be obtained without the need of the extra computational cost of the imputation process. However, when the amount of missing values is large (usually above 10%), the classifier seems to loose stability and the performance gets drastically worse the more missing values are added. This could be explained by the fact that when there are many contiguous windows missing, the Gaussian filter cannot deal with it, too much information is lost and the idea of derivatives is kind of pointless. In these cases, the use of an imputation method e.g. interpolation is recommended. In general, for the two analyzed patterns of missing values, that is RMV and RMF, all methods behaved similar. It can be observed that the type of pattern of the missing points did not have a strong influence in the performance of the methods. The main disturbing factor was the amount of missing values.

5   Conclusions

We have investigated two main approaches with the aim of dealing with the problem of missing values for the classification of multi-way data. The study was based on the Dissimilarity Representation approach, which consists in building classifiers on a space where objects are represented by their dissimilarities. As a first attempt, factorization techniques were applied to reconstruct the data before dissimilarities were computed. Their performance was good for small and large amounts of missing values, except in the cases where convergence could not be reached. Moreover, they imply an extra computational cost. Therefore, we studied as a second approach, the possibility of computing dissimilarities with the available data only. In this paper, as we experimented on continuous multi-way data, a modification of the Continuous Multi-way Shape measure was introduced in order to deal with missing attributes. This approach, has shown to work well for RMV and RMF patterns of missing values, it works well when they are present in small amounts(up to 10%). From that point on, classifiers performance deteriorates increasingly. We can then conclude that this approach is suitable for small amounts of missing data. However, the factorization approach should be more reliable for large amounts of missing values. Although experiments were carried out on three-way data only, the presented approaches can be extended to higher-order representations of objects.

References

[1] Mortensen, P.P., Bro, R.: Real time monitoring and chemical profiling of a cultivation process. Chemometr. Intell. Lab. 84(1-2), 106–113 (2005)

[2] Møller, J., Parolari, G., Gabba, L., Christensen, J., Skibsted, L.: Evaluated surface autofluorescence spectroscopy in order to measure age-related quality index of parma ham during processing. J. Agr. Food Chem. 51, 1224–1230 (2003)

[3] Tomasi, G., Bro, R.: PARAFAC and missing values. Chemometr. Intell. Lab. 75, 163–180 (2005)

[4] Kroonenberg, P.M.: Applied Multiway Data Analysis. John Wiley & Sons (2008)

[5] Acar, E., Dunlavy, D.M., Kolda, T.G., Mrup, M.: Scalable tensor factorizations for incomplete data. Chemometr. Intell. Lab. 106(1), 41–56 (2011)

[6] Walczak, B., Massart, D.: Dealing with missing data: Part I. Chemometr. Intell. Lab. 58, 15–27 (2001)

[7] Smilde, A.K., Bro, R., Geladi, P.: Multi-way Analysis. Applications in the chemical sciences. John Wiley & Sons, Inc. (2004)

[8] Pekalska, E., Duin, R.P.W.: The Dissimilarity Representation For Pattern Recognition. Foundations and Applications. World Scientific (2005)

[9] Porro-Muñoz, D., Duin, R.P.W., Talavera, I., Orozco-Alzate, M.: Classification of three-way data by the dissimilarity representation. Signal Processing 91(11), 2520–2529 (2011)

[10] Millán-Giraldo, M., Duin, R.P.W., Sánchez, J.S.: Dissimilarity-based classification of data with missing attributes. In: Proc. of CIP 2010, pp. 293–298 (2010)

[11] Porro-Muñoz, D., Duin, R.P.W., Orozco-Alzate, M., Talavera Bustamante, I.: Continuous multi-way shape measure for dissimilarity representation. In: Alvarez, L., Mejail, M., Gomez, L., Jacobo, J. (eds.) CIARP 2012. LNCS, vol. 7441, pp. 430–437. Springer, Heidelberg (2012)

[12] Lathauwer, L., De Moor, B.: From matrix to tensor: Multilinear algebra and signal processing. In: Proc. of the 4th International Conference on Mathematics in Signal Processing, Warwick, UK, vol. I, pp. 1–11 (1996)

[13] Gonzalez, R.C., Woods, R.E.: Digital Image Processing, 3rd edn. Prentice-Hall, Inc., Upper Saddle River (2006)

[14] Harshman, R.: Foundations of the Parafac procedure: models and conditions for an explanation multi-modal factor analysis. UCLA Working Papers in Phonetics, Los Angeles 16, 1–84 (1970)

[15] Acar, E., Bro, R., Schmidt, B.: New exploratory clustering tool. Journal of Chemomometrics 22, 91–100 (2008)

A New Distance for Data Sets
in a Reproducing Kernel Hilbert Space Context

Alberto Muñoz[1], Gabriel Martos[1], and Javier González[2]

[1] University Carlos III, Department of Statistics, Madrid, Spain
[2] J. Bernoulli Institute for Mathematics and Computer Science,
University of Groningen, The Netherlands
{alberto.munoz,gabrielalejandro.martos}@uc3m.es,
j.gonzalez.hernandez@rug.nl

Abstract. In this paper we define distance functions for data sets in a reproducing kernel Hilbert space (RKHS) context. To this aim we introduce kernels for data sets that provide a metrization of the power set. The proposed distances take into account the underlying generating probability distributions. In particular, we propose kernel distances that rely on the estimation of density level sets of the underlying data distributions, and that can be extended from data sets to probability measures. The performance of the proposed distances is tested on several simulated and real data sets.

1 Introduction

The study of distances between data sets lies at the core of many methods of analysis in image processing [9], genetics [1], time series [7], etc. In this paper we define distances between data sets that take into account the underlying data distribution. To this aim we will focus on the study of distances between probability measures (PM), also known as distributions. Classical examples of application of distances between PMs in Statistics are homogeneity tests, independence tests and goodness of fit test problems. These problems can be solved by choosing an appropriate distance between PM $e.g.$ the χ^2 or L_1 distance. Other examples of distances between PM can also be founded in Clustering, Image Analysis, Time Series Analysis, etc. For a review of interesting distances between probability distributions and theoretical results, see for instance [4]. In many practical situations the size of the available sample is small, and the use of purely non parametric estimators often results in a poor performance. Another important drawback in non-parametric density estimation is the high computation time and huge storage required. This motivates the need of seeking metrics for probability distributions that do not explicitly rely on the estimation of the corresponding distribution functions. In this work we elaborate on the idea of considering a kernel function for data points with reference to a distribution function, that will be extended to a kernel (and therefore to a distance) for data sets. This paper is organized as follows: In Section 2 we introduce kernel functions for data sets with uniform distributions. Section 3 introduces a new

J. Ruiz-Shulcloper and G. Sanniti di Baja (Eds.): CIARP 2013, Part I, LNCS 8258, pp. 222–229, 2013.

metric for general data sets based on the estimation of density level sets. Section 4 shows the performance of the proposed metric on simulated and real data sets.

2   A Kernel for Data Sets with Reference to a Distribution

Consider a measure space $(\mathcal{X}, \mathcal{F}, \mu)$, where $\mathcal{X}$ is the sample space (a compact set of a real vector space in this work), $\mathcal{F}$ is a σ-algebra of measurable subsets of $\mathcal{X}$ and $\mu : \mathcal{F} \to \mathbb{R}^+$ is the ambient σ-finite measure, the Lebesgue measure. A **probability measure** (PM) $\mathbb{P}$ is a σ-additive finite measure absolutely continuous w.r.t. μ that satisfies the three Kolmogorov axioms. By Radon-Nikodym theorem, there exists a measurable function $f_\mathbb{P} : \mathcal{X} \to \mathbb{R}^+$ (the density function) such that $P(A) = \int_A f_\mathbb{P} d\mu$, and $f_\mathbb{P} = \frac{dP}{d\mu}$ is the Radon-Nikodym derivative. From now on we focus on data sets generated from (unknown) PM. In Section 3 we will discuss the corresponding distributional distance measures. Consider two iid samples $A = s_n(\mathbb{P}) = \{x_i\}_{i=1}^n \in \mathcal{P}(\mathcal{X})$, where $\mathcal{P}(\mathcal{X})$ denotes the set of all subsets of $\mathcal{X}$ including the empty set and itself (the power set of $\mathcal{X}$), and $B = s_m(\mathbb{Q}) = \{y_j\}_{j=1}^m \in \mathcal{P}(\mathcal{X})$, generated from the density functions $f_\mathbb{P}$ and $f_\mathbb{Q}$, respectively and defined on the same measure space. Define $r_A = \min d(x_l, x_s)$, where $x_l, x_s \in A$. Then r_A gives the minimum resolution for data set A: If a point $z \in \mathcal{X}$ is located at a distance smaller than r_A from a point $x \in A$ then, taken $\mathbb{P}$ as reference measure, it is impossible to differentiate z from x. That is, it is not possible to reject the null hypothesis that z is generated from $\mathbb{P}$, given that z is closer to x than any other point from the same distribution. This suggests the following definition.

Definition 1. *Indistinguishability with respect to a distribution. Let $x \in A$, where A denotes a set of points generated from the probability measure $\mathbb{P}$, and $y \in \mathcal{X}$. We say that y is **indistinguishable** from x with respect to the measure $\mathbb{P}$ in the set A when $d(x, y) \leq r_A = \min d(x_l, x_s)$, where $x_l, x_s \in A$. We will denote this relationship as: $y \overset{A(\mathbb{P})}{=} x$.*

Given the sets $A = s_n(\mathbb{P})$ and $B = s_m(\mathbb{Q})$, we want to build kernel functions $K : X \times X \to [0, 1]$, such that $K(x, y) = 1$ when $y \overset{A(\mathbb{P})}{=} x$ or $x \overset{B(\mathbb{Q})}{=} y$, and $K(x, y) = 0$ if $y \overset{A(\mathbb{P})}{\neq} x$ and $x \overset{B(\mathbb{Q})}{\neq} y$. For this purpose we consider the following smooth indicator functions.

Definition 2. *Smooth indicator functions. Let $r > 0$ and $\gamma > 0$, define a family of smooth indicator functions with center in x as:*

$$f_{x,r,\gamma}(y) = \begin{cases} e^{-\frac{1}{(\|x-y\|^\gamma - r^\gamma)^2} + \frac{1}{r^2\gamma^2}} & \textit{if } \|x - y\| < r \\ 0 & \textit{otherwise.} \end{cases} \tag{1}$$

Of course, other definitions of $f_{x,r,\gamma}$ are possible. The smooth function $f_{x,r,\gamma}(y)$ act as a bump function with center in the coordinate point given by x: $f_{x,r,\gamma}(y) \approx 1$ for $y \in B_r(x)$, and $f_{x,r,\gamma}(y)$ decays to zero out of $B_r(x)$, depending on the shape parameter γ (see Fig. 1).

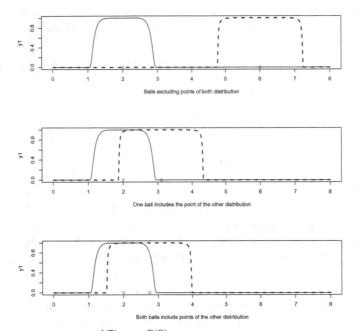

Fig. 1. Illustration of the $\overset{A(\mathbb{P})}{=}$ and $\overset{B(\mathbb{Q})}{=}$ relationship using smooth indicator functions

Definition 3. *Distributional indicator kernel.* *Given* $A = s_n(\mathbb{P})$ *and* $B = s_m(\mathbb{Q})$, *define* $K_{A,B} : \mathcal{X} \times \mathcal{X} \to [0,1]$ *by:*

$$K_{A,B}(x,y) = f_{x,r_A,\gamma}(y) + f_{y,r_B,\gamma}(x) - f_{x,r_A,\gamma}(y)f_{y,r_B,\gamma}(x), \qquad (2)$$

where $r_A = \min d(x_l, x_s)$, with $x_l, x_s \in A$, $r_B = \min d(y_l, y_s)$, with $y_l, y_s \in B$ and γ it is a shape parameter. Now, if $d(x,y) > r_A$ and $d(x,y) > r_B$ (Fig. 1, top) then $K_{A,B}(x,y) = 0$: $x \in A \backslash B$ w.r.t. $\mathbb{Q}$ and $y \in B \backslash A$ w.r.t. $\mathbb{P}$. If $d(x,y) > r_A$ but $d(x,y) < r_B$, then $y \in B \backslash A$ w.r.t. $\mathbb{P}$, but $x \overset{B(\mathbb{Q})}{=} y$ at radius r_B and $K_{A,B}(x,y) = 1$. If $d(x,y) < r_A$ but $d(x,y) > r_B$, then $x \in A \backslash B$ w.r.t. $\mathbb{Q}$, but $y \overset{A(\mathbb{P})}{=} x$ at radius r_A and $K_{A,B}(x,y) = 1$ (Fig. 1, center). Finally, if $d(x,y) < r_A$ and $d(x,y) < r_B$, then $K_{A,B}(x,y) = 1$ and $y \overset{A(\mathbb{P})}{=} x$ at radius r_A and $x \overset{B(\mathbb{Q})}{=} y$ at radius r_B (Fig. 1, bottom).

Definition 4. *Kernel for data sets.* *Given* $A = s_n(\mathbb{P})$ *and* $B = s_m(\mathbb{Q})$, *we consider kernels* $K : \mathcal{P}(\mathcal{X}) \times \mathcal{P}(\mathcal{X}) \to [0,1]$, *where* $\mathcal{P}(\mathcal{X})$ *denotes the power set of* $\mathcal{X}$, *and for* C *and* D *in* $\mathcal{P}(\mathcal{X})$, *define:*

$$K(C,D) = \sum_{x \in C} \sum_{y \in D} K_{A,B}(x,y). \qquad (3)$$

When $C = A$ and $D = B$, we can interpret $K(A,B)$ as a measure for $A \cap B$ by counting, using as equality operators $\overset{A(\mathbb{P})}{=}$ and $\overset{B(\mathbb{Q})}{=}$, the points 'in common':

$\mu_{K_{A,B}}(A \cap B) = K(A, B)$. Given the identity $A \cup B = \overbrace{(A - B) \cup (B - A)}^{A \Delta B} \cup (A \cap B)$, we will define $\mu_{K_{A,B}}(A \cup B) = N$, where $N = n + m = \#(A \cup B)$, is the counting measure of the set $A \cup B$. Therefore $\mu_{K_{A,B}}(A \Delta B) = N - \mu_{K_{A,B}}(A \cap B)$, and we can take this expression (dividing by N) as a definition for the distance between the sets A and B.

In the general case, $K(C, D)$ can be interpreted as a measure for $C \cap D$ by counting, using as equality operators $\overset{A(\mathbb{P})}{=}$ and $\overset{B(\mathbb{Q})}{=}$, the points 'in common': $\mu_{K_{A,B}}(C \cap D) = K(C, D)$. Therefore the respective distance between C and D obtained with the use of $K(C, D)$, is conditioned to a "resolution" level determined by the sets A and B (this is r_A and r_B).

Definition 5. *Distance between data sets.* *Given* $A = s_n(\mathbb{P})$ *and* $B = s_m(\mathbb{Q})$, *we define the kernels distance for* C *and* D *in* $\mathcal{P}(\mathcal{X})$:

$$d_K(C, D) = 1 - \frac{K(C, D)}{N}, \tag{4}$$

where $N = n_C + n_D = \#(C \cup D)$ *and represent the measure of the set* $C \cup D$.

It is straightforward to check that $d_K(C, D)$ is a semi-metric (using the equality operators $y \overset{A(\mathbb{P})}{=} x$ or $y \overset{B(\mathbb{Q})}{=} x$ where it corresponds). When $C = A$ and $D = B$ and the size of both sets increases, then: $\mu_{K_{A,B}}(A \cap B) \overset{n,m \to \infty}{\to} \mu(A \cap B)$ and $\mu_{K_{A,B}}(A \cup B) \overset{n,m \to \infty}{\to} \mu(A \cup B)$, therefore $\lim_{n,m \to \infty} d_K(A, B) = 1 - \frac{\mu(A \cap B)}{\mu(A \cup B)}$, that is the Jaccard distance for data sets.

3   A Metric for Data Sets Based on Estimation of Level Sets

Using constant radii in Eq. (1) to determine the "distinguishability" relationship between points is only adequate if we are working with the uniform PM. In this section we propose a solution to this problem by splitting each data set in density level sets, and then considering difference sets between consecutive density levels, for which density is approximately constant.

Consider the α-level sets defined by $S_\alpha(f_\mathbb{P}) = \{x \in X | f_\mathbb{P}(x) \geq \alpha\}$, where $P(S_\alpha(f_\mathbb{P})) = 1 - \nu$, where $f_\mathbb{P}$ is the density function and $0 < \nu < 1$. If we consider an ordered sequence $\alpha_1 < \ldots < \alpha_k$, then $S_{\alpha_{i+1}}(f_\mathbb{P}) \subseteq S_{\alpha_i}(f_\mathbb{P})$.

Let us define $A_i(\mathbb{P}) = S_{\alpha_i}(f_\mathbb{P}) - S_{\alpha_{i+1}}(f_\mathbb{P})$, $i \in \{1, \ldots, k - 1\}$. We can choose $\alpha_1 \simeq 0$ and $\alpha_k \geq \min\{\max_{x \in X} f_\mathbb{P}(x), \max_{x \in X} f_\mathbb{Q}(x)\}$; then $\bigcup_i A_i(\mathbb{P}) \simeq Supp(\mathbb{P}) = \{x \in X | f_\mathbb{P}(x) \neq 0\}$. Note that given the definition of the A_i, if $A_i(\mathbb{P}) = B_i(\mathbb{Q})$ for every i when $(n, m, k) \to \infty$, then $\mathbb{P} = \mathbb{Q}$. Given the definition of the A_i-level set, both $\mathbb{P}$ and $\mathbb{Q}$ are approximately constant on A_i and B_i level sets, respectively. Therefore the use of a constant radii is again adequate when we compare the distance between the sets A_i and B_i. To estimate level sets $\hat{S}_{\alpha_i}(f_\mathbb{P})$ from a data sample in this work we use the algorithm introduced in [5]. Next we take $\hat{A}_i(\mathbb{P}) = \hat{S}_{\alpha_{i+1}}(f_\mathbb{P}) - \hat{S}_{\alpha_i}(f_\mathbb{P})$, where $\hat{S}_{\alpha_i}(f_\mathbb{P})$ is estimated by R_n defined above.

Definition 6. *Weighted level-set distance.* *Consider data sets* $A = s_n(\mathbb{P})$ *and* $B = s_m(\mathbb{Q})$, *generated from PMs* $\mathbb{P}$ *and* $\mathbb{Q}$, *respectively. Choose a partition*

$\alpha_1 < \alpha_2 < \ldots < \alpha_k$, $\alpha_i \in (0, \min\{\max_{x \in X} f_{\mathbb{P}}(x), \max_{x \in X} f_{\mathbb{Q}}(x)\})$. *Then we define the weighted α-level set distances between the sets A and B by*

$$d(A, B) = \sum_{i=1}^{k-1} w_i d_K(A_i, B_i), \quad w_1, \ldots, w_{k-1} \in \mathbb{R}^+ \tag{5}$$

In the practice to compute the distance in Eq. (5), we have to use: $\hat{A}_i(\mathbb{P}) = \hat{S}_{\alpha_{i+1}}(f_{\mathbb{P}}) - \hat{S}_{\alpha_i}(f_{\mathbb{P}})$ the estimation of $A_i = S_{\alpha_{i+1}}(f_{\mathbb{P}}) - S_{\alpha_i}(f_{\mathbb{P}})$ based on set A; and the respective estimation for $\hat{B}_i(\mathbb{Q})$. In this paper we choose the weights by

$$w_i = \frac{1}{k} \sum_{x \in s_{\hat{A}_i(\mathbb{P})}}^{n_{\hat{A}_i(\mathbb{P})}} \sum_{y \in s_{\hat{B}_i(\mathbb{Q})}}^{n_{\hat{B}_i(\mathbb{Q})}} \frac{\left(1 - I_{r_{\hat{A}_i(\mathbb{P})}, r_{\hat{B}_i(\mathbb{Q})}}(x, y)\right) \parallel x - y \parallel_2}{(s_{\hat{B}_i(\mathbb{Q})} - \hat{A}_i(\mathbb{P})) \cup (s_{\hat{A}_i(\mathbb{P})} - \hat{B}_i(\mathbb{Q}))}, \tag{6}$$

where $s_{\mathbb{P}}$ and $s_{\mathbb{Q}}$ are the data samples corresponding to set of points/PMs $A(\mathbb{P})$ and $B(\mathbb{Q})$ respectively, $s_{\hat{A}_i(\mathbb{P})}$ and $s_{\hat{B}_i(\mathbb{Q})}$ denote the data samples that estimate $A_i(\mathbb{P})$ and $B_i(\mathbb{Q})$, respectively. $\hat{A}_i(\mathbb{P}) = \cup_{x \in s_{\hat{A}_i(\mathbb{P})}} B(x, r_{\hat{A}_i(\mathbb{P})})$, and $\hat{B}_i(\mathbb{Q}) = \cup_{y \in s_{\hat{B}_i(\mathbb{Q})}} B(y, r_{\hat{B}_i(\mathbb{Q})})$ are the covering estimations of the sets $A_i(\mathbb{P})$ and $B_i(\mathbb{Q})$ respectively, and $I_{r_{\hat{A}_i(\mathbb{P})}, r_{\hat{B}_i(\mathbb{Q})}}(x, y)$ is an indicator function that takes value 1 when y belongs to the covering estimation of the set $A_i(\mathbb{P})$, x belongs to the covering estimation of the set $B_i(\mathbb{Q})$ or both events happen, and value 0 otherwise. Note that the weight w_i is a weighted average of distances between a point of $s_{\hat{A}_i(\mathbb{P})}$ and a point of $s_{\hat{B}_i(\mathbb{Q})}$ where $\|x - y\|_2$ is taken into account only when $I_{r_{\hat{A}_i(\mathbb{P})}, r_{\hat{B}_i(\mathbb{Q})}}(x, y) = 0$. Other definitions of w_i are possible and give rise to different distance measures.

4   Experimental Work

The proposed distances are intrinsically non-parametric, so no tuning parameters have to be fixed or evaluated via simulation. The strategy to test the Weighted level-set distance (WLS) will be to compare it to other classical PM distances for some well known (and parametrized) distributions and for real data problems. We consider distances belonging to the main types of PMs metrics: Kullback-Leibler (KL) divergence [6] (f-divergence and also Bregman divergence), t-test (T) measure (Hotelling test in the multivariate case) and Energy distance [12]. For further details on the sample versions of the above distance functions and their computational subtleties see [6,11,12].

4.1   Synthetically Generated Data

Case I: Discrimination between Gaussian distributed sets of points with equal covariance structure

We quantify the ability of the considered set/PM distances to discriminate between multivariate normal distributed sets of points. To this end, we generate

Table 1. $\delta^*\sqrt{d}$ for a 5% type I and 10% type II errors

Metric	d: 1	2	3	4	5	10	15	20	50	100
KL	.870	.636	.433	.430	.402	.474	.542	.536	.495	.470
T	.490	.297	.286	.256	.246	.231	.201	.212	.193	.110
Energy	.460	.283	.284	.250	.257	.234	.213	.223	.198	.141
WLS	.490	.354	.277	.220	.224	.221	.174	.178	.134	.106

a data sample of size $100d$ from a $N(\mathbf{0}, \mathbf{I}_d)$ where d stands for dimension and then we generate 1000 iid data samples of size $100d$ from the same $N(\mathbf{0}, \mathbf{I}_d)$ distribution. Next we calculate the distances between each of these 1000 iid data samples and the first data sample to obtain the 95% distance percentile.

Now define $\boldsymbol{\delta} = \delta\mathbf{1} = \delta(1, \ldots, 1) \in \mathbb{R}^d$ and increase δ by small amounts (starting from 0). For each $\boldsymbol{\delta}$ we generate a data sample of size $100d$ from a $N(\mathbf{0} + \boldsymbol{\delta}, \mathbf{I}_d)$ distribution. If the distance under consideration for the displaced distribution data sample to the original data sample is larger than the 95% percentile we conclude that the present distance is able to discriminate between both populations and this is the value δ^* referenced in Table 1. To take into account the randomness in the experiment we repeat this process 100 times and fix δ^* to the present δ value if the distance is above the percentile in 90% of the cases. Thus we calculate the minimal value δ^* required for each metric in order to discriminate between populations with a 95% confidence level (type I error = 5%) and a 90% sensitivity level (type II error = 10%). In Table 1 we report the minimum distance ($\delta^*\sqrt{d}$) between distributions centers required to discriminate for each metric in several alternative dimensions, where small values implies better results. In the case of the T-distance for normal distributions we can use the Hotelling test to compute a p-value to fix the δ^* value.

The data chosen for this experiment are ideal for the use of the T statistics that, in fact, outperforms KL (results in Table 1). However, Energy distance works even better than T distance in dimensions 1 to 4 and WLS performs similarly (slightly better) to T (except for dimension 2) in dimensions upon 3.

Case II: Discrimination between Gaussian distributed sets of points with different covariance structure

In this experiment we consider again normal populations but different variance-covariance matrices. Define as expansion factor $\sigma \in \mathbb{R}$, which we gradually increase (starting from 0) in order to determine the smallest σ^* required for each metric in order to discriminate between the $100d$ sampled data points generated for the two distributions: $N(\mathbf{0}, \mathbf{I}_d)$ and $N(\mathbf{0}, (1+\sigma)\mathbf{I}_d)$. If the distance under consideration for the displaced distribution data sample to the original data sample is larger than the 95% percentile we conclude that the present distance is able to discriminate between both populations and this is the value $(1+\sigma^*)$ reported in Table 2. To take into account the randomness in the experiment we repeat it 100 times and fix σ^* to the present σ value if the distance is above the 90% percentile of the cases, as it was done in the previous experiment.

Table 2. $(1 + \sigma^*)$ for a 5% type I and 10% type II errors

Metric	dim: 1	2	3	4	5	10	15	20	50	100
KL	3.000	1.700	1.250	1.180	1.175	1.075	1.055	1.045	1.030	1.014
T	—	—	—	—	—	—	—	—	—	—
Energy	1.900	1.600	1.450	1.320	1.300	1.160	1.150	1.110	1.090	1.030
WLS	1.700	1.350	1.150	1.120	1.080	1.050	1.033	1.025	1.015	1.009

(a)   (b)

Fig. 2. Real image and sampled image of a leaf in the Tree Leaf Database

We can see here again that the proposed metric WLS is better than the competitors in all dimensions considered. There are no entries in Table 2 for the T distance because it was not able to distinguish between the considered populations in the considered dimensions.

4.2   Real Case-Study: Shape Classification

As an application of the preceding theory to the field of pattern recognition we consider a problem of shape classification, using the Tree Leaf Database [3]. We represent each leaf by a cloud of points in $\mathbb{R}^2$, as an example of the treatment given to a leaf consider the Fig. 2. For each image i of size $N_i \times M_i$, we generate a sample of size $N_i \times M_i$ from a uniform distribution and retain only those points which fall into the white region (image body) whose intensity gray level are larger than a fixed threshold (.99). This yield a representation of the leaf with around one thousand and two thousand points depending on the image. After rescaling and centering, we computed the 10×10 distance matrix (using the WLS distance and the Energy distance in this case) and the Multidimensional Scaling (MDS) plot in Fig. 3. It is clear that the WLS distance is able to better account for differences in shapes.

Future Work: Given a positive definite function $K : \mathcal{P}(X) \times \mathcal{P}(X) \to [0,1]$, as it is defined in Eq. (5), by Mercer's theorem there exists an Euclidean space $\mathcal{H}$ and a lifting map $\Phi : \mathcal{P}(X) \to \mathcal{H}$ such that $K(A,B) = \langle \Phi(A), \Phi(B) \rangle$ with $A, B \in \mathcal{P}(X)$ [8,10]. The study of the lifting map $\Phi : \mathcal{P}(X) \to \mathcal{H}$ is the object of our immediate research, in order to understand the geometry induced by the proposed metric and the asymptotic properties of the developed distances.

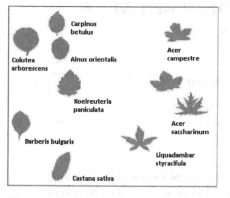
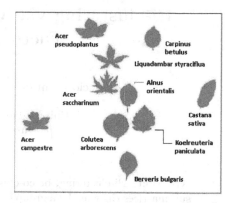

Fig. 3. MDS representation for leaf database based on WLS (a); Energy distance (b)

Acknowledgments. This work was partially supported by projects **MIC 2012/ 00084/00, ECO2012-38442, DGUCM 2008/00058/002** and **MEC 2007/04438/001**.

References

1. Ahlbrandt, C., Benson, G., Casey, W.: Minimal entropy probability paths between genome families. J. Math. Biol. 48(5), 563–590 (2004)
2. Dryden, I.L., Koloydenko, A., Zhou, D.: The Earth Mover's Distance as a Metric for Image Retrieval. Internat. Journal of Comp. Vision 40, 99–121 (2000)
3. Institute of Information Theory and Automation ASCR. LEAF - Tree Leaf Database. Prague, Czech Republic, http://zoi.utia.cas.cz/tree_leaves
4. Müller, A.: Integral Probability Metrics and Their Generating Classes of Functions. Advances in Applied Probability 29(2), 429–443 (1997)
5. Muñoz, A., Moguerza, J.M.: Estimation of High-Density Regions using One-Class Neighbor Machines. IEEE Trans. on Pattern Analysis and Machine Intelligence 28(3), 476–480 (2006)
6. Nguyen, X., Wainwright, M.J., Jordan, M.I.: Nonparametric Estimimation of the Likelihood and Divergence Functionals. In: IEEE International Symposium on Information Theory (2007)
7. Otey, E., Parthasarathy, S.: A dissimilarity measure for comparing subsets of data: application to multivariate time series. In: Fifth IEEE International Conference on Data Mining, pp. 101–112 (2005)
8. Phillips, J., Venkatasubramanian, S.: A gentle introduction to the kernel distance. arXiv preprint, arXiv:1103.1625 (2011)
9. Rubner, Y., Tomasi, C., Guibas, L.J.: A Metric for Distributions with Applications to Image Databases. In: Sixth IEEE Conf. on Computer Vision, pp. 59–66 (1998)
10. Sriperumbudur, B.K., Gretton, A., Fukumizu, K., Scholkopf, B.: Hilbert Space Embeddings and Metrics on Probability Measures. Journal of Machine Learning Research, 1297–1322 (2010)
11. Sriperumbudur, B.K., Fukumizu, K., Gretton, A., Scholkopf, B., Lanckriet, G.R.G.: Non-parametric estimation of integral probability metrics. In: International Symposium on Information Theory (2010)
12. Székely, G.J., Rizzo, M.L.: Testing for Equal Distributions in High Dimension. InterStat (2004)

Bi-clustering via MDL-Based Matrix Factorization

Ignacio Ramírez[1] and Mariano Tepper[2]

[1] Universidad de la República
[2] Duke University

Abstract. Bi-clustering, or co-clustering, refers to the task of finding sub-matrices (indexed by a group of columns and a group of rows) within a matrix such that the elements of each sub-matrix are related in some way, for example, that they are similar under some metric. As in traditional clustering, a crucial parameter in bi-clustering methods is the number of groups that one expects to find in the data, something which is not always available or easy to guess. The present paper proposes a novel method for performing bi-clustering based on the concept of low-rank sparse non-negative matrix factorization (S-NMF), with the additional benefit that the optimum rank k is chosen automatically using a minimum description length (MDL) selection procedure, which favors models which can represent the data with fewer bits. This MDL procedure is tested in combination with three different S-NMF algorithms, two of which are novel, on a simulated example in order to assess the validity of the procedure.

1 Introduction

Given a set of data vectors arranged as columns (rows) of a matrix, traditional data clustering corresponds to the task of finding groups of similar columns (rows) within that matrix. Bi-clustering, or co-clustering, refers to the task of finding sub-matrices (indexed by a group of columns and a group of rows) within a matrix such that the elements of each sub-matrix are related in some way. This idea has been widely applied in the last ten years as a powerful tool to analyze data of many kinds, a notorious example being micro-array analysis, where correlations between groups of genes and expression patterns are sought.

Finding the clusters usually involves identifying subsets of row and column indexes so that the indexed sub-matrices exhibit some regularity, for example, that their elements have a constant value, or that their rows, or columns, are identical. As examples of other measures of regularity, the reader can refer to [1]. As a more general problem (that applies to traditional clustering as well), the very number of clusters present in the data may not be known, or assumed, *a priori*.

The present work presents a method to perform bi-clustering under the hypothesis that each sub-matrix is a rank-1 component of the assignment matrix. Assuming that such components are non-negative, something usually required

J. Ruiz-Shulcloper and G. Sanniti di Baja (Eds.): CIARP 2013, Part I, LNCS 8258, pp. 230–237, 2013.

for the resulting models to have physical interpretability, leads to the well known concept of *non-negative matrix factorization* (NMF) [2]. Further assuming that the sub-matrices have a small number of non-zero elements leads to a *sparse* NMF model (S-NMF) [3].

The technique presented here combines S-NMF with a model selection technique, MDL [4], to *automatically infer the proper number of groups from the data*, an idea that has already been proposed for model selection in bi-clustering, albeit using a different formulation, in [5]. To perform S-NMF, we resort to two variants of the well known *sparse dictionary learning* paradigm [6,7], which is based on penalized regression subproblems to impose sparsity on the colums/rows of $\mathbf{U}/\mathbf{V}$, and the sparse SVD technique employed in [8]. We demonstrate the performance of the three resulting methods on a simulated experiment from computer vision [8].

Details on the involved techniques, as well as the formalization of the problem, and the relationship to prior art, are given in Section 2. We then develop our main contribution on Section 3, and show the performance of the developed technique on Section 4, leavning the conclusions to Section 5.

2   Background and Prior Art

Consider a data matrix $\mathbf{X} \in \mathbb{R}^{m \times n}$. We define $\mathcal{I} = \{1, 2, \ldots, m\}$ and $\mathcal{J} = \{1, d, \ldots, n\}$ as the sets of row and column indexes of $\mathbf{X}$ respectively. Given $I \subseteq \mathcal{I}$ and $J \subseteq \mathcal{J}$, we define a bi-cluster as the set $G = I \times J$, the Cartesian product of those two sets, and refer to the associated sub-matrix of $\mathbf{X}$ indexed by G, $\mathbf{X}_{[G]} = \{x_{ij}\}_{i \in I, j \in J}$. We define by $C = \{G_1, G_2, \ldots, G_c\}, G_k = I_k \times J_k$ the set of bi-clusters defined by some method. Note that $\{I_k : k = 1, \ldots, c\}$, $\{J_k : 1, \ldots c\}$ and C need not be partitions of, respectively, $\mathcal{I}$, $\mathcal{J}$ and $\mathcal{I} \times \mathcal{J}$; that is, bi-clusters may overlap.

Several techniques have been developed for performing bi-clustering. The differences among them being primarily the assumptions made about the data. We refer the reader to the recent surveys [1] for details on them. A number of them are based on the NMF idea [2], that is, that the data matrix $\mathbf{X}$ is the product of two other matrices $\mathbf{U} \in \mathbb{R}^{m \times p}$ and $\mathbf{V} \in \mathbb{R}^{p \times n}$ plus some perturbation $\mathbf{E}$, $\mathbf{X} = \mathbf{UV} + \mathbf{E}$. In the context of NMF-based bi-clustering, one usually associates each k-th cluster to a corresponding pair of column $\mathbf{u}_k$ and row $\mathbf{v}^k$ vectors (observe the indexing notation), so that the NMF decomposition is expressed as

$$\mathbf{X} = \sum_{k=1}^{c} \mathbf{u}_k \mathbf{v}^k + \mathbf{E} \tag{1}$$

The use of the general NMF model (1) stretches well beyond bi-clustering, so that the above formulation does not help in identifying the clusters, but only rank-1 components (each $\mathbf{u}_k \mathbf{v}^k$). In order to obtain a useful bi-clustering, one needs to further assume that only a few elements in $\mathbf{u}_k$ and $\mathbf{v}^k$ are non-zero, so that the support of such vectors define the index subsets, $I_k = \text{supp}(\mathbf{u})_k$ and

$J_k = \mathrm{supp}(\mathbf{v}^k)$. This leads to the idea of S-NMF, which admits several variants. One of them is the so-called *sparse modeling* one, where $\mathbf{V}$ is assumed column-sparse. The Sparse Principal Component Analysis (SPCA) technique developed in [9] belongs to this category. In the context of bi-clustering, the "all-sparse" technique developed in [3] has been applied for example in [10] with significant success. Finally, on the same line of work of this paper, [8] propose a multi-stage sparse SVD for bi-clustering with multi-model estimation as the target application.

In [3,10], sparsity is measured (and controlled) via a *sparseness* statistic which measures, indirectly, the number of non-zero entries in a data vector. The factorization problem is then expressed as an optimization problem constrained on the sparseness of the columns and rows of $\mathbf{U}$ and $\mathbf{V}$. The advantage of this approach is that sparsity is controlled in an indirect way that does not provide any types of guarantees regarding the recovery of correct sparse components in situations where those can be assumed to exist. Also, the degree of sparsity, as well as the number c of factors involved in the decomposition, are parameters which have a great impact on the effectiveness of the solution, and at the same time are challenging to tune.

3   Proposed Method

The main contribution of this work is an MDL-based method for selecting the optimum number of factors in an S-NMF decomposition which is guided by an objective criterion: to obtain a representation which yields the most compressed representation of the data. The method is similar in spirit to the also MDL-based [5], but uses exact codelengths for the data type at hand rather than an approximate expression for large sample sizes.

Our method is applied to three different numerical S-NMF techniques: the sparse SVD [11] used in [8], and two penalized regression-based dictionary learning methods, one using a ℓ_0 penalty, the other using a ℓ_1 regularizer. These are described next.

3.1   Sparse Matrix Factorization

Sparse SVD The standard SVD decomposition of a matrix $\mathbf{Y} \in \mathbb{R}^{m \times n}$ is given by $\mathbf{Y} = \mathbf{USV}^\mathsf{T}$, where $\mathbf{U}$ and $\mathbf{V}$ are orthonormal basis of $\mathbb{R}^m$ and $\mathbb{R}^n$ respectively, and $\mathbf{S}$ is a diagonal matrix of non-zero singular values. The sparse SVD [11] is a modification of the aforementioned decomposition where each column and row of $\mathbf{U}$ and $\mathbf{V}$ are forced to be sparse. This is a non-convex problem which is approximated by greedily extracting each i-th rank one component of $\mathbf{Y}$ as $\mathbf{u}_i\mathbf{v}_i^\mathsf{T}$ via the following formulation

$$(\mathbf{u}_i, \mathbf{v}_i) = \arg\min_{\alpha,\beta} \frac{1}{2} \|\mathbf{R}_i - \alpha\beta^\mathsf{T}\|_2 + \lambda_u \|\alpha\|_1 + \lambda_v \|\beta\|_1, \mathbf{R}_i = \mathbf{Y} - \sum_{l=1}^{i-1} \mathbf{u}_l\mathbf{v}_l^\mathsf{T}, \quad (2)$$

that is, the i-th rank one pair is obtained from the residual of $\mathbf{Y}$ after having extracted the previous $i - 1$ components.

Penalized Regression. Contrary to [3], and inspired by recent developments in sparse signal recovery (see [12] for a comprehensive review), we obtain sparse factors $\mathbf{U}$ and $\mathbf{V}$ by means of ℓ_ρ regularization,

$$(\hat{\mathbf{U}}, \hat{\mathbf{V}}) = \arg \min_{(\mathbf{U}, \mathbf{V})} \frac{1}{2} \|\mathbf{X} - \mathbf{U}\mathbf{V}\|_F^2 + \lambda_u \|\mathbf{U}\|_\rho + \lambda_v \|\mathbf{V}\|_\rho$$

$$\text{s.t.} \quad u_{ik} \geq 0, \ v_{kj} \geq 0 \ \forall i, j, k, \tag{3}$$

where $\|\cdot\|_F$ denotes Frobenius norm, and $\|\cdot\|_\rho$ denotes the ℓ_ρ norm of the vectorized matrix argument (that is, the sum of absolute values of the matrix). The problem (3) is non-convex in $(\mathbf{U}, \mathbf{V})$; but it is convex in $\mathbf{U}$ or $\mathbf{V}$ when the other is kept fixed when $\rho \geq 1$. As such, a common strategy to obtain a local minimum of (3) is to perform an alternate minimization between $\mathbf{U}$ and $\mathbf{V}$.

$$\mathbf{V}(t+1) = \arg \min_{\mathbf{V}} \frac{1}{2} \|\mathbf{X} - \mathbf{U}(t)\mathbf{V}\|_F^2 + \lambda_v \|\mathbf{V}\|_\rho \quad \text{s.t.} \quad v_{kj} \geq 0 \tag{4}$$

$$\mathbf{U}(t+1) = \arg \min_{\mathbf{U}} \frac{1}{2} \|\mathbf{X} - \mathbf{U}\mathbf{V}(t+1)\|_F^2 + \lambda_v \|\mathbf{U}\|_\rho \quad \text{s.t.} \quad u_{ik} \geq 0. \tag{5}$$

Note that the form of (5) is a transposed version of (4), so that both steps can be solved with exactly the same method. Note also that, in both cases, the problem is separable in the columns of $\mathbf{V}$ (rows of $\mathbf{U}$), which can greatly simplify the computations. For the case $\rho = 1$, we apply the Fast Iterative Soft Thresholding Algorithm (FISTA) [13] to each column of $\mathbf{V}$ (row of $\mathbf{U}$). For the case $\rho = 0$, we apply the Orthogonal Matching Pursuit (OMP) algorithm [14] to a constrained variant of (3) (and their corresponding alternate minimizations:

$$(\hat{\mathbf{U}}, \hat{\mathbf{V}}) = \arg \min_{(\mathbf{U}, \mathbf{V})} \frac{1}{2} \|\mathbf{X} - \mathbf{U}\mathbf{V}\|_F^2$$

$$\text{s.t.} \quad \|\mathbf{U}\|_\rho \leq \lambda_u \quad \|\mathbf{V}\|_\rho \leq \lambda_v, \quad u_{ik} \geq 0, \quad v_{kj} \geq 0, \quad \forall i, j, k, \tag{6}$$

3.2 Model Selection

As given above, all formulations (2) through (6) have three critical parameters to be dealt with: λ_u, λ_v and c, the number of factors (columns of $\mathbf{U}$, rows of $\mathbf{V}$). We select such values by posing the following model selection problem. (For simplicity of exposition, here we will consider $\lambda_u = \lambda_v = \lambda$, but in practice we optimize them independently). For a given pair of values (c, λ) we define a (local) solution to (3) as $(\mathbf{U}(c, \lambda), \mathbf{V}(c, \lambda), \mathbf{E}(c, \lambda))$. We then pose an hypothetical compression problem where the task is to describe $\mathbf{X}$ *losslessly* (that is, exactly) in terms of $(\mathbf{V}, \mathbf{U}, \mathbf{E})$. The model selection procedure then computes $(\mathbf{U}(c, \lambda), \mathbf{V}(c, \lambda), \mathbf{E}(c, \lambda))$ for different values of (c, λ) and keeps those that minimize the combined *codelenghts* (in bits) of those three components, $L(\mathbf{X}) = L(\mathbf{V}) + L(\mathbf{U}) + L(\mathbf{E})..$

From a modeling perspective, the bulk of the work at this point is to obtain expressions for the codelengths $L(\cdots)$ of each component. This is clearly a very data-dependent task. Here we will focus on the simple case of $\mathbf{X}$ being the binary assignment matrix used in the example of Section 4.

A first observation is that, since $\mathbf{X}$ is binary, the only error values that can occur are also binary, so that $\mathbf{E}$ will also be binary. More specifically, by denoting by $[[\cdot]]$ the element-wise binarization function that sets $[[a]] = 0$ if $a < 0.5$ and $[[a]] = 1$ otherwise, we can write $\mathbf{E} = \mathbf{X} \oplus [[\mathbf{UV}]]$. Under the usual assumption that the residual $\mathbf{E}$ is decorrelated, we then have that $\mathbf{E}$ can be described as a (one dimensional) IID Bernoulli sequence of values, which in turn can be efficiently described using an *enumerative code* [15].

As for $\mathbf{U}$ and $\mathbf{V}$, they may not be binary, but they are sparse. Furthermore, since their product will be binarized (thresholded) to produce an approximation to $\mathbf{X}$, we only need to describe them up to a precision q which suffices to preserve their binarized product. Therefore, we represent $\mathbf{U}$ (and $\mathbf{V}$) in two steps: first, the locations of the non-zero entries are encoded using the same enumerative code used for $\mathbf{E}$, and then the values of the non-zero entries are encoded using a uniform distribution between the integers 0 and Q_u (Q_v), where Q_u (Q_v) is the largest integer so that $qQ_u \geq \max \mathbf{U}$ (same for Q_v). Denoting by $\|\cdot\|_0$ the pseudo-norm that counts the number of non-zero elements in the argument, we then have a total cost function for the model selection problem:

$$L(\mathbf{X}) = \log_2 \binom{\|\mathbf{E}\|_0}{mn} + \log_2 mc + \log_2 cn$$
$$\log_2 \binom{\|\mathbf{U}\|_0}{mc} + \log_2(\|\mathbf{U}\|_0 Q_u) + \log_2 \binom{\|\mathbf{V}\|_0}{cn} + \log_2(\|\mathbf{V}\|_0 Q_v) \quad (7)$$

The total problem now involves the minimization of $L(\mathbf{X})$ in terms of three parameters: c, λ and q. The search for the best parameters is done in a nested fashion. Following a standard model selection approach, the order of the model (the number of clusters) c is the outermost loop, starting from $c = 0$, and increasing by one. For each fixed c, a solution is sought by optimizing for various values of λ and q. This part, in turn, is done by first obtaining a set of unquantized factors $\mathbf{V}$ and $\mathbf{U}$ for each candidate λ, and then evaluating (7) for different values of q. The innermost loop in q, and the evaluation of (7) are very fast operations. The real computational cost of the method comes from obtaining the unquantized pair $(\mathbf{U}, \mathbf{V})$ for each λ, which involves the alternating minimization algorithm (4)-(5), which are costly steps.

4   Experimental Results

Here we report on one of the simulated computer vision problems described in [8]. The task here is to find sets of aligned points which are mixed in a background of randomly scattered points. The ground truth consists of 11 line segments which are sampled (plus a small perturbation) 50 times, together with randomly sampled points, all within the 2D square $[-1, 1] \times [-1, 1]$. The total number of data points is 1100; those are shown in Fig. 1(b).

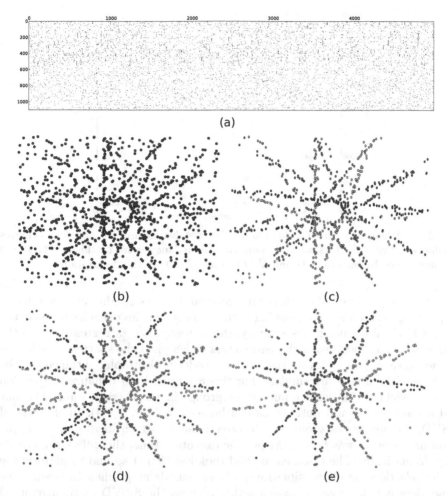

Fig. 1. Results for the line segment search problem. (a) Assignment data matrix, (b) data points, (c,d,e) final bi-clustering obtained using, respectively, ℓ_1, ℓ_0 and S-SVD: each color corresponds to one of the $c = 11$ blocks found by the algorithm. Each blocks groups together similar models (lines) which explain approximately the same points. Note that $c = 11$ is the correct number of total blocks as per the simulation. Here ℓ_0 (d) and S-SVD (e) give the best result, the latter yielding the correct number of clusters but including a few outliers, the former over-estimating the number of groups by $c = 13$ but doing a better job at rejecting outliers.

Each column j of the assignment matrix $\mathbf{X}$ (Figure 1(a)) is computed by selecting two points at random from the dataset, and setting x_{ij} to 1 or 0 if the i-th datapoint is respectively close (distance smaller than a given threshold τ) to the segment formed by those two points or not. This is performed $n = 5000$ times. A statistical tests is performed to remove all segments (columns of $\mathbf{X}$) for which the number of points assigned to them is too low (see [8] for details),

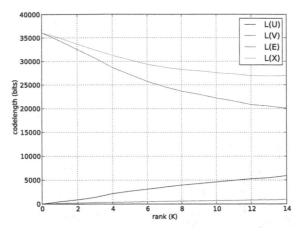

Fig. 2. Codelength vs rank for the sparse SVD case. Notice how the optimum achieves a balance between the bits saved by removing redundancy from **Y** (this is, $L(E)$) and the ones added by including **U** and **V** ($L(U)$ and $L(V)$) in the description.

and then the proposed algorithms are executed. Figures 1(c,d,e) are then drawn by plotting the points corresponding to the non-zero entries of each column of the matrix **U** obtained using, respectively, the ℓ_1 regression, ℓ_0 regression, and the sparse SVD methods, using the parameters which yield the shortest codelength in each case. Figure 2 shows the rank vs. codelength graphs obtained for the SVD case (the others are similar). For this example, both penalized regression methods yielded the correct number of groups in the original data (11), but had a tendency to add outliers, as can be seen in Figs. 2(c,d). In the case of S-SVD, the number of groups was over-estimated to 13 instead of 11, but the point assignments was better. As per the execution time, the different methods vary dramatically. The ℓ_0-based method took less than 1 second to perform the model selection for all possible ranges (all methods stop when increasing the range does not decrease the codelength), whereas the S-SVD method required about 30 seconds, and the ℓ_1 one required over an hour. The difference in speed here is due to ℓ_1-based optimization being much more expensive in general than ℓ_0 approximations. Clearly, which one is better will depend on the requirements of each case.

5   Conclusions

We have presented a novel method for bi-clustering that combines a non-negative matrix factorization with the powerful MDL model selection criterion for choosing the best model parameters. We have demonstrated the effectiveness of our approach for three different factorization methods. More results and a more in-depth analysis will be presented in a full article to be published elsewhere.

Acknowledgments. We acknowledge the support of Prof. Guillermo Sapiro from Duke University, Duke University, DHS/JHU and AFOSR.

References

1. Madeira, S., Oliveira, A.: Biclustering Algorithms for Biological Data Analysis: A Survey. IEEE Trans. CBB 1(1), 24–45 (2004)
2. Lee, D.D., Seung, H.S.: Learning the parts of objects by non-negative matrix factorization. Nature 401(6755), 7880–791 (1999)
3. Hoyer, P.: Non-negative matrix factorization with sparseness constraints. JMLR 5, 1457–1469 (2004)
4. Barron, A., Rissanen, J., Yu, B.: The minimum description length principle in coding and modeling. IEEE Trans. IT 44(6), 2743–2760 (1998)
5. Jornsten, R., Yu, B.: Simultaneous gene clustering and subset selection for sample classification via MDL. Bioinformatics 19(9), 1100–1109 (2003)
6. Olshausen, B.A., Field, D.J.: Sparse coding with an overcomplete basis set: A strategy employed by v1? Vision Research 37, 3311–3325 (1997)
7. Aharon, M., Elad, M., Bruckstein, A.: The K-SVD: An algorithm for designing of overcomplete dictionaries for sparse representations. IEEE Trans. SP 54(11), 4311–4322 (2006)
8. A bi-clustering formulation of multiple model estimation (submitted, 2013)
9. Zou, H., Hastie, T., Tibshirani, R.: Sparse Principal Component Analysis. Computational and Graphical Statistics 15(2), 265–286 (2006)
10. Hochreiter, S., Bodenhofer, U., Heusel, M., Mayr, A., Mitterecker, A., Kasim, A., Adetayo, K., Tatsiana, S., Suzy, V., Lin, D., Talloen, W., Bijnens, L., Shkedy, Z.: FABIA: factor analysis for biclustering acquisition. Bioinformatics 26(12), 1520–1527 (2010)
11. Lee, M., Shen, H., Huang, J.Z., Marron, J.S.: Biclustering via sparse singular value decomposition. Biometrics 66(4), 1087–1095 (2010)
12. Bruckstein, A.M., Donoho, D.L., Elad, M.: From Sparse Solutions of Systems of Equations to Sparse Modeling of Signals and Images. SIAM Review 51(1), 34–81 (2009)
13. Beck, A., Teboulle, M.: A Fast Iterative Shrinkage-Thresholding Algorithm for Linear Inverse Problems. SIAM Journal on Imaging Sciences 2(1), 183–202 (2009)
14. Pati, Y.C., Rezaiifar, R., Krishnaprasad, P.S.: Orthogonal Matching Pursuit: Recursive function approximation with applications to wavelet decomposition. In: Proc. 27th Ann. Asilomar Conf. Signals, Systems, and Computers (1993)
15. Cover, T.M.: Enumerative source coding. IEEE Trans. Inform. Theory 19, 73–77 (1973)

Kernel Spectral Clustering for Dynamic Data

Diego Hernán Peluffo-Ordóñez, Sergio García-Vega,
Andrés Marino Álvarez-Meza, and César Germán Castellanos-Domínguez

Universidad Nacional de Colombia, Sede Manizales
Signal Processing and Recognition Group
km 7 vía al Magdalena, Colombia
{dhpeluffoo,segarciave,amalvarezme,cgcastellanosd}@unal.edu.co
http://portal.manizales.unal.edu.co/gta/signal/

Abstract. This paper introduces a novel spectral clustering approach based on kernels to analyze time-varying data. Our approach is developed within a multiple kernel learning framework, which, in this case is assumed as a linear combination model. To perform such linear combination, weighting factors are estimated by a ranking procedure yielding a vector calculated from the eigenvectors-derived-clustering-method. Particularly, the method named kernel spectral clustering is considered. Proposed method is compared to some conventional spectral clustering techniques, namely, kernel k-means and min-cuts. Standard k-means as well. The clustering performance is quantified by the normalized mutual information and Adjusted Rand Index measures. Experimental results prove that proposed approach is an useful tool for both tracking and clustering dynamic data, being able to manage applications for human motion analysis.

Keywords: Dynamic data, kernels, support vector machines, spectral clustering.

1   Introduction

Undoubtedly, an emergent issue that has become of great interest today for the scientific community on pattern recognition and machine learning is the analysis of the evolutionary or dynamic behavior of time-varying data. There is a lot of highly important applications in which a dynamic analysis is needed, such as human motion analysis and people identification [1], image segmentation [2] and video analysis [3], among others. In this connection, clustering represents a good alternative since it allows for grouping and/or ranking data, mainly, when dealing with unlabeled problems. Due to its versatility, applicability and feasibility, it has been preferred in many approaches. In the literature, many recommended approaches the use of kernels since they allow to incorporate prior knowledge into the clustering procedure. However, the design of a whole kernel-based clustering scheme able to group time-varying data achieving a high accuracy is still an open issue. Taking advantage of kernel-based formulations, some works have been proposed to manage the temporal information for clustering, mainly in segmentation of human motion [4]. Other approaches include either the design of dynamic kernels for clustering [5] or a dynamic kernel principal component analysis (KPCA) based model [6]. Also, another study [7] introduces a variation of the primal

J. Ruiz-Shulcloper and G. Sanniti di Baja (Eds.): CIARP 2013, Part I, LNCS 8258, pp. 238–245, 2013.
© Springer-Verlag Berlin Heidelberg 2013

functional of a KPCA formulation for spectral clustering to incorporate the memory effect.

In this paper, aiming to consider the temporal effect of dynamic data, we introduce a spectral clustering approach based on multiple kernel learning. Our approach consists of a variation of the so-called kernel spectral clustering (KSC), introduced in [8], which is a KPCA formulation from least-square support vector machines for clustering being useful to group hardly separable data. It allows for out-of-samples extensions [9]. Multiple kernel learning (MKL) emerges from the premise that the learning can be enhanced when using a set of kernels instead of an unique kernel [10].The MKL here considered is a linear combination of kernels. Then, after computing the kernel matrices from an input data sequence – in which each data matrix represents a frame – , a cumulative kernel matrix is calculated as a linear combination of the previously obtained kernels. The weighting factors for such linear combinations are estimated by ranking each sample contained in the frame. Needed ranking is accomplished by combining the relevance procedure proposed in [11] as well as the MKL approach presented in [2]. This ranking approach is detailed in [12], in which it is used as a tracking approach. Experiments are carried out using a subject from Graphics Lab Motion Capture Database from Carnegie Mellon University. For comparison purposes, some conventional spectral clustering techniques are also considered, namely, kernel k-means (KKM) and min-cuts (MC) [13]. Also, standard k-means is considered. The normalized mutual information [14] and Adjusted Rand Index [15] metrics are used to quantify the clustering performance.

2   Kernel Spectral Clustering (KSC)

Let $X = [x_1^\top, \ldots, x_N^\top]^\top$ be a data matrix, where $X \in \mathbb{R}^{N \times d}$ and $x_i \in \mathbb{R}^d$, $\Phi \in \mathbb{R}^{N \times d_h}$, $\Phi = [\phi(x_1)^\top, \ldots, \phi(x_N)^\top]^\top$, $\phi(\cdot)$ is a function mapping data from the original dimension to a higher one d_h, that is $\phi(\cdot) : \mathbb{R}^d \to \mathbb{R}^{d_h}$. Then, projection matrix $E \in \mathbb{R}^{N \times n_e}$ is grounded in a latent variable model in the form $E = \Phi W + 1_N \otimes b^\top$, where $\otimes$ denotes the Kronecker product, vector b holds the bias terms and n_e denotes the number of considered support vectors. Therefore, the kernel spectral clustering introduced in [9] is aimed to maximize the following expression:

$$\max_{E, W, \Gamma} \quad \frac{1}{2N} \operatorname{tr}(E^\top V E \Gamma) - \frac{1}{2} \operatorname{tr}(W^\top W) \tag{1a}$$

$$\text{s.t.} \quad E = \Phi W + 1_N \otimes b^\top \tag{1b}$$

where $\operatorname{tr}(\cdot)$ denotes the trace, $\Gamma = \operatorname{Diag}([\gamma_1, \ldots, \gamma_{n_e}])$, $W \in \mathbb{R}^{d_h \times n_e}$, where $W = [w^{(1)}, \cdots, w^{(n_e)}]$ and $E \in \mathbb{R}^{N \times n_e}$, $E = [e^{(1)}, \cdots, e^{(n_e)}]$. Problem stated in (1), after forming a Lagrangian and applying the Karush-Kuhn-Tucker conditions becomes to the following dual problem:

$$A \Lambda = V H \Phi \Phi^\top A, \tag{2}$$

where $\Lambda = \operatorname{Diag}(\lambda_1, \ldots, \lambda_{n_e})$ is a diagonal matrix formed by the eigenvalues $\lambda_l = N/\gamma_l$, matrix $H \in \mathbb{R}^{N \times N}$ is the centering matrix that is defined as $H = I_N - 1/(1_N^\top V 1_N) 1_N 1_N^\top V$, where I_N a N-dimensional identity matrix.

From the Mercer's conditions, we have that $\boldsymbol{\Phi}\boldsymbol{\Phi}^\top = \boldsymbol{\Omega}$, where $\boldsymbol{\Omega} \in \mathbb{R}^{N \times N}$ is a kernel matrix such that its entries are given by $\Omega_{ij} = \mathcal{K}(\boldsymbol{x}_i, \boldsymbol{x}_j), i, j \in [N]$. Therefore, projections can be calculated as follows:

$$E = \boldsymbol{\Omega} A + \boldsymbol{1}_N \otimes \boldsymbol{b}^\top \qquad (3)$$

According to [9], by binaryzing the projection matrix E, we obtain a code book $\widetilde{E}$ as $\widetilde{E} = \operatorname{sgn}(E)$, where $\operatorname{sgn}(\cdot)$ is the sign function. Thus, its corresponding rows are codewords, which allow to form the clusters according to the minimal Hamming distance.

3   Dynamic Kernel Spectral Clustering

Dynamic Kernel Spectral Clustering (DKSC), which is an approach based on Kernel Spectral Clustering (KSC) and Multiple Kernel Learning (MKL), works, as follows: Given a sequence of data matrices $\{\boldsymbol{X}^{(1)}, \dots, \boldsymbol{X}^{(N_f)}\}$, being $\boldsymbol{X}^{(t)} = [\boldsymbol{x}_1^{(t)\top}, \dots, \boldsymbol{x}_N^{(t)\top}]^T$ the data matrix at instance time t, N_{fm} the number of input data (frames), then the corresponding kernel matrices are calculated $\{\boldsymbol{\Omega}^{(1)}, \dots, \boldsymbol{\Omega}^{(N_f)}\}$ with $\Omega_{ij}^{(t)} = \mathcal{K}(\boldsymbol{x}_i^{(t)}, \boldsymbol{x}_j^{(t)})$.

Afterwards, MKL is applied with the purpose to obtain accumulated kernel, as a result of the relation between kernel functions and weighting factors (calculated previously). Finally, assuming a certain number of clusters K, KSC is applied. Since the accumulated kernel matrix is used, the information of the frame at instance T contains the information of the previous ones. Hence, this approach can be called as dynamic.

3.1   Multiple Kernel Learning (MKL)

Here, multiple kernel learning is applied to obtain a linear combination of all the input kernel matrices until the current matrix. At instance T, the cumulative kernel matrix is computed as follows:

$$\check{\boldsymbol{\Omega}}^{(T)} = \sum_{t=1}^{T} \eta_t \boldsymbol{\Omega}^{(t)} \qquad (4)$$

where $\eta = [\eta_1, \dots, \eta_T]$ are the weighting factors or coefficients and $\boldsymbol{\Omega}^{(t)}$ is the kernel matrix associated to $\boldsymbol{X}^{(t)}$ such that $\Omega_{ij}^{(t)} = \mathcal{K}(\boldsymbol{x}_i^{(t)}, \boldsymbol{x}_j^{(t)})$. Nonetheless, the cumulative kernel matrix can be also calculated in a recursive fashion as: $\check{\boldsymbol{\Omega}}^{(T)} = \check{\boldsymbol{\Omega}}^{(T-1)} + \eta_T \boldsymbol{\Omega}^{(T)}$ with $\check{\boldsymbol{\Omega}}^{(0)} = \boldsymbol{0}_{N \times N}$.

3.2   Weighting Factors

The basic idea is to obtain the ranked values for samples, here, termed tracking vector that works as follow: first, we apply clustering to the input data by means KSC; at this step, it is necessary to establish manually the number of clusters previously and the kernel function, after we linearly project the high dimensional representation of input data (to obtain a sample relevance ranking process). Then, the projection matrix is obtained as a sparse solution of a quadratic optimization problem, where an energy term is maximized and, finally, a tracking vector is obtained by a linear combination of vectors solving such optimization problem.

Consider the frame matrix $\mathcal{X} \in \mathbb{R}^{N_f \times Nd}$ where, $\mathcal{X} = [\tilde{x}_1^\top, \dots, \tilde{x}_{N_f}^\top]^\top$ and $\tilde{x}_t = \text{vec}(X^{(t)})$. The corresponding kernel matrix can be expressed as $\widetilde{\Omega} \in \mathbb{R}^{N_f \times N_f}$ such that $\widetilde{\Omega}_{ij} = \mathcal{K}(\tilde{x}_i, \tilde{x}_j)$. Then, the high dimensional representation matrix $\widetilde{\Phi} \in \mathbb{R}^{N_f \times d_h}$ is $\widetilde{\Phi} = [\phi(\tilde{x}_1)^\top, \dots, \phi(\tilde{x}_{N_f})^\top]^\top$, where $\phi(\cdot) : \mathbb{R}^{Nd} \to \mathbb{R}^{d_h}$. Moreover, we assume a linear projection in the form $Z = \widetilde{\Phi}^\top U$, where $U \in \mathbb{R}^{N_f \times N_f}$ is an orthonormal matrix. Likewise, a lower rank representation of Z is assumed in the form $\widehat{Z} = \widetilde{\Phi}^\top \widehat{U}$, where $\widehat{U} \in \mathbb{R}^{N_f \times c(c<N_f)}$. Therefore, an energy maximization problem can be written as:

$$\max_{\widehat{U}} \ \text{tr}(\widehat{U}^\top \widetilde{\Omega} \widehat{U}) \quad \text{s.t.} \quad \widehat{U}^\top \widehat{U} = I_c \tag{5a}$$

Indeed, by using the kernel trick, we have $\text{tr}(\widehat{Z}^\top \widehat{Z}) = \text{tr}(\widehat{U}^\top \widetilde{\Omega} \widehat{U})$. Furthermore, the KSC allows centering matrix for frame matrix $\mathcal{X}$. Therefore, normalizing regarding the degree and centering both Z and $\widehat{Z}$, which means to pre-multiply $\widetilde{\Phi}$ by $\widetilde{L} \widetilde{V}^{-1/2}$, we can infer that $\text{tr}(\widehat{U}^\top \widetilde{\Omega} \widehat{U}) = \sum_{t=1}^c \tilde{\lambda}_t$, where $\widetilde{L}$ comes from the Cholesky decomposition of $\widetilde{H}$ such that $\widetilde{L}^\top \widetilde{L} = \widetilde{H}$ and $\tilde{\lambda}_l$ is the l-th eigenvalue obtained by KSC when applied over $\mathcal{X}$ with a determined number of clusters $\widetilde{K}$. Therefore, a feasible solution of the problem is $U = \widetilde{A}$, being $\widetilde{A} = [\tilde{\alpha}^{(1)}, \dots, \tilde{\alpha}^{(c)}]$ the corresponding eigenvector matrix. Thus, c is the same number of considered support vectors $\tilde{n}_e$.

We introduce a tracking vector $\eta \in \mathbb{R}^{N_f}$ as the solution of minimizing the dissimilarity term given by $\|\widetilde{\Phi} - \widehat{\Phi}\|_F^2$, subject to some orthogonality conditions, being $\widehat{\Phi}$ a lower-rank representation of $\widetilde{\Phi}$. Then, the ranked vector can be calculated by:

$$\eta = \sum_{\ell=1}^{\tilde{n}_e} \tilde{\lambda}_\ell \tilde{\alpha}^{(\ell)} \circ \tilde{\alpha}^{(\ell)} \tag{6}$$

where $\circ$ denotes Hadamard (element-wise) product. Accordingly, the ranking factor η_t is a single value representing an unique frame in a sequence. Notation $\tilde{a}$ means that variable a is related to $\widetilde{\Omega}$. Finally, it is possible to normalize the vector by multiplying it by $1/\max |\eta|$ to keep the entries of η ranged into the interval $[0,1]$.

3.3 Clustering

The proposed DKSC works as follows: Let $\{X^{(1)}, \dots, X^{(N_f)}\}$ be a sequence of data matrices, being N_f the number of frames, the corresponding kernel matrices are computed with $\Omega_{ij}^{(t)} = \mathcal{K}(x_i^{(t)}, x_j^{(t)})$. Then, the weighting factor η is calculated from equation 6 over the frame matrix $\mathcal{X}$. Further, we obtain the accumulated kernel matrices $\{\check{\Omega}^{(1)}, \dots, \check{\Omega}^{(N_f)}\}$ and, lastly, the KSC is applied over each pair $(X^{(t)}, \check{\Omega}^{(t)})$, where $t \in \{1, \dots, N_f\}$, achieving as a result the cluster assignment vector $\check{q}_{\text{train}}^{(t)}$.

4   Experimental Set-Up

4.1   Considered Database

Motion caption Database: The data used in this work was obtained from mocap.cs. cmu.edu. The database was created with funding from NSF EIA-0196217. In this work, we use the *subject #1* (progressive jump), for which the three first jumps are considered as shown Figure 1.

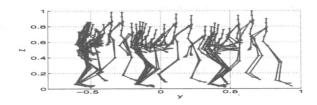

Fig. 1. Subject #1 (progressive jump)

Four frames are considered, where each frame $X^{(t)} \in \mathbb{R}^{160 \times 114}$ has rows containing the vectorization of coordinates X, Y, and Z of the subject's body points. Therefore $\hat{x}_i \in \mathbb{R}^{1 \times 18240}$ and $\mathcal{X} \in \mathbb{R}^{4 \times 18240}$. Data matrices from the above database are z-score normalized regarding their columns.

4.2   Applying DKSC

All the experiments are performed for a given set of initial parameters, that is, the number of clusters K per each frame and the kernel function parameter. To recognize three underlying movements in Motion Caption database (*subject #1*), parameter K is set to be 3. Kernel matrices associated to the data sequence are calculated by the local-scaled Gaussian kernel [16]. Then, each entry of kernel matrix related to frame t is given by: $\Omega_{ij}^{(t)} = \mathcal{K}(x_i, x_j) = \exp(-\|x_i - x_j\|_2^2/\sigma_i\sigma_j)$, where $\|\cdot\|$ denotes the Euclidean norm and the scale parameter σ_i is chosen as the Euclidean distance between the sample x_i and its corresponding m-th nearest neighbor. Free parameter m is empirically set as that one supplying the greatest Fisher's criterion value. For both databases, the value $m = 10$ is adjusted. To compute the lower-rank matrix $\hat{\Omega}$, a scaled Gaussian kernel is applied. Afterwards, the clustering for the pair $(\mathcal{X}, \hat{\Omega})$ is carried out by setting the number $K = N_{fm}$ whereas m is fixed as the entire closest number to $0.1N_{fm}$ in case of Motion Caption.

In order to numerically assess the performance of DKSC against other methods, we suggest an estimation of the ground truth. Since the tracking vector plotting depicts a concave mode for each identified dynamic event, we can suggest that the ground truth can be estimated by detecting the beginning and ending of each mode. In this sense, as seen from Fig. 2, we apply a Gaussian fitting process where each mean μ_k is located

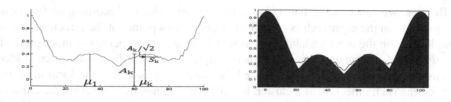

Fig. 2. Gaussian fitting process

at that entry t of η showing maximum value A_k. Likewise, the standard deviation s_k is the distance between μ_k and the entry corresponding to $A_k/\sqrt{2}$.

For comparison purposes, kernel K-means (KKM) and min-cuts(MC) are also considered [13], which are applied over the data sequence by considering the same MKL approach as considered for KSC. The clustering performance is evaluated by two metrics: normalized mutual information (NMI) [14] and Adjusted Rand Index (ARI) [15]. Both metrics return values ranged into the interval $[0, 1]$, where 1 is the best clustering performance.

5   Results and Discussion

Motion caption database has not a ground truth to apply label-based metric to assess the clustering performance. However, because weighting factors η are ranking values related to samples, we can consider each instant (man position) as a sample. Then, KSC can be applied to generate the eigenvectors needed to compute η. If analyzing each jump separately, corresponding η vectors should provide information about the clusters contained in the frame (jump). Figure 3 shows the η vector corresponding to each jump.

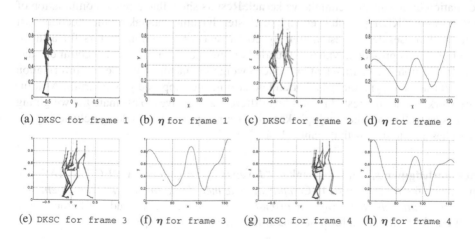

(a) DKSC for frame 1   (b) η for frame 1   (c) DKSC for frame 2   (d) η for frame 2

(e) DKSC for frame 3   (f) η for frame 3   (g) DKSC for frame 4   (h) η for frame 4

Fig. 3. MKL weighting factors

Besides, we can observe that η has a multi-modal shape. According to (6), η is computed from the eigenvectors $\alpha^{(l)}$. Such eigenvectors point out the direction where samples having the most variability measured in terms of a generalized inner product ($\Phi^\top \Phi$). Then, we can argue that each mode might represent a different cluster. Under this assumption, we obtain the reference label vectors by detecting the local minima, considering each inflection as a cluster. Results are obtained by comparing the clustering indicators of each method with the determined reference labels. It can be appreciated in Table 1 that our approach reaches greater values than the other methods, then in terms of NMI and ARI it is possible to affirm that DKSC and KSC are suitable approaches to cluster frames in this kind of applications.

Table 1. Clustering performance

Measure	Frame	Clustering Method			
		DKSC	KKM	KM	MC
NMI	1	0.6545	0.6583	0.6610	0.7537
	2	0.9046	0.9186	0.7527	0.9046
	3	0.8839	0.9028	0.6245	0.9045
	4	0.8533	0.8498	0.5993	0.5780
ARI	1	0.6583	0.6583	0.6800	0.6832
	2	0.9140	0.9304	0.7468	0.9140
	3	0.9054	0.9060	0.4372	0.9238
	4	0.8680	0.8542	0.4827	0.5101

6 Conclusions

A spectral clustering approach for time varying data is introduced. In this sense, the proposed approach is based on multiple kernel learning to keep the evolutionary information by means of a cumulative kernel. Results show that a linear combination of kernels as a MKL approach is enough to cluster dynamic data taking into account past information. Besides, an estimation for coefficients or weighting factors for a linear combination is provided, which is founded on the spectrum of kernel spectral clustering. In addition, we verified that introduced weighting factors give relevant information to both track the dynamic behavior and determine the supposed ground truth. As a future work, we are interested in studying different alternatives to estimate the weighting factors as well as another multiple kernel learning approaches to design clustering approaches able to deal with dynamic data.

Acknowledgments. Authors thank to *"Jóvenes Investigadores"* COLCIENCIAS program with the project entitled *"Comparativo de métodos kernel para agrupamiento espectral de datos desde un enfoque primal-dual"*(A comparative study of kernel-based methods for primal-dual formulations aimed spectral clustering).

References

1. Cong, D.N.T., Khoudour, L., Achard, C., Meurie, C., Lezoray, O.: People re-identification by spectral classification of silhouettes. Signal Processing 90(8), 2362–2374 (2010)
2. Rodrigues, M., Gama, J., Ferreira, C.A.: Identifying relationships in transactional data. In: Pavón, J., Duque-Méndez, N.D., Fuentes-Fernández, R. (eds.) IBERAMIA 2012. LNCS, vol. 7637, pp. 81–90. Springer, Heidelberg (2012)
3. Zhang, D.Q., Lin, C.Y., Chang, S.F., Smith, J.R.: Semantic video clustering across sources using bipartite spectral clustering. In: 2004 IEEE International Conference on Multimedia and Expo, ICME 2004, vol. 1, pp. 117–120. IEEE (2004)
4. Takács, B., Butler, S., Demiris, Y.: Multi-agent behaviour segmentation via spectral clustering. In: Proceedings of the AAAI-2007, PAIR Workshop, pp. 74–81 (2007)
5. Keshet, J., Bengio, S.: Automatic speech and speaker recognition: Large margin and kernel methods. Wiley (2009)
6. Maestri, M.L., Cassanello, M.C., Horowitz, G.I.: Kernel pca performance in processes with multiple operation modes. Chemical Product and Process Modeling 4(5), 7 (2009)
7. Langone, R., Alzate, C., Suykens, J.A.: Kernel spectral clustering with memory effect. Physica A: Statistical Mechanics and its Applications (2013)
8. Alzate, C., Suykens, J.A.K.: A weighted kernel PCA formulation with out-of-sample extensions for spectral clustering methods. In: International Joint Conference on Neural Networks, IJCNN 2006, pp. 138–144. IEEE (2006)
9. Alzate, C., Suykens, J.A.K.: Multiway spectral clustering with out-of-sample extensions through weighted kernel pca. IEEE Transactions on Pattern Analysis and Machine Intelligence 32(2), 335–347 (2010)
10. Huang, H.C., Chuang, Y.Y., Chen, C.S.: Multiple kernel fuzzy clustering. IEEE Transactions on Fuzzy Systems 20(1), 120–134 (2012)
11. Wolf, L., Shashua, A.: Feature selection for unsupervised and supervised inference: The emergence of sparsity in a weight-based approach. J. Mach. Learn. Res. 6, 1855–1887 (2005)
12. Peluffo-Ordóñez, D., García-Vega, S., Castellanos-Domínguez, C.G.: Kernel spectral clustering for motion tracking: A first approach. In: Ferrández Vicente, J.M., Álvarez Sánchez, J.R., de la Paz López, F., Toledo Moreo, F. J. (eds.) IWINAC 2013, Part I. LNCS, vol. 7930, pp. 264–273. Springer, Heidelberg (2013)
13. Guo, C., Zheng, S., Xie, Y., Hao, W.: A survey on spectral clustering. In: World Automation Congress (WAC), pp. 53–56. IEEE (2012)
14. Strehl, A., Ghosh, J.: Cluster ensembles - a knowledge reuse framework for combining multiple partitions. Journal of Machine Learning Research 3, 583–617 (2002)
15. Hubert, L., Arabie, P.: Comparing partitions. Journal of Classification 1(2), 193–218 (1985)
16. Zelnik-manor, L., Perona, P.: Self-tuning spectral clustering. In: Advances in Neural Information Processing Systems 17, pp. 1601–1608. MIT Press (2004)

Feature Space Reduction
for Graph-Based Image Classification

Niusvel Acosta-Mendoza[1,2,*], Andrés Gago-Alonso[1],
Jesús Ariel Carrasco-Ochoa[2], José Francisco Martínez-Trinidad[2],
and José E. Medina-Pagola[1]

[1] Advanced Technologies Application Center (CENATAV),
7a ♯ 21406 e/ 214 and 216, Siboney, Playa, CP: 12200, Havana, Cuba
{nacosta,agago,jmedina}@cenatav.co.cu
[2] National Institute of Astrophysics, Optics and Electronics (INAOE),
Luis Enrique Erro No. 1, Sta. María Tonantzintla, Puebla, CP: 72840, Mexico
{ariel,fmartine}@inaoep.mx

Abstract. Feature selection is an essential preprocessing step for classifiers with high dimensional training sets. In pattern recognition, feature
selection improves the performance of classification by reducing the feature space but preserving the classification capabilities of the original
feature space. Image classification using frequent approximate subgraph
mining (FASM) is an example where the benefits of features selections
are needed. This is due using frequent approximate subgraphs (FAS)
leads to high dimensional representations. In this paper, we explore the
use of feature selection algorithms in order to reduce the representation
of an image collection represented through FASs. In our results we report a dimensionality reduction of over 50% of the original features and
we get similar classification results than those reported by using all the
features.

Keywords: Approximate graph mining, approximate graph matching,
feature selection, graph-based classification.

1 Introduction

Finding a discriminative subset of features is essential when there are high dimensional representations. Feature selection algorithms allow improving classifiers performance by reducing the feature space and keeping discrimination
capabilities of the original representation. The main idea of these algorithms is
to calculate a subset of the input features by removing those with little or no
predictive information for classification [3–6, 10, 15, 17, 19]. These algorithms
can be arranged into three main groups: wrapper algorithms [3], filter algorithms [6, 10, 19] and embedded algorithms [5, 17]. Wrapper ones use a classifier
to evaluate feature subsets. The advantage of these algorithms is the interaction between the feature subset search and the classifier, but it is an expensive

---

* Corresponding author.

J. Ruiz-Shulcloper and G. Sanniti di Baja (Eds.): CIARP 2013, Part I, LNCS 8258, pp. 246–253, 2013.
© Springer-Verlag Berlin Heidelberg 2013

process. Filter ones evaluate the feature subsets without involving any classifier during selection and, generally, they are faster than wrapper algorithms. Embedded ones combine the advantage of wrappers and filters including some interaction with the classifier.

FASM has become a technique of great significance in mining tasks where the frequent subgraphs are computed considering data distortions. The usefulness of the patterns computed by these algorithms has been shown in different classification tasks [1, 2, 12, 14]; but only a few of them have been applied to image classification [1, 2] outperforming the results of exact algorithms [7, 18]. However, using a large number of graphs (patterns) as features could affect the performance of the classifiers, due to the high dimensionality of the representation of the images.

In this paper, we explore the use of feature selection to reduce the representation of an image collection represented through FASs. Experiments show that our proposal allows drastically reducing the dimensionality of feature vector while getting competitive results compared with the method that uses all the features for classification. On the other hand, to the best of our knowledge, this is the first work that uses a fusion of FASM and feature selection algorithms for image classification.

The organization of this paper is the following. In Section 2, some basic concepts are presented. In Section 3, we describe how the feature selection is included into the framework for image classification using FASM. Later, in Section 4, some experiments are shown in order to empirically validate the efficiency and accuracy of feature selection for feature space reduction in graph-based image classification. Finally, our conclusions and future directions are discussed in Section 5.

2   Background

This work is focused on collections of simple undirected labeled graphs. Henceforth, when we refer to a graph we are assuming this type of graphs.

A *labeled graph* in the domain of all possible labels $L = L_V \cup L_E$, where L_V and L_E are the label sets for vertices and edges respectively, is a 4-tuple, $G = (V, E, I, J)$, where V is a set whose elements are called *vertices*, $E \subseteq \{\{u,v\} \mid u, v \in V, u \neq v\}$ is a set whose elements are called *edges* (the edge $\{u,v\}$ connects the vertex u with the vertex v), $I : V \to L_V$ is a *labeling function* for assigning labels to vertices and $J : E \to L_E$ is a *labeling function* for assigning labels to edges.

Let $G_1 = (V_1, E_1, I_1, J_1)$ and $G_2 = (V_2, E_2, I_2, J_2)$ be two graphs, we say that G_1 is a *subgraph* of G_2 if $V_1 \subseteq V_2$, $E_1 \subseteq E_2$, $\forall u \in V_1, I_1(u) = I_2(u)$, and $\forall e \in E_1, J_1(e) = J_2(e)$. In this case, we use the notation $G_1 \subseteq G_2$ and we also say that G_2 is a *supergraph* of G_1.

Given two graphs G_1 and G_2, we say that f is an *isomorphism* between these graphs if $f : V_1 \to V_2$ is a bijective function, where: $\forall u \in V_1 : f(u) \in V_2 \wedge I_1(u) = I_2(f(u))$, and $\forall \{u,v\} \in E_1 : \{f(u), f(v)\} \in E_2 \wedge J_1(\{u,v\}) = J_2(\{f(u), f(v)\})$.

If there is an isomorphism between G_1 and G_2, we say that G_1 and G_2 are *isomorphic*. If G_1 is isomorphic to G_3 and $G_3 \subseteq G_2$, then we say that there is a *sub-isomorphism* between G_1 and G_2, and we also say that G_1 is sub-isomorphic to G_2.

Let $D = \{G_1, \ldots, G_{|D|}\}$ be a collection of graphs and G be a labeled graph in L, the *support* value of G in D is defined as the fraction of graphs $G_i \in D$, such that there is a sub-isomorphism between G and G_i. This value of support is obtained using the following equation: $supp(G, D) = |\{G_i \in D : G$ is sub-isomorphic to $G_i\}|/|D|$

Let Ω be the set of all possible labeled graphs in L, the *similarity* between two graphs $G_1, G_2 \in \Omega$ is defined as a function $sim : \Omega \times \Omega \to [0, 1]$. We say that the graphs are very different if $sim(G_1, G_2) = 0$, the higher the value of $sim(G_1, G_2)$ the more similar the graphs are, and if $sim(G_1, G_2) = 1$ then there is an isomorphism between these graphs.

As there are several correspondences between two graphs, $sim_{max}(G_1, G_2) = max\{sim(G_1, G_2)\}$ is defined as the highest value of similarity which can be obtained between the different correspondences of G_1 and G_2.

Let $D = \{G_1, \ldots, G_{|D|}\}$ be a graph collection and G be a labeled graph in L, the approximate support (denoted by appSupp) value of G in D, in terms of the similarity, is computed as: $appSupp(G, D) = \sum_{G_i \in D} sim_{max}(G, G_i)/|D|$.

When $appSupp(G, D) \geq \delta$, then G is a *frequent approximate subgraph* (FAS) in D. The value of the support threshold δ is in $[0, 1]$ since the similarity is defined in $[0, 1]$. *Frequent approximate subgraph mining* consists in finding all the FAS in a collection of graphs D, using a similarity function sim and a support threshold δ.

3   Proposed Framework

Given a pre-labeled image collection, we built a graph collection for representing these images, following the same approach proposed in [1]. The FAS are obtained from the graphs that represent the images in the collection, using a FASM algorithm. These patterns (FAS) are used as features for representing each image of the collection. In fact, feature vectors for the original images are built using such patterns, in the same way as in [1], taking into account the similarity of each image of the collection (represented as a graph) to each pattern. Later, these feature vectors are reduced by using a feature selection algorithm (information gain, chi-squared, and gain ratio feature evaluation) in order to take into account only the selected features for classification.

Following the main idea of [1], the proposed framework for graph-based image classification including feature selection consist of four modules (see Figure 1): representation module, pattern extraction module, feature selection module, and classification module. Representation, pattern extraction and classification modules are the same ones respectively used in [1]. The feature selection module is the main contribution of our proposal. This module is introduced in order to identify better features for representing the classes of the image collection than those used in [1].

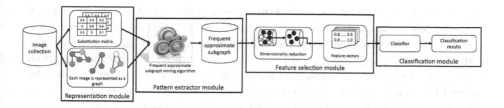

Fig. 1. The graph-based image classification framework proposed in this paper

4   Experiments

In this section, some experiments to show the impact of feature selection in graph-based image classification using FASM are presented. These experiments include a comparison between the framework for graph-based image classification including feature selection and the framework proposed in [1] which uses all the FASs for representing the images. The FASM algorithm, which we select to be used in the pattern extraction module for our experiments, is VEAM [1]. This decision was made based on the results reported in [1], where the use of patterns obtained taking into account distortion in vertex and edge labels, i.e. those computed by VEAM, are better for image classification than: those patterns found by APGM [14].

4.1   Databases

In order to compare the results obtained by our proposal against those reported in [1], the image collection used in this paper is the same. This collection consists of 700 images obtained by the Random image generator of Coenen[1]. These images are divided in two classes "landscape" and "seascape", according to their content. The process to represent these images as graphs is the same used in [1], which is based on quad-trees with 4 as depth limit for divisions. This collection was split into six sub-collections with different sizes: from 200 to 700 images with an increment of 100 images. All these collections contain 18 vertex labels, 24 edge labels and a mean graph size ranging between 43 to 47 in terms of the number of edges.

4.2   Experimental Results

The comparison presented in this section is performed over the graph collections detailed in Section 4.1. Once we have the FAS's computed by VEAM, a feature selection algorithm is used only once to obtain the feature subset that represents each class in the collection. Finally, this subset of features is used as input for a classifier using 10-fold cross-validation.

---

[1] www.csc.liv.ac.uk/~frans/KDD/Software/ImageGenerator/imageGenerator.html

In Table 1, six cells where each represents a collection database are shown. Each of these cells show a comparison between the number of features (patterns) used in the classification process. Four columns are grouped into each the mentioned cells, where the first of these columns shows the patterns computed by VEAM, the other three columns show the number of patterns that will be selected by each filter feature selector per each classifier algorithm. The number of features selected were obtained experimentally in a range [50,200], which resulted as the best options after carrying out several experiments. Finally, each classifier is specified in the last columns.

In our experiments, we use several classifiers to evaluate our proposal. These classifiers are of different nature: Support Vector Machine (SVM); Bayesian network (BayesNet); decision trees (J48graft); and boosting (AdaBoost). All these classifiers, except SVM, were taken from Weka v3.6.6 [9] using the default parameters. For SVM, we used the same libSVM used in [1]. Moreover, we use three filter feature selection algorithms: information gain (IG), chi-squared (CHI-Q), and gain ratio feature evaluation (GRAE). In these experiments, we compared the accuracy reached by selecting a feature subset computed by VEAM through a filter feature selector against the accuracy obtained by using all the features computed by VEAM as it is proposed in [1].

Table 1. Number of features used in the classification process

Coenen–200 ($\delta = 20\%$)				Coenen–300 ($\delta = 20\%$)				Coenen–400 ($\delta = 20\%$)				
All	IG	CHI-Q	GRAE	All	IG	CHI-Q	GRAE	All	IG	CHI-Q	GRAE	Classifier
	200	133	200		140	110	200		200	185	185	SVM
	110	80	95		125	110	125		125	80	65	BayesNet
340	155	125	155	374	140	50	140	433	140	150	150	AdaBoost
	133	110	110		125	140	155		125	110	140	J48graft
Coenen–500 ($\delta = 25\%$)				Coenen–600 ($\delta = 20\%$)				Coenen–700 ($\delta = 20\%$)				
All	IG	CHI-Q	GRAE	All	IG	CHI-Q	GRAE	All	IG	CHI-Q	GRAE	Classifier
	140	155	155		185	95	200		200	200	200	SVM
	65	50	50		155	65	50		65	80	65	BayesNet
238	155	101	110	498	95	80	125	864	65	65	155	AdaBoost
	95	101	95		65	200	125		200	200	200	J48graft

The results of our experiments are summarized in Table 2. This table is divided in two sub-tables, one for a pair of filter feature selectors. The first and second columns of these sub-tables show the name of the collection and the support threshold value that got the best results for this collection. The other eight columns are grouped in four, each group associated to a different supervised classifier, the first column in each group shows the accuracy obtained by using all the features (patterns) computed by VEAM, while the other three columns show the accuracy obtained by using a features selected by the filter feature selector specified in the top of the column.

As we can see in Table 2, the results achieved using our framework using feature selection are competitive in accuracy with those results using the framework proposed in [1], and it is important to highlight that our proposal uses less than 50% of features used by the framework proposed in [1] in most cases.

In addition, in Table 3 we present an statistical comparison of the tested classifiers using all the features (patterns) computed by VEAM against using the features selected by each one of the filter feature selectors. For this comparison, we use two significant statistical tests [8]: Holm [13], and Hommel [11] tests. The value for α used on these tests is 0.05.

Table 2. Accuracy results achieved using different classifiers in several graph (image) collections with and without the use of several feature selection algorithms.

Collection	δ	SVM (linear kernel)				BayesNet			
		All	IG	CHI-Q	GRAE	All	IG	CHI-Q	GRAE
Coenen–700	20%	95.86%	96.29%	**96.43%**	**96.43%**	90.29%	**94.57%**	**94.57%**	**94.57%**
Coenen–600	20%	95.83%	**96.50%**	96.17%	**96.50%**	91.17%	**94.83%**	94.67%	94.50%
Coenen–500	25%	97.20%	97.40%	**97.60%**	**97.60%**	90.60%	**94.80%**	**94.80%**	**94.80%**
Coenen–400	20%	96.75%	96.50%	96.75%	**97.25%**	93.25%	95.25%	**95.50%**	**95.50%**
Coenen–300	20%	**97.33%**	97.00%	97.00%	97.00%	88.33%	**95.00%**	**95.00%**	**95.00%**
Coenen–200	20%	97.50%	97.00%	95.50%	**97.50%**	88.00%	**94.50%**	**94.50%**	**94.50%**
Average		96.75%	96.78%	96.58%	**97.05%**	90.27%	94.83%	**94.84%**	94.81%

Collection	δ	AdaBoost				J48graft			
		All	IG	CHI-Q	GRAE	All	IG	CHI-Q	GRAE
Coenen–700	20%	94.14%	94.29%	**94.43%**	94.14%	96.14%	96.29%	**96.43%**	**96.43%**
Coenen–600	20%	92.67%	**94.33%**	94.17%	93.67%	95.67%	94.50%	**96.17%**	96.00%
Coenen–500	25%	94.80%	**94.80%**	**94.80%**	**94.80%**	95.80%	**96.60%**	96.40%	**96.60%**
Coenen–400	20%	94.50%	94.75%	94.75%	**95.25%**	94.50%	**96.00%**	95.75%	95.50%
Coenen–300	20%	95.00%	95.00%	**95.33%**	95.00%	94.33%	**96.00%**	94.67%	95.33%
Coenen–200	20%	94.00%	94.50%	**95.00%**	94.50%	91.50%	**95.00%**	**95.00%**	**95.00%**
Average		94.19%	94.61%	**94.75%**	94.56%	94.66%	95.73%	95.74%	**95.81%**

Table 3. Significant statistical tests (Holm and Hommel) using $\alpha = 0.05$ for different classifiers in several graph (image) collections using all the features computed by VEAM and using the features selected by the filter feature selectors.

Classifier	SVM	BayesNet	AdaBoost	J48graft
All vs. GRAE	–	GRAE	–	GRAE
All vs. CHI-Q	–	CHI-Q	CHI-Q	CHI-Q
All vs. IG	–	IG	IG	IG
IG vs. GRAE	–	–	–	–
CHI-Q vs. GRAE	–	–	–	–
IG vs. CHI-Q	–	–	–	–

In the first column of Table 3, "All" represents the approach using all features computed by VEAM while IG, CHI-Q and GRAE represent our approach using the feature selection through information gain, chi-squared, and gain ratio, respectively. The other columns show what approach is significantly better than the other one; the symbol "–" indicates that there is not a statistical significant difference between the results of both approaches.

As we can see from Tables 3 and 2, the use of the feature selection algorithm CHI-Q is the best option since in 75% of the results it is significantly better than "All", and using CHI-Q, the better classification accuracies are obtained in general. The other feature selection algorithms IG and GRAE outperform "All" in 75% and 50% of the results, respectively. And in general, IG, CHI-Q and

GRAE are significantly similar of the tests. Between CHI-Q and IG, we select CHI-Q as the best option because it had a better performance in term of the accuracy results.

5 Conclusions

In this paper, we propose the use of approximate subgraphs jointly with feature selection for image classification. To our best knowledge, this is the first work that performs such combination. Using a feature subset for representing the images in the collection allows us to drastically reduce the dimensionality of the feature vectors. This reduction was more than 50% in most cases. Moreover, our proposal is competitive in accuracy regarding the method that uses all the FASs.

As future work, we are going to study the identification of representative features (patterns) during the FASM process. Thus, only the discriminative patterns will be computed during the mining step, improving the effectiveness of FAS classifiers and reducing the runtime for the training stage.

Acknowledgment. This work was partly supported by the National Council of Science and Technology of Mexico (CONACyT) through the project grants CB2008-106443 and CB2008-106366; and the scholarship grant 287045.

References

1. Acosta-Mendoza, N., Gago-Alonso, A., Medina-Pagola, J.E.: Frequent Approximate Subgraphs as Features for Graph-Based Image Classification. Knowledge-Based Systems 27, 381–392 (2012)
2. Acosta-Mendoza, N., Morales-González, A., Gago-Alonso, A., García-Reyes, E.B., Medina-Pagola, J.E.: Image Classification Using Frequent Approximate Subgraphs. In: Alvarez, L., Mejail, M., Gomez, L., Jacobo, J. (eds.) CIARP 2012. LNCS, vol. 7441, pp. 292–299. Springer, Heidelberg (2012)
3. Bermejo, P., de la Ossa, L., Gámez, J.A., Miguel-Puerta, J.: Fast wrapper feature subset selection in high-dimensional datasets by means of filter re-ranking. Knowledge-Based Systems 25(1), 35–44 (2012)
4. Bolón-Canedo, V., Sánchez-Maroño, N., Alonso-Betanzos, A.: A review of feature selection methods on synthetic data. Knowledge and Information Systems 34(3), 483–519 (2013)
5. Duval, B., Hao, J.K., Hernandez, J.C.: A memetic algorithm for gene selection and molecular classification of cancer. In: Genetic and Evolutionary Computation Conference (GECCO 2009), pp. 201–208. ACM, Montreal (2009)
6. Ferreira, A.J., Figueiredo, M.A.T.: Efficient feature selection filters for high-dimensional data. Pattern Recognition Letters 33(13), 1794–1804 (2012)
7. Gago-Alonso, A., Carrasco-Ochoa, J.A., Medina-Pagola, J.E., Martínez-Trinidad, J.F.: Duplicate Candidate Elimination and Fast Support Calculation for Frequent Subgraph Mining. In: Corchado, E., Yin, H. (eds.) IDEAL 2009. LNCS, vol. 5788, pp. 292–299. Springer, Heidelberg (2009)

8. García, S., Herrera, F.: An Extension on "Statistical Comparisons of Classifiers over Multiple Data Sets" for all Pairwise Comparisons. Journal of Machine Learning Research 9, 2677–2694 (2008)
9. Hall, M., Frank, E., Holmes, G., Pfahringer, B., Reutemann, P., Witten, I.H.: The WEKA Data Mining Software: An Update. SIGKDD Explorations 11(1) (2009)
10. He, X., Cai, D., Niyogi, P.: Laplacian score for feature selection. Advances in Neural Information Processing Systems 18, 507–514 (2006)
11. Hommel, G.: A stagewise rejective multiple test procedure. Biometrika 75, 383–386 (1988)
12. Holder, L., Cook, D., Bunke, H.: Fuzzy substructure discovery. In: Proceedings of the 9th International Workshop on Machine Learning, San Francisco, CA, USA, pp. 218–223 (1992)
13. Holm, S.: A simple sequentially rejective multiple test procedure. Scandinavian Journal of Statistics 6, 65–70 (1979)
14. Jia, Y., Zhang, J., Huan, J.: An Efficient Graph-Mining Method for Complicated and Noisy Data with Real-World Applications. Knowledge Information Systems 28(2), 423–447 (2011)
15. Norshafarina, O.B., Fantimatufaridah, J.B., Mohd-Shahizan, O.B., Roliana, I.B.: Review of feature selection for solving classification problems. Journal of Research and Innovation in Information Systems, 54–60 (2013)
16. Pudil, P., Novovicova, J., Kittler, J.: Floating search methods in feature selection. Pattern Recognition Letters 15, 1119–1125 (1994)
17. Rodríguez-Bermúdez, G., García-Laencina, P.J., Roca-González, J., Roca-Dorda, J.: Efficient feature selection and linear discrimination of (eeg) signals. Neurocomputing 115(4), 161–165 (2013)
18. Yan, X., Huan, J.: gSpan: Graph-Based Substructure Pattern Mining. In: Proceedings International Conference on Data Mining, Maebashi, Japan, pp. 721–724 (2002)
19. Ye, Y., Wu, Q., Huang, J.Z., Ng, M.K., Li, X.: Stratified sampling for feature subspace selection in random forests for high dimensional data. Pattern Recognition 46(3), 769–787 (2013)

Mixed Data Balancing through Compact Sets Based Instance Selection

Yenny Villuendas-Rey[1] and María Matilde García-Lorenzo[2]

[1] Department of Computer Science, University of Ciego de Ávila, Carr. A Morón km 9 ½, Cuba
[2] Department of Computer Science, Universidad Central Marta Abreu of Las Villas, Carr. A Camajuaní, km 5 ½, Cuba
yenny@informatica.unica.cu, mmgarcia@uclv.edu.cu

Abstract. Learning in datasets that suffer from imbalanced class distribution is an important problem in Pattern Recognition. This paper introduces a novel algorithm for data balancing, based on compact set clustering of the majority class. The proposed algorithm is able to deal with mixed, as well as incomplete data, and with arbitrarily dissimilarity functions. Numerical experiments over repository databases show the high quality performance of the method proposed in this paper according to area under the ROC curve and imbalance ratio.

Keywords: imbalanced data, mixed data, supervised classification.

1 Introduction

The training dataset plays a key role for supervised classification. Training data allows building classifiers able to estimate the label or class of a new unseeing instance. Several researchers have pointed out that if the dataset has an approximately equal amount of instances for every class, the classifier can produce predictions that are more accurate [1]. However, in several real-world applications, it is not possible to obtain a training set with classes equally distributed. The class imbalance problem occurs when one or several classes (the majority classes) vastly outnumber the other classes (the minority classes), which are usually the most important classes and often with the highest misclassification costs.This problem is known as the problem of learning in imbalanced scenarios.

Learning in imbalanced scenarios poses challenges for supervised classifiers, such as Nearest Neighbor (NN). Several researchers have addressed the impact of data imbalance in NN performance [2, 3]. The problem of class imbalance has been addressed by numerous approaches at both algorithmic and data levels. At algorithmic level, the methods usually modify the learning algorithm to favor the detection of the minority class, while the solutions at data level obtain an approximately equally distributed data set, by means of re-sampling, either by oversampling the minority class [4] or undersampling the majority class [5-7]. Oversampling techniques create artificial objects of the minority class, and increase the computational cost of the

J. Ruiz-Shulcloper and G. Sanniti di Baja (Eds.): CIARP 2013, Part I, LNCS 8258, pp. 254–261, 2013.

learning algorithms, and the storage cost of the dataset, while undersampling techniques preserve minority class and obtains a small representation of majority class.

This paper proposes a novel algorithm for undersampling. The algorithm is based on Compact Sets (CS) structuralizations, and is able to deal with mixed and incomplete data. The use of CS based clustering allows selecting a highly representative set of the majority class, preserving the objects of minority class. The thorough experimental study carried out shows the significant performance gains of the proposed approach when compared to other state-of-the-art algorithms.

2   Compact Sets Based Data Balancing by Under-Sampling

One of the greatest challenges in undersampling techniques is to obtain a good representation of the majority class. Instead of using a classical prototype selection strategy, this paper introduces the idea of structuralize the majority class by means of compact sets, and then obtain the desired number of prototypes. Compact sets have been used successfully for prototype selection in mixed and incomplete data, and also for clustering [8, 9]. A compact set is a connected component of a Maximum Similarity Graph. A Maximum Similarity Graph is a directed graph, such as it connects each object with its most similar neighbors [10]. Formally, let be $G = (X, \theta)$ a MSG for a set of objects X, with arcs θ. Two objects $x_i, x_j \in X$ form an arc $(x_i, x_j) \in \theta$ if $\max_{x \in X}\{sim(x_i, x)\} = sim(x_i, x_j)$, where $sim(x_i, x_j)$ is a similarity function, usually $sim(x_i, x_j) = 1 - \Delta(x_i, x_j)$ and $\Delta(x_i, x_j)$ is a dissimilarity function. Each connected component of such graph is called a compact set. Compact sets are formed by highly similar instances, and allow structuralizing datasets. Formally, a subset $N \neq \emptyset$ of X is a β_0 compact set if and only if [10]:

$$a) \forall x_j \in X \left[x_i \in N \wedge \left(\begin{array}{c} \max_{\substack{x_k \in X \\ x_k \neq x_i}}\{sim(x_i, x_k)\} = sim(x_i, x_j) \geq \beta_0 \\ \vee \max_{\substack{x_k \in X \\ x_k \neq x_i}}\{sim(x_k, x_i)\} = sim(x_j, x_i) \geq \beta_0 \end{array} \right) \right] \Rightarrow x_j \in N$$

$$b) \forall x_i, x_j \in N, \exists x_{i_1}, \cdots, x_{i_q} \in N \left[\begin{array}{c} x_i = x_{i_1} \wedge x_j = x_{i_q} \wedge \forall p \{1, \cdots, q-1\} \\ \left[\begin{array}{c} \max_{\substack{x_t \in X \\ x_t \neq x_{i_p}}} \{sim(x_{i_p}, x_t)\} = sim(x_{i_p}, x_{i_{p+1}}) \geq \beta_0 \\ \vee \max_{\substack{x_t \in X \\ x_t \neq x_{i_p}}} \{sim(x_{i_{p+1}}, x_t)\} = sim(x_{i_{p+1}}, x_{i_p}) \geq \beta_0 \end{array} \right] \end{array} \right]$$

$c)$ Every isolated object is a compact set, degenerated.

The proposed algorithm, called CDB (Compact set based Data Balancing) starts by dividing the dataset into majority and minority classes (Figure 1 and 2). Then, it computes the compact sets of the majority class, and each is considered as a group. Next, for each group, it finds the more similar objects with respect to every other object in the group (holotype) to represent the group.

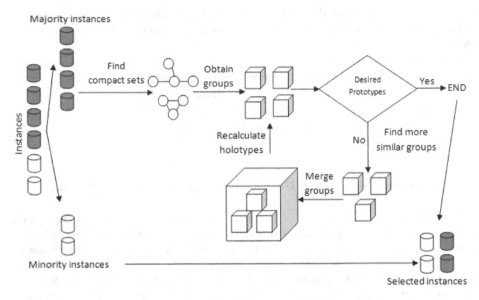

Fig. 1. Compact Set based Data Balancing algorithm (CDB).

The algorithm finds the most similar groups, and merges them, until the desired number of prototypes (groups) is reached. This proposal directly merges all possible groups which have less dissimilarity in a single step. This makes faster the merging process, and avoids order dependence.

Compact set based Data Balancing (CDB) algorithm
Inputs: I: set of instances, Δ: similarity function
Output: P: prototype set
1. $C = \phi, P = \phi$
2. Move the objects of I belonging to majority class to a set M, and add to P the remaining (minority) objects of I.
3. Create a maximum similarity graph of the objects in the set M using $\beta_0=0$ and Δ
4. Add to C each connected component of the graph created at step 3.
4.1. Select as cluster centre (holotype) the object that maximizes the overall similarity with respect to every object in the cluster
5. Merge all more similar groups, using as cluster similarity the similarity between cluster centers.
5.1. Recalculate cluster holotypes.
6. Repeat step 5, until $|C| \leq |P|$, that is, until the amount of clusters is less or equal to the amount of objects of minority class.
7. Add to P the holotypes of C
8. Return P

Fig. 2. Pseudocode of Compact set based Data Balancing (CBD) algorithm

The new compact set based algorithm differs from previously reported algorithms in the following: It clearly defines the amount of prototypes to select from majority class. It also deals with mixed and incomplete data, by using compact sets and a hierarchical approach that selects representative instances instead of constructing artificial ones. In addition, it uses the similarity between holotypes as intergroup similarity, avoiding additional instance similarity computation and it merges at each stage all groups selected as more similar, avoiding order-dependence.

3   Experimental Results

To compare the performance of the proposed algorithms, there were used 44 databases from the KEEL dataset repository [11].

Table 1. Databases used in the experiments

Databases	Att.	Instances	IR	Databases	Att.	Instances	IR
abalone9-18	8	2934	17	glass04-5	9	368	9
abalone19	8	16706	130	glass06-5	9	432	11
cleveland0-4	13	708	13	glass2-5	9	856	12
ecoli01-235	7	976	9	glass4-5	9	856	15
ecoli01-55	6	960	11	glass5-5	9	856	23
ecoli0137-26	7	1124	39	led7digit1	7	1772	11
ecoli0146-5	6	1120	13	page-blocks13-4	10	1888	16
ecoli0147-2356	7	1344	11	shuttlec0-4	9	7316	14
ecoli0147-56	6	1328	12	shuttlec2-4	8	516	21
ecoli0234-5	7	808	9	vowel0	13	3952	10
ecoli0267-35	7	896	9	yeast0256-3789	8	4016	9
ecoli034-5	7	800	9	yeast02579-368	8	4016	9
ecoli0346-5	7	820	9	yeast0359-78	8	2024	9
ecoli0347-56	7	1028	9	yeast05679-4	8	2112	9
ecoli046-5	6	812	9	yeast1-7	3	1836	14
ecoli067-35	7	888	9	yeast1289-7	8	3788	31
ecoli067-5	6	880	10	yeast1458-7	8	2772	22
ecoli4-5	7	1344	16	yeast2-4	8	3056	14
glass0146-2	9	820	11	yeast2-8	8	1928	23
glass015-2	9	688	9	yeast4	8	5936	28
glass016-2	9	768	10	yeast5	8	5936	33
glass016-5	9	736	19	yeast6	8	5936	41

These databases were modified from its original version, to obtain highly imbalanced data sets, having only one minority and one majority class [11]. The name of the datasets represents the index of minority and majority classes. Table 1 shows the characteristics of the selected databases. The second and third columns show the amount of attributes (Att.) and instances of the dataset, and the fourth, the Imbalance Ratio of each database. Imbalance Ratio (IR) is defined as the ratio between the instances count of majority class, with respect to the count of instances of minority class.

For numerical comparison, there were selected the HEOM (equation 1) dissimilarity function, proposed by Wilson and Martínez [12], which is able to deal with mixed and incomplete data.

$$HEOM(x,y) = \sqrt{\sum_{a=1}^{m} d_a(x_a, y_a)}, d_a = \begin{cases} 1 \\ overlap(x_a, y_a), \\ diff(x_a, y_a) \end{cases} \tag{1}$$

$$overlap(p,q) = \begin{cases} 0 & if\ p = q \\ 1 & in\ other\ case \end{cases}, diff(p,q) = |p - q|/max_a - min_a$$

In addition, the SEC [5], NCL [6], and GGE [7] algorithms were selected for comparison purposes, because they are among best undersampling algorithms for mixed data balancing. All algorithms were implemented in C# language, and the experiments were carried out in a laptop with 3.0GB of RAM and Intel Core i5 processor with 2.67HZ.

To compare the performance of the algorithms, it was used the area under the ROC curve (AUC).The Area under the ROC curve is another quality measure widely used to evaluate classifiers in problems with unequal costs, such as imbalanced problems. In [13] are shown some of the advantages of using the AUC measure over other quality measures, such as classifier error. To compute the AUC (equation 2) for a discrete classifier, a simple method is proposed in [14], based on a confusion matrix (table 2). It was also computed the Imbalance Ratio (IR) for every algorithm, in order to determine their effectiveness in balancing the datasets.

$$AUC = \frac{TPR+TNR}{2} \text{ where } TPR = (tp)/(tp + fp) \text{ and } TNR = (tn)/(tn + fn) \tag{2}$$

Table 2. Confusion matrix for two class problems

	Positive Prediction	Negative Prediction
Positive Class	True Positive (tp)	False Negative (fn)
Negative Class	False Positive (fp)	True Negative (tn)

Table 3 and 5 show the results according to AUC and Imbalance Ratio, respectively, in the testing phase. As shown in table 3, the proposed CDB algorithm obtains the highest area under the ROC curve in 28 databases, 16 of them above 0.9. These results show the high performance of the proposed method.

Table 3. AUC of the algorithms. In bold best results

Databases	NCL	SEC	GGE	CDB	Databases	NCL	SEC	GGE	CDB
abalone9-18	0.58	0.60	0.61	**0.83**	glass04-5	0.73	**0.81**	0.78	0.67
abalone19	0.50	0.50	0.50	**0.78**	glass06-5	0.67	0.70	0.65	**0.88**
cleveland0-4	0.74	0.83	0.73	**0.93**	glass2-5	0.51	0.50	0.46	**0.90**
ecoli01-235	0.76	0.73	0.77	**0.90**	glass4-5	0.48	0.53	0.51	**0.68**
ecoli01-55	0.87	0.86	**0.90**	**0.90**	glass5-5	0.69	0.71	0.67	**0.96**
ecoli0137-26	0.50	0.50	0.50	**0.88**	led7digit1	0.64	0.85	0.66	**1.00**
ecoli0146-5	0.87	0.89	0.90	**0.91**	page-blocks13-4	0.92	**0.96**	**0.96**	0.95
ecoli0147-2356	0.79	0.78	0.81	**0.90**	shuttlec0-4	**1.00**	**1.00**	**1.00**	0.99
ecoli0147-56	0.87	0.88	**0.91**	0.86	shuttlec2-4	0.95	**1.00**	0.95	0.75
ecoli0234-5	0.82	0.84	0.50	**0.93**	vowel0	0.94	**0.95**	0.94	0.86
ecoli0267-35	0.78	0.83	0.79	**0.86**	yeast0256-3789	0.70	**0.73**	0.72	0.72
ecoli034-5	0.82	0.82	0.57	**0.88**	yeast02579-368	0.81	0.82	**0.85**	0.79
ecoli0346-5	0.80	0.82	0.81	**0.91**	yeast0359-78	**0.67**	**0.67**	**0.67**	0.62
ecoli0347-56	0.50	0.50	0.50	**0.86**	yeast05679-4	0.67	0.69	**0.73**	0.64
ecoli046-5	0.87	**0.89**	0.88	0.86	yeast1-7	0.48	0.48	**0.63**	0.58
ecoli067-35	0.83	0.83	0.85	**0.93**	yeast1289-7	0.57	0.59	0.57	**0.90**
ecoli067-5	0.82	0.84	**0.85**	0.72	yeast1458-7	0.60	0.63	0.62	**0.77**
ecoli4-5	0.70	**0.74**	0.69	0.56	yeast2-4	0.50	0.73	0.73	**0.78**
glass0146-2	0.55	0.54	0.56	**0.66**	yeast2-8	0.72	0.71	0.70	**0.96**
glass015-2	0.53	0.52	0.50	**0.92**	yeast4	0.59	0.64	0.68	**0.80**
glass016-2	0.54	0.51	0.52	**0.94**	yeast5	0.73	0.79	**0.80**	0.66
glass016-5	0.64	0.66	0.67	**0.98**	yeast6	0.72	0.72	**0.75**	0.69

However, to determine the existence or not of significant differences in algorithm´s performance it was used the Wilcoxon test [15]. It was set as null hypothesis no difference in performance between the proposed method and every other algorithm, and as alternative hypothesis that CDB had better performance. It was set a significant value of 0.05, for a 95% of confidence. Table 4 summarizes the results of the Wilcoxon test, according to area under the ROC curve. The Wilcoxon test concludes the proposed method has significantly better performance than the other compared methods, according to the area under the ROC curve.

Table 4. Wilcoxon test comparing area under the ROC curve

CDB vs.	NCL	SEC	GGE
wins – looses – ties	31-13-0	29-15-0	26-17-1
probability	**0.000**	**0.001**	**0.001**

Table 5. Imbalance Ratio of the algorithms. In bold best results (near to 1).

Databases	NCL	SEC	GGE	CDB	Databases	NCL	SEC	GGE	CDB
abalone9-18	16.36	7.24	13.27	**1.00**	glass04-5	8.64	4.17	7.42	**1.00**
abalone19	129.3	31.7	126.1	**1.00**	glass06-5	10.50	5.69	8.44	**1.00**
cleveland0-4	12.29	3.17	11.69	**1.00**	glass2-5	11.35	7.26	7.93	**1.00**
ecoli01-235	8.95	2.72	8.50	**1.00**	glass4-5	15.06	5.85	12.85	**1.14**
ecoli01-55	10.76	2.81	10.66	**1.00**	glass5-5	22.22	9.17	21.08	**1.00**
ecoli0137-26	38.61	11.0	37.14	**1.00**	led7digit1	10.87	1.73	10.61	**1.00**
ecoli0146-5	12.76	3.26	12.69	**1.00**	page-blocks13-4	15.73	3.51	15.63	**1.00**
ecoli0147-2356	10.35	3.53	9.72	**1.00**	shuttlec0-4	13.85	0.04	13.87	**1.00**
ecoli0147-56	12.03	3.39	11.60	**1.00**	shuttlec2-4	20.00	**1.00**	20.50	**1.00**
ecoli0234-5	8.90	2.36	8.63	**1.00**	vowel0	9.92	1.81	9.68	**1.00**
ecoli0267-35	8.98	3.00	8.40	**1.00**	yeast0256-3789	9.04	4.76	7.35	**1.00**
ecoli02579-368	10.35				yeast02579-368	9.05	4.11	8.14	**1.00**
ecoli034-5	8.78	2.29	8.53	**1.00**	yeast02579-368	9.05	4.11	8.14	**1.00**
ecoli0346-5	9.04	2.49	8.79	**1.00**	yeast0359-78	8.93	4.86	6.94	**1.00**
ecoli0347-56	9.03	2.97	8.53	**1.00**	yeast05679-4	9.16	4.51	7.64	**1.00**
ecoli046-5	8.94	2.21	8.76	**1.00**	yeast1-7	14.13	5.48	12.32	**1.00**
ecoli067-35	8.89	2.91	8.35	**1.00**	yeast1289-7	30.38	15.00	27.73	**1.00**
ecoli067-5	9.79	3.16	9.18	**1.00**	yeast1458-7	21.90	11.42	18.88	**1.00**
ecoli4-5	15.56	4.60	14.88	**1.00**	yeast2-4	8.93	3.99	8.26	**1.00**
glass0146-2	10.79	6.69	7.94	**1.00**	yeast2-8	22.91	9.70	21.35	**1.00**
glass015-2	8.88	5.57	5.74	**1.00**	yeast4	27.90	11.27	25.98	**1.00**
glass016-2	10.01	6.28	7.19	**1.00**	yeast5	32.57	7.80	31.37	**1.00**
glass016-5	18.86	8.64	17.75	**1.00**	yeast6	41.09	14.93	38.79	**1.00**

As shown, CDB obtains a perfectly balanced dataset, in 43 of 44 databases, with only 1.14 of Imbalance Ratio in the glass4-5 database. These results confirm the proposed approach is able to obtain an adequate balance of data, without losing representative objects of majority class.

4   Conclusions

Prototype selection for data balancing is an important preprocessing step for learning in imbalance scenarios. In this paper, a novel method is introduced, using Compact Sets for hierarchical clustering of majority class. The method keeps minority objects, and selects representative objects of majority class, from compact sets structuralizations. The method is also able to deal with databases containing objects described by features no exclusively numeric or categorical. Experimental results carried out over several repository data show the high performance of the proposed method, which obtains a perfectly balanced datasets with high area under the ROC curve.

References

1. Weiss, G.M.: Learning with rare cases and small disjuncts. In: Proceedings of the International Conference on Machine Learning, ICML 2003, pp. 558–565 (2003)
2. Hand, D.J., Vinciotti, V.: Choosing k for two-class nearest neighbor classifiers with imbalanced classes. Pattern Recognition Letters 24, 1555–1562 (2003)
3. Zhang, J., Mani, I.: kNN approach to unbalanced data distribution: a case study involving information extraction. In: Proceedings of Workshop on Learning from Imbalanced Datasets (2003)
4. Moreno, J., Rodriguez, D., Sicilia, M.A., Riquelme, J.C., Ruiz, R.: SMOTE-I: improvement of SMOTE algorithm for minority classes balancing. In: Proceedings of Workshops of Software Engineering and Databases 3 (2009) (in Spanish)
5. García, V.: Distributions of non-balanced classes: metrics, complexity analysis and learning algorithms. PhD Dissertation Thesis, Department of Languages and Computer Systems, University Jaume I, Spain (2010)
6. Laurikkala, J.: Instance-based data reduction for improved identification of difficult small classes. Intelligent Data Analysis 6, 311–322 (2002)
7. Alejo, R., Valdovinos, R.M., García, V., Pacheco-Sanchez, J.H.: A hybrid method to face class overlap and class imbalance on neural networks and multi-class scenarios. Pattern Recognition Letters 34, 380–388 (2013)
8. García-Borroto, M., Ruiz-Shulcloper, J.: Selecting prototypes in Mixed and Incomplete data. In: Sanfeliu, A., Cortés, M.L. (eds.) CIARP 2005. LNCS, vol. 3773, pp. 450–459. Springer, Heidelberg (2005)
9. Villuendas-Rey, Y., Rey-Benguría, C., Caballero-Mota, Y., García-Lorenzo, M.M.: Nearest prototype classification of special school families based on hierarchical compact sets clustering. In: Pavón, J., Duque-Méndez, N.D., Fuentes-Fernández, R. (eds.) IBERAMIA 2012. LNCS, vol. 7637, pp. 662–671. Springer, Heidelberg (2012)
10. Ruiz-Shulcloper, J., Abidi, M.A.: Logical combinatorial Pattern Recognition: A review. In: Pandalai, S.G. (ed.) Recent Research Developments in Pattern Recognition. Transword Research Networks, pp. 133–176 (2002)
11. Alcalá-Fdez, J., Fernández, A., Luengo, J., Derrac, J., García, S., Sánchez, L., Herrera, F.: KEEL data-mining software tool: Data set repository, integration of algorithms and experimental analysis framework. Journal of Multiple-Valued Logic and Soft Computing 17, 255–287 (2011)
12. Wilson, R.D., Martinez, T.R.: Improved heterogeneous distance functions. Journal of Artificial Intelligence Research 6, 1–34 (1997)
13. Bradley, A.: The use of Area under the ROC curve in the evaluation of Machine Learning Algorithms. Pattern Recognition 30, 1145–1159 (1997)
14. Sokolova, M., Japkowicz, N., Szpakowicz, S.: Beyond Accuracy, F-Score and ROC: a family of Discriminant measures for Performance evaluations. In: Proceedings of the Australian Conference on Artificial Intelligence, pp. 1015–1021 (2006)
15. Demsar, J.: Statistical comparison of classifiers over multiple datasets. Journal of Machine Learning Research 7, 1–30 (2006)

An Empirical Study of Oversampling and Undersampling for Instance Selection Methods on Imbalance Datasets

Julio Hernandez, Jesús Ariel Carrasco-Ochoa,
and José Francisco Martínez-Trinidad

Instituto Nacional de Astrofísica Óptica y Electrónica, Computer Science
Department, Luis Enrique Erro No. 1, Sta. María Tonantzintla,
Puebla, CP 72840, Mexico
{julio.hernandez.t,ariel,fmartine}@ccc.inaoep.mx
http://ccc.inaoep.mx

Abstract. Instance selection methods get low accuracy in problems
with imbalanced databases. In the literature, the problem of imbalanced databases has been tackled applying oversampling or undersampling methods. Therefore, in this paper, we present an empirical study
about the use of oversampling and undersampling methods to improve
the accuracy of instance selection methods on imbalanced databases. We
apply different oversampling and undersampling methods jointly with
instance selectors over several public imbalanced databases. Our experimental results show that using oversampling and undersampling methods
significantly improves the accuracy for the minority class.

Keywords: supervised classification, instance selection, oversampling,
undersampling, imbalanced datasets.

1 Introduction

The classification process requires a training set T to create a model which will
be used to assign a class to unseen examples. Nevertheless, in a training sample
usually there are some redundant and/or noisy examples that are useless for the
classification process and they could negatively affect the classification accuracy
[1–3]. Instance selection (IS) is focused on this problem. The IS methods select
a subset S of the training set T such that S allows to get an accuracy as similar
as possible to the one computed using T [4].

In an ideal scenario the classes are balanced, that is, the number of instances
for each class are almost the same. But, some real world databases don't have
this property, i.e. their classes are imbalanced [5–7].

Instance selection algorithms have demonstrated to perform well when the
classes are balanced [3], however, this is not true for imbalanced datasets, instance selection algorithms get low accuracy in this kind of problems because
they tend to remove too many instances from the minority class, damaging
their performance [8, 9]. For this reason, in this paper we focus on the study

J. Ruiz-Shulcloper and G. Sanniti di Baja (Eds.): CIARP 2013, Part I, LNCS 8258, pp. 262–269, 2013.

of combining oversampling and undersampling methods with instance selection algorithms, in order to get good results in imbalanced problems.

This paper is divided in the following sections: Section 2, briefly describes the instance selection algorithms and oversampling and undersampling methods that will be used in our experiments. Section 3 presents the experimental results. Finally, section 4 provides some conclusions and future work.

2 Related Work

In the literature there have been reported several instance selection algorithms. Most of them are based on the KNN rule, for example DROP3 [10], IB3 [1], ICF [2]. Another group of instance selection algorithms, clearly different from the former, are those based on evolutionary algorithms, some examples of these methods are CHC [11], GGA [12], SGA[13]. More recently some instance selection algorithms for large databases have been proposed, which can be applied in problems where conventional IS algorithms, as those previously commented, cannot produce a solution in a reasonable time. For our study we have selected DROP3 as a representative of those algorithms based on KNN; CHC as a representative of algorithms based on evolutionary algorithms; and IRB [14] as a representative of IS algorithms for large datasets.

1. **DROP3** [10]: This algorithm is based on the concept of associate. The associates of an instance P are those instances such that P is one of their k nearest neighbors. First, DROP3 applies ENN [15] for noise-filtering over the initial training set T. Then, the remaining instances in T are sorted by the distance to their nearest enemy, which is the nearest instance with different class. DROP3 iteratively removes an instance P if the majority of its associates in T would be classified correctly without P.

2. **CHC** [11]: In [16] a comprehensive study of different evolutionary algorithms applied in the instance selection field is presented. From this study the CHC algorithm was able to achieve the best overall performance among the tested evolutionary algorithms. During each generation the CHC develops the following steps: (1) CHC uses a parent population of size n to generate an intermediate population of the same size, which are used to generate n potential offsprings. (2) Then, in a competition the best n chromosomes from the parent and offsprings population are selected to form the next generation.

3. **IRB** [14]: This algorithm tries to preserve the border instances (those located in a region where there are similar instances from different classes) by computing an instance ranking for each class based on the distance of each instance to border instances. This algorithm selects a predefined % of instances having high, medium and low values, in the ranking.

The described algorithms are not able to deal with imbalance datasets by itself. However, they maintain their reduction capabilities. One way to deal with the problem of imbalance dataset is applying some oversampling or undersampling techniques. Therefore, in this paper, we present an empirical study about the use of oversampling and undersampling methods to improve the accuracy of instance selection methods on imbalanced databases. For our study we have selected the following oversampling and undersampling methods, which are some of the most reported in the literature.

1. **Resample**: This oversampling method produces an uniform class distribution. Resample applies a random subsampling to the majority class and an oversampling, with replacement, to the minority class.
2. **Spread Subsampling**: This undersampling technique produces a random subsample of a database. The class distribution is adjusted through a random elimination of objects from the majority class.
3. **Synthetic Minority Over-sampling Technique** (SMOTE) [17]: This oversampling approach generates synthetic samples of the minority class based on nearest neighbors. The synthetic examples are generated computing the difference between feature vectors and their nearest neightbors, then this difference is multiplied by a random number between 0 and 1, and the result is added to the feature vector under consideration.

On the other hand, in [18] the One-sided method is proposed as an approach to instance selection over imbalanced datasets. The main idea of this work is to carry out instance selection only over the majority class leaving intact the minority class. Another approach to the same problem [19] involves that an instance can be choose more than once considering the number of nearest neighbours. The main idea of this work is to cover the same amount of space with fewer instances.

3   Experimental Results

For our experiments we use 18 databases taken from the KEEL repository [20]. Table 1 describes the used databases. The databases were sorted in ascending way according to their imbalance ratio (IR) computed as the ratio between the size of the majority and minority classes. As it is shown in Table 1 the imbalance ratio is very different for each database, for that reason we grouped the databases as: IR 1-3, IR 3-9 and IR > 9. It will allow us to analyze the behavior of oversampling and undersampling techniques, jointly with instance selection, depending of the imbalance ratio.

For each database, we performed 10 fold cross validation averaging the classification accuracy for the minority and majority classes separately as well as the global accuracy, in our experiments we also include the F-Measure.

We used the implementations of Resample, Spread Subsample and SMOTE taken from WEKA [21] with their default parameters, except for SMOTE where we adjusted the percentage parameter (-P) according with the imbalance ratio of each database (-P (IR * 100)). We used different percentage values because each minority class needs a different percentage of oversampling, for example, in the abalone database we have an imbalance ratio of 133, the minority class have only 28 examples, if we apply SMOTE with a fix percentage of 100 the result

Table 1. Characteristics of the databases used in the experiments. IR: the imbalance ratio; N.O.: number of objects; cl+: size of the majority class; cl-: size of the minority class.

Database	IR	N.O.	cl+	cl-	Database	IR	N.O.	cl+	cl-	Database	IR	N.O.	cl+	cl-
	IR 1-3					**IR 3-9**					**IR > 9**			
ionosphere	1.8	315	202	113	spliceie	3.2	2871	2180	691	ecoliom	15.8	302	284	18
pima	1.9	691	405	241	vehiclevan	3.3	761	582	179	abalone918	16.8	657	620	37
tic-tac-toe	1.9	862	564	298	ecolim	3.4	302	233	69	yeastme2	28.7	1335	1290	45
german	2.3	900	630	270	hepatitis	5.5	72	61	11	yeastme1	33.2	1335	1296	39
phoneme	2.4	4863	3436	1427	segment0	6.0	2077	1781	296	yeastexc	42.1	1335	1304	31
yeast	2.5	1335	949	386	ecolimu	8.7	302	271	31	abalone19	133.1	3756	3728	28

will be an imbalance database with an imbalance ratio very close to the original, in this case we needed an oversampling percentage of 13300% (133 * 100).

The implementations of KNN, DROP3 and CHC were taken from the KEEL software [22] and the implementation of IRB was supplied by the authors. The KNN algorithm with K = 1 is used as base line. For DROP3, CHC and KNN we used the default parameters in the KEEL software and for IRB we used the parameters suggested by the authors in [14].

For the One-sided prototype selection method [18] we followed the steps proposed by the authors. First, we apply DROP3, CHC or IRB over the whole database. The original examples of the minority class jointly with the examples selected by the IS algorithm in the majority class are used as training for the 1-NN classifier.

3.1 Experimental Comparison

Tables 2, 3 and 4 show the results of the experiments for the databases with imbalanced ratio 1-3, 3-9 and grater than 9, respectively. Each table is divided in two main columns, the right column presents the results of applying One-sided method and the left column presents the results of applying instance selection algorithms after oversampling or undersampling. In each sub-table the average accuracy for the minority and majority classes, the global accuracy, the F-Measure and the reduction percentage are reported. The numbers in bold represent the best results for the respective column and row.

The results for databases with IR in the interval 1-3 (see Table 2), show that applying an instance selection method (IS) followed by oversampling or undersampling always produces better results for minority class and global accuracy than applying the One-sided method. In terms of F-Measure it gets in most of the cases better results if an instance selection algorithm is applied after oversampling or undersampling in contrast to applying the One-sided method. These results show that IRB got the best accuracy for the minority class (and for global accuracy) with respect to CHC, DROP3 and KNN no matter if an oversampling or undersampling techniques is applied or not before applying IRB. However, SMOTE & IRB obtained the best results. On the other hand, although the accuracy for the majority class is greatly improved by One-sided, simultaneously,

Table 2. Experiment results for the databases with IR 1-3. Red.: reduction percentage, Acc+: Majority class Accuracy, Acc-: Minority class Accuracy, AccG: Global Accuracy, F-M: F-Measure

Selector	Without over or under sampling					One-sided					Resampling 300%				
	Red.	Acc-	Acc+	AccG.	F-M	Red.	Acc-	Acc+	AccG.	F-M	Red.	Acc-	Acc+	AccG.	F-M
KNN	0.00	0.66	0.79	0.74	0.54	0.00	0.66	0.79	0.74	0.54	0.00	0.61	0.81	0.75	0.59
CHC	0.99	0.65	0.79	**0.76**	0.54	0.68	0.37	**0.89**	0.43	0.53	0.99	0.56	0.84	**0.72**	0.61
DROP3	0.84	0.54	0.79	0.71	0.54	0.60	0.38	**0.85**	0.52	0.53	0.91	0.55	0.80	**0.71**	0.55
IRB	0.60	0.47	**0.92**	**0.78**	0.56	0.43	**0.54**	0.86	0.69	**0.62**	0.59	0.61	0.81	**0.75**	0.61

	SMOTE					SMOTE and One-sided					Resampling 300% and One-sided				
KNN	0.00	0.62	0.83	0.75	0.62	0.00	0.62	0.83	0.75	0.62	0.00	0.61	0.81	0.75	0.59
CHC	0.99	0.55	0.85	**0.71**	0.61	0.47	0.37	**0.90**	0.43	0.53	0.51	0.39	**0.95**	0.47	0.54
DROP3	0.82	0.51	0.81	**0.69**	0.56	0.38	0.45	**0.90**	0.61	**0.59**	0.47	0.39	**0.87**	0.53	0.54
IRB	0.59	0.74	0.79	**0.77**	**0.68**	0.40	0.53	**0.88**	0.67	0.60	0.45	0.50	**0.87**	0.66	**0.62**

	Spread Subsample					Spread Subsample and One-sided				
KNN	0.00	0.55	0.85	0.70	0.61	0.00	0.55	0.85	0.70	0.61
CHC	0.98	0.56	0.85	**0.72**	**0.62**	0.49	0.37	**0.93**	0.42	0.53
DROP3	0.79	0.50	0.81	**0.67**	0.56	0.45	0.42	**0.91**	0.56	**0.57**
IRB	0.60	0.70	0.78	**0.75**	**0.65**	0.41	0.50	**0.90**	0.63	0.62

Table 3. Experiment results for the databases with IR 3-9. Red.: reduction percentage, Acc+: Majority class Accuracy, Acc-: Minority class Accuracy, AccG: Global Accuracy, F-M: F-Measure

Selector	Without over or under sampling					One-sided					Resampling 300%				
	Red.	Acc-	Acc+	AccG.	F-M	Red.	Acc-	Acc+	AccG.	F-M	Red.	Acc-	Acc+	AccG.	F-M
KNN	0.00	0.61	0.94	0.87	0.63	0.00	0.61	0.94	0.87	0.63	0.00	0.61	0.93	0.87	0.64
CHC	0.98	0.65	0.92	**0.86**	**0.62**	0.80	0.28	**0.93**	0.49	0.42	0.99	0.61	0.95	**0.85**	**0.68**
DROP3	0.90	0.60	0.93	**0.84**	**0.65**	0.75	0.34	**0.96**	0.63	0.48	0.95	0.60	0.92	**0.84**	**0.64**
IRB	0.60	0.65	0.96	0.91	0.66	0.52	0.59	**0.96**	0.84	**0.67**	0.59	0.74	0.93	0.90	0.71

	SMOTE					SMOTE and One-sided					Resampling 300% and One-sided				
KNN	0.00	0.61	0.95	0.86	0.68	0.00	0.61	0.95	0.86	0.68	0.00	0.61	0.93	0.87	0.64
CHC	0.99	0.62	0.95	**0.86**	**0.70**	0.48	0.31	**0.99**	0.54	0.46	0.51	0.36	**0.98**	0.63	0.52
DROP3	0.90	0.59	0.91	**0.84**	**0.61**	0.42	0.42	**0.97**	0.73	0.57	0.49	0.35	**0.95**	0.64	0.50
IRB	0.60	0.91	0.90	**0.90**	**0.78**	0.43	0.52	**0.93**	0.85	0.56	0.46	0.61	**0.96**	0.86	0.68

	Spread Subsample					Spread Subsample and One-sided				
KNN	0.00	0.55	0.96	0.82	0.65	0.00	0.55	0.96	0.82	0.65
cline1-11 CHC	0.96	0.57	0.96	**0.83**	**0.67**	0.48	0.27	**0.98**	0.48	0.42
DROP3	0.84	0.55	0.93	**0.80**	**0.63**	0.40	0.37	**0.97**	0.65	0.52
IRB	0.63	0.89	0.86	**0.87**	**0.71**	0.45	0.48	**0.97**	0.77	0.61

Table 4. Experiment results for the databases with IR > 9. Red.: reduction percentage, Acc+: Majority class Accuracy, Acc-: Minority class Accuracy, AccG: Global Accuracy, F-M: F-Measure

Selector	Without over or under sampling					One-sided					Resampling 300%				
	Red.	Acc-	Acc+	AccG	F-M	Red.	Acc-	Acc+	AccG	F-M	Red.	Acc-	Acc+	AccG	F-M
KNN	0.00	0.45	0.98	0.97	0.41	0.00	0.45	0.98	0.97	0.41	0.00	0.41	0.98	0.97	0.41
CHC	0.99	0.41	0.98	0.97	0.35	0.96	0.07	0.97	0.32	0.13	0.99	0.33	0.99	0.90	0.41
DROP3	0.98	0.28	0.98	0.92	0.33	0.95	0.07	0.98	0.45	0.13	0.97	0.25	0.98	0.89	0.30
IRB	0.60	0.30	1.00	0.97	0.33	0.50	0.33	0.98	0.92	0.36	0.59	0.39	0.98	0.96	0.38
	SMOTE					SMOTE and One-sided					Resampling 300% and One-sided				
KNN	0.00	0.35	0.99	0.93	0.42	0.00	0.35	0.99	0.93	0.42	0.00	0.41	0.98	0.97	0.41
CHC	0.99	0.32	0.99	0.91	0.40	0.51	0.10	0.99	0.91	0.40	0.51	0.14	0.99	0.64	0.23
DROP3	0.94	0.28	0.98	0.91	0.33	0.48	0.18	0.99	0.73	0.26	0.51	0.07	0.98	0.44	0.13
IRB	0.59	0.66	0.92	0.91	0.38	0.40	0.28	0.99	0.85	0.36	0.48	0.42	0.98	0.96	0.44
	Spread Subsample					Spread Subsample and One-sided									
KNN	0.00	0.18	0.99	0.79	0.27	0.00	0.18	0.99	0.79	0.27					
CHC	0.95	0.21	0.99	0.82	0.31	0.47	0.08	1.00	0.36	0.14					
DROP3	0.82	0.18	0.99	0.77	0.27	0.40	0.11	0.99	0.55	0.19					
IRB	0.65	0.81	0.79	0.79	0.25	0.35	0.12	0.96	0.57	0.19					

it get a worse accuracy for the minority class, therefore the overall accuracy obtained by One-sided is far outweighed by the results obtained by applying oversampling or undersampling jointly with IS.

For databases with IR in the interval 3-9 (see Table 3), the results show that applying an IS method after oversampling or undersampling always produces better results for minority class and global accuracy than applying the One-sided method. In terms of F-Measure it gets in most of the cases better results if an instance selection algorithm is applied after oversampling or undersampling in contrast to applying the One-sided method. The same as in databases with IR in the interval 1-3. The results show that although IRB gets the lower reduction percentages, it outperformed the accuracy of the minority class, global accuracy and F-Measure with respect to CHC, DROP3 and KNN no matter if an oversampling or undersampling technique is applied before applying IRB. Again, as in databases with IR in the interval 1-3, SMOTE & IRB obtained the best results. On the other hand, the One-sided technique is far outweighed by the results obtained by applying oversampling or undersampling jointly with IS methods.

The results for databases with IR greater than 9 (see Table 4), show that applying an IS method after oversampling or undersampling always produces better results for the minority class and the global accuracy than applying the One-sided method. In this type of databases Spread Subsample & IRB obtained the best accuracies for the minority class. However, the best global accuracy was obtained by Resampling & IRB. The results show that the One-sided method is far outweighed by the results obtained by applying oversampling or undersampling jointly with an IS method.

4   Conclusions and Future Work

The instance selection methods are sensitive to imbalance databases. The main problem is that the minority class always obtains lower accuracy than the majority class. Only a few works have been proposed to deal with the imbalance problem on instance selection [18], however, there are some techniques based on oversampling and undersampling that can be combined with IS methods to improve the accuracy of the minority class.

The main contribution of this work is an empirical study of combining oversampling and undersampling techniques with some instance selection methods based on nearest neighbor rule (NN), evolutionary algorithms and ranking algorithms. The results show that this combination improves the accuracy of the minority class with respect to the original dataset. For imbalanced databases with an IR in the interval 1-9 the best option is to use SMOTE & IRB, for databases with an IR greater than 9 there are two main combinations: Resample & IRB, which obtains high global accuracy, and Spread Subsample & IRB, which obtains high accuracy for the minority class.

As future work, we plan to develop an instance selection algorithm to directly deal with imbalanced datasets.

Acknowledgment. This work was partly supported by the National Council of Science and Technology of Mexico (CONACyT) through the project grants CB2008-106443 and CB2008-106366.

References

1. Aha, D.W., Kibler, D., Albert, M.K.: Instance-Based Learning Algorithms. Mach. Learn. 6, 37–66 (1991)
2. Brighton, H., Mellish, C.: Advances in Instance Selection for Instance-Based Learning Algorithms. Data Min. Knowl. Discov. 6, 153–172 (2002)
3. Garcia, S., Derrac, J., Cano, J., Herrera, F.: Prototype Selection for Nearest Neighbor Classification: Taxonomy and Empirical Study. IEEE Trans. Pattern Anal. Mach. Intell. 34, 417–435 (2012)
4. Olvera-López, J.A., Carrasco-Ochoa, J.A., Martínez-Trinidad, J.F., Kittler, J.: A review of instance selection methods. Artif. Intell. Rev. 34, 133–143 (2010)
5. Estabrooks, A., Jo, T., Japkowicz, N.: A Multiple Resampling Method for Learning from Imbalanced Data Sets. Computational Intelligence 20, 18–36 (2004)
6. Chawla, N.V., Japkowicz, N., Kotcz, A.: Editorial: special issue on learning from imbalanced data sets. SIGKDD Explor. Newsl. 6, 1–6 (2004)
7. Sun, Y.M., Wong, A.K.C., Kamel, M.S.: Classification of imbalance data: A review. International Journal of Pattern Recognition and Artificial Intelligence 4, 687–719 (2009)
8. García-Pedrajas, N., Romero del Castillo, J.A., Ortiz-Boyer, D.: A cooperative co-evolutionary algorithm for instance selection for instance-based learning. Machine Learning 78, 381–420 (2010)
9. Batista, G.E.A.P.A., Prati, R.C., Monard, M.C.: A study of the behavior of several methods for balancing machine learning training data. SIGKDD Explor. Newsl. 6, 20–29 (2004)

10. Wilson, D.R., Martinez, T.R.: Reduction Techniques for Instance-Based Learning Algorithms. Mach. Learn. 30, 257–286 (2000)
11. Eshelman, L.J.: The CHC Adaptive Search Algorithm: How to Have Safe Search When Engaging in Nontraditional Genetic Recombination. In: Foundations of Genetic Algorithms, pp. 265–283. Morgan Kaufmann, San Francisco (1991)
12. Goldberg, D.E.: Genetic Algorithms in Search, Optimization and Machine Learning. Addison-Wesley Longman Publishing Co., Inc., Boston (1989)
13. Whitley, D.: The GENITOR algorithm and selection pressure: why rank-based allocation of reproductive trials is best. In: Proceedings of the Third International Conference on Genetic Algorithms, pp. 116–121. Morgan Kaufmann Publishers Inc. (1989)
14. Hernandez-Leal, P., Carrasco-Ochoa, J.A., Martínez-Trinidad, J.F., Olvera-Lopez, J.A.: InstanceRank based on borders for instance selection. Pattern Recogn. 46, 365–375 (2013)
15. Wilson, D.L.: Asymptotic Properties of Nearest Neighbor Rules Using Edited Data. IEEE Transactions on Systems, Man and Cybernetics 2, 408–421 (1972)
16. Cano, J.R., Herrera, F., Lozano, M.: Using evolutionary algorithms as instance selection for data reduction in KDD: an experimental study. Trans. Evol. Comp. 6, 561–575 (2003)
17. Chawla, N.V., Bowyer, K.W., Hall, L.O., Kegelmeyer, W.P.: SMOTE: synthetic minority over-sampling technique. J. Artif. Int. Res. 16, 321–357 (2002)
18. Millán-Giraldo, M., García, V., Sánchez, J.S.: One-sided prototype selection on class imbalanced dissimilarity matrices. In: Gimel'farb, G., Hancock, E., Imiya, A., Kuijper, A., Kudo, M., Omachi, S., Windeatt, T., Yamada, K. (eds.) SSPR & SPR 2012. LNCS, vol. 7626, pp. 391–399. Springer, Heidelberg (2012)
19. Pérez-Rodríguez, J., de Haro-García, A., García-Pedrajas, N.: Instance selection for class imbalanced problems by means of selecting instances more than once. In: Lozano, J.A., Gámez, J.A., Moreno, J.A. (eds.) CAEPIA 2011. LNCS, vol. 7023, pp. 104–113. Springer, Heidelberg (2011)
20. Alcalá-Fdez, J., Fernandez, A., Luengo, J., Derrac, J., García, S., Sánchez, L., Herrera, F.: KEEL Data-Mining Software Tool: Data Set Repository, Integration of Algorithms and Experimental Analysis Framework. Journal of Multiple-Valued Logic and Soft Computing 17, 255–287 (2011)
21. Estabrooks, A., Jo, T., Japkowicz, N.: A Multiple Resampling Method for Learning from Imbalanced Data Sets. Computational Intelligence 20, 18–36 (2004)
22. Jesús, A.-F., Alberto, F., Julián, L., Joaquín, D., Salvador, G.: KEEL Data-Mining Software Tool: Data Set Repository, Integration of Algorithms and Experimental Analysis Framework. Multiple-Valued Logic and Soft Computing 17, 255–287 (2011)

Learning Stability Features on Sigmoid Fuzzy Cognitive Maps through a Swarm Intelligence Approach

Gonzalo Nápoles[1,*], Rafael Bello[1], and Koen Vanhoof[2]

[1] Universidad Central "Marta Abreu" de Las Villas, Santa Clara, Cuba
[2] Hasselt University, Hasselt, Belgium
gnapoles@uclv.edu.cu

Abstract. Fuzzy Cognitive Maps (FCM) are a proper knowledge-based tool for modeling and simulation. They are denoted as directed weighted graphs with feedback allowing causal reasoning. According to the transformation function used for updating the activation value of concepts, FCM can be grouped in two large clusters: discrete and continuous. It is notable that FCM having discrete outputs never exhibit chaotic states, but this premise can not be ensured for FCM having continuous output. This paper proposes a learning methodology based on Swarm Intelligence for estimating the most adequate transformation function for each map neuron (concept). As a result, we can obtain FCM showing better stability properties, allowing better consistency in the hidden patterns codified by the map. The performance of the proposed methodology is studied by using six challenging FCM concerning the field of the HIV protein modeling.

Keywords: Fuzzy Cognitive Maps, Stability, Learning, Swarm Intelligence.

1 Introduction

The FCM theory [1] was introduced by B. Kosko as an improvement of the Cognitive Mapping which uses fuzzy reasoning in its knowledge representation scheme. From the structural point of view, FCM may be denoted as directed graphs with feedback, consisting of nodes and weighted arcs. Nodes or concepts are equivalent to neurons in connectionist models and represent variables of the modeled system; while weights associated to links denote the *causality* among concepts. In a FCM, each connection takes value in the range $[-1,1]$. It denotes the degree of causality between two nodes as a result of the quantification of a fuzzy linguistic variable [2-3], which is regularly assigned by experts at the modeling stage. The activation value of concepts is also fuzzy in nature and regularly takes values in the range $[0,1]$, although the scale $[-1,1]$ is also allowed. Hence, the higher the activation value, the stronger the influence of the concept over the system, which helps to understand the modeling.

In the past decade, FCM have gained considerable research interest and are widely used to analyze causal systems such as system control, decision making, management, risk analysis, text categorization, prediction, etc [4]. In order to increase the usability

---

* Corresponding author.

J. Ruiz-Shulcloper and G. Sanniti di Baja (Eds.): CIARP 2013, Part I, LNCS 8258, pp. 270–277, 2013.

of this knowledge-based approach, numerous researchers have developed learning algorithms [3], mainly varying the causal weight matrix. However, these approaches suppose that FCM are closed systems and they do not consider external influences, while other factors such as the FCM stability are ignored. On the other hand, as far as known, there not exist learning algorithms for enhancing the system stability once the causality is established. Based on these considerations, the main goal of this work is to introduce a new learning algorithm which is oriented to estimate the most adequate transformation function for each map concept, simulating the effect of ideal external stimulus over the neurons with the hope to improve the map stability. To do that, we use a Swarm Intelligence method to solve the related optimization task.

It is relevant to remark that the authors will be focused on sigmoid FCM, instead of discrete (binary o trivalent) maps. This remark is motivated by the benchmarking analysis discussed in [5] where results showed that the sigmoid function significantly outperforms the other functions, by using the same decision model. The rest of the paper is organized as follows: in next Section 2 the formulation of FCM is briefly described. In Section 3 we present the proposed learning algorithm which is oriented to compute the family of threshold functions improving the map convergence. After that, Section 4 introduces the experimental framework and also provides comments about the simulations. Finally, conclusions are given in Section 5.

2   Fuzzy Cognitive Maps

Without loss generality, a simple FCM can be defined using a 4-tuple (C, W, A, f) where $C = \{C_1, C_2, C_3, \dots, C_m\}$ is a set of m concepts of the graph, $W: (C_i, C_l) \rightarrow w_{il}$ is a function which associates a causal value $w_{il} \in [-1,1]$ to each pair of nodes (C_i, C_l), denoting the weight of the directed edge from C_i to C_l. In this context, it is important to notice that w_{il} represents the causality degree between the concepts C_i and C_l. Thus the weigh matrix $W_{m \times m}$ gathers the system causality which is frequently determined by experts. Likewise, $A: (C_i) \rightarrow A_i$ is a function that associates the activation degree $A_i \in \mathbb{R}$ to each concept C_i at the moment t $(t = 1,2, \dots, T)$. Finally, a transformation or threshold function $f: \mathbb{R} \rightarrow [0,1]$ is used to keep the activation value of concepts in the interval $[0,1]$. Following equation (1) shows the inference mechanism using the state vector A^0 as the initial configuration. This inference stage is iteratively repeated until a *hidden pattern* [6] or a maximal number of iterations T are reached.

$$A_{it+1} = f\left(\sum_{j=1}^{m} w_{ji} A_{it}\right), i \neq j \tag{1}$$

The most frequently used threshold functions [5] are: the bivalent function, the trivalent function, and the sigmoid variants. The effects on the selection of a specific function over the stability and inference capabilities of the FCM have been widely explored in [7]. From this work some important remarks were concluded:

- Discrete FCM (using a binary or trivalent function) never show chaotic behavior. It means that always a fixed-point attractor or a limit cycle will be detected in the map outputs. These states have the following behavior:

- o   Fixed-point attractor ($\exists t_k \in \mathbb{N} : A^{(t+1)} = A^{(t)}, \forall t > t_k$): the system produces the same output after the time t_k.
- o   Limit cycle ($\exists t_k, P \in \mathbb{N} : A^{(t+P)} = A^{(t)}, \forall t > t_k$): the same output or state vector is regularly observed with period T.

- Continuous FCM (using a sigmoid function) additionally may exhibit chaotic states, where the FCM model continues to produce different state vectors for successive cycles. In these situations the FCM can not stabilize.

In summary, from the algebraic point of view, the states characterizing the system are iteratively updated by multiplying the causal weight matrix, by the current state vector until a stopping condition is reached. Then the activation value of each concept is directly influenced by the values of the connected concepts with the appropriate weights, and also taking into account its previous value; showing the causal effect of changes on the concept's activation value on the whole map. That's why FCM theory is a suitable approach for handling modeling and simulation tasks.

3   Proposed Learning Methodology

In the literature several supervised and unsupervised learning algorithms have been proposed, mainly focused on the transformation of the causal weight matrix. As a brief categorization they can be gathered in three major groups [4]: Hebbian-based, population-based and hybrid approaches. On the other hand, Tsadiras[7] demonstrated that the inference capability of FCM may be strongly influenced by the selection of the concept's transformation function. Based on the Tsadiras' work, we conducted a set of empirical experiments using sigmoid FCM, where the parameter λ was changed as next equation (2) shows. Observe that in our simulations a custom amplification value for each map concept C_i is assumed. Results were quite promising: we observed that variations of factor λ_i lead to some changes on the map stability. Hence, it seems to be reasonable to suppose that a learning algorithm could helps to improve the map convergence, by solving the related real-parameter optimization problem.

$$f_i(x) = \frac{1}{1 + e^{-(x-0.5)\lambda_i}} \tag{2}$$

Before presenting the learning methodology, we need to answer the following question: how is affected the FCM inference mechanism by the inception of a function f_i for each node C_i? Normally FCM are considered as closed systems where external factors affecting the concepts are omitted. But, in many real world problems this perception will be inadequate and may affect the accuracy of simulations. For example, it is known that biological behavior on proteins not only depends on the amino acids interaction, but also depends on the external factors such as the chemical processes influencing the catalytic responses. Notice that such external factors may be modeled by using a function f_i for each neuron C_i (instead of the same function for all the neurons), ensuring better stability. It means that the activation value of a neuron C_i on the map will be now conditioned by the free interaction of the connected nodes and also by the steepness λ_i of its threshold function f_i which denotes the stimulus.

It should be mentioned that other works have been proposed to simulate external influence over the map concepts. For example, Stylios and Groumpos [8] introduced a new FCM model where each concept has an external output (bias), which influences each node with a weight and it is take n into account at the calculation rule. It is easy to perceive the similarity between the Stylios' model and our proposal, since both are oriented to simulate external influences over the neurons, although they use different implementations to do that. Of course, our approach leads to a different interpretation of the causal influences since the activation capability of each neuron (now influenced by its steepness λ_i) should be also considered. However, this aspect is not discussed in the paper since the authors prefer to be focused on the system stability.

Here, the learning step is focused on estimating an appropriate family of sigmoid functions ensuring certain stability features. More explicitly, we need to find a family of sigmoid functions $\{f_1(x), f_2(x), ..., f_m(x)\}$, where the ith function will be used for transforming the activation value of the ith concepts. In practice, it implies to find the steepness λ_i for each threshold function. With this purpose in mind, we use a Swarm Intelligence technique [9]. Particle Swarm Optimization (PSO) is a non-direct search method for solving challenging continuous problems [10], from a distributed point of view without any centralized control. In the standard PSO each agent (called particle) denotes a m-dimensional point in the solution space. For our optimization problem, m should be considered as the total number of nodes on the map. Hence, the ith position of each particle will correspond to the steepness λ_i of the ith function.

Particles adjust their position by using a combination of an attraction to the best solution that they individually have found, and an attraction to the best solution that any particle has found [3], imitating those who have a better performance. This search method has proven to be quite efficient for solving real-parameter optimization problems. However, the particle swarm is frequently attracted to local optima, causing premature convergence or stagnation configurations. For this reason, this paper uses a variant called PSO with Random Sampling in Variable Neighborhoods [11-12] which is capable to notably outperform the standard algorithm. Next equation (3) shows the objective function that should be minimized during the search steps.

$$\phi(f_1, f_2, f_3, ..., f_m) = \sum_{k=1}^{K} \sum_{i=1}^{m} \sum_{t=2}^{T} |A_{it}^k - A_{it-1}^k| \tag{3}$$

In the above function, K denotes the number of instances (historical data), m is the number of neurons, T denotes the maximal number of times, whereas A_{it}^k represents the activation value of the ith concept for the current time t, using the kth instance as initial condition. Here a simple instance is a sequence of values codifying the initial conditions of the system, and the corresponding response. In brief, during the learning step the algorithm attempts to reduce the global variability of the system response for each input sequence over the time. In this scheme a solution will be considered as no feasible if the system inference is negatively affected. It should be remarked that the weight matrix can not be modified during this process since our model is oriented to compute more stable maps once the causality estimation is done.

4   Simulations and Discussion

In order to validate the proposal discussed in the above section we use six previously adjusted FCM taken from the work of Grau and Nápoles [13-14]. Such maps describe the behavior of some HIV mutations related to their resistance to existing antiviral drugs. Accordingly, the authors described the HIV *protease* protein as a simple FCM where each sequence position[1] is taken as a map concept, while another node for the resistance target is also defined. Then, all the neurons are fully connected; also there exist causal links between each sequence position and the resistance concept. It means that the resistance is conditioned by the interaction of the amino acids once a specific mutation (simple or multiple) takes place, leading to different levels of resistance to the target drug. This model can not represent the external influences.

It is important to mention that each map denotes the protein behavior for a specific drug: Amprenavir (APV), Indinavir (IDV), Saquinavir (SQV), Nelfinavir (NFV), Ritonavir (RTV) and also Atazanavir (ATV). Each drug has associated a high-quality filtered datasets taken from [15] consisting in reported mutations and their resistance value. The configuration of the PSO-RSVN algorithm used as optimizer is fixed as follows: 40 particles as the population size, five variable neighborhoods ($m = 5$), 80 generations, and the allowed number of evaluations without progress is set to 20. In addition, the number of times of the FCM inference process is $T=100$.

As a first analysis the stability of the resistance node of each drug for a randomly selected mutation is measured. Figure 1, 2 and 3 show the activation value of the resistance over the time for two scenarios: the solid line represents the FCM response without any modification, whereas the dashed line denotes the FCM response using the family of sigmoid functions found by the learning method. From these simulations it is possible to conclude that our proposal induces better stability features over the drug resistance target. In this case, only the resistance node was monitored since it is the decision concept, allowing to predict whether a new mutation will be susceptible to the drug or not. Note that the system response changes for next drugs: IDV, RTV and ATV. In such cases the final classification rate does not suffer any change since the resistance target for a drug is measured in a certain range instead of using a single value. However, we noticed that some FCM achieve better accuracy.

For better understanding of this issue let us analyze the behavior of the selected mutation "FKLDVFMIIVVSVTVNML" for the map IDV. This sequence has high level of resistance for the drug IDV, which means that the higher the activation value of the resistance node, the better accuracy should report the model for this instance. In fact, in the figure 1a) the FCM inference process is able to compute higher resistance after applying the learning algorithm. As a partial conclusion, four behaviors from results may be observed: (1a-1b) it possible to compute better stability from stable maps, (2a-2b) we can obtain stable maps from maps exhibiting cyclic patterns, (3a) it is possible to compute more stable maps from chaotic systems, and (3b) we can obtain a map having stable features from a FCM exhibiting a chaotic behavior.

---

[1]   The protease sequence is defined by 99 amino acids where each position can be represented by its normalized contact energy [16]. In order to reduce the number of nodes in map, the authors use a subset of amino acids previously associated with resistance.

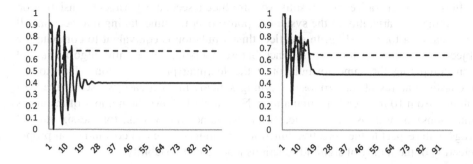

Fig. 1. Activation value of the resistance concept for a) drug IDV b) drug RTV. The *solid* line denotes the FCM response using the same function for all the neurons, whereas the *dashed* line represents the FCM output using the family of functions found by the learning scheme.

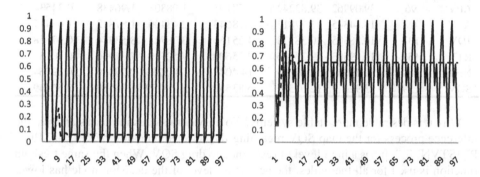

Fig. 2. Activation value of the resistance concept for a) drug ATV b) drug APV. The *solid* line denotes the FCM response using the same function for all the neurons, whereas the *dashed* line represents the FCM output using the family of functions found by the learning scheme.

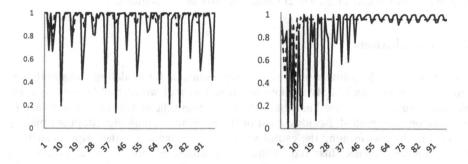

Fig. 3. Activation value of the resistance concept for a) drug SQV b) drug NFV. The *solid* line denotes the FCM response using the same function for all the neurons, whereas the *dashed* line represents the FCM output using the family of functions found by the learning scheme.

In order to generalize these results we introduce a second experiment consisting on computing the variability of the system response over the time, taking into account all historical data for each drug. In practice, this simulation is equivalent to compute the objective function (3) for each instance before applying the learning algorithm, and then computing the same formula once the learning process is done. Due to the stochastic features of the proposed learning scheme in each case we select the best solution from 10 independent simulations. Next table 1 shows the number of instances (mutations), as well as the average, mean and standard deviation for the six studied drugs with respect to the objective function. In summary, we can conclude that proper selection of the family of sigmoid functions lead to better stability.

Table 1. Variability of the system response over the time for all instances (mutations)

Drug	Mutations	Before			After		
		Average	Median	Std. deviation	Average	Median	Std. deviation
APV	96	39.09962	39.83242	1.57105	1.98303	1.96438	0.34534
ATV	69	13.84345	13.77815	2.18643	2.43406	1.87842	1.03477
IDV	137	10.58505	10.38378	4.25156	3.78721	3.53374	0.97868
RTV	151	19.19583	19.26046	0.75602	7.52529	7.37976	0.70137
NFV	204	19.59037	32.66005	14.4047	2.835233	2.78300	0.29764
SQV	139	13.92619	12.02521	6.83530	6.158739	6.30550	0.56349

Why it is desirable more stable systems? To answer this question let us analyze the inference process for the map SQV regarding the selected mutation "FKLDVFMIGV PVISTVNML". It has a high level of resistance to drug SQV. When the same treshold function is used for all the nodes, the activation level of the decision node has lower degree of resistance towards the end, and hence the sequence may be erroneously classified as susceptible. However, using the family of sigmoid functions found by the learning algorithm the final neuron is more stable, although the biological system remains cahotic. In a few words, after apliying the methodology discussed here, the map SQV will be more chance to correctly classify new mutations.

5   Conclusions

Fuzzy Cognitive Maps are a useful neurofuzzy technique for modeling and simulation which have been successfully applied to numerous real world problems. However, they are regularly considered as closed systems, where the effects of external factors over neurons are omitted. Besides, most of the existing learning algorithm are mainly oriented to the transforming the causal weight matrix, ignoring other aspects such as the system convergence. Inspired on these limitations, the present paper proposed a new learning approach for estimating the proper threshold function for each neuron in sigmoid FCM. It attempts to efficiently simulate the effects of external stimulus over the concepts, where the stability of the modeled system is the main goal. By doing so, we used a Swarm Intelligence based approach with diversity control, for computing better estimations during the optimization of the objective function.

In order to validate our proposal we used six FCM concerning the field of the HIV protein analysis. From these results we can definitely conclude that, after applying the learning methodology, adjusted FCM exhibit more stability. In addition, we observed that (i) it is possible to achieve better stability from stable maps, (ii) it is possible to compute stable maps from maps exhibiting cyclic patterns, (iii) it is possible to obtain more stable maps from chaotic systems, and finally (iv) it is possible to accomplish a stable map from a FCM exhibiting a chaotic behavior. In this sense more stable maps allows to extract more consistent patterns from the system behavior. The future work will be focused on studying the FCM convergence, but now from the point of view of the causal links characterizing the neurons interaction.

References

1. Kosko, B.: Fuzzy Cognitive Maps. Int. Journal of Man-Machine Studies 24, 65–75 (1986)
2. Kosko, B.: Neural Networks and Fuzzy systems, a dynamic system approach to machine intelligence. Prentice-Hall, Englewood Cliffs (1992)
3. Papageorgiou, E.P.: Learning Algorithms for Fuzzy Cognitive Maps—A Review Study. IEEE Tran. on Systems, Man, and Cybernetics 42, 150–163 (2012)
4. Papageorgiou, E.P.: Review study on Fuzzy Cognitive Maps and their applications during the last decade. In: IEEE International Conference on Fuzzy Systems, pp. 828–835 (2011)
5. Bueno, S., Salmeron, J.L.: Benchmarking main activation functions in Fuzzy cognitive maps. Expert Syst. Appl. 36, 5221–5229 (2009)
6. Kosko, B.: Hidden patterns in combined and adaptive knowledge networks. International Journal of Approximate Reasoning 2, 377–393 (1988)
7. Tsadiras, A.K.: Comparing the inference capabilities of binary, trivalent and sigmoid fuzzy cognitive maps. Information Science 178, 3880–3894 (2008)
8. Stylios, C.D., Groumpos, P.P.: Mathematical Formulation of Fuzzy Cognitive Maps. In: 7th Mediterranean Conference on Control and Automation, pp. 28–30 (1999)
9. Kennedy, J., Russell, C.E.: Swarm Intelligence. Morgan Kaufmann Publishers (2001)
10. Kennedy, J., Eberhart, R.: Particle Swarm Optimization. In: IEEE International Conference on Neural Networks, Australia, pp. 1942–1948 (1995)
11. Nápoles, G., Grau, I., Bello, R.: Particle Swarm Optimization with Random Sampling in Variable Neighbourhoods for solving Global Minimization Problems. In: Dorigo, M., Birattari, M., Blum, C., Christensen, A.L., Engelbrecht, A.P., Groß, R., Stützle, T. (eds.) ANTS 2012. LNCS, vol. 7461, pp. 352–353. Springer, Heidelberg (2012)
12. Nápoles, G., Grau, I., Bello, R.: Constricted Particle Swarm Optimization based Algorithm for Global Optimization. POLIBITS - Research Journal on Computer Science and Computer Engineering with Applications 46, 5–12 (2012)
13. Grau, I., Nápoles, G., León, M., Grau, R.: Fuzzy Cognitive Maps for Modelling, Predicting and Interpreting HIV Drug Resistance. In: Pavón, J., Duque-Méndez, N.D., Fuentes-Fernández, R. (eds.) IBERAMIA 2012. LNCS (LNAI), vol. 7637, pp. 31–40. Springer, Heidelberg (2012)
14. Nápoles, G., Grau, I., León, M., Grau, R.: Modelling, aggregation and simulation of a dynamic biological system through Fuzzy Cognitive Maps. In: Batyrshin, I., Mendoza, M.G. (eds.) MICAI 2012, Part II. LNCS, vol. 7630, pp. 188–199. Springer, Heidelberg (2013)
15. Stanford HIV Drug Resistance Database, http://hivdb.stanford.edu
16. Miyazawa, S., Jernigan, R.L.: Contacts energies Self-Consistent Estimation of Inter-Residue Protein Contact Energies Based on an Equilibrium Mixture Approximation of Residues. PROTEINS: Structure, Function, and Genetics 34, 49–68 (1999)

A Feature Set Decomposition Method
for the Construction of Multi-classifier Systems
Trained with High-Dimensional Data

Yoisel Campos[1], Roberto Estrada[1], Carlos Morell[2], and Francesc J. Ferri[3]

[1] Univ. de Holguín "Oscar Lucero Moya". Holguín, Cuba
campos.yoisel@gmail.com, restradal@facinf.uho.edu.cu
[2] Computer Science Dept. Univ. Central
"Marta Abreu" de Las Villas. Santa Clara, Cuba
cmorellp@uclv.edu.cu
[3] Dept. d'Informàtica Universitat de València València, Spain
francesc.ferri@uv.es

Abstract. Data mining for the discovery of novel, useful patterns, encounters obstacles when dealing with high-dimensional datasets, which have been documented as the "curse" of dimensionality. A strategy to deal with this issue is the decomposition of the input feature set to build a multi-classifier system. Standalone decomposition methods are rare and generally based on random selection. We propose a decomposition method which uses information theory tools to arrange input features into uncorrelated and relevant subsets. Experimental results show how this approach significantly outperforms three baseline decomposition methods, in terms of classification accuracy.

Keywords: multi-classifier systems, feature set decomposition, information theory.

1 Introduction

The technological advancement on the field of sensors and other measuring methodologies, has provoked the existence of processes which output data described by a large amount of features. These are often termed high-dimensional datasets and their distinctive quality is that the number m of features describing the data is far greater than the number N of data instances $(m \gg N)$.

Performing machine learning from such datasets is of high interest. Not only because of the inherent usefullness of discovering the underlying patterns, but also because frequently there is poor backgorund knowledge about the domains from where the data are drawn. Certain domains, e.g. genetic studies or biochemistry, yield datasets described by a number of features in the order of 10^4, while containing only a few hundred instances [14]. This extreme disproportion conducts to the appearance of certain fenomena affecting the performance of most machine learning algorithms, which is known in the literature as the "curse" of dimensionality [6].

J. Ruiz-Shulcloper and G. Sanniti di Baja (Eds.): CIARP 2013, Part I, LNCS 8258, pp. 278–285, 2013.

Many strategies have been applied to tackle this issue. One of them is the construction of multi-classifier systems (MCS) [2], where several complementary models are combined in some way to make predictions. For high-dimensional problems, MCS generally train each individual classifier using only a subset of the original data features, with the intention of reducing the effects of dimensionality.

Such an approach is the Random Subspace Method (RSM) for constructing decision forests [8], which introduced a general framework to deal with high-dimensional data. RSM iteratively selects random subsets of features from the original dataset (i.e. subspaces), which are then employed to train decision trees. This operation results in an ensemble of models trained with different projections of the data, whith the random subspacing ensuring diversity. This action of generating several subsets from an original feature set is commonly defined as "decomposition" [10].

However, there's no evidence to assert whether random decomposition is the most effective in terms of overall classification accuracy. Ideally, all features should be allocated inside a decomposition in a way that maximizes their combined usefullness. Some features will work well together, some will not because of redundancy or irrelevance.

In this paper, we explore the application of information theory tools to the decomposition task. After covering some fundamental concepts about feature set decomposition in Section 2, we present an information theoretic decomposer in Section 3, which is the main contribution of this work. Section 4 summarizes an experimental study where statistical tests show how our approach significantly outperforms 3 baseline methods, in terms of classification accuracy, over 19 high-dimensonal datasets.

2   Feature Set Decomposition for the Creation of Multi-classifiers

Decomposition methods are rarely found as an independent field of study. Usually a non-random decomposition strategy is developed as a secondary product of a certain ensemble construction method [11,9]. A tight integration between the different layers of a multi-classifier is of course desirable. But standalone decomposition methods [4] present their own advantages. According to Maimon and Rokach [10], some of these advantages are:

- Increase in classification performance, due to the simplification of the task.
- Scalabiliy to high-dimensional datasets.
- Flexibility in learning algorithm selection.

Given an inducer I, a combination method C and a training set S with input feature set $F = \{f_1, f_2, ..., f_m\}$ and a target feature c, the goal is to find an optimal decomposition D_{opt} of the input feature set F into n mutually exclusive subsets $D_i = \{d_{i1}, d_{i2}, ..., d_{ik}\} \mid d_{ij} \in F; i = 1, ..., n$ that are not necessarily exhaustive, such that the generalization error of the induced classifiers, combined using method C, will be minimized.

3   Information Theoretic Decomposition

Several machine learning techniques have been inspired on information theory concepts, especially in the field of feature selection. Some works have taken advantage of the usefulness of such concepts, to measure how much information a given description feature carries about the target feature. The root concept in this domain is the entropy of a feature X, $H(X)$. The entropy of a feature could be interpreted as the amount of uncertainty in drawing, at random, a value from it [12]. Furthermore, the conditional entropy between two given features $H(X|Y)$ expresses how much uncertainty remains about X, once Y is known. These two concepts are further combined to form other relational information measures, which prove to be very useful in assessing the interaction of features in a machine learning environment.

In particular, the Symmetrical Uncertainty (SU) and the Conditional Mutual Information (CMI) display some desirable properties. The success of applying these for attribute selection problems has been demonstrated in algorithms like FCBF[15] and CMIM[5].

SU describes how much information is shared by two given features. It is a normalized measure, with 1 indicating that the values in either feature can be predicted from the other and 0 indicating that X and Y are independent.

$$SU(X,Y) = 2 \left[\frac{H(X) - H(X|Y)}{H(X) + H(Y)} \right] \qquad (1)$$

CMI is an estimate of the amount of information shared between X and Y when Z is known. As shown in Equation 2, when the amount of information about X contained in Y is already given by Z, CMI equals 0 even if both Z and Y are informative and mutually independent.

$$CMI(X,Y|Z) = H(X|Z) - H(X|Y,Z) \qquad (2)$$

Regardless of the success in the application of the information theory approach in attribute selection algorithms, the selection problem essentially differs from the decomposition problem. Our goal will be to simultaneously construct the desired amount of feature subsets, so that the most appropriate subset will be determined for each feature analyzed.

For this information theoretic decomposition we will traverse 3 phases, each one aiming at a key aspect of multi-classifiers construction: relevance, diversity and non-redundancy. The whole procedure is summarized in Algorithm 1.

3.1   Phase A: Relevance

It is desirable that only informative features should be considered to form the decomposition. Hence, the first phase will ensure that non-informative features are excluded. To achieve this, all description features that show information independence from the target feature or class, will be removed.

Phase A will output a depurated feature set F', with $SU(f,c) > 0 \mid \forall f \in F'$.

3.2   Phase B: Diversity

It has been proved that individual classifiers with performance error under 0.5 and weakly correlated decisions, will display a higher performance when combined in an ensemble [2]. This weak correlation among the individual decisions is usually termed diversity and represents a key property on every ensemble.

Our depurated feature set F' will most likely contain some subset of highly relevant features which are also highly independent with regard to each other. Phase B will find these features and will designate them as "seeds", from which the decomposition subsets will grow. This is accomplished through an iterative procedure, where CMI is used to determine the usefulness and diversity of features. Starting from the most informative feature, at each iteration a new feature is selected, based on the amount of additional information it provides. It becomes a seed since it carries information about the class that is not already provided by the previously selected seeds.

Phase B outputs the features that will be used as seeds to build up the decomposition subsets. Their main property is that each one of them provides an amount of information about the class that complements the others. Our intuition is that such property should enhance the ensemble diversity, once the respective feature subsets are generated from uncorrelated seeds.

3.3   Phase C: Non-redundancy

As a final requirement, the decomposition must decide whether to include each description feature and where to allocate it. The main goal in this phase is to distribute features among subsets, in a way that optimizes their combined usefulness to predict the class. To achieve this, every feature should be allocated to the subset where it provides most information, i.e. where it is least redundant. Furthermore, a feature that is redundant in all subsets should not be considered.

We will define the amount of redundancy that a feature X introduces to a subset Z, as the maximum difference between the correlation of X to the members of Z and the relevance of X, as stated in Equation 3.

$$R(X, Z) = \max_{\forall z \in Z} [SU(X, z) - SU(X, c)] \tag{3}$$

Subsequently, a feature should be allocated to the subset where it introduces the least redundancy. To further increase the flexibility of the model, a threshold could be used to tolerate certain amount of redundancy. As a result, all target features are evaluated and either discarded or included in the most appropriate subset. This phase outputs the final decomposition D, which can then be applied to the original dataset to train an ensemble of n classifiers.

4   Experimental Study

In order to evaluate the performance of our information theoretic decomposer, we have tested this approach in an experimental setup. The objective is to determine

---

Algorithm 1. Information theoretic feature set decomposition (ITD)

Let F be the initial feature set ($c \in F$ is the target feature).
Let $D = \{D\}_{i=1}^{n}$ be the decomposition (n is the desired number of subsets) and let S be the set of seeds.
Let ξ be a redundancy threshold, with $\xi \in [-1, 1]$.

1. $F' = \{f \in F \mid SU(f, c) > 0\}$ // Phase A
2. $S \leftarrow \{\operatorname*{argmax}_{\forall f \in F'} SU(f, c)\}$ // Phase B
3. While $|S| < n$ do
   (a) $x = \operatorname*{argmax}_{\forall f \in F'} \left\{ \min_{\forall s \in S} CMI(f, c|s) \right\}$
   (b) $S \leftarrow S \cup \{x\}$
   (c) $F' \leftarrow F' - \{x\}$
4. $D_i \leftarrow s_i \mid s_i \in S; i = 1, 2, ..., n$
5. $\forall f \in F'$ // Phase C
   (a) $\mu = \operatorname*{argmin}_{i=1,...,n} R(f, D_i)$
   (b) If $R(f, D_\mu) < \xi$ then $D_\mu \leftarrow D_\mu \cup \{f\}$

---

how this method compares to other baseline decomposition methods in terms of classification accuracy, when working with high-dimensional datasets.

4.1   Datasets

There is a number of benchmark repositories on the web providing structured high-dimensional datasets. The experimental data for this study was composed from different sources.

The NIPS 2003 feature selection challenge [7] provided us with 3 datasets: "Arcene", "Dorothea" and "Gisette". The remaining 3 datasets presented for that challenge do not comply with the desired property of $m \gg N$. Furthermore, all 6 datasets from the basic track of the RSCTC 2010 challenge on mining DNA data for medical diagnosis [14] were included in our study. In addition, a group of 10 datasets from the Kent Ridge (KR) Bio-Medical Data Set Repository[1] were also included.

A preprocessing was needed in 3 of the KR datasets (DLBCL-NIH, DLBCL-Stanford and Prostate Tumor), where missing values were replaced by the per-class average of the corresponding feature values, although other more suited strategies will be tested in the future. Some interesting properties of the experimental data (Table 1) are: the variety in the number of classes (ranging from 2 to 7), the presence of unbalanced classes (in 13 out of the 19 datasets) and the variety in the number of features and instances.

---

[1] http://datam.i2r.astar.edu.sg/datasets/krbd/

4.2   Algorithms and Methods

The general procedure was to decompose the feature set in different ways to train a decision forest. The ensemble decision is then obtained through a standard average combination of the class posterior probabilities. Each decision tree was built using the C4.5 algorithm. For every decomposition method several values for the number of subsets were considered and tested: up to 50 at intervals of 5.

Table 1. Description of the experimental data (N is the number of instances, m denotes the number of features) and averaged accuracy rates of the methods. The best performances for each dataset are emphasized in bold. The threshold value (ξ) and number of subsets (s) corresponding to de best performances of ITD are also shown.

Dataset	N	m	RSM	IFCBF	CERP	ITD	s	ξ
Arcene	200	10000	0.74	0.77	**0.78**	**0.78**	30	0.2
Dorothea	350	100000	**0.76**	0.65	0.58	0.71	5	0.1
Gisette	1000	5000	**0.93**	0.92	**0.93**	**0.93**	10	0.5
E-GEOD-10334	123	54676	0.83	**0.85**	0.83	0.84	25	0.1
E-GEOD-5406	105	22284	**0.65**	**0.65**	0.63	**0.65**	15	0.1
E-GEOD-13425	95	22278	0.89	0.89	0.88	**0.90**	30	0.3
E-GEOD-13904	113	54676	0.40	0.41	0.40	**0.43**	20	0.3
E-GEOD-4290	89	54676	0.62	0.63	0.63	**0.64**	30	0.5
E-GEOD-9635	92	59005	0.52	0.53	0.55	**0.57**	25	0.5
ALL-AML Leukemia	72	7130	0.93	0.92	0.93	**0.96**	20	0.3
Breast Cancer	97	24482	0.64	0.67	**0.69**	**0.69**	30	0.1
Central Nervous System	60	7130	0.51	0.51	0.53	**0.55**	10	0.1
Colon Tumor	62	2001	0.75	0.75	**0.80**	0.79	20	0.1
DLBCL-NIH	240	7400	0.53	0.54	**0.57**	0.55	10	0.3
DLBCL-Stanford	47	4027	0.87	0.91	**0.93**	0.92	30	0.1
MLL Leukemia	72	12583	0.93	0.95	**0.96**	**0.96**	30	0.3
Lung cancer	181	12534	**0.98**	0.97	**0.98**	**0.98**	10	0.3
Prostate Tumor	136	12601	0.87	0.87	0.89	**0.90**	15	0.2
Stjude Leukemia	327	12559	0.76	0.79	0.76	**0.81**	10	0.1

We compared 4 decomposers:

- RSM, the Random Subspace Method [8], which builds subsets of randomly selected features and allows overlapping, i.e. a feature may appear in more than one subset. Three subspace sizes were tested, as proportions from the total: 0.1, 0.3 and 0.5.
- IFBCF, an iterative application of an attribute selection algorithm, in this case FCBF [15]. Each iteration builds a subset and the selected features are excluded from subsequent iterations. This particular algorithm was selected for its time efficiency and its similarity with our decomposer.
- CERP, Classification by Ensembles from Random Partitions [3], which is a successful decomposition method adapted from RSM. As its name states, this method randomly partitions the feature space, thus avoiding overlaps.

- ITD, our information theoretic decomposer, which also avoids feature over-laps. Redundancy threshold values we considered were: 0.1, 0.2, 0.3 and 0.5.

All implementations and tests were performed using Weka [13] 3.7.6. For the experimental scheme and statistical considerations, we followed what is recommended in a work from Demšar [1]. Five repetitions of a two-fold cross-validation (5x2cv) were performed for every combination of parameter values, with each algorithm over each dataset. The performance criterion was the balanced accuracy rate, recommended for experiments where unbalanced datasets are present [7]. A Friedman test was applied to determine whether significant differences in performance exist within the group of combination algorithms. Afterwards, the the Holm procedure was used as a *post-hoc* test, to help identifying those significant differences. All tests were performed with a 95% confidence level.

4.3   Experimental Results

The performance of each method over each dataset was computed averaging the 10 performance measurements resulting from the 5x2cv. The best performance of each method over each dataset was selected from the different parameter settings. As a result, ITD was ranked first in 14 datasets out of 19 (Table 1).

A Friedman test was performed, it yielded significant differences on the accuracies of the 4 methods ($p = 2.7408 \cdot 10^{-4}$). The Holm procedure rejected all 3 hypotheses that claim non-significant differences between ITD and the other methods (Table 2). Hence, ITD significantly outperforms the others.

Table 2. Average rankings of the algorithms according to the Friedman test and Holm procedure table for $\alpha = 0.05$

Algorithm	Ranking	p	Adjusted p	
ITD	1.50	-	-	-
CERP	2.37	0.03814	0.05	*rejected*
IFCBF	2.92	0.00069	0.025	*rejected*
RSM	3.21	$4.43 \cdot 10^{-5}$	0.0167	*rejected*

5   Conclusions and Future Work

Information theory tools may provide useful insight about the internal properties of a dataset. They reveal feature interactions that are present regardless of the machine learning algorithm or training procedure. This has been sucessfully exploited in the past on the field of attribute selection, accounting for fast and effective algorithms. The same logic can be applied to decompose the feature set in a way not so different from a filter algorithm for attribute selection.

The experimental and statisical results suggest that this intuition may lead to significantly superior performances. A decomposition method that takes into account the internal properties of the dataset will provide independence from the learning algorithm, enabling its use on different scenarios. In particular, this may prove useful when dealing with high-dimensional datasets, since these are often unmanageable in full size, as well as difficult to pre-process because of the unavailability of background knowledge on the domain.

We think there is potential behind this result. As a next step it is essential to test this decomposition method using other learning algorithms to train the ensemble members. Furthermore, a thorough study on the diversity of such generated decompositions will most likely reveal new interesting insights. Additionally, it is relevant to adapt the current approach so that it allows overlappings on the feature subsets, thus enabling useful features to be present in more than one subset, as long as it does not affect the overall diversity.

References

1. Demšar, J.: Statistical comparisons of classifiers over multiple data sets. Journal of Machine Learning Research 7, 1–30 (2006)
2. Dietterich, T.G.: Ensemble methods in machine learning. In: Kittler, J., Roli, F. (eds.) MCS 2000. LNCS, vol. 1857, pp. 1–15. Springer, Heidelberg (2000)
3. Ahn, H., et al.: Classiffication by ensembles from random partitions of high-dimensional data. Computational Statistics & Data Analysis 51, 6166–6179 (2007)
4. Hu, Q., et al.: Ensemble rough subspaces. Pattern Recognition 40, 3728–3739 (2007)
5. Fleuret, F.: Fast binary feature selection with conditional mutual information. Journal of Machine Learning Research 5, 1531–1555 (2004)
6. François, D.: High-dimensional data analysis: optimal metrics and feature selection. PhD thesis, Université Catholique de Louvain (2007)
7. Guyon, I., Gunn, S.R., Ben-Hur, A., Dror, G.: Design and analysis of the NIPS 2003 challenge. In: Guyon, I., Nikravesh, M., Gunn, S., Zadeh, L.A. (eds.) Feature Extraction. STUDFUZZ, vol. 207, pp. 237–263. Springer, Heidelberg (2006)
8. Ho, T.K.: The random subspace method for constructing decision forests. IEEE Transactions on Pattern Analysis and Machine Intelligence 20, 832–844 (1998)
9. Liao, Y., Moody, J.: Constructing heterogeneous committees via input feature grouping. In: Advances in Neural Information Processing Systems, vol. 12, pp. 921–927 (2000)
10. Maimon, O., Rokach, L.: Decomposition methodology for knowledge discovery and data mining. World Scientific (2005)
11. Tahir, M.A., Smith, J.: Creating diverse nearest-neighbour ensembles using simultaneous metaheuristic feature selection. Pattern Recognition Letters 31(11), 1470–1480 (2010)
12. Torkkola, K.: Information-Theoretic Methods. In: Guyon, I., Nikravesh, M., Gunn, S., Zadeh, L.A. (eds.) Feature Extraction. STUDFUZZ, vol. 207, pp. 167–185. Springer, Heidelberg (2009)
13. Witten, I.H., Frank, E.: Data Mining: Practical Machine Learning Tools and Techniques, 3rd edn. Morgan Kaufmann Publishers (2011)
14. Wojnarski, M., et al.: RSCTC'2010 discovery challenge: Mining DNA microarray data for medical diagnosis and treatment. In: Szczuka, M., Kryszkiewicz, M., Ramanna, S., Jensen, R., Hu, Q. (eds.) RSCTC 2010. LNCS (LNAI), vol. 6086, pp. 4–19. Springer, Heidelberg (2010)
15. Yu, L., Liu, H.: Feature selection for high-dimensional data: A fast correlation-based filter solution. In: Machine Learning, ICML 2003, Washington, DC, USA, August 21-24, pp. 856–863 (2003)

On Stopping Rules
in Dependency-Aware Feature Ranking

Petr Somol[1,2], Jiří Grim[2], Jiří Filip[2], and Pavel Pudil[1]

[1] Faculty of Management, Prague University of Economics, Czech Republic
[2] Institute of Information Theory and Automation of the AS CR, Czech Republic

Abstract. Feature Selection in very-high-dimensional or small sample problems is particularly prone to computational and robustness complications. It is common to resort to feature ranking approaches only or to randomization techniques. A recent novel approach to the randomization idea in form of Dependency-Aware Feature Ranking (DAF) has shown great potential in tackling these problems well. Its original definition, however, leaves several technical questions open. In this paper we address one of these questions: how to define stopping rules of the randomized computation that stands at the core of the DAF method. We define stopping rules that are easier to interpret and show that the number of randomly generated probes does not need to be extensive.

Keywords: dimensionality reduction, feature selection, randomization, stopping rule.

1 Introduction

Feature selection (FS) is one of dimensionality reduction techniques, that preserves meaning of the selected original data features, while irrelevant features are discarded. Assume a general pattern recognition problem (typically a classification or clustering problem) in N-dimensional feature space. In the particular case of classification, some objects described by means of features $f_1, f_2, \ldots, f_N$ (real valued or discrete) are to be classified into one of a finite number of mutually exclusive classes. The common initial step in classifier design is to choose a reasonably small subset of informative features by using a feature selection method. The first step in solving the FS problem involves choosing appropriate method based on the knowledge (or lack of therein) of available training data properties. The key decision to be made involves the choice of the criterion and the search algorithm capable of optimizing such a criterion. Note that feature subset search is potentially an expensive combinatorial problem as the number of candidate subsets is very high. The search is stopped according to chosen stopping rule; it can be defined in terms of achieved completeness of search, criterion convergence threshold, subset size limit, time, etc.

In recent years the focus of feature selection research is moving from the relatively well covered area of low-to-mid-dimensional recognition problems towards very-high-dimensional problems [1]. As the high-dimensional FS is susceptible

J. Ruiz-Shulcloper and G. Sanniti di Baja (Eds.): CIARP 2013, Part I, LNCS 8258, pp. 286–293, 2013.

to problems arising from insufficient sample size and computational complexity, the FS methods often prefer simpler analysis ignoring inter-feature dependencies, e.g., based on feature ranking [2]. This simplifications is commonly assumed less harmful than obtaining misleading information through serious estimation errors due to over-fitting. The computational complexity can be reduced by resorting to randomized methods, however, this is counterbalanced by loss of optimality due to a user-defined time restriction of the search process. An example of such techniques is Relief algorithm [3] based on a simple idea of repeated randomized sampling of one pattern followed by feature weights update. Combinations of randomized and greedy algorithms [4] seems to be better suited for high-dimensional tasks, than randomized methods based on Genetic algorithms, Simulated Annealing, and Tabu Search [5], which provide strong optimization mechanism, at the cost of long converge times. Method's over-fitting has been tackled by a random restriction of inter-feature dependencies evaluation by repeatable running FS process on various random subspaces in [6].

Finally a combination of ranking and randomization called Dependency-Aware Feature Ranking has been introduced in [7]. The idea of individually best ranking is generalized to evaluate features contributions in a sequence of randomly generated feature subsets. The method has been shown capable of selecting features reliably even in settings where standard feature techniques fail due to problem complexity or over-fitting issues and where individual feature ranking results are unsatisfactory. Several open questions, however, remain with respect to DAF applicability, that have not been addressed in [7]. The two most practically important are: a) *What is the right final subset size?*, and b) *How long is it necessary to let the random probe generation process run?*

The problem to specify the optimal number of features to be selected, is closely related to the number of available data, dimension of the feature space and also to the underlying classification complexity. It is well known that in case of infinitely large training sets we should use all features since by omitting features the classifier performance cannot be improved. If a multidimensional training set were not large enough then most classifiers would tend to over-fit with the resulting poor classification performance on the independent test data. In such a case the generalizing property of the classifier could be improved by selecting a subset of informative features. Obviously, the optimal choice of the final reduced dimensionality depends on the size of the training data set and the complexity of the underlying classification problem. In this sense the question a) is beyond the scope of this paper since the size of the training data set is not considered explicitly. For a more detailed discussion of dimensionality problems in the context of standard individual feature ranking see e.g. [8]. In the following we investigate some aspects of question b), i.e., we discuss different options specifying the stopping rule of the feature ordering process.

2   Dependency-Aware Feature Ranking

Denoting F the set of all features $F = \{f_1, f_2, \ldots, f_N\}$ we assume that for each subset of features $S \subset F$ a feature selection criterion $J(\cdot)$ can be used as a measure of quality of S. We assume the criterion $J(\cdot)$ to be bounded according to the most feature selection criteria (estimates of classification accuracy are typically bounded by [0,1]).

The starting point of dependency-aware feature ranking is a randomly generated sequence of feature subsets to be denoted *probe* subsets $\mathbb{S} = \{S_1, S_2, \ldots, S_K\}$, $S_j \subset F$, $j = 1, 2, \ldots, K$, where each subset is evaluated by the criterion function $J(\cdot)$. For details on probe generation see [7].

Given a sufficiently large sequence of feature subsets $\mathbb{S}$, we can utilize the information contained in the criterion values $J(S_1), J(S_2), \ldots, J(S_K)$ to assess how each feature adds to the criterion value. Therefore, we compare the quality of probe subsets containing f with the quality of probe subsets not including f.

We compute the mean quality μ_f of subsets $S \in \mathbb{S}$ containing the considered feature

$$\mu_f = \frac{1}{|\mathbb{S}_f|} \sum_{S \in \mathbb{S}_f} J(S), \quad \mathbb{S}_f = \{S \in \mathbb{S} : f \in S\} \tag{1}$$

and the mean quality $\bar{\mu}_f$ of subsets $S \in \mathbb{S}$ not containing the considered feature f:

$$\bar{\mu}_f = \frac{1}{|\bar{\mathbb{S}}_f|} \sum_{S \in \bar{\mathbb{S}}_f} J(S), \quad \bar{\mathbb{S}}_f = \{S \in \mathbb{S} : f \notin S\} \tag{2}$$

with the aim to use the difference of both values as a criterion for ranking the features:

$$DAF(f) = \mu_f - \bar{\mu}_f, \quad f \in F. \tag{3}$$

The sequence of generated probe subsets can be arbitrarily long but the number of possible probes is finite. The probe subsets are generated randomly according to some fixed rules, for example the number of features in the subset may be fixed or bounded. If we denote $\mathbb{A}$ the class of admissible subsets which may occur in the sequence then, in view of the random generating procedure, the admissible subsets $S \in \mathbb{A}$ will occur in the sequence $\mathbb{S}$ repeatedly according to some fixed probabilities $\alpha(S)$. Thus, in long sequences of probes the admissible subsets $S \in \mathbb{A}$ will occur in $\mathbb{S}$ with the relative frequencies approaching $\alpha(S)$.

Like Eq. (1), (2) we denote $\mathbb{A}_f$ the class of admissible sets containing feature $f \in F$ and $\bar{\mathbb{A}}_f$ the class of admissible sets not containing feature f

$$\mathbb{A}_f = \{S \in \mathbb{A} : f \in S\}, \quad \bar{\mathbb{A}}_f = \{S \in \mathbb{A} : f \notin S\}, \quad f \in F. \tag{4}$$

It can be seen that, in view of above considerations, both the mean quality μ_f and $\bar{\mu}_f$ converge to some finite limit values. Considering Eq. (5) we can write

$$\lim_{|\mathbb{S}_f| \to \infty} \mu_f = \lim_{|\mathbb{S}_f| \to \infty} \frac{1}{|\mathbb{S}_f|} \sum_{S \in \mathbb{S}_f} J(S) = \sum_{S \in \mathbb{A}_f} \alpha_f(S) J(S) = \mu^* \tag{5}$$

where $\alpha_f(S)$ is the probability that the admissible subsets $S \in \mathbb{A}_f$ occur in the sequence $\mathbb{S}_f$ and μ^* is the corresponding limit value of μ_f. Similarly we can write analogous limit expression for the mean quality $\bar{\mu}_f$:

$$\lim_{|\bar{\mathbb{S}}_f| \to \infty} \bar{\mu}_f = \lim_{|\bar{\mathbb{S}}_f| \to \infty} \frac{1}{|\bar{\mathbb{S}}_f|} \sum_{S \in \bar{\mathbb{S}}_f} J(S) = \sum_{S \in \bar{\mathbb{A}}_f} \bar{\alpha}_f(S) J(S) = \bar{\mu}^* \tag{6}$$

with $\bar{\alpha}_f(S)$ denoting the occurrence probability of $S \in \bar{\mathbb{A}}_f$ in the sequence $\bar{\mathbb{S}}_f$. Consequently, the criterion value $DAF(f)$ has a finite limit for any $f \in F$:

$$\lim_{|\mathbb{S}_f| \to \infty} DAF(f) = \mu_f^* - \bar{\mu}_f^*, \quad f \in F. \tag{7}$$

It has been shown in [7] that selecting features according to highest DAF coefficients leads to significantly better results then selecting features according to individually best criterion values. This makes the method well suitable for scenarios where individual feature evaluation had been considered the only viable choice (i.e., very high-dimensional or small sample size problems).

In paper [7] the question of when to stop the process of randomized probe generation (i.e., what is the right value of K) is not specifically addressed. All presented results have been obtained using the ad-hoc stopping rules. The first obvious rule is a *user-specified time limit*, i.e., the computation is stopped after a pre-specified time limit. Here it is hoped that the number of probes that are evaluated in the time limit is sufficient with respect to the given problem. There is almost no way of guessing what time limit should suffice, except the generally applicable advice that the more time can be invested, the more accurate predictions can be made. Another problem here is the dependence on particular hardware, different computers would manage significantly different number of probes within the same time. The second trivial rule is a *user-specified limit of the number of probes*, i.e, the computation is stopped after a pre-specified number of probes has been investigated. Specifying the minimum necessary number of probes is as unreliable as specifying the time limit. Although this is independent on particular computer settings, there is still no guidance or interpretation available that would help to adjust the setting for particular problem.

3   Design of Novel Stopping Rules

In this section we consider two natural stopping rules that have not been considered in paper [7]. Both of them are based on evaluating a *function of change* while adding probes, which then can be thresholded to find the moment to stop.

Stopping Condition 1. *Change of Feature Order.* The adding of probes and recalculating DAF coefficients for each feature leads to changes in ordering of all features according to their DAF coefficients. Defining a threshold on the change would allow to stop adding probes when the ordering is not changing substantially any more.

Definition 1. *Let C denote the function to evaluate difference in feature ordering yielded by evaluating DAF coefficient in systems $\mathbb{S}_1$ and $\mathbb{S}_2$ where $\mathbb{S}_1 \subset \mathbb{S}_2$. Denoting $DAF(f)^{\mathbb{S}}$ the DAF coefficient of feature f computed on system $\mathbb{S}$, and assuming that features have been ordered according to descending $DAF(f)^{\mathbb{S}}$ values and the index of feature f in such ordering is denoted $DAF(f)_{idx}^{\mathbb{S}}$, we define $C[\mathbb{S}_1, \mathbb{S}_2] = \frac{1}{N} \sum_{f=1}^{N} |DAF(f)_{idx}^{\mathbb{S}_1} - DAF(f)_{idx}^{\mathbb{S}_2}|$.*

In Definition 1 we average the change in position in DAF-based ordering of features when a certain number of probes has been added to system $\mathbb{S}_1$ to obtain system $\mathbb{S}_2$. Naturally, with decreasing change in DAF based ordering of features we could assume at some point that no more probe adding is needed as it would not affect the resulting feature ranking.

In Stopping Condition 1 we assume the value of C asymptotically decreases with increasing $\mathbb{S}$ size. However, this may not be always true.

Proposition 1. *Assume we keep adding equally large groups of random probes to systems of subsets so as to obtain a series of systems $\mathbb{S}_1 \subset \mathbb{S}_2 \subset \mathbb{S}_3 \ldots$. For any $i \geq 1$ the value $C[\mathbb{S}_i, \mathbb{S}_{i+1}]$ can be arbitrary, there is no guarantee of it going close to zero. As a consequence, there is no guarantee that C would fall below given threshold when adding probes to a system of subsets indefinitely.*

Proof. The problem here is the fact that arbitrarily small change of DAF value can cause feature ordering to change. Imagine all features in the given problem to be equal. The feature selection criterion used to evaluate each probe would yield slightly different values for different probes because the estimate is done from finite training data susceptible to sampling errors. The process of computing DAF values would produce for each feature a DAF coefficient that would be arbitrarily close to each other, in some cases equal. Adding a probe could at any time cause an arbitrarily small change (possibly decreasing with the number of probes), but any arbitrarily small nonzero change would be capable of change DAF coefficient values of two features and change their mutual order.

It seems Stopping Condition 1 is thus useless in general case. We will test it, however, in our experiments as well, as the convergence problem should not show up in cases when a sufficient distinction among features can be identified.

Stopping Condition 2. *Change of Average DAF value.* The adding of probes and recalculating DAF coefficients for each feature leads to changes in DAF coefficient value for some or all features. Assuming that these changes would decrease with increasing number of probes, it should be possible to define a threshold on DAF value change to specify when the change is to be considered small enough to justify stopping the process.

Definition 2. *Let $C2$ denote the function to evaluate difference in average DAF coefficient values over all features, yielded by evaluating DAF coefficient in systems $\mathbb{S}_1$ and $\mathbb{S}_2$ where $\mathbb{S}_1 \subset \mathbb{S}_2$. Denoting $DAF(f)^{\mathbb{S}}$ the DAF coefficient of feature f computed on system $\mathbb{S}$, we define $C2[\mathbb{S}_1, \mathbb{S}_2] = \frac{1}{N} \sum_{f=1}^{N} |DAF(f)^{\mathbb{S}_1} - DAF(f)^{\mathbb{S}_2}|$.*

In Definition 2 we average the change in DAF coefficient values of features when a certain number of probes has been added to system $\mathbb{S}_1$ to obtain system $\mathbb{S}_2$. Naturally, with decreasing change in DAF coefficient values we could assume at some point that no more probe adding is needed as it would not affect the resulting feature ranking. Concerning the convergence properties of $C2$ we proof the following Lemma.

Lemma 1. *Assume we keep adding equally large groups of random probes to systems of subsets so as to obtain a series of systems $\mathbb{S}_1 \subset \mathbb{S}_2 \subset \mathbb{S}_3 \ldots$. Then, for arbitrarily small threshold value $t > 0$ there exists a size of subset system $\mathbb{S}$ (number of probes) p so that for any $i > j > p$ it is true that $C2[\mathbb{S}_i, \mathbb{S}_j] < t$.*

Proof. The proof is a simple consequence of the Bolzano-Cauchy theorem. The sequence of $DAF(f)^{\mathbb{S}}$ coefficients converges with the increasing number of probes in $\mathbb{S}$ and the same holds for the finite sum of coefficients $\sum_{f=1}^{N} DAF(f)^{\mathbb{S}}$. Therefore the corresponding Bolzano-Cauchy condition is satisfied which directly implies the assertion of the Lemma.

The remaining problem with Stopping Condition 2 is the necessity by user to specify a threshold based on DAF coefficient values. this may still be difficult to interpret. Therefore, we suggest to set relative instead of absolute threshold. The relative change can be evaluated with respect to the first recorded change in probe adding process. For this and also for computational reasons it is practical to evaluate function $C2$ not after each probe addition but after the addition of several probes.

Stopping Condition 2a. *Relative Change of Average DAF value.* The adding of probes to system of subsets $\mathbb{S}$ and recalculating DAF coefficients for each feature after the additions leads to changes in DAF coefficient value for some or all features. Stop probe adding when for the k-th added probe it is true that $\frac{C2[\mathbb{S}_k, \mathbb{S}_{k+1}]}{C2[\mathbb{S}_1, \mathbb{S}_2]} < t$ for a pre-specified threshold t.

In this case the threshold represents limit on the proportional change in average DAF coefficient values. In the next section we show on examples how the values C and $C2$ correspond with classification accuracy throughout the probe addition process.

4   Experimental Evaluation

We illustrate the proposed stopping rules on two datasets: Reuters-21578 text categorization benchmark data[1] (33 classes, 10105 features) and artificial Madelon data [9] (2 classes, 500 features, out of which 20 are informative and 480 noise). Our experiment setup followed the setup described in [7]. With Reuters data we used the estimated accuracy of linear SVM; both as probe evaluating criterion and the eventual evaluation of the quality of selected subsets. With Madelon data we used 3-NN for the same purpose.

Figures 1 and 2 show a 3D graph showing the achieved classification accuracy on independent test data at various stages of probe-adding process. As DAF ranking does not decide about the number of features, the d axis in graph represents results for various subset sizes obtained by using the first d best features according the current DAF coefficients. Both Figures 1 and 2 show very quick improvement of classification accuracy after a small number of initially added

---

[1] http://www.daviddlewis.com/resources/testcollections/reuters21578

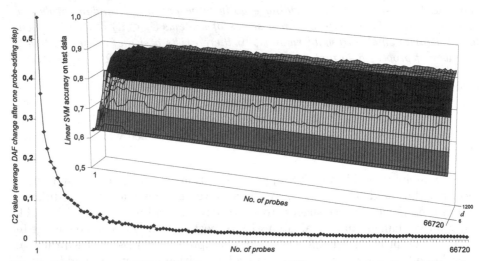

Fig. 1. Reuters data - SVM Classifier accuracy and $C2$ convergence during DAF probe generation

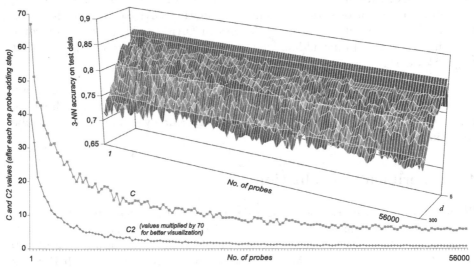

Fig. 2. Madelon data - 3-NN Classifier accuracy and C and $C2$ convergence during DAF probe generation

probes, most of the remaining process of probe adding later led to very slow improvement (Fig. 1) or negligible improvements but stabilization (visible in Fig. 2 at least for subset sizes around 20 representing the informative features).

The experiments serve primarily to illustrate the behavior of functions C and $C2$ with respect to growing number of probes being added to $\mathbb{S}$. The C and $C2$ have not been computed after each single added probe but after each 400-th probe. This is to compensate for the fact that adding a single probe can not affect all features (probe size was limited to 200 features).

The function C converged very slowly in the case of Madelon data. Reaching a point of no changes in feature ordering proved unrealistic in this case of 500-dimensional data; with higher-dimensional Reuters data we did not even attempt. The function $C2$ though converges reasonably fast as can be seen in both experiments. The question of what would be the practical threshold can not be answered unanimously for the general case, but in all our experiments (on 5 different datasets from which only 2 are presented here) it showed practical to set the threshold roughly to $\frac{C2[S_k,S_{k+1}]}{C2[S_1,S_2]} < 0.01$, i.e., to stop when $C2$ values decrease roughly to 1% of their initial value.

5 Conclusions

We have investigated alternative stopping rules in Dependency-Aware Feature Ranking. We have shown that thresholding the averaged change in DAF value when adding probes to the considered subset system is preferable to other stopping rules in terms of interpretability, especially in cases when there is lack of knowledge of the underlying data. We have also demonstrated that DAF is fairly robust and does not require excessive numbers of randomized probes (as expressed by change evaluating functions) in order to produce feature ranking that works well in independent test case.

Acknowledgements. This work has been supported by the Czech Science Foundation grants P403/12/1557 and P103/11/0335.

References

1. Fan, J., Li, R.: Statistical challenges with high dimensionality: Feature selection in knowledge discovery (2006)
2. Kuncheva, L.I.: A stability index for feature selection. In: Proc. 25th IASTED International Multi-Conference, AIAP 2007, pp. 390–395. ACTA Press (2007)
3. Kononenko, I.: Estimating attributes: Analysis and extensions of RELIEF. In: Bergadano, F., De Raedt, L. (eds.) ECML 1994. LNCS, vol. 784, pp. 171–182. Springer, Heidelberg (1994)
4. Gheyas, I.A., Smith, L.S.: Feature subset selection in large dimensionality domains. Pattern Recognition 43(1), 5–13 (2010)
5. Glover, F.W., Kochenberger, G.A. (eds.): Handbook of Metaheuristics. Int. Series in Operations Research & Management Science, vol. 57. Springer (2003)
6. Lai, C., Reinders, M.J.T., Wessels, L.: Random subspace method for multivariate feature selection. Pattern Recogn. Lett. 27(10), 1067–1076 (2006)
7. Somol, P., Grim, J., Pudil, P.: Fast dependency-aware feature selection in very-high-dimensional pattern recognition. In: Proceedings of the IEEE International Conference on Systems, Man and Cybernetics (SMC), pp. 502–509. IEEE (2011)
8. Liu, H., Motoda, H.: Feature Selection for Knowledge Discovery and Data Mining. Kluwer Academic Publishers, Norwell (1998)
9. Newman, D., Hettich, S., Blake, C., Merz, C.: UCI repository of machine learning databases (1998)

Towards Cluster-Based Prototype Sets for Classification in the Dissimilarity Space

Yenisel Plasencia-Calaña[1,2], Mauricio Orozco-Alzate[3],
Edel García-Reyes[1], and Robert P.W. Duin[2]

[1] Advanced Technologies Application Center. 7ma A ♯ 21406,
Playa, Havana - 12200, Cuba
{yplasencia,egarcia}@cenatav.co.cu
[2] Faculty of Electrical Engineering, Mathematics and Computer Sciences,
Delft University of Technology, The Netherlands
r.duin@ieee.org
[3] Departamento de Informática y Computación, Universidad Nacional de Colombia -
Sede Manizales. Kilómetro 7 vía al Aeropuerto, Campus La Nubia – Bloque Q,
Piso 2, Manizales, Colombia
morozcoa@unal.edu.co

Abstract. The selection of prototypes for the dissimilarity space is a
key aspect to overcome problems related to the curse of dimensionality
and computational burden. How to properly define and select the prototypes is still an open issue. In this paper, we propose the selection
of clusters as prototypes to create low-dimensional spaces. Experimental results show that the proposed approach is useful in the problems
presented. Especially, the use of the minimum distances to clusters for
representation provides good results.

Keywords: dissimilarity space, prototype selection, cluster-based
prototypes.

1 Introduction

The representation of objects is crucial for the success of a pattern recognition
system. The feature space representation is the most common approach since a
large number of techniques can be used. Dissimilarity representations [1] arose
as an alternative and have been showing a good performance in several problems, where the dissimilarities may be computed by directly matching original
objects [1] or on top of feature representations [2]. Three main approaches are
presented in [1], the most promising being the dissimilarity space (DS).

In the DS, an object is represented by a vector of dissimilarities with other
objects called prototypes. If a large set of prototypes is used, it leads to a high-
dimensionality of the DS implying that computational costs of classification are
increased as well as storage costs. In addition, a high-dimensionality leads to
problems related to the "curse of dimensionality" and small sample sizes. Furthermore, high-dimensional representations are likely to contain noise since the
intrinsic dimensionality of the data is usually small, leading to overfitting.

J. Ruiz-Shulcloper and G. Sanniti di Baja (Eds.): CIARP 2013, Part I, LNCS 8258, pp. 294–301, 2013.

Prototype selection is a way to overcome these drawbacks. It has been studied [3] for reducing dimensions of DS with encouraging results. Several methods have been proposed such as Kcentres, Forward Selection (FS), Editing and Condensing, among others [3]. In these studies, the selected prototypes are objects. However, some efforts are also put in a different direction and, instead of objects, linear models are built, selecting out some of them for representation [4]. These studies showed that it is a feasible alternative to use a small number of carefully selected feature lines as prototypes instead of the original objects.

In this paper we study the selection of clusters for the generation of a low-dimensional generalized dissimilarity space (GDS). Our hypothesis is that clusters may be useful to obtain low-dimensional GDSs in case datasets are structured in clusters. A similar approach was presented in [5], however it was specifically developed for graph distances while our research is not restricted to graphs. Besides, they do not take into account the selection of the best clusters, while our goal is to find the clusters which allow a good classification with a decreased dimension of the space. We also included the subspace distance to clusters. Different approaches to compute the distances of the training and test objects to the clusters are presented. The paper is divided as follows. Section 2 introduces the DS and prototype selection. Section 3 describes the construction of the datasets based on cluster distances. Experimental results and discussions are provided in Sec. 4 followed by concluding remarks in Sec. 5.

2   Dissimilarity Space

The DS was conceived with the purpose to address classification of data represented by dissimilarities that may be non-Euclidean or even non-metric. The dissimilarities of a training set X with a set of prototypes $R = \{r_1, ..., r_k\}$ are interpreted as coordinates in the DS. Thereby, the number of prototypes selected determines the dimension of the space. The DS was postulated as a Euclidean vector space, making suitable the use of statistical classifiers. The set of prototypes may satisfy $R \subseteq X$ or $R \cap X = \emptyset$. Once R is selected by any prototype selector, the dissimilarities of both training and test objects with R are computed. Let x be any training or test object and d a suitable dissimilarity measure for the problem at hand, the representation d_x of the object in the dissimilarity space is:

$$d_x = [d(x, r_1) \ d(x, r_2) \ ... \ d(x, r_k)]. \tag{1}$$

2.1   Prototype Selection

Many approaches have been considered [2,3] for the selection of prototypes in the DS. Variants of wrapper or supervised methods [3] have been proposed. Other approaches are considered that use the distances or distribution of the prototypes over the dataset [2]; note that in these cases the class labels of the prototypes may not be needed. An interesting option is the genetic algorithm

(GA) presented in [6]. The GA is an evolutionary method which uses heuristics in order to evolve an initial set of solutions (sets of prototypes) to better ones by using operations such as mutation and reproduction. Moreover, it is adequate to handle non-metric dissimilarities and it can find complicated relationships between the prototypes. For these reasons we propose to use a GA to select the clusters together with the leave-one-out nearest neighbor (LOO 1-NN) error in the DS as selection criterion. We adopt the same parameters for the GA as in [6]. Clusters present nice properties that good prototypes must have. For example, they do not provide redundant information since redundant or close objects must lie together in the same cluster and they cover the representation space better than a small set of objects.

3   Construction of Models Based on Clusters

In this section we describe our methodology to construct the new dissimilarity datasets based on cluster distances computed from the originally given dissimilarities. In this study, the clusters are created per class by the Affinity Propagation algorithm [7]. In the clustering process representatives and their corresponding clusters emerge from a message-passing procedure between pairs of samples until stopping criteria are met. This method is reported to provide good clustering results. Furthermore, it is also of our convenience that it semi-automatically selects the proper number of clusters, emerging from the message-passing procedure but also from a user preference of the cluster representatives. The original dissimilarities must be transformed into similarities in order to apply the clustering procedure. We set the preferences for each object (i.e. the potential to be selected as cluster center) equal to the median similarity.

Different types of distances are used to measure the resemblance of objects with clusters such as: the minimum, maximum, average and subspace distances. The minimum distance is computed as the distance between the object and its nearest object in the cluster. The maximum distance is defined as the distance between the object and its farthest object in the cluster. The average distance is defined as the average of the distances between the object and all the cluster objects. The subspace distance is explained more carefully. Theory about it is sparse in the literature [8,9], especially for the case of data given in terms of non-metric dissimilarities. Therefore, one contribution of this paper is to describe the methodology to compute the (speeded-up) distance of objects to subspaces when data is provided in terms of non-metric dissimilarities.

The methodology to compute the subspace distance to clusters is as follows. First, a subspace is created for every cluster in order to compute the subspace distances. To achieve this, the set of dissimilarities is transformed into equivalent dot products (which can be interpreted as similarities) and centered according to the "double-centering" formula for each cluster:

$$S_{ij} = -\frac{1}{2}\left(D_{ij}^2 - \frac{1}{n}C_i - \frac{1}{n}C_j + \frac{1}{n^2}C_iC_j\right), \tag{2}$$

where D_{ij} is the dissimilarity between the cluster objects x_i and x_j, $C_i = \sum_j D_{ij}^2$, which is the i-th row sum of the dissimilarity matrix for the cluster objects, n is the number of objects in the cluster, and S_{ij} are the centered dot products. The eigendecomposition of S is performed and eigenvectors are sorted in descendent manner according to their eigenvalues. Only the eigenvectors associated with eigenvalues $\lambda > 0$ are used to compute the projections of new points to the subspace via the *Nyström* formula [10].

Each embedding coordinate of a cluster object x_i used to compute the kernel is given by $e_{ik} = \sqrt{\lambda_k} v_{ik}$ as for multidimensional scaling (MDS) [8], where λ_k is the k-th eigenvalue and v_{ik} is the i-th element of the k-th eigenvector of S, but the embedding for a new point is obtained via the *Nyström* approximation which is interpreted as the Kernel PCA projection [9] using S as the kernel matrix. The *Nyström* formula was generalized for extending MDS as suggested in [9], therefore, each embedding coordinate e_{ik} is computed by:

$$e_{ik}(x) = \frac{\sqrt{\lambda_k}}{\lambda_k} \sum_{i=1}^{n} v_{ik} S(x, x_i), \tag{3}$$

where x_i are the cluster objects and $S(x, x_i)$ is computed from a continuous version of the "double-centering" formula:

$$S(x, x_i) = -\frac{1}{2} \left(d(x, x_i)^2 - \frac{1}{n} \sum_j d(x, x_j)^2 - \frac{1}{n} \sum_j D_{ij}^2 + \frac{1}{n^2} \sum_{ij} D_{ij}^2 \right). \tag{4}$$

$S(x, x_i)$ is a data-dependent kernel where $d(\cdot, \cdot)$ is the dissimilarity function. This *Nyström* embedding is applied to speed-up the embedding computation instead of recomputing the eigendecomposition including x in the whole process. However, in our case, the embedding is not directly used, instead, the embedding coordinates are used to compute the distance to the subspace. The squared subspace distance $d_L(x, L)^2$ is formulated as the difference between the squared length of the vector (its squared norm) given by $S(x, x)$ and the length of its projection on the space via *Nyström*:

$$d_L(x, L)^2 = S(x, x) - \sum_{k=1}^{m} \left(\frac{\sqrt{\lambda_k}}{\lambda_k} \sum_{i=1}^{n} v_{ik} S(x, x_i) \right)^2. \tag{5}$$

4   Experimental Results

4.1   Datasets and Experimental Setup

The dissimilarity datasets were selected for the experiments based on the existence of clusters in the data. The Ionosphere dataset consists in radar data [11] where the $L1$ distance is used. The Kimia dataset is based on the shape contexts descriptor [12] computed for the Kimia shapes data [13]. The dissimilarity is based on sums of matching costs for the best matching points defining two shapes, plus the amount of transformation needed to align the shapes. The dissimilarity data set Chickenpieces-20-60 [14] is composed by edit distances from string representations of the angles between segments defining the contours of chicken pieces images. The Ringnorm dataset is the one presented in [15]; it is originally a 20-dimensional, 2-class data, where the first class is normally distributed with zero mean and covariance matrix 4 times the identity. The second class has unit covariance matrix and mean close to zero. We use only the first 2 features and the $L2$ distance. The characteristics of the datasets as well as the cardinality of the training sets used are presented in Table 1.

Table 1. Properties of the datasets used in this study, Symm. and Metric refers to whether the data is symmetric or metric, the $|T|$ column refers to the training set cardinality used for the experiments

Datasets	# Classes	# Obj. per class	Symm.	Metric	$|T|$
Ionosphere	2	225,126	yes	yes	140
Kimia	18	18×12	no	no	90
Rings	2	440,449	yes	yes	222
ChickenPieces-20-60	5	117,76,96,61,96	no	no	158

As classifier we used the support vector machine (SVM) classifier. For the SVM we used a linear kernel and a fixed appropriately selected cost parameter $C = 1$. Note that despite the fact that the curse of dimensionality was mentioned as a limitation of high-dimensional spaces, the SVM classifier is able to handle high dimensions well. This makes our comparisons more fair for the high-dimensional representations. However, the limitation was mentioned since in many applications people may want to use classifiers that suffer from the curse of dimensionality and resorting to low-dimensional representations by prototype selection is one option to overcome the problem. Our proposals are the following cluster-based methods: selection by GA of clusters created using minimum, maximum, average and subspace distances of training objects to the clusters. The cluster-based methods are compared with some of the best prototype selectors presented in the literature (which select objects as prototypes), with representatives of unsupervised and supervised methods: Forward selection [3] optimizing the LOO 1-NN error in the DS, Kcentres prototype selector [3], random selection, selection by GA of the best clusters centers, and selection by GA of the best prototypes from the whole candidate set. In addition, we compared the approach using all candidate objects as prototypes.

A set of 5 to 20 prototype clusters/objects are selected. However, the total number returned by the affinity propagation is about 25 clusters. Averaged errors and standard deviations over 30 experiments are reported in Table 2 for the dimension where the best result was obtained. Objects in each dataset are randomly split 30 times into training, representation, and test sets. Clusters are computed on the representation set which also contains the candidate objects for prototypes, the best clusters and objects are selected optimizing the criteria for the training set by which the classifiers are trained, and the final classification errors are computed for the test sets. We performed a t-test to find if the differences between the mean errors of the best overall result and the mean errors achieved by the other approaches was statistically significant, the level of significance used is 0.05. In the case that a cluster-based method was the best, the statistical significance is computed with respect to the non cluster-based approaches.

Table 2. Mean and standard deviation of errors over 30 experiments. The best overall result is reported for each dataset with the corresponding results of the other methods for the same dimension of the space (in parenthesis). When the difference of the best result with the other standard approaches is statistically significant, it is reported in bold.

Selectors \ Datasets	Ionosph(15)	Kimia(20)	Rings(20)	Chicken Pieces(20)
Clusters minimum	**0.063 ± 0.028**	**0.047 ± 0.032**	0.265 ± 0.0205	0.11 ± 0.025
Clusters maximum	0.09 ± 0.029	0.11 ± 0.054	**0.263 ± 0.0236**	0.15 ± 0.028
Clusters average	0.072 ± 0.023	0.06 ± 0.045	0.274 ± 0.0181	0.09 ± 0.024
Clusters subspace	0.073 ± 0.022	0.07 ± 0.048	0.276 ± 0.0193	0.088 ± 0.023
Random	0.086 ± 0.026	0.12 ± 0.057	0.274 ± 0.0181	0.17 ± 0.039
GA (whole set)	0.082 ± 0.028	0.1 ± 0.043	0.274 ± 0.0181	0.16 ± 0.028
GA (cluster centres)	0.085 ± 0.032	0.094 ± 0.05	0.275 ± 0.0177	0.15 ± 0.029
Forward selection	0.09 ± 0.027	0.12 ± 0.054	0.274 ± 0.0184	0.16 ± 0.036
Kcentres	0.082 ± 0.029	0.13 ± 0.061	0.274 ± 0.0181	0.15 ± 0.036
All	0.083 ± 0.033	0.068 ± 0.042	0.274 ± 0.0181	**0.077 ± 0.017**

4.2   Results and Discussion

In Table 2 it can be seen that classification results in the GDS generated by selected clusters outperform the classification results in DS with selected objects as prototypes for the same dimensions of the spaces. For the Ionosphere and Kimia datasets the best method uses clusters with minimum distance, this is in agreement with previous findings for graph dissimilarities in [5]. In the Ionosphere and Kimia datasets, the selection of clusters using maximum distance is usually among the worse alternatives. This may be expected since it may be very sensitive to outliers. However, in the Rings dataset the clusters based on maximum distances provide the best overall result. In the case of Chicken Pieces, the best results are obtained using all objects as prototypes, perhaps because this dataset has a high intrinsic dimension (176) according to the number of significant eigenvalues of the covariance matrix in the DS. Therefore, in order to obtain good results, high-dimensional spaces are needed. However, the average and subspace distance to clusters outperformed the other approaches that create low-dimensional spaces.

Cluster-based approaches create irregular kernels which nonlinearly map the data to the GDS in a better way than the object-based approaches for the same dimensions. We computed the nonlinear mapping for the Rings data from the underlying feature space to a Hilbert space using a second degree polynomial kernel and applied SVM classification with this kernel and regularization parameter optimized. We corroborate that the results were very similar to the ones obtained using clusters in the dissimilarity space. Cluster-based prototypes allow one to apply linear classifiers with good results to originally nonlinear data. The same can be achieved by kernels and SVM if the dissimilarities are Euclidean (they are transformed to the equivalent kernel). However, the original SVM will not work anymore for a non-Euclidean dissimilarity matrix but a nonlinear mapping to the DS or GDS can still be achieved for non-Euclidean data (e.g. the Kimia dataset).

The main disadvantage of using cluster-based prototypes compared to object-based prototypes for spaces of the same dimension is the computational cost, since, when using clusters, more dissimilarities must be measured. In this case, for training and test objects, the dissimilarities with all the objects in the clusters must be computed in order to find the minimum, maximum and average dissimilarity. However, when compared to the approach using all objects as prototypes, the computational cost of the cluster-based approach is smaller because some clusters are discarded in the selection process and, thereby, less dissimilarity computations are made for training and test objects. Since the dissimilarity matrix is computed in advance before prototype selection is executed, the proposed approach as well as the standard prototype selection methods have limitations in case of very large datasets. This remains open for further research.

5   Conclusions

For the selection of prototypes not only the optimization method and criterion used are important, but also how the prototypes are devised is vital. We found that clusters may be useful to obtain low-dimensional GDSs in the case of datasets that present clusters. Our approach is useful for problems where the use of cluster-based prototypes make sense according to the data distribution. Note that our results hold for small and moderate training set sizes. When large training sets are available, they may compensate for bad mappings using objects as prototypes.

In general, we found that the minimum, average and subspace distances to clusters perform well in real-world datasets. However, there is no "best" approach among the cluster-based methods, it seems that the best option depends on specific data characteristics. Our intuition is that the minimum distance seems to be more meaningful for measuring distances with sets of objects with a shape such as the clusters. The cluster-based approaches improve the results of using DS of the same dimension but created by selected objects as well as DS using all the objects as prototypes (high-dimensional). Future works will be devoted to study the sensitivity to the choice of different clustering methods as well as the influence of numbers and sizes of the clusters.

References

1. Pekalska, E., Duin, R.P.W.: The Dissimilarity Representation for Pattern Recognition: Foundations and Applications (Machine Perception and Artificial Intelligence). World Scientific Publishing Co., Inc., River Edge (2005)
2. Lozano, M., Sotoca, J.M., Sánchez, J.S., Pla, F., Pekalska, E., Duin, R.P.W.: Experimental study on prototype optimisation algorithms for prototype-based classification in vector spaces. Pattern Recogn. 39(10), 1827–1838 (2006)
3. Pekalska, E., Duin, R.P.W., Paclík, P.: Prototype selection for dissimilarity-based classifiers. Pattern Recogn. 39(2), 189–208 (2006)
4. Plasencia-Calaña, Y., Orozco-Alzate, M., García-Reyes, E., Duin, R.P.W.: Selecting feature lines in generalized dissimilarity representations for pattern recognition. Digit. Signal Process. 23(3), 902–911 (2013)
5. Riesen, K., Bunke, H.: Graph classification by means of Lipschitz embedding. Trans. Sys. Man Cyber. Part B 39(6), 1472–1483 (2009)
6. Plasencia-Calaña, Y., García-Reyes, E., Orozco-Alzate, M., Duin, R.P.W.: Prototype selection for dissimilarity representation by a genetic algorithm. In: Proceedings of the 20th International Conference on Pattern Recognition, ICPR 2010, pp. 177–180. IEEE Computer Society, Washington, DC (2010)
7. Frey, B.J.J., Dueck, D.: Clustering by passing messages between data points. Science 315, 972–976 (2007)
8. Cox, T.F., Cox, M.: Multidimensional Scaling, 2nd edn. Chapman and Hall/CRC (2000)
9. Bengio, Y., Paiement, J.F., Vincent, P., Delalleau, O., Roux, N.L., Ouimet, M.: Out-of-sample extensions for LLE, Isomap, MDS, Eigenmaps, and Spectral Clustering. In: Advances in Neural Information Processing Systems, pp. 177–184. MIT Press (2003)
10. Baker, C.T.H.: The numerical treatment of integral equations. Clarendon Press, Oxford (1977)
11. Sigillito, V.G., Wing, S.P., Hutton, L.V., Baker, K.B.: Classification of radar returns from the ionosphere using neural networks. Johns Hopkins APL Technical Digest, 262–266 (1989)
12. Belongie, S., Malik, J., Puzicha, J.: Shape matching and object recognition using shape contexts. IEEE Trans. Pattern Anal. Mach. Intell. 24(4), 509–522 (2002)
13. Sebastian, T.B., Klein, P.N., Kimia, B.B.: Recognition of shapes by editing their shock graphs. IEEE Trans. Pattern Anal. Mach. Intell. 26(5), 550–571 (2004)
14. Bunke, H., Buhler, U.: Applications of approximate string matching to 2D shape recognition. Pattern Recogn. 26(12), 1797–1812 (1993)
15. Breiman, L.: Bias, Variance, and Arcing Classifiers. Technical report, University of California, Berkeley (1996)

Easy Categorization of Attributes in Decision Tables Based on Basic Binary Discernibility Matrix

Manuel S. Lazo-Cortés[1], José Francisco Martínez-Trinidad[1],
Jesús Ariel Carrasco-Ochoa[1], and Guillermo Sánchez-Díaz[2]

[1] Instituto Nacional de Astrofísica, Óptica y Electrónica, Puebla, México
{mlazo,ariel,fmartine}@ccc.inaoep.mx
[2] Universidad Autónoma de San Luis Potosí, San Luis Potosí, México
guillermo.sanchez@uaslp.mx

Abstract. Attribute reduction is an important issue in classification problems. This paper proposes a novel method for categorizing attributes in a decision table based on transforming the binary discernibility matrix into a simpler one called basic binary discernibility matrix. The effectiveness of the method is theoretically demonstrated. Experiments show application results of the proposed method.

Keywords: Attribute reduction, rough sets, reduct, binary discernibility matrix.

1   Introduction

Attribute reduction is an important issue in classification problems. The accuracy of many classification algorithms depends on the quality of selected attributes. Rough set [1] approach for attribute reduction is based on reducts, which are in fact minimal sets of attributes that preserve some necessary amount of information.

This paper investigates the problem of categorizing attributes, identifying the set of attributes that are present in all reducts (core); such attributes are called indispensable attributes. Those attributes that belong to at least one reduct are called relevant and the remaining attributes are called superfluous or redundant. For a given decision table, the problem of searching for all relevant (also called reductive [2] or semi-core [3]) attributes becomes the problem of determining the union of all reducts of a given decision table, or determining the set of all redundant attributes of a decision table.

Several papers face the problem of attribute reduction by finding redundant attributes, in [4] an updated review about research on attribute reduction is presented, however there is no reference about the use of the binary representation of the discernibility matrix.

In this paper, we present a new approach for categorizing attributes by using a binary representation of the discernibility matrix. This approach could be useful to reduce the search space for computing all reducts. The binary discernibility matrix, introduced by Felix and Ushio [5] plays an important role in the solution of the

J. Ruiz-Shulcloper and G. Sanniti di Baja (Eds.): CIARP 2013, Part I, LNCS 8258, pp. 302–310, 2013.

problem of categorizing attributes. First, we describe the binary discernibility matrix and some of its properties, then based on some properties of a special type of binary discernibility matrix we present a characterization of both indispensable and super-fluous attributes. The remaining relevant attributes are determined by exclusion.

The structure of this paper is as follows. Section 2 presents some basic concepts in rough set theory. Section 3 presents the theoretical study of the properties that allow establishing the categorization of the attributes from the basic binary discernibility matrix. In section 4, we introduce a new method for categorizing attributes, as well as a demonstration of its effectiveness. In section 5 we present some experiments. Final-ly conclusions are presented in section 6.

2   Basic Concepts

In this section, we review some basic concepts of the Rough Set Theory [6]. In many data analysis applications, information and knowledge are stored and represented as a decision table because this table provides a convenient way to describe a finite set of objects, within a universe, through a finite set of attributes.

Definition 1 *(decision table): A decision table is a tuple* $S = (U; A_t = A_t^* \cup \{d\}, \{V_a \mid a \in A_t\}, \{I_a \mid a \in A_t\})$, *where* A_t^* *is a set of descriptive attributes and d is a decision attribute indicating the decision class for each object in the universe.* U *is a finite non-empty set of objects,* V_a *is a non-empty set of values for each attribute* $a \in A_t$, *and* $I_a : U \rightarrow V_a$ *is an information function that maps an object in U to exactly one value in* V_a.

The decision attribute allows us to partition the universe into blocks determined by possible decisions. Usually, these blocks are called classes.

Definition 2 *(decision class): For* $k \in V_d$, *a decision class is defined as* $U_k = \{u \in U : I_d(u) = k\}$.

Let us denote the cardinality of U_k by m_k; so $|U_k| = m_k$. We will also denote $\{d\}$ as D.

Definition 3 *(indiscernibility relation): Given a subset of attributes* $A \subseteq A_t^*$, *the indiscernibility relation* $IND(A|D) \subseteq U \times U$ *is defined by:*

$$IND(A|D) = \{(x, y) \in U \times U \mid \forall a \in A, [I_a(x) = I_a(y)] \vee [I_d(x) = I_d(y)]\}.$$

The indiscernibility relation consists of all object pairs that cannot be distinguished (indiscernible) based on the set A of conditional attributes $(A \subseteq A_t^*)$ or share the same decision class. Based on the relative indiscernibility relation, Pawlak defined a reduct as a minimal set of attributes that keeps the indiscernibility relation $IND(A_t^*)$ un-changed [6].

Definition 4 *(reduct for a decision table): Given a decision table S, an attribute set* $R \subseteq A_t^*$ *is called a reduct, if R satisfies the following two conditions:*

(i) $IND(R \mid D) = IND(A_t^* \mid D)$; *if R satisfies (i) it is a super reduct.*

(ii)   *For any* $a \in R, IND((R - \{a\}) \mid D) \neq IND(A_t^* \mid D)$.

The set of all reducts of an information table S is denoted by $RED(S)$.

3   The Discernibility Matrix and the Discernibility Function

Two objects are discernible if their values are different in at least one attribute. Skowron and Rauszer suggested a matrix representation for storing the sets of attributes that discern pairs of objects, called discernibility matrix [7].

Definition 5 (discernibility matrix): Given a decision table S, its discernibility matrix $M = (M[x,y])_{|U| \times |U|}$ is defined as $M[x,y] = \{a \in A_t^* | [I_a(x) \neq I_a(y)] \wedge [I_d(x) \neq I_d(y)]\}$.

The meaning of $M[x,y]$ is that objects x and y can be distinguished by any attribute in $M[x,y]$. The pair (x,y) can be discerned if $M[x,y] \neq \emptyset$. A discernibility matrix M is symmetric, i.e., $M[x,y] = M[y,x]$, and $M[x,x] = \emptyset$. Therefore, it is sufficient to consider only the lower triangle or the upper triangle of the matrix.

Example 1. Table 1 shows an example of a decision table, its discernibility matrix M (only lower triangle) is shown in (1).

Table 1. A decision table

U	x_1	x_2	x_3	x_4	x_5	d
u_1	2	1	1	1	1	0
u_2	1	1	1	2	1	0
u_3	1	2	1	1	1	1
u_4	0	1	4	1	1	1
u_5	2	2	3	3	3	1

$$
M = \begin{vmatrix}
\emptyset & & & \\
\{x_1, x_2\} & & & \\
\{x_1, x_3\} & \{x_2, x_4\} & & \\
\{x_2, x_3, x_4, x_5\} & \{x_1, x_3, x_4\} & \emptyset & \\
& \{x_1, x_2, x_3, x_4, x_5\} & \emptyset & \emptyset
\end{vmatrix} \tag{1}
$$

Let S be a decision table $S = (U; A_t = A_t^* \cup \{d\}, \{V_a \mid a \in A_t\}, \{I_a \mid a \in A_t\})$, and let us define for each attribute a in A_t a dissimilarity function φ_a as follows:

$$
\varphi_a : V_a \times V_a \rightarrow \{0,1\} \quad : \varphi_a(x,y) = \begin{cases} 0 & if\ x = y \\ 1 & otherwise \end{cases}
$$

Applying these dissimilarity functions to all possible pairs of objects belonging to different classes in S, a binary discernibility matrix, denoted by M^{01} can be built. This concept was previously introduced by Felix and Ushio[5].

Definition 6 (binary discernibility matrix): Given a decision table S, its binary discernibility matrix M^{01} is a $m \times n$ matrix, in which each row is defined by $(\varphi_1(I_1(u), I_1(v)), \varphi_2(I_2(u), I_2(v)), \ldots, \varphi_n(I_n(u), I_n(v)))$, being u, $v \in U$ belonging to different decision classes. $n = |A_t^*|$ and $m = \sum_{i=1}^{|V_d|-1} \sum_{j=i+1}^{|V_d|} m_i \cdot m_j$.

After defining the binary discernibility matrix, the authors in [5] highlighted the following properties:

1.   If a row only contains 0's, it means that the corresponding pair of objects are indiscernible even when using the whole set A_t^*, in this case the decision table is inconsistent.

2.   If a column only contains 1's, then the corresponding attribute is capable of distinguishing all objects pairs belonging to different classes. In such a case, a reduct was found, and since it has only one attribute, we can say that it is a minimal reduct.

3.   If a column has only 0's, then the attribute is completely irrelevant because it is unable to distinguish any pair of objects by itself.

4.   If a row in the matrix has only one 1, then the corresponding attribute is the only one able to distinguish that pair of objects and so it is indispensable.

The definition of binary discernibility matrix and the properties above outlined are the starting point for the method proposed in this work.

Obviously, taking into account property 1, rows containing only 0's are not considered. So, actually m is an upper bound of the number of rows.

Example 2. *As an example, we can build the binary discernibility matrix for the decision table shown in Table 1.*

$$M^{01} = \begin{array}{c c c c c c} & x_1 & x_2 & x_3 & x_4 & x_5 \\ & \begin{vmatrix} 1 & 1 & 0 & 0 & 0 \\ 1 & 0 & 1 & 0 & 0 \\ 0 & 1 & 1 & 1 & 1 \\ 0 & 1 & 0 & 1 & 0 \\ 1 & 0 & 1 & 1 & 0 \\ 1 & 1 & 1 & 1 & 1 \end{vmatrix} \end{array} \qquad (2)$$

This matrix has 6 rows, the same amount of non-empty attribute sets that are in the discernibility matrix in (1). First row is equivalent to $\{x_1,x_2\}$, second row is equivalent to $\{x_1,x_3\}$ and so on, until the last row which is equivalent to $\{x_1,x_2,x_3,x_4,x_5\}$. Therefore both matrices contain the same information.

From now on, we interpret some concepts and properties from this matrix. Since the discernibility matrix is just focused on the ability of attribute subsets to distinguish objects belonging to different classes, we conclude that usually this matrix contains redundant information.

In this paper, we describe a simple way to eliminate redundant information in M in terms of its ability to discern.

Definition 7 *(basic row): Let $f = (f_1, f_2, ..., f_n)$ and $f' = (f'_1, f'_2, ..., f'_n)$ two rows in M^{01}, we say that f is a sub row of f' if for each column $j=1,2,...,n$: $f_j \leq f'_j$ and for at least one index the inequality is strict. We say that a row f in M^{01} is a basic row if no row of the matrix is a sub row of f.*

Definition 8 *(basic binary discernibility matrix): Let M^{01} be a binary discernibility matrix, the basic binary discernibility matrix (bbdm) $M^{(01)}$ is defined as the sub-matrix of M^{01} formed only by the basic rows (without repetitions).*

Example 3. *For the binary discernibility matrix M^{01} (2), we have the following bbdm*

$$M^{(01)} = \begin{vmatrix} 1 & 1 & 0 & 0 & 0 \\ 1 & 0 & 1 & 0 & 0 \\ 0 & 1 & 0 & 1 & 0 \end{vmatrix} \qquad (3)$$

From a discernibility matrix, Skowron and Rauszer [7] define the discernibility function.

Definition 9 *(discernibility function): The discernibility function of a discernibility matrix is defined as* $f(M) = \bigwedge\{\bigvee(M[x,y])|\forall x,y \in U, M[x,y] \neq \emptyset\}$.

Starting from the binary discernibility matrix, it is very easy to obtain the discernibility function $f(M)$. If instead of it, we consider the bbdm, then we obtain an equivalent simplified discernibility function.

The discernibility function can be used to state an important result regarding the set of reducts of a decision table, as it is shown by the following theorem.

Theorem 1. [7] *The reduct set problem is equivalent to the problem of transforming the discernibility function to a reduced disjunctive form (RDF). Each term of the RDF is called a prime implicant. Given the discernibility matrix M of a decision table S, an attribute set* $R = \{a_1, \ldots, a_p\}$ *is a reduct iff the conjunction of all attributes in R, denoted as* $a_1 \wedge \ldots \wedge a_p$, *is a prime implicant of* $f(M)$.

In order to derive the RDF, the discernibility function $f(M)$ is transformed by using the absorption and distribution laws.

Based on Theorem 1, Skowron and Rauszer [7] also suggested an alternative characterization of a reduct in terms of the discernibility matrix which provides a convenient way to test if a subset of attributes is a reduct. However, they neither offer a method to compute a reduct nor a way to determine whether an attribute is reductive or not.

Using definitions and notations introduced here, we can state the following equivalent theorem:

Theorem 2. *Given the bbdm* $M^{(01)}$ *of a decision table, an attribute set B is a reduct iff*

(i) $\forall f \in M^{(01)}$ $\sum_{i=1}^{n}(\delta_B{}^i \cdot f_i) \neq 0$.

(ii) $\forall j = 1, \ldots, n$ $(\delta_B{}^j = 1) \Rightarrow \exists f \in M^{(01)} : f_j = 1 \wedge \sum_{i=1}^{n}(\delta_B{}^i \cdot f_i) = 1$

being δ_B *the characteristic vector of B, defined as follows:*

$$\delta_B = (\delta_B{}^1, \delta_B{}^2, \ldots, \delta_B{}^n) \text{ where } \delta_B{}^i = \begin{cases} 1 & if \ a_i \in B \\ 0 & if \ a_i \notin B \end{cases} \quad i = 1, 2, \ldots, n.$$

Condition (i) means that B is a super reduct; (ii) means that each attribute is necessary.

Proof is rather immediate and omitted for space reasons.

4   Attribute Categorization

In this section, we introduce the categorization of attributes and establish a method to categorize them from the bbdm in an easy way.

Definition 10: *Let* $S = (U; A_t = A_t^* \cup \{d\}, \{V_a \mid a \in A_t\}, \{I_a \mid a \in A_t\})$ *be a decision table, let* $a \in A_t^*$

    (i) the attribute a is a core (or an indispensable) attribute iff it belongs to all reducts of S. The set of all core attributes is denoted by Core(S).

(ii) the attribute a is superfluous (or redundant) iff it does not belong to any reduct of S. We denote the set of all superfluous attributes by Spf(S).
(iii) the attribute a is relevant iff it belongs to at least one reduct.

Obviously, all indispensable attributes are relevant. The set of all relevant attributes is denoted by Rlv(S).

We have that $Core(S) \subseteq R \subseteq Rlv(S)$ for any reduct $R \in RED(S)$. Let $Rem(S) = Rlv(S) - Core(S)$, then A_t^* is partitioned into $A_t^* = Core(S) \cup Rem(S) \cup Spf(S)$.

Below, we enunciate and prove some theorems that allow us to carry out this partition.

Theorem 3. *Let $S = (U; A_t = A_t^* \cup \{d\}, \{V_a \mid a \in A_t\}, \{I_a \mid a \in A_t\})$ be a decision table and let $M^{(01)}$ be its bbdm. An attribute a_j is indispensable iff $M^{(01)}$ contains a row*
$$f \text{ such that } f_i = \begin{cases} 1 & \text{if } i = j \\ 0 & \text{if } i \neq j \end{cases}.$$
Proof: ($\Leftarrow$) Let f be a row in $M^{(01)}$ such that $f_j = 1$ and all remaining co-ordinates are 0's, and suppose that B is a reduct such that $a_j \notin B$, i.e. $\delta_B{}^1 = 0$, then $\sum_{i=1}^{n}(\delta_B{}^i \cdot f_i) = 0$ and from theorem 2 *(i)* B is not a super reduct which contradicts the supposition. Then we conclude that if such row exists a_j is indispensable.

($\Rightarrow$) Let a_j be an indispensable attribute, then $\forall R \in RED(S)$ $a_j \in B$ (i.e. $\delta_B{}^j = 1$) and $B' = B - \{a_j\}$ is not a reduct. From theorem 2 *(i)* we have that $\forall f \in M^{(01)}$ $\sum_{i=1}^{n}(\delta_B{}^i \cdot f_i) \neq 0$ but B' does not fulfill this condition. It means that there exists a row f in $M^{(01)}$ such that $\sum_{i=1}^{n}(\delta_B^i \cdot f_i) \neq 0$ and $\sum_{i=1}^{n}(\delta_{B'}^i \cdot f_i) = 0$. Since B and B' only differ in a_j, these sums only differ in the j-th terms which are $\delta_B^j \cdot f_j$ and $\delta_{B'}^j \cdot f_j$ respectively. By hypothesis $\delta_B^j = 1$ then we can conclude that $f_j = 1$ and $f_i = 0$ for all $i \neq j$. The proof is complete.

Theorem 4. *Let $S = (U; A_t = A_t^* \cup \{d\}, \{V_a \mid a \in A_t\}, \{I_a \mid a \in A_t\})$ be a decision table and let $M^{(01)}$ its bbdm. An attribute a_j is superfluous iff the corresponding column in $M^{(01)}$ has only 0's.*
Proof: ($\Leftarrow$) Suppose that B is a reduct containing a_j and let $B' = B - \{a_j\}$. From theorem 2 *(i)* we have that $\forall f \in M^{(01)}$ $\sum_{i=1}^{n}(\delta_B{}^i \cdot f_i) \neq 0$.

Let j be the index of the column corresponding to a_j in $M^{(01)}$. By hypothesis $\forall f \in M^{(01)}$ $f_j = 0$, then B' fulfills condition *(i)* of theorem 2 and it means that B' is a super reduct which contradicts the supposition. We conclude that a_j is redundant.

($\Rightarrow$) Now suppose that a_j is redundant, it means that a_j does not belong to any reduct. If a_j is not able to discern any pair of objects belonging to different classes, its corresponding column in M^{01} has only 0's and of course also in $M^{(01)}$. More interesting is the case when a_j discerns at least a pair of objects but it does not belong to any reduct. In this case, it turns out that all disjunctions containing a_j in the discernibility function are absorbed and therefore ultimately a_j does not appear in any prime implicant. As the construction of the bbdm is based precisely on the law of absorption, if a_j is not in any reduct, the corresponding column in $M^{(01)}$ will contain only 0's.

It is important to emphasize that this property is not held in M. If the corresponding column in M is fully of 0's, the attribute is superfluous, but the reciprocal is not true. This is one of the most important contributions of using the bbdm instead of the original binary discernibility matrix, since eliminating redundant attributes reduces the space dimension which may facilitate several tasks, for example computing all reducts.

Corollary. *Let* $S = (U; A_t = A_t^* \cup \{d\}, \{V_a \mid a \in A_t\}, \{I_a \mid a \in A_t\})$ *be a decision table and let* $M^{(01)}$ *its bbdm. An attribute* a_j *is relevant iff the corresponding column in* $M^{(01)}$ *contains at least one 1.*

Based on the above theorems the proposed method for categorizing the attributes is as follows: given a decision table, first compute the binary discernibility matrix, and then compute the bbdm. Columns containing only 0´s correspond to redundant attributes, all other attributes are relevant. Each row in bbdm containing only one 1 determines that the attribute corresponding to that 1 is indispensable. Thus we have the attributes categorized as indispensable, relevant, and superfluous.

Example 4. Let S be the decision table in Table 1. $RED(S) = \{\{x_1,x_2\},\{x_1,x_4\},\{x_2,x_3\}\}$, $Core(S)=\emptyset$, $Rem(S)=\{x_1,x_2,x_3,x_4\}$ and $Spf(S)=\{x_5\}$.

The main contribution of the proposed method is that without calculating all the reducts, it allows, by analyzing easy properties over the bbdm, obtaining the same categorization that we would get after computing all the reducts (see $M^{(01)}$ (3)). Notice that the column corresponding to x_5 in $M^{(01)}$ (3) has only 0's but in M^{01} (2) this column has 0's and 1's.

5   Experiments

In order to show the application of the proposed method, ten datasets from the UCI machine learning repository [8] were used. Table 2 shows information about these datasets: name, number of attributes, objects and classes respectively. Last column shows the size of the bbdm.

Table 2. Datasets information

N.	Dataset	Attributes	Objects	Classes	$M^{(01)}$ size
1	iris	4	150	3	6×4
2	krkopt	6	28056	18	6×6
3	mushroom	22	8124	2	39×22
4	nursery	8	12960	5	8×8
5	yeast	8	1484	10	9×8
6	zoo	17	101	7	14×17
7	adult	14	30162	2	8×14
8	australian	14	690	2	23×14
9	krvskp	36	3196	2	29×36
10	shuttle	9	43500	7	8×9

Table 3 shows the results of categorization for these ten datasets. Columns contain indexes of attributes belonging to Core, Spf and Rem sets respectively.

Table 3. Attribute categorization for the ten datasets

N.	Core(S)	Spf(S)	Rem(S)
1	Ø	Ø	{1,2,3,4}
2	{1,2,3,4,5,6}	Ø	Ø
3	Ø	{1,16}	{2,3,4,5,6,7,8,9,10,11,12,13,14, 15,17,18,19,20,21,22}
4	{1,2,3,4,5,6,7,8}	Ø	Ø
5	{7}	{5,6}	{1,2,3,4,8}
6	{1,7,14}	{3,6,16}	{2,4,5,8,9,10,11,12,13,15,17}
7	{1,2,3,7,8,11,13}	{6,9,10, 12,14}	{4,5}
8	{2}	Ø	{1,3,4,5,6,7,8,9,10,11,12,13,14}
9	{1,3,4,5,6,7,10,12,13,15,16,17,18,20,21,23,2 4,25,26,27,28,30,31,33,34,35,36}	{2,8,14, 19,29}	{9,11,22,32}
10	{2}	{6}	{1,3,4,5,7,8,9}

6   Conclusions

In this paper, we present an easy method to categorize attributes in a decision table. This method is based on the concept of basic binary discernibility matrix (bbdm), which is a simplification of the classical binary discernibility matrix. Once the bbdm is obtained, attributes are immediately categorized. Experiments show that our proposed method is very simple and effective. Moreover, the effectiveness of the method has been theoretically demonstrated.

Acknowledgements. This work was partly supported by the National Council of Science and Technology of Mexico (CONACyT) through the project grants CB2008-106443 and CB2008-106366.

References

1. Pawlak, Z.: Rough sets. International Journal of Computer Information and Science 11, 341–356 (1982)
2. Nguyen, L.G., Nguyen, H.S.: On elimination of redundant attributes in decision tables. In: Ganzha, M., Maciaszek, L., Paprzucki, M. (eds.) Proceedings of the Federated Conference on Computer Science and Information Systems, pp. 317–322. IEEE Computer Society Press, Alamitos (2012)
3. Hashemi, R.R., Bahrami, A., Smith, M., Young, S.: Identification of Core, Semi-Core and Redundant Attributes of a Dataset. In: Eighth International Conference on Information Technology: New Generations, pp. 580–584. IEEE Computer Society, Washington, DC (2011)
4. Linyuan, G., Yanyun, C., Jianlin, Q.: Research advances of attribute reduction based on rough sets. In: 9th International Conference on Fuzzy Systems and Knowledge Discovery (FSKD), pp. 143–247. IEEE (2012)
5. Felix, R., Ushio, T.: Rough sets-based machine learning using a binary discernibility matrix. In: Meech, J.A., Veiga, M.M., Smith, M.H., LeClair, S.R. (eds.) Proceedings of the Second International Conference on Intelligent Processing and Manufacturing of Materials, pp. 299–305. IEEE Press, New York (1999)

6. Pawlak, Z.: Rough Sets: Theoretical Aspects of Reasoning About Data. Kluwer Academic Publishers, Dordrecht (1991)
7. Skowron, A., Rauszer, C.: The discernibility matrices and functions in information systems. In: Slowiński, R. (ed.) Intelligent Decision Support, Handbook of Applications and Advances of the Rough Sets Theory. Kluwer, Dordrecht (1992)
8. Bache, K., Lichman, M.: UCI Machine Learning Repository. University of California, School of Information and Computer Science, Irvine, CA (2013), http://archive.ics.uci.edu/ml

Comparing Quality Measures
for Contrast Pattern Classifiers

Milton García-Borroto[1], Octavio Loyola-Gonzalez[1,2],
José Francisco Martínez-Trinidad[2], and Jesús Ariel Carrasco-Ochoa[2]

[1] Centro de Bioplantas. Carretera a Moron km 9, Ciego de Avila, Cuba
{mil,octavioloyola}@bioplantas.cu
[2] Instituto Nacional de Astrofísica, Óptica y Electrónica. Luis Enrique Erro No. 1,
Sta. María Tonanzintla, Puebla, México,C.P. 72840
{ariel,fmartine}@ccc.inaoep.mx

Abstract. Contrast pattern miners and contrast pattern classifiers typically use a quality measure to evaluate the discriminative power of a pattern. Since many quality measures exist, it is important to perform comparative studies among them. Nevertheless, previous studies mostly compare measures based on how they impact the classification accuracy. In this paper, we introduce a comparative study of quality measures over different aspects: accuracy using the whole training set, accuracy using pattern subsets, and accuracy and compression for filtering patterns. Experiments over 10 quality measures in 25 repository databases show that there is a huge correlation among different quality measures and that the most accurate quality measures are not appropriate in contexts like pattern filtering.

Keywords: quality evaluation, contrast patterns, emerging patterns.

1 Introduction

A supervised classifier predicts the class of a query object based on the relationships it finds among its description and the descriptions of the objects in the training sample. An accurate prediction is an important component of the classifier behavior, but in some domains the classifier and its results should be also easily understandable by the user. In some cases, the lack of comprehensibility may cause a reluctance to use certain classifiers. For example, when credit has been denied to a customer, the Equal Credit Opportunity Act of the US requires the financial institution to provide the reasons for rejecting the application; indefinite or vague reasons for denial are illegal [1].

Most understandable classifiers are based on patterns, which are expressions defined in some language that describe some properties of an object collection. An important family of understandable and accurate classifiers is based on *contrast patterns* [2]. A contrast pattern is a pattern that describes differences between two given datasets. Then, if a contrast pattern appears in a query object, it can be taken as an evidence towards the pattern class.

J. Ruiz-Shulcloper and G. Sanniti di Baja (Eds.): CIARP 2013, Part I, LNCS 8258, pp. 311–318, 2013.
© Springer-Verlag Berlin Heidelberg 2013

Algorithms for finding contrast patterns or for classification based on contrast patterns usually employ a quality measure for evaluating the discriminative power of a pattern [3]. Since many authors have introduced different quality measures, it is important to perform both theoretical and experimental studies, in order to help users to select the appropriate one for a given task. Nevertheless, most published studies present comparisons mainly based on the classifier accuracy [4]. In this paper, we introduce a comparative study about a set of quality measures for contrast patterns over the following aspects:

- Accuracy using the whole training sample
- Accuracy using percentages of the best evaluated patterns
- Ability to be used to filter patterns:
  - Accuracy using a classifier based on aggregated support
  - Compression ratio

Additionally, we perform a correlation study that reveals that all the studied quality functions can be grouped into four groups. Functions in the same group have so similar behaviour that it is enough to use one of them in future comparative studies. This result is consistent with other results shown in this paper.

2   Quality Measures

In this section, we succinctly describe the quality measures used in this paper. More details can be found on each associated reference. Lets define the function count($pattern, set$) as the number of objects in set containing $pattern$, and the function

$$\text{support}(pattern, set) = \frac{\text{count}(pattern, set)}{|set|}$$

as the ratio of objects in set containing $pattern$. We also consider, for a given universe U, $|U| = N$, $|I| = \text{count}(I, U)$, $\neg I$ as the pattern negation, and $|\neg I| = \text{count}(\neg I, U) = N - |I|$.

A quality measure $q(I, D_p, D_n) \to R$ returns a value, which is larger while the pattern I better discriminates objects between the positive class D_p and the negative class D_n (both classes form a partition of the universe $U = D_p \cup D_N, D_p \cap D_N = \emptyset$). In this paper, we investigate the following quality measures:

Confidence. $Conf = \text{count}(I, D_p)/\text{count}(I, U)$, predictive ability of the pattern for the positive class [5].

Growth Rate. $GR = \text{support}(I, D_p)/\text{support}(I, D_n)$, ratio of the positive and negative class supports [6].

Support Difference. $SupDif = \text{support}(I, D_p) - \text{support}(I, D_n)$, support difference between positive and negative classes [7].

Odds Ratio. $Odds = \frac{\text{support}(I,D_p)/(1-\text{support}(I,D_p))}{\text{support}(I,D_n)/(1-\text{support}(I,D_n))}$, ratio of the pattern odds from D_p to D_n [8].

Gain. $Gain = \text{support}(I, D_p)(\log \frac{\text{support}(I,D_p)}{\text{support}(I,U)} - \log \frac{|D_p|}{|U|})$ [9].

Length. $Length = 1/|I|$, inverse of the number of items in $|I|$. We use the inverse because shorter patterns are more desirable for discrimination [10].

Chi-square. $\chi^2 = \sum_{X \in \{I, \neg I\}} \sum_{Y \in \{D_p, D_n\}} \frac{(count(X,Y) - E(X,Y))^2}{E(X,Y)}$, where $E(X,Y)$ is the expected frequency count of pattern X in class Y. This measure assesses how significantly different is a pattern support with respect to the universe support [7].

Mutual Information. Estimates how correlated is the pattern distribution with respect to the expected pattern frequencies per class [5].

$$MI = \sum_{X \in \{I, \neg I\}} \sum_{Y \in \{D_p, D_n\}} \frac{count(X,Y)}{N} \log \frac{count(X,Y)/N}{|X||Y|/N^2}$$

Weighted Relative Accuracy. $WRACC = \frac{|I|}{|D_p| + |D_n|} (\frac{count(I,D_p)}{|I|} - \frac{|D_p|}{N})$, used in the subgroup discovery field [11].

Strength. $Strength = \frac{support^2(I, D_P)}{support(I, D_p)\, support(I, D_n)}$ measures how strongly the pattern appearance indicates the class of the query instance containing it. [12]

Although most of these quality measures were defined for two-class problems, we use them in multi-class problems using the one-vs-rest approach [13]

3 Comparing Quality Functions

Accuracy Comparison. A good quality measure should assign higher evaluations to patterns that contribute more to the correct classification of query objects. That is why it is frequent to evaluate quality measures using the accuracy of a supervised classifier, which uses the measure information during the classification process. Nevertheless, in a contrast pattern classifier there are many parameters that impact the classifier accuracy like thresholds, aggregation scheme, and normalization procedures, among others. Then, using the classifier accuracy as an estimation of the behavior of the quality measure can be error prone.

To minimize the parameter influence in the classification accuracy, we perform the accuracy comparison using a simple classification algorithm. This algorithm assigns O to the class with the maximum aggregated support, calculated with the top-quality patterns from those contained in O. As this classifier is mostly based on the quality values, we expect that accuracy differences are mostly due to the specific quality measure behavior. In this way, we can safely estimate the behavior of the quality measure based on the accuracy. The pseudocode of the algorithm is the following:

Input: Set of patterns P, quality function q, query object O
Output: Class assigned to O

1. $S \longleftarrow$ patterns in P contained in O
2. $MaxQual \longleftarrow \text{argmax}_s(q(s))$
3. $S' \longleftarrow \{s \in S : q(s) = MaxQual\}$
4. **return** class with maximum aggregated support of patterns in S'

Accuracy Comparison Using a Pattern Subset. If we use a small subset of the pattern collection in a supervised classifier, the global classifier accuracy usually deteriorates. This behavior is mainly due to query objects that do not contain any pattern, causing classifier abstention to appear. If we select a percentage of the best patterns, using some quality measure, we expect the best quality measure to obtain the highest accuracy.

Filtering Patterns. Most pattern filtering methods iterate through the pattern collection, selecting those that fulfill some criterion. To obtain a subset with the best patterns, the pattern collection is sorted according to some quality measure. In this section, we evaluate the ability of quality measures to be used in a pattern filtering procedure. We use the following filtering algorithm:

> **Input:** Set of patterns P, quality function q, training sample T
> **Output:** Selected patterns R

1. $R \longleftarrow \emptyset$
2. **foreach** $o \in T$
   (a) Find $S =$ patterns in P contained in o
   (b) **if** $S \cap R = \emptyset$ **then** add to R the pattern in S with the highest q value
3. **return** R

The filtering algorithm uses a greedy heuristic to find the smallest pattern subset covering the full training sample, selecting the pattern with the highest quality evaluation. In this way, the best quality measure is expected to obtain the smallest and most accurate filtered subset.

4   Experimental Results

Experimental Setup. For mining patterns, we use LCMine miner [14], pruning each decision tree in order to obtain non pure patterns. LCMiner extracts patterns from a collection of decision trees, induced using a particular diversity generation procedure. For comparing the accuracy of a classifier based on emerging patterns, we perform a Friedman test with all the results [15]. Then, when we find significant differences, we perform the Bergmann-Hommel dynamic post-hoc, because it is more powerful than the classical Nemenyi and Holm procedures [16]. Post-hoc results are shown using *critical distance* (CD) diagrams, which present the order of the classifier accuracy, the magnitude of differences between them, and the significance of the observed differences in a compact form [15]. In a CD diagram, the rightmost classifier is the best classifier, while two classifiers sharing a thick line means they have statistically similar behavior. We use a 2 times 5 fold cross validation procedure averaging results, as suggested in [15].

All databases used for experiments were taken from the UCI repository of Machine Learning [17]. We selected small databases with balanced classes, because emerging pattern classifiers are very sensitive to class imbalance [18]. According to the feature type, there are pure numerical, pure categorical, and mixed databases. The number of features ranges from 4 to 60. Databases are *breast-cancer, breast-w, cleveland, colic, credit-a, credit-g, crx, cylinder-bands, diabetes, haberman, heart-c, heart-h, heart-statlog, hepatitis, ionosphere, iris, labor, lung-cancer, sonar, tae, tic-tac-toe, vote, wdbc, wine,* and *wpbc.*

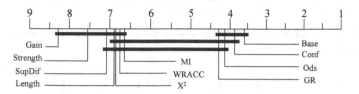

Fig. 1. CD diagram for accuracy comparisons

Accuracy Comparison. Results of the accuracy comparison (Figure 1) reveals that the quality measures Conf, Odds, and GR obtain the most accurate classifier. Their results are statistically similar to the base classifier, which uses the whole pattern collection to achieve classification. The good behavior of GR is not surprising, because it has been used as quality function in many papers. Additionally, it is used in the definition of *emerging patterns* [6], which are contrast patterns whose GR is above certain threshold.

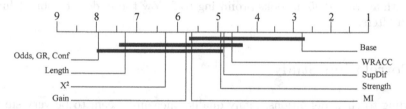

Fig. 2. CD diagram for accuracy comparisons taking the 10% of the best patterns

Accuracy Comparison Using a Pattern Subset. To compare accuracies using pattern subsets, we created pattern collections containing different percentages of the whole collection. We finally chose 10%, because it is the lowest value where accuracies are significantly similar to the unfiltered classifier, so the filtering procedure does not significantly deteriorates the classifier. Results shown in Figure 2 reveal an outcome not consistent with Figure 1, because the top accurate classifiers like Conf, GR and Odds had the worst behavior. To explain this behavior we must realize that Conf, GR and Odds returns the same value on all patterns having zero support on the negative class. In this way, a pattern with support $(1,0)$ is considered as good as a pattern with support $(0.001, 0)$. On the other hand, the quality measures with the best results like WRACC, SupDif and Strength can easily differentiate among them, assigning the former a significant higher quality value.

Filtering Patterns. Figures 3 and 4 show the accuracy and compression ratio results from the pattern filtering experiment. Results are consistent with those

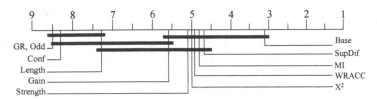

Fig. 3. CD diagram for accuracy comparisons with filtered pattern subset using each quality measure

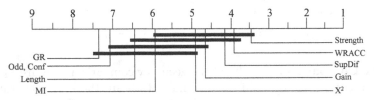

Fig. 4. CD diagram for compression ratio of the filtering procedure using each quality measure

previously shown, being the most accurate quality measures those that distinguish among single class patterns. As the compression ratio ranges from 0.01 to 0.10, with average 0.05, it looks promising to follow these ideas to obtain future pattern filters.

5   Correlation Study

According to their definitions, many quality measures seem to be very similar, being most of them variations of other measures. Additionally, during the analysis of the experiments, we also realize that many quality measures behave very similarly in all the experiments and databases. That is why we performed a two-way Pearson correlations analysis using the quality values extracted from all the emerging patterns per database. A Pearson correlation is a measure of association between two numerical variables. Pearson values range from -1 (perfect negative correlation) to 1 (perfect positive correlation). Since the results are highly consistent among all databases, we only show in Table 1 the results in *colic* database.

Correlation results allows us to cluster measures in four different groups, with very high inner correlations and very low outer correlations. These groups are completely consistent with other experimental results presented in this paper. The groups are the following:

Group 1. Conf, GR, Odds
Group 2. WRACC, Gain, SupDif, Strength, MI
Group 3. Length
Group 4. χ^2

Table 1. Non-trivial correlations among quality functions on *colic* database. An "X" appears where qualities have correlations above 0.75

	χ^2	Conf	Gain	GR	Length	MI	Odds	Strength	SupDif	WRACC
χ^2										
Conf				X			X			
Gain						X		X	X	X
GR		X					X			
Length										
MI			X					X	X	X
Ods		X		X						
Strength			X			X			X	X
SupDif			X			X		X		X
WRACC			X			X		X	X	

This clustering information can be useful in at least two tasks. First, we can simplify future researches on quality measures, using a single quality measure per cluster. Second, we can take a single quality measure per cluster to obtain a diverse measure collection, which can be used in some combination schemes.

6   Conclusions

In this paper, we present a comparative study about a set of quality measures for contrast patterns, which are used to evaluate the discriminative power of a pattern. We have addressed the necessity to provide theoretical and experimental comparisons to help users select among the existing measures, since previous studies lack comparisons over different relevant aspects.

After analysing experiments over 10 quality measures in 25 repository databases, we lead to the following conclusions:

- Many quality measures are strongly correlated, obtaining very similar results among them. Quality measures used in this paper can be grouped in four clusters: **Group1**={Conf, GR, Ods}, **Group2**={WRACC, Gain, Supdif, Strength, MI}, **Group3**{Length}, and **Group4**={χ^2}.
- On most databases, quality measures in Group1 are better estimations of the real pattern value for classification.
- Quality measures in Group1 can be very inaccurate in domains like pattern filtering, because they cannot distinguish among patterns supported by a single class

References

1. Martens, D., Baesens, B., Gestel, T.V., Vanthienen, J.: Comprehensible credit scoring models using rule extraction from support vector machines. European Journal of Operational Research 183(3), 1466–1476 (2007)

2. Dong, G.: Overview of Results on Contrast Mining and Applications. In: Dong, G., Bailey, J. (eds.) Contrast Data Mining: Concepts, Algorithms, and Applications, pp. 353–362. Chapman & Hall/CRC, United States of America (2012)

3. Fang, G., Wang, W., Oatley, B., Ness, B.V., Steinbach, M., Kumar, V.: Characterizing discriminative patterns. Computing Research Repository, abs/1102.4 (2011)

4. An, A., Cercone, N.: Rule quality measures for rule induction systems: Description and evaluation. Computational Intelligence 17(3), 409–424 (2001)

5. Bailey, J.: Statistical Measures for Contrast Patterns. In: Dong, G., Bailey, J. (eds.) Contrast Data Mining: Concepts, Algorithms, and Applications, pp. 13–20. Chapman & Hall/CRC, United States of America (2012)

6. Dong, G., Li, J.: Efficient mining of emerging patterns: Discovering trends and differences. In: ACM International Conference on Knowledge Discovery and Data Mining (KDD), pp. 43–52 (1999)

7. Bay, S.D., Pazzani, M.J.: Detecting change in categorical data: Mining contrast sets. In: ACM International Conference on Knowledge Discovery and Data Mining (KDD), pp. 302–306 (1999)

8. Li, J., Yang, Q.: Strong compound-risk factors: Efficient discovery through emerging patterns and contrast sets. IEEE Transactions on Information Technology in Biomedicine 11(5), 544–552 (2007)

9. Yin, X., Han, J.: CPAR: Classification based on predictive association rules. In: SIAM International Conference on Data Mining, SDM (2003)

10. Li, J., Li, H., Wong, L., Pei, J., Dong, G.: Minimum description length principle: Generators are preferable to closed patterns. In: 21st National Conf. on AI, pp. 409–414 (2006)

11. Lavrac, N., Kavsek, B., Flach, P.A., Todorovski, L.: Subgroup discovery with cn2-sd. Journal of Machine Learning Research with CN2-SD 5, 153–188 (2004)

12. Ramamohanarao, K., Fan, H.: Patterns based classifiers. World Wide Web 10, 71–83 (2007)

13. Abudawood, T., Flach, P.: Evaluation measures for multi-class subgroup discovery. In: Buntine, W., Grobelnik, M., Mladenić, D., Shawe-Taylor, J. (eds.) ECML PKDD 2009, Part I. LNCS (LNAI), vol. 5781, pp. 35–50. Springer, Heidelberg (2009)

14. García-Borroto, M., Martínez-Trinidad, J.F., Carrasco-Ochoa, J.A., Medina-Pérez, M.A., Ruiz-Shulcloper, J.: LCMine: An efficient algorithm for mining discriminative regularities and its application in supervised classification. Pattern Recognition 43(9), 3025–3034 (2010)

15. Demsar, J.: Statistical comparisons of classifiers over multiple data sets. J. Mach. Learn. Res. 7, 1–30 (2006)

16. García, S., Herrera, F., Shawe-Taylor, J.: An extension on statistical comparisons of classifiers over multiple data sets for all pairwise comparisons. Journal of Machine Learning Research 9 (2008)

17. Merz, C.J., Murphy, P.M.: Uci repository of machine learning databases, Technical report, Department of Information and Computer Science, University of California at Irvine (1998)

18. Loyola-González, O., García-Borroto, M., Medina-Pérez, M.A., Martínez-Trinidad, J.F., Carrasco-Ochoa, J.A., De Ita, G.: An Empirical Study of Oversampling and Undersampling Methods for LCMine an Emerging Pattern Based Classifier. In: Carrasco-Ochoa, J.A., Martínez-Trinidad, J.F., Rodríguez, J.S., di Baja, G.S. (eds.) MCPR 2013. LNCS, vol. 7914, pp. 264–273. Springer, Heidelberg (2013)

Selecting Features with SVM

Jacek Rzeniewicz and Julian Szymański

Department of Computer Systems Architecture,
Gdańsk University of Technology, Poland
jrzeniewicz@gmail.com, julian.szymanski@eti.pg.gda.pl

Abstract. A common problem with feature selection is to establish how many features should be retained at least so that important information is not lost. We describe a method for choosing this number that makes use of Support Vector Machines. The method is based on controlling an angle by which the decision hyperplane is tilt due to feature selection.

Experiments were performed on three text datasets generated from a Wikipedia dump. Amount of retained information was estimated by classification accuracy. Even though the method is parametric, we show that, as opposed to other methods, once its parameter is chosen it can be applied to a number of similar problems (e.g. one value can be used for various datasets originating from Wikipedia). For a constant value of the parameter, dimensionality was reduced by from 78% to 90%, depending on the data set. Relative accuracy drop due to feature removal was less than 0.5% in those experiments.

Keywords: feature selection, SVM, documents categorization.

1 Introduction

Commonly known feature selection methods for automatic text processing, like mutual information and information gain [1] [2] or SVM-based approaches [3], define ranking algorithms that allow to order features from most to least informative. However, those methods do not specify how many features must be retained for a particular set of data so that classification accuracy is preserved. This number can be determined by cross validation, yet such a solution is computationally very expensive unless the data set is small. Often either final dimensionality is fixed a priori, only features ranked above certain threshold are retained, or the number of selected features depends on vectors' density [4].

In this paper we would like to propose a different approach to deciding how many features to retain. The method is based on Support Vector Machines (SVM) [5] [6], requiring a hyperplane trained on all features. Similarly to other widely used schemes, it has a single parameter, yet we argue that it is much easier to find its correct value than in case of feature weight threshold or the final dimensionallity itself. It is worth noting that our approach does not enforce any particular ranking method. On the other hand, since it requires a hyperplane separating the classes, it would be a natural choice to take that hyperplane into account when ranking features.

J. Ruiz-Shulcloper and G. Sanniti di Baja (Eds.): CIARP 2013, Part I, LNCS 8258, pp. 319–325, 2013.
© Springer-Verlag Berlin Heidelberg 2013

Much of our current work is related to processing text data obtained from Wikipedia dumps. We work on a large-scale, distributed multilabel text classifier [7] based on the LIBLINEAR library [8] and one-vs-all approach that allows to categorize a textual data into Wikipedia categories. In this context we managed to successfully apply the feature selection method described here.

In the next section we will describe the feature selection method in detail. In section 3 results of experiments conducted using presented method will be shown, and we will conclude in section 4.

2   Feature Selection

One of the method's prerequisites is an SVM-trained hyperplane separating between some two classes. A normal to this hyperplane will be denoted by $\boldsymbol{w}$, while w_i will mean an ith component of $\boldsymbol{w}$ referring to feature i. Also a feature ranking is required in form of a vector $\boldsymbol{r}$ where r_i denotes ith feature's rank. Number of retained features is set to minimum k satisfying inequality 1:

$$\cos \gamma^{(k)} \geq 1 - \alpha \tag{1}$$

where $\alpha \in [0, 1]$ is the method's parameter defining the accepted level of distortion between original hyperplane and the one obtained after feature selection, and γ is a following angle:

$$\gamma^{(k)} = \angle \left(\boldsymbol{w}, \boldsymbol{w}^{(k)} \right) \tag{2}$$

where $\boldsymbol{w}^{(k)}$ is a vector defined as below:

$$\boldsymbol{w}^{(k)}{}_i = \begin{cases} w_i & \text{if } r_i \text{ is among } k \text{ top components of } \boldsymbol{r} \\ 0 & \text{otherwise} \end{cases} \tag{3}$$

A simple way to obtain $\boldsymbol{r}$ is to use naive SVM ranking. For some input $\boldsymbol{x}$, prediction of a label can be computed as $\operatorname{sgn}\left(\boldsymbol{x}^T \cdot \boldsymbol{w} + b\right)$, where b is a bias term. The larger value of w_i is, the more presence of feature i inclines the classifier to predict positive class; the smaller (negative) it gets, the bigger ith feature contribution towards negative class. When w_i is close to 0, it has minor influence on the output meaning that feature i is not imporant in this context. Therefore naive SVM ranking can be defined as below:

$$r_i = |w_i| \tag{4}$$

However, in presence of highly corelated features it may be beneficial to apply Recursive Feature Elimination (RFE) [3]. In this iterative approach one feature is neglected in each run after a new SVM is trained on a working set of features. Ranking obtained this way, as opposed to naive approach, does not undervalue groups of correlated features. Note that ranking $\boldsymbol{r}$ is not limited to the two

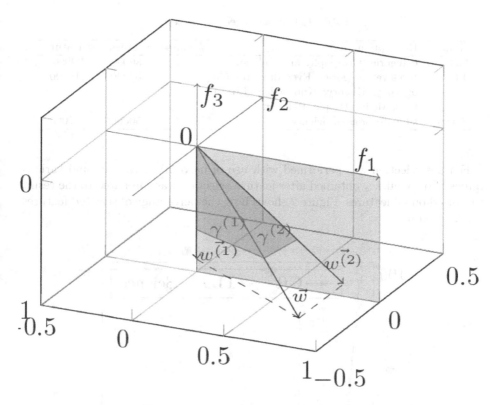

Fig. 1. Feature selection – toy example

approaches mentioned above. Features may be ranked in any way and exact rank values are not important since r is only required to order features.

Figure 1 presents a toy feature selection scenario for a dataset of three features f_1, f_2, f_3. It was assumed that the trained hyperplane has normal vector $\boldsymbol{w} = [0.8; -0.35; -0.9]$ and naive SVM ranking was applied: $\boldsymbol{r} = [0.8; 0.35; 0.9]$ implying that features ordered by their ranks are f_3, f_1, f_2. In such case $\boldsymbol{w}^{(2)} = [0.8; 0; -0.9]$ and $\boldsymbol{w}^{(2)} = [0; 0; -0.9]$. If α was set to 0.05, $k = 2$ features would be retained as $\cos\gamma^{(2)} \approx 0.96 \geq 1 - \alpha$ and $\cos\gamma^{(1)} \approx 0.72 < 1 - \alpha$.

3   Experiments

MATRIX'u application [9] was used to generate representations of three datasets originating from a Simple Wikipedia dump. Stemmed words were used as features and documents were expressed in vector space model with TF-IDF weighting. Features were then scaled to the range $[0.15, 1]$. The datasets are described in Table 1.

Table 1. Datasets used in the tests

Name	Description	# classes	# objects	# features
GR	categories Geography and Religion	2	36000	90000
TL	top level categories: Everyday Life, Geography, History, Knowledge, Literature, Media, People, Religion	8	50000	115000
Science	subcategories of Science	29	50000	117000

Feature selection was performed with use of naive SVM ranking and various values of α. Accuracy obtained after feature selection was compared to the result measured on all features. Figure 2 shows how the percentage of selected features depends on α.

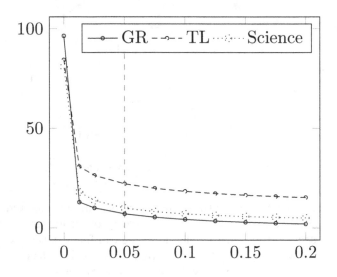

Fig. 2. Average percent of retained features (per hyperplane) as a function of the parameter α

For each of the data sets there is a distinct elbow point: the number of features drops considerably for $\alpha = 0.0125$ and stabilizes around $\alpha = 0.05$. Percentages of retained features differ among the data sets. In Figure 3 the accuracy drop (measured performing 10-fold cross validation) is displayed. Note that relation between the relative accuracy and α is linear, and slopes of those lines differ depend on how many classes there are in a dataset. According to these results, the proposed approach to feature selection requires little parameter adjustment. For the considered data sets the only parameter of the described model universally yields good results for the steady value of $\alpha = 0.05$.

A by-product of this feature selection method is the information that can be easily inferred from the vector w. Having ordered the features by w_i one can find

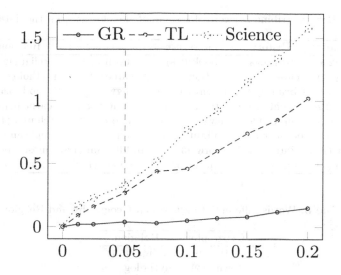

Fig. 3. Relative F_1-score accuracy drop as a function of α (percentage)

out what are the most descriptive features of a related class, which can be useful for debugging purposes. Table 2 presents keywords that are the most specific to some of the classes from the dataset TL. The words in the table are malformed due to stemming. Similarly, features most differentiating between two classes can be inspected this way – Table 3 presents words that are the most useful to tell Geography and Religion pages apart. Finally Table 4 lists features which are the most specific to category Mathematics as well as keywords indicating scientific categories other than math.

4 Discussion

We described a method for choosing the number of features that should be retained based on the hyperplane tilt angle caused by feature selection. This method is parametrized by a single parameter α, however in our experiments on Wikipedia good results were achieved for constant value $\alpha = 0.05$.

According to the conducted experiments, the method for selecting number of features allows for significant dimensionality reduction while preserving classification accuracy. Dimensionality of the datasets was decreased by from 78% to 90% while the relative accuracy drop was less than 0.5%. With a single parameter value across various datasets containing different numbers of classes, we obtained satisfying dimensionality reduction. We plan to compare this technique to other known approaches in order to evaluate the order of features resulting from the ranking function [10].

The datasets differed in terms of "classification difficulty" (to distinguish between articles about geography and pages about religion is easier than to tell

Table 2. Best describing keywords for some of the classes from the dataset TL

Geography	History	Literature	People	Religion
town (2.9)	born (3.8)	book (5.8)	born (4.5)	religi (12.8)
river (2.7)	career (2.3)	fiction (4.9)	career (2.3)	mytholog (7.3)
city (2.6)	february (2.2)	screenwrit (4.1)	songwrit (2.2)	god (5.6)
island (2.2)	event (2.1)	treati (3.8)	ethnic (1.8)	cathedr (5.1)
county (2.0)	june (1.9)	newspap (3.8)	wrote (1.7)	church (4.5)
motto (1.9)	october (1.9)	diktat (3.0)	tribe (1.7)	anglican (4.3)
district (1.9)	military (1.7)	orig (3.0)	middleham (1.6)	mosqu (4.2)
chicago (1.9)	single (1.7)	epistl (3.0)	spous (1.5)	islam (4.2)

Table 3. Words differentiating between Geography and Religion

Geography	Religion
citi (6.9)	religi (15.1)
town (4.2)	mytholog (6.5)
district (4.1)	god (6.2)
born (4.0)	christian (5.5)
armenian (3.8)	islam (5.2)
region (3.7)	cathedr (4.9)
area (3.7)	bibl (4.8)
river (3.7)	pope (4.2)
capit (3.7)	church (4.2)
franc (3.5)	jewish (3.9)

Table 4. Keywords specific to the category Mathematics along with the words indicating other subcategories of Science

Mathematics	
+	-
mathemat (15.3)	fear (7.6)
number (7.1)	citi (6.9)
geometri (5.5)	comput (5.1)
math (5.3)	superscript (4.8)
algebra (4.7)	water (4.6)
actuari (4.6)	state (4.6)
arithmet (4.6)	town (4.6)
statist (4.4)	cyril (4.5)
function (4.2)	birth (4.2)

some scientific topics apart). Feature selection resulted in various numbers of retained features as well as various cut off thresholds. Such results would not be possible if the final dimensionality was fixed a priori or if only features ranked above some constant threshold were retained.

Of course it would be easy to construct datasets for which optimal α would be vastly different. However, for groups of similar problems – in our case all problems origined in some areas of Wikipedia – good results can be obtained using constant value of α.

Acknowledgments. The work has been supported by the Polish Ministry of Science and Higher Education under research grant N N 516 432338.

References

1. Yang, Y., Pedersen, J.O.: A comparative study on feature selection in text categorization. In: Proceedings of the Fourteenth International Conference on Machine Learning, ICML 1997, pp. 412–420. Morgan Kaufmann Publishers Inc., San Francisco (1997)
2. Chen, J., Huang, H., Tian, S., Qu, Y.: Feature selection for text classification with naïve bayes. Expert Systems with Applications 36(3), 5432–5435 (2009)
3. Guyon, I., Weston, J., Barnhill, S., Vapnik, V.: Gene selection for cancer classification using support vector machines. Mach. Learn. 46(1-3), 389–422 (2002)
4. Brank, J., Grobelnik, M.: Feature selection using linear support vector machines (2002)
5. Hearst, M.A., Dumais, S.T., Osman, E., Platt, J., Scholkopf, B.: Support vector machines. IEEE Intelligent Systems and their Applications 13(4), 18–28 (1998)
6. Neumann, J., Schnörr, C., Steidl, G.: Combined svm-based feature selection and classification. Machine Learning 61(1-3), 129–150 (2005)
7. Rzeniewicz, J.: Analysis methods for intercategorial links. Master's thesis, Gdansk University of Technology (2013)
8. Fan, R.-E., Chang, K.-W., Hsieh, C.-J., Wang, X.-R., Lin, C.-J.: Liblinear: A library for large linear classification. J. Mach. Learn. Res. 9, 1871–1874 (2008)
9. Szymański, J.: Wikipedia Articles Representation with Matrix'u. In: Hota, C., Srimani, P.K. (eds.) ICDCIT 2013. LNCS, vol. 7753, pp. 500–510. Springer, Heidelberg (2013)
10. Balicki, J., Krawczyk, H., Rymko, Ł., Szymański, J.: Selection of Relevant Features for Text Classification with K-NN. In: Rutkowski, L., Korytkowski, M., Scherer, R., Tadeusiewicz, R., Zadeh, L.A., Zurada, J.M. (eds.) ICAISC 2013, Part II. LNCS (LNAI), vol. 7895, pp. 477–488. Springer, Heidelberg (2013)

Benchmarking Datasets for Breast Cancer Computer-Aided Diagnosis (CADx)

Daniel Cardoso Moura[1], Miguel Angel Guevara López[2,1], Pedro Cunha[1],
Naimy González de Posada[1], Raúl Ramos Pollan[3], Isabel Ramos[4],
Joana Pinheiro Loureiro[4], Inês C. Moreira[4], Bruno M. Ferreira de Araújo[4],
and Teresa Cardoso Fernandes[4]

[1] INEGI - Institute of Mechanical Engineering and Industrial Management,
Faculty of Engineering, University of Porto, Portugal
{dmoura,mguevaral,pcunha,nposada}@inegi.up.pt
[2] DETI - Department of Electronics, Telecommunications and Informatics,
University of Aveiro, Portugal
mguevaral@ua.pt
[3] Universidad Industrial de Santander, Bucaramanga, Colombia
rramosp@unal.edu.co
[4] FMUP-HSJ – Faculty of Medicine – Centro Hospitalar São João, University of Porto, Portugal
radiologia.hsj@mail.telepac.pt,
{joanaploureiro,ines.c.moreira}@gmail.com,
{bruno.araujo,teresafernandes}@hsjoao.minsaude.pt

Abstract. Designing reliable computer-aided diagnosis (CADx) systems based on data extracted from breast images and patient data to provide a second opinion to radiologists is still a challenging and yet unsolved problem. This paper proposes two benchmarking datasets (one of them representative of low resolution digitized Film Mammography images and the other one representative of high resolution Full Field Digital Mammography images) aimed to (1) modeling and exploring machine learning classifiers (MLC); (2) evaluating the impact of mammography image resolution on MLC; and (3) comparing the performance of breast cancer CADx methods. Also, we include a comparative study of four groups of image-based descriptors (intensity, texture, multi-scale texture and spatial distribution of the gradient), and combine them with patient's clinical data to classify masses. Finally, we demonstrate that this combination of clinical data and image descriptors is advantageous in most CADx scenarios.

Keywords: Breast cancer, image-based descriptors, clinical data, machine learning classifiers, computer-aided diagnosis (CADx), histograms of gradient divergence.

1 Introduction

According to the World Health Organization, breast cancer is the second most common form of cancer in the world, with a prediction of over 1.5 million diagnoses in 2010 and causing more than half a million deaths per year [1]. At present, there are no

J. Ruiz-Shulcloper and G. Sanniti di Baja (Eds.): CIARP 2013, Part I, LNCS 8258, pp. 326–333, 2013.
© Springer-Verlag Berlin Heidelberg 2013

effective ways to prevent breast cancer, because its cause remains unknown. However, efficient diagnosis of breast cancer in its early stages can give women better chances of full recovery. Screening mammography is the primary imaging modality for early detection of breast cancer because it is the only method of breast imaging that consistently has been found to decrease breast cancer-related mortality [2].

Double reading of mammograms (two radiologists read the same mammogram) has been advocated to reduce the proportion of missed cancers. But the workload and costs associated with double reading are high. Therefore, many research institutions have focused their efforts in applications of Computer-Aided Diagnosis (CADx) approaches combining mammography image-based descriptors and associated metadata, being the correct patterns classification of breast cancer an important real-world medical problem. For this reason, the use of Machine Learning Classifiers (MLC) in breast cancer diagnosis is gradually increasing [3]. MLC can explain complex relationships in the data and constitute the backbone of biomedical data analysis on high dimensional quantitative data provided by the state-of-the-art medical imaging and high-throughput biology technologies [4].

While several produced mammography-based breast cancer databases (public or private) have been reported [1], [5-12], currently, the information included in these databases presents some undesirable issues: a) lesions are not exactly identified; b) are incomplete in terms of available features (pre-computed image-based descriptors and clinical data); c) have a reduced number of annotated patient's cases; and/or d) the database is private and cannot be used as reference. Altogether, these issues make it difficult producing golden standard datasets assembling properly extracted information of breast cancer lesions (biopsy proven) for assessing and comparing the performance of machine learning classifiers (MLC) and Breast Cancer CADx methods.

In preceding works, first we made an exploration of mammography-based MLC [13] and hereafter we made an evaluation of several groups of mammography image-based descriptors, clinical data, and combinations of both types of data for classifying microcalcifications, masses and all lesions together on two different Film mammography-based datasets [14]. As result, we obtained MLC with high performance and it was proposed a novel image-based descriptor that is especially designed for round-shape objects, such as masses, the Histograms of Gradient Divergence (HGD).

This paper proposes two benchmarking datasets (one of them representative of low resolution Film Mammography images and the other one representative of high resolution Full Field Digital Mammography (FFDM) images) aimed to: (1) modeling and exploring machine learning classifiers (MLC); (2) evaluating the impact of mammography image resolution on MLC; and (3) comparing the performance of breast cancer CADx developed methods. Also, it is included a comparative study of four groups of image-based descriptors (intensity, texture, multi-scale texture and spatial distribution of the gradient), and their combination with patient's clinical data to classify masses. The two benchmarking datasets used in this work are available for public domain at the Breast Cancer Digital Repository (BCDR – http://bcdr.inegi.up.pt) and it is the first experiment made on the FFDM-based dataset (BCDR-D01).

2   Materials and Methods

2.1   Benchmarking Datasets

The two benchmarking datasets proposed here were extracted from the Breast Cancer Digital Repository (BCDR). The BCDR is a wide-ranging annotated public repository composed by Breast Cancer patients' cases of the northern region of Portugal.

BCDR is subdivided in two different repositories: (1) a Film Mammography-based Repository (BCDR-FM) and (2) a Full Field Digital Mammography-based Repository (BCDR-DM). Both repositories were created with anonymous cases from medical archives (complying with current privacy regulations as they are also used to teach regular and postgraduate medical students) supplied by the Faculty of Medicine – Centro Hospitalar São João, at University of Porto (FMUP-HSJ). BCDR provides normal and annotated patients cases of breast cancer including mammography lesions outlines, anomalies observed by radiologists, pre-computed image-based descriptors as well as related clinical data.

The BCDR-FM is composed by 1010 (998 female and 12 male) patients cases (with ages between 20 and 90 years old), including 1125 studies, 3703 mediolateral oblique (MLO) and craniocaudal (CC) mammography incidences and 1044 identified lesions clinically described (820 already identified in MLO and/or CC views). With this, 1517 segmentations were manually made and BI-RADS classified by specialized radiologists. MLO and CC images are grey-level digitized mammograms with a resolution of 720 (width) by 1168 (height) pixels and a bit depth of 8 bits per pixel, saved in the TIFF format.

The BCDR-DM, still in construction, at the time of writing is composed by 724 (723 female and 1 male) Portuguese patients cases (with ages between 27 and 92 years old), including 1042 studies, 3612 MLO and/or CC mammography incidences and 452 lesions clinically described (already identified in MLO and CC views). With this, 818 segmentations were manually made and BI-RADS classified by specialized radiologists. The MLO and CC images are grey-level mammograms with a resolution of 3328 (width) by 4084 (height) or 2560 (width) by 3328 (height) pixels, depending on the compression plate used in the acquisition (according to the breast size of the patient). The bit depth is 14 bits per pixel and the images are saved in the TIFF format.

The **BCDR-F01** dataset is built from BCDR-FM and is formed by 200 lesions: 100 benign and 100 malignant (biopsy proven) and it is composed by a total of 358 features vectors (184 instances related to the 100 benign lesions and 174 instances related to the 100 malignant lesions).

The **BCDR-D01** dataset is built from BCDR-DM and is formed by 79 lesions: 49 benign and 30 malignant (biopsy proven) and it is composed by 143 features vectors (86 instances related to the 49 benign lesions and 57 instances related to the 30 malignant lesions).

Both datasets (currently, available for download at the BCDR website) are composed by instances of the same clinical, intensity, texture, multi-scale texture and spatial distribution of the gradient features. Clinical features include the patient age, breast density and a set of selected binary attributes for indicating abnormalities observed by radiologists, namely masses, microcalcifications, calcifications (other than microcalcifications), axillary adenopathies, architectural distortions, and stroma distortions. Thus, the clinical data for each instance of the datasets is formed by a total of 8 attributes per instance: 6 binary attributes related to observed abnormalities, an ordinal attribute for breast density, and a numerical attribute that contains the patient age at the time of the study. The same group of image-based features (intensity, texture, multi-scale texture and spatial distribution of the gradient) that we reported in [14] were utilized here, namely, Intensity statistics, Histogram measures, Invariant moments, Zernike moments, Haralick features, Grey-level run length (GLRL) analysis, grey-level differences matrix (GLDM), Gabor filter banks, Wavelets, Curvelets, Histograms of Oriented Gradient (HOG), and Histograms of Gradient Divergence (HGD). For the sake of brevity, the reader is addressed to [14] for a formal description of the descriptors and the range of parameters evaluated. All descriptors were computed from rectangular patches of the lesions that were generated by extracting the part of the mammogram within the bounding box of the outlines provided by both datasets.

2.2   Evaluation of the Benchmarking Datasets

For evaluating the datasets, and delivering baseline benchmarks for CADx, an experiment was conducted for classifying masses.

Classification was performed using several machine learning classifiers available on Weka version 3.6 [15], namely Support Vector Machines (SVM), Random Forests (RF), Logistic Model Trees (LMT), K Nearest Neighbours (KNN), and Naive Bayes (NB). For all classifiers with the exception of NB (which is parameterless), 3-fold cross-validation was performed on the training set for optimizing the classifiers parameters. Linear SVM was chosen for simplicity and speed with regulation parameter C ranging from 10^{-2} to 10^3. The number of trees of RF was optimized between 50 and 400, with each tree having $\log_2(A) + 1$ randomly selected attributes, where A is the number of attributes available in the current dataset. On LMT the number of boosting iterations was also optimized. Finally, the number of neighbours (K) of KNN varied from 1 to 20, and the contribution of each neighbour was always weighted by the distance to the instance being classified. For all classifiers, attribute range normalization [0..1] was performed as pre-processing with the minimum and maximum values of the attributes found in the training set and then applied to both train and test sets.

The evaluation measure used was the Area Under the Curve of the Receiver Operator Characteristic (AUC). Resampling without replacing was performed 50 times for each view (MLO and CC) resulting in 100 runs per experiment to provide different splits across training and test sets, with 80% of the cases randomly selected for training the classifier, and the remaining 20% used for test. The two views were trained and tested independently to prevent biasing results and finally the AUCs from both views were merged resulting in a total of 100 evaluations per experiment. When comparing descriptors, the best combination of parameters' values and classifier was used. Comparisons between the experiments were based on the median AUC of the 100 runs (mAUC) and were supported by Wilcoxon signed rank tests to determine wheth-er differences have statistical evidence ($p < 0.05$). The experiment was done for both BCDR-F01 and BCDR-D01 datasets, for all descriptors including and excluding clin-ical data, and for all classifiers.

3   Results and Discusion

Results for the BCDR-F01 were previously published on [14] and are included here for reference and comparison with BCDR-D01. On the BCDR-F01 dataset (Fig.1), the standalone clinical data had a performance of mAUC=0.829, and was only outper-formed by HGD (mAUC=0.860, p<0.001). When combining clinical data with image descriptors, four descriptors (Intensity Histograms, Zernike, GLRL and GLDM) did not show evidence of increasing the performance of standalone clinical data. All the remainder descriptors outperformed clinical data (p<0.028), with HGD being the best (mAUC=0.894). HGD performance was significantly superior to all the remainder (p<0.024). All descriptors significantly improved performance (p<0.001) when com-bined with clinical data.

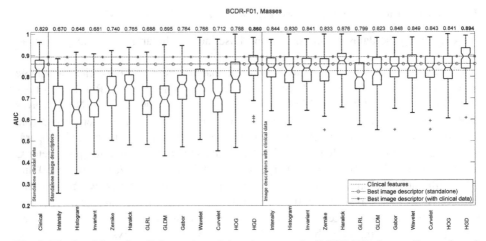

Fig. 1. Final rankings for all the evaluated descriptors on the BCDR-F01 dataset (image-based standalone and image-based combined with clinical data)

On the BCDR-D01 dataset (Fig.2), in contrast to the previous dataset, the standalone clinical data was outperformed by all descriptors (p<0.001). It was observed that this difference was mainly explained by an increase of performance of the image descriptors on the BCDR-D01 dataset, rather than a decrease of performance of the standalone clinical data. Haralick features scored the highest score with mAUC=0.938, and both Wavelets and HGD did not show statistical evidence of significant differences to Haralick features, with p=0.943 and p= 0.710 respectively. When clinical data is combined with the image descriports, Haralick features remains the descriptor with the highest score (mAUC=0.965), with Wavelets (p=0.241), Curvelets (p=0.889) and HGD (p=0.585) not showing statistical evidence of significant differences to Haralick features. All descriptors significantly improved performance (p<0.003) when combined with clinical data, with the exception of GLDM and HOG.

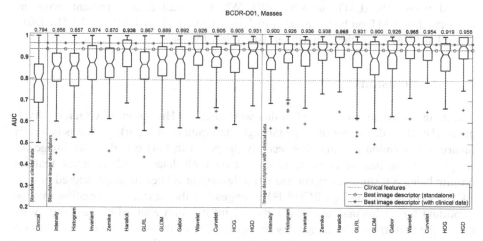

Fig. 2. Final rankings for all the evaluated descriptors on the BCDR-D01 dataset (image-based standalone and image-based combined with clinical data)

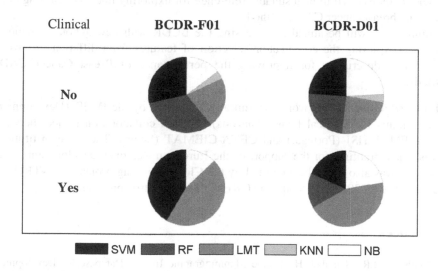

Fig. 3. Distribution of wins among classifiers on both datasets in the absence and presence of clinical data. A classifier scores a win for each time it enables to reach the best result for a given descriptor or when there is no evidence of significant differences to the best results (Wilcoxon test, p>0.05).

Regarding the performance, it can be observed (Fig. 3) that the performance of classifiers is more sensible to the absence or presence of clinical data, rather than to the dataset that was used BCDR-FM (Film) vs BCDR-DM (digital). KNN scored the worst results with performances ranging from 0% to 3% of the wins. When clinical data is not included in the datasets, the frequence of wins is equaly distributed by all the remainder classifiers on BCDR-D01 with 24% of wins, while on BCDR-F01 ranged from 21% (LMT) to 32% (RF). When clinical data is present, wins are dominated by LMT on both datasets (46% on BCDR-F01, and 44% on BCDR-D01), as well as SVM in the the film dataset with 42% of wins.

4   Conclusions

The main contributions observed in this work are: (1) Histogram of Gradient Divergence (HGD), a descriptor of shape through the gradient of the image that is naturally invariant to rotation and that was recently proposed in [14] was the only image descriptor scoring best or comparable to best on both datasets; (2) Haralick features despite being a texture descriptor and not a descriptor related to shape, scored best on BCDR-D01 and second on BCDR-F01, suggesting that texture information may be important for evaluating masses; (3) clinical information enabled to significantly increase the performance of image descriptors in 92% of the cases; (4) the relative performance of the classifiers is similar for the two datasets, then it is possible to expect that image resolution is not critical; and (5) the Breast Cancer Digital Repository (BCDR) demonstrated to be a suitable reference for exploring machine learning classifiers and breast cancer CADx methods.

Future work will be aimed at increasing the BCDR with new annotated patients cases and exploring the combination/selection of features from different groups of image-based descriptors for improving the performance of Breast Cancer CADx methods.

Acknowledgements. This work was initially supported by the IMED (Development of Algorithms for Medical Image Analysis) research collaboration project between INEGI, FMUP-HSJ (Portugal) and CETA-CIEMAT (Spain). The three institutions express their gratitude for the support of the European Regional Development Fund. This work was also partially supported by the Cloud Thinking project (CENTRO-07-ST24-FEDER-002031), co-funded by QREN, "Mais Centro" program.

References

1. Matheus, B.R., Schiabel, H.: Online Mammographic Images Database for Development and Comparison of CAD Schemes. Journal of Digital Imaging 24(3), 500–506 (2011)
2. Christoyianni, I., Dermatas, E., Kokkinakis, G.: Fast detection of masses in computer-aided mammography. IEEE Signal Processing Magazine 17(1), 54–64 (2000)
3. Marcano-Cedeño, A., Quintanilla-Domínguez, J., Andina, D.: WBCD breast cancer database classification applying artificial metaplasticity neural network. Expert Systems with Applications 38(8), 9573–9579 (2011)
4. Ramos-Pollan, R., Guevara-Lopez, M.A., Oliveira, E.: A software framework for building biomedical machine learning classifiers through grid computing resources. J. Med. Syst. 36(4), 2245–2257 (2012)

5. Antoniou, Z.C., et al.: A web-accessible mammographic image database dedicated to combined training and evaluation of radiologists and machines. In: 9th International Conference on Information Technology and Applications in Biomedicine, ITAB 2009 (2009)
6. de Oliveira, J., et al.: MammoSVD: A content-based image retrieval system using a reference database of mammographies. In: 22nd IEEE International Symposium on Computer-Based Medical Systems, CBMS 2009 (2009)
7. Oliveira, J.E.E., et al.: Toward a standard reference database for computer-aided mammography. In: Proceeding 6915 Medical Imaging 2008: Computer-Aided Diagnosis (2008)
8. Heath, M., et al.: Current status of the digital database for screening mammography. In: Digital Mammography, pp. 457–460. Kluwer Academic Publishers (1998)
9. Markey, M.K., et al.: Self-organizing map for cluster analysis of a breast cancer database. Artificial Intelligence in Medicine 27(2), 113–127 (2003)
10. Nishikawa, R.M.: Mammographic databases. Breast Dis. 10(3-4), 137–150 (1998)
11. Suckling, J.: The Mammographic Image Analysis Society Digital Mammogram Database in Exerpta Medica. International Congress Series, vol. 1069, pp. 375–378 (1994)
12. Moreira, I.C., et al.: INbreast: Toward a Full-field Digital Mammographic Database. Academic Radiology 19(2), 236–248 (2012)
13. Ramos-Pollan, R., et al.: Discovering mammography-based machine learning classifiers for breast cancer diagnosis. J. Med. Syst. 36(4), 2259–2269 (2012)
14. Moura, D., Guevara López, M.: An evaluation of image descriptors combined with clinical data for breast cancer diagnosis. International Journal of Computer Assisted Radiology and Surgery, 1–14 (2013)
15. Hall, M., et al.: The WEKA data mining software: an update. SIGKDD Explorations 11(1), 10–18 (2009)

Managing Imbalanced Data Sets in Multi-label Problems: A Case Study with the SMOTE Algorithm

Andrés Felipe Giraldo-Forero[1], Jorge Alberto Jaramillo-Garzón[1,2],
José Francisco Ruiz-Muñoz[1], and César Germán Castellanos-Domínguez[1]

[1] Signal Processing and Recognition Group, Universidad Nacional de Colombia,
Campus la Nubia, Km 7 vía al Magdalena, Manizales, Colombia
[2] Grupo de Máquinas Inteligentes y Reconocimiento de Patrones - MIRP,
Instituto Tecnológico Metropolitano, Cll 54A No 30-01, Medellín, Colombia
{afgiraldofo,jaramillog,jfruizmu,cgcastellanosd}@unal.edu.co

Abstract. Multi-label learning has been becoming an increasingly active area into the machine learning community since a wide variety of real world problems are naturally multi-labeled. However, it is not uncommon to find disparities among the number of samples of each class, which constitutes an additional challenge for the learning algorithm. SMOTE is an oversampling technique that has been successfully applied for balancing single-labeled data sets, but has not been used in multi-label frameworks so far. In this work, several strategies are proposed and compared in order to generate synthetic samples for balancing data sets in the training of multi-label algorithms. Results show that a correct selection of seed samples for oversampling improves the classification performance of multi-label algorithms. The uniform generation oversampling, provides an efficient methodology for a wide scope of real world problems.

1 Introduction

Multi-label learning refers to classification problems where each sample can be associated to more than one class at the same time. A high number of real world applications such as image classification [1] or protein sequence annotation [2] are multi-labeled. Methods for classifying multi-label data can be grouped into two categories: transformation of the problem and adaptation of the algorithm [3]. The former kind of methods searches to transform the multi-label problem into a single-label one. For that purpose, they employ intuitive strategies such as considering each different set of labels in the multi-label data set as a single label [1] or learning one binary classifier for each different label (one-against-all) [4]. Although those strategies have reached acceptable performances and they are very commonly used nowadays, none of them considers existing correlations among classes, thus discarding potentially useful information that could help to properly solve the problem.

On the other hand, methods based on adaptation of the algorithm are intended to modify existing algorithms in order to explode those correlations among classes.

J. Ruiz-Shulcloper and G. Sanniti di Baja (Eds.): CIARP 2013, Part I, LNCS 8258, pp. 334–342, 2013.

Some of the most recent and successful general purpose algorithms in this category are ML-KNN [5], ML-LOC [6], and TRAM [7]. However, it is common to find that the number of elements belonging to each class significantly differ from each other. This "class imbalance" is a well known problem for most standard algorithms that assume balanced class distributions and thus, when presented with complex imbalanced data sets, fail to properly represent the distributive characteristics of the data and provide unfavorable accuracies [8]. Common strategies to manage imbalanced data comprise sub-sampling and over-sampling methods. Among them, SMOTE (Synthetic Minority Over-sampling Technique) [9] is an oversampling tool that has been successfully applied to several real world problems, but has not been applied so far to multi-label algorithms. Moreover, standard SMOTE does not consider correlations among classes and therefore it only could generate synthetic samples belonging to single classes. Although some studies have tackled the balance of classes in multi-label problems [10,11], these follow follow a scheme one vs all to adapt the balancing technique, lossing information about the correlations that exist between the classes. In [12] the imbalance is treated from the classification point of view, causing lack of flexibility of the method when this is intended to be adapted to other classifiers.

This work presents a series of strategies for applying class balance tools in conjunction with multi-label algorithms. The strategies are tested over several real-world problems, proving to be a valuable tool to improve classification performance in multi-label problems. The rest of the paper is organized as follows: section II presents the basis of SMOTE; section III explains the proposed strategies to apply SMOTE in conjunction with multi-label algorithms. Experimental framework and results are shown in section IV and discussion and conclusions are presented in sections V and VI, respectively.

2 Synthetic Minority Oversampling Technique - Smote

Basic strategies to manage class imbalance are: random sub-sampling and random over-sampling. However, these techniques provide disappointing results in several cases because the former one causes lose of potentially useful information, while the latter induces overfitting due to the exact replication of samples. As an alternative to improve these limitations, SMOTE [9] is an over-sampling strategy that avoids the overfitting because synthetic samples are not exact copies of the original ones. Instead, synthetic samples are interpolated along the line segments connecting seed samples, forcing the decision region of the minority class to become more general. Algorithm 1 describes this procedure.

3 Proposed Framework for Balancing Multi-label Data

Generating synthetic data from multi-labeled instances requires a careful selection of inputs for the SMOTE algorithm. For explanatory purposes, consider a set of training samples associated to a set of three possible labels $\mathcal{T} = \{(\mathbf{x}_i, \mathbf{y}_i)\}$, $i = 1, 2, \ldots, m$, with $\mathbf{x}_i \in \mathbb{R}^d$ and $\mathbf{y}_i \subseteq \mathcal{Y}$, being $\mathcal{Y} = \{a, b, c\}$. Let $\mathcal{T}_\gamma \subset \mathcal{T}$,

---

Algorithm 1. SMOTE $(\mathcal{S}, r, k)$

Input: $\mathcal{S}$: Seed samples, samples of the minority class $\mathbf{x}_i \in \mathbb{R}^d$, $i = 1, 2, \ldots, m$
Input: r: Imbalance percentage
Input: k: Number of nearest neighbors
1: **for** $i = 1, 2, ..., m$ **do**
2:      Compute distances $\|\mathbf{x}_i - \mathbf{x}_j\|_2, \forall i \neq j$
3:      Find the k nearest neighbors asociated to the k minimum distances
4:      Compute the number of synthetic samples to be generated from $\mathbf{x}_i$,
         $n = \text{round}(r/100)$
5:      **for** $z = 1, 2, ..., n$ **do**
6:         Select a random integer ε between 1 and k
7:         Draw a random vector from a uniform multivarite distribution $\boldsymbol{\lambda} \sim \mathcal{U}_d(0, 1)$
8:         Compute the synthetic sample $\mathbf{s}_i^z = \boldsymbol{\lambda} \circ (\mathbf{x}_i - \mathbf{x}_\varepsilon) + \mathbf{x}_i$ where $\circ$ is the
            Hadamard product between vectors
9:      **end for**
10: **end for**
11: **return** The set of $n \times m$ synthetic samples $\{s_i^z\}$, $i = 1, 2, \ldots, m_-$, $z = 1, 2, \ldots, n$

$\gamma \in \mathcal{Y}$, be the set of samples associated to a given class, $\mathcal{T}_\gamma = \{(\mathbf{x}_i, \mathbf{y}_i) | \gamma \in \mathbf{y}_i\}$. Balancing the classes means generating a number of synthetic samples of the three classes such that $|\mathcal{T}_a| = |\mathcal{T}_b| = |\mathcal{T}_c|$, where $| \cdot |$ denotes the number of elements of the set.

Three strategies are proposed in order to apply SMOTE to imbalanced multi-label data. In the first place, it is important to properly define the set of seed samples for each class, $\mathcal{S}_\gamma \subseteq \mathcal{T}_\gamma$, $\gamma \in \mathcal{Y}$. Strategies are depicted with graphs in figures 1 2 3, highlighting in each case the nodes of the graph corresponding to seed samples of the class a. After defining the set of seed samples, the second input parameter of the SMOTE algorithm is the imbalance percentage r. The imbalance percentage r_a drives the decision of how many synthetic samples from class a must be generated (known as over-sampling). Equations (2), (4) and (6) show the calculus for strategies OG, PG and UG, respectively.

One-against-All Generation The first strategy, depicted in figure 1, is defined as a "one-against-all generation" (OG). In this case, all the samples belonging to the minoritary class are considered as seed samples, that is, seed samples of class a are defined on equation (1)

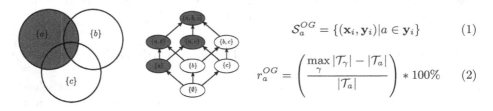

$$\mathcal{S}_a^{OG} = \{(\mathbf{x}_i, \mathbf{y}_i) | a \in \mathbf{y}_i\} \qquad (1)$$

$$r_a^{OG} = \left(\frac{\max_\gamma |\mathcal{T}_\gamma| - |\mathcal{T}_a|}{|\mathcal{T}_a|} \right) * 100\% \qquad (2)$$

Fig. 1. one-against-all generation

This strategy is inspired from transformation method called binary relevance, used in [4]. This approach is widely employed, however, it is criticized for not taking into account the correlation between classes.

Pure Samples Generation The second strategy, termed "pure samples generation" (PG) is depicted in figure 2. It takes as seed samples only those samples associated to a single label. Thus, the seed samples for class a are selected according to equation 3.

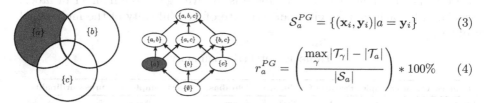

$$\mathcal{S}_a^{PG} = \{(\mathbf{x}_i, \mathbf{y}_i) | a = \mathbf{y}_i\} \qquad (3)$$

$$r_a^{PG} = \left(\frac{\max_\gamma |\mathcal{T}_\gamma| - |\mathcal{T}_a|}{|\mathcal{S}_a|}\right) * 100\% \qquad (4)$$

Fig. 2. pure samples generation

This strategy is inspired from transformation method called PT2 described in [3], those were used successfully in problems with low cardinality levels.

Uniform Generation. The third strategy, depicted in figure 3 divides the whole set $\mathcal{T}_a$ into several subsets, and over-samples each set individually. The subsets are defined on , by each different set of labels and are depicted in figure 3 with different intensities of green. This strategy is termed "uniform generation" (UG).

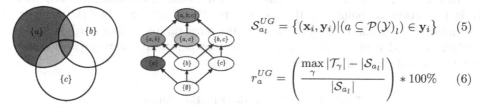

$$\mathcal{S}_{a_l}^{UG} = \{(\mathbf{x}_i, \mathbf{y}_i) | (a \subseteq \mathcal{P}(\mathcal{Y})_l) \in \mathbf{y}_i\} \qquad (5)$$

$$r_a^{UG} = \left(\frac{\max_\gamma |\mathcal{T}_\gamma| - |\mathcal{S}_{a_l}|}{|\mathcal{S}_{a_l}|}\right) * 100\% \qquad (6)$$

Fig. 3. uniform generation

4 Experimental Setup

Experiments were performed over four datasets from the MULAN [13] repository and a fifth dataset from [14]. The first dataset, *Emotion*, comprises 593 songs belonging to several music genres. The second dataset, *Scene*, is a natural scene classification problem [1]. It consists of 2407 natural scene images belonging to six different classes. The third dataset, the *Enron* database, is a subset of the Enron email corpus [15], including 1702 emails with 53 possible labels. Each message was labeled by two people, but no claims of consistency, comprehensiveness, nor generality are made about these labelings. Due to the large number of classes, only those that have more than 300 samples were selected. Also, the principal component analysis (PCA) was used in order to decrease the number of features. The fourth dataset, *Image*, consists of 2000 natural scene images, where a set of labels is artificially assigned to each image. The number of images belonging to more than one class (e.g. sea+sunset) comprises over 22% of the dataset [14]. Finally, the *Yeast* database is designed to predict functional classes in the genome of yeast *Saccharomyces cerevisiae*. The whole data set has 2417 instances of genes and 14 possible class labels; only the classes 1, 3, 4, 5 and 6 are considered and the first 250 principal components were used as features. Table 1 summarizes the datasets. The cardinality of the database is an average of the number of labels associated to each sample, given an estimate of the difficulty of the multi-label problem.

Table 1. Databases summary

Database	Classes	Samples	Features	Cardinality	Database	Classes	Samples	Features	Cardinality
Emotion	6	593	72	1.869	Image	5	2000	135	1.24
Scene	6	2407	294	1.074	Yeast	14	2417	103	4.237
Enron	52	1702	1001	3.378					

The strategies are used in conjunction with three state-of-the-art multi-label methods: TRAM, ML-KNN and ML-LOC. Parameters are fixed for all the datasets as: 10 nearest neighbors for the first two methods (values suggested in [5, 7]), and $\lambda_1 = 1$, $\lambda_2 = 100$, $m = 15$ for ML-LOC (suggested by [6]). A lineal kernel is used for evading extra tuning parameters. The number of nearest neighbors for SMOTE is set to 5, by literature recommendations [9].

All the reported results are obtained with a 10-fold cross-validation scheme. It is important to point out that, since the Yeast database has the highest cardinality and some of its classes have no pure samples (samples belonging exclusively to that class), the "pure samples regeneration" strategy (PG) could not be applied for such database.

Table 2. Results for the Emotion dataset

Classifier	Measure	WO	OG	PG	UG
ML-kNN	H_loss ↓	0.197 ± 0.020	0.255 ± 0.021 ∘	0.239 ± 0.019 ∘	0.207 ± 0.019 ∘
	$F\_measure$ ↑	0.621 ± 0.037	0.459 ± 0.051 ∘	0.536 ± 0.041 ∘	0.646 ± 0.030 •
	G_mean ↑	0.700 ± 0.031	0.567 ± 0.046 ∘	0.635 ± 0.035 ∘	0.734 ± 0.029 •
	$Recall$ ↑	0.596 ± 0.050	0.401 ± 0.053 ∘	0.480 ± 0.047 ∘	0.646 ± 0.051 •
TRAM	H_loss ↓	0.218 ± 0.022	0.247 ± 0.027 ∘	0.240 ± 0.026 ∘	0.218 ± 0.026
	$F\_measure$ ↑	0.640 ± 0.032	0.540 ± 0.045 ∘	0.579 ± 0.044 ∘	0.652 ± 0.040
	G_mean ↑	0.729 ± 0.028	0.649 ± 0.035 ∘	0.678 ± 0.035 ∘	0.743 ± 0.035 •
	$Recall$ ↑	0.656 ± 0.037	0.496 ± 0.042 ∘	0.546 ± 0.047 ∘	0.683 ± 0.050 •
MLLOC	H_loss ↓	0.248 ± 0.024	0.285 ± 0.023 ∘	0.255 ± 0.022	0.253 ± 0.016
	$F\_measure$ ↑	0.450 ± 0.076	0.231 ± 0.074 ∘	0.424 ± 0.070 ∘	0.471 ± 0.045
	G_mean ↑	0.545 ± 0.074	0.313 ± 0.089 ∘	0.520 ± 0.067 ∘	0.574 ± 0.046
	$Recall$ ↑	0.389 ± 0.074	0.166 ± 0.062 ∘	0.345 ± 0.070 ∘	0.413 ± 0.051

Table 3. Results for the Scene dataset

Classifier	Measure	WO	OG	PG	UG
ML-kNN	H_loss ↓	0.086 ± 0.009	0.089 ± 0.008 ∘	0.087 ± 0.008	0.087 ± 0.008
	$F\_measure$ ↑	0.742 ± 0.028	0.731 ± 0.025 ∘	0.738 ± 0.026	0.741 ± 0.026
	G_mean ↑	0.812 ± 0.020	0.807 ± 0.018 ∘	0.815 ± 0.019	0.817 ± 0.019
	$Recall$ ↑	0.691 ± 0.031	0.688 ± 0.026	0.701 ± 0.029 •	0.705 ± 0.030 •
TRAM	H_loss ↓	0.090 ± 0.010	0.093 ± 0.009	0.092 ± 0.010	0.092 ± 0.010
	$F\_measure$ ↑	0.746 ± 0.027	0.736 ± 0.027 ∘	0.740 ± 0.029	0.740 ± 0.028
	G_mean ↑	0.831 ± 0.019	0.825 ± 0.018 ∘	0.828 ± 0.018	0.829 ± 0.019
	$Recall$ ↑	0.730 ± 0.028	0.725 ± 0.027	0.729 ± 0.026	0.731 ± 0.028
MLLOC	H_loss ↓	0.155 ± 0.009	0.153 ± 0.008	0.152 ± 0.008 •	0.151 ± 0.006 •
	$F\_measure$ ↑	0.355 ± 0.047	0.339 ± 0.051	0.356 ± 0.045	0.350 ± 0.043
	G_mean ↑	0.463 ± 0.049	0.441 ± 0.053 ∘	0.456 ± 0.048	0.453 ± 0.046
	$Recall$ ↑	0.270 ± 0.045	0.256 ± 0.048	0.274 ± 0.043	0.265 ± 0.040

Table 4. Results for the Enron dataset

Classifier	Measure	WO	OG	PG	UG
ML-kNN	H_loss ↓	0.325 ± 0.021	0.393 ± 0.017 ∘	0.356 ± 0.019 ∘	0.336 ± 0.023 ∘
	$F\_measure$ ↑	0.458 ± 0.036	0.283 ± 0.033 ∘	0.385 ± 0.032 ∘	0.533 ± 0.041 •
	G_mean ↑	0.528 ± 0.033	0.391 ± 0.034 ∘	0.496 ± 0.026 ∘	0.616 ± 0.031 •
	$Recall$ ↑	0.402 ± 0.044	0.255 ± 0.034 ∘	0.301 ± 0.027 ∘	0.509 ± 0.049 •
TRAM	H_loss ↓	0.268 ± 0.021	0.361 ± 0.020 ∘	0.321 ± 0.025 ∘	0.288 ± 0.016 ∘
	$F\_measure$ ↑	0.623 ± 0.026	0.491 ± 0.029 ∘	0.554 ± 0.029 ∘	0.633 ± 0.021 •
	G_mean ↑	0.664 ± 0.023	0.607 ± 0.023 ∘	0.646 ± 0.026 ∘	0.696 ± 0.018 •
	$Recall$ ↑	0.618 ± 0.024	0.500 ± 0.024 ∘	0.550 ± 0.032 ∘	0.670 ± 0.025 •
MLLOC	H_loss ↓	0.299 ± 0.016	0.347 ± 0.025 ∘	0.317 ± 0.021 ∘	0.306 ± 0.020
	$F\_measure$ ↑	0.556 ± 0.042	0.425 ± 0.051 ∘	0.507 ± 0.039 ∘	0.572 ± 0.039
	G_mean ↑	0.601 ± 0.043	0.530 ± 0.046 ∘	0.588 ± 0.038	0.624 ± 0.039 •
	$Recall$ ↑	0.540 ± 0.047	0.340 ± 0.045 ∘	0.446 ± 0.050 ∘	0.572 ± 0.055 •

5 Results and Discussion

For comparison purposes, all test are also performed without over-sampling (WO).
Tables 2, 3, 4, 5 and 6 show the results for the *Emotions, Scene, Enron Image* and
Yeast datasets, respectively. Tables show Hamming Loss (H_loss), F-meausure
($F\_measure$), Geometric mean (G_mean) and Recall ($Recall$) defined below.

$$F\_measure = \frac{1}{Q} \sum_{i \in \mathcal{T}} 2 \frac{|h(x_j) \cap \mathbf{Y}_i|}{|\mathbf{Y}_i \setminus h(x_j)| + 2|h(x_j) \cap \mathbf{Y}_i| + |h(x_j) \setminus \mathbf{Y}_i|}$$

$$H\_loss = \frac{1}{Q(n-m)} \sum_{i \in \mathcal{T}} |h(x_j) \Delta \mathbf{Y}_i| \qquad Recall = \frac{1}{Q} \sum_{i \in \mathcal{T}} \left(\frac{|h(x_j) \cap \mathbf{Y}_i|}{|h(x_j) \cap \mathbf{Y}_i| + |\mathbf{Y}_i \setminus h(x_j)|} \right)$$

$$G\_mean = \frac{1}{Q} \sum_{i \in \mathcal{T}} \sqrt{\frac{|h(x_j) \cap \mathbf{Y}_i| |h(x_j)^c \cap \mathbf{Y}_i^c|}{(|h(x_j) \cap \mathbf{Y}_i| + |\mathbf{Y}_i \setminus h(x_j)|)(|h(x_j) \setminus \mathbf{Y}_i| + |h(x_j)^c \cap \mathbf{Y}_i^c|)}}$$

where $\setminus$, Δ, ^{c}, $|.|$, $h(x_j)$, $\mathbf{Y}_i$ stands for the difference and symmetric difference
between two sets, complement and the cardinality of the set, the set of labels
predicted, the set of real labels, respectively; and Q is the number of labels.

Table 5. Results for the Image dataset

Classifier	Measure	WO	OG	PG	UG
ML-kNN	$H\_loss \downarrow$	0.197 ± 0.010	0.201 ± 0.010 ○	0.200 ± 0.011 ○	0.202 ± 0.011 ○
	$F\_measure \uparrow$	0.470 ± 0.029	0.458 ± 0.033	0.471 ± 0.037	0.481 ± 0.040
	$G\_mean \uparrow$	0.580 ± 0.025	0.575 ± 0.029	0.586 ± 0.032	0.598 ± 0.035 ●
	$Recall \uparrow$	0.374 ± 0.033	0.380 ± 0.033	0.394 ± 0.040 ●	0.404 ± 0.047 ●
TRAM	$H\_loss \downarrow$	0.218 ± 0.015	0.220 ± 0.014 ○	0.218 ± 0.016	0.222 ± 0.017 ○
	$F\_measure \uparrow$	0.531 ± 0.031	0.517 ± 0.029 ○	0.524 ± 0.034 ○	0.526 ± 0.035
	$G\_mean \uparrow$	0.657 ± 0.025	0.649 ± 0.023 ○	0.655 ± 0.027	0.658 ± 0.027
	$Recall \uparrow$	0.496 ± 0.032	0.488 ± 0.029	0.494 ± 0.035	0.502 ± 0.036
MLLOC	$H\_loss \downarrow$	0.231 ± 0.011	0.230 ± 0.010	0.230 ± 0.009	0.228 ± 0.011
	$F\_measure \uparrow$	0.161 ± 0.063	0.153 ± 0.058	0.150 ± 0.058	0.181 ± 0.058
	$G\_mean \uparrow$	0.249 ± 0.068	0.240 ± 0.064	0.239 ± 0.060	0.273 ± 0.065
	$Recall \uparrow$	0.104 ± 0.047	0.099 ± 0.046	0.096 ± 0.046	0.119 ± 0.045

Table 6. Results for the Yeast dataset

Classifier	Measure	WO	OG	UG
ML-kNN	$H\_loss \downarrow$	0.240 ± 0.013	0.273 ± 0.015 ○	0.269 ± 0.016 ○
	$F\_measure \uparrow$	0.575 ± 0.028	0.505 ± 0.033 ○	0.590 ± 0.029 ●
	$G\_mean \uparrow$	0.648 ± 0.023	0.598 ± 0.027 ○	0.674 ± 0.024 ●
	$Recall \uparrow$	0.491 ± 0.031	0.400 ± 0.037 ○	0.554 ± 0.039 ●
TRAM	$H\_loss \downarrow$	0.272 ± 0.016	0.295 ± 0.017 ○	0.288 ± 0.017 ○
	$F\_measure \uparrow$	0.598 ± 0.024	0.551 ± 0.028 ○	0.601 ± 0.023
	$G\_mean \uparrow$	0.671 ± 0.02	0.645 ± 0.023 ○	0.685 ± 0.020 ●
	$Recall \uparrow$	0.609 ± 0.023	0.518 ± 0.027 ○	0.623 ± 0.025 ●
MLLOC	$H\_loss \downarrow$	0.319 ± 0.019	0.346 ± 0.017 ○	0.319 ± 0.018
	$F\_measure \uparrow$	0.298 ± 0.068	0.153 ± 0.075 ○	0.307 ± 0.057
	$G\_mean \uparrow$	0.386 ± 0.070	0.245 ± 0.087 ○	0.394 ± 0.062
	$Recall \uparrow$	0.237 ± 0.058	0.101 ± 0.055 ○	0.246 ± 0.053

All tables depict (mean ± sd) for each metric. Additionally, ●(○) indicate wich strategy is significantly higer (lower) than WO strategy, based on paired t−test at 95% significance level. ↑(↓) implies the larger (smaller), the better.

Strategies OG and PG decrement the performance of classification, presumably due to the fact that this strategy is only capable of generating synthetic samples belonging to a single class instead of truly synthetic samples belonging to multiple classes. In addition PG presents a decrease respecting to the performance without over-sampling, possibly by the inability of this strategy to generate samples with multiple labels, fact that results in the lack of exploitation of the correlations between classes. Generation strategies based on OG, PG and UG showed similar behaviors when applied to datasets with low cardinality (low number of labels per sample), as it can be seen in Table 3, with variations of less 2% in the performance for three classifier. The experiments carried out in this paper show that the performance of ML-KNN can be significantly improved when a balance of classes is made, due to the fact that the prior probabilities on the Bayesian decision rule are computed from relative frequencies of samples and are thus the minority class loses prominence.

6   Conclusions

Three strategies for managing imbalanced data sets in multi-label problems are proposed. Experimental analyses on several real-world problems showed that "uniform generation" and classification by TRAM, achieved high performance on four of five tasks. Also, "uniform generation" is the most efficient strategy for multi-label datasets with high cardinality, while 'pure samples generation" and "one against all" induce noise to the classification. It is important to note that the proposed strategies can also be implemented with other class-balance techniques based on classifier ensembles or undersampling. As future work, a broader study including several class-balance methods can be conducted. Also, further studies are needed for computing the optimal number of synthetic samples.

Acknowledgements. This work was partially funded by the Research office (DIMA) at the Universidad Nacional de Colombia at Manizales and (COLCIENCIAS) through grant No.111952128388.

References

1. Boutell, M., Luo, J., Shen, X., Brown, C.: Learning multi-label scene classification. Pattern Recognition 37(9), 1757–1771 (2004)
2. Elisseeff, A.: Kernel methods for multi-labelled classification and categorical regression problems. In: Advances in Neural Information Processing (2002)
3. Tsoumakas, G., Katakis, I.: Multi-label classification: An overview. International Journal of Data Warehousing and Mining 3(3), 1–13 (2007)
4. Jaramillo-Garzón, J.A., et al.: Predictability of protein subcellular locations by pattern recognition techniques. In: EMBC-IEEE (2010)
5. Zhang, M., Zhou, Z.: ML-KNN: A lazy learning approach to multi-label learning. Pattern Recognition 40(7), 2038–2048 (2007)
6. Huang, S.J., Zhou, Z.H.: Multi-Label Learning by Exploiting Label Correlations Locally. In: IAAA (2012)
7. Kong, X., Ng, M., Zhou, Z.: Transductive Multi-Label Learning via Label Set Propagation. IEEE Transactions on Knowledge and Data Engineering, 1–14 (2011)
8. He, H., Garcia, E.: Learning from imbalanced data. IEEE Transactions on Knowledge and Data Engineering 21(9), 1263–1284 (2009)
9. Chawla, N., Bowyer, K., Hall, L.: SMOTE: synthetic minority over-sampling technique. Journal of Artificial 16 (2002)
10. Tahir, M.A., Kittler, et al.: Inverse random under sampling for class imbalance problem and its application to multi-label classification. Pattern Recognition (2012)
11. Dendamrongvit, S., Kubat, M.: Undersampling approach for imbalanced training sets and induction from multi-label text-categorization domains. In: Theeramunkong, T., Nattee, C., Adeodato, P.J.L., Chawla, N., Christen, P., Lenca, P., Poon, J., Williams, G. (eds.) PAKDD Workshops 2009. LNCS, vol. 5669, pp. 40–52. Springer, Heidelberg (2010)

12. Chen, K., Liang Lu, B.: Efficient classification of multilabel and imbalanced data using min-max modular classifiers. In: The International Joint Conference on Neural Networks (IJCNN 2006), pp. 1770–1775 (2006)
13. Tsoumakas, G., Vilcek, J., Spyromitros, E., Vlahavas, I.: Mulan: A java library for multi-label learning. Journal of Machine Learning Research 1, 1–48 (2010)
14. Zhou, Z.-H., Zhang, M.: Multi-instance multi-label learning with application to scene classification. In: Advances in Neural Information Processing Systems (2007)
15. Klimt, B., Yang, Y.: Introducing the Enron Corpus. Machine Learning (2004)

Online Matrix Factorization
for Space Embedding Multilabel Annotation

Sebastian Otálora-Montenegro,
Santiago A. Pérez-Rubiano, and Fabio A. González

MindLab Research Group, Universidad Nacional de Colombia, Bogotá, Colombia
{jsotaloram,saaperezru,fagonzalezo}@unal.edu.co

Abstract. The paper presents an online matrix factorization algorithm for multilabel learning. This method addresses the multi-label annotation problem finding a joint embedding that represents both instances and labels in a common latent space. An important characteristic of the novel method is its scalability, which is a consequence of its formulation as an online learning algorithm. The method was systematically evaluated in different standard datasets and compared against state-of-the-art space embedding multi-label learning algorithms showing competitive results.

1 Introduction

The multilabel learning problem consists in inducing a function, from a set of labeled instances, that assigns one or more labels to a new instance. Formally, given a set of labels $\mathcal{L} = \{\lambda_1, \lambda_2, \ldots, \lambda_m\}$ and a set of instances $\mathcal{D} = \{x_i, y_i\}_{i=1\ldots n}$, where $x_i \in \mathcal{X}, y_i \subset \mathcal{L}$, with $l = |\mathcal{L}| > 1$, find a function $f : \mathcal{X} \to P(\mathcal{L})$. This is in contrast with the multi class learning problem where a given instance is associated with one and only one of the $|\mathcal{L}|$ labels. Instances are usually represented in a k-dimensional real space, i.e. $\mathcal{X} = R^k$, while the labels are usually represented using a l-dimensional vector space model, i.e. a subset of $\mathcal{L}$ is described by binary vector $y \in \{0,1\}^l$ such that for $i = 1, \ldots, l$, $y_j[i] = 1$ if and only if the j-th instance has the i-th label associated with it.

The multi-label learning problem arises in areas such as semantic labeling of images and video, text classification, music categorization and functional genomics among others [9]. Several methods to address this problem have been proposed during the last years. Many of these methods transform the problem to a conventional classification problem. For instance, multiples classifiers are trained, one binary classifier per label, then a new instance is labeled by independently applying the set of classifiers. The problem with this class of approaches is that usually they do not scale well when there is a large number of labels and/or instances [9]. A possible strategy to deal with the large number of labels is to find a compact representation of them by using, for instance, a dimensionality reduction method. This approach is followed by multi-label latent space embedding (MLLSE) methods, which have recently shown competitive results [8,7,6].

J. Ruiz-Shulcloper and G. Sanniti di Baja (Eds.): CIARP 2013, Part I, LNCS 8258, pp. 343–350, 2013.

LSE methods find a low-dimensional latent space, $\mathcal{S} = R^s$ with $s << k$ or $s << l$, where labels, and in some case instances, are embedded. This embedding is expected to preserve and highlight correlation information from each space and to remove irrelevant, redundant or noisy data, while at the same time reducing computational and space complexities of the learning algorithms. The main disadvantage of this method is that usually the dimensionality of the shared space is a parameter to be tuned.

MLLSE methods use different strategies to find the latent space: principal component analysis, canonical correlation analysis, compressive sensing, among others. Some of these methods do not scale well to large datasets. This paper presents an MLLSE method, which is able to deal with large datasets thanks to the fact that it uses an online learning strategy. Our method embeds both the instances and the labels in a common latent space, which makes it able to exploit the labels structure and to find instance-instance, label-label and instance-label correlations.

The paper is organized as follows: Section 2 reviews the related work, Section 3 introduces the details of the new method, Section 4 presents the experimental evaluation of the method, and Section 5 discusses the conclusions as well as the future work.

2   Related Work

MLLSE models are characterized by the usage of a latent space where either the representation of the labels, the instances or both are embedded. This embedding is done to (1) reduce the dimensionality of the data and eventually reduce the computational and spatial complexities of the learning algorithms and to (2) extract and exploit hidden structures which rise from the correlation patterns present in real world datasets.

Among MLLSE models there is a subset that has been recently called feature-unaware [3]. These subset of methods only embed the labels' space but not the instances' space. Some examples of feature-unaware models are Compressive Sensing (CS)[4] and Principal Label Space Transformation (PLST)[8]. These models can be characterized by their definition of two functions: a label embedding function $f_L : \{0,1\}^l \rightarrow R^s$ and a reconstruction function $f_S : R^s \rightarrow \{0,1\}^l$. The function f_L goes from the original space of labels to the compact embedded representation and the function f_S reconstructs the original labels given the embedded representation. The labels embedding function is designed to exploit the correlation information and find semantic factors presents in the labels representation data, while the reconstruction function is designed to minimize the loss of information (as measured by a reconstruction error). Using the embedding, s linear regressors $f_i : \chi \rightarrow R$ are found and used later to predict the embedding of the labels of new unseen instances as $F(x) = (f_1(x), \ldots, f_s(x))$. This prediction is then translated into a labels representation using the reconstruction function.

In CS [4] the goal is to learn to predict compressed label vectors using linear regressors, under the assumption that the labels vector y are sparse. The embedding function is determined by random projections that allow the embedded labels to fulfill some sparseness requirements that reduce the number of linear regressors to learn. The reconstruction function on the other hand is posed as an optimization problem, also called the decoding problem, and so adds computational complexity to the overall multi labeling process.

In PLST [8] the embedding function is defined as $f_L(y) = Vy$ and the recovery function is defined as $f_S(h) = V^T h$, where V is obtained by solving the optimization problem $\min_{V^T V = I} \|Z - V^T V Z\|$, with $Z = Y - \frac{1}{n} Y 11^T$, and 1 being a vector of ones. This minimizes the reconstruction error in the reconstruction function. In this model the reconstruction function consists in just a multiplication by a precomputed projector, in contrast with the decoding problem faced by CS.

There are two problems with feature-unaware models: (1) the information provided by the correlation between the instances' data and the labels' data is ignored as the dimensionality reduction is only applied to the labels' space, and (2) the curse of dimensionality is still present as the instances' space is not reduced. Reducing only the instances' space would have the same issues and so it is natural to think in models that embed both the labels and the instances into the same low-dimensional space.

In contrast with feature-unaware models, there are feature-aware models, which take into account both the instances and labels data when inducing the mappings to a latent space. Therefore an instances' embedding function $f_K : \mathcal{R}^k \to \mathcal{R}^s$ is learned in addition to the labels' embedding function and the reconstruction function. Examples of this models are multilabel max-margin embedding (MME) [6] and multilabel canonical correlation analysis (CCA) [7].

CCA [7] looks for a latent space in which the instances' and the labels' embedding correlation is maximized. The method proposed in [3] embeds the instances into the latent space to learn a binary relevance model in which a binary classifier is trained for each label, i.e. the labels' embeddings to the latent space are not further used and so there's no recovery function here.

In MME [6] both the instances and the labels are embedded into a shared latent space, where the distance between a given instance embedding and its associated labels' embedding is smaller than the distance between the instance embedding and other unrelated labels' embeddings in the dataset, i.e. $\forall j \neq i$ $f_K(x_i)^T f_L(y_i) - f_K(x_i)^T f_L(y_j)$ is maximized. Once such latent space is found MME predicts the labels of a new instance by embedding it to the latent space and then recovering the labels representation using the reconstruction function.

There are several MLLSE methods based on non-negative matrix factorization, those methods includes asymmetric and mixed NMF [2] and another variations like structure preserving NMF [5] that could be adapted to multilabel learning, however, they impose more constraints on the embedding space that usually leads to an addition of complexity to the original NMF model.

Our method simultaneously addresses both the embedding problem and the label representation reconstruction problem using a common formulation based on matrix factorization, which is solved using an efficient online learning strategy.

3   Online Matrix Factorization Multilabel Classification

Let $X \in R^{k \times n}$ be the instances representation matrix, with n the number of instances and k the dimensionality of the instances space, and $Y \in R^{l \times n}$ be the label indicator matrix with l the number of labels and $Y_{ij} = 1$ if and only if the i-th label is assigned to the j-th instance.

The proposed method has two stages, a learning stage and a prediction stage. In the learning stage the method assumes that there is a latent space, $L = \mathbb{R}^s$, where both instances and labels have a common representation. Lets $H \in \mathbb{R}^{s \times n}$ be the latent representation matrix, then X may be obtained from H by a transformation:

$$X = PH$$

In the same way, the label indicator matrix may be obtained from H by the transformation:

$$Y = QH$$

The goal of the learning stage is to find P, Q and H. This is accomplish by solving the following unconstrained optimization problem:

$$\min_{P,Q,H} (1 - \alpha)\|X - PH\|_F^2 + \alpha\|Y - QH\|_F^2 + \lambda(\|P\|_F^2 + \|Q\|_F^2 + \|H\|_F^2) \quad (1)$$

where α controls the relative importance of instance reconstruction with respect to label reconstruction during the embedding learning, and λ controls the relative importance of the regularization term, which penalizes large values (measured by the Frobenious norm) in matrices P and Q preventing overfitting.

The H matrix contains a compact representation of each instance, which is expected to encode a unique semantic representation of the instance, from which the label or instance information may be reconstructed using the Q and P transformations respectively.

In the prediction stage, the latent representation of a new unseen instance x is calculated using the the learned model (matrices P and Q) and solving the optimization problem:

$$h = \arg\min \|x - Ph\|_F^2 + \xi\|h\|_F^2 \quad (2)$$

From the latent representation h of the sample we calculate the corresponding labels using the Q matrix, i.e. the predicted labels representation for the new instance would be $y = Qh$. So, once the model is learned, the embedding function of our model consists in solving the convex optimization problem of Eq. 2, while the recovery function consists in multiplying by a projection matrix Q.

The algorithm 1 solves the optimization problem in Eq. 1 using an online learning strategy based on stochastic gradient descent. This requires the objective function to be formulated as a per-sample loss function as follows:

$$f(x_i, y_i, P, Q, h_i) = (1 - \alpha)\|x_i - Ph_i\|_F^2 + \alpha\|y_i - Qh_i\|_F^2 + \lambda(\|P\|_F^2 + \|Q\|_F^2) \quad (3)$$

In each step, the algorithm processes a sample (x_i, y_i) by calculating the gradient of f, ∇f, and moving the parameters P and Q in the opposite direction:

$$g_P(x_i, P, Q, h_i, \alpha, \lambda) = \nabla_P f(x_i, y_i, P, Q, h_i) = \lambda P - (1 - \alpha)(x_i - Ph_i)h_i^T$$

$$g_Q(y_i, P, Q, h_i, \alpha, \lambda) = \nabla_Q f(x_i, y_i, P, Q, h_i) = \lambda Q - \alpha(y_i - Qh_i)h_i^T$$

Algorithm 1. Learning stage

Precondition: $X \in \mathcal{R}^{k \times n}$ and $Y \in \mathcal{R}^{l \times n}$

  function TRAIN($X, Y, s, \lambda, epochs$)

    $P^{(0)} \leftarrow$ RANDOM-MATRIX(k,s)

    $Q^{(0)} \leftarrow$ RANDOM-MATRIX(l,s)

    $h^{(0)} \leftarrow$ RANDOM-MATRIX(s,1)

    $gamma \leftarrow 1$

    for $j \leftarrow 1$ to $epochs$ **do**

      for $i \leftarrow 1$ to n **do**

        $x, y \leftarrow$ SAMPLE-WITHOUT-REPLACEMENT(X,Y)

        $P^{(i*j)} \leftarrow P^{(i*j)-1} - \gamma g_P(x, \lambda, P^{(i*j)-1}, Q^{(i*j)-1}, h^{(i*j)-1})$

        $Q^{(i*j)} \leftarrow Q^{(i*j)-1} - \gamma g_Q f(y, \lambda, P^{(i*j)-1}, Q^{(i*j)-1}, h^{(i*j)-1})$

        $h^{(i*j)} \leftarrow (\lambda I_r + {P^{(i*j)}}^T P^{(i*j)} + {Q^{(i*j)}}^T Q^{(i*j)})^{-1}(P^T x + Q^T y)$

        $\gamma \leftarrow \frac{\gamma}{1+i\gamma\lambda j}$

      end for

    RESTART-SAMPLING()

    end for

    return $P^{epochs \times n}, Q^{epochs \times n}$

  end function

In Algorithm 1 the details of the training algorithm are shown. The algorithm randomly samples pairs (instance,labels) from the dataset $\mathcal{D}$ and updates P and Q the gradient of per-instance loss function f (Eq. 3). The vector h is updated using the closed-form solution to the optimization problem with respect to h. At every update only one sample is processed, in contrast with batch gradient descent algorithms where the whole dataset is processed during each update, therefore the memory usage is proportional to the size of one sample and the size of the matrices P and Q. This makes the algorithm suitable for large-scale applications. The algorithm can be easily extended to process not just one sample but a small sampled subset of the dataset, a minibatch, on each iteration. This has shown good results on online factorization algorithms [1].

In this algorithm the learning rate γ is updated on each iteration to improve the convergence rate as it is usual in SGD algorithms. The $epochs$ parameter indicates the number of times that each sample from the dataset will be processed. This parameter is analogous to the number of iterations of a batch gradient descent algorithm.

In Algorithm 2 the prediction algorithm is detailed. A new instance is embedded into the latent space by solving the problem in eq 2, to later recover its label representation. However the predicted representation is not necessarily a binary one because our model does not restricts it to be, but we can interpret this representation as a label ranking and then either selecting the top m ranked labels (letting m be close to the average number of labels of each instance in the training data set) or using a threshold value to decide for each label whether it is selected or not. For the experimental evaluation of our method we evaluate both approaches and selected the best one using cross-validation.

Algorithm 2. Prediction stage

> **function** PREDICT(x, P, Q, xi, $param$)
> $\quad h \leftarrow (\xi I_r + P^{(i)^T} P^{(i)})^{-1}(P^T x)$
> $\quad y \leftarrow Qh$
> $\quad L \leftarrow SELECT - TOP(param, y)$ $\qquad\qquad$ ▷ Or THRESHOLD(param,y)
> $\quad$ **return** L
> **end function**

The parameter $param$ might either be an integer for the top selection case or a real for the thresholding case. The $THRESHOLD(param, y)$ procedure returns a list of the indices of the labels with a rank value in y bigger than $param$. The procedure SELECT-TOP(m, y) will return the index of the elements of m largest elements of y, SAMPLE-WITHOUT-REPLACEMENT(X, Y) will sample a pair (instance, labels) from the dataset, represented by the pair (X, Y), and store in x the instance and in y the labels representation. Subsequent calls to SAMPLE-WITHOUT-REPLACEMENT will not return the same values as before, unless the RESTART-SAMPLING procedure is invoked.

4   Experimental Evaluation

The method was evaluated on 5 standard multilabel datasets (described in Table 1) distributed by the *mulan* framework authors [10]. Results were compared against 7 MLLSE algorithms: CCA, OVA, MME, CS, PLST, and two batch non-negative matrix factorization techniques: Assymetric Non-negative Matrix Factorization (ANMF) and Mixed Non-negative Matrix Factorization (MNMF) [2]. We used the implementation kindly provided by the authors of [6] to compare it with our algorithm on the larger Mediamill dataset.

We used the same experimental setup as in [6], i.e. a random 5-fold cross validation schema for all experiments. One important parameter of our algorithm is the weight parameter α, which controls the relative importance of instances and labels. This parameter was experimentally tuned. The weight α has been experimentally shown to have low values, giving more importance to the label data. This can be seen as a consequence of the semantic richness underlying the

Table 1. Datasets considered in our experimental setup. The label cardinality is the average number of labels per instance.

Dataset	Labels	Examples	Features	Label Cardinality
Medical	45	978	1449	1.245
Corel5k	374	5000	500	3.522
Bibtex	159	7395	1836	2.402
Scene	6	2407	294	1.074
MediaMill	101	43907	120	4.376

words used for annotation. In the reconstruction of the label vector for the test instances a range of thresholds were evaluated according to the range of values of the reconstructed vector, so we assign 1 to the label j of the instance x^n if $x_j^n > threshold$. In a similar way we choose the top-k labels for each test sample selecting the highest k label values in the reconstruction of the labels vector.

Table 2 reports the performance of each method in terms of the micro f-measure. In all the cases, the presented method shows a competitive performance, obtaining in three of the five datasets the best one. ANMF and MNMF are based on ideas similar to the ones that support our method, learning a joint embedding space for instances and labels. In ANMF a compact label space is learned as a semantic basis for the joint embedding space, and in MNMF a concatenation of the label and instance matrices is made to learn the embedding space, also the instance and label matrices are weighted according to a parameter α for weight the contribution to of each representation to the embedding space representation. Both algorithms have the drawback that are not suitable for large scale datasets, since them handle the whole matrices X and Y becoming unfeasible to store in RAM for huge datasets. In contrast, the proposed method scales very well to large datasets thanks to its formulation as an online learning algorithm.

Table 2. Performance of each method in terms of f-measure, in parentheses the embedding space dimension. Results in bold are the best ones for each dataset. Results for OVA, CCA, CS and PLST correspond to the ones reported in [6].

	Corel5k	Scene	Bibtex	Medical	Mediamill
OVA	0.112	0.617	0.372	0.732	—
CCA[7]	0.150	0.610	0.404	0.404	—
CS[4]	0.086 (50)	0.499 (6)	0.332 (50)	0.499(50)	—
PLST[8]	0.074 (50)	0.539 (6)	0.283 (50)	0.539 (50)	—
MME[6]	0.178 (50)	**0.698** (6)	0.403 (50)	0.808 (70)	0.199 (350)
ANMF[2]	0.210 (30)	0.678 (10)	0.297 (140)	0.679 (70)	0.496 (350)
MNMF[2]	0.240 (35)	0.697 (10)	0.376 (140)	0.690 (350)	**0.510** (350)
Our Method	**0.26337** (40)	0.691 (10)	**0.436** (140)	**0.896** (70)	0.503 (350)

5   Conclusions

We have presented a novel latent space embedding method for multi label annotation which learns a joint embedding space using an online matrix factorization formulation that can deal with large datasets. The method was compared against state-of-art MLLSE methods showing competitive results, especially on data sets with a large number of annotations. This might be due to the semantic richness of the information in the labels space. This is an aspect that we plan to explore in more detail in the future as well as to compare it against recent online methods for multi labeling in web-scale datasets.

Acknowledgments. This work was supported by Colciencias grant 566 "Jóvenes Investigadores 2012" and partially funded by the following projects: Colciencias "Anotación Automática y Recuperación por Contenido de Imágenes Radiológicas Usando Semántica Latente", "Diseño e implementación de un sistema de cómputo sobre recursos heterogéneos para la identificación de estructuras atmosféricas en predicción climatológica" and LACCIR "Multimodal Image Retrieval to Support Medical Case-Based Scientific Literature Search".

References

1. Caicedo, J.C., González, F.A.: Multimodal fusion for image retrieval using matrix factorization. In: Proceedings of the 2nd ACM International Conference on Multimedia Retrieval, ICMR 2012, pp. 56:1–56:8. ACM, New York (2012)
2. Caicedo, J.C., González, F.A., Jaafar, B.-A., Olfa, N.: Multimodal Representation, Indexing, Automated Annotation and Retrieval of Image Collections via Non-negative Matrix Factorization. Neurocomputing 76(1) (2012)
3. Chen, Y.-N., Lin, H.-T.: Feature-aware label space dimension reduction for multi-label classification. In: Advances in Neural Information Processing Systems 25, pp. 1538–1546 (2012)
4. Hsu, D., Kakade, S.M., Langford, J., Zhang, T.: Multi-label prediction via compressed sensing. arXiv preprint arXiv:0902.1284 (2009)
5. Li, Z., Liu, J., Lu, H.: Structure preserving non-negative matrix factorization for dimensionality reduction. Computer Vision and Image Understanding 117(9), 1175–1189 (2013)
6. Park, S., Choi, S.: Max-margin embedding for multi-label learning. Pattern Recognition Letters (2012)
7. Sun, L., Ji, S., Ye, J.: Canonical correlation analysis for multilabel classification: a least-squares formulation, extensions, and analysis. IEEE Transactions on Pattern Analysis and Machine Intelligence 33(1), 194–200 (2011)
8. Tai, F., Lin, H.-T.: Multilabel classification with principal label space transformation. Neural Computation 24(9), 2508–2542 (2012)
9. Tsoumakas, G., Katakis, I., Vlahavas, I.: Mining multi-label data. In: Data Mining and Knowledge Discovery Handbook, pp. 667–685. Springer (2010)
10. Tsoumakas, G., Spyromitros-Xioufis, E., Vilcek, J., Vlahavas, I.: Mulan: A java library for multi-label learning. Journal of Machine Learning Research 12, 2411–2414 (2011)

A Theoretical and Practical Framework for Assessing the Computational Behavior of Typical Testor-Finding Algorithms*

Eduardo Alba-Cabrera[1], Julio Ibarra-Fiallo[1], and Salvador Godoy-Calderon[2]

[1] Universidad San Francisco de Quito, Colegio de Ciencias e Ingeniería,
Diego de Robles y Vía Interoceánica, Quito, Ecuador
[2] Instituto Politécnico Nacional-Centro de Investigación en Computación (CIC)
Av. Juan de Dios Bátiz, Esq. Miguel Othón de Mendizábal. Col. Nueva
Industrial Vallejo. D.F., México
{ealba,jibarra}@usfq.edu.ec, sgodoyc@cic.ipn.mx
http://www.usfq.edu.ec,
http://www.cic.ipn.mx

Abstract. Although the general relevance of Testor Theory as the theoretical ground for useful feature selection procedures is well known, there are no practical means, nor any standard methodologies, for assessing the behavior of a testor-finding algorithm when faced with specific circumstances. In this work, we present a practical framework, with proven theoretical foundation, for assessing the behavior of both deterministic and meta-heuristic testor-finding algorithms when faced with specific phenomena.

Keywords: Feature selection, testor theory, typical testor algorithms.

1 Introduction

A matrix A is called Boolean if all its entries are 0 or 1. Let $\mathcal{R}_A = \{a_1, ..., a_m\}$ and $\mathcal{C}_A = \{x_1, ...x_n\}$ be the set of rows and the set of columns of A, respectively. Two rows of $\mathcal{R}_A$, a_p and a_q, are incomparable if $(\exists i) [a_{pi} \geq a_{qi}] \wedge (\exists j) [a_{qj} \geq a_{pj}]$.

A row is called a basic row if it is incomparable with any other row from $\mathcal{R}_A$. A Boolean matrix is called a basic matrix if it is composed exclusively of basic rows. $T \subseteq \mathcal{C}_A$ is a testor in A if the submatrix $A|_T$, obtained by eliminating from A all columns not in the subset T, doesn't have any zero rows. Also, T is a typical testor if no subset of T can be found that is also a testor in A.

Typical testors play an important role in solving some feature selection [4] [14], diagnosis of diseases [8], text categorization [10], document summarization [9] and document clustering [6]. The concept of typical testor has been extended and generalized in several ways [5]. The problem of finding the set $\Psi^*(A)$ of all typical

---

* This research was supported by Collaboration Grants from Universidad San Francisco de Quito, Ecuador. The third author is also grateful for the finantial support by Instituto Politécnico Nacional and CONACyT, México, particularly through project SIP-20130932

J. Ruiz-Shulcloper and G. Sanniti di Baja (Eds.): CIARP 2013, Part I, LNCS 8258, pp. 351–358, 2013.

testors in a basic matrix A is an old problem that has had an important development in the last ten years. To support this statement, consider the number of published papers with new algorithms related to this problem [3] [13] [7] [12].

There are two classes of typical testor-finding algorithms (TTAs): deterministic and meta-heuristic. Deterministic algorithms guarantee that they will find all typical testors at the expense of an exponential complexity. On the other hand, meta-heuristic algorithms have no guarantee to find all the typical testors in a given problem, but they are feasible to be used on extremely large search spaces [1] [3]. The complexity of deterministic TTAs has not been sufficiently studied. This lack of sufficient study can be regarded as the cause of why most published works about TTAs fail, in the opinion of the authors of this paper, to properly justify their selection of basic matrices for comparative performance experimentation between different algorithms. On one hand, since the number of matrices selected for experimentation is considerably low, the obtained results lack statistical significance. On the other hand, by not using a specific criterion for selecting test matrices and testing any new algorithm with the same matrices the characteristic behavior of each algorithm in the presence of certain stereotypical phenomena is not captured.

However, a formal and convenient strategy for selecting matrices for algorithm testing is certainly viable. In [2], a feasible strategy for studying the behavior of the TTAs was presented for the first time. That strategy was based on the construction of test matrices (TM) which are basic matrices whose sets of typical testors can be determined in advance. This property allows the assessment of the behavior of the computational implementation of any deterministic TTA, as well as the validation of the answer completeness of any meta-heuristic TTA. Since both the amount of typical testors and their length can be preset, TMs can be generated for studying the behavior of an algorithm varying only one parameter at a time. For example, we can consider the exponential increase in the number of matrix rows with only a linear increase in the number of typical testors, or the opposite phenomenon, a linear increase in the number of matrix rows, resulting in an exponential growth of the number of typical testors.

In this paper, we worked along two main directions. First, we significantly extended the theoretical framework of the TM strategy to allow the generation of a whole new set of TMs that are more flexible and versatile. Second, we show how TMs can be used to study the behavior of a TTA in the presence of specific phenomena. We also selected three previously published TTAs, tested them against specific TMs, and reported and discussed the obtained results.

2   Theoretical Background

Let $A = [a_{ij}]_{m \times n}$ and $B = [b_{ij}]_{m' \times n'}$ be two basic matrices. In [2] the operators ϕ and θ were defined on pairs of matrices A and B. The result of a φ operation is a new Boolean matrix obtained by concatenating two basic matrices with the same number of rows. The resulting matrix has exactly the same number of rows of A and B, but it has $n + n'$ columns (the sum of the number of columns from

A and B). On the other hand, the θ operator produces a new matrix having $m \times m'$ rows (the product of the number of rows in A and B), and also having $n + n'$ columns.

One important property of the φ and θ operators is that, when applied to basic matrices, the resulting matrix is also basic, since it preserves the portion of the matrix that guarantees incomparability of the rows. Moreover, it can be demonstrated that if A, B and C are basic matrices, the φ operator is associative. As a consequence, we will write $\varphi^N(A)$ to represent the resulting matrix of applying the φ operator to the matrix A N times. Likewise, the θ operator is also associative, so we will write $\theta^N(A)$ to represent the result of applying the θ operator consecutively N times.

Now, let $C_A = \{x_1, ... x_n\}$ be the set of columns in a basic matrix A, and let $x_j \in C_A$. We will write $[x_j]_N$ to denote the class of all columns in A exactly equal to x_j in $\varphi^N(A)$. In other words, $[x_j]_N = \{x_j, x_{j+n}, ..., x_{j+(N-1)n}\}$.

Given $S \subseteq C_A$ and $S = \{x_{j_1}, ..., x_{j_s}\}$, $[S]_N$ will denote the set of all subsets of columns from $\varphi^N(A)$ that can be obtained by replacing one or more columns in S with any other column in the same class, that is, $[S]_N = [x_{j_1}]_N \times ... \times [x_{j_s}]_N$. Then it is easy to verify that $|[S]_N| = N^s = N^{|S|}$.

Therefore, if A and B are basic matrices such that the sets $\Psi^*(A)$ and $\Psi^*(B)$ of all typical testors are known, then the next two propositions establish how the sets $\Psi^*(\varphi^N(A))$ and $\Psi^*(\theta(A, B))$ can be obtained from them.

Proposition 1. $\Psi^*(\varphi^N(A)) = \{[T]_N \mid T \in \Psi^*(A)\}$.

Proposition 2. $\Psi^*(\theta(A, B)) = \Psi^*(A) \cup \Psi^*(B)$.

Proposition 1 is proved by observing that, with the exception of the order of the columns, the submatrices in $\varphi^N(A)$ that form the elements of $[T]_N$ are always identical to $A|_T$. This is, because a column in T can only be replaced by another from the same class, and therefore all elements in $[T]_N$ are, by definition, typical testors. Now, let's make the assumption that some typical testor $S = \{x_{j_1}, ..., x_{j_s}\}$ exists outside $\{[T]_N \mid T \in \Psi^*(A)\}$. There must be at least one column of S that is not part of A. Lets replace all columns in S with the column from A within their same equivalence class. Then we would have a contradiction, because the resulting submatrix must determine a typical testor, which must be in A, and therefore S must be in $[T]_N$.

In order to prove Proposition 2, it is enough to observe that if we identify in $\theta(A, B)$ the columns from A and from B, and we eliminate repeated rows in each set, we end up with the original matrices A and B. Therefore, the set of typical testors in A and B is preserved in $\theta(A, B)$. Also, we cannot find any testor in $\theta(A, B)$ with columns of both matrices, because if the selected columns were testors in A or in B, then we would be constructing supersets of testors, and they would not be typical any more. On the other hand, if the selected columns were not testors, the following reasoning applies:

Let S_A and S_B be sets of non-testor columns from A and B respectively. Let also a be the row from A with zeros in the columns of S_A , and let b be the row from B with zeros in the columns of S_B. Since the row $[ab]$ is in $\theta(A, B)$ the

Table 1. Test Matrices $\varphi^N (B)$ and $\theta^N (\theta (A, B))$

N	Rows	Cols	$\Psi^* \left(\varphi^N (B) \right)$	N	Rows	Cols	$\Psi^* \left(\theta^N (\theta (A, B)) \right)$
1	4	5	4	1	16	10	8
2	4	10	18	2	256	20	16
...	...	...	...	...	...	...	...
N	4	$2N$	$N + 2N^2 + N^3$	N	16^N	$2N$	$8N$

submatrix of $\theta (A, B)$, formed by $S_A \cup S_B$ must also have a row with zeros, and therefore it cannot be a testor.

So, we have that $|\{[T]_N \mid T \in \Psi^*(A)\}| = \sum_{T \in \Psi^*(A)} [T]_N = \sum_{T \in \Psi^*(A)} N^{|T|}$, and also that within $\theta (A, B)$, $\Psi^*(A) \cap \Psi^*(B) =$. These two properties allow us to state the following corollaries from Propositions 1 and 2.

Corollary 1. $\left| \Psi^* \left(\varphi^N (A) \right) \right| = \sum_{T \in \Psi^*(A)} N^{|T|}$

Corollary 2. $|\Psi^* (\theta (A, B))| = |\Psi^*(A)| + |\Psi^*(B)|$

Example 1. Let $A = \begin{matrix} x_1\,x_2\,x_3\,x_4\,x_5 \\ \begin{bmatrix} 1 & 0 & 0 & 0 & 0 \\ 0 & 0 & 1 & 0 & 1 \\ 0 & 1 & 0 & 1 & 1 \\ 0 & 1 & 1 & 0 & 0 \end{bmatrix} \end{matrix}$ and $B = \begin{matrix} x_6\,x_7\,x_8\,x_9\,x_{10} \\ \begin{bmatrix} 1 & 1 & 1 & 0 & 0 \\ 1 & 1 & 0 & 0 & 1 \\ 1 & 0 & 1 & 1 & 0 \\ 1 & 0 & 1 & 0 & 1 \end{bmatrix} \end{matrix}$

We can verify that $\Psi^*(A) = \{\{x_1, x_2, x_3\}, \{x_1, x_2, x_5\}, \{x_1, x_3, x_4\}, \{x_1, x_3, x_5\}\}$, and $\Psi^*(B) = \{\{x_6\}, \{x_8, x_{10}\}, \{x_7, x_9, x_{10}\}, \{x_7, x_8\}\}$. Note that A has 4 typical testors of length 3. By using Corollary 1 above, we know that $\left| \Psi^* \left(\varphi^3 (A) \right) \right| = 4 * 3^3 = 108$. Likewise, since B has one typical testor of length 1, two of length 2, and one of length 3, we can establish using the same corollary that $\left| \Psi^* \left(\varphi^3 (B) \right) \right| = 3^1 + 2 * 3^2 + 3^3 = 48$. We can also determine how many typical testors to expect in $\theta (A, B)$ using corollary 2: $|\Psi^* (\theta (A, B))| = 8$.

Test matrices allow us to control particular aspects that we wish to study regarding the performance of a TTA. In Table 1, the effect of appying the operator φ^N to matrix B from example 1 is shown. As can be seen, the generated matrices preserve the same number of rows, while the number of columns increase linearly; but the resulting number of typical testors grows according to a cubic polynomial.

If one wishes to assess the effect of an exponential growth in the number of rows while sustaining a linear behavior of both the number of columns and the number of typical testors, then one would only need to use the test matrix $\theta^N (\theta (A, B))$ with A and B being exactly those from example 1. The resulting behavior of such test is shown in Table 1.

3   Taxonomy and Nature of TTAs

Deterministic TTAs can be classified in two sets: external and internal. External TTAs always set an order to test the power set of columns in the basic matrix.

Following that order, each subset of columns is tested to determine if it is a typical testor or not. However, the test process is not an exhaustive search over the power set. Some properties of each tested subset allow the TTA to infer which other successive subsets, following the established order, cannot be typical testors, and therefore it is not worthwhile to test them. The act of bypassing the test of some subsets of columns is commonly referred to as *jumping*. In general, the selected order for traversing the power set of columns, along with the magnitude of the jumps (i.e. the number of subsets not tested), and the specific procedure applied to a subset for testing if it is a typical testor or not, determine the behavior of an external TTA.

On the other hand, internal TTAs do not test the power set of columns in a basic matrix. Their strategy lies in iteratively selecting the entries in the basic matrix and using them to construct typical testor candidates. An extended version of this work, which includes analysis and comparison of experimental results, both on internal and external TTAs as [7], is being prepared. In order to meet the space requirements, this work will exclusively show results obtained with experiments on external TTAS.

Three external TTAs were selected for experimentation with representative TMs. These algorithms are *BT* [11], *LEX* [13], and *FastCTExt* [12]. In the next section, all the above mentioned algorithms are tested against specifically selected families of TMs, and the obtained results discussed.

4   Experimental Results

As an example of how the TMs framework can be used for TTA testing purposes, we designed specific experiments to asses the TTA's performance when facing different phenomena. For each experiment, a custom-designed TM was created with a specific combination of the θ and φ operators, applied to the A and B matrices, as well as some identity matrices. Identity matrices are denoted by I_N, where N is the dimension of the identity matrix.

All experiments were run on an Intel i7 processor, with 4GB in RAM. However, since the ultimate goal of this work is to promote the usefulness of the proposed framework, and not to rigorously test each algorithm, absolute execution times as well as the hardware platform, are not relevant. For the intended goal, relative execution times are sufficient.

The first set of experiments was designed with successive powers of the φ operator, applied to the identity matrix I_5. Each one of those operations generates a basic matrix with 5 rows, but with a linearly increasing number of columns, and with a number of typical testors equal to the selected power of φ raised to the power of the dimension of the matrix (5) . Algorithms *LEX* and *FastCTExt* were tested against each matrix, and in order to asses the resulting performance in each case, their execution times are recorded relative to the time needed for solving the first experiment (the one described in the first row of the table). Table 2 summarizes all the experiments performed.

As in the reports from several research works, Table 2 shows that the performance of the *LEX* and *BT* algorithms are clearly below that of the *FastCTExt*

Table 2. Relative execution times of the LEX, $FastCTExt$, and BT algorithms when facing powers of the φ operator, applied to the identity matrix I_5.

#	Test Matrix	Rows	Cols	$|\Psi^*|$	LEX	FastCTExt	BT
1	$\varphi^1\,(I_5)$	5	5	1	x	y	z
2	$\varphi^2\,(I_5)$	5	10	32	$4x$	y	$2z$
3	$\varphi^3\,(I_5)$	5	15	243	$22x$	$9y$	$87z$
4	$\varphi^4\,(I_5)$	5	20	1024	$86x$	$31y$	$2,113z$
5	$\varphi^5\,(I_5)$	5	25	3,125	$246x$	$90y$	$37,246z$

algorithm. However, the fundamental premise of this work is that without using a practical test framework capable of generating a wide diversity of phenomena, it is not possible to identify performance bottlenecks and special cases where a different processing technique is needed. As concrete evidence of this premise, the reader should consider the next set of experiments, where different combinations of the θ and φ operators applied to the reference matrices are used to induce specific test phenomena for the same algorithms. Table 3, summarizes the basic matrix phenomena that both algorithms were confronted with. Like in the previous set of experiments, all execution times are expressed relative to the time recorded in the first experiment.

As recorded in Table 3, the LEX algorithm turns out to be far more sensible to an increase in the number of columns of the basic matrix than to an increase in its number of rows. When the number of rows is kept constant and the number of columns and typical testors only slightly increase (rows 2, 3, 5, 6 & 7), the execution time also stays approximately the same. However, when the number of rows is doubled, and the number of columns (and typical testors) is kept constant (rows 4, 7 & 10), LEX's execution times almost doubles.

The $FastCTExt$ algorithm roughly follows the same behavior pattern, although experiments show it to be even more sensitive to the same phenomenon than the LEX algorithm. Rows 9 and 10, in Table 3, show the exact quantification for this phenomenon. By observing rows 9 and 10, it seems obvious that when doubling the number of columns and typical testors (from 46 to 96

Table 3. Relative execution times of the LEX and $FastCTExt$ algorithms when facing alternate powers of θ and φ operators

#	Test Matrix	Rows	Cols	$|\Psi^*|$	LEX	FastCTExt
1	$S_1 = \theta\,(A, B)$	16	10	8	x	y
2	$S_2 = \varphi^2\,(S_1)$	16	20	50	$17x$	$22y$
3	$S_3 = \theta\,(S_2, \theta^2\,(I_1))$	16	22	52	$17x$	$23y$
4	$S_4 = \theta\,(S_2, \theta^{20}\,(I_1))$	16	40	70	$18x$	$40y$
5	$S_5 = \theta\,(S_2, I_2)$	32	22	51	$54x$	$65y$
6	$S_6 = \varphi^2\,(S_5)$	32	44	360	$2,009x$	$4,245y$
7	$S_7 = \theta\,(S_6, \theta^2\,(I_1))$	32	46	362	$2,021x$	$4,321y$
8	$S_8 = \theta\,(S_6, \theta^{44}\,(I_1))$	32	88	404	$2,044x$	$5,113y$
9	$S_9 = \theta\,(S_6, I_2)$	64	46	361	$5,466x$	$11,671y$
10	$S_{10} = \varphi^2\,(S_9)$	64	92	2716	$486,052x$	$2,147,293y$

Table 4. Relative execution times of the LEX, $FastCTExt$, and BT algorithms using identity matrices of different sizes

#	Test Matrix	Rows	Cols	$|\Psi^*|$	LEX	$FastCTExt$	BT
1	I_5	5	5	1	x	y	z
2	I_{10}	10	10	1	$25x$	$7y$	$0.25z$
3	I_{15}	15	15	1	$885x$	$231y$	$0.5z$
4	I_{20}	20	20	1	$35,574x$	$7,758y$	$0.5z$
5	I_{25}	25	25	1	$1428772x$	$259,945y$	$0.75z$

columns), LEX's execution times increases by a factor 88, while $FastCTExt$'s time increases to 296 times that of the previous experiment. The same behavior, in a lesser magnitude, can also be observed in rows 3 and 4 of the same table.

For the last set of experiments, a comparison of the three studied algorithms is performed, using simple identity matrices. The results are summarized in Table 4. Clearly, an identity matrix has only one typical testor, regardless of its dimension. Surprisingly enough, the BT algorithm turns out to have the best performance, far beyond those of the LEX and $FastCTExt$ algorithms. This particular behavior could not be observed without the proposed framework.

5   Conclusions and Recommendations

Deterministic TTAs, as previously discussed, are guaranteed to find the complete set of typical testors in a basic matrix. The order in which a TTA traverses the search space, as well as the particular pre-search procedures it applies to the basic matrix, ultimately determine its behavior and general performance. However, the TTA's sensitivity to specific phenomena, such as the growth in rows, columns, or typical testors on the basic matrix is, in general, not sufficiently assessed.

We have presented a theoretical and practical framework that allows a researcher to test a TTA against specific pre-designed phenomena. The combination of θ and φ operators, in conjunction with sufficiently studied basic matrices, turns out to be a versatile tool for generating almost any conceivable phenomenon a researcher could wish a TTA to confront. The behavior observed during those tests can potentially yield enough information for identifying performance bottle-necks, and help design the appropriate fine-tuning procedures.

Meta-heuristic TTA's, on the other hand, are pseudo-random search procedures that, by nature, don't offer enough guarantees about the completeness of the resulting typical testors set. In order to validate these kind of TTA's, a wise course of action is to test the TTA against sufficiently studied basic matrices (those for which the total number of typical testors is known in advance). Matrices that satisfy such requirements are generally small ones, not suited for serious testing purposes. The TM framework herein proposed allows the generation, based on one original matrix, of increasingly larger matrices, with any desired dimensions, for which the total number of typical testors is always known.

In conclusion, TTA testing, under realistic conditions, appears to be a valuable asset for advancing the general state-of-the-art in pattern recognition.

By providing practical means for testing both deterministic and meta-heuristic TTAs, the TM framework seems to fullfill the current gap between theoretical developments and practical implementations.

References

1. Alba-Cabrera, É., Santana, R., Ochoa-Rodriguez, A., Lazo-Cortes, M.: Finding typical testors by using an evolutionary strategy. In: Proceedings of the V Ibero American Symposium on Pattern Recognition, pp. 267–278 (2000)
2. Alba, E., Guilcapi, D., Ibarra, J.: New strategies for evaluating the performance of typical testor algorithms. In: Alvarez, L., Mejail, M., Gomez, L., Jacobo, J. (eds.) CIARP 2012. LNCS, vol. 7441, pp. 813–820. Springer, Heidelberg (2012)
3. Diaz-Sanchez, G., Piza-Davila, I., Sanchez-Diaz, G., Mora-Gonzalez, M., Reyes-Cardenas, O., Cardenas-Tristan, A., Aguirre-Salado, C.: Typical Testors Generation Based on an Evolutionary Algorithm. In: Alagar, V.S., Nivat, M. (eds.) AMAST 1995. LNCS, vol. 936, pp. 58–65. Springer, Heidelberg (1995)
4. Lazo-Cortes, M., Ruiz-Shulcloper, J.: Determining the feature relevance for non classically described objects and a new algorithm to compute typical fuzzy testors. Pattern Recognition Letters 16, 1259–1265 (1995)
5. Lazo-Cortes, M., Ruiz-Shulcloper, J., Alba-Cabrera, E.: An overview of the evolution of the concept of testor. Pattern Recognition 34(4), 753–762 (2001)
6. Li, F., Zhu, Q.: Document clustering in research literature based on NMF and testor theory. Journal of Software 6(1), 78–82 (2011)
7. Lias-Rodríguez, A., Pons-Porrata, A.: BR: A New Method for Computing All Typical Testors. In: Bayro-Corrochano, E., Eklundh, J.-O. (eds.) CIARP 2009. LNCS, vol. 5856, pp. 433–440. Springer, Heidelberg (2009)
8. Ortiz-Posadas, M., Martinez-Trinidad, F., Ruiz-Shulcloper, J.: A new approach to diferential diagnosis of diseases. International Journal of Biomedical Computing 40(3), 179–185 (2001)
9. Pons-Porrata, A., Ruiz-Shulcloper, J., Berlanga-Llavori, R.: A method for the automatic summarization of topic-based clusters of documents. In: Sanfeliu, A., Ruiz-Shulcloper, J. (eds.) CIARP 2003. LNCS, vol. 2905, pp. 596–603. Springer, Heidelberg (2003)
10. Pons-Porrata, A., Gil-García, R., Berlanga-Llavori, R.: Using Typical Testors for Feature Selection in Text Categorization. In: Rueda, L., Mery, D., Kittler, J. (eds.) CIARP 2007. LNCS, vol. 4756, pp. 643–652. Springer, Heidelberg (2007)
11. Ruiz-Shulcloper, J., Bravo, M., Aguila, F.: Algoritmos BT y TB para el cálculo de todos los tests típicos. Revista Ciencias Matemáticas 6(2) (1982)
12. Sanchez-Diaz, G., Lazo-Cortes, M., Piza-Davila, I.: A fast implementation for the typical testor property identication based on an accumulative binary tuple. International Journal of Computational Intelligence Systems 5(6) (2012)
13. Santiesteban-Alganza, Y., Pons-Porrata, A.: LEX: A new algorithm for calculating typical testors. Revista Ciencias Matematicas 21(1), 85–95 (2003)
14. Vázquez, R., Godoy-Calderon, S.: Using testor theory to reduce the dimension of neural network models. Special Issue in Neural Networks and Associative Memories 28, 93–103 (2007)

A NSGA Based Approach
for Content Based Image Retrieval

Salvador Moreno-Picot, Francesc J. Ferri, and Miguel Arevalillo-Herráez

Department of Computer Science, University of Valencia
Avda.de la Universidad s/n. 46100-Burjasot, Spain
salvador.moreno@uv.es

Abstract. The purpose of CBIR (Content Based Image Retrieval) systems is to allow users to retrieve pictures related to a semantic concept of their interest, when no other information but the images themselves is available. Commonly, a series of images are presented to the user, who judges on their relevance. Several different models have been proposed to help the construction of interactive systems based on relevance feedback. Some of these models consider that an optimal query point exists, and focus on adapting the similarity measure and moving the query point so that it appears close to the relevant results and far from those which are non-relevant. This implies a strong causality between the low level features and the semantic content of the images, an assumption which does not hold true in most cases. In this paper, we propose a novel method that considers the search as a multi-objective optimization problem. Each objective consists of minimizing the distance to one of the images the user has considered relevant. Representatives of the Pareto set are considered as points of interest in the search space, and parallel searches are performed for each point of interest. Results are then combined and presented to the user. A comparatively good performance has been obtained when evaluated against other baseline methods.

1 Introduction

Usually, a CBIR system represents the images in the repository as a multi-dimensional feature vector extracted from a series of low level descriptors, such as color, texture or shape. The perceptual similarity between two pictures is then quantified in terms of a distance/similarity function defined on the corresponding multi-dimensional feature space. A major problem with CBIR systems is the so called "semantic gap", which refers to difficulty of translation of user's intentions into similarities amongst low level features. Relevance feedback, a technique inherited from traditional information retrieval, has been used to increase the efficiency of CBIR systems helping to induce high level semantic contents from low level descriptors. When relevance feedback is used, a search is considered an iterative process. At each iteration, the system retrieves a series of images ordered according to a pre-defined similarity measure, and requires user interaction to mark the relevant and non relevant retrievals. This data is used to adapt the similarity measure and produce a new set of results, repeating the process until the desired picture is found.

Relevance feedback has been a major topic of research during the last two decades (see [1, 2]). First methods were based on adapting the similarity measure and moving

J. Ruiz-Shulcloper and G. Sanniti di Baja (Eds.): CIARP 2013, Part I, LNCS 8258, pp. 359–366, 2013.

the query point so that more emphasis is placed on relevant elements and less on irrelevant ones [3–5]. This type of techniques use the user's judgments to dynamically adjust the weights of each feature, and to produce a new query point that represents his/her interest in a more reliable way. In general, these are the fastest techniques, but they assume the existence of a unique query point. A large number of probabilistic methods have also been proposed *e.g.* [6–8]. Most of these are based on estimating posteriori probabilities from the prior probabilities and the relevance judgments provided by the user. One particular way to estimate these probabilities is by using nearest-neighbour estimators [9, 10]. The use of supervised learning techniques has also been a major trend in the development of relevance feedback mechanisms. In this context, SVMs (Support Vector Machines) have been widely used [11–13], despite the difficulties associated with fine-tuning the retrieval systems choosing the optimal set of parameters for the SVM [9]. Other successful approaches to CBIR include the use of fuzzy sets [14], self organized maps [15] or evolutionary computation [16] to determine the degree of relevance of each image in the database.

In this paper, we propose a novel technique which considers the search as a multi-objective optimization problem. Each positive selection constitutes an objective, and the search space is explored to find a representative set of trade-off solutions between the objectives. Then, each member of this representative set is chosen as a seed, and the search proceeds concurrently at each seed. By using this method, the search not only takes place in regions surrounding the relevant selections but also in others areas in between. This is in contrast to many other existing techniques, which concentrate the search only on regions around known positive samples.

The remainder of the paper is organized as follows. First the technique proposed is explained in section 2. Then , the approach is evaluated in section 3. Finally, some conclusions are drawn in section 4.

2   The Algorithm

2.1   Problem Formulation

Let us consider the discrete solution space of all M images stored in the repository and denote it by $\{Im_1, Im_2, \ldots, Im_M\}$. Let us also denote the set of P relevant user selections by $\{Im_1^+, \ldots, Im_P^+\}$, and the non-relevant selections by $\{Im_1^-, \ldots, Im_N^-\}$. Let us assume that a similarity function s exists which produces an estimate of the resemblance between any pair of images.

Let us also consider a set of P objectives $\{o_1, o_2, \ldots o_p\}$ for each image Im_x, and define each objective o_i as the similarity between the image and the corresponding relevant user selection Im_i^+. The similarity function s can then be used to measure the degree of satisfaction of the objective o_i as $s(Im_x, Im_i^+)$. This formulation allows us to consider each of the M images in the repository as a potential solution to the problem, and the similarity to each of the P relevant selections as a different objective which should be maximized.

When a problem has multiple objectives, several optimal solutions may co-exist. These are all possible non-dominated solutions to the problem. A solution is said to be non-dominated if there is no other solution which simultaneously satisfies all the objectives better. In the absence of any further information, these cannot be said to be worse than any other. The set of all non-dominated solutions to a problem is commonly referred to as the Pareto optimal set.

The calculation of the Pareto optimal set may yield a large number of non-dominated solutions, specially for large numbers of relevant selections. In general, this implies that it would not be possible to show the entire set to the user. For this reason, we chose conveniently scattered representative samples from the Pareto optimal set. In addition, trade-off solutions which are closer to a negative selection than to a positive one are removed, according to the principles of a nearest neighbor classifier. The remaining ones are treated as seeds for potential regions of interest. Then, a ranking is produced for each seed. These are computed by sorting all images in the repository by their similarity to the seed, according to the function s. The rankings are finally combined iteratively, by taking one element from each ranking at each round.

2.2 Implementation

Determining the Pareto optimal set in a discrete solution space is a simple but also a time consuming operation. Every solution has to be compared against the rest and, in the worst case, it takes $O(P \cdot M^2)$, with P representing the number of objectives (positive selections) and M the number of solutions evaluated (the number of images in the database). With usual values of M in CBIR systems, this cost becomes prohibitive.

An alternative is to assume a continuous search space and use a MOEA (Multi-Objective Evolutionary Algorithm) to determine a spread of solutions along a set which is close to the true Pareto optimal front. The algorithm NSGA-II [17] has been chosen for this purpose. Despite that this algorithm does not perform best with a large number of objectives [18], it provides a spread set of solutions which is sufficient for our purpose.

In addition, the use of this approach provides two major advantages. In the one hand, the parameterless diversity preservation mechanism of NSGA-II provides a representative spread set of solutions directly, with as many elements as the population size used. This means that the optimal Pareto set does not need to be post-processed to obtain the desired representative set of spread solutions. In the other hand, the stopping criteria can be decided so that the response time is kept within reasonable limits.

In our implementation, the feature vectors of the positive solutions are provided as an input (these are known to be part of the optimal Pareto set), and the genetic algorithm generates a set of feature vectors that represent the optimal Pareto set. Negative selections in previous iterations of the same search are accumulated and a restriction is imposed on potential solutions to the problem. They have to be closer to a positive than to a negative selection, as determined by the similarity function s. If this is not the case, the potential solution is discarded. To avoid inconsistent solutions or solutions outside the border of the multi-dimensional search space, all feature vectors produced in the process are repaired so that their features are all in range and histogram descriptors add to the appropriate amount. To this end, out of range values are replaced by the nearest valid value and histograms are linearly scaled so that all components add to one.

Once the representative set of spread solutions has been determined, each of its members is used as a seed to drive the search process. Separate rankings are built for each feature vector in the set. To build the final ordering, these are visited iteratively until no elements are left. At each iteration, the top element from each ranking is extracted, and added to the final ordering if it is not already present. Observe that, for the simplest case when a single picture is selected as relevant, the optimal Pareto set would be the image itself, and all pictures in the repository would be ranked according to their similarity to this image.

3   Evaluation

To evaluate the results, an experimental set-up similar to those reported in [9] and [19] has been implemented. These systems use classified databases and simulate user judgment according to the class information available. In our case, a fixed number of images were chosen at random from each class, avoiding repetitions, and these were submitted as targets to the system. At each iteration, the system made automatic judgments on the first 50 images returned by the algorithm. Images which belong to the same class as the target were considered relevant and any other non relevant.

We compare the results obtained with this algorithm to those obtained by using other existing techniques, namely a) a classical feature weighting and query movement approach, implemented as presented in [5]; and b) an engine that uses similar principles to those used in the PicSOM system [20]. From now on, these algorithms will be referred to as the Query movement and the SOM-based approaches respectively. The SOM-based approach uses 64x64 SOMs for the first repository and 16x16 SOMs for the second. Because of the relatively small size of the repositories, standard SOMs have replaced the hierarchical SOMs used in the original publication. To allow for a fair comparison, these two algorithm have been adapted to work with the same feature sets. Note that although the results obtained with SOM approach may not be generalizable (the performance depends on the size of the maps and the low pass filter applied), they provide an indicative baseline for comparison purposes.

To test the approach for different database systems two different collections have been used:

- The first repository is composed of 30 000 pictures from the Corel database. These were manually classified into 71 themes and used for evaluation purposes in [21]. This collection has been the largest found for which class information is available and can be obtained from the KDD-UCI repository (http://kdd.ics.uci.edu/databases/CorelFeatures), together with a set of 4 descriptors, namely: (a) a nine component vector with the mean, standard deviation and skewness for each hue, saturation and value in the HSV color space; (b) a 16 component vector with the second angular moment, the contrast, the inverse difference moment and the entropy for the co-ocurrence in the horizontal, vertical, and two diagonal directions; (c) a 32 component vector representing the 4 x 2 color HS histograms for each of the resulting sub-images after one horizontal and one vertical split; and (d) a 32 component vector with the 8 x 4 color HS histogram for the entire picture.

- A second smaller repository composed of 1 508 pictures, classified into a total of 29 categories. Some of these were extracted from the Web and some others were taken by the authors. The features used in this case were: (a) a 30 component vector with the 10×3 HS histogram (b) two 10 component vectors with the granulometries[22], calculated using a horizontal and a vertical segment as the structuring elements (each for a different feature vector).

In both repositories, (dis)similarity between features is estimated by using the histogram intersection on the color histogram vectors and the Euclidean distance on the rest. Results have been measured in terms of precision at a cutoff value, and precision vs recall curves, the most common methods to present results in the context of CBIR [1]. Precision is defined as the percentage of relevant images in the set of pictures retrieved, and it is usually expressed as a value in the range $[0, 1]$. Recall represents the percentage of the relevant images that are retrieved. When measuring precision at a cutoff value n, the precision is measured over the set composed of the first n images retrieved. We have chosen $n = 50$ as the area of interest. In table 1, the results for the multi-objective technique and those for the query movement algorithm and the SOM-based approaches are presented. To facilitate the comparison, this same data is also shown in Figure 1. The numbers shown are the average over a large number of searches. In particular, a total of 1 420 searches were performed on the first repository (20 queries for each class), and 1 022 on the second (50 per class, except for those classes containing less than 50 images). To diminish the possible variabilities introduced by the random selection of targets and by potentially unguided searches when no relevant images are selected, we have forced that there is at least one relevant sample in between the first 50 images in the initial order of pictures, and all techniques have been evaluated using the same list of targets and the same initial orderings.

Figure 2 shows the precision vs recall graphs at each iteration, properly scaled to the areas of interest, for the two databases considered. The two plots in figures 1 and 2 evidence the robustness of the method as a relevance feedback mechanism. In both repositories, the number of relevant results in between the first 50 retrievals significantly increases at each iteration. Unlike the query movement approach, the algorithm is able to maintain several concurrent search areas and discover new regions of interest as the search progresses.

Table 1. Precision obtained at a cutoff value of 50 for each of the algorithms considered in the cases of the Large and Small repositories

	Algorithm	Iteration									
		1	2	3	4	5	6	7	8	9	10
Large	Multi-objective	0.1656	0.2716	0.3540	0.4193	0.4721	0.5174	0.5551	0.5861	0.6119	0.6345
	Query-movement	0.1434	0.1826	0.1958	0.2007	0.2074	0.2082	0.2118	0.2139	0.2171	0.2193
	SOM-based	0.1346	0.1928	0.1965	0.2055	0.2048	0.2125	0.2098	0.2167	0.2126	0.2190
Small	Multi-objective	0.3531	0.4963	0.5749	0.6216	0.6534	0.6754	0.6914	0.7046	0.7151	0.7244
	Query-movement	0.3247	0.3425	0.3596	0.3461	0.3646	0.3461	0.3656	0.3491	0.3643	0.3513
	SOM-based	0.3208	0.3428	0.3580	0.3308	0.3522	0.3307	0.3548	0.3339	0.3544	0.3341

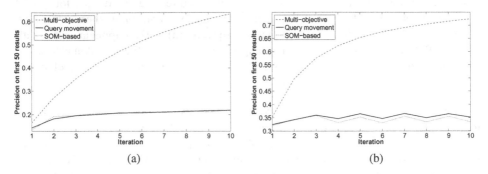

Fig. 1. Precision at a cutoff value of 50 for the three algorithms compared. (a) in the large repository; (b) in the small repository.

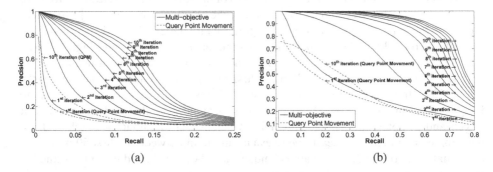

Fig. 2. Precision vs recall graphs at each iteration. (a) in the large repository; (b) in the small repository.

4   Conclusions

A relevance feedback method based on formulating the CBIR problem from a multi-objective optimization perspective has been presented in this paper. The main advantage of the method is that it is able to simultaneously explore regions around the relevant selections and others which are in between them. This allows the method to recover images in regions that other methods would not explore. Results show that the method performs reasonably well on two manually classified repositories of different characteristics.

One major drawback of the technique is the relatively high computational time involved in the calculation of the pareto optimal sets. Despite that the number of iterations may be adjusted to keep the response time under reasonable limits, the query movement and SOM-based approaches are considerably faster. As an illustrative figure, and fixing the response time as 1 second for the method proposed, running time becomes two to three order of magnitude higher than for the other two methods in the comparison. The study of alternative methods to compute the pareto optimal front is still an issue under investigation, and may yield important improvements in retrieval performance and/or execution time. Currently, further work is directed towards a more detailed characterization of the way this method behaves in order to integrate this and other more powerful strategies into a combined scheme.

Acknowledgments. We would like to thank Dr. G. Giacinto for his help by facilitating the manually performed classification of the 30 000 images repository. This work has been partially funded by FEDER and Spanish Government through projects TIN2011-29221-C03-02, TIN2009-14205-C04-03, and Consolider Ingenio 2010 CSD07-00018.

References

1. Thomee, B., Lew, M.S.: Interactive search in image retrieval: a survey. International Journal of Multimedia Information Retrieval 1(2), 71–86 (2012)
2. Datta, R., Joshi, D., Li, J., Wang, J.Z.: Image retrieval: Ideas, influences, and trends of the new age. ACM Computing Surveys 40(2), 1–60 (2008)
3. Ishikawa, Y., Subramanya, R., Faloutsos, C.: Mindreader: Querying databases through multiple examples. In: Proc. 24th Int. Conf. Very Large Data Bases, VLDB, New York, USA, pp. 433–438 (1998)
4. Rui, Y., Huang, S., Ortega, M., Mehrotra, S.: Relevance feeback: a power tool for interactive content-based image retrieval. IEEE Transaction on Circuits and Video Technology 8(5), 644–655 (1998)
5. Ciocca, G., Schettini, R.: A relevance feedback mechanism for content-based image retrieval. Information Processing and Management 35(1), 605–632 (1999)
6. de Freitas, N., Brochu, E., Barnard, K., Duygulu, P., Forsyth, D.: Bayesian models for massive multimedia databases: a new frontier. Technical Report TR-2003-5, Department of Computer Science, University of British Columbia (2003)
7. Vasconcelos, N., Lippman, A.: Learning from user feedback in image retrieval systems. In: Proceedings of Advances in Neural Information Processing Systems (NIPS 1999), Denver, Colo, USA, pp. 977–986 (November-December 1999)
8. Arevalillo-Herráez, M., Ferri, F.J., Domingo, J.: A naive relevance feedback model for content-based image retrieval using multiple similarity measures. Pattern Recognition 43(3), 619–629 (2010)
9. Giacinto, G.: A nearest-neighbor approach to relevance feedback in content based image retrieval. In: Proceedings of the 6th ACM International Conference on Image and Video Retrieval (CIVR 2007), Amsterdam, The Netherlands, pp. 456–463. ACM Press (1993)
10. Arevalillo-Herraez, M., Ferri, F.J.: Interactive image retrieval using smoothed nearest neighbor estimates. In: Hancock, E.R., Wilson, R.C., Windeatt, T., Ulusoy, I., Escolano, F. (eds.) SSPR&SPR 2010. LNCS, vol. 6218, pp. 708–717. Springer, Heidelberg (2010)
11. Zhou, X.S., Huang, T.S.: Small sample learning during multimedia retrieval using biasmap. In: Proceedings of the IEEE Conference on Computer Vision and Pattern Recognition, pp. 11–17 (2001)
12. Chen, Y., Zhou, X.S., Huang, T.S.: One-class svm for learning in image retrieval. In: Proceedings of the IEEE International Conference on Image Processing, pp. 34–37 (2001)
13. Tao, D., Tang, X., Li, X.: Which components are important for interactive image searching? IEEE Transactions on Circuits and Systems for Video Technology 18(1), 3–11 (2008)
14. Arevalillo-Herráez, M., Zacarés, M., Benavent, X., de Ves, E.: A relevance feedback CBIR algorithm based on fuzzy sets. Signal Processing: Image Communication 23(7), 490–504 (2008)

15. Koskela, M., Laaksonen, J., Oja, E.: Use of image subset features in image retrieval with self-organizing maps. In: Enser, P.G.B., Kompatsiaris, Y., O'Connor, N.E., Smeaton, A.F., Smeulders, A.W.M. (eds.) CIVR 2004. LNCS, vol. 3115, pp. 508–516. Springer, Heidelberg (2004)

16. Arevalillo-Herráez, M., Ferri, F.J., Moreno-Picot, S.: Distance-based relevance feedback using a hybrid interactive genetic algorithm for image retrieval. Applied Soft Computing 11(2), 1782–1791 (2011)

17. Deb, K., Pratap, A., Agarwal, S., Meyarivan, T.: A fast and elitist multiobjective genetic algorithm: Nsga. Transactions on Evolutionary Computation 6(2) (April 2002)

18. Pighetti, R., Pallez, D., Precioso, F.: Hybdrid content based image retrieval combining multi-objective interactive genetic algorithm and svm. In: 2012 21st International Conference on Pattern Recognition (ICPR), pp. 2849–2852 (2012)

19. Müller, H., Müller, W., Squirre, D.M.: Automated benchmarking in content based image retrieval. In: IEEE International Conference on Multimedia and Expo, pp. 321–324 (2001)

20. Laaksonen, J., Koskela, M., Oja, E.: Picsom-self-organizing image retrieval with mpeg-7 content descriptors. IEEE Transactions on Neural Networks 13(4), 841–853 (2002)

21. Giacinto, G., Roli, F.: Nearest-prototype relevance feedback for content based image retrieval. In: ICPR 2004: Proceedings of the 17th International Conference on Pattern Recognition, vol. 2, pp. 989–992. IEEE Computer Society, Washington, DC (2004)

22. Soille, P.: Morphological Image Analysis: Principles and Applications. Springer, Berlin (2003)

Large Scale Image Indexing
Using Online Non-negative Semantic Embedding

Jorge A. Vanegas and Fabio A. González

MindLab Research Group, Universidad Nacional de Colombia, Bogotá, Colombia
{javanegasr,fagonzalezo}@unal.edu.co

Abstract. This paper presents a novel method to address the problem of indexing a large set of images taking advantage of associated multimodal content such
as text or tags. The method finds relationships between the visual and text modalities enriching the image content representation to improve the performance of
content-based image search.

This method finds a mapping that connects visual and text information that
allows to project new (annotated and unannotated) images to the space defined
by semantic annotations, this new representation can be used to search into the
collection using a query-by-example strategy and to annotate new unannotated
images. The principal advantage of the proposed method is its formulation as an
online learning algorithm, which can scale to deal with large image collections.
The experimental evaluation shows that the proposed method, in comparison with
several baseline methods, is faster and consumes less memory, keeping a competitive performance in content-based image search.

1 Introduction

Large online collections of images are becoming common, thanks to the fast advance
in acquisition, storage and communication technology. These collections are potential
source of knowledge, but an effective and efficient access to them is fundamental to
harness this potential. The classic way to search for images is by typing keywords on
a search engine, but in many cases it is desirable to search by providing an example
image. This approach, called content-based image retrieval, has been studied during the
last two decades resulting in important progress . However, it is well known that matching visual features alone may lead to results with lack of semantic validity [16]. In this
paper we address the problem of indexing the visual content of an image collection,
enriching it with the semantic information provided by text annotations. The method
presented in this papers learns relationships between visual features and text keywords
co-occurring in images. A successful strategy to find these relationships is to build a
common semantic representation space where both image and text content are embedded. This has been previously approached using different methods: Latent Semantic
Analysis (LSA) [8], Latent Dirichlet Allocation (LDA) [1], Non-negative Matrix Factorization (NMF) [4] and Non-negative Semantic Embedding (NSE) [19], among others. The main drawback of most semantic learning strategies is that the algorithms are
memory and computation intensive [7]. In order to address this drawback, it is proposed

J. Ruiz-Shulcloper and G. Sanniti di Baja (Eds.): CIARP 2013, Part I, LNCS 8258, pp. 367–374, 2013.

a reformulation of the NSE algorithm as an online learning process, which scales up to data collections with a vast amount of samples.

This work presents two main contributions: first, a reformulation of the NSE algorithm to make it scalable to large image collections, and second, an experimental evaluation of the algorithm performance in a content-based image retrieval task. The rest of this paper is organized as follows: Section 2 discusses the related work; Section 3 introduces the proposed method called Online Non-negative Semantic Embedding (ONSE); Section 4 presents the experimental evaluation; and, finally, Section 5 presents some concluding remarks.

2   Related Work

The strategy of finding relationships between visual and text representations has been extensively studied in the last years, specially focused in the task of image annotation. However many of the proposed algorithms have been designed without considering a large scale setup [15,10,11]. In some cases, these algorithms can be scaled up by relying on parallelized implementations and assuming the availability of abundant computational resources. However, this can be expensive, tricky and hard to accomplish.

There are some works that try to make semantic embedding approaches suitable for large scale collections. For example, Hsan et al. [18] propose to utilize multi-modality cues by incorporating visual and textual information as embedded objects, by using a simple linear projection to approximate the embedding functions, solving a non-smooth convex optimization problem. Their goal is to make the method (called Modified Multistage Convex Relaxation, MMCR) suitable for large scale image collections by reformulating the basic algorithm in some way that is possible to reduce the time complexity and the amount of storage, achieving a significant reduction in time complexity. Also, Jason Weston et al. [20] present a scalable architecture, proposing methods that learn to represent images and annotations jointly in a low dimension embedding space. To make training time efficient, they propose a loss function based in stochastic gradient descent (SGD) approach. Likewise, Juan Caicedo et al. [6] propose multimodal matrix factorization algorithms based on SGD to decompose a training data set, and find correspondences between visual patterns and text terms in large image collection.

The proposed algorithm in this work is based on a stochastic gradient descent approach, which, according to the work of Bottou [2], requires very little time to reach a predefined expected risk. This makes the strategy suitable for large scale learning problems, providing guarantees about convergence and scalability [2,3].

3   Online Non-negative Semantic Embedding Model

When the image associated text has a rich and clean semantic interpretation (e.g. tags provided by experts), the text representation may be used directly as the semantic space. So the problem of finding a common semantic representation for both visual and text content is reduced to map the visual content to the semantic space defined by the tags. A method that follows this strategy is the Non-negative Semantic Embedding (NSE) [19].

3.1   Non-negative Semantic Embedding

If the visual and semantic representations are vectors, a database of images can be represented with two matrices by joining the corresponding vectors of visual and semantic features as columns of the matrices. Let $V \in \mathbb{R}^{n \times l}$ be the matrix of visual features, where n is the number of visual patterns in the bag of features representations and l the number of images in the collection, and let $T \in \mathbb{R}^{m \times l}$ be the matrix of text terms, with m the number of keywords in the terms dictionary. NSE is used when we assume that the semantic encoding is already known, and we use it to index and represent all images in the collection. We formulate this problem as finding a linear transformation of the visual data imposing a non negativity constraint on the solution: $V \approx ST; S \geq 0$. Where, $S \in \mathbb{R}^{n \times m}$ is the transformation matrix representing the relationships between the visual and text modalities. The non-negativity constraint in this case enforces an additive reconstruction of visual features, since vectors in the matrix S can be thought of as parts of images that are combined according to the presence of associated labels. Notice that the vectors in S can be interpreted as the visual features related to each text term. Our purpose is to solve the problem under an online formulation using stochastic gradient descent, which is a gradient descent optimization method for minimizing an objective function that is written as a sum of differentiable functions. In this context, we can formulate the problem of semantic embedding as the optimization problem of $\min_{S \geq 0} d(V, ST)$. Where, $d(.,.)$ is a function that measures the difference between V and ST. The purpose is to find S that minimize this difference.

3.2   Kullback-Leibler Divergence Optimization

A popular measure function for NMF is the generalized Kullback-Leibler divergence between V and ST [14], Although the KL-divergence equation is not symmetric, and therefore, it is not strictly a distance metric. This allows to take advantage of the normalized visual and text representation that can be interpreted as probability distributions. Zhirong Yang et. al [21] show that projected gradient methods based in for KL-divergence runs faster and yields better approximation than others widely used NMF algorithms. The updating rule for gradient descent approach with τ as the index of iterations and γ as the step size is:

$$S_{\tau+1} = S_\tau + \gamma \left[\left(\frac{V}{ST} - [1]_{n \times l} \right) T^\mathsf{T} \right] . \tag{1}$$

This algorithm requires a non-negativity restriction that can be incorporated by using a projected gradient strategy. The projection function maps a point back to the feasible region in each iteration [13], updating the current solution S_τ to $S_{\tau+1}$ by the following rule:

$$S_{\tau+1} = P[S_\tau - \gamma \nabla f(S_\tau)]; \quad P[s_{ij}] = \begin{cases} s_{ij} & if\ s_{ij} \geq 0, \\ 0 & if\ s_{ij} < 0, \end{cases} . \tag{2}$$

3.3   Online Formulation

The idea of online learning using stochastic approximations is to compute the new solution for each unknown in the problem using a single data sample at a time.

Algoritmo 1. Online Non-negative Semantic Embedding

---

input S^0: Initial transformation matrix, γ_0: initial step size, N: number of iterations

for $k = 1$ **to** N **do**

    1. Step size calculation: $\gamma_k = \gamma_0/(1 + \gamma_0 \lambda k)$

    2. Update transformation matrix: $S_{\tau+1} = P\left[S_\tau - \gamma_k \left[\left(\frac{v_\tau}{S_\tau t_\tau} - [1]_{n \times m}\right) t_\tau^T\right]\right]$

end for

return $S_{\tau+1}$

Then, we can scan large data sets without memory restrictions. The updating rule has to be reformulated in such a way that it only depends on the τ-th sample (v_t, t_t, visual and text features for the τ-th image). The updating rule is reformulated as follows:

$$S_{\tau+1} = S_\tau + \gamma \left[\left(\frac{v_\tau}{S_\tau t_\tau} - [1]_{n \times 1}\right) t_\tau^T\right] . \tag{3}$$

The resulting algorithm (Algorithm 1) starts by randomly initialization of the transformation matrix. Each iteration consists on updating the transformation matrix from an observed pair of visual and text features randomly obtained. The step size used in this algorithm is a decreasing rate [2] that depends on the number of iterations and an initial learning rate γ_0. A small variation of this algorithm is obtained by using several samples at each iteration instead of using only one. Experimental results show faster execution when using mini-batches instead of single examples, and also a better numerical stability for the solution.

3.4 Image Indexing and Search

A special indexing case is when images do not have attached text. An example of this situation is when users are interested in searching the database using example images as queries. A new image without text can be projected to the semantic space by finding the pseudo-inverse of the transformation matrix (S^+) .

$$t = S^+ v; \quad S^+ = \left(S^T S + \beta I\right)^{-1} S^T . \tag{4}$$

where, v is the visual representation of the new image, t is the semantic representation and β is a regularization parameter. In this way we can searching the database using an inferred text representation based in its visual features. This pseudo-inverse matrix has to be preprocessed only once and storing in memory, making very efficient the process of projection for a new image. Finally, the ranking function for semantic search is based on the histogram intersection similarity[17].

4   Experiments and Results

4.1   Datasets

The performance of the proposed algorithm was evaluated using three different datasets with different sizes:

Carcinoma dataset. The Carcinoma dataset is a histopathology image collection that has been used to diagnose a special kind of skin cancer known as basal-cell carcinoma

[5]. It is composed of 1,502 images that were studied and annotated by pathologists to highlight various tissue structures and relevant diagnostic information, elaborating a list with 18 terms. These images were acquired at various magnification levels, including 8X, 10X and 20X, and stored at 1280×1024 pixels. The list of keywords includes terms like micro-nodules, elastosis, and fibrosis, among others.

Histology Dataset. The Histology dataset is composed of 2,641 images extracted from an atlas of histology for the study of the four fundamental tissues [19]. The collection includes photographs of histology in different magnification factors (10X, 20X and 40X). The resolution of these images is about 800×500 pixels. Each of these images was annotated by an expert, indicating the biological system and organs that can be observed. The total number of different keywords in this data set is 46.

MIRFlickr 25000 Dataset. The MIRFlickr-25000 image dataset is composed of 25,000 pictures downloaded from the popular online photo sharing service Flickr. These photos were collected directly from the web, to provide a realistic dataset for image retrieval research, with high-resolution images and associated metadata [12]. This image collection has been manually annotated using a set of 38 semantic terms.

4.2 Experimental Setup

We conducted retrieval experiments under the query-by-example paradigm. In all datasets 20% of images were randomly selected as queries and the remaining images were used as the target collection to find relevant images. We performed automatic experiments by sending a query to the system and evaluating the relevance of the results. A ranked image in the results list is considered relevant if it shares at least one keyword with the query. The evaluation was done using traditional measures of image retrieval, including precision at 10 and mean average precision (MAP).

Image Features. In all datasets we build a bag-of-features representation, with the following characteristics: Patches of 8×8 pixels are extracted from a set of training images with an overlap of 4 pixels along the x and y axes. The DCT (Discrete Cosine Transform) transform is applied in each of the 3 RGB channels to extract the largest 21 coefficients. (DCT-based visual codewords has been found to be an effective representation for microscopy image analysis [9]). A k-means clustering is applied to build a dictionary. For Carcinoma and Histology datasets we use 500 visual terms and for MIRFlickr we select a dictionary of 2000 features (larger dictionaries do not provide significant improvements, but just more computational load). Once the vocabulary has been built, every image in the collection goes through the patch extraction process. Each patch from an image is linked to one visual term in the dictionary using a nearest neighbor criterion. Finally, the histogram of frequencies is constructed for each image.

Text Annotations. In these data sets the text annotations are clean and clearly defined terms from a technical vocabulary and these represent directly the semantic space. We build semantic vectors following a boolean approach, assigning 1 to the terms attached to an image and 0 otherwise. This leads to 46-dimensional binary vectors, for text representation in the Histology dataset, 18-dimensional binary vectors for Carcinoma dataset and 39-dimensional binary vectors for Flickr.

4.3 Retrieval Performance

In order to evaluate the performance of the proposed algorithm, we compare the proposed online algorithm with the classical NSE and the MMCR (Modified Multi-stage Convex Relaxation) proposed by Hsan et. al [18]. Although the MMCR algorithm was proposed mainly for annotation, it is possible to use its semantic score vector as a new representation for retrieval task.

Parameter Tuning. The proposed algorithm has a set of parameters that can impact the quality of the resulting model. Improper settings of these parameters may cause the algorithm converge slowly or diverge. So, as preliminary evaluation, we perform an exploration of these parameters by retrieval experiments using cross-validation 10 fold in the subset of 80% of the images that were not selected as queries. And, we select the configuration that perform better in average in all folds (Table 1).

Table 1. Results of parameter tuning for Online Non-negative Semantic Embedding (ONSE)

	Carcinoma				Histology				MIRFlickr		
λ_0	γ	β	Mini-batch size	λ_0	γ	β	Mini-batch size	λ_0	γ	β	Mini-batch size
2^{-5}	2^{-2}	2^4	16	2^{-6}	2^{-3}	2	16	2^{-8}	2^{-10}	2	32

Once, we had found the better configuration, we evaluate the proposed algorithm with the remaining 20% of images as test. So we use this 20% of images as queries and the 80% as finding objective. Table 2 summarizes the findings of our experimental results. In all cases, a general improvement over visual baseline (direct visual matching using visual representation) is shown in MAP measure. And, with the exception of the Histology dataset NSE, ONSE-KL and MMCR algorithms, present a very similar performance.

Table 2. Image retrieval performance. Reported measures are Mean Average Precision (MAP) and Precision at the first 10 results (P@10).

Algorithm	Carcinoma		Histology		MIRFlickr	
	MAP	P@10	MAP	P@10	MAP	P@10
Visual	0.2236	0.3503	0.2107	0.6104	0.2505	0.4931
MMCR [18]	0.3146	0.3322	0.5346	0.6030	0.3670	0.5063
NSE [19]	0.3265	0.3249	0.4025	0.4148	0.3672	0.5079
ONSE	0.3171	0.3651	0.3594	0.4439	0.3674	0.5065

4.4 Computational Load

Table 3 shows the average time consumption for the training phase. Reported times are the result of running all algorithms 5 times in a computer with 4 GB of ram memory and a CPU at 2.4Ghz using only one core. The size of each dataset is also reported to observe how the algorithm complexity grows. NSE algorithm take about 5 seconds to process the Carcinoma dataset, 9 to process the Histology collection and finally increases to

Table 3. Time consumption in training phase: Time required for each epoch (Epoch Avg. Time) and the total average time required until convergence (Total Avg. Time). The algorithm presented in this paper (ONSE) is compared against MMCR [18] and NSE [19].

Dataset	Size	Algorithm	Epochs	Epoch Avg. Time (sec)	Total Avg. Time (sec)
Carcinoma	1502	MMCR	8	0.2854	2.1878
		NSE	130	0.0411	5.3442
		ONSE	4	**0.0836**	**0.3345**
Histology	2641	MMCR	10	1.5351	14.2029
		NSE	90	0.1009	9.0869
		ONSE	4	**0.3027**	**1.2086**
MIRFlickr	25000	MMCR	10	283.4327	2834,3278
		NSE	200	2.4701	494.017
		ONSE	2	**13.755497**	**27.2188**

494 seconds for MIRFlickr. MMCR have the most time consuming, requiring about 2 seconds for Carcinoma 14 for Histology and 2834 for MIRFlickr. In contrast, the ONSE algorithm only requires 0.3 seconds for Carcinoma, 1.2 for Histology and 27 for MIRFlickr. Thus for MIRFlickr dataset, ONSE algorithm is 18 times faster than NSE and 104 times faster than MMCR.

The main reason for the reduction of training time, is, that the number of required epochs until the ONSE algorithm converges is reduced drastically (convergence in all algorithms is verified by means of a minimum threshold required to improve the error in each epoch). For instance, in the carcinoma dataset the NSE algorithm required 130 full scans to the training set and the online version only needed 4. In general, Bottou [3] shows that for a small collection, it is necessary to use very few epochs and for large collections, one full scan is enough. Furthermore, the proposed algorithm reduces the memory requirements, since the only element necessary to keep in memory is the transformation matrix, since visual and textual samples used in each update can be discarded,.

5 Conclusions

We presented an approach for large image indexing that takes advantage of text annotations to provide a semantic representation space where the visual content of images is embedded. This approach is a reformulation of NSE as an online learning algorithm allowing to deal with large collections of data, achieving a significantly reduction in memory requirements and computational load, but keeping a competitive retrieval performance.

Acknowledgements. This work was partially funded by projects Anotación Automática y Recuperación por Contenido de Imágenes Radiológicas Usando Semántica Latente, No. 110152128803 by Colciencias 0521-2010, Diseño e implementación de un sistema de cómputo sobre recursos heterogéneos para la identificación de estructuras atmosféricas en predicción climatológica, No. 1225-569-34920 by Colciencias 0213-2013 and Multimodal Image Retrieval to Support Medical Case-Based Scientific Literature Search, ID R1212LAC006 by Microsoft Research LACCIR.

References

1. Barnard, K., Duygulu, P., Forsyth, D., De Freitas, N., Blei, D.M., Kandola, J., Hofmann, T., Poggio, T., Shawe-Taylor, J.: Matching words and pictures. JMLR 3, 1107–1135 (2003)
2. Bottou, L.: Large-scale machine learning with stochastic gradient descent. In: COMPSTAT 2010, Paris, France, pp. 177–187. Springer (August 2010)
3. Bottou, L., LeCun, Y.: Large scale online learning. In: NIPS (2003)
4. Caicedo, J.C., BenAbdallah, J., González, F.A., Nasraoui, O.: Multimodal representation, indexing, automated annotation and retrieval of image collections via non-negative matrix factorization. Neurocomput. 76(1), 50–60 (2012)
5. Caicedo, J.C., Cruz, A., Gonzalez, F.A.: Histopathology image classification using bag of features and kernel functions. In: Combi, C., Shahar, Y., Abu-Hanna, A. (eds.) AIME 2009. LNCS, vol. 5651, pp. 126–135. Springer, Heidelberg (2009)
6. Caicedo, J.C., González, F.A.: Online matrix factorization for multimodal image retrieval. In: Alvarez, L., Mejail, M., Gomez, L., Jacobo, J. (eds.) CIARP 2012. LNCS, vol. 7441, pp. 340–347. Springer, Heidelberg (2012)
7. Chandrika, P., Jawahar, C.V.: Multi modal semantic indexing for image retrieval. In: CIVR 2010, pp. 342–349. ACM, New York (2010)
8. Chen, Q., Tai, X., Jiang, B., Li, G., Zhao, J.: Medical image retrieval based on latent semantic indexing. In: CSSE 2008, pp. 561–564. IEEE Computer Society, Washington, DC (2008)
9. Cruz-Roa, A., Caicedo, J.C., González, F.A.: Visual pattern mining in histology image collections using bag of features. AIME 52(2), 91–106 (2011)
10. Fang, C., Torresani, L.: Measuring image distances via embedding in a semantic manifold. In: Fitzgibbon, A., Lazebnik, S., Perona, P., Sato, Y., Schmid, C. (eds.) ECCV 2012, Part IV. LNCS, vol. 7575, pp. 402–415. Springer, Heidelberg (2012)
11. Guillaumin, M., Mensink, T., Verbeek, J., Schmid, C.: Tagprop: Discriminative metric learning in nearest neighbor models for image auto-annotation. In: ICCV (2009)
12. Huiskes, M.J., Lew, M.S.: The mir flickr retrieval evaluation. In: MIR 2008. ACM, New York (2008)
13. Jen Lin, C.: Projected gradient methods for non-negative matrix factorization. Raport Instytutowy, Neural Computation (2007)
14. Lee, D.D., Seung, H.S.: Algorithms for non-negative matrix factorization. In: NIPS, pp. 556–562. MIT Press (2000)
15. Makadia, A., Pavlovic, V., Kumar, S.: A new baseline for image annotation. In: Forsyth, D., Torr, P., Zisserman, A. (eds.) ECCV 2008, Part III. LNCS, vol. 5304, pp. 316–329. Springer, Heidelberg (2008)
16. Smeulders, A.W.M., Worring, M., Santini, S., Gupta, A., Jain, R.: Content-based image retrieval at the end of the early years. TPAMI 22(12), 1349–1380 (2000)
17. Swain, M.J., Ballard, D.H.: Color indexing. IJCV 7, 11–32 (1991)
18. Tsai, M.-H., Wang, J., Zhang, T., Gong, Y., Huang, T.S.: Learning semantic embedding at a large scale. In: ICIP, pp. 2497–2500 (2011)
19. Vanegas, J.A., Caicedo, J.C., González, F.A., Romero, E.: Histology image indexing using a non-negative semantic embedding. In: Müller, H., Greenspan, H., Syeda-Mahmood, T. (eds.) MCBR-CDS 2011. LNCS, vol. 7075, pp. 80–91. Springer, Heidelberg (2012)
20. Weston, J., Bengio, S., Usunier, N.: Large scale image annotation: Learning to rank with joint word-image embeddings. In: ECML (2010)
21. Yang, Z., Zhang, H., Yuan, Z., Oja, E.: Kullback-leibler divergence for nonnegative matrix factorization. In: Honkela, T. (ed.) ICANN 2011, Part I. LNCS, vol. 6791, pp. 250–257. Springer, Heidelberg (2011)

Using Boundary Conditions for Combining Multiple Descriptors in Similarity Based Queries

Rodrigo F. Barroso[1], Marcelo Ponciano-Silva[3,2],
Agma Juci Machado Traina[2], and Renato Bueno[1]

[1] Computer Science Dept, UFSCar, São Carlos-SP, Brazil
[2] Computer Science Dept, ICMC-USP, São Carlos-SP, Brazil
[3] Computer Science Dept, IFTM, Uberaba-MG, Brazil

Abstract. Queries dealing with complex data, such as images, face semantic problems that might compromise results quality. Such problems have their source on the differences found between the semantic interpretation of the data and their low level machine code representation. The descriptors utilized in such representation translate intrinsic characteristics of the data (usually color, shape and texture) into qualifying attributes. Different descriptors represent different intrinsic characteristics that can get different aspects of the data while processing a similarity comparison among them. Therefore, the use of multiple descriptors tends to improve data separation and categorization, if compared to the use of a single descriptor. Another relevant fact is that some specific intrinsic characteristics are essential for identifying a subset of the data. Based on such premises, this work proposes the use of boundary conditions to identify image subsets and then use the best descriptor combination for each of these subsets aimed at decreasing the existing "semantic gap". Throughout the conducted experiments, the use of the proposed technique had better results when compared to individual descriptor use (employing the same boundary conditions) and to various descriptors combination without the use of boundary conditions.

Keywords: CBIR, multiple descriptor combination, similarity queries.

1 Introduction

The need for storing and manipulating non-traditional data (such as images, video and audio among others) is becoming very common in a variety of computer systems, thus managing and retrieving such data in an effective and efficient way is more necessary than ever. Such data are commonly called complex data. The similarity found between element pairs of such complex data is one of the most useful approach to manipulate such data and indicates how similar or distinct an object is in relation to another. In such similarity queries, the comparison is not done using the complex data elements directly but, instead, a set of features that were extracted from such data. Features extraction algorithms are commonly applied to data generating the so called feature vectors which are

J. Ruiz-Shulcloper and G. Sanniti di Baja (Eds.): CIARP 2013, Part I, LNCS 8258, pp. 375–382, 2013.

used to represent the data in further processing. In the case of images, the most used features are related to texture, shape or color distribution. Comparison is done by applying distance functions over the feature vectors of two element pairs resulting in a numeric value that determines the distance (dissimilarity) between such elements. A basic means to compute similarity queries is employing the Content-Based Retrieval (CBR) techniques, or, in the case of images, the Content-Based Image Retrieval (CBIR). One of the major challenges found in CBIR is to reduce the semantic gap [1] which is characterized by the divergence between the low level image characteristics found by the extraction algorithms and the semantic interpretation of the same image made by a human being.

Besides finding the best combination between the features extractor and an appropriate distance function [2,3], the use of more than one intrinsic characteristic while comparing elements tend to present better results while reducing such semantic gap [4,3]. Furthermore, different subsets of data in a same larger set can be better represented by different characteristics [5,6].

Based on all principles above, this work proposes the use of boundary conditions in order to find subsets of similar data inside a larger data set thus allowing the choice of the best combination of multiple descriptors in each given subset. The expected result is a reduction on the aforementioned semantic gap while running similarity based queries against data in each subset.

The remainder of the paper is organized as follows. Section 2 presents the background and correlated work. Section 3 shows this works proposal and Section 4, in its turn, shows the experiments performed and the discussion about the results found. Finally, Section 5 present the papers final remarks.

2   Background and Related Work

2.1   Similarity Queries and Semantic Gap

Content Based Image Retrieval is supported by similarity queries which commonly make use of feature vectors. Such vectors, normally extracted in an automatic way, contain low level characteristics, such as color distribution, shape and texture, which aim at representing the image contents. To compare those images, the similarity between element pairs is calculated through the use of a distance function between each images feature vectors. A small distance value corresponds to a high similarity degree. A descriptor comprises a features extractor and a distance function [3]. The main similarity query operators [7] are kNN Queries (giving an element as query center, the k nearest neighbors are returned) and Range Queries (giving an element as query center and a radius, all elements positioned inside a given distance (radius) are returned).

There exist many difficulties inherent to content based image retrieval systems. The decision about what is found similar compared to what is found not similar can be subjective thus generating a perceptual variation among system users. The very own search by similarity mechanism using feature vectors assuming similar data would render results not compatible to reality. Such difficulties are directly tied to the semantic gap mentioned before [1].

2.2   Multiple Descriptors Combination

The multiple descriptors combination approach in CBIR has been demonstrating a great capacity for leveraging results accuracy in similarity queries [8,4,5,3] and such fact has its explanation on the complimentary nature of each images visual characteristics. By using multiple descriptors, the CBIR systems try to mimic human behavior on a similar image interpretation task where various image aspects (such as color, texture or shape) are compared simultaneously. Many works proposed different ways to perform multiple descriptors combination [4,5,9,10,8]. In [4], fractal dimension analysis is used to determine the intrinsic data correlation, then using it to normalize the contribution among the multiple descriptors on the similarity calculations between the elements.

Other proposals use a relevance feedback [9,10,8] in an attempt to capture the users similarity perception using his/her interactions in the system and reflecting them in the similarity calculation. In [8], a weighted calculation is done and each multiple descriptors weight is interactively changed according to the indication of the relevant images. In [9], together with the relevance feedback, functions are generated using a genetic programming algorithm what generates more complex functions that would better calculate each elements similarity [3]. Genetic programming algorithms are also used in [11] to combine local and global descriptors.

In its majority, the approaches for combining multiple descriptors dont consider the fact that distinct intrinsic characteristics (or their combination) can better identify different data subsets.

2.3   Boundary Conditions

The use of boundary conditions allows delimitating subsets of data inside the data as a whole. In this work, we understand boundary conditions for image similarity queries as any information associated to the images that can be used for estimating limits for subsets of images in a way that data in a subset can be better highlighted by a descriptor or a combination of specific descriptors. For medical imaging queries, for example, we can quote as boundary conditions items like the diagnose hypothesis mentioned by the medical doctor in the moment an exam is requested, radiological findings included by a radiologist, or even the exam type, among others.

In [6] a perceptual parameter was included in the medical imaging similarity queries. It has been verified that in a same database, there are image subsets that could be better represented by different individual descriptors thus increasing results precision. The authors proposed the use of triads formed by the perceptual parameter, features extractor and distance function. As boundary condition to subset limitation, the radiological finding has been used, i.e., some visual characteristic found by the specialist usually related to some diagnostic hypothesis. For each subset delimited by this boundary condition the best individual descriptor was defined experimentally. Further experimentation demonstrated that the use of this perceptual parameter had leveraged similarity queries results quality and helped reducing the semantic gap.

In [5] it had been shown that different subsets (or classes) of images were better represented by the combination of multiple descriptors with distinct weights. As illustrated in Figure 1 (adapted from [5]), queries using images from class B as query center had better precision levels when higher weight values were used to the texture descriptor than the shape descriptor. An opposite result had been found while considering only images pertaining to class A, and its similar to the average result while considering all images in the subset.

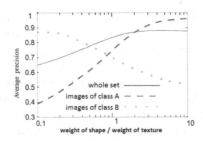

Fig. 1. Average precision with descriptors weight variation (adapted from[5])

3 Proposed Method: Multiple Descriptors Combination Using Boundary Conditions

In this work we propose the use of boundary conditions to delimitate subsets of images and, for each subset, the establishment of the best combination of multiple descriptors to be used in subsequent similarity queries.

Such descriptors combination establishment is done in an initial training phase. Later in the process, while executing a query, the boundary condition is used to identify (or estimate) the subset where the query center image is part of, so the best descriptors combination for that particular subset can be used.

A boundary condition for the larger image set must be defined first in an attempt to delimitate images subsets that have similar behavior in similarity queries. A domain application specialist is responsible for choosing such boundary condition definition considering the query objectives to be obtained while running such queries against the data set. Taking as example medical imaging applications, the boundary conditions can be defined using its associated data, like the diagnose hypothesis given by the medical specialist while requesting the exam, as well as from an initial analysis of the images provided by a specialist who can pre-classify then based in any radiological finding.

After the boundary condition is defined, the next step is to find the best descriptors combination where pre-classified images are used in this training phase and the outcome is a relation of the best descriptors combination for each boundary condition. It is worth mentioning that the criteria used as boundary condition does not need to be the same used for image classification. As a simple example, the patients sex can be used as a boundary condition while the images used for training were classified according to the illness identified in the image.

In this case, the multiple descriptors combination to be found would be the ones that better highlight the illness being considered (classes) to each image subset gathered using the boundary condition (men and women).

To demonstrate the proposed methods validity, during the training phase it has been used a simple linear combination algorithm so an exhaustive search for the best descriptors combination could be performed. Despite that, the proposed method can be used with almost any multiple descriptors combination method that can generate a valid descriptors combination in a data set.

4   Experiments

Two experiments (using two different data bases) are presented in this paper. Both image sets used were made available by the Clinical Hospital of the Medical School of Ribeirão Preto, Universidade de São Paulo, Brazil. The results evaluation was based in precision and recall curves[12].

4.1   Experiment 1: Lung Computed Tomography Exam Images

In this first experiment, a collection of 247 images related to lung computed tomography (CT) exams were classified by specialists in 6 classes according to radiologic findings: emphysema, consolidation, ground-glass opacity, inter-lobular septal thickening, honeycombing and normal (no findings). As boundary condition, the physicians perception has been used according to each finding: homogenous and non-homogenous increase of attenuation, inter-lobular fissures, and low attenuation with and without well defined lobule walls [6]. The extracted features were related to color [6] (high histogram, low histogram, traditional histogram) and texture (Haralick [13]).

Initially, through experimentation, descriptors with the best results were chosen (shown in Figure 2) and then the best descriptors combination for the whole set. Distinct distance function types were evaluated for each feature vector, namely the Minkowski family functions and Canberra [2]. Following, the best descriptor for each subset delimited by the boundary conditions was chosen and then triads were formed from the association between them [6]. As a final step, for each subset formed using the boundary conditions it has been calculated the best descriptors combination using the linear combination algorithm. This way, we have the final result with an ideal descriptors combination associated to each subset delimited by each of the boundary conditions.

Figure 2a) depicts the precision curves versus the recall found on the best individual descriptors for the whole set, the best individual descriptors for each boundary condition, the best combination considering the whole set and the best combination defined for each boundary condition. For the definition of the best descriptor and the best combinations, only 25% of recall was considered. The proposed technique obtained better results in all recall levels.

Figure 2b) presents the average precision for the same procedures, but now analyzing all recall levels for triad and descriptors combination definition. The

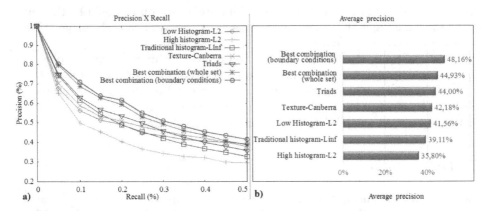

Fig. 2. CT for lung examination. a) Precision vs Recall curves. b) Average Precision. Comparison between individual descriptors, individual descriptors using boundary conditions, descriptors combination for the whole set, and descriptors combination using boundary conditions (proposed technique).

multiple descriptors combination proposed resulted in better results, with average precision next to 6.5% superior to the one obtained using descriptors combination without the boundary conditions and 14.2% better average precision obtained through the best individual descriptor use.

4.2   Experiment 2: MR Images

A set of 704 images acquired by magnetic resonance (MRI) was used to perform the second experiment, where each image was pre-classified in 40 classes according to the body region, vision plan, and cut over position they covered. As boundary condition, it has been used the exam type that generated the image: Angiogram, Axial and Coronal abdomen, Axial, Coronal and Sagittal head, Axial pelvis and Sagittal spine. The extracted features were related to color (traditional histogram), texture (Haralick) and shape (256 first Zernike moments [14]). Through the experiments, three descriptors presenting better results over the whole data (shown in Figure 3) and the triad (best descriptor associated to the boundary condition) have been defined. All recall levels in this experiment have been analyzed in order to define the triad and the best multiple descriptors combination.

Figure 3a) presents precision versus recall curves and Figure 3b) presents average precision found by each individual descriptor, individual descriptors defined for each boundary condition, best combination considering the whole set and best combination defined for each boundary condition. As it can be verified in Figure 3a), and as occurred in the first experiment, the proposed method presented better results in all recall levels and, according to Figure 3b), the average precision of the proposed method was also superior with approximately 9% gain in relation to the boundary conditions chosen for a single descriptor.

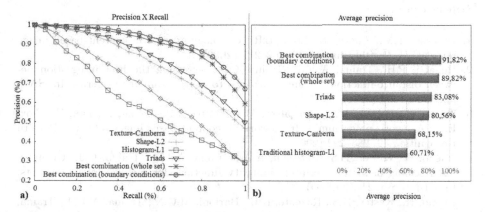

Fig. 3. Magnetic resonance images. a) Precision vs Recall curves. b) Average Precision. Comparison between individual descriptors, individual descriptors using boundary conditions, descriptors combination for the whole set, and descriptors combination using boundary conditions (proposed technique).

5   Conclusion

This paper proposed a technique that chooses the best combination of multiple descriptors for each subset in a large data set. The similar subsets were found by use of boundary conditions. This new methodology sought to simulate human perception during images analysis for purposes of comparison among them.

In the presented experiments, the proposed technique was compared with the main techniques used in CBIR found in the literature. These were: 1) use of individual descriptors for the entire set of images 2) use of a combination of descriptors for the entire set of images and 3) use of individual descriptors for each selected subsets of images, delimited by the boundary conditions. The proposed technique achieved better results in all the experiments, showing that the automatic comparison of images should consider all relevant visual aspects, each with its specific balancing to the presented context.

The use of a single descriptor for content search limited the comparison to just one criterion of similarity. On the other hand, the use of multiple descriptors for the entire set of images disregards the visual properties intrinsic to each subset delimited by the boundary conditions. Thus, the analysis presented in this paper showed a new field of research in CBIR systems, with approach to the perception of similarity of the users of these systems. The results show how promising is the use of boundary conditions for combining multiple descriptors for similarity queries on medical images.

Acknowledgments. We thank FAPESP, CAPES, CNPq and the INCT INCod for the financial support.

References

1. Deserno, T.M., Antani, S., Long, L.R.: Ontology of gaps in content-based image retrieval. J. Digital Imaging 22, 202–215 (2009)
2. Bugatti, P.H., Traina, A.J.M., Traina, C.J.: Assessing the best integration between distance-function and image-feature to answer similarity queries. In: SAC, pp. 1225–1230 (2008)
3. Torres, R., Falcão, A.X., Gonçalves, M.A., Papa, J.P., Zhang, B., Fan, W., Fox, E.A.: A genetic programming framework for content-based image retrieval. Pattern Recognition 42, 283–292 (2009)
4. Bueno, R., Kaster, D.S., Paterlini, A.A., Traina, A.J.M., Traina, C.J.: Unsupervised scaling of multi-descriptor similarity functions for medical image datasets. In: CBMS, pp. 24–31 (2009)
5. Bueno, R., Kaster, D.S., Razente, H.L., Barioni, M.C.N., Traina, A.J.M., Traina, C.J.: Using visual analysis to weight multiple signatures to discriminate complex data. In: IV, pp. 282–287 (2011)
6. Ponciano-Silva, M., Traina, A.J.M., Azevedo-Marques, P.M., Felipe, J.C., Traina, C.J.: Including the perceptual parameter to tune the retrieval ability of pulmonary cbir systems. In: CBMS, pp. 8–17 (2009)
7. Zezula, P., Amato, G., Dohnal, V., Batko, M.: Similarity Search - The Metric Space Approach. Advances in Database Systems, vol. 32. Kluwer (2006)
8. Rui, Y., Huang, T.S., Ortega, M., Mehrotra, S.: Relevance feedback: a power tool for interactive content-based image retrieval. IEEE Trans. Circuits Syst. Video Techn. 8, 644–655 (1998)
9. Ferreira, C.D., dos Santos, J.A., Torres, R., Gonçalves, M.A., Rezende, R.C., Fan, W.: Relevance feedback based on genetic programming for image retrieval. Pattern Recognition Letters 32, 27–37 (2011)
10. Arevalillo-Herráez, M., Ferri, F.J., Domingo, J.: A naive relevance feedback model for content-based image retrieval using multiple similarity measures. Pattern Recognition 43, 619–629 (2010)
11. Andrade, F.S.P., Almeida, J., Pedrini, H., da S.Torres, R.: Fusion of local and global descriptors for content-based image and video retrieval. In: Alvarez, L., Mejail, M., Gomez, L., Jacobo, J. (eds.) CIARP 2012. LNCS, vol. 7441, pp. 845–853. Springer, Heidelberg (2012)
12. Baeza-Yates, R.A., Ribeiro-Neto, B.A.: Modern Information Retrieval. ACM Press/Addison-Wesley (1999)
13. Haralick, R., Shanmugam, K., Dinstein, I.: Textural features for image classification. IEEE Trans. on Systems, Man and Cybernetics SMC-3, 610–621 (1973)
14. Khotanzad, A., Hong, Y.H.: Invariant image recognition by zernike moments. IEEE Trans. Pattern Anal. Mach. Intell. 12, 489–497 (1990)

Stopping Criterion
for the Mean Shift Iterative Algorithm

Yasel Garcés Suárez, Esley Torres, Osvaldo Pereira,
Claudia Pérez, and Roberto Rogríguez

Institute of Cybernetics, Mathematics and Physics, Havana, Cuba
{ygarces,esley,rrm}@icimaf.cu

Abstract. Image segmentation is a critical step in computer vision tasks constituting an essential issue for pattern recognition and visual interpretation. In this paper, we propose a new stopping criterion for the mean shift iterative algorithm by using images defined in $\mathbb{Z}_n$ ring, with the goal of reaching a better segmentation. We carried out also a study on the weak and strong of equivalence classes between two images. An analysis on the convergence with this new stopping criterion is carried out too.

1 Introduction

Many techniques and algorithms have been proposed for digital image segmentation. Unfortunately, traditional segmentation techniques using low-level, such as thresholding, histograms or other conventional operations are rigid methods. Automation of these classical approximations is difficult due to the complexity in shape and variability within each individual object in the image. Mean Shift (MSH) is a robust technique which has been applied in many computer vision tasks. MSH as an iterative algorithm has been used in many works by using the entropy as a stopping criterion [4–8].

Entropy is an essential function in information theory and has special uses for images data, e.g., restoring images, detecting contours, segmenting images and many other applications [9, 10]. However, in the field of images, the range of properties of this function could be increased if the images would be defined in $\mathbb{Z}_n$ rings.

In this paper, we compare the stability of iterative MSH algorithm using a new stopping criterion based on ring theory with respect to the stopping criterion used in [4–7]. The remainder of the paper is organized as follows: Theoretical aspects related with the entropy and the defined images in $\mathbb{Z}_n$ ring are exposed in Section 2. Here, a special attention is dedicated to the benefits of image entropy in the $\mathbb{Z}_n$ ring. Section 3 shows the experimental results, comparisons and discussion. And finally the most important conclusions are given in the last section.

2 Theoretical Aspects: Entropy

Entropy is a measure of unpredictability or information content. In the space of the digital images the entropy is defined as [1].

J. Ruiz-Shulcloper and G. Sanniti di Baja (Eds.): CIARP 2013, Part I, LNCS 8258, pp. 383–390, 2013.
© Springer-Verlag Berlin Heidelberg 2013

Definition 1 (Image Entropy). *The entropy of the image* $\mathcal{A}$ *is defined by*

$$E(\mathcal{A}) = -\sum_{x=0}^{2^B-1} p_x log_2 p_x, \tag{1}$$

where B *is the total quantity of bits of the digitized image* $\mathcal{A}$ *and* $p(x)$ *is the probability of occurrence of a gray-level value. By agreement* $log_2(0) = 0$.

In recent works [4–7] the entropy is an important point to define a stopping criterion for a segmentation algorithm based on an iterative computation of the mean shift filtering. In [4–7] the stopping criterion is

$$\nu(\mathcal{A}, \mathcal{B}) = |E(\mathcal{A}) - E(\mathcal{B})|. \tag{2}$$

$E(\cdot)$ is the function of entropy and the algorithm is stopped when $\nu(\mathcal{A}_k, \mathcal{A}_{k-1}) \leq \epsilon$. Here ϵ and k are respectively the threshold to stop the iterations and the number of iterations.

Definition 2 (Weak equivalent in Images). *Two images* $\mathcal{A}$ *and* $\mathcal{B}$ *are weakly equivalents if*

$$E(\mathcal{A}) = E(\mathcal{B}).$$

We denote the weak equivalent between $\mathcal{A}$ *and* $\mathcal{B}$ *using* $\mathcal{A} \asymp \mathcal{B}$.

Trivial implication is:

$$\mathcal{A} \asymp \mathcal{B} \Longleftrightarrow \nu(\mathcal{A}, \mathcal{B}) = 0.$$

Note that using the Definition 2 the stopping criterion defined in (2) is a measure to know when two images are close to be weakly equivalents.

Figure 1 shows two different images of 64×64. A reasonable stopping criterion should present a big difference between Figure 1(a) and Figure 1(b). However, by using the expression (2), we obtain that $\nu(Figure\ 1(a),\ Figure\ 1(b)) = 0$.

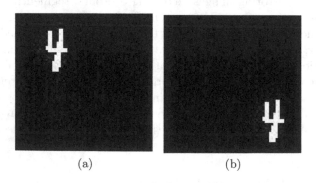

(a)   (b)

Fig. 1. Dissimilar Images

The defined stopping criterion in (2) never consider the spacial information between the images $\mathcal{A}$ and $\mathcal{B}$. For this reason, it is possible to have two very different images and to obtain a small value by using (2).

This is a strong reason to consider that the defined stopping criterion in (2) is not appropriate and provide instability in the iterative mean shift algorithm. For this reason, it is necessary to consider other stopping criterion that provides a better performance.

It is natural to think that two images are close if their subtraction is close to zero. The problem of this idea is that, in general, when the subtraction gives negative values many authors consider to truncate to zero these elements. This consideration, in general, does not describe the difference between both images, and in some cases, it is possible to lose important information.

For this reason, it is necessary to define a structure such that the operations between two images are intern.

Definition 3 ($\mathbb{Z}_n$ Ring). *The $\mathbb{Z}_n$ ring is the partition of the set of integers $\mathbb{Z}$ in which the elements are related by the congruence module n.*

Mathematically speaking, we say that a is in the class of b ($a \in C_b$) if a is related by ($\sim$) with b, where

$$a \sim b \Longleftrightarrow a \equiv b(mod\ n) \overset{def}{\Longleftrightarrow} (b - a) \in n\mathbb{Z}, \quad \text{where}$$
$$n\mathbb{Z} = \{0, n, 2n, \ldots\} \quad \text{and} \quad n \in \mathbb{Z} \quad \text{is fixed.}$$

Consequently $\mathbb{Z}_n = \{C_0, C_1, \ldots, C_{n-1}\}$.

If we translate the structure of the $\mathbb{Z}_n$ ring to the set of images of size $k \times m$ where the pixel values are less that $n - 1$ and we denote this set as $G_{k \times m}(\mathbb{Z}_n)$, we obtain the next result.

Theorem 1. *The set $G_{k \times m}(\mathbb{Z}_n)(+, \cdot)$, where $(+)$ and $(\cdot)$ are respectively the pixel-by-pixel sum and multiplication in $\mathbb{Z}_n$, has a ring structure.*

Proof. As the pixels of the image are in $\mathbb{Z}_n$, this has satisfies the ring axioms. The operation between two images was defined pixel by pixel, then is trivial that $G_{k \times m}(\mathbb{Z}_n)$ under the operations $(+, \cdot)$ of the $\mathbb{Z}_n$ ring inherits the ring structure. $\square$

In this moment, we have an important structure where we can operate with the images. In the ring $G_{k \times m}(\mathbb{Z}_n)(+, \cdot)$ the sum, subtraction or multiplication of two images always is an image.

Definition 4 (Strong Equivalence). *Two images $\mathcal{A}, \mathcal{B} \in G_{k \times m}(\mathbb{Z}_n)(+, \cdot)$ are strongly equivalents if*

$$\mathcal{A} = \mathcal{S} + \mathcal{B},$$

where $\mathcal{S}$ is a scalar image. We denote the strong equivalence between $\mathcal{A}$ and $\mathcal{B}$ as $\mathcal{A} \cong \mathcal{B}$.

Note that if $\mathcal{A} = \mathcal{S} + \mathcal{B} \Rightarrow \exists\ \overline{\mathcal{S}}\ |\ \mathcal{B} = \overline{\mathcal{S}} + \mathcal{A}$ and $\overline{\mathcal{S}} = -(\mathcal{S})$, where $-(\mathcal{S})$ is the additive inverse of $\mathcal{S}$. This is calculated using the inverse of each pixels of $\mathcal{S}$ in $\mathbb{Z}_n$.

Theorem 2. *If two images $\mathcal{A}$ and $\mathcal{B}$ are strongly equivalents then they are weakly equivalents.*

Proof. If $\mathcal{A}$ and $\mathcal{B}$ are strongly equivalents then $\mathcal{A} = \mathcal{S} + \mathcal{B}$ where $\mathcal{S}$ is a scalar image. Then $E(\mathcal{A}) = E(\mathcal{S} + \mathcal{B})$ but $\mathcal{S}$ is a scalar image and for this reason the sum $\mathcal{S} + \mathcal{B}$ only change in $\mathcal{B}$ the intensity of each pixel but don't change the number of different intensities or the frequency of each intensity in the image. Then, $E(\mathcal{S} + \mathcal{B}) = E(\mathcal{B})$. Finally we obtain that $E(\mathcal{A}) = E(\mathcal{B})$ and they are weakly equivalents. □

Note that the shown images in Figure 1 are weakly equivalents, but they are not strongly equivalents. This is an example that in general $\mathcal{A} \asymp \mathcal{B} \not\Rightarrow \mathcal{A} \cong \mathcal{B}$.

Definition 5 (Natural Entropy Distance). *Let $\mathcal{A}$ and $\mathcal{B}$ two images, then the natural entropy distance is defined by*

$$\hat{\nu}(\mathcal{A}, \mathcal{B}) = E(\mathcal{A} + (-\mathcal{B})). \tag{3}$$

Remark 1. Remember that $-(\mathcal{B})$ is the additive inverse of $\mathcal{B}$ and this is calculated using the inverse of each pixel of $\mathcal{B}$ in $\mathbb{Z}_n$.

If it are considered the images of Figure 1, the results show that

$$\hat{\nu}(Figure\ 1(a),\ Figure\ 1(b)) = 0.2514.$$

The next theorem is an important characterization of the strong equivalent among images.

Theorem 3. *Two images $\mathcal{A}$ and $\mathcal{B}$ are strongly equivalent if and only if $\hat{\nu}(\mathcal{A}, \mathcal{B}) = 0$.*

Proof. If $\mathcal{A}$ and $\mathcal{B}$ are strongly equivalents $\mathcal{A} = \mathcal{S} + \mathcal{B}$ where $\mathcal{S}$ is the scalar image. Then we have

$$\begin{aligned}
\hat{\nu}(\mathcal{A}, \mathcal{B}) &= E(\mathcal{A} + (-\mathcal{B})) &&\text{replacing}\quad \mathcal{A} = \mathcal{S} + \mathcal{B} \\
&= E(\mathcal{S} + \mathcal{B} + (-\mathcal{B})) \\
&= E(\mathcal{S}) = 0.
\end{aligned}$$

$E(\mathcal{S}) = 0$ because $\mathcal{S}$ is a scalar image. It is demonstrated that $\mathcal{A} \cong \mathcal{B} \Rightarrow \hat{\nu}(\mathcal{A}, \mathcal{B}) = 0$.
On the other hand if $\hat{\nu}(\mathcal{A}, \mathcal{B}) = 0 \Rightarrow \mathcal{A} + (-\mathcal{B}) = \mathcal{S}$, where $\mathcal{S}$ is a scalar image. Adding $\mathcal{B}$ in the last equation we obtain that $\mathcal{A} = \mathcal{S} + \mathcal{B}$, therefore $\hat{\nu}(\mathcal{A}, \mathcal{B}) = 0 \Rightarrow \mathcal{A} \cong \mathcal{B}$. □

Taking in consideration the good properties that, in general, the natural entropy distance has (see Definition 5), one sees logical to take the condition (3) as the new stopping criterion of the iterative mean shift algorithm. Explicitly, the new stopping criterion is

$$E(\mathcal{A}_k + (-\mathcal{A}_{k-1})) \leq \epsilon, \tag{4}$$

where ϵ and k are respectively the threshold to stop the iterations and the number of iterations.

3   Experiments and Results

Image segmentation, that is, classification of the image gray-level values into homogeneous areas is recognized to be one of the most important step in any image analysis system. Homogeneity, in general, is defined as similarity among the pixel values, where a piecewise constant model is enforced over the image [3].

The principal goal of this section is to evaluate the new stopping criterion in the iterative mean shift algorithm and to prove that, in general, with this new stopping criterion the algorithm have better stability. For this reason, comparisons with other segmentation approaches will not be carried out. In [5] were compared the obtained results with the mean shift iterative algorithm through the old stopping criterion with other segmentation methods. We used three different images for the experiments. The first image (" Bird") have low frequency, the second ("Baboon") have high frequency and in the image "Montage" has mixture low and high frequencies.

All segmentation experiments were carried out by using a uniform kernel [4, 6]. In order to be effective the comparison between the old and the new stopping criterion, we use the same value of hr and hs in the iterative mean shift algorithm ($hr = 12$, $hs = 15$). The value of hs is related to the spatial resolution of the analysis, while the value hr defines the range resolution. In the case of the new stopping criterion, we use the stopping threshold $\epsilon = 0.9$ and when the old stopping criterion was used, we selected $\epsilon = 0.0175$, this values are selected based to the segmentation level that we want obtain in each case.

Figure 2 shows the segmentation of the three images. Observe that, in all cases, the iterative mean shift algorithm had better result when was used the new stopping criterion.

When one compares Figures 2(b) and 2(c), in the part corresponding to the face or breast of the bird a more homogeneous area, with the new stopping criterion (see arrows in Figure 2(c)), it was obtained. Observe that, with the old stopping criterion the segmentation gives regions where different gray levels are originated. However, these regions really should have only one gray level. For example, Figure 2(e) and 2(f) show that the segmentation is more homogeneous when the new stopping criterion was used (see the arrows). In the case of the "Montage" image one can see that, in Figure 2(i) exists many regions that contains different gray levels when these regions really should have one gray level (see for example the face of Lenna, the circles and the breast of the bird). These good results are obtained because the defined new stopping criterion through the natural distance between images in expression (4) offers greater stability to the mean shift iterative algorithm.

Figure 3 shows the profile of the obtained segmented images by using both stopping criteria[1]. The plates that appear in Figure 3(b) and 3(d) are indicative of equal intensity levels. In both graphics the abrupt falls of an intensity to other represent the different regions in the segmented image. Note that, in Figure 3(b) exists, in the same region of the segmentation, least variation of the pixel

---

[1] We show only the profile of one image for reasons of space, but the results in the other images were similar.

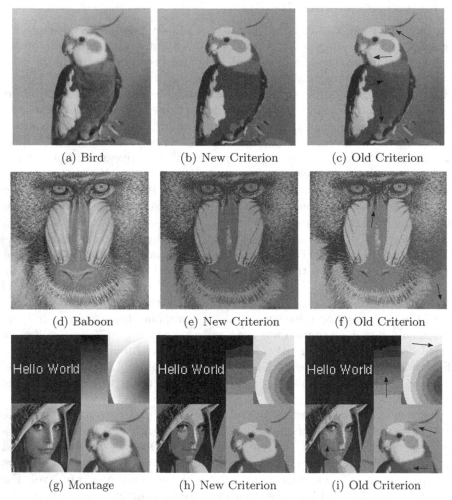

Fig. 2. Segmentation of the experimental images. In the first column are show the original images; in the second, the segmentation using the new stopping criterion and in the third column are the segmented images using the old stopping criterion.

intensities with regard to Figure 3(d). This illustrates that, in this case the segmentation was better when the new stopping criterion was used.

Figure 4 shows the performance of the two stopping criterion in the experimental images. In the "x" axis appears the iterations of the mean shift algorithm and in the "y" axis is shown the obtained values by the stopping criterion in each iteration of the algorithm.

The graphics of iterations of the new stopping criterion (Figure 4(a), 4(b), 4(c)) show a smooth behavior; that is, the stopping criterion has a stable performance through the iterative mean shift algorithm. The new stopping criterion

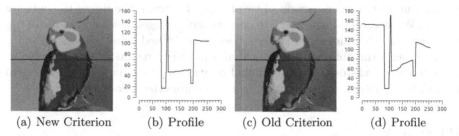

| (a) New Criterion | (b) Profile | (c) Old Criterion | (d) Profile |

Fig. 3. An intensity profile through of a segmented image. Profile is indicated by a line. (a) and (c) are the segmented images and (b) and (d) are the profile of (a) and (c) respectively.

not only has good theoretical properties, but also, in the practice, has very good behavior.

On the other hand, if we analyze the old stopping criterion in the experimental images (Figure 4(d), 4(e), 4(f)), we can see that the performance in the mean shift algorithm is unstable. In general, we have this type of situation when the stopping criterion defined in (2) is used. This can originate bad segmented images.

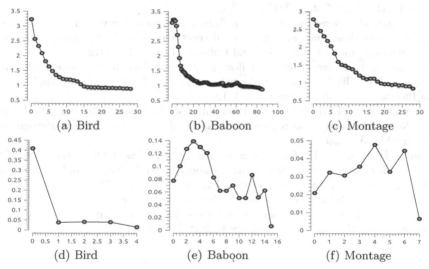

Fig. 4. Stopping criterion. In the first row appears the performance of the new stopping criterion and in the second, it is shown the old stopping criterion in correspondence with the experimental images.

4   Conclusions

In this work, a new stopping criterion, for the iterative mean shift algorithm, based on the ring theory was proposed. The new stopping criterion establishes a new measure for the comparison of two images based on the use of the entropy concept. We introduced a new way to operate with images based on the use of the ring structure. The rings in the images space were defined using the concept of $\mathbb{Z}_n$ rings. Through the obtained theoretical and practical results, it was possible to prove that the new stopping criterion had very good performance in the iterative mean shift algorithm, and in general, is more stable that the old criterion [4–7].

References

1. Shannon, C.: A Mathematical Theory of Communication. Bell System Technology Journal 27, 370–423, 623–656 (1948)
2. Comaniciu, D.I.: Nonparametric Robust Method for Computer Vision. Thesis New Brunswick, Rutgers, The State University of New Jersey (2000)
3. Comaniciu, D., Meer, P.: Mean Shift: A Robust Approach toward Feature Space Analysis. IEEE Transactions on Pattern Analysis and Machine Intelligence 24(5), 1–18 (2002)
4. Rodriguez, R., Torres, E., Sossa, J.H.: Image Segmentation based on an Iterative Computation of the Mean Shift Filtering for different values of window sizes. International Journal of Imaging and Robotics 6(A11) 1–19 (2011)
5. Rodriguez, R., Suarez, A.G., Sossa, J.H.: A Segmentation Algorithm based on an Iterative Computation of the Mean Shift Filtering. Journal Intelligent & Robotic System 63(3-4), 447–463 (2011)
6. Rodriguez, R., Torres, E., Sossa, J.H.: Image Segmentation via an Iterative Algorithm of the Mean Shift Filtering for Different Values of the Stopping Threshold. International Journal of Imaging and Robotics 7(6), 1–19 (2012)
7. Rodriguez, R.: Binarization of medical images based on the recursive application of mean shift filtering: Another algorithm. Journal of Advanced and Applications in Bioinformatics and Chemistry I, 1–12 (2008)
8. Dominguez, D., Rodriguez, R.: Convergence of the Mean Shift using the Linfinity Norm in Image Segmentation. International Journal of Pattern Recognition Research 1, 3–4 (2011)
9. Zhang, H., Fritts, J.E., Goldma, S.A.: An Entropy-based Objective Evaluation Method for Image Segmentation, Storage and Retrieval Methods and Applications for Multimedia. In: Proceeding of the SPIE, vol. 5307, pp. 38–49 (2003)
10. Suyash, P., Whitake, R.: Higher-Order Image Statistics for Unsupervised, Information-Theoretic, Adaptive, Image Filtering. IEEE Transactions on Pattern Analysis and Machine Intelligence 28(3), 364–376 (2006)

Evolutionary Optimisation of JPEG2000 Part 2 Wavelet Packet Structures for Polar Iris Image Compression

Jutta Hämmerle-Uhl, Michael Karnutsch, and Andreas Uhl

Multimedia Signal Processing and Security Lab
Department of Computer Sciences, University of Salzburg, Austria
uhl@cosy.sbg.ac.at

Abstract. The impact of using evolutionary optimised wavelet subband stuctures as allowed in JPEG2000 Part 2 in polar iris image compression is investigated. The recognition performance of two different feature extraction schemes applied to correspondingly compressed images is compared to the usage of the dyadic decomposition structure of JPEG2000 Part 1 in the compression stage. Recognition performance is significantly improved, provided that the image set used in evolutionary optimisation and actual application is identical. Generalisation to different settings (individuals, sample acquisition conditions, feature extraction techniques) is found to be low.

1 Introduction

The International Organization for Standardization (ISO) specifies iris biometric data to be recorded and stored in (raw) image form (ISO/IEC FDIS 19794-6), rather than in extracted templates (e.g. iris-codes). On the one hand, such deployments benefit from future improvements (e.g. in feature extraction stage) which can be easily incorporated, without re-enrollment of registered users. On the other hand, since biometric templates may depend on patent-registered algorithms, databases of raw images enable more interoperability and vendor neutrality [1, 2]. These facts motivate detailed investigations and optimisations of image compression on iris biometrics in order to provide an efficient storage and rapid transmission of biometric records. Furthermore, the application of low- powered mobile sensors for image acquisition, e.g. mobile phones, raises the need for reducing the amount of transmitted data. There are two options in iris recognition: the acquired sample data can be compressed and transfered as it has been obtained by the sensor (termed "rectilinear images"), or the iris texture strip as obtained from prior segmentation and log-polar mapping (termed "polar iris image") may be compressed and transfered. The second option obviously trades off the higher computational cost at the sensor (segmentation + compression) for a minimisation of the transfered data amount.

The certainly most relevant standard for compressing image data relevant in biometric systems is the ISO/IEC 19794 standard on Biometric Data Interchange Formats where only JPEG2000 is included for lossy compression. In literature on compressing iris imagery, rectilinear [1, 2, 3] as well as polar [2, 4] iris sample data has been considered. With respect to employed compression technology, we find JPEG [1, 2] JPEG2000 [1, 2, 3, 4], JPEG XR, and other general purpose compression techniques [2] being investigated.

J. Ruiz-Shulcloper and G. Sanniti di Baja (Eds.): CIARP 2013, Part I, LNCS 8258, pp. 391–398, 2013.

In biometrics, wavelet packet based image compression schemes have been applied before in the area of fingerprint recognition (e.g. [5, 6]) due to the high frequency nature of the ridge and valley pattern in fingerprint imagery. Eventually, similar to fingerprint images, image features important for iris template matching might reside in high or mid frequency parts of the iris texture, which could be represented better by adapted wavelet packet structures.

In this work, we employ wavelet packet decomposition structures for the compression of polar iris images using JPEG2000 Part 2 technology. Recent work [7] showed that common subband structure selection selection strategies including rate-distortion optimising ones are not very successful as compared to the dyadic decomposition scheme (defined in the Part 1 of the JPEG2000 standard suite). Therefore, in this work, evolutionary optimisation is applied to select subband structures where recognition performance is used as optimisation criterion (while much simpler criteria are used in [7]). In Section 2, we review the use of wavelet packets in JPEG2000 and discuss various subband structure selection strategies inlcuding the evolutionary approach used in this paper. Section 3 provides experimental results for two different iris recognition schemes while Section 4 concludes the paper.

2   Wavelet Packet Selection and JPEG2000

The use of adapted wavelet packet bases for image compression purposes has been subject to investigation since the introduction of the first adaptation technique called "best basis algorithm". Due to the high number of wavelet packet bases (*wpb*) (i.e., for a decomposition depth d, the number is $Q_d = Q_{d-1}^4 + 1$ with $Q_0 = 1$), exhaustive search is infeasible which has lead to the development of various *wpb* selection strategies. The employment of rate-distortion optimization criteria for *wpb* subband structure selection has been first demonstrated for classical wavelet image coding schemes, but has been extended later to zero-tree based compression algorithms [8] and to JPEG2000 in recent work [9]. While JPEG2000 Part 1 is restricted to the pyramidal wavelet transform (fixed dyadic decomposition), JPEG2000 Part 2 facilitates the use of more general wavelet packet subband structures [10] (besides the specification of user-defined wavelet filters and other advanced coding options).

All the so far described *wpb* selection schemes have failed to significantly improve iris recognition performance as compared to dyadic decomposition [7]. Therefore, we want to directly optimise recognition performance instead of optimising certain cost functions usually targeted towards rate/distortion performance. However, common *wpb* selection schemes rely on the independent evaluation of cost functions on single *wpb* subbands, which is not possible when recognition performance of a certain *wpb* has to be assessed. In earlier work [11], we have used genetic algorithms to assess the degree of optimality and to further optimize *wpb* subband structues. This approach is adopted for the present study where the fitness function of the evolutionary approach rating a single *wpb* is set to be a parameter describing recognition performance after compressing the data to JPEG2000 format using the corresponding *wpb*, i.e. the equal error rate (EER).

Genetic algorithms are random search procedures guided by evolutionary principles suited for vast search spaces, where parameter optimisation problems need to be solved.

A key issue to apply the generic approach to the *wpb* subband structure selection task is to find a suitable representation of the *wpb* and to adapt genetic operators to the *wpb* tree structures [11]. The *wpb* can also be considered as a quadtree which needs to be transformed into a "flat" representation: in adopting principles of the heap sort algorithm, a string b of finite length L over a binary alphabet $\{0, 1\}$ is used. With a particular bit k set to 1, the corresponding subband is decomposed, otherwise the index k is set to 0 and the decomposition stops in this part of the tree. Determining the indices for the corresponding subbands is accomplished by $k'_m = 4 * k + m, 1 \leq m \leq 4$. After having chosen two particular individuals for being candidates for the next generation, a kind of genetical material interchange is performed. Classical one- or two-point crossover operators cannot be applied since in general, the resulting bitstrings do not correspond to valid *wpb*. Therefore, sub-tree based crossover has been introduced [11] which exchanges sub-trees and maintains a valid tree structure. Other genetic operators like mutation and selection can be applied in a standard manner. For selection, we apply *roulette wheel selection* (where the probability of an individual i for being chosen to be a candicate for the next generation is $p_i = f_i / \sum_{j=1}^{N} f_j$; f_i is the fitness value of the individual i and is N the total number of individuals per generation) as well as *tournament selection* (where the best m out of k randomly chosen individuals are selected for the next generation).

3 Experiments

3.1 Experimental Settings

As sample data, we use the public CASIA V3 Interval database consisting of 2639 images from 391 eye classes with 320×280 pixels and eight-bit grey value. These are extracted into polar iris images with 512×64 pixels, which act as the base for the following compression and subsequent iris recognition algorithms. For the evolutionary optimisation, the first 59 classes (555 images) were used, while the remaining data is used for intra-database verification. For cross-database verification, the first 555 images (i.e. 111 classes) of the IITD Iris Database version 1.0 are used, polar iris images are extracted into the same size.

Experimental results with respect to JPEG2000 Part 1 & 2 compression have been generated using a custom implementation of *wpb* selection strategies based on the JJ2000 reference implementation [9]. Bitrates 0.2bpp, 0.4bpp, 0.8bpp and 1.5bpp are considered. Both templates involved in biometric matching, the one generated from the sample data and the one from the database, are derived from images compressed to the same bitrate.

It is crucial to assess the effects of compressing iris samples using different iris recognition schemes since it can be expected that different feature extraction strategies will react differently when being confronted with compression artefacts and reduced image quality in general. We use custom implementations of two feature extraction techniques (for a description of our implementation of preprocessing, feature extraction, and matching see [2]). Both implementations are available in USIT (University of Salzburg Iris-Toolkit at http://wavelab.at. The first scheme has been developed by Ko *et al.* [12] and extracts spatial domain features, while the second approach has been designed by Monro *et al.* [13] and relies on DCT-derived features.

Evolutionary optimisation is started with 50 initial individuals (*wpb*) in the first generation which are derived from results using techniques in [7]. After determining the fitness values (difference to the EER, which the dyadic decomposition at depth three achieves), either roulette wheel selection or tournament selection (with $k = 5$ and $m = 2$) is applied. Subsequently, tree crossover is repeatedly applied to two selected *wpb* in order to generate two new individuals for the next generation and finally, mutation is applied to each bit in the *wpb* representation of the new generation with a probability of 0.01. This procedure is repeated over 50 generations.

In case of cross-bitrate optimisation (i.e. searching for *wpb* superior to the dyadic case for more then just a single bitrate), the *wpb* fitness is the number of bitrates, at which the particular *wpb* outperforms the dyadic case, and as a second value either the mean or the standard deviation of the relative EER for the bitrates (0.2bpp, 0.4bpp, 0.8bpp, 1.5bpp) is considered. In this case, only roulette wheel selection is applied.

3.2 Experimental Results

Figs. 1 and 2 are meant for illustrating the evolutionary process. On the x-axis, the 50 generations are shown whereas on the y-axis the fitness values are given (a point in the plot corresponds to the value of a single individual – *wpb*). Below the two graphs (left: roulette wheel selection, right: tournament selection) three *wpb* are shown: the one corresponding to the "best" *wpb* in the initial generation in the middle, and the final "winning" individuals of the last respective generations left and right to it.

When considering the EER of the two recognition schemes under JPEG2000 Part 1 compression for the four bitrates 0.2bpp, 0.4bpp, 0.8bpp, and 1.5bpp (i.e. ($EER(Ko) =$

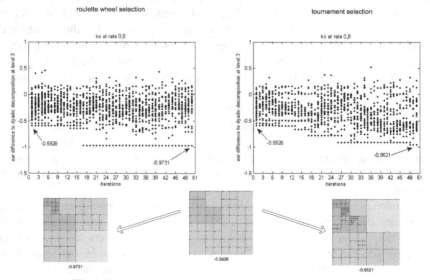

Fig. 1. Evolvement of *wpb* for Ko *et al.* recognition @ 0.8 bpp

$9.28, 9.51, 9.40, 9.18, EER(Monro) = 2.24, 1.40, 1.35, 1.36$), the improvements of 0.97 (Ko @ 0.8bpp, roulette wheel selection) and 0.77 (Monro @ 0.2bpp, roulette wheel selection) can be rated clearly significant.

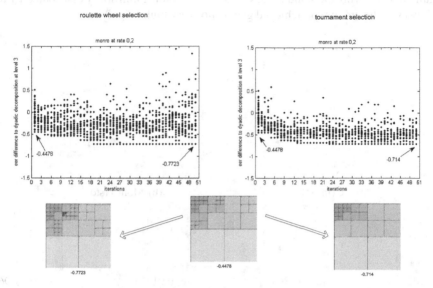

Fig. 2. Evolvement of *wpb* for Monro *et al.* @ 0.2 bpp

Table 1 provides the overall view. For each bitrate considered, JPEG2000 Part 2 compression is able to significantly outperform the dyadic JPEG2000 Part 1 scheme. While for the Ko *et al.* recognition algorithm improvements are distributed rather uniformly over different bitrates, for Monro *et al.* the case 0.2bpp shows the highest optimisation potential (EER is reduced from 2.24 to 1.47 !). In all but a single case, roulette wheele selection exhibits superior results to tournament selection.

Table 1. Results of the individual bitrate optimizations (improvements in terms of EER)

Ko *et al.*	0.2 *bpp*	0.4 *bpp*	0.8 *bpp*	1.5 *bpp*
Roulette wheel selection	-0.5401	-0.8154	-0.9731	-0.6233
Tournament selection	-0.4817	-0.7940	-0.9521	-0.544

Monro *et al.*	0.2 *bpp*	0.4 *bpp*	0.8 *bpp*	1.5 *bpp*
Roulette wheel selection	-0.7723	-0.2531	-0.2621	-0.1000
Tournament selection	-0.7140	-0.1564	-0.2368	-0.1437

Having seen the potential of optimisation to a single target bitrate, the question arises natually if there exist *wpb* which outperform the dyadic decomposition for several bitrates (we stick to the four bitrates defined before) – "cross-bitrate optimisation". The answer is "yes", as illustrated in Fig. 3. Figs. 3.a - 3.b show the gain in EER (y-axis) of the top-six *wpb* individuals for the four target bitrates (x-axis). We clearly see that we succeed with our optimisation, but the improvements are less distinct as compared to the optimisation for a single bitrate. For Ko *et al.* recognition, optimisation with respect to the mean EER gain leads to several *wpb* which improve over the dyadic case for all bitrates considered (see Fig. 3.a). For the Monro *et al.* scheme (Fig. 3.b), the fitness function involving the standard deviation leads to some uniformly distributed EER gain, however, the amount of achieved gain is not very high (Fig. 3.b).

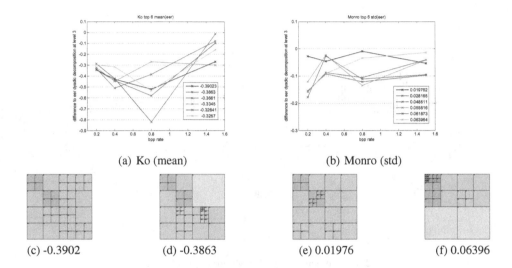

(a) Ko (mean)   (b) Monro (std)

(c) -0.3902   (d) -0.3863   (e) 0.01976   (f) 0.06396

Fig. 3. Cross-bitrate optimisation results

Fig. 3.c – Fig. 3.f illustrate some of the evolved *wpb*, the value in the corresponding caption is the cost function value (mean or standard deviation of EER gain). The first two *wpb* correspond to Fig. 3.a – while they look fairly different overall, at least the LL-band decompsition (top left quater) is identical (which is the case for all but one of those top-six results). The last two *wpb* correspond to Fig. 3.b – they do not exhibit structural similarity among each other nor to the *wpb* considered before.

The aim of the following investigations is to verify if the behaviour of the optimised *wpb* generalise to different scenarios. First we look into intra-database verification, i.e., we apply the *wpb* optimised on the first part of the CASIA V3 Interval dataset for a specific target bitrate to the remaining part of the database using the same bitrate. Consequently, no evolutionary optimisation is involved in the following experiments, the results of which are shown in Table 2.

Results clearly indicate that the results do not at all generalise. While for some specific settings we still observe significant EER improvements as compared to the JPEG2000 Part 1 dyadic scheme (e.g. Ko *et al.* with roulette wheel selection @ 0.4bpp or Monro *et al.* with tournament selection @ 0.2bpp), for most scenarios the EER gain is not significant, in some cases EER even clearly degenerates (e.g. Monro *et al.* with roulette wheel selection @ 0.2bpp).

Table 3 shows the results of the cross-database verification, where the *wpb* optimised on a part of the CASIA V3 Interval database are applied to a part of the IITD database. As expected (when considering the previous results), results do not generalise as well.

Table 2. Results of intra-database verification (individual bitrate optimizations, improvements in terms of EER)

Ko *et al.*	0.2 *bpp*	0.4 *bpp*	0.8 *bpp*	1.5 *bpp*
Roulette wheel selection	-0.0874	-0.2529	-0.0143	-0.1541
Tournament selection	-0.2282	-0.1012	0.0264	-0.0075

Monro *et al.*	0.2 *bpp*	0.4 *bpp*	0.8 *bpp*	1.5 *bpp*
Roulette wheel selection	0.3974	0.0158	-0.0711	-0.0105
Tournament selection	-0.1514	-0.0867	-0.1074	-0.0041

Interestingly, at least for roulette wheel selection a sight gain is observed for all bitrates and both recognition algorithms but given the amount of improvement (especiall for the Monro *et al.* scheme) this seems to be a random phenonemon only.

Table 3. Results of cross-database verification (individual bitrate optimizations, improvements in terms of EER)

Ko *et al.* , IITD	0.2 *bpp*	0.4 *bpp*	0.8 *bpp*	1.5 *bpp*
Roulette wheel selection	-0.2063	-0.1103	-0.3951	-0.1541
Tournament selection	-0.3471	0.0414	-0.3543	-0.0075

Monro *et al.* , IITD	0.2 *bpp*	0.4 *bpp*	0.8 *bpp*	1.5 *bpp*
Roulette wheel selection	-0.3494	-0.0888	-0.0451	-0.1461
Tournament selection	-0.1806	0.1846	0.0145	0.0697

Finally, we apply the *wpb* optimised for one iris recognition scheme using the other scheme. The dataset of the intra-database verification is used, while optimisation has been done on the first part of the CASIA V3 Interval dataset as before. Results are displayed in Table 4 which show that in about half the cases, EER is degenerated.

Table 4. Results of cross-algorithm verification (individual bitrate optimizations, improvements in terms of EER)

Ko verifies Monro	0.2 *bpp*	0.4 *bpp*	0.8 *bpp*	1.5 *bpp*
Roulette wheel selection	0.1539	-0.1360	0.3710	0.0123
Tournament selection	0.1807	-0.7029	-0.1833	0.0416

Monro verifies Ko	0.2 *bpp*	0.4 *bpp*	0.8 *bpp*	1.5 *bpp*
Roulette wheel selection	0.2761	0.1444	-0.0406	0.0623
Tournament selection	-0.0169	0.1501	-0.071	-0.0050

4   Conclusion

The obtained results show that evolutionary optimisation of wavelet packet subband structures in JPEG2000 with respect to a fixed target bitrate is possible and leads to a significant gain in terms of EER as compared to the dyadic JPEG2000 Part 1 decomposition. Also optimisation for a set of bitrates is possible, however, the gain in EER is clearly lower as compared to the individual bitrate optimisation strategy. Our results also show that the computed wavelet packet subband stuctures are highly tuned to the dataset used in the optimisation – results do neither generalise to a different sample database (different capturing conditions) nor to a different subset of the database used for optimisation (different individuals). Furthermore, results are highly specific for the recognition algorithm they have been optimized for and do not at all carry over to a different feature extraction and matching scheme. Thus, the proposed approach can be used for a closed application with a fixed user set – a verification scenario as it is expected at border control with multi-national passports obviously cannot be supported. For such a scenario with dynamically varying user group it is best to stick to the fixed pyramidal decomposition of JPEG2000.

References

[1] Daugman, J., Downing, C.: Effect of severe image compression on iris recognition performance. IEEE Transactions on Information Forensics and Security 3(1), 52–61 (2008)

[2] Rathgeb, C., Uhl, A., Wild, P.: Iris Recognition: From Segmentation to Template Security. Advances in Information Security, vol. 59. Springer (2013)

[3] Ives, R.W., Broussard, R.P., Kennell, L.R., Soldan, D.L.: Effects of image compression on iris recognition system performance. Journal of Electronic Imaging 17, 011015 (2008), doi:10.1117/1.2891313

[4] Rakshit, S., Monro, D.: An evaluation of image sampling and compression for human iris recognition. IEEE Transactions on Information Forensics and Security 2(3), 605–612 (2007)

[5] Kasaei, S., Deriche, M., Boashash, B.: A novel fingerprint image compression technique using wavelet packets and pyramid lattice vector quantization. IEEE Transactions on Image Processing 12(11), 1365–1378 (2002)

[6] Bradley, J.N., Brislawn, C.M., Hopper, T.: The FBI wavelet/scalar quantization standard for gray-scale fingerprint image compression. In: SPIE Proceedings, Visual Information Processing II, Orlando, FL, USA, vol. 1961, pp. 293–304 (April 1993)

[7] Hämmerle-Uhl, J., Karnutsch, M., Uhl, A.: Recognition impact of JPEG2000 part 2 wavelet packet subband structures in polar iris image compression. In: Zovko-Cihlar, B., Rupp, M., Mecklenbräuker, C. (eds.) Proceedings of the 19th International Conference on Systems, Signals and Image Processing (IWSSIP 2012), pp. 13–16 (2012)

[8] Rajpoot, N.M., Wilson, R.G., Meyer, F.G., Coifman, R.R.: Adaptive wavelet packet basis selection for zerotree image coding. IEEE Transactions on Image Processing 12(12), 1460–1472 (2003)

[9] Stütz, T., Uhl, A.: Efficient and rate-distortion optimal wavelet packet basis selection in JPEG2000. IEEE Transactions on Multimedia 14(2), 264–277 (2012)

[10] Taubman, D., Marcellin, M.: JPEG2000 — Image Compression Fundamentals, Standards and Practice. Kluwer Academic Publishers (2002)

[11] Schell, T., Uhl, A.: Optimization and assessment of wavelet packet decompositions with evolutionary computation. EURASIP Journal on Applied Signal Processing 2003(8), 806–813 (2003)

[12] Ko, J.G., Gil, Y.H., Yoo, J.H., Chung, K.I.: A novel and efficient feature extraction method for iris recognition. ETRI Journal 29(3), 399–401 (2007)

[13] Monro, D., Rakshit, S., Zhang, D.: DCT-based iris recognition. IEEE Transactions on Pattern Analysis and Machine Intelligence 29(4), 586–595 (2007)

Improving Image Segmentation for Boosting Image Annotation with Irregular Pyramids

Annette Morales-González[1], Edel García-Reyes[1], and Luis Enrique Sucar[2]

[1] Advanced Technologies Application Center. 7a # 21812 b/ 218 and 222,
Rpto. Siboney, Playa, P.C. 12200, La Habana, Cuba
{amorales,egarcia}@cenatav.co.cu
[2] Instituto Nacional de Astrofísica, Óptica y Electrónica, Puebla, Mexico
esucar@ccc.inaoep.mx

Abstract. Image Segmentation and Automatic Image Annotation are two research fields usually addressed independently. Treating these problems simultaneously and taking advantage of each other's information may improve their individual results. In this work our ultimate goal is image annotation, which we perform using the hierarchical structure of irregular pyramids. We propose a new criterion to create new segmentation levels in the pyramid using low-level cues and semantic information coming from the annotation step. Later, we use the improved segmentation to obtain better annotation results in an iterative way across the hierarchy. We perform experiments in a subset of the Corel dataset, showing the relevance of combining both processes to improve the results of the final annotation.

Keywords: image annotation, image segmentation, irregular pyramids.

1 Introduction

Automatic image segmentation and annotation are two prominent fields in Computer Vision, that are usually addressed individually, disregarding the benefits they can provide to each other. Image segmentation based only on low-level cues (without prior knowledge of the object being segmented) is insufficient to delineate objects due to the semantic gap. Image segmentation presupposes an abstraction process of low-level features and when it is not guided by a semantic interpretation of the segments, the resulting partition is dependant on the defined mathematical equivalence relation. Also, Automatic Image Annotation (AIA) will not provide good results if the underlying segmentation is not correct (i.e. instances of different classes are merged together in a region, boundaries of objects are lost).

In the literature, some works have addressed these two problems together. In [1] the author proposes an object recognition scheme that involves a hierarchy (tree) of class-specific object parts (fragments). He combines a recognition process with a top-down segmentation, where the latter process takes advantage of the classification information, but not the other way around. In [2] they propose

J. Ruiz-Shulcloper and G. Sanniti di Baja (Eds.): CIARP 2013, Part I, LNCS 8258, pp. 399–406, 2013.
© Springer-Verlag Berlin Heidelberg 2013

to use a hierarchy of segmentations to guide a selective search for improving object classification results, but the segmentation is based only on low level cues. The same happens in [3] and [4], where a hierarchy of segmentations is used for object detection and image annotation respectively, but semantic information is not used in the segmentation process. In [5] they combine four segmentation algorithms to obtain an enhanced partition, and they refine classification in this partition by using classification information from the initial partitions. Yet, there is no contribution of the semantic information to improve the segmentation. In [6] they perform detection and segmentation simultaneously, allowing cross information between these processes, but they need ground truth segmentations at training stage and the proposal is intended for detecting/segmenting specific objects in the images.

In this work we use an idea similar to the one presented in [4] to perform AIA using irregular pyramids [7], but we propose an iterative process where the segmentation hierarchy is rebuilt and improved using the classification information obtained from the annotation process in each level of the pyramid. Our ultimate goal is to improve the results of image annotation. We show in the experiments performed on the CorelA dataset how much the synergy between segmentation and annotation can contribute to this task, improving almost in 5% the reported accuracy in this collection. Our contributions are (1) the introduction of a new criterion to create new levels in the irregular pyramid, combining semantic and low-level information and (2) the proposal of an iterative process where segmentation is improved using the annotation results of the previous level, and each new segmentation level is annotated taking the advantages of a better partition.

2 Introduction to Irregular Pyramids

A Region Adjacency Graph (RAG) that represents an image is a graph $G = (V, E)$, whose vertices (V) represent regions, and the edges (E) represent adjacency relations between them. An irregular pyramid [7] is composed by a set of successively reduced RAGs, (being the base level the high resolution input image). When we build an irregular pyramid [8] from an image, each level represents a partition of the pixel set into cells, i.e. connected subsets of pixels. On the base level (level 0) of the pyramid, the cells represent single pixels and the neighborhood of the cells is defined by the 4-connectivity of pixels. A cell on level k (parent) is a union of neighboring cells on level $k - 1$ (children). Each graph is built from the graph below by selecting a set of surviving vertices and mapping each non surviving vertex to a surviving one. Each surviving vertex represents all the non surviving vertices mapped to it and becomes their father [7]. At any level these parent-child relations may be iterated down to the base level and the set of descendants of one vertex in the base level is named its receptive field (RF). Within the irregular pyramid framework the reduction process is performed by a set of edge contractions. The edge contraction collapses two adjacent vertices into one vertex and removes the edge. This set is called a Contraction Kernel (CK) [7][8]. The contraction of the graph reduces the number of vertices while maintaining the connections to other vertices.

3   Proposed Approach

3.1   Automatic Image Annotation Using Hierarchical Random Fields

In order to annotate regions in an image, we use the method proposed by [4]. In this work they use a base classifier to classify image regions based only on low-level features of these regions. After this first classification step, a Markov Random Field (MRF) is constructed for every level of the irregular pyramid. In addition to using the spatial Markovian neighborhood (defined by all the vertices adjacent to one vertex), they proposed to include a hierarchical Markovian neighborhood (composed by the father, in level $k+1$ of the pyramid, and children, in level $k-1$ of a vertex). This hierarchical MRF structure is used to improve the initial annotation by using contextual information from the adjacent regions and hierarchical information from regions in adjacent levels.

First, this annotation process is performed bottom-up. All the MRFs are solved starting from the lowest level using only information from the children regions in level $k-1$. After the top level is reached, the annotation is reconsidered again, and all the MRFs are computed once more in a top-down process, now with information from father and children regions in adjacent levels.

3.2   Improving Segmentation Based on Annotation Results

The approach presented in [4] is limited in terms of annotation accuracy because of the underlying image segmentation. In the irregular pyramid implementation employed in [4], the only criterion for deciding whether two regions must be joined for the next level is based on the similarity between the average color of each region. The average color of the regions is a feature that becomes less and less discriminative as regions grow bigger. We believe that the combination of low-level cues and semantic information resulting from the annotation step can improve the image segmentation and ultimately, the final annotation results.

For this task we are proposing to modify the criterion employed to create the Contraction Kernels (CK) by using the classification information at each level and the edge information extracted from each image. We propose to compute a value $V_{contract}$ that will label every edge at every level of the pyramid and will combine a semantic measure V_S and a low-level measure V_B.

For computing the semantic value $V_S(i,j)$ between vertices v_i and v_j, we use the information of the classes obtained and the prior probability given by the base classifier. For each vertex v_i, after the classification step (and correction using the MRF) we have the following information:

- A class C_i^{MRF} assigned to vertex v_i after the MRF was solved.
- The prior probability that the base classifier obtained for this class in this vertex $P(C_i^{MRF})$.
- A list of all the n classes $[C_{i,1}^{BC}, C_{i,2}^{BC}, ..., C_{i,n}^{BC}]$, ordered by the prior probability of each class for representing vertex v_i, obtained with the base classifier

(BC). In this way, we can notice that class $C_{i,1}^{BC}$ was the one assigned finally to vertex v_i by the BC.

– A list of all the prior probabilities $[P(C_{i,1}^{BC}), P(C_{i,2}^{BC}), \dots, P(C_{i,n}^{BC})]$ obtained with the BC to v_i for each class.

The first thing to do is to check whether the classes annotated for v_i and v_j are the same. If this is the case, the value of $V_S(i,j)$ is the sum of the probabilities given by the base classifier for these classes. If the classes are different, there is a chance that the base classifier made a misclassification, therefore, we check the confidence of the class assigned to these vertices. The confidence of the classification is a logical value (true/false) given by Equation 1.

$$Confidence(C_i^{MRF}) = [(P(C_{i,1}^{BC}) - P(C_{i,2}^{BC})) > \delta] \tag{1}$$

We consider that there is confidence in the classification of vertex v_i with class C_i^{MRF} if the difference between the two highest probabilities assigned by the base classifier for this vertex, is bigger than a threshold δ. If there is confidence in the classification of both vertices, the value of $V_S(i,j)$ will be -1, indicating that semantically, these two vertices should not be joined. But if the classification for one of the vertices has no confidence, we check whether the first or second class assigned to it with higher probabilities are the same of the other vertex class, and if this happens, we sum up the probabilities for those classes to obtain $V_S(i,j)$ (depicted in Equation 2 with the name of $MisclassValue(i,j)$).

$$MisclassValue(i,j) = \begin{cases} P(C_i^{MRF}) + P(C_{j,1}^{BC}) & \text{if } C_i^{MRF} = C_{j,1}^{BC} \\ P(C_i^{MRF}) + P(C_{j,2}^{BC}) & \text{if } C_i^{MRF} = C_{j,2}^{BC} \\ -1 & \text{otherwise} \end{cases} \tag{2}$$

The process for computing $V_S(i,j)$ can be summarized in Equation 3:

$$V_S(i,j) = \begin{cases} P(C_i^{MRF}) + P(C_j^{MRF}) & \text{if } C_i^{MRF} = C_j^{MRF} \\ MisclassValue(i,j) & \text{if } Confidence(C_i^{MRF}) = 0 \\ MisclassValue(j,i) & \text{if } Confidence(C_j^{MRF}) = 0 \\ -1 & \text{otherwise} \end{cases} \tag{3}$$

Based on the above explanation, it can be noticed that $V_S(i,j)$ intuitively represents the likelihood for two adjacent regions of being of the same class, and therefore, the likelihood for joining them given this information.

On the other hand, the value $V_B(i,j)$ represents intuitively the likelihood of joining vertices v_i and v_j taking into account the boundary information when they are two separate regions and when they are combined into a single region. For this, we use the Canny edge detector [9] to find the edges for each image, and we use the resulting edge mask to evaluate the convenience of joining two adjacent regions. We will call the set of edge pixels in the Canny mask B_{Canny}. The set of edge pixels corresponding to the boundary of the receptive field (RF) of vertex v_i is B_i and the set of edge pixels resulting from joining the RFs of v_i and v_j is $B_{i\cup j}$. We compute in the first place how many pixels of $B_{i\cup j}$ match the edge pixels in B_{Canny} (Equation 4), and then we find the intersection between the edge pixels in B_{Canny} and the union of B_i and B_j (Equation 5).

$$B_1(i,j) = |B_{i\cup j} \cap B_{Canny}| \quad (4) \qquad B_2(i,j) = |(B_i \cup B_j) \cap B_{Canny}| \quad (5)$$

We propose to compute $V_B(i,j)$ as shown in Equation 6. In this case, we can notice that if $B_2(i,j) > B_1(i,j)$, there is a boundary between the regions of v_i and v_j that is present in the Canny edge mask, and that would be removed if these two regions were joined. This is not desirable, since this is a boundary that we would like to preserve, therefore in this case the value of $V_B(i,j)$ is -1, invalidating the contraction of these two vertices. Otherwise, the value of $V_B(i,j)$ is the relation between $B_{i\cup j}$ and the intersection of $B_{i\cup j}$ with B_{Canny}, i.e, intuitively how many edge pixels of the joint regions representing v_i and v_j match the Canny mask, with respect to the total edge pixels of the union. If all the edge pixels from the union of the two regions are present in the Canny mask, the value $V_B(i,j)$ will be 1.

$$V_B(i,j) = \begin{cases} -1 & \text{if } B_2(i,j) > B_1(i,j) \\ \frac{B_1(i,j)}{|B_{i\cup j}|} & \text{otherwise} \end{cases} \quad (6)$$

Once we have $V_S(i,j)$ and $V_B(i,j)$, we can compute $V_{contract}(i,j)$ as expressed in Equation 7, using a weight (α) to balance the importance of each type of information.

$$V_{contract}(i,j) = \begin{cases} 0 & \text{if } V_S(i,j) = -1 \text{ or } \\ & V_B(i,j) = -1 \\ \alpha V_S(i,j) + (1-\alpha)V_B(i,j) & \text{otherwise} \end{cases} \quad (7)$$

Once we compute $V_{contract}$ for every edge in the graph, in order to create the new CKs, each surviving vertex will use this information to select which of its adjacent vertices is more likely to be joined with it. The biggest value of $V_{contract}$ corresponds with the edge with best conditions to be contracted, given the semantic and boundary information employed. If $V_{contract}$ is 0, that edge will never be contracted, either because the vertices it connects have different semantic classes or because there is a boundary between the underlying regions that must be preserved. The combination process is illustrated in Figure 1.

Using this contraction criterion, a new level will be created. This is part of an iterative process where a level is first annotated with a base classifier, then this classification is refined by solving the associated MRF and finally the new CKs are found using the classification and boundary information, giving birth to a new level of segmentation. All the process will be repeated until we reach a level where no more contractions are allowed.

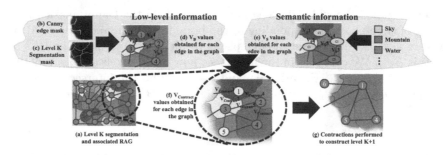

Fig. 1. Combination of the low-level and the semantic information for building a new segmentation level. In (f), white vertices are the surviving ones, and they use the $V_{Contract}$ value to determine which non-surviving vertex will be merged to it.

4   Experiments

We ran experiments on a subset of the Corel image collection (CorelA) developed by [10]. This dataset contains 205 natural scene images split into two subsets with 137 images for training and 68 images for testing. All images have been segmented and manually annotated with 22 classes.

We compute irregular pyramids for all the images, with an average of 20 levels per image. We consider that image over-segmentation is sufficient to perform efficient classification of small objects or object parts, therefore we start our process from level 10 of the original pyramids. In [4] and [11] they use KNN as base classifier We chose for our proposal to use a more sophisticated base classifier, in this case, Random Forests [12]. In order to train the base classifier, we used the ground truth annotations of this dataset, i.e. a group of regions per image, each one manually annotated with a class label. To perform the base classification on the test set, we use the training information to classify all the regions at level 10 of the test image pyramid, then we compute the MRF associated to this level and find the new CKs to construct a whole new level 11. This process will be repeated until reaching level 20 for all pyramids. We measured the annotation accuracy at pixel level for every segmentation level of each test image, with respect to the ground truth labels. Following the idea of [13], we used as visual features for each vertex (region) of each graph, the quantization of the RGB values in 16 bins per channel, yielding a 48-dimensional color histogram, and a local binary pattern (LBP) histogram to characterize texture in the region. The value of δ was set to 0.3 empirically.

In Table 1 we can see a comparison among the annotation results obtained using the base classifier Random Forest (RF) alone, the results from the HMRF-Pyr algorithm [4], which keeps the original pyramid levels of segmentation throughout the annotation process, and our proposal HMRF-PyrSeg, which uses the same annotation method of HMR-Pyr, but improves the segmentation by creating new levels. In [4] they use KNN as base classifier, with 32% of annotation accuracy, and after the HMRF-Pyr method is applied, they improved the results up to 44.6%. Nevertheless, as shown in Table 1, when we use a better base

Table 1. Results obtained in the CorelA subset for each level of the pyramid

Algorithm	Pyramid levels										
	10	11	12	13	14	15	16	17	18	19	20
RF (base classifier)	37.3%	38.5%	39.7%	40.7%	41.7%	42.6%	43.1%	43.1%	42.7%	42.2%	41.6%
HMRF-Pyr	39.7%	40.4%	41.2%	42.0%	42.7%	43.3%	43.7%	44.1%	44.4%	44.6%	44.8%
HMRF-PyrSeg	**48.7%**	**48.7%**	**48.9%**	**49.3%**	**49.7%**	**49.9%**	**50.0%**	**50.2%**	**50.3%**	**50.4%**	**50.4%**

classifier for HMRF-Pyr, the relative improvement decreases (being 3.2% the highest improvement). Since the base classifier does a better job, there is less room for refining the annotation given the underlaying image representation. We chose to modify the image segmentation by creating new levels that would take into account the annotation results from the level below, and therefore, it is possible to obtain much better annotation results with respect to the base classifier.

In Table 2 we can see a comparison of our approach with other methods that were tested on this dataset, in terms of overall accuracy. To illustrate the improvement of segmentation, in Figure 2 we show the best segmented levels for one sample image using HMRF-Pyr and HMRF-PyrSeg. With these results we can notice the relevance of having a better underlying segmentation during the process of image annotation and how these two processes can be combined to take advantage of each other's feedback for improving their results.

Table 2. Comparison with other methods in the CorelA subset. Second row shows the accuracy of each algorithm.

Algorithm	gML1o [10]	MRFs AREK [11]	HMRF-Pyr [4]	HMRF-PyrSeg
Overall accuracy	36.2%	45.6%	44.6%	**50.4%**

Original Image   Ground Truth   HMRF-Pyr   HMRF-PyrSeg

Fig. 2. Example segmentation result using HMRF-Pyr and HMRF-PyrSeg. Colors represent different classes. (Best seen in color)

5   Conclusions

In this paper we proposed an approach that combines image annotation and segmentation in an iterative and hierarchical way. The segmentation step is improved using semantic information coming from a previous annotation and the subsequent annotation takes advantages of a better partition. As experimental results showed, this synergy can boost the final results of image annotation.

In a future work we plan to make experiments showing the improvements in image segmentation, as an alternative goal of this combination.

References

1. Ullman, S.: Object recognition and segmentation by a fragment-based hierarchy. Trends in Cognitive Sciences 11(2), 58–64 (2007)
2. van de Sande, K.E.A., Uijlings, J.R.R., Gevers, T., Smeulders, A.W.M.: Segmentation as selective search for object recognition. In: Proceedings of ICCV 2011, pp. 1879–1886. IEEE Computer Society (2011)
3. Akcay, H.G., Aksoy, S.: Automated detection of objects using multiple hierarchical segmentations. In: IGARSS, pp. 1468–1471. IEEE (2007)
4. Morales-González, A., García-Reyes, E., Sucar, L.E.: Hierarchical markov random fields with irregular pyramids for improving image annotation. In: Pavón, J., Duque-Méndez, N.D., Fuentes-Fernández, R. (eds.) IBERAMIA 2012. LNCS, vol. 7637, pp. 521–530. Springer, Heidelberg (2012)
5. Vieux, R., Benois-Pineau, J., Domenger, J.P., Braquelaire, A.: Segmentation-based multi-class semantic object detection. Multimedia Tools Appl. 60(2), 305–326 (2012)
6. Torrent, A., Lladó, X., Freixenet, J., Torralba, A.: A boosting approach for the simultaneous detection and segmentation of generic objects. Pattern Recogn. Lett. 34(13), 1490–1498 (2013)
7. Brun, L., Kropatsch, W.: Contains and inside relationships within combinatorial pyramids. Pattern Recogn. 39(4), 515–526 (2006)
8. Haxhimusa, Y., Kropatsch, W.G.: Hierarchy of partitions with dual graph contraction. In: Michaelis, B., Krell, G. (eds.) DAGM 2003. LNCS, vol. 2781, pp. 338–345. Springer, Heidelberg (2003)
9. Canny, J.: A computational approach to edge detection. IEEE Trans. Pattern Anal. Mach. Intell. 8(6), 679–698 (1986)
10. Carbonetto, P.: Unsupervised statistical models for general object recognition. Tech. Rep., The Faculty of Graduate Studies, Department of Computer Science, The University of British Columbia, West Mall Vancouver, BC Canada (2003)
11. Hernández-Gracidas, C., Sucar, L.E.: Markov random fields and spatial information to improve automatic image annotation. In: Mery, D., Rueda, L. (eds.) PSIVT 2007. LNCS, vol. 4872, pp. 879–892. Springer, Heidelberg (2007)
12. Breiman, L.: Random forests. Mach. Learn. 45(1), 5–32 (2001)
13. Morales-González, A., García-Reyes, E.B.: Simple object recognition based on spatial relations and visual features represented using irregular pyramids. Multimedia Tools Appl. 63(3), 875–897 (2013)

Implementation of Non Local Means Filter in GPUs*

Adrián Márques and Alvaro Pardo

Universidad Catolica del Uruguay, Montevideo 11600, Uruguay
adrian.marques@gmail.com, apardo@ucu.edu.uy

Abstract. In this paper, we review some alternatives to reduce the computational complexity of the Non-Local Means image filter and present a CUDA-based implementation of it for GPUs, comparing its performance on different GPUs and with respect to reference CPU implementations. Starting from a naive CUDA implementation, we describe different aspects of CUDA and the algorithm itself that can be leveraged to decrease the execution time. Our GPU implementation achieved speedups of up to 35.8x with respect to our reduced-complexity reference implementation on the CPU, and more than 700x over a plain CPU implementation.

Keywords: Image denoising, Non-Local Means, GPU, CUDA.

1 Introduction

In this work we focus on the implementation in GPU of the Non-Local Means (NLM) image filter[3] which proposes to compute the output pixels as a weighted average of all pixels in the image (in practice for all pixels inside a given search region). The weights reflect the similarity between pixels and the novelty of the method is that this similarity is based on the distance between patches centered at pixels being processed. If $I(x)$ is the value of the input image at pixel x and S_x is a rectangular search region centered at pixel x the output of the NLM filter is computed with the following equation: $\hat{I}(x) = \frac{\sum_{y \in S_x} w(x,y) I(y)}{\sum_{y \in S_x} w(x,y)}$ where the weights $w(x,y)$ measure the similarity between patches N_x and N_y of size $(2W + 1) \times (2W + 1)$ centered at x and y respectively. This similarity is computed as: $w(x,y) = \exp(-\|N_x - N_y\|_2^2 / h^2)$ with h a parameter that controls the aperture of the weighting function. We assume a search region with range $[-S, S]^2$. The computational cost of a naive implementation of NLM is $O(N^2 (2S + 1)^2 (2W + 1)^2))$ where N is the size of the image (N rows and columns), $(2S + 1)^2$ is the number of pixels in S_x and $(2W + 1)^2$ is the number patch pixels. To alleviate the computational cost of the NLM filter several authors proposed different strategies to speed up the algorithm. These strategies can be classified into two categories. On the one hand the ones that propose approximations to the original NLM

---

* ANII FMV200913042 and SticAmsud MMVPSCV. Thanks to P. Ezzatti and E. Dufrechou from Univ. de la Republica for discussions and running our code on their machines.

J. Ruiz-Shulcloper and G. Sanniti di Baja (Eds.): CIARP 2013, Part I, LNCS 8258, pp. 407–414, 2013.

that allow the reduction of the computation cost [8,7]. On the other hand, there are solutions that reduce the computational cost while implementing the same filter [5,4]. Here, we review these references that inspired our work for the GPU implementation.

In [4] Condat proposes an elegant solution to lower the computational cost using convolutions. The first observation is the following. If the pixel y is expressed using a displacement vector starting from pixel x as $y = x + dx$ then the weights fulfill $w(x, x + dx) = w(y, y - dx)$. Therefore, there is no need to compute both weights. The second modification involves swapping the loops in x and dx and dividing the computation of the weights in two steps. First, compute an image with square differences: $u(x; dx) = (I(x) - I(x + dx))^2$ Second, using the image $u(x; dx)$, the weights are expressed using convolutions as:

$$w(x, x + dx) = \exp(-v(x)/h^2), \quad v(dx) = \sum_{x \in N} u(x; dx) = u(x; dx) * g$$

where g is a square kernel of size $(2W + 1)^2$. Condat's algorithm is:

```
Î(.),  C(.)  =  0
for all dx in halved search region
   compute the image u(x)  =  ( I(x)  −  I(x + dx) )²
   compute the exponents v(x)  =  u(x) * g
   for all pixels x
      w(x + dx)  =  exp( −v(x)/h² )
      Î(x) + =  w(x + dx)I(x + dx); Î(x + dx) + =   w(x + dx)I(x)
      C(x) + =  w(x + dx); C(x + dx) + =  w(x + dx)
for all pixels x
   Î(x)  =  Î(x)/C(x)
```

The computational cost of this algorithm is $O(N^2(2S + 1)^2(2W + 1))$ which implies a reduction of $(2W + 1)$. If the convolution with g is implemented with a IIR filter this cost can be further reduced to $O(N^2(2S + 1)^2)$. A similar solution was presented in [5] by Darbon et. al., where they also express the differences between patches as a convolution and calculate them using integral images. This alternative has a computational cost $O(4N^2S^2)$ which is independent of the patch size (does not depend on W).

In this work we evaluate a GPU implementation of Condat's algorithm and study different optimizations at the GPU level. For comparison purposes we also implemented CPU versions of Condat's and Darbon's proposals.

2   GPUs

Modern GPUs are very efficient in parallel processing of computer graphics data but also with any other type of data that can take advantage of the parallel nature of the GPUs. The manufacturers of the GPUs realized the power of this technology in fields beyond computer graphics and introduced programming models that transform the GPU units into more general computing devices. Image and video processing are two examples where the application of GPUs gives many benefits and great reductions in computational time. Since GPUs are basically consumer electronics products they are very competitive in terms of price. The programming models provided by the manufacturers are transparent to the hardware specifications to allow the end user to upgrade the hardware to increase computational power without the need to modify the software. NVIDIA was the first company to introduce a general-purpose programming model with the release of CUDA and recently other companies joined efforts around the OpenCL standard.

Several authors have proposed NLM implementations for GPUs. In [2] the authors divide the image in blocks and calculate weights only for the central pixel, assigning that weight to all pixels within the block. Although their proposed method does reduce the computational complexity of the algorithm, it does so by sacrificing denoising performance, since this coarse weight approximation can introduce artifacts at the edges in the image. This same implementation is evaluated in [9].

In [10], a CUDA implementation of NLM for CT scans is presented that takes no steps to reduce the computational complexity of the algorithm. The authors' main contribution towards runtime optimization is exploiting the shared memory space to prefetch and then access the image data rather than reading from global memory multiple times, since the former can be accessed much faster than the latter. However, shared memory is a limited resource that restricts the number of thread blocks that can be run concurrently on a streaming multiprocessor, and the proposed approach does not extend well when processing color images or video. In [6], the authors present a DirectX implementation that, just as Condat's and Darbon's, exploits the fact that the differences between patches can be calculated as a convolution.

3   Proposed Implementation

There are many resources available to learn CUDA programming, and coding an initial version of a parallel application can be very easy. However, to get the most of the GPU, a deeper understanding of the underlying architecture is usually required and at this point the learning curve grows steeper. In this article we describe each of these improvements so that they may serve as an introductory guide to others that may be getting started with implementing image processing applications in CUDA.

Naive Implementation: This consists in a straightforward implementation of Condat's algorithm. Host code controls the iteration through the search region while GPU kernel functions are invoked for displaced image subtraction, separable convolution, addition of weighted pixel contribution and finally division of the contributions by the total summed weights. The pseudo code for this approach is described below. For the separable convolution, we used the CUDA Toolkit sample code described in [1]. The other kernels are straightforward implementations of their CPU counterparts. The only addition is that, since a thread with linearized index x updates $\hat{I}(x)$ and $C(x)$ as well as $\hat{I}(x + dx)$ and $C(x + dx)$, we introduced another pair of accumulation and summed weight images $\hat{I}_{sym}$ and C_{sym} to store the symmetric contributions and thus eliminate concurrency overwrite issues between threads.

$\hat{I}(x), \ \hat{I}\_sym \ = \ 0, \ C, \ C\_sym \ = \ 0$
for all dx **in halved search region**
$\quad u \ = \ displaced\_image\_substraction\_kernel(I, \ dx)$
$\quad v \ = \ separable\_convolution\_kernel(u)$
$\quad (\hat{I}, \ \hat{I}\_sym, \ C, \ C\_sym) \ += \ add\_weighted\_pixel\_contributions\_kernel(I, \ v, \ dx)$
$\hat{I}(x) \ = \ weight\_normalization\_kernel(\hat{I}(x), \ \hat{I}\_sym, \ C(x), \ C\_sym)$

Coalescing Memory Access: On many GPU applications, memory access can have a great impact on performance. Reads and writes to global memory can be coalesced (meaning grouped into a single transaction) when the threads in a warp access the memory addresses in predefined patterns. These patterns can vary depending on the CUDA architecture, with 1.0 and 1.1 being the most restrictive and relaxing into more permissive models from 1.2 to 2.x and 3.x versions. In CUDA 1.0 and 1.1, successive threads in a half-warp must access consecutive 4, 8, or 16-byte words, with the first word located in a memory address aligned to the size of the transaction. In order to coalesce most global memory reads, we allocated the memory for our images using the function $cudaMallocPitch()$ and $cudaMemcpy2D()$ rather than $cudaMalloc()$ and $cudaMemcpy()$. The former pads (if necessary) the allocation to ensure that the addresses of the rows of 2D arrays will meet the alignment requirements for coalescing. Since we replicate the border of the processed images, we also had to make sure that the size of the replicated border was a multiple of 16 for our card with CUDA 1.1 and of 32 for our cards with CUDA 2.0 or higher, in order to assure memory alignment when working within the border. After coalescing global memory access in this manner, a speedup of 1.5x over the naive GPU implementation was obtained.

Using 2D Textures for Remaining Unaligned Reads: After the modifications described above, all reads and writes of threads with linearized index x to pixels with the same index will be coalesced. However, the kernels that compute image subtraction and addition of weighted pixel contributions also perform accesses that remain uncoalesced to pixels indexed as $x + dx$. We therefore explored using textures to accelerate these read operations. The texture memory space is read-only and resides in device memory but is cached, so a texture fetch will cost one memory read from the texture cache rather than global memory unless a cache miss occurs, in which case the cost will then be a read from global memory. Since this cache is optimized for 2D spatial locality, higher bandwidth can be achieved by using textures if memory reads by threads in the same warp do not follow the access patterns required for memory transaction coalescing but the read addresses are close together in 2D. By using textures to read displaced pixel values, the speedup factor over the previous implementation was of 1.2x.

As an alternative to texture fetches for unaligned memory access, we experimented with prefetching the data to shared memory using a coalesced memory access pattern to then operate on the data in shared memory. However, due to the overhead introduced by the prefetching code and that we only used the prefetched data once per kernel, using textures remained the faster option.

Coalescing Remaining Write Operations: At this point, writes of the contributions and weights of displaced pixels to $\hat{I}_{sym}(x+dx)$ and $C_{sym}(x+dx)$ still remained uncoalesced. However, if instead of each thread using $w(x)$ to update indexes x and $x+dx$ we change to updating only x using $w(x)$ and $w(x-dx)$ as noted in [6], all writes can be coalesced. Furthermore, the need for a second set of images to keep track of symmetric weighted contributions and weights dissapears as well, since each thread will now update a single image index. Under this strategy, in order to avoid reevaluations of the exponential function, the convolution kernel has to be trivially modified to calculate the weights of each pixel as a last step. This modification resulted in a further speedup factor of 2.3x.

4   Results

All of the reported NLM implementations operate on color float images. Table 1 details the execution times and speedups obtained for each of the GPU implementation variants mentioned in section 3, with 4.1x being the final speedup factor obtained over the naive GPU implementation. These results were obtained on a Quadro FX 770M card with compute capability 1.1. Following CUDA versions introduced global memory caching that may provide a higher bandwidth than texture fetches if the accessed elements are present on the cache, which may yield different speedup factors than these.

Table 2 lists execution times for the different algorithm variants we implemented on the CPU and our current GPU version. Since the purpose of the CPU implementations was to provide easily reproducible and comparable baseline execution times, straightforward implementations with no particular code optimizations were employed. The fastest implementation on the CPU was Condat's alternative, which represented a 11.8x improvement over the implementation that only exploits weight symmetry. In turn, the GPU version was 32.4x faster than its CPU counterpart (Condat) and an impressive 717.9x faster than the naive CPU implementation, but the latter is hardly a fair comparison.

We experimented with running the algorithm on different cards, obtaining the same execution times for a Quadro FX 770M and a GT 430, in spite of the latter having 3 times as many cores as the former. This is caused by the algorithm being bandwidth-bound rather than compute-bound and both cards having the same memory bandwidth of 25.6 GB/sec. For the GTX 480, with 133.9 GB/sec, and the GTX 680, with 192.2 GB/sec, execution times were 8.7x and 10.7x respectively faster than with the previous cards. Thread block dimensions were set to maximize occupancy. In order to comply with memory access coalescing

Table 1. Execution times and speedup factors over the naive GPU implementation for all tested GPU implementation alternatives. Listed results correspond to 512x512 images with a 21x21 search window and 9x9 patches.

GPU implementation alternative	Execution Time (sec)	Speedup vs. Naive Implementation
Naive Implementation	3.09	1x
Coalescing memory access	2.06	1.5x
Using 2D textures for unaligned reads	1.72	1.8x
Coalescing remaining write operations	0.73	4.1x

Table 2. Execution times and speedup factors for a 720x480 image with a 21x21 search window and 9x9 patches. The CPU used was an Intel Core Intel Core i7 2600 CPU @ 3.40GHz. The GPU implementation was run on a NVIDIA GeForce GTX 680 card.

NLM implementation alternative	Execution Time (ms)	Speedup vs. Naive Implementation
CPU 1: Naive Implementation	63,180	1x
CPU 2: Using symmetric weights	33,688	1.9x
CPU 3: Darbon (integral images)	4,789	13.2x
CPU 4: Condat (separable convolution)	2,851	22.2x
GPU Final implementation	88	717.9x

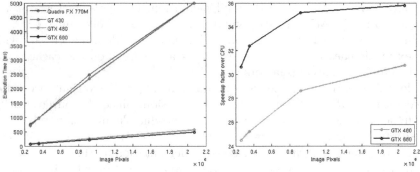

Fig. 1. Left: Execution times per image pixels for different GPUs on images of size 512x512, 720x480, 1200x720 and 1920x1080. **Right:** GPU speedup factor over an Intel Core i7 2600 @ 3.40GHz CPU for the different test image sizes.

patterns, the block width was set to 16 for the Quadro FX 770M, which has compute capability 1.1, and to 32 for the other cards.

Figure 1 (left) illustrates execution times for NLM running on images of different sizes over the different GPU cards. For these image sizes and the best two cards, the speedup factor obtained over the CPU implementation of Condat's method is plotted on the right. The speedup factor increases with image size, leveling off for larger images, and varies between 24.5x and 30.7x for the GTX 480 and between 30.6x and 35.8x for the GTX 680.

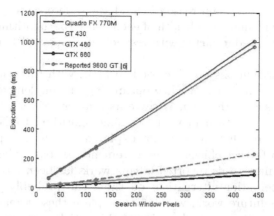

Fig. 2. Execution times per pixels in search window for windows of size 5x5, 7x7, 11x11 and 21x21. Image size remained fixed at 720x480 and patch size at 9x9.

Figure 2 illustrates the execution times when varying the search window's size. Since the algorithm calculates the differences between patches using a separable convolution, changing the patch size hardly affects execution time. The execution times reported in [6] for their DirectX-based implementation, which also exploits the use of a convolution to calculate the distances between image patches, are included among the results presented in figure 2. A more direct comparison was not possible, but when adjusting for the maximum memory bandwidth of the cards, the results in 2 seem to be up to 2x faster than our current implementation. The difference may lie in that they mention computing the convolution as a moving average, whereas we compute the separable convolution. We will evaluate whether we can improve on this point.

5 Conclusions

In this paper we have presented a CUDA-based GPU implementation of NLM that reduces its computational complexity by calculating the differences between images patches as a separable convolution. This variant still produces the same result as the original algorithm, as opposed to the CUDA implementation proposed in [2], which calculates weights for only a subset of image pixels and assigns the same weight within image blocks. It is also faster than the alternative described in [10], since in that case the authors do not reduce the algorithm's computational complexity. The implementation that can be more closely compared to our work is the DirectX-based one presented in [6], which seems to suggest that we could still improve upon our convolution computation to achieve higher speedups.

With respect to our CPU reference implementation, a speedup factor of 3.5x was obtained with the Quadro FX 770M and GeForce GT 430 cards, and up to 30x and 35x speedups were obtained with the comparatively more powerful GTX

480 and GTX 680. The main reason behind the difference in performance between cards is the memory bandwidth of each, since the algorithm is bandwidth-limited. The final speedup factor with respect to a naive CPU implementation was of 718x.

One of the contributions we have tried to make with this paper has been to report each step we have taken while optimizing our implementation, starting from the most basic, so that it may serve as a quick reference for people that are just starting to port their image processing algorithms to CUDA.

It should be noted that we have not explored yet all concepts that we believe may lead to further efficiency improvements. In particular, our access to the better-performing cards reported in this work has been recent, and further exploring implementation alternatives on them can probably yield additional optimizations. As future work, we plan to explore these remaining promising modifications and write a revised version of this article more focused on serving as an quick introduction to CUDA optimization for image processing tasks based on the NLM case study.

References

1. Podlozhnyuk, V., Kharlamov, A.: Image convolution with CUDA. Technical report. NVIDIA, Inc., Santa Clara (2007)
2. Podlozhnyuk, V., Kharlamov, A.: Image denoising. Technical report. NVIDIA, Inc., Santa Clara (2007)
3. Buades, A., Coll, B., Morel, J.M.: A non-local algorithm for image denoising. In: CVPR, pp. 60–65 (2005)
4. Condat, L.: A simple trick to speed up the non-local means. Technical report
5. Darbon, J., Cunha, A., Chan, T., Osher, S., Jensen, G.: Fast nonlocal filtering applied to electron cryomicroscopy. In: ISBI, pp. 1331–1334 (2008)
6. Goossens, B., Luong, H., Aelterman, J., Pižurica, A., Philips, W.: A GPU-accelerated real-time NLMeans algorithm for denoising color video sequences. In: Blanc-Talon, J., Bone, D., Philips, W., Popescu, D., Scheunders, P. (eds.) ACIVS 2010, Part II. LNCS, vol. 6475, pp. 46–57. Springer, Heidelberg (2010)
7. Orchard, J., Ebrahimi, M., Wong, A.: Efficient nonlocal-means denoising using the SVD. In: ICIP, pp. 1732–1735 (2008)
8. Tasdizen, T.: Principal neighborhood dictionaries for nonlocal means image denoising. IEEE Trans. on Image Process. 18(12), 2649–2660 (2009)
9. Wu, H., Zhang, W.-H., Gao, D.-Z., Yin, X.-D., Chen, Y., Wang, W.-D.: Fast CT image processing using parallelized non-local means. Journal of Medical and Biological Eng. 31(6), 437–441 (2011)
10. Mueller, K., Zheng, Z., Xu, W.: Performance tuning for CUDA-accelerated neighborhood denoising filters. In: Workshop on High Performance Image Reconstruction (July 2011)

Wide-Angle Lens Distortion Correction Using Division Models

Miguel Alemán-Flores, Luis Alvarez, Luis Gomez, and Daniel Santana-Cedrés

CTIM (Centro de Tecnologías de la Imagen),
Universidad de Las Palmas de Gran Canaria, Spain
{maleman,lalvarez,lgomez,dsantana}@ctim.es
http://www.ctim.es

Abstract. In this paper we propose a new method to automatically correct wide-angle lens distortion from the distorted lines generated by the projection on the image of 3D straight lines. We have to deal with two major problems: on the one hand, wide-angle lenses produce a strong distortion, which makes the detection of distorted lines a particularly difficult task. On the other hand, the usual single parameter polynomial lens distortion models is not able to manage such a strong distortion. We propose an extension of the Hough transform by adding a distortion parameter to detect the distorted lines, and division lens distortion models to manage wide-angle lens distortion. We present some experiments on synthetic and real images to show the ability of the proposed approach to automatically correct this type of distortion. A comparison with a state-of-the-art method is also included to show the benefits of our method.

Keywords: lens distortion, wide-angle lens, Hough transform, line detection.

1 Introduction

Wide-angle lenses are specially suited for some computer vision tasks, such as real-time tracking, surveillance, close range photogrammetry or even for simple aesthetic purposes. The main advantage these lenses offer is that they provide a wide view up to 180 degrees. However, the strong distortion produced by these lenses may cause severe problems, not only visually, but also for further processing in applications such as object detection, recognition and classification.

To model the lens distortion, we consider radial distortion models given by the expression:

$$\begin{pmatrix} \hat{x} - x_c \\ \hat{y} - y_c \end{pmatrix} = L(r) \begin{pmatrix} x - x_c \\ y - y_c \end{pmatrix}, \tag{1}$$

where (x, y) is the original (distorted) point, $(\hat{x}, \hat{y})$ is the corrected (undistorted) point, (x_c, y_c) is the center of the camera distortion model, $L(r)$ is the function which defines the shape of the distortion model and $r = \sqrt{(x - x_c)^2 + (y - y_c)^2}$.

J. Ruiz-Shulcloper and G. Sanniti di Baja (Eds.): CIARP 2013, Part I, LNCS 8258, pp. 415–422, 2013.

According to the choice of function $L(r)$, there exist two widely accepted types of lens distortion models: the polynomial model and the division model.

The polynomial model, or simple radial distortion model [10], is formulated as:

$$L(r) = 1 + k_1 r^2 + k_2 r^4 + ..., \qquad (2)$$

where the set $\mathbf{k} = (k_1, ..., k_{N_k})^T$ contains the distortion parameters estimated from image measurements, usually by means of non-linear optimization techniques. The two-parameter model is the usual approach, due to its simplicity and accuracy [12], [1]. Alvarez, Gomez and Sendra [1] proposed an algebraic method suitable for correcting significant radial distortion which is highly efficient in terms of computational cost. An on-line demo of the implementation of this algebraic method can be found in [2].

Camera calibration is a topic of interest in Computer Vision which, in order to be efficient, requires including the distortion into the camera model. Most calibration techniques rely on the linear pinhole camera and use a calibration pattern to establish a point-to-point correspondence between 2D and 3D points (see a review on camera calibration in [14]). In this applications, the polynomial model with only one distortion parameter, k_1 (*one-parameter model*), achieves an accuracy around 0.1 pixels in image space using lenses exhibiting large distortion [7], [8]. However, [7] also indicates that for cases of strong radial distortion, the one-parameter model is not recommended.

The division model has initially been proposed by [13], but it has received special attention after the more recent research by Fitzgibbon [9]. It is formulated as:

$$L(r) = \frac{1}{1 + k_1 r^2 + k_2 r^4 + ...}. \qquad (3)$$

The main advantage of the division model is the requirement of fewer terms than the polynomial model for the case of severe distortion. Therefore, the division model seems to be more adequate for wide-angle lenses (see a recent review on distortion models for wide-angle lenses in [11]). Additionally, when using only one distortion parameter, its inversion is simpler, since it requires finding the roots of a second degree polynomial instead of a third degree polynomial. In fact, a single parameter version of the division model is normally used.

For both models, $L(r)$ can be estimated by considering that 3D lines in the image must be projected onto 2D straight lines, and minimizing the distortion error, which is given by the sum of the squares of the distances from the points to the lines [7].

Once a lens distortion model has been selected, we must decide how to apply it. Some methods rely on the human-supervised identification of some known straight lines in one or more images [3], [4], [15]. As a consequence of the human intervention, these methods are robust, independent of the camera parameters, and require no calibration patterns. However, for the same reason, these methods are slow and tedious for the case of dealing with large sets of images.

New approaches have recently appeared to eliminate human intervention. In [6] and [5], an automatic radial estimation method is discussed. This method works on a single image and no human intervention or special calibration pattern are required. The method applies the one-parameter Fitzgibbon's division model to estimate the distortion from a set of automatically detected non-overlapping circular arcs within the image. The main limitation of the method is that each circular arc has to be a collection of contiguous points in the image and, therefore, the method fails if there are no such arcs.

In this paper, we propose a new unsupervised method which makes use of the one-parameter division model to correct, from a single image, the radial distortion caused by a wide-angle lens. We first automatically detect the distorted lines within the image by adapting the usual Hough transform to our problem. The adaptation consists in embedding the radial distortion parameter into the Hough parametric space to tackle the detection of the longest arcs (*distorted lines*) within the image. From the improved Hough transform, we obtain a collection of distorted lines and an initial value for the distortion parameter k_1. Next, we optimize this parameter by minimizing the distance of the corrected line points to straight lines.

2   A Hough Space Including a Division Lens Distortion Parameter

In order to correct the distortion, we need to estimate the magnitude and sign of the distortion parameter and, to this aim, we can rely on the information provided by line primitives. Line primitives are searched in the edge image which is computed using any edge detector. One of the most commonly used techniques to extract lines in an edge image is the Hough transform, which searches for the most reliable candidates within a certain space. This space is usually a two-dimensional space which considers the possible values for the orientation and the distance to the origin of the candidate lines. Each edge point votes for those lines which could contain this point, and the lines which receive the highest scores are considered the most reliable ones.

However, this technique does not consider the influence of the distortion in the alignment of the edge points, in such a way that straight lines are split into different segments due to the effect of the distortion. For this reason, we propose to include a new dimension in the Hough space, namely the distortion parameter. For practical reasons, instead of considering the distortion parameter value itself in the Hough space, we make use of the percentage of correction obtained with that value, which is given by:

$$p = (\tilde{r}_{max} - r_{max})/r_{max}, \tag{4}$$

where r_{max} is the distance from the center of distortion to the furthest point in the original image, and $\tilde{r}_{max}$ is the same distance, but after applying the distortion model. This way, the parameter p is easier to interpret than the distortion parameter itself. Another advantage of using p as an extra parameter in

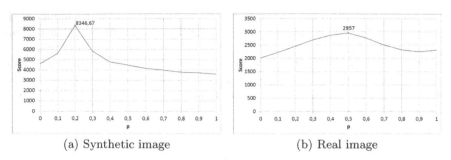

(a) Synthetic image   (b) Real image

Fig. 1. Values of the maximum in the voting space with respect to the percentage of correction for the images in (a) the synthetic image in Fig. 2 and (b) the real image in Fig. 3 using the modified Hough transform and division lens distortion model

the Hough space is that it does not depend on the image resolution. When we use single parameter division models the relation between parameter p and k_1 is straightforward and it is given by the expression :

$$k_1 = \frac{-p}{(1+p)r_{max}^2}. \tag{5}$$

To reduce the number of points which vote and the number of lines that each edge point votes for, we first estimate the magnitude and orientation of the edge for every edge point. Only those points where the magnitude of the gradient is higher than a certain threshold are considered. Afterward, we select, for every value of p and every edge point, those lines which, after being corrected according to the distortion model associated to this value of p, are close enough to the point and present an orientation which is similar to the orientation of the edge in that point. Furthermore, the vote of a point for a line depends on how close they are, and is given by $v = 1/(1+d)$, where d is the distance from the point to the line.

In the Hough space, the different lines may have different orientations and distances to the origin. Nevertheless, they should all have the same value of the distortion parameter (i.e. the same value of p), since it is a single value for the whole image. This means that we must not search for the best candidates individually, but for the value of p which concentrates the largest number of significant lines.

Figure 1 illustrates how the maximum of the voting score varies within the Hough space according to the percentage of correction determined by the distortion parameter.

Once we have searched for the best value of p within the three-dimensional Hough space, we refine it to obtain a more accurate approximation. To this aim, by using standard optimization techniques (gradient descent method) we minimize the following error function:

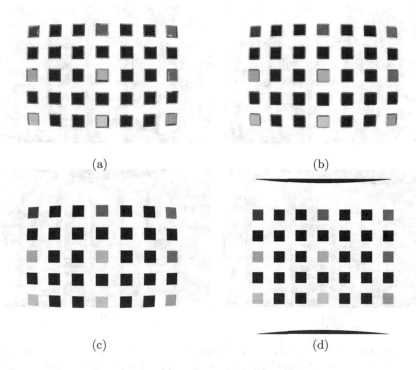

(a)   (b)

(c)   (d)

Fig. 2. Lens distortion correction for a test image: (a) lines detected using the Bukhari-Dailey method, (b) lines detected using the proposed method, (c) undistorted image using the Bukhari-Dailey method, and (d) undistorted image using the proposed method.

$$E\left(p\right) = \sum_{j}^{Nl} \sum_{i}^{Np(j)} dist\left(\overline{x}_{ji}, line_j\right)^2 \tag{6}$$

Nl is the number of lines, $Np(j)$ is the number of points of the jth line and $\overline{x}_{ji}$ are the points associated to $line_j$. This error measures how distant the points are from their respective lines, so that the lower this value, the better the matching.

3   Experimental Results

We have tested our model in some images showing wide-angle lens distortion and we have compared the results with those obtained using the Bukhari-Dailey method [5]. We have used the code avaliable on F. Bukhari's web page[1].

Figure 2 (1024×683 pixels) presents the results for a synthetic image. It consists of a calibration pattern in which the radial distortion has been simulated using a division model. The magnitude of such distortion is 20% ($p = 0.2$). Figure 2(a) shows the arcs detected using the Bukhari-Dailey method, whereas

---

[1] http://www.cs.ait.ac.th/vgl/faisal/downloads.html

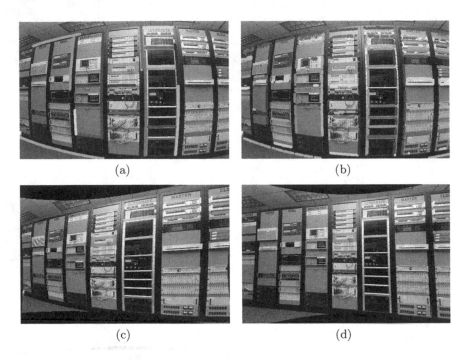

(a) (b)

(c) (d)

Fig. 3. Lens distortion correction for a real image: (a) lines detected using the Bukhari-Dailey method, (b) lines detected using the proposed method, (c) undistorted image using the Bukhari-Dailey method, and (d) undistorted image using the proposed method

the lines detected using the proposed method (modified Hough transform and division model) are shown in Fig. 2(b). We have represented each line using a different color to identify them. In both cases, from the detected arcs or distorted lines, the distortion is estimated and the images are corrected. Figure 2(c) illustrates the result using the Bukhari-Dailey method, whereas Fig. 2(d) presents the corrected image using the proposed method. As observed, the Bukhari-Dailey method splits those lines where points are not contiguous, while the proposed method is able to identify a single line from different disconnected segments (see, for instance, how the edges of the squares in the same row or column are not associated using the Bukhari-Dailey method, but are properly linked using our method). Since longer lines provide more useful information than shorter ones, this results in a better distortion estimation for the proposed method.

Figure 3 (640×425 pixels)[2] illustrates the same experiment on a real image with a strong distortion. Figure 3(a) shows the arcs detected using the Bukhari-Dailey method. As observed, when different segments of the same line are visible, this method is not able to associate them (see for instance the lower green line, which is not continued on the right side of the image), but the proposed method associates them into the same line (see Fig. 3(b)). For this case, the corrected

---

[2] US Air Force CC0 http://commons.wikimedia.org/wiki/File:Usno-amc.jpg

Table 1. Number of lines, number of points, CPU time and percentage of correction for Fig. 2 and 3 using the Bukhari-Dailey method and the proposed method

Figure	Measure	Bukhari-Dailey	Our method
Figure 2 (synthetic image)	No. of arcs	306	24
	No. of points	11,255	9,033
	CPU time (sec.)	79.611	7.844
	% correction	0	19.9555
Figure 3 (real image)	No. of arcs	22	22
	No. of points	2,894	3,651
	CPU time (sec.)	57.41	3.209
	% correction	63.3116	49.9186

image using the proposed method is also better than that obtained by means of the Bukhari-Dailey method (compare Fig. 3(c) and Fig. 3(d)).

Table 1 shows some quantitative results. If we analyze the results for the calibration pattern, we can observe two important advantages of our method. First, the number of lines which have been identified is 24, which is exactly the number of lines within the image. Nevertheless, the Bukhari-Dailey method extracts a higher number of lines, since each one of them has been split in many segments. Second, the percentage of correction obtained with our method is very close to the real value (20%). In this case the Bukhari-Dailey method does not provide a good result (0% of correction), probably because the obtained segments are too small to properly estimate the distortion model. Concerning the total amount of points of the arcs obtained by both methods, the Bukhari-Dailey method obtains more points (11,255 points in all) than our method (9,033 points) probably due to the spurious arcs extracted by the Bukhari-Dailey method.

For the real image, both methods have identified the same number of lines, but those obtained by our method are longer (3,651 points in all) and they have not been split. Regarding the computational cost, in the experiments presented, our method is about 10 times faster than the one proposed by Bukhari-Dailey.

4   Conclusions

In this paper we propose a new method to automatically correct wide-angle lens distortion. The main novelty of the paper is the combination of an improved 3D Hough space, which includes the distortion parameter to detect distorted lines, and the division distortion model which is able to manage the strong distortion produced by wide-angle lenses. We present some experiments which show that the proposed method properly corrects the lens distortion in the case of wide-angle lenses and outperforms the results obtained in [5] specially in the case where the distorted lines are not contiguous arcs in the image.

Acknowledgement. This work has been partially supported by the MICINN project reference MTM2010-17615 (Ministry of Science and Innovation, Spain).

References

1. Alvarez, L., Gomez, L., Sendra, R.: An algebraic approach to lens distortion by line rectification. Journal of Mathematical Imaging and Vision 39(1), 36–50 (2008)
2. Alvarez, L., Gomez, L., Sendra, R.: Algebraic lens distortion model estimation. Image Processing On Line (2010), http://www.ipol.im
3. Alvarez, L., Gomez, L., Sendra, R.: Accurate depth dependent lens distortion models: an application to planar view scenarios. Journal of Mathematical Imaging and Vision 39(1), 75–85 (2011)
4. Brown, D.: Close-range camera calibration. Photogrammetric Engineering 37(8), 855–866 (1971)
5. Bukhari, F., Dailey, M.: Automatic radial distortion estimation from a single image. Journal of Mathematical Imaging and Vision 45(1), 31–45 (2012)
6. Bukhari, F., Dailey, M.N.: Robust radial distortion from a single image. In: Bebis, G., et al. (eds.) ISVC 2010, Part II. LNCS, vol. 6454, pp. 11–20. Springer, Heidelberg (2010)
7. Devernay, F., Faugeras, O.: Straight lines have to be straight. Machine Vision and Applications 13(1), 14–24 (2001)
8. Faugeras, O., Toscani, G.: Structure from motion using the reconstruction and reprojection technique. In: Proc. IEEE Workshop on Computer Vision, pp. 345–348. IEEE Computer Society (November-December 1987)
9. Fitzgibbon, A.W.: Simultaneous linear estimation of multiple view geometry and lens distortion. In: Proc. IEEE International Conference on Computer Vision and Pattern Recognition, pp. 125–132 (2001)
10. Hartley, R.I., Zisserman, A.: Multiple view geometry in computer vision. Cambridge University Press (2004)
11. Hughes, C., Glavin, M., Jones, E., Denny, P.: Review of geometric distortion compensation in fish-eye cameras. In: IET Irish Signals and Systems Conference (ISSC 2008), Galway, Ireland, pp. 162–167 (2008)
12. Kang, S.: Radial distortion snakes. Proc. IEICE Transactions on Information and Systems, 1603–1611 (2000)
13. Lenz, R.: Linsenfehlerkorrigierte Eichung von Halbleiterkameras mit Standardobjektiven für hochgenaue 3D - Messungen in Echtzeit. In: Paulus, E. (ed.) Mustererkennung 1987, Informatik-Fachberichte, vol. 149, pp. 212–216. Springer, Heidelberg (1987)
14. Salvi, J., Armangu, X., Batlle, J.: A comparative review of camera calibrating methods with accuracy evaluation. Pattern Recognition Letters 35(7), 1617–1635 (2002)
15. Wang, A., Qiu, T., Shao, L.: A simple method to radial distortion correction with centre of distortion estimation. Journal of Mathematical Imaging and Vision 35(3), 165–172 (2009)

Current Trends in the Algebraic Image Analysis: A Survey

Igor Gurevich, Yulia Trusova, and Vera Yashina

Dorodnicyn Computing Centre, Russian Academy of Sciences,
Moscow, The Russian Federation
{igourevi,ytrusova}@ccas.ru, werayashina@gmail.com

Abstract. Survey. The main goal of the Algebraic Approach is the design of a unified scheme for the representation of objects for the purposes of their recognition and the transformation of such representations in the suitable algebraic structures. It makes possible to develop corresponding regular structures ready for analysis by algebraic, geometrical and topological techniques. Development of this line of image analysis and pattern recognition is of crucial importance for automated image mining and application problems solving. It is selected and briefly characterized main aspects of current state of the image analysis algebraization. Special attention is paid to the recent results of the Russian mathematical school.

Keywords: Image analysis, image algebras, descriptive approach, pattern recognition, image representations.

1 Introduction

Automation of image processing, analysis, estimating and understanding is one of the crucial points of theoretical computer science having decisive importance for applications.

The specificity, complexity and difficulties of image analysis and estimation (IAE) problems stem from necessity to achieve some balance between such highly contradictory factors as goals and tasks of a problem solving, the nature of visual perception, ways and means of an image acquisition, formation, reproduction and rendering, and mathematical, computational and technological means allowable for the IAE.

The mathematical theory of image analysis is not finished and is passing through a developing stage. It is only recently came understanding that only intensive creating of comprehensive mathematical theory of image analysis and recognition (in addition to the mathematical theory of pattern recognition) could bring a real opportunity to solve efficiently application problems via extracting from images the information necessary for intellectual decision making.

A new approach to analyzing and estimating information represented in the form of images - the Descriptive Approach to Image Analysis and Understanding (DA) by I.B.Gurevich [2, 6, 14-16] is based on the specialization of the "Algebraic Approach to Pattern Recognition and Classification Problems Solving" by Yu. I. Zhuravlev [43] for the case when the initial information is represented in the form of images.

J. Ruiz-Shulcloper and G. Sanniti di Baja (Eds.): CIARP 2013, Part I, LNCS 8258, pp. 423–430, 2013.

2   State of the Art of the Mathematical Theory of Image Analysis

To automate image mining, we need an integrated approach to implement the potential of mathematical apparatus being used in transforming and analyzing information represented in the form of images.

Image mining now tends to multiplicity (multi-algorithmic and multi-model modes) and to fusion of the results. It means that several different algorithms are applied in parallel to process the same model and several different models of the same initial data are used to solve the problem and then the results are fused to obtain the most accurate solution. Yu.I.Zhuravlev obtained the first and fundamental results in this area in 1970s [43].

From 1990s, the most part of pattern recognition applications and considerable part of research in artificial intelligence deal with images. As a result, new technical tools emerged to obtain information that allow representing of recorded and accumulated data in the form of images and the image recognition itself became more popular as the powerful and efficient methodology to process and analyze data mathematically and to detect hidden regularities.

There are a lot of internal scientific problems that have arisen within image recognition. First of all, these imply algebraizing the image recognition theory, arranging image recognition algorithms, estimating the algorithmic complexity of the image recognition problem, automating the synthesis of the corresponding efficient procedures, formalizing the description of the image as a recognition object, etc. These problems form the base of the mathematical agenda of the descriptive theory of image recognition developed using the ideas of the Algebraic Approach to Pattern Recognition and Classification.

There are three main issues one needs to overcome when dealing with images: 1) to describe images; 2) to develop, study and optimize the selection of mathematical methods and tools for data processing under image recognition; 3) to implement mathematical methods of image analysis via software and hardware means.

3   Algebraization of Pattern Recognition and Image Analysis

This section contains steps of the algebraization in image analysis fundamentals and the basic theories of pattern recognition, image algebras.

By now, image analysis and evaluation have a wide experience gained in applying mathematical methods from different sections of mathematics, computer science and physics, in particular algebra, geometry, discrete mathematics, mathematical logic, probability theory, mathematical statistics, mathematical analysis, mathematical theory of pattern recognition, digital signal processing, and optics.

However we still need a regular basis to arrange and choose suitable methods of image analysis, represent in an unified way the processed data (images), construct mathematical models of images designed for recognition problems, and, on the whole, to introduce the universal language for unified description of images and transformations over them.

The necessity to solve complex recognition and specialized image languages generated attention to formal descriptions–models of initial data and formalization of descriptions of procedures of their transformation in the area of pattern recognition (and especially in image recognition in 1960s). As the substantial achievements in this "descriptive" line of R&D we should mention publications by A. Rosenfeld [34], T. Evans [12], R. Narasimhan [29], R. Kirsh [21], A. Shaw [37], H. Barrow, A. Ambler, and R. Burstall [1], S. Kaneff [20].

In 1970s Yu.I.Zhuravlev proposed "The Algebraic Approach to Recognition and Classification Problems" [43], where he defined formalization methods for describing heuristic algorithms of pattern recognition and proposed the universal structure of recognition algorithms. In the same years, U. Grenander stated his "Pattern Theory" [18], where he considered methods of data representation and transformation in recognition problems in terms of regular combinatorial structures, leveraging algebraic and probabilistic apparatus. M.Pavel [31] introduced "Theory of Categories Techniques in Pattern Recognition", to describe pattern recognition algorithms via transforms of initial data preserving its class membership.

The Russian mathematical school also has important original results on algebraic tools for pattern recognition and image analysis in. There are algebras on algorithms, algebraic multiple classifiers, algebraic committees of algorithms, combinatorial algorithms for recognition of 2-D data [1], descriptive image models, 2-D formal grammars [34].

In the framework of scientific school of Yu.I.Zhuravlev several essential results were obtained by V.L.Matrosov [26], K.V.Rudakov [35] and V.D.Mazurov [27]. There are significant number of results concerned with algebraic methods of analysis and estimation of information represented as signals (G.Labunec [22], Ya.A.Furman [13], V.M.Chernov [4]).

Algebraization of pattern recognition and image analysis has attracted and continues to attract the attention of many researchers. First of all – the development of algebraic construction for image analysis and processing – formal grammars, cellular automata, mathematical morphology, image algebras, multiple algorithms, descriptive approach.

The idea of constructing a unified language for concepts and operations used in image processing appeared for the first time in works of Unger [42], who suggested to parallelize algorithms for processing and image analysis on computers with cellular architecture.

Mathematical morphology by G. Matheron [25] and J.Serra [36] became a starting point for a new mathematical wave in image analysis. Serra and Sternberg [39] were the first to succeed in constructing an integrated algebraic theory of processing and image analysis on the basis of mathematical morphology. It is believed [28] that it was precisely Sternberg who introduced the term "image algebra" in the current standard sense. The final version of image algebras (IA) was Standard Image Algebra by G.Ritter [32] (algebraic presentation of image analysis and processing operations).

Descriptive Image Algebras (DIA) is created as a new IA provided possibility to operate with main image models and with basic models of procedure of transforms, which lead to effective synthesis and realization of basic procedures of formal image description, processing, analysis and recognition. DIA is introduced by I.B.Gurevich and developed by him and his pupils I.V.Koryabkina, I.A.Jernova, A.A.Myagkov, A.A.Nefedov, Y.O.Trusova, V.V.Yashina [14-16].

In the history of algebraization we should mention: J.von Neumann [30], S.Unger [42] (studies of interactive image transformations in cellular space); M. Duff, D. Watson, T. Fountain, and G. Shaw [10] (a cellular logic array for image Processing); A. Rosenfeld [33] (digital topology); H.Minkowski and H.Hadwiger (pixel neighborhood arithmetic and mathematical morphology); G.Matheron, J.Serra, S.Sternberg [25, 36, 39] (a coherent algebraic theory specifically designed for image processing and image analysis - mathematical morphology); S. Sternberg [39] (the first to use the term "image algebra"); P. Maragos [24] (introduced a new theory unifying a large class of linear and nonlinear systems under the theory of mathematical morphology); L. Davidson [9] (completed the mathematical foundation of mathematical morphology by formulating its embedding into the lattice algebra known as Mini-Max algebra); G.Ritter [32] (Image Algebra); I.B.Gurevich [15] (Descriptive Image Algebra); T.R. Crimmins and W.M. Brown, R.M. Haralick, L. Shapiro, R.W. Schafer, J. Goutsias, L. Koskinen and Jaako Astola, E.R. Dougherty, P.D. Gader, M.A. Khabou, A. Koldobsky, B. Radunacu, M.Grana, F.X. Albizuri, P. Sussner [7,8,10,11,19,40] (recent papers on mathematical morphology and image algebras).

4   Descriptive Approach to Image Analysis and Understanding

This section contains a brief description of the principal features of the DA needed to understand the meaning of the introduction of the conceptual apparatus and schemes of synthesis of image models proposed to formalize and systematize the methods and forms of image representation.

By the middle of 1990s, it became obvious that for the development of image analysis and recognition, it is critical to: 1) understand the nature of the initial information – images, 2) find methods of image representation and description that allow constructing image models designed for recognition problems, 3) establish the mathematical language designed for unified description of image models and their transformations that allow constructing image models and solving recognition problems; 4) construct models to solve recognition problems in the form of standard algorithmic schemes that allow, in the general case, moving from the initial image to its model and from the model to the sought solution.

The DA gives an unified conceptual structure that helps to develop and implement these models and the mathematical language [14-17]. The main DA purpose is to structure and standardize different methods, operations and representations used in image recognition and analysis. The DA provides the conceptual and mathematical basis for image mining, with its axiomatic and formal configurations giving the ways and tools to represent and describe images to be analyzed and evaluated.

Experience in the development of the mathematical theory of image analysis and its use to solve applied problems shows that, when working with images, it is necessary to solve problems that arise in connection with the three basic issues of image analysis: 1) the description of images; 2) the development, exploration, and optimization of the selection of mathematical methods and tools for information processing in the analysis of images; 3) the hardware and software implementation of the mathematical methods of image analysis.

Mathematical foundations of the DA are as follows: 1) the algebraization of the extraction of information from images; 2) the specialization of the Zhuravlev algebra to the case of representation of recognition source data in the form of images; 3) a standard language for describing the procedures of the analysis and recognition of images (DIA) [14-16]; 4) the mathematical formulation of the problem of image recognition; 5) mathematical theories of image analysis and pattern recognition; 6) a model of the process for solving a standard problem of image recognition. The main objects and means of the DA are: 1) images; 2) a universal language (DIA); 3) 2 types of descriptive models: a) an image model; b) a model for solving procedures of problems of image recognition and their implementation; 4) descriptive algebraic schemes of image representation (DASIR); 5) multi-model and multi-aspect representations of images, which are based on generating descriptive trees (GDT) [14-16].

The basic methodological principles of the DA are: 1) the algebraization of the image analysis; 2) the standardization of the representation of problems of analysis and recognition of images; 3) the conceptualization and formalization of phases through which the image passes during transformation while the recognition problem is solved; 4) the classification and specification of admissible models of images (descriptive image model - DIM); 5) RIRF; 6) the use of the standard algebraic language of DIA for describing models of images and procedures for their construction and transformation;7) the combination of algorithms in the multi-algorithmic schemes; 8) the use of multi-model and multi-aspect representations of images; 9) the construction and use of a basic model of the solution process for the standard problem of image recognition; 10) the definition and use of non-classical mathematical theory for the recognition of new formulations of problems of analyzing and recognizing images.

5   Ontology-Based Approach to Image Analysis

The automation of image analysis assumes that researchers and users of different qualifications have at their disposal not only a standardized technology of automation, but also a system supporting this technology, which accumulates and uses knowledge on image processing, analysis and evaluation and provides adequate structural and functional possibilities for supporting the more intelligent choice and synthesis of methods and algorithms. The automated system (AS) for image analysis must combine the possibilities of the instrumental environment for image processing and analysis and a knowledge-based system. Therefore, one of its main components is a knowledge base. Knowledge bases usually contain modules of universal knowledge, which are not related to any subject domain and knowledge modules related to a certain subject domain. The AS must provide software implementation of the hierarchies of classes of the main objects used in image analysis, have a specialized user interface, contain a library of algorithms that allow one to solve the main problems of image analysis and understanding with the help of efficient computational procedures, and provide accumulation and structuring of knowledge and experience in the domain of image analysis and understanding.

The need of efficient knowledge representation facilities can be fulfilled by using a suite of ontologies, For example, in [23], an approach devoted to semantic image interpretation for complex object classification purposes is proposed. The work described in [5] addresses the problem of explicit representation of objectives when developing image processing applications. The proposed framework demonstrates that ontology-based content representation can be used as an effective way for hierarchical and goal-directed inference in high-level visual analysis tasks.

In [6], a novel knowledge-oriented approach to image analysis based on the use of thesauruses and ontologies as tools for representation of knowledge, which are necessary for making intelligent decisions on the basis of information extracted from images, is proposed. The main contribution of this work is the development of a sufficiently detailed and well-structured Image Analysis Ontology. As a main source of the information about concepts the Image Analysis Thesaurus (IAT) [2] has been used. The important feature of the IAT is a novel hierarchical classification of tasks and algorithms for image processing, analysis and recognition.

6   Conclusions

The main deduction from the analysis of current trends in mathematical image analysis is necessity of a new algebraic language for describing and representing of image processing and understanding procedures and models. The new image algebra has to make possible: a) processing of images as objects of analysis and recognition; b) operations on image models and on models of procedures for image transformations; c) implementation of the procedures for image modifications both as operations and operands of the new image algebras for construction of compositions of basic models of procedures. The future research will be mostly devoted to constructing of image formal descriptions, i.e. to the Image Formalization Space and, in particular, to a) its topological properties; b) embedding of descriptive algorithmic schemes for image analysis into this space.

Acknowledgments. This work was supported in part by the Russian Foundation for Basic Research (projects Nos. 11-01-00990, 12-07-31123) and by the Presidium of the Russian Academy of Sciences within the Program "Information, Control, and Intelligent Technologies and Systems" (project No. 204) and the Program of the Division of Mathematical Sciences, of the Russian Academy of Sciences "Algebraic and Combinatorial Methods of New Generation Mathematical Cybernetics and Information Systems".

References

1. Barrow, H.G., Ambler, A.P., Burstall, R.M.: Some Techniques for Recognizing Structures in Pictures. In: Watanabe, S. (ed.) Proceedings of the International Conference on Frontiers of Pattern Recognition, pp. 1–30. Academic Press (1972)
2. Beloozerov, V.N., Gurevich, I.B., Gurevich, N.G., Murashov, D.M., Trusova, Y.O.: Thesaurus for Image Analysis: Basic Version. In: Pattern Recognition and Image Analysis: Advances in Mathematical Theory and Applications, vol. 13(4), pp. 556–569. Pleiades Publishing, Inc. (2003)

3. Bloehdorn, S., et al.: Semantic Annotation of Images and Videos for Multimedia Analysis. In: Gómez-Pérez, A., Euzenat, J. (eds.) ESWC 2005. LNCS, vol. 3532, pp. 592–607. Springer, Heidelberg (2005)

4. Chernov, V.M.: Clifford Algebras Are Group Algebras Projections. In: Bayro-Corrochano, E., Sobczyk, G. (eds.) Advances in Geometric Algebra with Applications in Science and Engineering, pp. 467–482. Birkhauser, Boston (2001)

5. Clouard, R., Renouf, A., Revenu, M.: An Ontology-Based Model for Representing Image Processing Application Objectives. International Journal of Pattern Recognition and Artificial Intelligence 24(8), 1181–1208 (2010)

6. Colantonio, S., Gurevich, I., Pieri, G., Salvetti, O., Trusova, Y.: Ontology-Based Framework to Image Mining. In: Gurevich, I., Niemann, H., Salvetti, O. (eds.) Image Mining Theory and Applications: Proceedings of the 2nd International Workshop on Image Mining Theory and Applications (in conjunction with VISIGRAPP 2009), pp. 11–19. INSTICC Press, Lisboa (2009)

7. Crespo, J., Serra, J., Schaffer, R.W.: Graph-based Morphological Filtering and Segmentation. In: Proc. 6th Symp. Pattern Recognition and Image Analysis, Cordoba, pp. 80–87 (1995)

8. Crimmins, T., Brown, W.: Image Algebra and Automatic Shape Recognition. IEEE Transactions on Aerospace and Electronic Systems 21(1), 60–69 (1985)

9. Davidson, J.L.: Classification of Lattice Transformations in Image Processing. Computer Vision, Graphics, and Image Processing: Image Understanding 57(3), 283–306 (1993)

10. Duff, M.J.B., Watson, D.M., Fountain, T.J., Shaw, G.K.: A Cellular Logic Array for Image Processing. Pattern Recognition 5(3), 229–247 (1973)

11. Dougherty, E.R.: A Homogeneous Unification of Image Algebra. Part I: The Homogenous Algebra, part II: Unification of Image Algebra. Imaging Science 33(4), 136–143, 144–149 (1989)

12. Evans, T.G.: Descriptive Pattern Analysis Techniques: Potentialities and Problems. In: The Proceedings of the International Conference on Methodologies of Pattern Recognition, pp. 149–157. Academic Press (1969)

13. Furman, Y.A.: Parallel Recognition of Different Classes of Patterns. Pattern Recognition and Image Analysis 19(3), 380–393 (2009)

14. Gurevich, I.B., Yashina, V.V.: Operations of Descriptive Image Algebras with One Ring. Pattern Recognition and Image Analysis: Advances in Mathematical Theory and Applications 16(3), 298–328 (2006)

15. Gurevich, I.B., Yashina, V.V.: Computer-Aided Image Analysis Based on the Concepts of Invariance and Equivalence. Pattern Recognition and Image Analysis: Advances in Mathematical Theory and Applications 16(4), 564–589 (2006)

16. Gurevich, I.B., Yashina, V.V.: Descriptive Approach to Image Analysis: Image Formalization Space. Pattern Recognition and Image Analysis: Advances in Mathematical Theory and Applications 22(4), 495–518 (2012)

17. Gader, P.D., Khabou, M.A., Koldobsky, A.: Morphological Regularization Neural Networks. Pattern Recognition 33, 935–944 (2000)

18. Grenander, U.: Elements of Pattern Theory. The Johns Hopkins University Press (1996)

19. Haralick, R., Shapiro, L., Lee, J.: Morphological Edge Detection. IEEE J. Robotics and Automation RA-3(1), 142–157 (1987)

20. Kaneff, S.: Pattern Cognition and the Organization of Information. In: Watanabe, S. (ed.) The Proceedings of the International Conference on Frontiers of Pattern Recognition, pp. 193–222. Academic Press (1972)

21. Kirsh, R.: Computer Interpretation of English Text and Picture Patterns. IEEE-TEC EC-13(4) (1964)
22. Labunec, V.G.: Algebraic Theory of Signals and Systems (Digital Signal Processing). Krasnoyarsk University (1984)
23. Maillot, N., Thonnat, M., Boucher, A.: Towards ontology-based cognitive vision. Machine Vision and Applications 16, 33–40 (2004)
24. Maragos, P.: Algebraic and PDE Approaches for Lattice Scale-Spaces with Global Constraints. International Journal of Computer Vision 52(2/3), 121–137 (2003)
25. Matheron, G.: Random Sets and Integral Geometry. Wiley, New York (1975)
26. Matrosov, V.L.: The Capacity of Polynomial Expansions of a Set of Algorithms for Calculating Estimates. USSR, Comput. Maths. Math. Phys. 24(1), 79–87 (1985)
27. Mazurov, V.D., Khachai, M.Y.: Parallel Computations and Committee Constructions. Journal Automation and Remote Control 68(5), 912–921 (2007)
28. Miller, P.: Development of a Mathematical Structure for Image Processing: Optical division tech. report. Perkin-Elmer (1983)
29. Narasimhan, R.: Picture Languages. In: Kaneff, S. (ed.) Picture Language Machines, pp. 1–30. Academic Press (1970)
30. von Neumann, J.: The General Logical Theory of Automata. In: Celebral Mechenism in Behavior: The Hixon Symposium. John Wiley & Sons (1951)
31. Pavel, M.: Fundamentals of Pattern Recognition. Marcell, Dekker, Inc., New York (1989)
32. Ritter, G.X.: Image Algebra. Center for computer vision and visualization, Department of Computer and Information science and Engineering, University of Florida, Gainesville, FL 32611 (2001)
33. Rosenfeld, A.: Digital Topology. American Math Monthly, 86 (1979)
34. Rosenfeld, A.: Picture Languages. Formal Models for Picture Recognition. Academic Press (1979)
35. Rudakov, K.V.: Universal and local constraints in the problem of correction of heuristic algorithms. Cybernetics 23(2), 181–186 (1987)
36. Serra, J.: Image Analysis and Mathematical Morphology. Academic Press (1982)
37. Shaw, A.: A Proposed Language for the Formal Description of Pictures. CGS Memo, 28, Stanford University (1967)
38. Schlesinger, M., Hlavac, V.: Ten Lectures on Statistical and Structural Pattern Recognition. In: Computational Imaging and Vision, vol. 24, 520 p. Kluwer Academic Publishers, Dordrecht (2002)
39. Sternberg, S.R.: Grayscale Morphology. Computer Vision, Graphics and Image Processing 35(3), 333–355 (1986)
40. Sussner, P.: Observations on Morphological Associative Memories and the Kernel Method. Neurocomputing 31, 167–183 (2000)
41. Town, C.: Ontological inference for image and video analysis. Machine Vision and Applications 17(2), 94–115 (2006)
42. Unger, S.H.: A Computer Oriented Toward Spatial Problems. Proceedings of the IRE 46, 1744–1750 (1958)
43. Zhuravlev, Y.I.: An Algebraic Approach to Recognition and Classification Problems. Pattern Recognition and Image Analysis: Advances in Mathematical Theory and Applications 8, 59–100 (1998)

Combining Texture and Shape Descriptors for Bioimages Classification: A Case of Study in ImageCLEF Dataset*

Anderson Brilhador, Thiago P. Colonhezi,
Pedro H. Bugatti, and Fabrício M. Lopes

Federal University of Technology - Paraná, Brazil
{pbugatti,fabricio}@utfpr.edu.br

Abstract. Nowadays a huge volume of data (e.g. images and videos) are daily generated in several areas. The importance of this subject has led to a new paradigm known as eScience. In this scenario, the biological image domain emerges as an important research area given the great impact that it can leads in real solutions and people's lives. On the other hand, to cope with this massive data it is necessary to integrate into the same environment not only several techniques involving image processing, description and classification, but also feature selection methods. Hence, in the present paper we propose a new framework capable to join these techniques in a single and efficient pipeline, in order to characterize biological images. Experiments, performed with the ImageCLEF dataset, have shown that the proposed framework presented notable results, reaching up to 87.5% of accuracy regarding the plant species classification, which is highly relevant and a non-trivial task.

Keywords: image descriptors, feature selection, classification, pattern recognition.

1 Introduction

Currently the digitization of information is becoming more common, generating a massive volume of data, leading to a new paradigm of data analysis known as eScience [1]. In 2011 it was estimated that the amount of information in the digital universe exceeded 1.8 zettabytes [2]. Among these data are largely digital content such as images and videos. However, these contents can only become useful when accessed efficiently, meaning not only fast, but also accurate. Therefore, it is needed new computational tools to retrieve and index these great volume of generated data.

The recovery of data can occur in textual form, through the inclusion of identifiers known as *tags*. Although, the *tags* inclusion have the advantage of indexing and retrieving multimedia content quickly, it is required to be given the textual information for each content. This task may lead to inconsistencies because it depends on the human perception. If the *tag* inclusion is incorrect, incomplete or not done, the content is not indexed properly, and consequently it

---

* This work has been supported by Fundação Araucária and CNPq.

J. Ruiz-Shulcloper and G. Sanniti di Baja (Eds.): CIARP 2013, Part I, LNCS 8258, pp. 431–438, 2013.

will not be recovered correctly. On the other hand, the retrieval of images based on its content eliminates the human interaction and the allocation of *tags* is done automatically. This process is based on extracting measures or features of the content, which is used to perform the indexing and retrieval of a particular object. A major challenge in this process is to generate features that really represent the data and consequently establish a classifier in order to correctly identify the data under analyses.

In this scenario, emerges an important research area known as Bioimage informatics [3], which focuses attention on developing new techniques for image processing, data mining, database and visualization in order to extract, compare, search and manage the biological knowledge in data-intensive problems. Regarding bioimages, there is an important challenge called the CLEF Cross Language Image Retrieval Track (ImageCLEF) [4]. This challenge illustrates the importance of the image retrieval in the actual data-intensive scenario. In particular, the biological diversity is very significant both in relation to the genetic potential as compared to the number of species and ecosystems. Considering plant biodiversity, the Amazon Rainforest holds the largest reserves of medicinal plants in the world. Then, there is a great necessity to recognize the flora through fast and efficient computational methods in order to deal with big data scenarios.

This paper presents an efficient framework for bioimage processing, feature extraction and classification, based on its texture and shape descriptors, which are combined in order to classify the input images. In this way, the performance of the proposed methodology was evaluated based on ImageCLEF [4] database by using several image features and classification techniques for this task, which are presented in the following sections.

2   Background

2.1   Feature Extraction

The feature extraction is defined as the entire set of operations for image processing and analysis performed in order to obtain numerical values that characterize the images or parts of them. It can also be defined as the capture of the most relevant information from a data given as input. The features extracted from the images can be based on three main classes: color, texture and shape.

The shape descriptors are measures of the boundaries, such as chain code, circularity, width, perimeter and area. The Fourier descriptor is widely used as a shape descriptor through its coefficients. The Fourier coefficients represents a global information of the curvature extracted from the image, which can be used to compare objects, because these coefficients are invariant to rotation, translation and scale. This invariance is achieved by applying simple transformations to the Fourier coefficients [5]. In this way, the Fourier coefficients from object boundary [6] was adopted in this work.

The color descriptors are based on the spectral radiation emitted or reflected by the objects, quantified by the intensity of the pixels in different spectral bands.

In this work, it was not adopted color descriptors by the nature of application in images of leaves, which have little variation in this feature.

The texture is an important descriptor used to identify objects in a digital image. The Haralick descriptors [7] use the distribution of gray levels and co-occurrence matrices to evaluate the different textures, which can be defined as: thin, thick, smooth, wavy, irregular or linear. Another method for texture analysis was proposed by Chao-Bing Lin and Quan [8], called Quantized Compound Change Histogram (QCCH). In this method, given a particular pixel the main idea is to check all gray level variations from its neighbors in the four directions. The differences of intensities in each direction are used for the construction of a histogram. By considering the variation of the intensities, this approach is free from variation between rotation and translation of the image. The Haralick and QCCH descriptors were adopted in the present work.

2.2   Image Classification

The classification is a way to analyse the data set and extracting models that lead to a category (class). The classification process can be defined in two paradigms: supervised learning, in which is known the classes for each available sample and unsupervised learning, in which the samples has no indication about its class.

The supervised learning is commonly divided into two tasks. The first task is called training, in which the classifier is constructed to determine the classes of the input objects from their attributes [9]. The second task is the classification, in which the model created in the first task is applied in order to define the classes for the input samples. There are a wide variety of supervised learning methods. In order to explore some important methods available in the literature the following classifiers: K-NN (K-nearest neighbor) [10], NB (Naive Bayes) [11], MLP (Multilayer Perceptron) [12], RF (Random Forest) [13], J4.8 [14] and SVM (Support Vector Machines) [15] were considered in this work.

In addition, the classifiers can be combined with the adaptive boosting strategy, which can be defined as a machine learning algorithm used to improve the performance of other learning algorithms [16]. In order to evaluate the performance of such technique, it was also considered in this work.

2.3   Feature Selection

The feature selection approach has been investigated, mainly in pattern recognition area, since the 70s [17]. By considering the big data scenario, the feature selection techniques has become essential in many knowledge areas [18–21].

Regarding pattern recognition, the feature selection aims to reduce the volume of features, i.e. the feature space, keeping the maximum of the source information as possible, in order to reduce the computational cost and to increase the accuracy of the classifier. Other aspects may be useful such as to increase the comprehensibility of the classification model and to increase the robustness of learning.

An important consideration in feature selection methods [22] is that much of the search assumes the monotonicity principle, i.e. increasing the number of attributes improves the performance of the classifier. However, adding more features the estimation error also increases, because the number of samples needed for constructing a suitable model.

A well known feature selection technique is the so-called correlation feature selection (CFS) [23]. This technique evaluates the subset of features by considering the consistency measure, seeking for combinations of attributes whose values split the data into subsets associated with a majority class. For a feature fit in this condition, the technique seeks for features that have a high correlation with the observed class and features not correlated among themselves, considering not only the feature individually, but also the relation among them.

3   Proposed Approach

After the image dataset definition it was performed the segmentation of the desired object from the image. Once the segmentation process is not the main focus of this paper, it was applied the baseline thresholding method proposed by Otsu [24]. Its basic principle is to select a threshold that maximizes the variance between classes (foreground and background).

The next step was the extraction of the image features as related in Sec. 2.1. It was developed in Java technology a framework to perform the extraction of the adopted image features from an input image, which is freely available[1].

The image features are extracted from each sample and was built a feature vector with 218 positions, as follows: [1 - 52] Haralick, [53 - 92] QCCH and [93 - 218] Fourier coefficients. Each image has an unique feature vector, which will be considered for its classification (see Sec. 5).

The final step is the classification of the image data set by applying the methods described in Sec. 2.2. In face of the number of the extracted image features, a feature selection was adopted as a filter step before the classification (Sec. 2.3). Besides, the adaptive boosting strategy was also performed with the classifiers.

4   Measuring Effectiveness

In order to evaluate the performance, it is necessary to perform the classification and to compare the results with the correct class for each sample. An approach commonly used in this task is the cross-validation or k-fold cross validation, in which the image data set is splitted in k folds, $D_1, D_1, \ldots, D_k$ of equal size. Then, the training and test set is performed k times in order to evaluate the performance of the classifier. More specifically, one fold D_i is used for test and the remaining folds are used for training. The overall accuracy is calculated by averaging the results obtained at each step, thus achieving an estimation of the quality of knowledge generated by the classification model and allowing statistical analyses.

After performing the test, it is also possible to obtain statistical values for measure the performance of the classifier such as *Precision*, *recall* and receiver operating characteristic (ROC) curve [25].

---

[1] http://code.google.com/p/jimagefeature/

4.1   Image Dataset Description

The ImageCLEF 2012 [26] image dataset was adopted in this work in order to evaluate the proposed methodology by considering the plant identification species from its leaves. The image dataset includes $n = 126$ different species of trees located in the French Mediterranean area, the total number of samples available is 11,527, which are subdivided into three categories of images: scan (57%), scan-like (24%) and free natural photos(19%).

The scan category was adopted in this work, which contains 4870 images divided unevenly among the 126 species (classes). In order to normalize the distribution among classes, it was applied the following procedure: (1) it was calculated the average x of images for each species e_i, $i = 1, \ldots, n$; (2) by considering this average value, it was observed the quantity of images in each specie (q_i) was greater than x. The species with lower quantity of samples, i.e. $q_i < x$, were excluded for not having enough samples. This pre-processing led to a balanced number of samples for each species. As a result, the pre-processed image dataset was reduced to 3,582 samples distributed in 54 different species.

5   Results

The first round of experiments was performed in order to evaluate the contribution of each class of the adopted descriptors (shape and texture). The correlation-based feature approach was applied to the complete feature vector (see Sec. 3) before the classification methods. As a result, the features were selected in order to build a new feature vector as shown in Table 1.

Table 1. Feature vector composition by considering all features and the feature selection results

Descriptors	All Features	Selected Features
Haralick	52 (24%)	11 (20%)
QCCH	40 (18%)	20 (37%)
Fourier	126 (58%)	23 (43%)
Total	**218**	**54**

These results points out that the texture features are slightly more relevant than shape descriptors with respect to the number of selected features. However, the feature selection indicates that both were important. The texture features have 58% and the shape descriptors have the 42% of the selected features.

The second round of experiments was performed in order to investigate the behavior of the adopted classifiers by considering all features, the filtered feature vector and the the Adaptive Boosting technique. Table 2 presents the average results by adopting the 10-fold cross validation approach for each configuration. It is important to notice that the SVM classifier presented the best performance over all configuration, achieving 87,5% of precision when all features were applied. The MLP and Random Forest classifiers showed slightly lower results. However, these results were achieved only after performing the feature selection and adaBoost approaches, respectively, indicating the robustness of the SVM classifier. The J4.8, Random Forest methods had a significant improvement when using the feature selection and adaBoost approaches. Surprisingly, the MLP classifier showed no improvement when combined with the AdaBoost approach. The K-NN and Naive Bayes showed similar results for all adopted variations.

Table 2. Performance comparison among the adopted classifiers by considering all features, the selected features and the selected features with adaBoost technique in terms of the precision measure

Classifier	all features	selected features	adaBoost
K-NN	78.9%	82.6%	82.6%
Naive Bayes	76.8%	78.9%	78.9%
J4.8	67.1%	68.3%	84.1%
Random Forest	77.0%	81.1%	**87.1%**
MLP	50.9%	**83.9%**	83.3%
SVM	**87.5%**	83.2%	86.5%

In order to evaluate the performance of the classifiers regarding the better and the worst classified species, the five species with better and worst results were selected in Tables 3 and 4 respectively. Figure 1 shows an example for each of the species listed in Tables 3 and 4.

Table 3. The five better classified species

Id	Class	K-NN Precision	K-NN ROC	NB Precision	NB ROC	J48 Precision	J48 ROC	RF Precision	RF ROC	MLP Precision	MLP ROC	SVM Precision	SVM ROC
(a)	Daphne-cneorum	1	0,992	1	0,985	0,988	0,999	0,988	1	0,975	1	1	1
(b)	Buxus-sempervirens	0,978	0,999	0,983	0,998	0,972	1	0,978	1	0,962	1	0,972	1
(c)	Juniperus-oxycedrus	0,988	1	0,987	0,997	0,963	1	0,988	1	0,898	1	0,975	1
(d)	Albizia-julibrissin	1	1	0,886	0,999	1	1	0,951	1	0,95	0,999	1	0,993
(e)	Nerium-oleander	0,978	0,993	0,965	0,988	0,966	0,996	0,966	0,998	0,925	0,999	0,977	0,997

Table 4. The five worst classified species

Id	Class	K-NN Precision	K-NN ROC	NB Precision	NB ROC	J48 Precision	J48 ROC	RF Precision	RF ROC	MLP Precision	MLP ROC	SVM Precision	SVM ROC
(f)	Ginkgo-biloba	0,784	0,788	0,515	0,911	0,7	0,985	0,871	0,983	0,583	0,959	0,795	0,974
(g)	Acer-campestre	0,795	0,857	0,515	0,906	0,789	0,956	0,696	0,986	0,707	0,954	0,688	0,979
(h)	Arbutus-unedo	0,562	0,866	0,791	0,782	0,662	0,963	0,593	0,975	0,667	0,953	0,788	0,969
(i)	Laurus-nobilis	0,661	0,926	0,508	0,882	0,681	0,993	0,765	0,99	0,694	0,961	0,706	0,988
(j)	Fraxinus-angustifolia	0,464	0,704	0,712	0,795	0,676	0,99	0,803	0,988	0,615	0,982	0,662	0,932

(a)   (b)   (c)   (d)   (e)   (f)   (g)   (h)   (i)   (j)

Fig. 1. Samples of the better and worst classified species accordingly Tables 3 and 4

By considering the five better classified species (a–e), it was observed that they have similar features of texture and shape. For instance, the *Daphne cneorum* (a) and *Juniperus oxycedrus* (c) species present similar shape features, but have different texture features being the first roughened and the second smooth. Only the *Albizia-julibrissin* has different texture and shape from other species.

The five worst classified species (f–j) show similar texture and shape features as in the case of the species *Arbutus unedo* (h) and *Laurus nobilis* (i) increasing the difficulty in classification between them. Another case is the *Fraxinus angustifolia* (j), because it varies greatly in shape making very difficult to establish a pattern for this class, the same variation occurs with the species *Ginkgo biloba* (f) and *Acer campestre* (g).

6 Conclusion

This paper presents a novel and flexible framework for Bioimage processing, feature extraction and classification. The proposed framework combines texture-based and shape-based features improving in a great extent the classification accuracy of biological images. Furthermore, it not only allows an easy addition of new methods for processing, description and classification of images, but also provides the evaluation of such methods under the same conditions. It is important to highlight that the great majority of works in the literature neglects this issue. Another point addressed by the proposed approach is related to the high dimensionality of the feature vectors. In order to mitigate this problem we embedded a feature selection method into it.

As shown in the experiments section, the proposed approach presented notable results by considering the plant species classification, reaching up to 87.5% of accuracy in the overall case. Considering each one the species it reached, in many cases, up to 100% of accuracy. Moreover, the dimensionality of the feature vectors was reduced about 4 times less dimensions, diminishing the classification computational cost. Hence, this testifies the usefulness of the proposed approach in real biological applications.

Future work includes to apply the proposed framework to other biological image datasets, to include color-based features and join new steps in the proposed framework, such as unsupervised classification. It is also planned as a future work to apply non-parametric tests for statistical comparisons of classifiers as described in [27].

References

1. Gray, J.: Jim gray on escience: a transformed scientific method. The Fourth Paradigm: Data-intensive Scientific Discovery (2009)
2. Gantz, J., Reinsel, D.: Extracting value from chaos. IDC iView, 1–12 (2011)
3. Peng, H.: Bioimage informatics: a new area of engineering biology. Bioinformatics 24(17), 1827–1836 (2008)
4. Müller, H., Clough, P., Deselaers, T., Caputo, B.: ImageCLEF: Experimental Evaluation in VIsual Information Retrieval, vol. 32. Springer (2010)

5. Bartolini, I., Ciaccia, P., Patella, M.: Warp: Accurate retrieval of shapes using phase of fourier descriptors and time warping distance. IEEE Transactions on Pattern Analysis and Machine Intelligence 27(1), 142–147 (2005)
6. da Fontoura Costa, L., Cesar Jr., R.M.: Shape analysis and classification: theory and practice, 2nd edn. CRC Press (2010)
7. Attig, A., Perner, P.: A comparison between haralick's texture descriptor and the texture descriptor based on random sets for biological images. In: Perner, P. (ed.) MLDM 2011. LNCS, vol. 6871, pp. 524–538. Springer, Heidelberg (2011)
8. Huang, C.B., Liu, Q.: An orientation independent texture descriptor for image retrieval. In: Int. Conf. on Communic., Circ. and Systems, pp. 772–776. IEEE (2007)
9. Han, J., Kamber, M.: Data mining: concepts and techniques. Morgan Kaufmann (2006)
10. Aha, D.W., Kibler, D., Albert, M.K.: Instance-based learning algorithms. Machine Learning 6(1), 37–66 (1991)
11. Lewis, D.D.: Naive (bayes) at forty: The independence assumption in information retrieval. In: Nédellec, C., Rouveirol, C. (eds.) ECML 1998. LNCS, vol. 1398, pp. 4–15. Springer, Heidelberg (1998)
12. Gardner, M., Dorling, S.: Artificial neural networks–a review of applications in the atmospheric sciences. Atmospheric Environment 32(14-15), 2627–2636 (1998)
13. Statistics, L.B., Breiman, L.: Random forests. Machine Learning, 5–32 (2001)
14. Quinlan, J.R.: C4.5: Programs for Machine Learning. Morgan Kaufmann (1993)
15. Abe, S.: Support vector machines for pattern classification. Springer (2010)
16. Freund, Y., Schapire, R.E.: A decision-theoretic generalization of on-line learning and an application to boosting. In: Vitányi, P.M.B. (ed.) EuroCOLT 1995. LNCS, vol. 904, pp. 23–37. Springer, Heidelberg (1995)
17. Mucciardi, A.N., Gose, E.E.: A comparison of seven techniques for choosing subsets of pattern recognition properties. IEEE Trans. on Comp. 100(9), 1023–1031 (1971)
18. Lopes, F.M., Martins Jr., D.C., Cesar Jr., R.M.: Feature selection environment for genomic applications. BMC Bioinformatics 9(1), 451 (2008)
19. Lopes, F.M., de Oliveira, E.A., Cesar Jr., R.M.: Analysis of the GRNs inference by using Tsallis entropy and a feature selection approach. In: Bayro-Corrochano, E., Eklundh, J.-O. (eds.) CIARP 2009. LNCS, vol. 5856, pp. 473–480. Springer, Heidelberg (2009)
20. Lopes, F.M., Martins Jr., D.C., Barrera, J., Cesar Jr., R.M.: SFFS-MR: A floating search strategy for GRNs inference. In: Dijkstra, T.M.H., Tsivtsivadze, E., Marchiori, E., Heskes, T. (eds.) PRIB 2010. LNCS, vol. 6282, pp. 407–418. Springer, Heidelberg (2010)
21. Pinto, S.C.D., Mena-Chalco, J.P., Lopes, F.M., Velho, L., Cesar Jr., R.M.: 3D facial expression analysis by using 2D and 3D wavelet transforms. In: ICIP, pp. 1281–1284 (2011)
22. John, G.H., Kohavi, R., Pfleger, K., et al.: Irrelevant features and the subset selection problem. In: 11th Int. Conf. on Machine Learning, pp. 121–129 (1994)
23. Hall, M.A.: Correlation-based feature selection for machine learning. PhD thesis, The University of Waikato (1999)
24. Sahoo, P.K., Soltani, S., Wong, A.: A survey of thresholding techniques. Computer Vision, Graphics, and Image Processing 41(2), 233–260 (1988)
25. Davis, J., Goadrich, M.: The relationship between precision-recall and roc curves. In: 23rd International Conference on Machine Learning, pp. 233–240. ACM (2006)
26. Goëau, H., Bonnet, P., Joly, A., Yahiaoui, I., Barthélémy, D., Boujemaa, N., Molino, J.: The ImageCLEF 2012 Plant Identification Task (2012)
27. Demšar, J.: Statistical comparisons of classifiers over multiple data sets. J. Mach. Learn. Res. 7, 1–30 (2006)

CWMA: Circular Window Matching Algorithm

Daniel Miramontes-Jaramillo[1], Vitaly Kober[1], and Víctor Hugo Díaz-Ramírez[2]

[1] CICESE, Ensenada, B.C. 22860, México
dmiramon@cicese.edu.mx, vkober@cicese.mx
[2] CITEDI-IPN, Tijuana, B.C. 22510, México
vhdiaz@citedi.mx

Abstract. Various vision applications exploit matching algorithms to locate a target object in a scene image. A new fast matching algorithm based on recursive calculation of oriented gradient histograms over several circular sliding windows is presented. In order to speed up the algorithm pyramidal image decomposition technique and parallel implementation with modern multicore processors are utilized. The proposed fast algorithm yields a good invariance performance for both in-plane and out-of-plane rotations of a scene image. Computer results obtained with the proposed algorithm are presented and compared with those of common algorithms in terms of matching accuracy and processing time.

1 Introduction

Recently numerous matching algorithms using features or keypoints were proposed. Among them, Scale Invariant Feature Transform (SIFT) [1] and Speeded-Up Robust Features (SURF) [2] are the most popular algorithms. These basic algorithms and their variants [3,4,5] can be used as references for comparison with new matching methods. Although feature-based matching methods are popular, template matching algorithms are an attractive alternative for real-time applications [6,7]. Template matching filters possess a good formal basis and can be implemented by exploiting massive parallelism in hybrid optodigital systems [6,8] or in high-performance digital hardware such as graphic processing units (GPU) [7,9] or field programmable gate arrays (FPGA) [10] at high speed. Another approach is a combination of feature-based and template matching algorithms. For example, Scale Invariant Compressed Histogram Transform (SICHT) [11] uses the Histograms of Oriented Gradients (HoG) [12] calculated in a moving window as features. In this paper we present a fast hybrid algorithm for a reliable matching that recursively calculates the histograms of oriented gradients in several sliding circular windows. The shape of sliding windows helps us to obtain a pretty good invariance to in-plane/out-of-plane image rotations with a slight scaling. The algorithm can be easily implemented using modern technology of multi-core processors. The performance of the proposed algorithm in a test database is compared with that of SIFT and SURF algorithms in terms of matching accuracy and processing time.

J. Ruiz-Shulcloper and G. Sanniti di Baja (Eds.): CIARP 2013, Part I, LNCS 8258, pp. 439–446, 2013.
© Springer-Verlag Berlin Heidelberg 2013

2 Proposed Approach

First, let us define a set of circular windows $\{W_i,\ i=1,...,M\}$ in a reference image as a set of the following closed disks:

$$W_i = \left\{ (x,y) \in \mathbb{R}^2 : (x - x_i)^2 + (y - y_i)^2 \le r_i \right\}, \tag{1}$$

where (x_i, y_i) are coordinates of the center and r_i is the radius of the ith disk. The circular windows with possible overlapping fill inside an object of interest in the reference image as shown in Fig. 1. The disks form a geometric structure that runs across a scene image. The histograms of oriented gradients are calculated in circular areas and further used for matching. It is interesting to note that at any position of the structure each disk contains image area that is unchangeable during rotation; therefore, the histogram of oriented gradients computed in a circular window is also invariant to rotation. Moreover, in order to obtain a high accuracy of matching relative positions of the disks described by the center distances and center-to-center angles should be taken into account. It is recommendable to choose a minimum number of equal disks with a radius to fill inside as much as possible the reference object. Actually, numerous experiments have showed that the number M of circular windows may be chosen from 2 to 4 to yield the matching performance comparable with that of the SIFT.

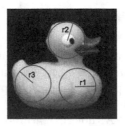

Fig. 1. Set of circular windows calculated from an object

Histograms of Oriented Gradients are good features for matching [12] because they possess a good discriminant capability and robust to small image deformations such as rotation and scale. First, at each position of the ith circular window on a scene image we compute gradients inside the window with the help of the Sobel operator [13]. Next, using the gradient magnitudes $\{Mag_i (x,y) : (x,y) \in W_i\}$ and orientation values quantized for Q levels $\{\varphi_i (x,y) : (x,y) \in W_i\}$, the histogram of oriented gradients can be computed as follows:

$$HoG_i (\alpha) = \begin{cases} \displaystyle\sum_{(x,y)\in W_i} \delta (\alpha - \varphi_i (x,y)), & Mag_i (x,y) \ge Med \\ 0, & otherwise, \end{cases} \tag{2}$$

where $\alpha = \{0, ..., Q-1\}$ are histogram values (bins), Med is the median value of image pixels inside of the circular window, and $\delta(z) = \begin{cases} 1, & z = 0 \\ 0, & otherwise \end{cases}$ is the Kronecker delta function. Note that the calculation in Eq.(2) requires approximately $\lceil \pi r_i^2 \rceil$ addition operations. In order to reduce computational complexity the calculation of the histograms at the sliding window position k can be performed in a recursive manner as follows:

$$HoG_i^k(\alpha) = HoG_i^{k-1}(\alpha) - \sum_{(x,y) \in OutP_i^{k-1}} \delta\left(\alpha - Out\varphi_i^{k-1}(x,y)\right) \tag{3}$$

$$+ \sum_{(x,y) \in InP_i^k} \delta\left(\alpha - In\varphi_i^k(x,y)\right)$$

where $OutP_i^{k-1}$ is a set of outgoing orientation values whose pixels belong to the half of the perimeter of the sliding window at step $k-1$, that is,

$$\left\{ Out\varphi_i^{k-1}(x,y) = \begin{cases} \varphi_i^{k-1}(x,y), & Mag_i^{k-1}(x,y) \geq Med^{k-1} \\ 0, & otherwise \end{cases} \right. : \tag{4}$$

$$(x,y) \in OutP_i^{k-1} \bigg\};$$

InP_i^k is a set of incoming orientation values whose pixels belong to the half of the perimeter of the sliding window at step k given by

$$\left\{ In\varphi_i^k(x,y) = \begin{cases} \varphi_i^k(x,y), & Mag_i^k(x,y) \geq Med^k \\ 0, & otherwise \end{cases} \right. : \tag{5}$$

$$(x,y) \in InP_i^k \bigg\}.$$

The computational complexity of this calculation is approximately $\lceil 2\pi r_i \rceil$ addition operations. Fig. 2 shows the recursive update of the histogram along columns. The recursive calculation can be used along columns as well as along rows. To provide rotation invariance a cyclic shift of the histogram moving a dominant orientation was proposed [11]. However, if there are several dominant orientations in the histogram owing to noise, this method does not work properly.

Another drawback is the method does not take into account scale invariance. To overcome these disadvantages, we utilize a normalized correlation operation for comparison of the histograms of the reference and scene images. Let us compute a centered and normalized histogram of oriented gradients of the reference as follows:

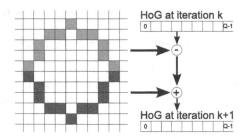

Fig. 2. Recursive histogram update

$$\overline{HoG_i^R}(\alpha) = \frac{HoG_i^R(\alpha) - Mean^R}{\sqrt{Var^R}}, \tag{6}$$

where $Mean^R$ and Var^R are sample mean and variance of the histogram, respectively.

The correlation output for the ith circular window at position k can be computed with the help of the fast Inverse Fourier Transform [13] as follows:

$$C_i^k(\alpha) = IFT\left[\frac{HS_i^k(\omega)HR_i^*(\omega)}{\sqrt{Q\sum_{q=0}^{Q-1}\left(HoG_i^k(q)\right)^2 - \left(HS_i^k(0)\right)^2}}\right], \tag{7}$$

where $HS_i^k(\omega)$ is the Fourier Transform of the histogram of oriented gradients inside of the ith circular window over the scene image and $HR_i(\omega)$ is the Fourier Transform of $\overline{HoG_i^R}(\alpha)$; the asterisk denotes complex conjugate. The correlation peak is a measure of similarity of the two histograms, which can be obtained as follows:

$$P_i^k = \max_\alpha\left\{C_i^k(\alpha)\right\}. \tag{8}$$

The correlation peaks are in the range of $[-1, 1]$. It is of interest to note that the normalized correlation peaks possess two important properties: first, invariance to rotation because a cyclic shift of the histogram values corresponds to a cyclic shift of the correlation output and does not change the correlation peak value; second, the normalization in Eqs.(6) and (7) helps us to take into account a slight scale difference between the reference and scene images. Computation of the centered and normalized histograms for all circular windows over the reference image as well as the Fourier Transforms can be done as preprocessing. A block diagram of the proposed one-pass matching algorithm is shown in Fig. 3.

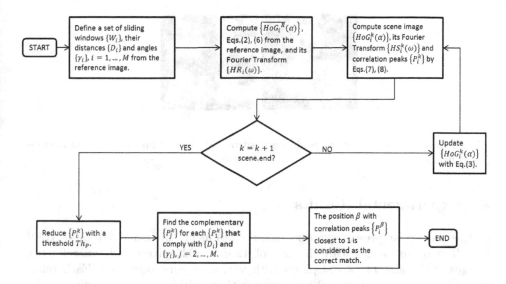

Fig. 3. Block diagram of the algorithm

In order to accelerate the proposed algorithm a decomposition technique [14] is exploited. As shown in Fig 4, an image can be decomposed in a set of small images by decimating in each direction depending on a decomposition level L; i. e. when $L = 2$, the image is divided in 4 similar images that can reconstruct the original image by performing the inverse process, in a similar way, if $L = 3$ there are 9 images, and so on.

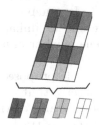

Fig. 4. Ilustration of a pyramidal decompostition with level 2 of an image

After selecting the decomposition level, two sets of small images from a scene and reference images are formed. Next, the described algorithm in the preceding section is applied only to one pair of the images. A set of decomposed images are shown in Fig. 5.

The speed-up is achieved by the spatial search in a smaller scene image.

Fig. 5. Level 2 of reference image decomposition: a) original image, b) set of decomposed images

3   Experimental Results

In this section we present experimental results using the image database ALOI [15]. Ten scene images with the size of 1280×1024 pixels and ten reference images of the size 144×144 pixels with varied objects were used. Each reference object is located at 100 random positions within the scene images. The performance of the proposed algorithm was compared with that of popular SIFT and SURF algorithms, the parameters of such algorithms are the ones proposed by Lowe [1] and Bay [2]. The algorithms are tested in different conditions such as in-plane/out-of-plane rotations and a slight scaling. The performance is evaluated in terms of the number of correct matches and processing time. The proposed algorithm referred to as CWMA uses two circular windows in each object with a radius r (depends on the size of object). For a better matching we use $Q = 64$ bins instead of 9 bins as proposed in [12]. The parameters of the algorithms are as follows: $M = 2$, $Q = 64$, $Th_p = 0.7$, $L = \{1, 2, 4\}$. The performance of the tested algorithms for in-plane/out-of-plane rotation is shown in Fig. 6. It can be seen that the CWMA yields the best in-plane rotation invariance and a similar performance with that of the SIFT for out-of-plane rotation. The number in parenthesis is the decomposition level.

Figure 7 illustrates tolerance of the proposed algorithm to image scaling in the range of $[0.8, 1.2]$. One may observe that the performance of the CWMA is pretty good for slight image upscaling and downscaling. So, the algorithm can be utilized in real-life application such as tracking.

Finally, the performance of the tested algorithms in terms of processing time is shown in Fig. 8. A standard PC with an Intel Core i7 processor with 3.2 GHz and 8 GB of RAM was used. The implementation of the SIFT and the SURF is taken from the open library OpenCV with Intel multithreading library TBB. The proposed algorithm was also implemented with OpenCV with multithreading from OpenMP library. We see that the proposed algorithm with a pyramidal decomposition performs close to the SURF and outperforms the SIFT.

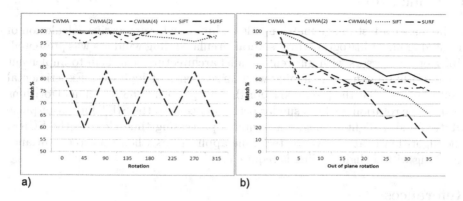

Fig. 6. Matching results for: a) in-plane rotation, b) out-of-plane rotation

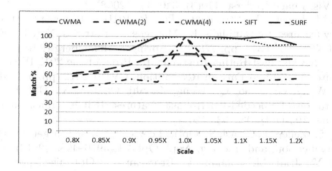

Fig. 7. Matching results for a slight scaling

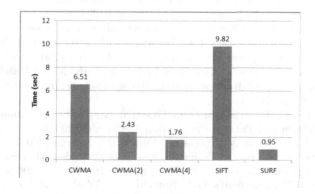

Fig. 8. Processing time of tested algorithms

4   Conclusion

In this paper a fast image matching algorithm based on recursive calculation of oriented gradient histograms over several circular sliding windows was presented. Multicore processors with inherent parallel architectures can help to implement the algorithm for image matching with large scenes at high rate. Experimental results showed that the proposed algorithm outperforms the common algorithms for in-plane rotation, yields a similar performance with the SIFT for out-of-plane rotation and a slight scaling, and requires processing time close to the SURF. The algorithm is attractive for real-time applications when rotation invariance matching with a slight scaling is required.

References

1. Lowe, D.G.: Object recognition from local scale-invariant features. In: Proc. Int. Conference on Computer Vision, vol. 2, pp. 1150–1157 (1999)
2. Bay, H., Ess, A., Tuytelaars, T., Van Gool, L.: SURF: Speeded Up Robust Features. Comput. Vis. Image Underst. 110(3), 346–359 (2008)
3. Calonder, M., Lepetit, V., Strecha, C., Fua, P.: BRIEF: Binary robust independent elementary features. In: Daniilidis, K., Maragos, P., Paragios, N. (eds.) ECCV 2010, Part IV. LNCS, vol. 6314, pp. 778–792. Springer, Heidelberg (2010)
4. Ortiz, R.: FREAK: Fast Retina Keypoint. In: Proc. of the 2012 IEEE Conference on Computer Vision and Pattern Recognition, CVPR 2012, pp. 510–517 (2012)
5. Liao, C., Wang, G., Miao, Q., Wang, Z., Shi, C., Lin, X.: DSP-Based Parallel Implementation of Speeded-Up Robust Features. IEICE Trans. on Information and Systems E94-D(4), 930–933 (2011)
6. Manzurv, T., Zeller, J., Serati, S.: Optical correlator based target detection, recognition, classification, and tracking. Appl. Opt. 51, 4976–4983 (2012)
7. Ouerhani, Y., Jridi, M., Alfalou, A., Brosseau, C.: Optimized preprocessing input plane GPU implementation of an optical face recognition technique using a segmented phase only composite filter. Opt. Comm. 289, 33–44 (2013)
8. Diaz-Ramirez, V.H., Kober, V.: Adaptive phase-input joint transform correlator. Appl. Opt. 46(26), 6543–6551 (2007)
9. Sanders, J., Kandrot, E.: CUDA by Example: An Introduction to General-Purpose GPU Programming. Addison-Wesley Professional (2010)
10. Rice, K.L., Taha, T.M., Chowdhury, A.M., Awwal, A.A.S., Woodard, D.L.: Design and acceleration of phase-only filter-based optical pattern recognition for fingerprint identification. Optical Engineering 48(11), 117–206 (2009)
11. Zalesky, B.A., Lukashevich, P.V.: Scale Invariant Algorithm to Match Regions on Aero or Satellite Images. In: Proc. Pattern Recognition and Information Processing, vol. 11, pp. 25–30 (2011)
12. Dalal, N., Triggs, B.: Histograms of Oriented Gradients for Human Detection. Computer Vision and Pattern Recognition 1, 886–893 (2005)
13. Pratt, W.K.: Digital Image Processing. John Wiley & Sons (2007)
14. López-Martınez, J.L., Kober, V.: Fast image restoration algorithm based on camera microscanning. In: Proc. SPIE, vol. 7443, pp. 744310–744315 (2009)
15. Geusebroek, J.M., Burghouts, G.J., Smeulders, A.W.M.: The Amsterdam library of object images. Int. J. Computer Vision. 61(1), 103–112 (2005), http://staff.science.uva.nl/~aloi/

A Histogram-Based Approach
to Mathematical Line Segmentation

Mohamed Alkalai and Volker Sorge

School of Computer Science, University of Birmingham
{M.A.Alkalai,V.Sorge}@cs.bham.ac.uk

Abstract. In document analysis line segmentation is a necessary pre-requisite step for further analysing of textual components. While much work has been devoted to line segmentation of regular text documents, this work can not be easily adopted to documents that contain specialist components such as tables or mathematical expressions. In this paper we concentrate on a line segmentation technique for documents containing mathematical expressions, which, due to their two dimensional structure are often comprised of multiple distinct lines. We present an approach to line segmentation in the presence of mathematics that is based on a set of histogram measures and heuristics considering vertical and horizontal distances of characters only. The method also provides a technique to distinguish consecutive lines that are vertically overlapped but belong to different mathematical expressions. Experiments on data sets of 200 and 1000 maths pages, respectively, show a high rate of accuracy.

1 Introduction

Line segmentation is a prerequisite step for structural analysis of both printed and handwritten documents. While much work has been done for text line segmentation of documents containing primarily text only. The developed techniques such as projection profile cutting [3,2], smearing [6], grouping [4] or seam carving [5], rely to some extent on the fact that in regular text documents generally lines can be clearly separated by detecting consecutive whitespace between them.

For documents containing mathematical expressions, however, these techniques do not suffice due to the occurrence of particular artifacts of mathematical notations such as math accents, the limits of sum symbols, etc. that, while actually constituting a single line, can appear spatially lay out over more than one separable line. And while there exists quite a body of work on the segmentation of mathematical documents, this work is generally more concerned with the identification and separation of mathematical structures from surrounding text and their subsequent layout analysis [8].

In this paper we present a math line recognition algorithm that is reliable independent of knowledge on any peculiarities of mathematical expressions (Sec. 2). It is based on spatial considerations only, thus avoiding committing to premature errors, that stem from considering actual content such as symbols or fonts. In particular, we use a histogram-based approach, considering horizontal spaces

J. Ruiz-Shulcloper and G. Sanniti di Baja (Eds.): CIARP 2013, Part I, LNCS 8258, pp. 447–455, 2013.

between glyphs in lines of a page, in order to classify lines into two types: principal and non-principal, where the former are lines in their own right, while the latter are only parts of mathematical expressions and should be merged with neighbouring lines. In addition to this technique we have developed a set of heuristics using simple yet effective measures for correction of classification errors as well as to separate lines that share vertically overlapping characters but that belong to distinct mathematical expressions. We demonstrate the effectiveness of our approach by presenting experiments on two distinct data sets containing 200 and 1000 pages from mathematical documents, where we achieve an accuracy rate of 96.9% and 98.6%, respectively for line detection (Sec. 3). A previous version of the algorithm, that in particularly did not allow for splitting lines with vertical overlap, has been successfully applied in experiments to improve the identification rate of mathematical expressions was presented in [1].

2   A Histogrammatic Approach to Line Segmentation

The basic idea of our approach is to detect all possible individual lines first and then merge neighbouring lines into single lines likely to contain mathematical expressions. Thereby we rely neither on knowledge of the content of lines, font information nor vertical distance. Instead we use a histogrammatic measure on space within a single line. We then employ simple height considerations to detect lines that have not been correctly classified to be merged or not merged. In a final step, each line that is classified to be merged is clustered with its closest line as long as they are horizontally overlapped. In summary our procedure consists of the following steps:

1. *Initial line separation* by vertical cuts (cf. [7]).
2. *Detect and split lines* with vertically overlapping characters.
3. *Initial classification of lines* into principal and non-principal, where the latter should be merged with the former.
4. *Improvement of classification* using two measures based on character height.
5. *Merge* non-principal with neighbouring principal lines to obtain final lines.

We now define the concepts of our procedure more formally. Step 1 is given by the following three definitions.

Definition 1 (Bounding Box). *Let g be a glyph, then the limits of its bounding box are defined by $l(g), r(g), t(g), b(g)$ representing left, right, top and bottom limit respectively. We also have $l < r$ and $t < b$.*

Definition 2 (Vertical and Horizontal Overlap). *Let g_1, g_2 be two glyphs. We say g_1 overlaps vertically with g_2 if we have $[t(g_1), b(g_1)] \cap [t(g_2), b(g_2)] \neq \emptyset$, where $[t(g), b(g)]$ is the interval defined by the top and bottom limit of glyph g.*
Similarly we define horizontal overlap of two glyphs g_1, g_2 by $[l(g_1), r(g_1)] \cap [l(g_2), r(g_2)] \neq \emptyset$.

We can now define a line using the vertical overlap on a set of glyphs.

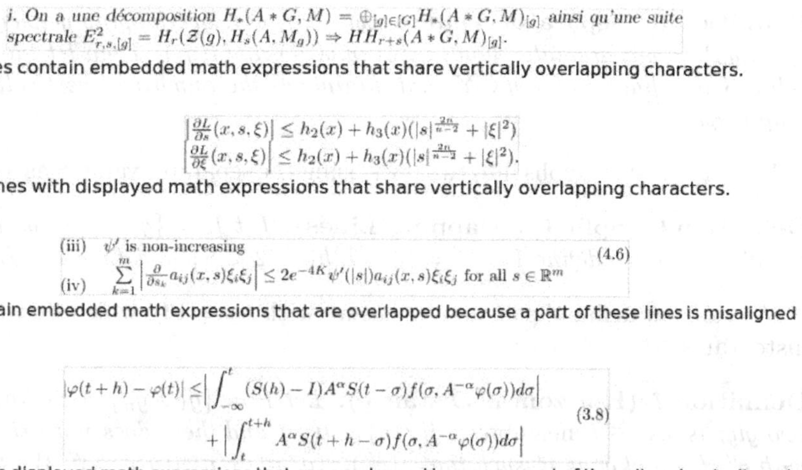

i. On a une décomposition $H_*(A * G, M) = \bigoplus_{[g] \in [G]} H_*(A * G, M)_{[g]}$ ainsi qu'une suite spectrale $E^2_{r,s,[g]} = H_r(\mathcal{Z}(g), H_s(A, M_g)) \Rightarrow HH_{r+s}(A * G, M)_{[g]}$.

(a) Lines contain embedded math expressions that share vertically overlapping characters.

$$\left|\frac{\partial L}{\partial s}(x, s, \xi)\right| \le h_2(x) + h_3(x)(|s|^{\frac{2n}{a-2}} + |\xi|^2)$$
$$\left|\frac{\partial L}{\partial \xi}(x, s, \xi)\right| \le h_2(x) + h_3(x)(|s|^{\frac{2n}{n-2}} + |\xi|^2).$$

(b) Lines with displayed math expressions that share vertically overlapping characters.

(iii) ψ' is non-increasing   (4.6)

(iv) $\sum_{k=1}^{m} \left|\frac{\partial}{\partial s_k} a_{ij}(x, s)\xi_i\xi_j\right| \le 2e^{-4K}\psi'(|s|)a_{ij}(x, s)\xi_i\xi_j$ for all $s \in \mathbb{R}^m$

(c) Lines contain embedded math expressions that are overlapped because a part of these lines is misaligned

$$|\varphi(t + h) - \varphi(t)| \le \left|\int_{-\infty}^{t} (S(h) - I)A^{\alpha}S(t - \sigma)f(\sigma, A^{-\alpha}\varphi(\sigma))d\sigma\right|$$
$$+ \left|\int_{t}^{t+h} A^{\alpha}S(t + h - \sigma)f(\sigma, A^{-\alpha}\varphi(\sigma))d\sigma\right| \quad (3.8)$$

(d) Lines with displayed math expressions that are overlapped because a part of these lines is misaligned

Fig. 1. Examples of different types of lines overlapping

Definition 3 (Line). *Let $G = \{g_1....g_n\}$ be a set of glyphs. We call a $L \subseteq G$ a line if for every $g \in L$ there is a $h \in L$ such that g and h overlap vertically and there is no $g \in G \setminus L$ that overlaps vertically with any element in L.*

Since this initial step separates lines that share vertically overlapping characters as one line. For examples of different types of overlaps see Fig. 1. Therefore, we perform a post-processing step to detect and split those lines, which is formalised in the next three definitions:

Definition 4 (Detect Overlapping Line). *Let $L = \{g_1....g_m\}$ be a line where the glyphs are sorted in ascending order according to $l(g)$ and m. We split L if the following conditions are satisfied:*

(i) *Neighbouring glyphs $g_1, g_2 \in L$ horizontally overlap such that $[l(g_1), r(g_1)] \cap [l(g_2), r(g_2)] \ne \emptyset$.*

(ii) *The same two neighbouring glyphs $g_1, g_2 \in L$ not both vertically overlap with any $g \in L$ where $g \ne g_1$ and $g \ne g_2$ such that $[t(g_1), b(g_1)] \cap [t(g_2), b(g_2)] \cap [t(g), b(g)] \ne \{g_1, g_2, g\}$.*

(iii) *$h(g_1) < (t(g_2) - b(g_1))$ and $h(g_2) < (t(g_2) - b(g_1))$ where h is the height of glyphs such that $h = b(g) - t(g)$.*

(iv) *$h(g_1) > (w(g_1)/2)$ and $h(g_2) > (w(g_2)/2)$ where w is the width of glyphs such that $w = r(g) - l(g)$.*

We then split the line into two lines by using a threshold that is determined by horizontally projecting lines across the whole vertical distance between the two overlapping glyphs, using the y-coordinate value of the line that crosses the least number of glyphs.

Definition 5 (Separator Value). *Let $g_1, g_2 \in L$ overlapping glyphs, and $Y = \{y_1....y_n\}$ be y-coordinate values between $b(g_1)$ and $t(g_2)$. Then let the separator value S is defined as the $y \in Y$ that minimises the number of vertically overlapping glyphs.*

We then cluster glyphs into two lines using the separator value S as a threshold.

Definition 6 (Split Overlapping Lines). *Let $L = \{g_1....g_m\}$ be the line to be split. Then we define $L_{above} = \{g \in L | h(g)/2 < S\}$ and $L_{below} = L \setminus L_{above}$.*

We can now define the distance measure with respect to which we will consider histograms.

Definition 7 (Horizontal Distance). *Let $L = \{g_1....g_n\}$ be a line. We call two glyphs $g, g' \in L$ neighbours if $r(g) < l(g')$ and there does not exist a $g'' \in L$ with $g'' \neq g$ and $g'' \neq g'$ such that $[l(g''), r(g'')] \cap [r(g), l(g')] = \emptyset$. We then define the horizontal distance d between two neighbouring glyphs g, g' as $d(g, g') = l(g') - r(g)$.*

Observe that in the above definition we define distances only for elements in the line that do not overlap horizontally. Thus the distances represent the actual whitespace in lines.

The distance measure from the previous definition allows us now to compute a histogram that captures the horizontal distances between glyphs in lines for the entire page. Figure 2 shows two examples for the histograms, where the x-axis denotes the values for the distance measure d in pixels and the y-axis the number of occurrences of a particular distance. Note, that when building the histogram, we deliberately omit all the values where no distance occurs or in other words, where the y value is equal to 0.

We can observe a general pattern in these histograms: They can be split into two parts by a global minimum that is roughly in the middle of the x-axis. This leaves two parts, each with a global maximum. Furthermore in the right part one can identify a further global minimum. While this can be at the very end of the x-axis it usually is not. We call these two minimal points v_1 and v_2, respectively, and use them to define classification of lines as follows:

Definition 8 (Principal Lines). *Let L be a line. We call L a principal line if there exists two neighbouring glyphs $g, h \in L$ with $v_1 \leq d(g, h) \leq v_2$. Otherwise L is a non-principal line.*

The intuition behind this definition is that the values in the histogram less than v_1 represent distances between single characters in a word or a mathematical expression, whereas the area between v_1 and v_2 represents the distance between single words, which generally do not occur in lines that only constitute part of a mathematical formula, for example, those consisting of limit expression of a sum.

While the measure alone already yields good results, it can be improved upon by considering a simple ratio between glyph heights of principal and non-principal lines.

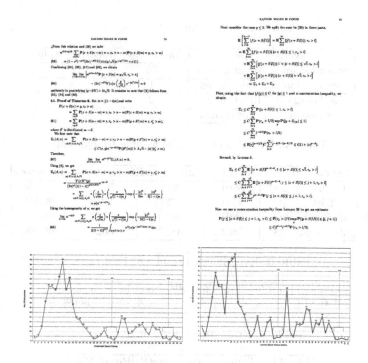

Fig. 2. Examples of pages and their histogram of the gap between glyphs

Definition 9 (Height Ratio). *Let L_1 and L_2 be two consecutive lines, such that L_1 is a non-principle line and L_2 is the nearest principle line to L_1. If $\max_{g \in L_1}[b(g) - t(g)] > \frac{1}{T}\max_{g \in L_2}[b(g) - t(g)]$, where $1 \le T \le 2$ then L_1 is converted into a principal line.*

Observe that the value for the parameter T is fixed and determined empirically by experiments in on a small sample set.

Since the previous step tackles only the problem of wrongly classified principal lines, we also need to define a corrective instrument to detect non-principal lines that have wrongly been classified as principal lines. This is achieved as follows:

Definition 10 (Non-principal Height Bound). *Let $L_n = \{n_1, n_2, ...n_l\}$ be the set of non-principal lines of a page and $L_p = \{p_1, p_2, ...p_k\}$ be the principal lines of the same page.*

Then we define the non-principal height bound *as the maximum height of all non-principal lines M as*

$$M = \max_{n \in L_n} |b'(n) - t'(n)|,$$

where t' and b' are the top and bottom limits of L respectively, such that $t'(n) = \min_{g \in n} t(g)$ and $b'(n) = \max_{g \in n} b(g)$.

Any $p \in L_p$ is converted to a non-principal line, if and only if, $[b'(p) - t'(p)] \le M$.

Table 1. Results for vertical splitting

Overlap Type		Correct Split	Incorrect Split
embedded math	direct overlap	36	2
expression	misaligned	1	0
display math	direct overlap	2	2
expression	misaligned	2	0

Table 2. Experimental results for line recognition

Method	Pages.	Total line	Lines found	Correct lines	Accuracy
Vert. Cuts	200	5801	6987	5015	86.4%
Hori. Dist.	200	5801	5727	5265	90.7%
Height Ratio	200	5801	5910	5587	96.3%
Height Bound	200	5801	5863	5625	96.9%

Table 3. Experimental results of 1000 pages

Pages.	Total line	Lines found	Correct lines	Accuracy
1000	34146	34526	33678	98.6%

Table 4. Evaluation results of 1000 pages

Line Type	Precision(P)	Recall(R)
Principal Line	99.39%	99.15%
Non-principal Line	93.87%	81.49%

Once the classification of lines is finished, in the final step we merge non-principal lines with their horizontally closest neighbouring principal line, but only if there exists horizontal overlapping between them. If not, the non-principal line is converted to a principle line.

Definition 11 (Merging Lines). *Let N and P be non-principal and principal lines respectively, such that P is the nearest neighbour of N. Let l' and r' be the left and right limits of L respectively, such that, $l' = \min_{g \in L} l(g)$ and $r' = \max_{g \in L} r(g)$. If $l'(P) < r'(N)$ and $r'(P) > l'(N)$ then N and P are merged. Otherwise, N is converted to P.*

3   Experimental Results and Discussion

We have run experiments on two datasets of 200 and 1000 pages, respectively, taken from a wide variety of mathematical documents. Before discussing the results of our overall procedure we first present the results of the line separation step alone. Our dataset contained 36 pages with lines that share vertically overlapping characters. These lines were effectively of two types: text lines with embedded math expressions and lines with display math expressions. Each of the two categories are further divided into two sub-categories: lines that overlap because of at least one overlapping glyph and lines that overlap because a part of these lines is misaligned. (See Figure 1 for examples of the four types.)

Table 1 shows the results of the splitting step. Observe that the two lines that are incorrectly split fail due to characters being wrongly clustered to either of the two result lines, which suggests that some improvement on our separator threshold method should be investigated in the future.

In terms of experiments of the overall procedure we have carried out initial experiments on 200 pages. These pages are taken from 12 documents comprising a mixture of books and journal articles. Table 2 presents the experimental results for this dataset. We have compared using simple vertical cuts, with our techniques of using the horizontal distance measure introduced in Def. 7 as well as using additionally the height ratio defined in Def. 9 and the non-principal height bound defined in Def. 10. As height ratio parameter we have set $T = 1.7$, a value that was experimentally determined on a small independent sample set.

Altogether we manually identified 5801 lines in the 200 pages of the dataset. We compare this number with the number of lines found altogether and the number of lines identified correctly, that is, those lines corresponding to the actual line as manually identified in the dataset.

Not surprisingly simple vertical cuts results in a larger number of lines and, as there is no subsequent merging of lines, in a relatively low accuracy of 86.4%. Using the horizontal distance measure improves this accuracy, however, in general merging too many lines. This is corrected by the addition of the height ratio that re-classifies some of the lines incorrectly assumed to be non-principal as principal lines. As a consequence we get a slightly higher number of lines but also a higher accuracy of 96.3%. A further slight improvement in this accuracy to 96.9% is obtained using the height bound.

To further examine the robustness of our technique and in particular to rule out that there was overfitted to our original data set we have experimented with a second independent and larger data set. The data set contains 1000 pages composed from more than 60 mathematical papers different of our original set.

We ran our technique on this second larger data set and then manually checked the results by painstakingly going through every page line by line. Consequently we have done this comparison only for the full classification including both height ratio and height bound correction. And while we can not rule out some classification mistakes due to human error we are very confident that the experimental results given in Table 3 are accurate.

Table 3 demonstrates that although, the data set is five times the size of the previous one our classification results remain stable. In fact, one can see that in comparison with table 2 we have even a increase of recognition rate by approximately 2%. This result gives us confidence about the effectiveness of our technique even on large datasets and documents.

Further evaluation is shown in table 4. Precision (P) and recall (R) measurements are used. As can be seen, the (P) and (R) percentages for principal line are close and high since there are 33186 correct principal lines and a very small number of incorrect ones. For non-principal lines, the percentages are not as high as the fronter lines. However, one can still claim that these results are very promising in comparison with the Vertical Cuts results where all non-principal lines are not recognized.

For the lines that were not identified, it is possible to categorise the recognition error into two types.

Incorrect Non-principal Lines: The most common error stems from classifying a line with respect to the horizontal distance measure as a principal line that should actually be non-principal. This is the case when there is a gap between two neighbouring glyphs that satisfies the horizontal distance condition. Below are some examples show several cases of errors taken directly from our dataset.

$$\leq C \sum_{i=1}^{\infty} \sum_{j=1}^{\sqrt{i}} E[|x + S(l) \dots \qquad \widetilde{B_i}\widetilde{B_{i+1}}\widetilde{B_i} = 2\widetilde{M_i} + \dots$$

Although, the first expression should be detected as a single line, the limits under the two summation symbols are at a distance that coincides with the distance identified by the histogram for the entire page. Likewise, in the second expression, also taken from our dataset, the tilde accents have a similar distance.

Incorrect Principal Lines: This error occurs when a line is initially classified as non-principal line as it does not contain any glyph gaps that coincide with the distance measure derived from the histogram. Examples of these lines are those with single words, page numbers, single expressions etc. While these can be corrected by the height ratio, sometimes they are not as they do not satisfy the ratio condition. Below is an example taken from our dataset.

$$+\tfrac{3}{5}\left(V_1^{k-1,k,2}(n;(1)).(L_{n-3}^{k-1,k,2} - L_3^{k-1.k.2})\right)$$
$$12$$

Here the page number 12 is merged as a non-principal line to the expression above, as firstly it does not exhibit a glyph gap satisfying the distance measure and secondly its height is significantly smaller as the height of the open parenthesis in the mathematical expression.

4   Conclusions

In this paper, we presented a line detection technique that is geared towards documents that contain a large number of complex mathematical expressions. Our approach can not only deal with detecting compound lines that consist of combination of several independent lines separated by vertical whitespace, but we also have most recently added a method to detect and split math lines that share vertically overlapping characters. The procedure exploits only simple spatial features in a histogrammatic approach, avoiding the use of many parameters that need to be fine tuned or relying on statistical data from large sample sets. Our experiments show that we nevertheless get a high rate of accuracy in detecting correct lines. The algorithm currently serves as a basis for our work on layout analysis of tabular mathematical expressions.

References

1. Alkalai, M., Baker, J., Sorge, V., Lin, X.: Improving formula analysis with line and mathematics identification. In: Proc. of ICDAR (to appear, 2013)
2. Boussellaa, W., Zahour, A., El Abed, H., BenAbdelhafid, A., Alimi, A.: Unsupervised block covering analysis for text-line segmentation of arabic ancient handwritten document images. In: ICPR, pp. 1929–1932 (2010)
3. Marti, U., Bunke, H.: On the influence of vocabulary size and language models in unconstrained handwritten text recognition. In: Proc. of ICDAR 2001, pp. 260–265. IEEE Computer Society (2001)
4. O'Gorman, L.: The document spectrum for page layout analysis. IEEE Transactions on Pattern Analysis and Machine Intelligence 15(11), 1162–1173 (1993)
5. Saabni, R., El-Sana, J.: Language-independent text lines extraction using seam carving. In: Document Analysis and Recognition, pp. 563–568. IEEE Computer Society (2011)
6. Wong, K., Casey, R., Wahl, F.: Document analysis system. IBM Journal of Research and Development 26(6), 647–656 (1982)
7. Zanibbi, R.: Recognition of mathematics notation via computer using baseline structure. Technical report, Queen's University, Kingston, Canada (2000)
8. Zanibbi, R., Blostein, D.: Recognition and retrieval of mathematical expressions. IJDAR 15(4), 331–357 (2012)

Cleaning Up Multiple Detections Caused by Sliding Window Based Object Detectors

Arne Ehlers, Björn Scheuermann, Florian Baumann, and Bodo Rosenhahn

Institut für Informationsverarbeitung (TNT)
Leibniz Universität Hannover, Germany
lastname@tnt.uni-hannover.de

Abstract. Object detection is an important and challenging task in computer vision. In cascaded detectors, a scanned image is passed through a cascade in which all stage detectors have to classify a found object positively. Common detection algorithms use a sliding window approach, resulting in multiple detections of an object. Thus, the merging of multiple detections is a crucial step in post-processing which has a high impact on the final detection performance. First, this paper proposes a novel method for merging multiple detections that exploits intra-cascade confidences using Dempster's Theory of Evidence. The evidence theory allows hereby to model confidence and uncertainty information to compute the overall confidence measure for a detection. Second, this confidence measure is applied to improve the accuracy of the determined object position. The proposed method is evaluated on public object detection benchmarks and is shown to improve the detection performance.

1 Introduction

Object detection is a widely used application in computer vision and has been intensively studied. Most detectors used in computer vision have been trained by a machine learning algorithm. Especially the cascaded object detector proposed by Viola & Jones [1] which employs the AdaBoost [2] machine learning algorithm is very successful. Object detectors are commonly applied by a sliding window which scans the scene image on shifted positions and varied scales. This frequently results in multiple detections of an object at slightly shifted and scaled positions. In a post-processing step, these multiple detections have to be combined to determine the final object position and scale. Often only little effort is spend on detection merging and simple methods are applied. Although this subtask has a strong impact on the overall accuracy of the detection framework and the results achieved in benchmarks. E.g., Viola & Jones in [1] merge all overlapping detection windows to one detection. But this approach easily leads to worse results in case of increasing numbers of detections, in particular if detections on large scales are involved. Everingham et al. [3] thus reported in the PASCAL VOC Challenge that the measured average precision steeply dropped for all participating methods when they tightened the tolerances for correct detections on the "car" class.

In this work, a novel method for merging multiple detections is proposed. Dempster's Theory of Evidence is applied to combine confidence values similar to Real AdaBoost [4] and uncertainty information that is available in a cascaded detector. In this

J. Ruiz-Shulcloper and G. Sanniti di Baja (Eds.): CIARP 2013, Part I, LNCS 8258, pp. 456–463, 2013.
© Springer-Verlag Berlin Heidelberg 2013

way intra-cascade information is exploited in an improved merging of multiple detections during post-processing. Huang et al.[5] introduced a nested classifier to inherit classification confidences in detection cascades. But their approach is confined to the classification step and requires a retraining. This paper proposes a novel confidence measure which is in addition applied to refine the position and scale of merged detections. It is shown that the proposed confidence gives an appropriate measure to distinguish the reliability of detections. As a post-processing step, the proposed method is easily applicable in other object detection frameworks without the need of retraining the object classifiers. Hence, other object detection frameworks could benefit from the proposed detection merging.

2 Merging Multiple Detections Based on Dempster's Theory

In this Section, the proposed strategies on merging detections are described in detail. The required methods of machine learning, object detection and evidence theory are briefly discussed in advance.

2.1 Cascaded Classifier

The object detection framework used in this work utilizes a cascaded classifier as introduced by Viola & Jones [1] and illustrated in Figure 1. Each stage of this cascaded classifier consists of a strong classifier that is created using the AdaBoost machine learning algorithm [2]. Hence in a cascade of S stages, S strong classifier have to decide positively for a scanned sub-window x to be classified as an object. Any of these candidate sub-windows is then further processed in the post-processing step in which the merging of multiple detections is done.

Each strong classifier $H_s(x) = \sum_{t=1}^{T_s} \alpha_{s,t} h_{s,t}(x), s \in 1 \ldots S$ is composed of an ensemble of T_s weak classifiers $h_{s,t}$ which have been selected in the training phase of the AdaBoost algorithm. Each weak classifier returns 0 or 1 in case of a negative or positive classification, respectively. These ensembles decide in a weighted majority vote in which each weak classifier $h_{s,t}$ supports its decision by an assigned weight $\alpha_{s,t}$ that represents the classification error of that weak classifier in training. Thus, the maximum positive classification of a strong classifier is given by $H_{s,max} = \sum_{t=1}^{T_s} \alpha_{s,t}$ and the decision threshold of AdaBoost is the weighted majority $\tau_s = \frac{1}{2} \sum_{t=1}^{T_s} \alpha_{s,t}$.

AdaBoost's decision threshold aims at a low error rate on the training set without differentiating between positive and negative training examples. But due to the rejection opportunity of each cascade stage, a very high true positive rate is primarily desired. Hence according to [1], a subsequently adjusted threshold τ_s is used to maintain a very high true positive rate accepting an also high false positive rate.

2.2 Dempster-Shafer Theory of Evidence

In this section Dempster's theory of evidence is briefly described. It is utilized in the proposed method to model intra-cascade decision confidences and uncertainties. The Dempster-Shafer theory of evidence was introduced in 1968 by A. P. Dempster [6] and

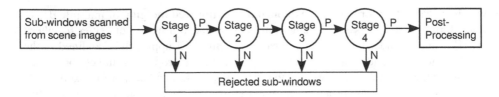

Fig. 1. Detection cascade: Evaluated sub-window have to be positively classified (P) and passed by all cascade stages to be considered as a found object. Each cascade stage can reject a sub-window if it is negatively classified (N) and thus prevents its processing by the following stages.

later in 1976 expanded by G. Shafer [7]. Evidence theory can be interpreted as a generalization of Bayesian theory that directly allows the representation of uncertainty and inaccuracy information. The key element of the evidence theory is the definition of a mass function on a hypotheses set Ω. Let a hypotheses set be denoted by Ω and composed of n single mutually exclusive subsets Ω_i written as $\Omega = \{\Omega_1, \Omega_2, \ldots, \Omega_n\}$. For each element A of the power set $\wp(\Omega)$ a mass function $m(A)$ is defined that expresses the proportion of all evidence assigned to this hypothesis. Hence, the mass function m represents a degree of confidence and is defined as $m : \wp(\Omega) \rightarrow [0, 1]$. Furthermore, the following conditions have to be fulfilled by the mass function:

$$(i) \quad m(\emptyset) = 0 \quad (ii) \quad \sum_{A_n \subseteq \Omega} m(A_n) = 1 . \tag{1}$$

Mass functions in evidence theory describe the totality of belief as opposed to Bayesian probability functions. This belief can be associated with single and composed sets of hypotheses allowing for a higher level of abstraction. The so-called additivity rule $p(A) + p(\overline{A}) = 1$ is in contrast to Bayesian theory not generally valid in Dempster-Shafer evidence theory. This means that if $m(A) < 1$, the remaining evidence $1 - m(A)$ does not necessarily claim its negation $\overline{A}$.

Dempster's Rule of Combination. In order to combine information from different stages of the detection cascade, *Dempster's rule of combination* is applied. Dempster's rule combines two mass functions that are defined within the same frame of discernment but belong to independent bodies of evidence. Let m_1 and m_2 be two mass functions associated to such independent bodies of evidence. Then Dempster's rule defines the new body of evidence by the mass function

$$m(A) = m_1(A) \otimes m_2(A) = \frac{\displaystyle\sum_{B \cap C = A} m_1(B) m_2(C)}{1 - \displaystyle\sum_{B \cap C = \emptyset} m_1(B) m_2(C)} . \tag{2}$$

The denominator in Equation (2) works as a normalization factor that ignores the conflicting evidence. Hence, Dempster's rule of combination focuses on the measure of agreement between two bodies of evidence. Dempster's rule is associative and thus can be used to iteratively combine evidences obtained from arbitrary number of classifiers.

2.3 Joint Confidence Based on Dempster-Shafer

In the proposed application of joining intra-cascade confidences, the frame of discernment is defined as $\Omega = \{TP, FP\}$ containing the set of hypotheses supporting a true positive (TP) and a false positive (FP) decision, respectively. The uncertainty of each cascade stage s is modeled by $m_s(\Omega)$ with respect to its size:

$$m_s(\Omega) = 1 - \frac{T_s}{\sum_{s=1}^{S} T_s} \tag{3}$$

This leads to a higher belief into stages that consist of larger number of weak classifiers.

The mass functions, expressing the proportion of evidence of a stage s, for true positive or false positive decisions are defined by:

$$m_s(TP) = \frac{H_s(x) - \tau_s}{H_{s,max} - \tau_s}(1 - m_s(\Omega)), \tag{4}$$

$$m_s(FP) = \left(1 - \frac{H_s(x) - \tau_s}{H_{s,max} - \tau_s}\right)(1 - m_s(\Omega)) \tag{5}$$

This results in higher stage confidence when the difference between the response of the strong classifier and the decision threshold grows. Using Dempster's rule of combination the stage confidences for a detection D_i are joined by

$$m_{D_i}(TP) = m_1(TP) \otimes m_2(TP) \otimes \cdots \otimes m_S(TP) \tag{6}$$

to gain an overall detection confidence.

2.4 Confidence-Based Detection Merging

Merging of multiple detection commonly takes place in the post-processing step of an object detection framework. The position and scale information of the candidate subwindows has to be processed to determine the true object location.

In this work, the candidate detections are first clustered using the Meanshift algorithm [8,9] as the number of true objects and thus desired clusters is unknown in advance. The i-th candidate detection is hereby defined as a four-dimensional vector $D_i = (x_i, y_i, \gamma_i, \delta_i)^\top$ which represents the combined position $(x_i, y_i)^\top$ and scale $(\gamma_i, \delta_i)^\top$ in x and y-dimension. The set of n candidate detections is partitioned by the Meanshift algorithm in four-dimensional space into $k \leq n$ sets $\mathbf{C} = \{C_1, C_2, \ldots, C_k\}$ of clusters. The merged detections are then set as the cluster centers of the k clusters in $\mathbf{C}$ and a simple confidence of the k-th cluster is given by its cluster size $|C_k|$.

To improve the performance of the object detector, this paper proposes two enhancements to the detection merging. First, the detection confidences given by Equation (6) are exploited to define the Dempster-Shafer based confidence of the k-th cluster as $\Gamma_k = \sum_{D_i \in C_k} m_{D_i}(TP)$. Second, these confidences of detections associated to one cluster are utilized to refine the position and scale of the cluster center. In this way the Dempster-Shafer refined position/scale of the k-th cluster is defined by:

$$D'_k = \frac{1}{\Gamma_k} \sum_{D_i \in C_k} D_i m_{D_i}(TP) \tag{7}$$

(a)   (b)   (c)

Fig. 2. Example images showing detections of our method on the three evaluated data sets: MIT+CMU [11], FDDB [10] and UIUC lateral car database [12]

3   Experimental Results

In this section, cascaded classifiers are applied by a sliding window to data sets for face and lateral car detection. The acquired multiple detections are post-processed using different merging strategies and results are presented for the Face Detection Data Set and Benchmark (FDDB) [10], the MIT+CMU frontal face database [11] and the UIUC lateral car database [12]. Figure 2 exemplary shows detections found by our method in the evaluated data sets.

3.1   Face Detection

For the detection of faces, a classifier is trained on the "MPLap GENKI-4K" database from the Machine Perception Laboratory in California [13] that consists of 4000 faces under different facial expressions. The obtained strong cascaded classifier consists of 10 stages and 593 weak classifiers in total.

Experiments Incorporating Confidence. The first experiments are conducted using the Face Detection Data Set and Benchmark [10] that contains 5171 faces in 2845 images. This data set also provides an evaluation tool for a consistent comparison of the performance of competing methods. Evaluations generated by this tool for different face detectors are available on the project web page[1]. The evaluation procedure requires multiple detections to be priorly merged to single detections that have an assigned confidence value. In descending order, each unique confidence value is then selected as a threshold and the true positive rate and total false positives are calculated considering all merged detections that have a greater confidence. In this way, a ROC curve is constructed that presents the detection performance.

The inspection of the detection confidence enables the separate evaluation of two contributions in the proposed approach: The confidence computation based on Dempster-Shafer theory of evidence and the position and scale refinement using these confidences.

Figure 3 presents the detection results for different strategies on merging multiple detections. The performance of the Viola & Jones detector in OpenCV, supplied by the FDDB project page, is presented as a baseline result. But the primary topic of this work

---

[1] http://vis-www.cs.umass.edu/fddb/results.html

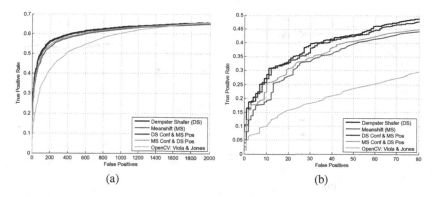

Fig. 3. ROC curve presenting the detection performance on FDDB [10] for different approaches on merging multiple detections. Confidence calculation and position/scale refinement based on Dempster-Shafer (DS) is compared to Meanshift-based confidence and position/scale (MS) and mixed approaches using Dempster-Shafer only for confidence and position/scale, respectively. The performance of the Viola & Jones implementation in OpenCV is presented as a baseline result. The shown range is (a) up to saturation and (b) a detailed view.

is the impact of the pre-processing step of multiple detection merging and not the comparison to different object detection methods. The proposed method (DS) is compared to an approach that only exploits the preceding Meanshift clustering (MS). For this, the number of detections forming each cluster is utilized as the confidence value. In addition, the results of two mixed approaches are presented that use Dempster-Shafer only for confidence calculation and position/scale refinement, respectively. The detailed view in Figure 3(b) demonstrates that, although the same detector is used, the performance can be significantly improved by about 5% in terms of true positive rate. It can be also observed from the blue curve in Figure 3(b) that the proposed confidence computation causes the biggest part of the improvement. This demonstrates that the Dempster-Shafer confidence gives an appropriate measure to distinguish the reliability of detections. The position/scale refinement slightly improves the detection performance, indicating that the trained classifier is not detecting symmetrically around the true object location. The proposed refinement can rectify that bias presenting improved results in the green curve of Figure 3(b).

Experiments on Position/Scale Refinement. Additional experiments are performed on the MIT+CMU frontal face database [11] which consists of 130 grayscale images containing 511 faces. The image database is partially noisy and blurred and contains several difficult samples like comics, line drawings and a binary raster image and thus is, despite its age, still challenging. This test set gives ground truth information on the position and scale of the faces but no evaluation tool is provided. Hence, the evaluation against ground truth is done by a built-in function of the detection framework that governs the ROC curve by a threshold multiplier in the detection process instead of exploiting confidence values.

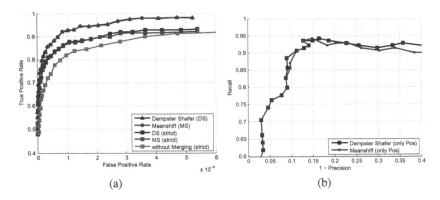

Fig. 4. (a) ROC curve presenting the detection performance on the MIT+CMU frontal face database [11]. The effect of the position/scale refinement using Dempster-Shafer is compared to Meanshift clustering in the case of loosened and stricter ground truth tolerances. Additionally results when omitting multiple detection merging are presented. (b) ROC curve presenting the detection performance on the UIUC lateral car database [12]. The effect of the additional position/scale refinement using Dempster-Shafer is compared to merging multiple detections by Meanshift clustering.

For this reason, Figure 4(a) shows only the impact of the position/scale refinement. In addition, results for completely omitting the post-processing are presented as the built-in evaluation does not require the merging of multiple detections. The general benefit of the post-processing can be observed from the improved results compared to the approach without merging multiple detections. During the merging process detection outliers are suppressed that are outside the ground truth tolerances. The detector performance only slightly benefits from the position/scale refinement. This is partly a consequence of the properties of the MIT+CMU frontal face database that contains many very small faces but provides no subpixel accuracy in the ground truth data. As the accuracy of the detections position and scale has no influence on the ROC curve as long as they are inside the tolerances, additional results for stricter tolerances are presented by the curves labeled as strict. These curves reveal a slight improvement due to the proposed position/scale refinement even on this unfavourable test set.

3.2 Lateral Car Detection

To evaluate an additional object class, experiments are conducted on the UIUC lateral car database [12]. This database provides a training set containing 1050 grayscale images (550 cars and 500 non-car images). In addition, images for single and multi-scale tests are contained as well as an evaluation tool for the calculation of precision and recall. Figure 4(b) compares the detection results achieved when merging multiple detections by Meanshift clustering and the proposed position/scale refinement using Dempster-Shafer confidences. The evaluation tool does not consider detection confidences but requires multiple detections to be merged to a single detection in advance. Hence, a concentration on only the impact of the position/scale refinement is predetermined. In this experiment, that utilizes a different object class, an improvement of the detection performance can be observed due to the position/scale refinement. This indicates that the car classifier as well does not detect symmetrically around the true object location but introduces a bias that can be rectified by the proposed method.

4   Conclusion

This paper presents a novel method for merging multiple detections which exploits classification information available in cascaded detectors. Two enhancements are proposed. First, Dempster-Shafer theory of evidence is applied to model a confidence measure which incorporates intra-cascade decision confidences and uncertainties. Second, a method is presented to refine the position and scale of merged detections based on these confidence measures. These methods can be easily integrated in existing detection frameworks to improve performance without retraining of typical cascaded detectors. Results are presented for a recent benchmark on unconstrained face detection (FDDB), the MIT+CMU face and the UIUC car database. The refinement of position and scale solely results in a slight improvement in detection performance. In addition, the proposed confidence measure shows an improvement of 5% in true positive rate for applications that consider detection confidences. This demonstrates that Dempster-Shafer theory of evidence is a powerful technique to model and exploit intra-cascade confidences.

References

1. Viola, P., Jones, M.J.: Robust real-time face detection. International Journal of Computer Vision 57(2), 137–154 (2004)
2. Freund, Y., Schapire, R.E.: Experiments with a new boosting algorithm. In: Machine Learning: Proceedings of the Thirteenth International Conference, pp. 148–156 (1996)
3. Everingham, M., Van Gool, L., Williams, C.K., Winn, J., Zisserman, A.: The pascal visual object classes (voc) challenge. International Journal of Computer Vision 88(2) (2010)
4. Schapire, R.E., Singer, Y.: Improved boosting algorithms using confidence-rated predictions. Machine Learning 37(3), 297–336 (1999)
5. Huang, C., Al, H., Wu, B., Lao, S.: Boosting nested cascade detector for multi-view face detection. In: Pattern Recognition, ICPR 2004 (2004)
6. Dempster, A.P.: A generalization of bayesian inference. Journal of the Royal Statistical Society. Series B (Methodological) 30(2), 205–247 (1968)
7. Shafer, G.: A mathematical theory of evidence, vol. 1. Princeton University Press, Princeton (1976)
8. Cheng, Y.: Mean shift, mode seeking, and clustering. IEEE Trans. Pattern Anal. Mach. Intell. 17(8), 790–799 (1995)
9. Comaniciu, D., Meer, P.: Mean shift: A robust approach toward feature space analysis. IEEE Trans. Pattern Anal. Mach. Intell. 24(5), 603–619 (2002)
10. Jain, V., Learned-Miller, E.: Fddb: A benchmark for face detection in unconstrained settings. Technical Report UM-CS-2010-009, University of Massachusetts, Amherst (2010)
11. Sung, K.K., Poggio, T., Rowley, H.A., Baluja, S., Kanade, T.: MIT+CMU frontal face dataset a, b and c. MIT+CMU (1998)
12. Agarwal, S., Awan, A., Roth, D.: UIUC image database for car detection (2002)
13. TheMPLab GENKI Database, u.S., http://mplab.ucsd.edu

A Differential Method for Representing Spinal MRI for Perceptual-CBIR

Marcelo Ponciano-Silva[1,2], Pedro H. Bugatti[3], Rafael M. Reis[4],
Paulo M. Azevedo-Marques[4], Marcello H. Nogueira-Barbosa[4],
Caetano Traina-Jr.[1], and Agma Juci Machado Traina[1]

[1] Department of Computer Science, University of São Paulo at São Carlos, Brazil
[2] Fed. Inst. of Education, Science and Technology of the Triângulo Mineiro, Brazil
[3] Dept. of Computer Engineering, Fed. Tech. University of Paraná, Brazil
[4] School of Medicine of University of São Paulo at Ribeirão Preto, Brazil
{ponciano,pbugatti,agma,caetano}@icmc.usp.br,
{pmarques,rafael,marcello}@fmrp.usp.br

Abstract. Image exams are a fundamental tool in health care for decision making. A challenge in Content-based image retrieval (CBIR) is to provide a timely answer that complies with the specialist's expectation. There are different systems with different techniques to CBIR in literature. However, even with so much research, there are still particular challenges to be overcame, such as the semantic gap. In this paper, we presented a new spinal-image comparison method based on the perception of specialists during his/her analysis of spine lesions. We take advantage of a color extractor and propose a shape descriptor considering the visual patterns that the radiologists use to recognize anomalies in images. The experiments shown that our approach achieved promising results, testifying that the automatic comparison of images should consider all relevant visual aspects and comparisons' criteria, which are defined by the specialists.

Keywords: Content-Based Medical Image Retrieval, Features Extraction, Spinal Images.

1 Introduction

X-Ray images, Magnetic Resonance Imagining (MRI) and Computed Tomography (CT) provide fundamental information for making an accurate diagnosis. In many situations, when a specialist gets a new image to analyze, having information and knowledge from similar cases can be very helpful. All these similar images are stored and organized by a system such as a Picture Archiving and Communication Systems (PACS). A PACS [7] consists of a set of computational systems able of providing storage, retrieval, distribution and presentation of images for physicians and medical staff in a Medical Center. One of its sub-systems allows specialists to have access to an automatic retrieval of similar cases based only on the intrinsic content of the image. These similar-cases retrieval sub-systems use Content-Based Image Retrieval (CBIR) techniques [14].

J. Ruiz-Shulcloper and G. Sanniti di Baja (Eds.): CIARP 2013, Part I, LNCS 8258, pp. 464–471, 2013.
© Springer-Verlag Berlin Heidelberg 2013

There are different systems that provide different techniques and algorithms to CBIR area of Spine. The Lister Hill National Center for Biomedical Communications department with the National Library of Medicine (NLM) is developing a CBIR for pathologies in the spine. This system supports hybrid queries, text-based and content-based of X-Ray images. The feature extraction is performed on Regions of Interest - ROIs (vertebral bodies), working with shape descriptors where each ROI is compared separately to each other [1,16]. There is also a tool developed for the Web, called SPIRS, which works on X-Ray images of the spine and makes a comparison between the separate ROIs [6]. Another study, focused on Spine MRI, uses statistical methods as Haralick features and texture spectrum spine MRI features for image feature extraction. This method is global, considering the entire image as the object for feature extraction. Thus, a single feature vector represents each image being used to compare it with another image contained in the base, in this case, to support diagnosis and treatment of scoliosis [9]. Another work allows automatically extracting specific measures from spine curvature of x-ray images from patients with scoliosis [10]. In addition to these, there are also others generic systems, such as IRMA [5] and the ASSERT [12], among others, that can also incorporate specific techniques to the images discussed in this paper. CBIR tools have been extensively explored in several areas of medicine. However, even with so much research, there are particular challenges to be overcame in each specific area. The main one is the Semantic Gap [3], expressed as the difference between what the specialist considers as similar and what is offered as similar by the system. One of the techniques used to reduce this gap is to use of Perceptual-Parameters to guide the query according to well-defined user's Criteria of Similarity [11]. However, to reach this level, there is the need to establish *comparison methods* compatible with the methods used by the radiologists in clinical practice and, therefore, to approximate the CBIR technique to the method identified.

In this paper we propose a spinal-image's comparison method based on the perception of the specialist during his/her analysis of lesions in the Lumbar Spine on MR images. To consolidate our proposal, we take advantage of a color extractor and propose a shape extractor to bring the CBIR to the way of the comparison performed by the physician during the process of analyzing images. The proposed approach achieved better results in the experiments, showing that the automatic comparison of images should consider all relevant visual aspects and criteria of comparison, defined by the specialist in a specific context.

2   Related Concepts

In the present section we show a set of significant visual patterns used as a similarity criterion for differentiating vertebral compression fractures - VCFs (focus of this work) as well as the traditional algorithms employed to extract the features to quantify the similarity between the images.

2.1   Similarity Criterion for VCFs

The practice of evidence-based medicine within radiology is growing and provides an important mechanism by which to facilitate further advancement of evidence based radiology. The goal of this practice is formalizing and standardizing image interpretation and results communication [15]. Studying this interpretation allows to identify a set of significant visual predictors used by radiologists for differentiating VCFs and, with this knowledge to establish a criteria for comparing spinal images. Some diseases are characterized by the presence of known alterations in the normal vertebral body structure. The physicians call these alterations as *radiological findings*. Each radiological finding is related to visual feature parameters. For this work we listed some issues the radiologists analyze in spine images and for each issue it was specified what the radiologists look for in the image to help identifying a finding (see Figure 1).

Finding	Pathophysiological Description	Visual Characteristics	Example
Vertebral Body Deformity	- Weakening of the trabecular bone of the vertebra and the consequent compression of the vertebral body. Trabecular bone is impacting against itself	- Proportional Flattening: anterior equivalent to posterior - Decrease the Vertebra "height"	
		- Flattening of Superior endplate involvement. Change in shape	
		- Flattening of Inferior endplate involvement. Change in shape	
Presence of Vertebral Signal	- Replacement of Fat from Vertebral Body by Edema	- Change in Vertebral Color. - Fat (normal) in MRI is bright, but the edema is opaque (dark): Distribution Homogeneous	
		- Change in Vertebral Color. - Fat (normal) in MRI is bright, but the edema is opaque (dark): Distribution Diffuse	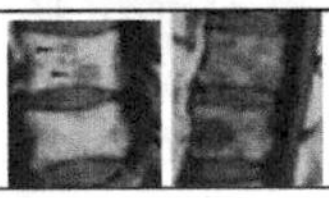

Fig. 1. Findings and visual characteristics

2.2 Feature Extraction

The feature vectors extracted from the medical images is the one of the key aspects for the similarity comparison between such images. To represent the similarity criterions showed in Subsection 2.1 we used the color and shape descriptors described as follows.

Color Descriptors. There are several methods to describe color features from images. The traditional gray-level histogram is one of the most applied one. However, some works have shown more robust alternatives to the color representation. One of this is an interesting feature extractor, called the Border/Interior Classification (BIC) [13]. This color descriptor uses the RGB color space uniformly quantized in a given number of colors (e.g. each pixel represented by 6 bits). It presents a compact representation and consists in classifying the image pixels in edge-pixels or interior-pixels. Thus, it divides the image in two histograms. A pixel is classified as border if it is at the border of the image itself or if at least one of its 4-neighbors (top, bottom, left and right) has a different quantized color. A pixel is classified as interior if its 4-neighbors have the same quantized color. In the final step both histograms are merged, generating the image feature vector.

Shape Descriptors. Shape is one of the most important feature extracted from an image. For instance, in medical images shape-based features play a major role from describing the malignancy of tumor nodules to vertebral fractures. The Zernike moments [8] are a relevant shape-based features that employ the general theory of moments joined with the Zernike polynomials.

3   Proposed Approach

In this paper, we consider a search engine based on the radiologist's analysis as a Method Based on Human Perception (Perceptual-Based). The specialist's comparison method, when he/she is comparing two images, are not usually explored in the design of traditional CBIR systems. With the goal of bringing the CBIR system to the perception of the specialist, we questioned several radiologists about how they compare images that have the findings described in Subsection 2.1. After that, we developed ways to represent the visual aspects described for each finding. As a result of questioning, we got the proposals described as follows.

3.1   Spine-Based Feature Extraction

To represent the similarity criterions showed in Subsection 2.1 and aimed at employing the descriptors listed in Subsection 2.2, we propose the following color and shape descriptors.

Vertebral Body Color Descriptor. The BIC, presented in subsection 2.2, was designed for traditional RGB images. The medical images are usually in gray levels, with 16 bits per pixel. This format gives the images up to 4096 gray levels. Furthermore, the interior of objects found in medical images does not always have the same intensity (same pixel value). A slight variation in these gray levels within the same object can be considered normal in this context. Thus, using BIC can bring losses in traditional representation of the image, due to a possible misclassification between edge and interior.

Because of this observation, we have changed the way the pixel classification between interior/border, proposing the BIC-Med. With BIC-Med, the pixel is classified as border if at least one of its 4-neighbors (top, bottom, left and right) has a variation of quantized gray-level greater than a given threshold. A pixel is classified the interior if all its 4-neighbors have a variation less than or equal to a given threshold. In the final step both histograms are merged, generating the image feature vector. The threshold for the experiments of this work was 20% of the gray level of each pixel. This color variation value was chosen empirically based on an already established culture among physicians about the variation between the vertebrae images, as is presented below.

Vertebral Body Shape Descriptor. The shape features extractor proposed in this work was created based on the method of analysis of vertebral bodies' fractures proposed by Genant et al. [4]. The method is based on a given score from zero to three, considering the difference between the maximum and minimum measurement of the anterior (AH), central (CH) and posterior (PH) vertebral body heights. It is assigned a score value of 0 (normal) to the percentage difference less than 20%, until score 3 (severe fracture) to percentage difference greater than 40%. Thus, the feature vector of the proposed extractor, called VertebralBody-RelativeShape (VB-RelativeShape), is composed of the relative proportion between the anterior, central and posterior vertebral body heights. That is, each vertebral body is represented by the proportion of three measurements. They are: AH/CH, AH/PH, CH/PH.

3.2   Perceptual Spinal Based Method

The images A_1, A_2 and A_3 of Figure 2 are quite similar. However, if you make a global comparison between them, will probably find images A_2 and A_3 more similar to each other. However, if you consider only the focusöf this specific domain (see A'_1, A'_2 and A'_3), images A_1 and A_2 would be considered more similar to each other. This example characterizes the difference between what the specialist believes to be similar and that the system can deem to be similar (i.e., the semantic gap). Probably a descriptor of color or texture applied to the entire image (Global-Based) would erroneously return images A_2 and A_3 as the most similar ones.

On the other hand, in an attempt to reduce this semantic gap, many studies use ROIs for performing the comparison between images (ROIs-Based). However, although this method really brings good results, through graphs of precision and recall, it still has a gap in what occurs naturally during the expert analysis. The radiologist spots variations in ROIs contrasting them with neighboring regions. Not to mention that when comparing two images, 1) scoring ROIs is extra work to be performed by the radiologist and 2) When considering only similar ROIs, the

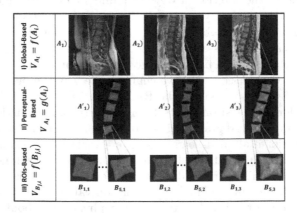

Fig. 2. Different methods (visions) for comparing images

physician may come across images that have different ROIs representing (as is the case of Vertebral Bodies) having normal and non-normal ROIs in the same image.

In order to adapt the feature extraction for something close to the concept of similarity perceived by radiologists, we propose a method that considers the local characteristics (ROI-based), but, composed into a single feature vector. Thus, each vertebra belonging to the analyzed image is compared to the equivalent vertebra on another image. Thus, the similarity between two images is not only calculated by the similarity of a single ROI, but considering the variation of all the neighbors.

4   Experiments and Results

To evaluate the proposed method, we have generated precision and recall (P&R) graphs [2]. Precision is the percentage of relevant images actually returned in the query among the total number of images returned in the query. Recall is the percentage of relevant images actually returned in the query among the total number of relevant images for a given query. For the dataset analyzed, all images of each class were employed as query centers.

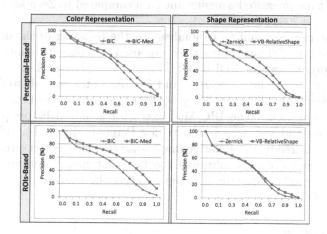

Fig. 3. Precision Vs. Recall graphs for Color and Shape representation

To perform the experiments we have used an image dataset, provided by the Hospital of our university (HCRP). The dataset consists of 171 images separated by the specialists into two distinct classes (83 normal images and 88 images with VCFs). To enable the Spinal-based experiments, radiologists and residents from HCRP provided a manual segmentation of the lumbar vertebral bodies. And to enable the ROI-based experiments, we used this manual segmentation to create a data set with 855 ROIs.

Analyzing the feature descriptor proposed in this work, both showed better performance when compared with traditional ones. This comparison was performed using data 171 images, through the Perceptual-based proposed method,

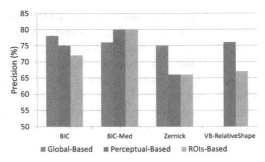

Fig. 4. Extractors' precision with different approaches considering the area under the Precision Vs.Recall graph in the first 50% of recall

and the base 855 ROIs (ROI-based) as shown in Figure 3. Comparing the extractors color, the BIC-Med precision was higher than 80% in the first 20% of recall, while the traditional BIC has not reached this level. For shape extractors, considering the ROI-based methodology, both VB-RelativeShape and Zernike performed very similar. However, when analyzing with the focus on the Perceptual-based method, the precision of the two extractors improved and the VB-RelativeShape presented a significant gain compared to Zernike (about 10% better in the first 20% of recall).

Another interesting result to be analyzed is the behavior of the different descriptors regarding different ways they are used to compare images (Global-Based, Perceptual-based or ROI-based). Figure 4 illustrates their performance in the different approaches. The BIC and Zernike extractors showed are more focuses to analysis global image. They both lost performance when used in segmented images or ROIs. The BIC-Med extractor achieved better precision in almost all cases and was representative for Perceptual-Based and the ROIs-based retrieval. Already VB-RelativeShape showed much better precision with the proposed methodology, confirming the fact that specific features of shape, in this context, are best described as representing the whole neighborhood, not just a single ROI.

5 Conclusions

In this paper, we presented a new approach to deal with the semantic gap. We propose a spinal-image's comparison method based on the perception of specialist during his/her analysis of lesions in the Lumbar Spine on MR images. The proposed approach gathers from the physicians the visual patterns they use to recognize anomalies in images and apply them on building feature extractors based on these visual patterns. We took advantage of color extractor and propose a new shape extractor to bring the CBIR to the way of the comparison performed by the physician during the process of analyzing the images. The proposed approach achieved better results in the experiments, showing that the automatic comparison of images should consider all relevant visual aspects and criteria of comparison, defined by specialist in a specific context.

Acknowledgments. We thank FAPESP, CAPES, CNPq and the INCT INCod for the financial support.

References

1. Antani, S., Lee, D.J., Long, L.R., Thoma, G.R.: Evaluation of shape similarity measurement methods for spine X-ray images. J. Visual Communication and Image Representation 15(3), 285–302 (2004)
2. Baeza-Yates, R.A., Ribeiro-Neto, B.A.: Modern Information Retrieval - the concepts and technology behind search, 2nd edn. Pearson Education Ltd., Harlow (2011)
3. Deserno, T.M., Antani, A., Long, L.R.: Ontology of Gaps in Content-Based Image Retrieval. J. Digital Imaging 22(2), 202–215 (2009)
4. Genant, H.K., Wu, C.Y., van Kuijk, C., Nevitt, M.C.: Vertebral fracture assessment using a semiquantitative technique. J. of Bone and Mineral Research: The Official J. of the American Society for Bone and Mineral Research 8(9), 1137–1148 (1993)
5. Güld, M.O., Thies, C., Fischer, B., Lehmann, T.M.: A generic concept for the implementation of medical image retrieval systems. I. J. Medical Informatics 76(2-3), 252–259 (2007)
6. Hsu, W., Antani, S., Long, L.R., Neve, L., Thoma, G.R.: SPIRS: A Web-based image retrieval system for large biomedical databases. I. J. Medical Informatics 78 (S1) S13–S24 (2009)
7. Huang, H.K.: PACS and Imaging Informatics: Basic Principles and Applications, 2nd edn. Wiley-Blackwell, Hoboken (2010)
8. Khotanzad, A., Hong, Y.H.: Invariant Image Recognition by Zernike Moments. IEEE Trans. Pattern Anal. Mach. Intell. 12(5), 489–497 (1990)
9. Kumaran, N., Bhavani, R.: Spine MRI Image Retrieval using Texture Features. I. J. of Computer Applications 46(24), 1–7 (2012)
10. Medina, J.M., Jaime-Castillo, S., Jiménez, E.: A DICOM viewer with flexible image retrieval to support diagnosis and treatment of scoliosis. Expert Syst. Appl. 39(10), 8799–8808 (2012)
11. Ponciano-Silva, M., Traina, A.J.M., Azevedo-Marques, P.M., Felipe, J.C., Traina, C.J.: Including the perceptual parameter to tune the retrieval ability of pulmonary cbir systems. In: CBMS, pp. 8–17 (2009)
12. Shyu, C.R., Brodley, C.E., Kak, A.C., Kosaka, A., Aisen, A.M., Broderick, L.S.: ASSERT: A Physician-in-the-Loop Content-Based Retrieval System for HRCT Image Databases. Comp. Vision and Image Understanding 75(1-2), 111–132 (1999)
13. Stehling, R.O., Nascimento, M.A., Falcão, A.X.: A compact and efficient image retrieval approach based on border/interior pixel classification. In: CIKM, pp. 102–109 (2002)
14. Town, C.: Content-Based and Similarity-Based Querying for Broad-Usage Medical Image Retrieval. In: Sidhu, A.S., Dhillon, S.K. (eds.) Advances in Biomedical Infrastructure 2013. SCI, vol. 477, pp. 63–76. Springer, Heidelberg (2013)
15. Wang, K.C., Jeanmenne, A., Weber, G.M., Thawait, S.K., Carrino, J.A.: An Online Evidence-Based Decision Support System for Distinguishing Benign from Malignant Vertebral Compression Fractures by Magnetic Resonance Imaging Feature Analysis. J. Digital Imaging 24(3), 507–515 (2011)
16. Xue, Z., Long, L.R., Antani, S., Thoma, G.R.: Spine X-ray image retrieval using partial vertebral boundaries. In: CBMS, pp. 1–6 (2011)

Image Segmentation Using Active Contours and Evidential Distance

Foued Derraz[1,3], Antonio Pinti[4,5], Miloud Boussahla[3],
Laurent Peyrodie[2], and Hechmi Toumi[5]

[1] Facult Libre de Mdicine
Institut Catholique de Lille
Universit Catholique de Lille
46 rue du Port de Lille, France
foued.derraz@icl-lille.fr
[2] Hautes Etudes d'Ingenieur
Universit Catholique de Lille
46 rue du Port de Lille, France
laurent.peyrodie@hei.fr
[3] Telecommunication Laboratory
Technology Faculty
Abou Bekr Belkaid University, Tlemcen, Algeria
BP 230, Tlemcen 13000, Algeria
m_boussahla@mail.univ-tlemcen.dz
[4] ENSIAME UVHC, Universite de Valenciennes, France
antonio.pinti@univvalenciennes.fr
[5] A5 EA 4708, I3MTO, CHRO 1, rue Porte Madeleine, 45032, Orlans, France
hechmi.toumi@univ-orleans.fr

Abstract. We proposed a new segmentation based on Active Contours
(AC) for vector-valued image that incorporates evidential distance. The
proposed method combine both Belief Functions (BFs) and probability
functions in the Bhattacharyya distance framework. This formulation allows all features issued from vector-valued image and guide the evolution
of AC using an inside/outside descriptor. The imprecision caused by the
variation of the contrast issued from the multiple channels is incorporated
in the BFs as weighted parameters. We demonstrated the performance of
the proposed algorithm using some challenging color biomedical images.

Keywords: Active Contours, Characteristic function, Belief Function,
Bhattacharyya distance ,Dempster Shafer rule.

1 Introduction

Segmentation based AC models presents several challenges that are mainly related to image noise, poor contrast, weak or missing boundaries between imaged
objects, inhomogeneities, etc. One way to overcome these difficulties is to exploit the prior knowledge in order to constrain the segmentation process. Due
occlusion or texture this is often not appropriate to delineate object regions.

J. Ruiz-Shulcloper and G. Sanniti di Baja (Eds.): CIARP 2013, Part I, LNCS 8258, pp. 472–479, 2013.

Statistical knowledge [4,20] and additional information such as texture [4] can improved the segmentation based AC models for vector-valued image [3,22]. Another reason for failed segmentations is due local or global minimizer for AC models [2]. To overcomes these difficulties, the evidential framework appears to be a new way to improve segmentation based AC models for vector valued images [19,12,21]. The Dempster Shafer (DS) framework [7] has been combined with either a simple thresholding [19], a clustering algorithm [14], a region merging algorithm [12] or with an AC algorithm [21]. In this paper we propose to use the evidential framework [7] to combine several information sources and incorporates them in the formulation of the AC models. The fusion of this information from different feature channels, e.g., color channels and texture offers an alternative to the Bayesian framework. Instead to fuse separated probability densities, the evidential framework allows both inaccuracy and uncertainty. This concept is represented using BFs [7,5,8,1] which is particularly well suited to represent information from partial and unreliable knowledge. To use BFs as an alternative to probability in segmentation process can be very helpful in reducing uncertainties and imprecisions using conjunctive combination of neighboring pixels. First, it allows us to reduce the noise and secondly, to highlight conflicting areas mainly present at the transition between regions where the contours occurs. In addition, BFs has the advantage to manipulate not only singletons but also disjunctions. This gives the ability to explicitly to represent both uncertainties and imprecisions. The disjunctive combination allows transferring both uncertain and imprecise information on disjunctions [7,1]. Then, the conjunctive combination is applied to reduce uncertainties due to noise while maintaining representation of imprecise information at the boundaries between areas on disjunctions. In this paper, we proposed to incorporate the BFs in the formulation of the AC models. In Section 2, we review of the AC models based Vector-valued image segmentation in total variation framework, which is the basis for our segmentation framework. In section 3, we formulated our AC models in evidential framework. Experimental results in Section 4 demonstrate the advantages of the proposed method.

2   Globally Active Contours for Vector-Valued Image in Evidential Framework

The evidential framework is provided through the definition of the plausibility (Pl) and belief (Bel) function [7,8], which are both derived from a mass function (m). For the frame of discernment $\Omega_{II} = \{\Omega_1, \Omega_2, ..., \Omega_n\}$, composed of n single mutually exclusive subsets Ω_i, the mass function is defined by $m : 2^\Omega \to [0,1]$.

$$m(\emptyset) = 0$$

$$\sum_{\Omega_i \subseteq \Omega} m(\Omega_i) = 1; \quad Bel(\Omega) = \sum_{\Omega_i \subseteq \Omega_{II}} m(\Omega_i) = 1$$

$$Pl(\Omega) = \sum_{\Omega_i \cap \Omega_{II} \neq \emptyset} m(\Omega_i)$$

(1)

The relation between mass function, Bel and Pel can be described as fellows:

$$m\left(\Omega_i\right) \leq Bel\left(\Omega_i\right) \leq p\left(\Omega_i\right) \leq Pl\left(\Omega_i\right) \tag{2}$$

When $m\left(\Omega\right) > 0$, Ω is a so called focal element [12,7]. The independent masses m_m are defined within the same frame of discernment as:

$$m\left(\Omega_{i=\{1,\dots,n\}}\right) = m_1\left(\Omega_{i=\{1,\dots,n\}}\right) \otimes m_2\left(\Omega_{i=\{1,\dots,n\}}\right) \cdots \\ \otimes m_m\left(\Omega_{i=\{1,\dots,n\}}\right) \tag{3}$$

The total belief assigned to a focal element Ω_i is equal to the belief strictly placed on the foreground region Ω_i. Then Belief Function (Bel) can expressed as:

$$Bel\left(\Omega_i\right) = m\left(\Omega_i\right) \tag{4}$$

This relation can be very helpful in the formulation of our AC model. The segmentation based AC for vector Valued image $\mathbf{I}$ consists in finding one or more regions Ω from $\mathbf{I}$. In this framework, we search for the domain Ω or the partition of the image $P\left(\Omega\right)$ that maximizes the Bhattacharyya distance [15,9] between Bel associated to the inside/outside region or minimizing the criterion:

$$\partial\hat{\Omega} = \arg\min \left\{ \underbrace{\log\left(\frac{1}{p\left(P\left(\Omega\right)\right)}\right)}_{E_b(\partial\Omega)} + \underbrace{\sum_{j=1}^{m}\lambda_{in}^j \int_{R+} \sqrt{m_{in}^j\left(\Omega\right)p_{out}^j}}_{E_{data}(I,\Omega)} \\ + \underbrace{\sum_{j=1}^{m}\lambda_{out}^j \int_{R+} \sqrt{m_{out}^j\left(\Omega\right)p_{in}^j}}_{E_{data}(I,\Omega)} \right\} \tag{5}$$

Similairely as in [21], we used the definitions proposed in [1] to define mass function for all image channels I_j as:

$$m_{j=\{1,\dots,m\}}\left(\Omega_{in/out}\right) = p_{in/out}^{j=\{1,\dots,m\}}$$
$$m_{j=\{1,\dots,m\}}\left(\Omega\right) = 1 - p_{in}^{j=\{1,\dots,m\}} + p_{out}^{j=\{1,\dots,m\}} \tag{6}$$
$$m_{j=\{1,\dots,m\}}\left(\emptyset\right) = 0$$

The pdfs p_{in}^j and p_{out}^j are estimated for all channels using Parzen kernel [17]. Our proposed method uses the total belief committed to foreground or back ground region. In the next section we proposed a fast version of our segmentation algorithm.

3   Fast Algorithm Based on Split Bregman

The Split Bregman method [2,10] is an efficient optimization technique for solving L^1 regularized problems and has good convergence properties [2,10]. In order to find a contour minimizing AC energy functional, the Split Bregman method [11] will separate the L^1 and L^2 norm, by introducing a vectorial variable d and imposing constraints on the segmentation problem. This results in the following segmentation problem:

$$
\min_{\chi,d} \ (E(\chi,d)) = \int_{\Omega} |d(\mathbf{x})|\, d\mathbf{x} + \sum_{j=1}^{m} \lambda_{in}^{j} \int_{\Omega} V_{Belief}^{in} \chi
$$

$$
+ \sum_{j=1}^{m} \lambda_{out}^{j} \int_{\Omega} V_{Belief}^{out} \chi \tag{7}
$$

This constrained segmentation problem can be transformed to an unconstrained segmentation problem by adding a quadratic penalty function. This function only approximates the constraint $d = \nabla\chi$. However, by using a Split Bregman technique [11], this constraint can be enforced exactly in an efficient way. An extra vector, b^k is added to the penalty function (7). Then the following two unconstrained steps are iteratively solved by:

$$
\begin{cases}
(\chi^{k+1}, d^{k+1}) = \arg\min
\begin{cases}
\int_{\Omega_0} |d| + \sum_{j=1}^{m} \lambda_{in}^{j} \int_{\Omega} V_{Belief}^{in} \chi + \\
+ \sum_{j=1}^{m} \lambda_{out}^{j} \int_{\Omega} V_{Belief}^{out} \chi + \\
\frac{\mu}{2} \int_{\Omega_0} |d - \nabla\chi^k - b^k|^2
\end{cases} \\
b^{k+1} = b^k + \nabla\chi^{k+1} - d^{k+1}
\end{cases} \tag{8}
$$

where μ is a weighting parameter. The first step requires optimizing for two different vectors. We approximate these optimal vectors by alternating between χ and d independently:

$$
\begin{cases}
\chi^{k+1} = \arg\min
\begin{cases}
\int_{\Omega_0} |d| + \sum_{j=1}^{m} \lambda_{in}^{j} \int_{\Omega} V_{Belief}^{in} \chi + \\
\sum_{j=1}^{m} \lambda_{out}^{j} \int_{\Omega} V_{Belief}^{out} \chi + \\
\frac{\mu}{2} \int_{\Omega_0} |d - \nabla\chi^k - b^k|^2
\end{cases} \\
d^{k+1} = \arg\min_{d^k} \left\{ \int_{\Omega_0} |d^k| + \frac{\mu}{2} \int_{\Omega_0} |d^k - \nabla\chi^k - b^k|^2 \right\} \\
b^{k+1} = b^k + \nabla\chi^{k+1} - d^{k+1}
\end{cases} \tag{9}
$$

This problem can be optimized by solving a set of Euler-Lagrange equations. For each element χ^{k+1} of the optimal $\hat{\chi}$, the following optimality condition should be satisfied :

$$
\underbrace{\left(\Delta - \frac{1}{\mu}\sum_{j=1}^{m} \lambda_{in}^{j} V_{Belief}^{in} - \frac{1}{\mu}\sum_{j=1}^{m} \lambda_{out}^{j} V_{Belief}^{out} \right)}_{A} \chi^k = \underbrace{div\left(b^k - d^k\right)}_{C} \tag{10}
$$

Note that this system of equations can be written as $A\chi = C$. In [6] they proposed to solve this linear system using the Kyrlov subspace method. The solution of equation (10) is unconstrained, i.e. χ does not have to lie in the interval $[0,1]$. If $\chi \in [0,1]$, the constrained optimum $\chi \in \{0,1\}$, since a quadratic function is monotonic in an interval which does not contain its extremum. Then the constrained optimum can be calculated as follows [10,6]:

$$\hat{\chi} = \max\{\min\{\chi, 1\}, 0\} \tag{11}$$

Finally, the minimizing solution d^{k+1} is given by soft-thresholding:

$$d^{k+1} = \frac{\nabla\chi^{k+1} + b^k}{|\nabla\chi^{k+1} + b^k|} \max\left(|\nabla\chi^{k+1} + b^k| - \frac{1}{\mu}, 0\right) \tag{12}$$

Note that this results in a minimizer which values are between 0 and 1, and the final active contour curve is given by the boundary of:

$$\eta_\sigma(\hat{\chi}) = \begin{cases} 1 & if \sigma < \hat{\chi}^{final} \leq 1 \\ 0 & 0 \leq \hat{\chi}^{final} \leq \sigma \end{cases} \tag{13}$$

In algorithm below an overview of the complete segmentation. Our segmentation model is initialized using an initial curve χ^0. Given the parameters d^0, b^0, V_{Belief}^{in} and V_{Belief}^{out} and for the set parameters λ_{in}, λ_{out}, μ, and σ, the Kl function solves equation (10) to update primal variable χ. The dual variable d^{k+1} is shrink iteratively. The final segmentation is given by $\left\{ \mathbf{x} \in \Omega | \chi(\mathbf{x})^{final} \geq \frac{1}{2} \right\}$.

4   Results

The proposed method was tested on a dataset [18,16] which contained both 914 color images acquired from 52 patients. These images have a definition of 1280 pixels/line for 1008 lines/image and are lossless compressed images. To illustrate and demonstrates the accuracy of our segmentation method, we present some results of our method and compare them to segmentation done by the traditional AC model based vector value image and the model proposed in [21]. The three methods are evaluated on 10 color images taken form the dataset [18,16] using F-measure criterion[13]. Traditional segmentation and method in [21] are initialized by contour curve around the object to be segmented, our method is free initialization and the segmentation done by the three method are presented for three challenging images (see Figure.1).

The accuracy of the segmentation is represented in term of Precision/Recall [13]. The proposed method give the best segmentation and the F-measure is better then the other methods (see Table.1).

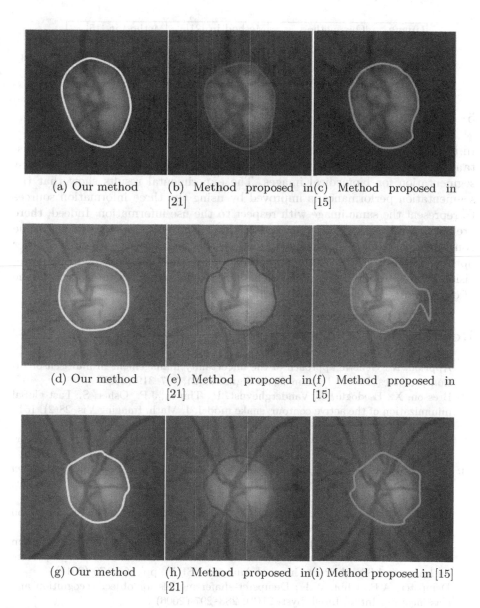

(a) Our method   (b) Method proposed in(c) Method proposed in
                        [21]   [15]

(d) Our method   (e) Method proposed in(f) Method proposed in
                        [21]   [15]

(g) Our method   (h) Method proposed in(i) Method proposed in [15]
                        [21]

Fig. 1. Images taken from the dataset [16]. The from the left to right, en yellow color
color segmentation done by our segmentation model, in red color segmentation done by
the model proposed in [21] and green color, the segmentation done by the traditional
model proposed in [15].

Table 1. Quantitative evaluation of the segmentation using F-measure

Image	Our method	Method in [21]	Method in [15]
Image 1	0.82	0.81	0.81
Image 2	0.79	0.76	0.77
Image 3	0.83	0.79	0.75

5 Conclusion

In this paper, we have investigate the use of the BFs in the Bhattacharyya distance framework. The results have shown that proposed approach give the best segmentation for biomedical images. The experimental results show that the segmentation performance is improved by using the three information sources to represent the same image with respect to the use information. Indeed, there are some drawbacks of our proposed method. The proposed is very high time consuming for calculating the mass functions. Furthermore, the research of other optimal models to estimate the mass functions in the DS theory and the imprecision coming from different images channels are an important perspective issue of our work.

References

1. Appriou, A.: Generic approach of the uncertainty management in multisensor fusion processes. Revue Traitement du Signal 22(2), 307–319 (2005)
2. Bresson, X., Esedoglu, S., Vandergheynst, P., Thiran, J.P., Osher, S.: Fast global minimization of the active contour/snake model. J. Math. Imaging Vis. 28(2), 151–167 (2007)
3. Chan, T.F., Sandberg, B.Y., Vese, L.A.: Active contours without edges for vector-valued images. Journal of Vis. Communi. and Image Repres. 11, 130–141 (2000)
4. Cremers, D., Rousson, M., Deriche, R.: A review of statistical approaches to level set segmentation: Integrating color, texture, motion and shape. Int. J. Comput. Vision 72(2), 195–215 (2007)
5. Cuzzolin, F.: A geometric approach to the theory of evidence. IEEE Trans. on Syst., Man, and Cyber., Part C 38(4), 522–534 (2008)
6. De Vylder, J., Rooms, F., Philips, W.: Convex formulation and global optimization for multimodal active contour segmentation. In: 2011 7th International Symposium on Image and Signal Processing and Analysis (ISPA), pp. 165–170 (2011)
7. Dempster, A.P., Chiu, W.F.: Dempster-shafer models for object recognition and classification. Int. J. Intell. Syst. 21(3), 283–297 (2006)
8. Denoeux, T.: Maximum likelihood estimation from uncertain data in the belief function framework. IEEE Trans. Knowl. Data Eng. 25(1), 119–130 (2013)
9. Derraz, F., Taleb-Ahmed, A., Pinti, A., Peyrodie, L., Betrouni, N., Chikh, A., Bereksi-Reguig, F.: Fast unsupervised texture segmentation using active contours model driven by bhattacharyya gradient flow. In: Bayro-Corrochano, E., Eklundh, J.-O. (eds.) CIARP 2009. LNCS, vol. 5856, pp. 193–200. Springer, Heidelberg (2009)

10. Goldstein, T., Bresson, X., Osher, S.: Geometric applications of the split bregman method: Segmentation and surface reconstruction. J. Sci. Comput. 45(1-3), 272–293 (2010)

11. Goldstein, T., Osher, S.: The split bregman method for l1-regularized problems. SIAM J. Img. Sci. 2(2), 323–343 (2009)

12. Lelandais, B., Gardin, I., Mouchard, L., Vera, P., Ruan, S.: Using belief function theory to deal with uncertainties and imprecisions in image processing. In: Denœux, T., Masson, M.-H. (eds.) Belief Functions: Theory & Appl. AISC, vol. 164, pp. 197–204. Springer, Heidelberg (2012)

13. Martin, D.R., Fowlkes, C.C., Malik, J.: Learning to detect natural image boundaries using local brightness, color, and texture cues. IEEE Trans. Pattern Anal. Mach. Intell. 26(5), 530–549 (2004)

14. Masson, M.-H., Denoeux, T.: Ecm: An evidential version of the fuzzy c. Pattern Recognition 41(4), 1384–1397 (2008)

15. Michailovich, O., Rathi, Y., Tannenbaum, A.: Image segmentation using active contours driven by the bhattacharyya gradient flow. IEEE Transactions on Image Processing 16(11), 2787–2801 (2007)

16. Niemeijer, M., van Ginneken, B., Cree, M., Mizutani, A., Quellec, G., Sanchez, C., Zhang, B., Hornero, R., Lamard, M., Muramatsu, C., Wu, X., Cazuguel, G., You, J., Mayo, A., Li, Q., Hatanaka, Y., Cochener, B., Roux, C., Karray, F., Garcia, M., Fujita, H., Abramoff, M.: Retinopathy online challenge: Automatic detection of microaneurysms in digital color fundus photographs. IEEE Transactions on Medical Imaging 29(1), 185–195 (2010)

17. Parzen, E.: On estimation of a probability density function and mode. The Annals of Mathematical Statistics 33(3), 1065–1076 (1962)

18. Quellec, G., Lamard, M., Josselin, P., Cazuguel, G., Cochener, B., Roux, C.: Optimal wavelet transform for the detection of microaneurysms in retina photographs. IEEE Transactions on Medical Imaging 27(9), 1230–1241 (2008)

19. Rombaut, M., Zhu, Y.M.: Study of dempster–shafer theory for image segmentation applications. Image and Vision Computing 20(1), 15–23 (2002)

20. Rousson, M., Paragios, N.: Prior knowledge, level set representations & visual grouping. Int. J. Comput. Vision 76(3), 231–243 (2008)

21. Scheuermann, B., Rosenhahn, B.: Feature quarrels: The dempster-shafer evidence theory for image segmentation using a variational framework. In: Kimmel, R., Klette, R., Sugimoto, A. (eds.) ACCV 2010, Part II. LNCS, vol. 6493, pp. 426–439. Springer, Heidelberg (2011)

22. Tschumperle, D., Deriche, R.: Vector-valued image regularization with pdes: a common framework for different applications. IEEE Trans. Pattern Anal. Mach. Intell. 27(4), 506–517 (April)

Threshold Estimation in Energy-Based Methods for Segmenting Birdsong Recordings

José Francisco Ruiz-Muñoz[1], Mauricio Orozco-Alzate[1,2],
and César Germán Castellanos-Domínguez[1]

[1] Grupo de Procesamiento y Reconocimiento de Señales, Universidad Nacional de
Colombia - Sede Manizales, km 7 vía al aeropuerto, Manizales (Caldas), Colombia
[2] Departamento de Informática y Computación, Universidad Nacional de Colombia -
Sede Manizales, km 7 vía al aeropuerto, Manizales (Caldas), Colombia
{jfruizmu,morozcoa,cgcastellanosd}@unal.edu.co

Abstract. Monitoring wildlife populations is important to assess ecosystem health, attend environmental protection activities and undertake research studies about ecology. However, the traditional techniques are temporally and spatially limited; in order to extract information quickly and accurately about the current state of the environment, processing and recognition of acoustic signals are used. In the literature, several research studies about automatic classification of species through their vocalizations are found; however, in many of them the segmentation carried out in the preprocessing stage is briefly mentioned and, therefore, it is difficult to be reproduced by other researchers. This paper is specifically focused on detection of regions of interest in the audio recordings. A methodology for threshold estimation in segmentation techniques based on energy of a frequency band of a birdsong recording is described. Experiments were carried out using chunks taken from the RMBL-Robin database; results showed that a good performance of segmentation can be obtained by computing a threshold as a linear function where the independent variable is the estimated noise.

Keywords: Audio signal processing and recognition, segmentation, bioacoustics.

1 Introduction

Technology for automatic classification of animal vocalizations is a useful tool in research studies on taxonomy, ecology and conservation as well as for attending activities of environmental monitoring. Traditional technologies for assessing ecosystem health, such as line transects or fixed-radius point counts, are spatial and time consuming, often imply expensive and exhausting journeys, and could be disruptive to the habitat under observation; thereby, in order to avoid those inconveniences, an automated system would be desired [1]. Particularly, researchers are interested in analyzing birdsongs because birds are widely distributed in nature, relatively easy to detect by their vocalizations and they have

J. Ruiz-Shulcloper and G. Sanniti di Baja (Eds.): CIARP 2013, Part I, LNCS 8258, pp. 480–487, 2013.

great knowledge of the biology of most species. Furthermore, there is a commercial interest in developing this type of systems due to the large and increasing number of birdwatchers worldwide [2]; additionally, this technology is ideal for impact studies and environmental management plans that are frequently required by authorities in many countries.

The problem of classifying bird species from an audio recording is a typical signal recognition problem [3], therefore in many studies, stages of signal preprocessing, feature extraction and classification are included. The first one includes the segmentation of vocalizations into smaller recognition units [4]. Sometimes it is done manually, and sometimes automatically; nevertheless, automatic recognition should not require manual segmentation. Even if classification is the aim in some papers, it is mentioned that a complete automatic recognition system should include the automatic detection of intervals of interest [5] because accurate segmentation is fundamental for successful classification systems [3].

Segmentation algorithms have been developed using energy and entropy as criteria to identify the onset and offset times of the regions of interest [5–7]. This process is simple in ideal conditions [3]; if vocalization call is the only sound in the recording, an increase in energy reveals a region of interest. In real conditions, the signal is degraded due to the many sources of sound in a recording, e.g., wind streams, background noise from other animals and surrounding events.

In this paper, it is proposed a non-supervised segmentation method of birdsong recordings. The signal energy is calculated from a frequency band extracted from the Short-time Fourier transform (STFT) —it can be considered as an image known as spectrogram: a representation of the intensity of a sound as a function of time and frequency [2, 6]. The output of the method is a binary signal in function of time, where time instants of interest are marked with "one" and non-interest time instants with "zero". Despite segmentation methods are essential in many studies about this topic, it is not clear how similar their outputs are to manual segmentations. Such a judgement must be based on objective performance estimation measurements; a number of them are presented in Section 2.4. Three ways of threshold estimation are compared: optimal in each case, linear function of estimated noise (parameter computed by least squares) and the segmentation technique used in [4].

2 Material and Methods

The proposed segmentation method is shown in Fig. 1. Basically, it consists in detecting regions with the highest energies in frequencies where the sound of interest typically exhibits its components.

2.1 Time-Frequency Analysis

Time-frequency analysis of a signal can be carried out through the STFT, namely, the Fourier transform per frame of a signal. STFT is a representation of the distribution of acoustic energy across frequencies and over time. Often,

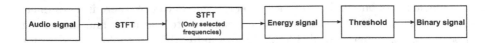

Fig. 1. Flow diagram of the proposed segmentation method

the time is graphically represented in the horizontal axis and frequency in the vertical one, and the amount of power detected is represented as the intensity at each time-frequency point, as follows:

$$
\mathbf{S} = [s_{ij}]_{N \times M} = \begin{bmatrix} P_0(f_0) & P_1(f_0) & \cdots & P_{M-1}(f_0) \\ P_0(f_1) & P_1(f_1) & \cdots & P_{M-1}(f_1) \\ P_0(f_2) & P_1(f_2) & \cdots & P_{M-1}(f_2) \\ \vdots & \vdots & \ddots & \vdots \\ P_0(f_{N-1}) & P_1(f_{N-1}) & \cdots & P_{M-1}(f_{N-1}) \end{bmatrix} \tag{1}
$$

where $i = 0, 1, ..., N-1$ corresponds to the frequency indexes and $j = 0, 1, ..., M-1$ to the time.

2.2 Energy Signal

A smoothed energy signal is computed taking only frequencies selected in the spectrogram (it requires *a priori* knowledge). When the segmentation is done in a limited frequency band, with minimum frequency f_l and maximum frequency f_h, a sub-matrix $\hat{\mathbf{S}} = [\hat{s}_{ij}]_{\hat{N} \times M}$ ($\hat{N} \leq N$) is taken from the STFT representation, such that elements in $\mathbf{S}$ corresponding to $f < f_l$ and $f > f_h$ are discarded. Energy signal is computed as:

$$
E_j = \frac{1}{\hat{N}} \sum_{i=0}^{i=\hat{N}-1} \hat{s}_{ij}^2, \tag{2}
$$

where the energy vector from (3) is obtained.

$$
\mathbf{E} = [E_0, \ E_1, \ ..., \ E_{M-1}] \tag{3}
$$

A smoothed energy signal $\hat{\mathbf{E}} = [\hat{E}_0 \ \hat{E}_1 ... \ \hat{E}_{M-1}]$ is obtained using the convolution operator and a Hann window $\mathbf{w} = \frac{1}{\sum_{i=0}^{l-1} w_i}[w_0 \ w_1 ... \ w_{l-1}]$ of size l, where $w_i = 0.54 - 0.46\cos(2\pi i/(l-1))$ to $i = 0, ..., l-1$:

$$
\hat{E}_j = (\mathbf{E} * \mathbf{w})[j] = \sum_{i=0}^{i=l-1} E_n \hat{w}_i, \tag{4}
$$

with $j = 0, 1, ..., M-1$.

The normalized energy signal is:

$$\hat{\mathbf{E}}_{norm} = 10 \log\left(\frac{\hat{\mathbf{E}}}{\mathrm{argmax}\{\hat{\mathbf{E}}\}}\right), \tag{5}$$

so that the maximum element of $\hat{\mathbf{E}}_{norm}$ is equal to zero (0).

2.3 Binary Signal

Assuming that vocalizations are present in regions where the energy signal $\hat{\mathbf{E}}_{norm}$ has the highest values, a threshold T_{dB} is used to build a binary function $\mathbf{B} = [B_0, B_1, ..., B_{M-1}]$ so:

$$B_i = \begin{cases} 1 & \text{if } \hat{E}_{norm\ i} > T_{dB} \\ 0 & \text{otherwise} \end{cases} \tag{6}$$

for $i = 0, ..., M - 1$.

2.4 Performance

Let $T = [t_0, t_1, ..., t_{M-1}]$ be a vector of time instants and $\mathbf{A} = [A_0, A_1, ..., A_{M-1}]$ a reference binary signal manually labeled, where $A_i = 1$ if the time instant t_i in the recording is considered as a point of interest and $A_i = 0$ otherwise; and $\mathbf{B} = [B_0, B_1, ..., B_{M-1}]$ is a binary signal resulting from a segmentation process as is indicated in Section 2.3. Recall rate (R) and precision rate (P) were chosen to measure the performance, following the same evaluation protocol used in [8]; the first one relates the number of points of interest correctly detected or hits (N_h, it is the total of points where $A_i = B_i = 1$) with the number of real points of interest (N_r, it is the total of points where $A_i = 1$), according with a manual segmentation; and the second one relates N_h with the number of detected points (N_d, it is the total of points where $B_i = 1$), so:

$$R = \frac{N_h}{N_r} \times 100\%, \quad P = \frac{N_h}{N_d} \times 100\%. \tag{7}$$

A measure that combines the two previous ones is the Euclidean distance between the point (R,P) in Cartesian coordinates and the point (100,100):

$$d_T(R, P) = \sqrt{(100 - R)^2 + (100 - P)^2}, \tag{8}$$

where the best segmentation corresponds to 0 and the worst one to 100.

Other measure that combines R and P is the F1 Score, it is defined as:

$$\text{F1 Score} = \frac{2PR}{P+R} \tag{9}$$

2.5   Estimating the Optimum Threshold

Threshold level is important because it is used to mark the boundaries between chosen and discarded segments. In [4] it is suggested to choose as threshold half of the noise level N_{dB} (computed by an iterative method, see Section 3) of the energy signal normalized with the maximum value 0 dB.

Intuitively, it is expected that when the T_{dB} value is changed in (6) from N_{dB} until 0 dB, R starts in 100 and tends to 0 and P starts in 0 and tends to 100 (assuming that at least the maximum energy point is considered of interest). Therefore, the best T_{dB} is considered the one that minimizes (8), as follows: if $\mathbf{T}_{dB} = [T_{dB\ 0},\ T_{dB\ 1},\ ...,\ T_{dB\ k}]$, where $T_{dB\ 0} = 0$ and $T_{dB\ k} = N_{dB}$, and the corresponding $\mathbf{R} = [R_0,\ R_1,\ ...,\ R_k]$ and $\mathbf{P} = [P_0,\ P_1,\ ...,\ P_k]$, the optimal threshold (T_{opt}) is $T_{dB\ i}$ for which $d_T(R_k, P_k)$ is minimum.

3   Experimental Setup

The objective in this section is to find a rule to estimate a threshold in order to obtain good segmentation. Experiments were done by following the steps listed below:

- Signal energy was estimated from audio recording chunks with the following features: STFTs representations computed using 512 points in each block of time with an overlap of 256 points; a sub-matrix was estimated, as described in Section 2.2, with $f_l = 1000$ Hz and $f_h = 5000$ Hz because the pitch information of the Robin ranges from 1500 to 4500 Hz [8]. The normalized and smoothed energy signal (see (5)) was estimated using a Hann window of size 20.
- N_{dB} is computed: the initial N_{dB} is set to the lowest $\hat{\mathbf{E}}_{norm}$ level and updated as the mean from gaps between regions where $\hat{\mathbf{E}}_{norm} < N_{dB}/2$ until the previous and current values of N_{dB} not vary more than 1 dB.
- T_{opt} is estimated as it is explained in Section 2.5: segmentation was carried out to several levels of threshold $\mathbf{T}_{dB}$, 20 steps from 0 to the minimum of $\hat{\mathbf{E}}_{norm}$. The element of $\mathbf{T}_{dB}$ with the best performance is chosen as T_{opt}.
- Threshold in function of N_{dB} is computed using least squares: this method consists in minimizing the expression $\left\| \hat{y} - [\hat{x}\ 1]\,[m\ \ c]^T \right\|^2$, where $\hat{x}$ and $\hat{y}$ are vectors that represents points in a Cartesian coordinate system, and m and c are the parameters of the linear equation $f(x) = mx + c$ computed in the regression; N_{dB} and T_{opt} for each chunk were taken as $\hat{x}$ and $\hat{y}$ respectively. Implementation was done using the numerical package of Python "Numpy"; the command `numpy.linalg.lstsq` was used.

3.1   Dataset

Experiments were carried out using a set of chunks of the RMBL-Robin database, which can be downloaded from http://www.ee.ucla.edu/~weichu/bird/. It is

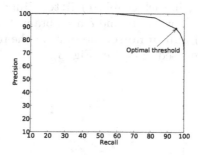

Fig. 2. P-R curve from a segment of recording

a set of recordings of Robin bird songs collected at the Rocky Mountain Biological Laboratory near Crested Butte, Colorado (USA) in the summer of 2009 [8]. Recordings are corrupted by environmental background noises and human voices. This dataset was selected in this research because timing boundaries of syllables were annotated by experts. Although noise and intensity levels vary considerably between recordings, it was assumed that they are relatively constant over chunks of approximately 10 seconds of duration as considered in [6]. Therefore, experiments were carried out using 20 segments of 10 s approximately, extracted from 10 recordings. Names of the selected recordings and time intervals are specified in Table 1.

Table 1. Chunks selected from the RMBL-Robin database

Name of file .wav	Start time	End time
A-01june09-0702-robin.wav	0	10
A-30may09-0729-robin.wav	24	36
C-30may09-0826-robin.wav	0	12
C-31may09-0608-robin.wav	9	19
E-01june09-0537-robin.wav	0	12
E-01june09-0543-robin.wav	0	9
G-08june09-0517-robin.wav	0	12
H-08june09-0507-robin.wav	12	23
H-08june09-0512-robin.wav	0	10
H-09june09-0518-robin.wav	14	26
L-03june09-1905-robin.wav	9	21
L-12june09-0728-robin.wav	0	11
S-09june09-1953-robin.wav	2	15
U-03june09-1813-robin.wav	4	16
U-03june09-1815-robin.wav	10	24
W-03june09-1905-robin.wav	0	9
W-08june09-0733-robin.wav	49	63
W-09june09-1902-robin.wav	4	15
X-04june09-0615-robin.wav	5	15
X-14june09-0518-robin.wav	6	24

3.2 Results

Table 2 shows the performance obtained in segmentation experiments. Two methods of threshold estimation were compared with the performance obtained for segmentation with T_{opt} in each chunk: 1) **fitted line:** threshold in function of N_{dB} ($T_{dB} = m \ N_{dB} + c$), where m and c are obtained with the regression as explained in Section 3; 2) **half of noise:** the same as the previous case but with $m = 0.5$ and $c = 0$, as proposed in [4] (see Fig. 3).

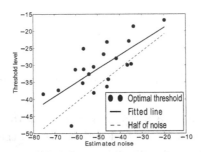

Fig. 3. Graphical representation of optimal threshold estimated in each chunk and the linear functions obtained by the linear regression (fitted line) and taken the threshold equals to $N_{dB}/2$ (half of noise)

Notice in Table 2 that, according to d_T and F1 Score measures, with threshold regression it is obtained a better performance than the one using the method of [4] (half of N_{dB}). With threshold estimation as half of N_{dB} a good P was obtained, even better than with optimum threshold by chunk, nevertheless P decays considerably.

Table 2. Comparison between performance obtained by computing the threshold as a linear function of N_{dB}, and the optimal threshold estimated by each chunk. If the performance measure is next to ↑: the better the bigger; analogously, if it is next to ↓: the better the lower.

	R ↑	P ↑	d_T ↓	F1 Score ↑	Parameters estimated
Fitted line	**90.3**	80.7	**21.3**	**85.2**	m=0.4; c=-10.9
Half of N_{dB}	76.0	**89.8**	26.1	82.3	m=0.5; c=0
Optimum threshold (Reference)	91.1	85.4	17.1	88.2	

4   Conclusions

A detailed segmentation methodology for birdsong recordings was presented. It is based on energy of a frequency band, is straightforward and provides a good performance. The proposed threshold estimation technique consists in computing it in function of background noise from a linear regression. Performance methods are described and results are compared with the optimum threshold heuristically computed for each chunk and with the threshold estimation method from [4].

Several research studies about automated species recognition are not rigorous in the description of the segmentation stage, even when they clarify that their methods work well when the classification objects are correctly detected [5,9,10]. However, the system confidence depends on both event detection and classification algorithms; therefore, the two stages should be explained in detail, including appropriate evidence of performance.

Birdsongs often have a gramatical structure, where the basic building blocks are called syllables [2] and which have been used as recognition objects in many studies; as future work it is proposed to use a merge and delete criterion particularly to detect these units. Furthermore, other representations different to the energy might be explored, e.g., the entropy and other criteria to detect regions of interest; tuning of the new parameters might be carried out based on the performance measures used in this research.

Acknowledgments. This research was supported by "Programa Nacional de Formación de Investigadores COLCIENCIAS 2012" and "Convocatoria de apoyo a la movilidad de estudiantes de la FIA 2013-2014 de la Universidad Nacional de Colombia - Sede Manizales".

References

1. Trifa, V.M., Girod, L., Collier, T., Blumstein, D.T., Taylor, C.E.: Automated wildlife monitoring using self-configuring sensor networks deployed in natural habitats. In: International Symposium on Artificial Life and Robotics (AROB 2007), Beppu, Japan (2007)
2. Harma, A.: Automatic identification of bird species based on sinusoidal modeling of syllables. In: 2003 IEEE International Conference on Acoustics, Speech, and Signal Processing (ICASSP). IEEE (2003)
3. Neal, L., Briggs, F., Raich, R., Fern, X.Z.: Time-frequency segmentation of bird song in noisy acoustic environments. In: 2011 IEEE International Conference on Acoustics, Speech and Signal Processing (ICASSP), pp. 2012–2015 (2011)
4. Fagerlund, S.: Bird species recognition using support vector machines. EURASIP Journal on Advances in Signal Processing 2007 (2007)
5. Trifa, V.M., Kirschel, A.N.G., Taylor, C.E., Vallejo, E.E.: Automated species recognition of antbirds in a Mexican rainforest using hidden Markov models. The Journal of the Acoustical Society of America 123(4), 2424–2431 (2008)
6. Briggs, F., Fern, X., Raich, R.: Acoustic classification of bird species from syllables: an empirical study. Technical report, Oregon State University (2009)
7. Stowell, D., Plumbley, M.D.: Birdsong and C4DM: A survey of UK birdsong and machine recognition for music researchers. Technical report (2011)
8. Chu, W., Blumstein, D.T.: Noise robust bird song detection using syllable pattern-based hidden Markov models. In: 2011 IEEE International Conference on Acoustics, Speech and Signal Processing (ICASSP), pp. 345–348 (2011)
9. Hao, Y., Campana, B., Keogh, E.: Monitoring and Mining Animal Sounds in Visual Space. Journal of Insect Behavior 26(4), 466–493 (2012)
10. Huang, C.J., Yang, Y.J., Yang, D.X., Chen, Y.J.: Frog classification using machine learning techniques. Expert Systems with Applications 36(2), 3737–3743 (2009)

Detection of Periodic Signals in Noise Based on Higher-Order Statistics Joined to Convolution Process and Spectral Analysis

Miguel Enrique Iglesias Martínez and Fidel Ernesto Hernández Montero

Universidad de Pinar del Río Hermanos Saíz Montes de Oca,
Departamento de Telecomunicaciones, Calle Martí Final No. 270,
esquina 27 de Noviembre, Pinar del Río, Cuba, C.P 20100
migueliglesias2010@gmail.com, fidel@tele.upr.edu.cu

Abstract. This paper refers to the application of higher-order statistical signal processing techniques (cumulant calculation) on Gaussian noise cancellation. The performed procedure, joined to a convolution process and Fast Fourier Transform (FFT) application, results in the complete estimation (i.e., amplitude, frequency and phase recovery) of any corrupted periodic signal. Whereas tone frequency estimation is performed by 4th-order cumulant calculation, phase recovery is achieved by the convolution of the cumulant calculation and the corrupted signal. At last, the original signal amplitude is recovered by means of modification of the resulting amplitude spectrum. In this paper, higher-order statistics foundations are presented and the validation of the proposed algorithm is revealed in both theoretical and practical sense. Obtained results are highly satisfactory.

Keywords: Higher-Order Statistics, Noise Cancellation, Convolution, Fourier Transform.

1 Introduction

Methods for noise cancellation using higher-order statistics, in particular those based on cumulants, have demonstrated to be very effective [1]. This is mainly due to the properties that state, from one hand, that higher-order cumulants of a normal distribution random signal is 0 and, on the other hand, that cumulant of the sum of signals is equal to the sum of the cumulants of each signal, then higher-order cumulant of a signal corrupted by normal distribution random signal (noise) is equal to the higher-order cumulant of the signal without noise.

Several works have been approached to the harmonics retrieval problem [2], [3] and [4]. However all of these papers only reach to recover harmonic amplitude and frequency; phase cannot be retrieved. Other works, as in [5] and [6], use higher-order statistics (fourth-order cumulant) for adaptive estimation of amplitude and frequency of harmonics in real zero-mean random signals. Some methods, developed for phase

J. Ruiz-Shulcloper and G. Sanniti di Baja (Eds.): CIARP 2013, Part I, LNCS 8258, pp. 488–495, 2013.

estimation, are based on higher-order spectra [7] [8] and Bayes Theorem [9]. However, tools proposed in these works exhibit a high computational complexity (higher-order spectral parameters are results of multidimensional functions calculation) that makes them no suitable for practical use and cannot be directly or simply applied on the problem of estimation of amplitude, frequency and phase of a periodic signal in noise.

Methods for phase estimation using Polyspectrum Slice [10] have also been reported but these ones are just approached to phase recovery in linear time-invariant systems, thus they are out of the scope of this work. In order to obtain a complete algorithm for periodic signals estimation corrupted by noise, a new algorithm is proposed in this work.

2   Removing Noise from Periodic Signal through Higher-Order Statistics

For real value signals, in the problem that concerns removing noise from harmonic signal, observed data is described as follows:

$$y(t) = \sum_{k=1}^{N} A_k \cos(w_k t + \phi_k) + w(t) = x(t) + w(t) \qquad (1)$$

where $x(t)$ is the useful signal (signal to be detected) and $w(t)$ is additive zero mean Gaussian noise. Besides, A_k, f_k and ϕ_k are the amplitude, frequency and phase, respectively, of the signal. Since higher-order cumulants of a zero mean Gaussian noise is equal to zero, the estimation of cumulants for noise cancellation can be made starting from the third order, but from [11] all third-order cumulants of complex harmonic are always zero. Consequently this research continues with the use of fourth-order cumulant.

2.1   Fourth-Order Cumulant Calculation

For a zero-mean stationary random process $z(t)$, and for $k=3,4$, the kth order cumulant of $z(t)$ can be defined in term of its joint moments as [12]:

$$C_k^z(\tau_1, \tau_2, ..., \tau_{k-1}) = E\{z(\tau_1)...z(\tau_{k-1})\} - E\{g(\tau_1)...g(\tau_{k-1})\} \qquad (2)$$

Where $g(t)$ is a Gaussian random process with the same second-order statistic as $z(t)$. If $z(t)$ is Gaussian, the cumulants are all zero. Then, for zero-mean real random variables the fourth-order cumulant can be calculated in agreement to [12] as follows:

$$C_4^z(\tau_1, \tau_2, \tau_3) = E\{z(t) \cdot z(t + \tau_1) \cdot z(t + \tau_2) \cdot z(t + \tau_3)\}$$

$$- C_2^z(\tau_1) \cdot C_2^z(\tau_2 - \tau_3) - C_2^z(\tau_2) \cdot C_2^z(\tau_3 - \tau_1) - C_2^z(\tau_3) \cdot C_2^z(\tau_1 - \tau_2) \qquad (3)$$

According to the process described in equation (1), since $w(t)$ is a zero-mean Gaussian random signal, $C_4^w(\tau_1,\tau_2,\tau_3)=0$. Then, $C_4^y(\tau_1,\tau_2,\tau_3)=C_4^x(\tau_1,\tau_2,\tau_3)$.

Using equation (3) and working with only the one-dimensional component of the fourth-order cumulant, $C_4^y(\tau_1,0,0)$, by setting $\tau_2=\tau_3=0$, leads to a result similar to that obtained in [11] by setting $\tau_1=\tau_2=\tau_3=\tau$. This one-dimensional component contains original amplitude and frequency of the signal to detect, $x(t)$, although the phase is missed; on the other hand, the noise is entirely removed:

$$C_4^y(\tau_1,0,0)=E\{x(t)^3\cdot x(t+\tau_1)\}-3\cdot E\{x(t)\cdot x(t+\tau_1)\}\cdot E\{x^2(t)\} \qquad (4)$$

Then, developing the left term of the equation (4) by substituting $x(t)$ declared in (1):

$$E\{x(t)^3\cdot x(t+\tau_1)\}=\int_{-\pi}^{\pi}g(x)\cdot f_\varphi(\phi)d\phi$$

$$=\sum_{k=1}^{N}\frac{3A_k^{\,4}}{8}\cos(w_k\tau_1) \qquad (5)$$

Substituting, in the equation (6), the result obtained in the expression (5):

$$C_4^y(\tau_1,0,0)=\sum_{k=1}^{N}\frac{3A_k^{\,4}}{8}\cos(w_k\tau_1)-\sum_{k=1}^{N}\frac{3A_k^{\,4}}{4}\cos(w_k\tau_1) \qquad (6)$$

obtaining as result (similar to that obtained in [11]):

$$C_4^y(\tau_1,0,0)=\sum_{k=1}^{N}-\frac{3A_k^{\,4}}{8}\cos(w_k\tau_1) \qquad (7)$$

It is clear from equation (7), that the waveform of the original signal is not preserved, which is due to the loss of the phase information of the original signal in the noise cancellation procedure. This is the problem to face in the following section.

3   Phase Recovery Method

In order to preserve the phase information of the original signal (deterministic) in $C_4^y(\tau_1,0,0)$, a method based on the convolution between corrupted signal, y(t), and $C_4^y(\tau_1,0,0)$ is proposed. In order to theoretically prove the proposed method, let $a(t)$ be a sinusoidal signal corrupted by Gaussian noise,

$a(t) = \sum_{k=1}^{N} A_k \cos(w_k t + \phi_k) + w(t)$, and $b(t)$, the one-dimensional 4th-order

cumulative of the corrupted signal, $C_4^y(\tau_1, 0, 0) = \sum_{k=1}^{N} -\frac{3A_k^4}{8}\cos(w_k \tau_1)$,

(i.e., an equivalent of the free-noise periodic signal, the phase of which is equal to 0).
The convolution procedure is developed as follows:

$$Conv_{ab} = \lim_{T \to \infty} \frac{1}{T} \int_{-T/2}^{T/2} a(t) \cdot b(-t + \tau)dt \tag{8}$$

$$= \int_{-T/2}^{T/2} \sum_{k=1}^{N} [A_k \cos(w_k t + \phi_k) + w(t)][-\frac{3A_k^4}{8}\cos(-w_k t + w_k \tau)]dt$$

$$= \int_{-T/2}^{T/2} \sum_{k=1}^{N} -\frac{3A_k^5}{8}\cos(w_k t + \phi_k) \cdot \cos(-w_k t + w_k \tau)dt$$

$$+ \int_{-T/2}^{T/2} \sum_{k=1}^{N} -\frac{3A_k^4}{8}\cos(-w_k t + w_k \tau) \cdot w(t)dt$$

$$Conv_{ab} = \sum_{k=1}^{N} -\frac{3A_k^5}{16}\cos(w_k \tau + \phi_k) \tag{9}$$

Equation (9) reveals that an equivalent of the original periodic signal, preserving phase information, is achieved.

4   Spectral Amplitude Estimation

As it can be seen in (9), the original harmonic amplitudes are affected during the whole process by a non linear factor equivalent to:

$$A_i = A_o \sqrt[5]{\frac{16}{3}} \tag{10}$$

where A_i represents the original signal amplitude and A_o correspond to the output signal amplitude. This represents a problem because each amplitude of harmonics in x(t) must be independently corrected by itself. Then, in order to fix the original amplitude of harmonics in the periodic signal, in this paper every individual harmonic component is individually adjusted in the amplitude spectrum.   The process involves calculating the FFT of the signal resulting from the convolution process, and then, applying expression (10) on every single spectral component. Then, the resulting spectral vector is anti transformed, leading to the original signal with noise removed. This spectral adjustment carries on an important inconvenience since noise brought out by the FFT application is also adjusted (depending on its magnitude, this noise could indeed be amplified). In practice, this inconvenience can be reduced by anti transforming the zero-mean adjusted spectrum instead of the original adjusted spectrum. The method diagram can be observed in figure 1.

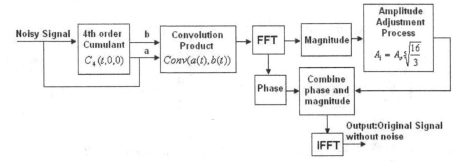

Fig. 1. Block Diagram of the Proposed Algorithm

5   Experimental Results

First, in order to verify the effectiveness of the proposed algorithm, an experiment using a multitone signal was performed. In this case, the superposition of six tones with different amplitudes (0.4, 0.5, 0.6, 0.6, 0.3, 0.1), frequencies (50 Hz, 200 Hz, 400 Hz, 400 Hz, 600 Hz and 700 Hz) and phases ($\pi/4$ rad, $\pi/6$ rad, $\pi/3$ rad, $\pi/2$ rad, $\pi/12$ rad and π rad), corrupted by zero-mean Gaussian noise, was generated. Figure 2a and 2b show the corrupted signal and its spectrum, and the obtained results, applying the proposed algorithm on this signal, are shown in figure 2c.

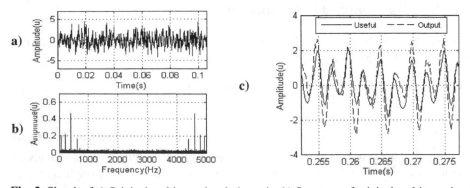

Fig. 2. Sketch of a) Original multitone signal plus noise b) Spectrum of original multitone signal plus noise. c) Comparison between useful signal (uncontaminated signal) and output signal

- Periodic rectangular and triangular pulses.

A train of rectangular pulses and a train of triangular pulses were also used during experimentations. The temporal approach of these signals in Fourier series representation can be described through equation (11, rectangular pulses) and (12, triangular pulses) respectively. Figure 3a and 3b show the noisy rectangular pulse and its spectrum, and a comparison between such an output signal and the desired signal is shown in figure 3c. Furthermore, the figure 4a and 4b shows the noisy triangular pulse and its spectrum, and in the figure 4c it is shown a comparison between the signal at the noise canceller output and the original periodic signal.

$$x(t) = \frac{4A}{\pi} \sum_{n=1}^{P} \frac{1}{2n-1} \sin((2n-1)w_c t + \phi) \tag{11}$$

$$x(t) = \frac{8A}{\pi^2} \sum_{n=1}^{P} \frac{(-1)^{((2n-1)-1)/2}}{(2n-1)^2} \sin((2n-1)w_c t + \phi) \tag{12}$$

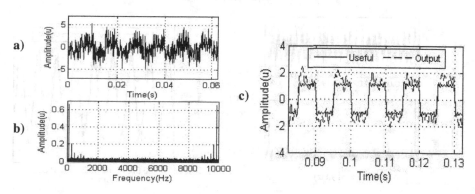

Fig. 3. Sketch of a) Noisy rectangular pulse b) Noisy rectangular pulse spectrum c) Comparison between useful signal (uncontaminated signal) and output signal

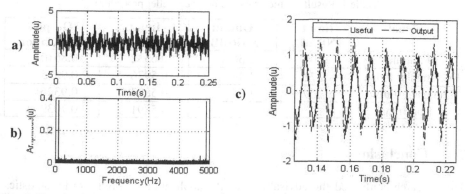

Fig. 4. Sketch of a) Noisy triangular pulse b) Noisy triangular pulse spectrum c) Comparison between useful signal (uncontaminated signal) and output signal

6   Working with Real Signals

This noise cancellation procedure was also applied on real experimental signals. In this case, a signal corresponding to the vibration produced by an unbalanced shaft, as part of an experimental rig, was processed. Since shaft rotates at constant speed, the sensed vibration is periodic by nature. The signal was digitized by a data acquisition system based on an A/D converter, 10 bits resolution, with sampling frequency equals to 20 kHz. Gaussian noise was generated in Matlab and added to the sensor signal. The resulting signal was given at the noise canceller input. Figure 5a and 5b show the sensor signal plus noise and its spectrum, and in the Figure 5c it is shown the output signal and the desired signal. In this experiment, only the correlation index was computed in order to quantify the effectiveness of the noise cancellation procedure; in fact, computation of the SNR at the noise canceller input and output is hard to be accurately achieved. Table 1 summarizes all the results, verifying the effectiveness of the proposed algorithm.

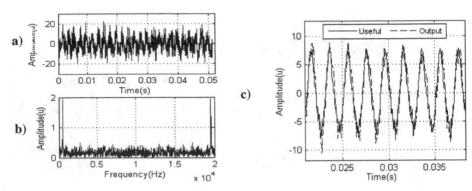

Fig. 5. Sketch of a) Sensor signal plus noise b) Spectrum of sensor signal plus noise c) Comparison between original sensor signal (useful signal) and output signal

Table 1. Results of the proposed noise canceller procedure

Signal	Input SNR(dB)	Output SNR(dB)	Input Correlation	Output Correlation
Multitone	− 3.99	2.36	0.6332	0.8610
Rectangular Pulse	− 5.72	1.44	0.5976	0.9575
Triangular Pulse	− 6.09	1.54	0.5883	0.9326
Sensor Signal	-	-	0.5891	0.7039

7   Conclusions

This research confirmed the advisability of the application of higher-order statistics combined to a convolution process and Fast Fourier Transform, for detection of periodic signals in noise (Gaussian noise). In this work, the use of 4th-order cumulant, was proposed and argued. Experimental results performed in Matlab were presented using real and simulate signals, revealing not only the benefits of this application but also the problem it carries on. This problem was clearly defined as the loss of signal phase information because of the noise cancellation procedure. In order to solve this problem, a convolution procedure was proposed. Finally, an amplitude spectral manipulation was performed in order to restore the original amplitude of each spectral component. Results revealed a high effectiveness, given by the significant signal-to-noise rate enhancement achieved, preserving the amplitude, frequency and phase information of the signals to be detected.

References

1. Howard, R.M.: Principles of Random Signal Analysis and Low Noise Design. John Wiley & Sons Ltd. (2009)
2. Swami, A., Mendel, J.M.: Cumulant-Based Approach to the Harmonic Retrieval Problem. In: International Conference on Acoustics, Speech, and Signal Processing, ICASSP 1988, April 11-14, vol. 4, pp. 2264–2267 (1988)
3. Swami, A., Mendel, J.M.: Cumulant-Based Approach to Harmonic Retrieval and Related Problems. IEEE Transactions on Signal Processing 39(5), 1099–1109 (1991)
4. Le, T.H., Clediere, J., Serviere, C., Lacoume, J.L.: Noise Reduction in Side Channel Attack Using Fourth-Order Cumulant. IEEE Transactions on Information Forensics and Security 2(4), 710–720 (2007)
5. Zhang, Y., Wang, S.-X.: A Hybrid Approach to Harmonic Retrieval in Non-Gaussian Noise Using Fourth-Order Moment and Autocorrelation. In: Fourth International Conference on Signal Processing, ICSP 1998, vol. 1, pp. 411–414 (1998)
6. Blagouchine, I.V., Moreau, E.: Unbiased Adaptive Estimations of the Fourth-Order Cumulant for Real Random Zero-Mean Signal. IEEE Transactions on Signal Processing 57(9), 3330–3346 (2009)
7. Narasimhan, S.V., Basumallick, N., Chaitanya, R.: Improved Phase Estimation Based on Complete Bispectrum and Modified Group Delay. Signal, Image and Video Processing 2(3), 261–274 (2008)
8. Geng, M., Liang, H., Wang, J.: Research on Methods of Higher-order Statistics for Phase Difference Detection and Frequency Estimation. In: 4th International Congress on Image and Signal Processing, Shanghai, vol. 4, pp. 2189–2193 (2011)
9. Sacchi, M.D., Ulrych, T.J., Walker, C.J.: Interpolation and extrapolation using a high-resolution discrete Fourier transform. IEEE Transactions on Signal Processing 46(1), 31–38 (1998)
10. Kachenoura, A., Albera, L., Bellanger, J.-J., Senhadji, L.: Non-Minimum Phase Identification Based on Higher Order Spectrum Slices. IEEE Transactions on Signal Processing 56(5), 1821–1829 (2008)
11. Nikias, C.L., Mendel, J.M.: Signal Processsing with Higher-Order Spectra. IEEE Signal Processing Magazine 10(3), 10–37 (1993)
12. Molí, S., Josep M.: Técnicas de Speech Enhancement Considerando Estadísticas de Orden Superior, Tesis Doctoral, Barcelona, Junio (1995),
    http://hdl.handle.net/10803/6943

Hierarchical Models for Rescoring Graphs vs. Full Integration

Raquel Justo* and M. Inés Torres

Dpto. Electricidad y Electrónica, Universidad del País Vasco (UPV/EHU), Spain

Abstract. In this work, we explore the integration of hierarchical Language Models (HLMs) in different modules of a Spoken Dialog System. First of all, HLMs are integrated into the Automatic Speech Recognition system. In order to carry out this integration, within the recognition process, finite-state machines were considered. This approach was compared to a two step decoding process in which HLMs are used to rescore a graph. Then, HLMs were also used for Language Understanding (LU) purposes. Two architectures were compared theoretically and empirically in both ASR and LU modules.

Keywords: finite-state machines, language models, automatic speech recognition, language understanding.

1 Introduction

In a classical pattern recognition problem the maximization of posterior probability $P(\bar{w}|\bar{x})$ allows to get the most likely sequence of symbols $\bar{w}$, that matches a given sequence of input observations $\bar{x}$, according to eq (1).

$$\hat{\bar{w}} = \arg\max_{\bar{w}} P(\bar{w}|\bar{x}) = \arg\max_{\bar{w}} P(\bar{w})P(\bar{x}|\bar{w}) \tag{1}$$

Automatic Speech Recognition (ASR) is a classical pattern recognition problem in which the term $P(\bar{w})$ corresponds to the prior probability of a word sequence and it is commonly estimated by a Language Model (LM), while $P(\bar{x}|\bar{w})$ is estimated by an Acoustic Model (AM), typically a Hidden Markov Model.

If we focus on $P(\bar{w})$, word n-gram LMs are the most widely used approach in ASR systems. However, a large amount of training material, that is not always available, is needed to get a robust estimations of the parameters of such models. Therefore, different alternatives like Hierarchical Language Models (HLMs) based on classes of phrases could be adopted. This approach has been successfully employed in ASR systems for restricted domain applications [6]. However, the integration of this kind of complex models into the ASR system is an important issue that has to be solved. Usually, decoders can deal with standard word-based LMs, but when complex LMs need to be used two possible alternatives can be considered: 1) a *decoupled architecure* consisting of a two-step

---
* This work has been partially supported by the Gov. of the Basque Country under grant IT685-13 and by the Spanish CICYT under grant TIN2011-28169-C05-04.

J. Ruiz-Shulcloper and G. Sanniti di Baja (Eds.): CIARP 2013, Part I, LNCS 8258, pp. 496–503, 2013.

process with a word graph rescoring [9,2] or 2) an *integrated architecture* where the decoder has to be modified to integrate the LM into the recognition process.

An ASR system employs different knowledge sources to carry out the recognition process such as acoustic, phonetic, lexical and syntactic knowledge. Each of this sources adds complexity to the decoding algorithm. AT&T laboratories presented an approach that simplifies the integration of different knowledge sources into the ASR system by using Stochastic Finite State Transducers (SFST) [8,3,1]. Newer architectures have also been recently provided for large vocabulary ASR [10]. The *integrated architecture* employed in this work takes advantage of the same idea, that is, the composition of finite-state machines, which model each knowledge source, to build a dynamic search network. This architecture was previously described in [7] and it is compared to a decoupled architecture.

On the other hand, HLMs can also be used to deal with a Language Understanding (LU) procedure that is devoted to extracting semantic information from a text sentence.

The contribution of this paper is twofold: first, it provides a full theoretical description of the two architectures, i.e. fully integrated HLMs vs. HLMs for graphs rescoring. Then, these approaches are theoretically and empirically evaluated for both ASR and LU purposes in a Spanish Spoken Dialogue task. The paper is organized as follows: in Section 2 the employed LMs are briefly described. Then, in Section 3 a full theoretical description of the two architectures is given for ASR and LU tasks; and a theoretical comparison between them is given. Finally, Section 4 and Section 5 summarizes the obtained results and the extracted conclusions.

2   HLMs Based on Classes of Phrases

In this section we present the different LMs that were used in this work. All of them were defined as Stochastic Finite State models. Specifically, we used *k-Testable in the Strict Sense* (k-TSS) LMs, which are a subclass of regular languages and have been successfully proposed for natural language processing applications [11]. They have been considered as a syntactic approach of the n-gram LMs under certain conditions. First of all a classical word k-TSS LM was considered (M_w), where the probability of a sequence of N words ($\bar{w}$), is obtained considering the history of previous $k_w - 1$ words as shown in eq. (2).

$$P(\bar{w}) \simeq P_{M_w}(\bar{w}) = \prod_{i=1}^{N} P(w_i|w_{i-k_w+1}^{i-1}) \qquad (2)$$

Then two different approaches for HLMs (M_{sw}, M_{sl}) were considered [6]. In the **first approach**, M_{sw}, a set of classes made up of phrases constituted by not linked words is used. In this way, the probability of a word sequence ($\bar{w}$) can be computed by means of eq. (3), where the segmentation (s) and classification ($\bar{c}$) of a word sequence are considered as hidden variables:

$$P(\bar{w}) = \sum_{\forall \bar{c} \in \Sigma_c^*} \sum_{\forall s \in \mathcal{S}(\bar{w})} P(\bar{w}, \bar{c}, s) = \sum_{\forall \bar{c} \in \Sigma_c^*} \sum_{\forall s \in \mathcal{S}(\bar{w})} P(\bar{w}|s, \bar{c})P(s|\bar{c})P(\bar{c}) \qquad (3)$$

being Σ_c^* the set of all possible $\bar{c}$ given an a-priori defined $\Sigma_c = \{c_i\}$ alphabet of classes and being $S(\bar{w})$ the set of all possible segmentations of a given $\bar{w}$.

Then, assuming the following approaches: a k-TSS model to estimate the term $P(\bar{c})$ (k_c-1 stands for the considered history of classes), $P(s|\bar{c}) \simeq \alpha$ and $P(\bar{w}|s,\bar{c})$ estimated with zero order models ($k_{cw} - 1$ stands for the maximum length of the word history considered in each class), eq. (3) is rewritten as follows:

$$P(\bar{w}) \simeq \alpha \sum_{\forall \bar{c} \in \Sigma_c^*} \sum_{\forall s \in \mathcal{S}(\bar{w})} \prod_{i=1}^{T} \left[\left[\prod_{j=a_{i-1}+1}^{a_i} P(w_j|w_{j-k_{cw}+1}^{j-1}, c_i) \right] P(c_i|c_{i-k_c+1}^{i-1}) \right] \tag{4}$$

According to this, $N_c + 1$ (N_c is the size of the set of classes) SFSA are needed to represent the M_{sw} model: one for each class considering the relations among words inside the classes, $P(w_j|w_{j-k_{cw}+1}^{j-1}, c_i)$, and an additional one that takes into account the relations among classes, $P(c_i|c_{i-k_c+1}^{i-1})$.

In the **second approach**, M_{sl}, classes are made up of phrases constituted by linked words, $\bar{l}$. Thus, the probability of $\bar{w}$ is given now by eq. (5)

$$P(\bar{w}) = \sum_{\forall \bar{c} \in \Sigma_c^*} \sum_{\forall \bar{l} \in \Sigma_l^*} P(\bar{w}, \bar{c}, \bar{l}) = \sum_{\forall \bar{c} \in \Sigma_c^*} \sum_{\forall \bar{l} \in \Sigma_l^*} P(\bar{w}|\bar{l}, \bar{c}) P(\bar{l}|\bar{c}) P(\bar{c}) \tag{5}$$

where Σ_c^* is the set comprising all possible class sequences for the given Σ_c alphabet of classes and Σ_l^* is the set of all possible sequences of l_i phrases. Assuming that $P(\bar{c})$ is estimated using a k-TSS model, that $P(\bar{l}|\bar{c})$ is estimated using zero-order models and finally, $P(\bar{w}|\bar{l}, \bar{c})$ is equal to 1 when $\bar{l}$ and $\bar{c}$ are compatible with $\bar{w}$ and 0 otherwise, the eq. (5) can be rewritten as eq. (6).

$$P(\bar{w}) \simeq \sum_{\forall \bar{c} \in \mathcal{C}} \sum_{\forall \bar{l} \in \mathcal{L}_{\bar{c}}(\bar{w})} \prod_{i=1}^{T} \left[P(l_i|c_i) P(c_i|c_{i-k_c+1}^{i-1}) \right] \tag{6}$$

$N_c + 1$ SFSA are needed again to represent the M_{sl} model: one that takes into account the relations among classes, $P(c_i|c_{i-k_c+1}^{i-1})$, and N_c additional SFSA that, in this case, stands for 1-TSS models, $P(l_i|c_i)$.

3   HLMs into ASR and LU Systems

When considering the **ASR system**, we want to carry out the recognition process by using the HLMs (M_{sw} and M_{sl}) defined above through two different architectures. First of all, an **integrated architecture** was considered. In this case, we took advantage of the use of k-TSS LMs. These models can be represented by SFSA, which can be easily composed with each other and with other automata. When considering the integration of complex HLMs there is not only one automaton associated to each LM but $N_c + 1$ different SFSA are needed, as described in Section 2. Thus, for doing the integration of the different SFSA a dynamic composition was carried out, in the same way the different models involved in the recognition process (LM, AM and lexical models) are integrated into the search network for a classical word k-TSS LM.

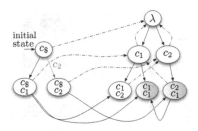

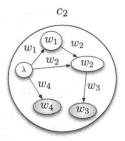

Fig. 1. SFSA that considers the relations among classes (shaded states correspond to final states)

Fig. 2. Specific SFSA for a c_2 class (final states are shaded)

Let us show an example to illustrate this method for the M_{sw} model. Being $\Sigma_c = \{c_1, c_2\}$ a two-class vocabulary made up of phrases, where $c_1 = \{w_1, w_1\ w_1\}$ and $c_2 = \{w_2\ w_3, w_1\ w_2\ w_3, w_4\}$, Fig 1 and Fig 2 represent the automata that take into account the relations among classes, and the specific automaton associated to class c2, respectively. Then, when the search network is built dynamically and the transition probabilities between words are needed (red arrows in Fig. 3) not only one but the two SFSA associated to the LM have to be consulted.

In this case, the probability of a word sequence is given by eq. (3) and the most likely word sequence is estimated according to the Viterbi algorithm:

$$\hat{w} \simeq \arg\max_{\forall \bar{w} \in \Sigma_w^*} \left[\max_{\forall \bar{c} \in \Sigma_c^*} \max_{\forall s \in S_c(\bar{w})} \max_{\bar{n}} P(\bar{x}, \bar{n} | \bar{w}, \bar{c}, s) P(\bar{w} | \bar{c}, s) P(s | \bar{c}) P(\bar{c}) \right] \quad (7)$$

where $\bar{n}$ is a path of the search network that is associated to a specific classification $\bar{c}$, to a specific segmentation s and to a specific word sequence $\bar{w}$. Let us point out that in the decoding process all the probabilities associated to the M_{sw} model, as well as to lexical models and AMs, are involved. When considering M_{sl} model, a similar process is carried out, but in this case the SFSA associated to each class is a 1-TSS model and the Viterbi algorithm leads to the following $\hat{w}$:

$$\hat{w} \simeq \arg\max_{\forall \bar{w} \in \Sigma_w^*} \left[\max_{\forall \bar{c} \in \Sigma_c^*} \max_{\forall \bar{l} \in \Sigma_l^*} \max_{\bar{n}} P(\bar{x}, \bar{n} | \bar{w}, \bar{c}, \bar{l}) P(\bar{w} | \bar{c}, \bar{l}) P(\bar{l} | \bar{c}) P(\bar{c}) \right] \quad (8)$$

On the other hand, a **decoupled architecture** is considered when the recognition process is carried out by means of a two-pass decoder. First of all, we employ an standard decoder into which a classical word k-TSS LM (M_w) is integrated. However, the decoder's output is not a word sequence ($\hat{w}$), but a word-graph [5]. This word-graph produces a set of hypotheses denoted by $\Gamma_G(\bar{x})$, where $\Gamma_G(\bar{x}) \subset \Sigma_w^*$, being Σ_w the alphabet of words. Once the word-graph has been obtained, we can now extract the $\mathcal{N}$-best list, $\mathcal{L}_\mathcal{N}(\bar{x}) = \{\hat{\bar{w}}_1, \hat{\bar{w}}_2, \ldots, \hat{\bar{w}}_\mathcal{N}\}$, with its corresponding scores $\mathcal{P}_\mathcal{N}(\bar{x}) = \{P(\hat{\bar{w}}_1 | \bar{x}), P(\hat{\bar{w}}_2 | \bar{x}), \ldots, P(\hat{\bar{w}}_\mathcal{N} | \bar{x})\}$ where $\hat{\bar{w}}_i \in \mathcal{L}_\mathcal{N}(\bar{x})$, as shown in eq. (9) and (10).

$$\hat{\bar{w}}_i \simeq \arg\max_{\forall \bar{w} \in \mathcal{L}_{i-1}^c(\bar{x})} P(\bar{x} | \bar{w}) P_{M_w}(\bar{w}) \simeq \arg\max_{\forall \bar{w} \in \mathcal{L}_{i-1}^c(\bar{x})} \left[\max_{\bar{n}} P(\bar{x}, \bar{n} | \bar{w}) P_{M_w}(\bar{w}) \right] \quad (9)$$

$$P(\hat{\bar{w}}_i | \bar{x}) \simeq P(\bar{x} | \hat{\bar{w}}_i) P_{M_w}(\hat{\bar{w}}_i) \simeq \max_{\forall \bar{w} \in \mathcal{L}_{i-1}^c(\bar{x})} \left[\max_{\bar{n}} P(\bar{x}, \bar{n} | \bar{w}) P_{M_w}(\bar{w}) \right] \quad (10)$$

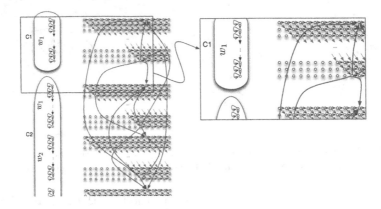

Fig. 3. Dynamic search network for M_{sw} model

being $\mathcal{L}_{i-1}^c(\bar{x}) = \Gamma_G(\bar{x}) - \mathcal{L}_{i-1}(\bar{x})$; that is, the i-th best word sequence would be chosen among those hypotheses that are in $\Gamma_G(\bar{x})$ but without considering the ones that are already in the $(i-1)$-best list $(\mathcal{L}_{i-1}(\bar{x}))$.

Then, the HLM of choice (M_{sw} or M_{sl}) is employed to produce a new score for the obtained hypotheses (see eq. (3)). A linear combination of this score and the one given in eq. (10) yields a final score, which is used to reorder the list again. Thus, we finally obtain a new best hypothesis (the system's output) when the HLM is used, as eq. (11) shows for the M_{sw} model.

$$\hat{\hat{w}} \simeq \underset{\hat{w}_i \in \mathcal{L}_N(\bar{x})}{\arg\max} \left[P(\hat{w}_i|\bar{x}) + \alpha P_{M_{sw}}(\hat{w}_i) \right] \tag{11}$$

However, in the present work the sum over all $\bar{c}$ and s is approaches by the maximum value. Therefore, eq. (11) can be rewritten as eq. (12) and in a similar way, $\hat{\hat{w}}$ would be estimated for M_{sl} as eq. (13) shows:

$$\hat{\hat{w}} \simeq \underset{\hat{w}_i \in \mathcal{L}_N(\bar{x})}{\arg\max} \left[P(\hat{w}_i|\bar{x}) + \alpha \max_{\forall \bar{c} \in \Sigma_c^*} \max_{\forall s \in \mathcal{S}_c(\hat{w}_i)} P(\hat{w}_i|s, \bar{c}) P(s|\bar{c}) P(\bar{c}) \right] \tag{12}$$

$$\hat{\hat{w}} \simeq \underset{\hat{w}_i \in \mathcal{L}_N(\bar{x})}{\arg\max} \left[P(\hat{w}_i|\bar{x}) + \alpha \max_{\forall \bar{c} \in \Sigma_c^*} \max_{\forall \bar{l} \in \Sigma_l^*} P(\hat{w}_i|\bar{l}, \bar{c}) P(\bar{l}|\bar{c}) P(\bar{c}) \right] \tag{13}$$

If we compare eq. (12) and (13) with eq. (7) and (8), respectively, some differences can be observed. Here, the probabilities associated to M_w LM are taken into account in the search network, providing $P(\hat{w}_i|\bar{x})$ values and then, the HLM is considered a posteriori. Although this architecture tries to simulate the integration of the model into the ASR system, the recognition process is not guided by the LM of choice. Turning to eq. (10) and (12), two maximization processes can be clearly differentiated. In the first one (eq. (10)), the recognition process with M_w is carried out and this LM together with lexical and acoustic models contribute to the local decisions until the final result is reached (an $\mathcal{N}$-best list $(\mathcal{L}_N(\bar{x}))$, in this case). Then, in the second maximization process (see eq. (12)) a hypothesis is chosen from among those that are in the list, according to the probability provided by the HLM. In this process the acoustic and lexical models do not take part in the decision-making process in any way. Furthermore, the result obtained with the *decoupled architecture* will always be limited by the best result that an M_w model could provide using a word graph (oracle result), because it is selected from among those that are in $\mathcal{L}_N(\bar{x})$. On the other hand, this kind of integration enables us to use a simple standard decoder, while all the model's complexity is considered a posteriori, what could be very interesting in large-vocabulary ASR. When the *integrated architecture* is employed instead, a single maximization process is carried out, as can be seen in eq. (7), where lexical models and AMs along with the M_{sw} model contribute to the local decision making until the resulting word sequence is obtained. The same happens with the M_{sl} model (see eq.(8)).

In this work, we also propose to use hierarchical models within the **LU module**. When HLMs are integrated into the ASR system by using the *integrated architecture*, the Viterbi algorithm provides an estimation of the most-likely word sequence, as shown in eq. (7) and (8). However, these equations can be rewritten as eq. (14) and (15) respectively. Consequently, the word sequence, class sequence and segmentation associated to the most-likely sequence of states $\bar{n}$ can all be obtained simultaneously from the Viterbi algorithm.

$$\left[\hat{\bar{w}}, \hat{\bar{c}}, \hat{s}\right] \simeq \underset{\forall \bar{w} \in \Sigma_w^*, \forall \bar{c} \in \Sigma_c^*, \forall s \in \mathcal{S}_c(\bar{w})}{\arg \max} \left[\max_{\bar{n}} P(\bar{x}, \bar{n}|\bar{w}, \bar{c}, s)P(\bar{w}|\bar{c}, s)P(s|\bar{c})P(\bar{c})\right] \quad (14)$$

$$\left[\hat{\bar{w}}, \hat{\bar{c}}, \hat{\bar{l}}\right] \simeq \underset{\forall \bar{w} \in \Sigma_w^*, \forall \bar{c} \in \Sigma_c^*, \forall \bar{l} \in \Sigma_l^*}{\arg \max} \left[\max_{\bar{n}} P(\bar{x}, \bar{n}|\bar{w}, \bar{c}, \bar{l})P(\bar{w}|\bar{c}, \bar{l})P(s|\bar{c})P(\bar{c})\right] \quad (15)$$

Thus, if our set of classes is obtained using a semantically motivated criterion, the semantic information associated to the word sequence will be retrieved during the recognition process. Therefore, when using the HLMs and the integrated ASR architecture, the speech recognition and understanding processes could be merged into a single step, thus speeding up the interventions of the dialogue system. Furthermore, the semantic, acoustic and language information contribute to the local decisions-making process throughout the search space until the output word sequence and class sequence are obtained. Thus, more accurate results could be attained regarding both words and classes.

In the same way, when HLMs are employed, the *decoupled architecture* can also be used to obtain the semantic information associated to a word sequence. Once the $\mathcal{N}$-best list $\mathcal{L}_N(\bar{x})$ has been obtained, all the possible s and $\bar{c}$ associated to each hypothesis can be inferred. Using the hierarchical model of choice (M_{sw} or M_{sl}), a probability $P(\hat{\bar{w}}_i)$ is associated to each hypothesis according to eq. (3) and eq. (5) for M_{sw} and M_{sl} models respectively.

Then, a linear combination of this probability and $P(\hat{\bar{w}}_i|\bar{x})$ is computed taking into account that in this work the sum over all different s and $\bar{c}$ is approximated by the maximum. Finally, the class sequence associated to the best new score is provided in the output as eq. (16) and (17) show for the M_{sw} and M_{sl} models respectively.

$$\left[\hat{\bar{w}}, \hat{\bar{c}}, \hat{s}\right] \simeq \underset{\forall \hat{\bar{w}}_i \in \mathcal{L}_N(\bar{x}), \forall \bar{c} \in \Sigma_c^*, \forall s \in \mathcal{S}_c(\hat{\bar{w}}_i)}{\arg \max} \left[P(\hat{\bar{w}}_i|\bar{x}) + \alpha \, P(\hat{\bar{w}}_i|s, \bar{c})P(s|\bar{c})P(\bar{c})\right] \quad (16)$$

$$\left[\hat{w}, \hat{c}, \hat{\bar{l}}\right] \simeq \underset{\forall \hat{w}_i \in \mathcal{L}_N(\bar{x}), \forall \bar{c} \in \Sigma_c^*, \forall \bar{l} \in \Sigma_l^*}{\arg \max} \left[P(\hat{w}_i|\bar{x}) + \alpha\, P(\hat{w}_i|\bar{l}, \bar{c}) P(\bar{l}|\bar{c}) P(\bar{c})\right] \qquad (17)$$

4   Experimental Results

In order to evaluate the approaches presented in this work a speech based conversational interface is considered. It consists of a virtual butler service that would be installed at home to control and provide information about electrical appliances. The system was developed within the framework of the GENIO project [4], which was partially supported by FAGOR. In this context a Spanish corpus (Domolab) was acquired with the specific features described in Table 1.

First of all, M_{sw} and M_{sl} models were evaluated when they were integrated into the ASR system. The two different architectures proposed in this work were considered here for comparison purposes and the results are shown in Table 2. From this table it can be concluded that hierarchical M_{sw} and M_{sl} models attain a better ASR system performance than the classical M_w one, when using either integration method. However, the *decoupled architecture* provides slightly worst WER values than the integrated one for M_{sw}. Note that the lowest WER that can be achieved with the M_w model through the word graph (oracle WER) is higher than the WER obtained with the integrated M_{sw}. Thus, a rescoring procedure cannot outdo this result.

We also evaluated HLMs within a LU task. Note that 40 manually-chosen, task-dependent semantic classes made up of phrases, specifically those employed in the LU module of the dialogue system, were used to build HLMs in both experiments. The evaluation was carried out in terms of the *Category Error Rate* (CER) and it is also presented in Table 2. CER is measured in the same way the WER is, but considering the class sequences provided by the system and the classified reference sentences. Table 2 shows that both architectures provide better CER values than the baseline M_w model. Regarding this M_w model, CER values were obtained by classifying both the reference sentences and the sentences obtained with the ASR system and an M_w model. Consequently, it can be concluded that the extraction of the semantic information can benefit from the use of hierarchical models. Moreover, the percentage improvement associated

Table 1. Features of Domolab corpus

		Domolab
Training	Sentences	44,236
	Diff. sent.	43,962
	Words	349,890
	Vocab.	357
Test	Sentences	1,617
	Words	9,660
	Vocab.	325

Table 2. WER and CER results for M_w, M_{sw} and M_{sl} models using different architectures

		M_w		M_{sw}	M_{sl}
		1-best	oracle		
WER	Int. Arch.	6.04	-	5.14	5.4
(%)	Dec. Arch.	6.04	5.23	5.34	5.35
CER	Int. Arch.	8.68	-	7.18	7.06
(%)	Dec. Arch.	8.68	5.93	7.12	6.98

to the use of HLMs with regard to M_w model, is greater when considering CER values than when considering WER values (e.g. 14.9% vs. 17.28% for M_{sw} model and integrated architecture). Thus, the CER improvement is not only due to a better recognized sentence, but the semantic information involved in the HLMs is helping to provide a better CER result.

Regarding the two different architectures very similar performance values are achieved. However, when using *integrated architecture* all the processes (recognition and LU) can be carried out in only one step. Instead, *decoupled architecture* makes it possible to use HLMs to carry out the LU process over the outputs of different ASR systems.

5 Concluding Remarks

In this work the integration of complex HLMs into ASR systems was explored by making use of two different architectures, an integrated one and a decoupled one. The obtained results show that HLMs provide better ASR performance for both architectures. On the other hand, HLMs can also be used in a LU module. Different experiments were carried out in order to evaluate this task and the results show that this process can benefit from the use of hierarchical models.

References

1. Caseiro, D., Trancoso, I.: A specialized on-the-fly algorithm for lexicon and language model composition. IEEE TASLP 14(4), 1281–1291 (2006)
2. Chung, E., Jeon, H.B., Park, J.G., Lee, Y.K.: Lattice rescoring for speech recognition using large scale distributed language models. In: Proceedings of COLING, pp. 217–224 (2012)
3. Dolfing, H.J.G.A., Hetherington, I.L.: Incremental language models for speech recognition using finite-state transducers. In: Proceedings of IEEE ASRU, pp. 194–197. Madonna di Campiglio, Italy (2001)
4. GENIO: Gestor Embebido Natural de Interfaz Oral. INTEK project. Industry Department. Basque Government (2006)
5. Justo, R., Pérez, A., Torres, M.I.: Impact of the approaches involved on word-graph derivation from the ASR system. In: Vitrià, J., Sanches, J.M., Hernández, M. (eds.) IbPRIA 2011. LNCS, vol. 6669, pp. 668–675. Springer, Heidelberg (2011)
6. Justo, R., Torres, M.I.: Phrase classes in two-level language models for asr. Pattern Analysis & Applications 12(4), 427–437 (2009)
7. Justo, R., Torres, M.I.: Using finite state models for the integration of hierarchical LMS into ASR systems. In: Martínez-Trinidad, J.F., Carrasco-Ochoa, J.A., Ben-Youssef Brants, C., Hancock, E.R. (eds.) MCPR 2011. LNCS, vol. 6718, pp. 332–340. Springer, Heidelberg (2011)
8. Pereira, F., Riley, M.D.: Speech recognition by composition of weighted finite automata. In: Finite-State Language Processing, pp. 431–453. MIT Press (1996)
9. Rastrow, A., Dredze, M., Khudanpur, S.: Fast syntactic analysis for statistical language modeling via substructure sharing and uptraining. In: Proceedings of ACL 2012, Stroudsburg, PA, USA, pp. 175–183 (2012)
10. Siniscalchi, S.M., Svendsen, T., Lee, C.H.: A bottom-up modular search approach to large vocabulary continuous speech recognition. IEEE TASLP 21(4), 786–797 (2013)
11. Torres, M.I., Casacuberta, F.: Stochastic k-tss bi-languages for machine translation. In: Proceedings of FSMNLP, pp. 98–106. ACL (2011)

A Phonetic-Based Approach
to Query-by-Example Spoken Term Detection

Lluís-F. Hurtado, Marcos Calvo, Jon Ander Gómez,
Fernando García, and Emilio Sanchis

Departament de Sistemes Informàtics i Computació
Universitat Politècnica de València
{lhurtado,mcalvo,jon,fgarcia,esanchis}@dsic.upv.es

Abstract. Query-by-Example Spoken Term Detection (QbE-STD) tasks are usually addressed by representing speech signals as a sequence of feature vectors by means of a parametrization step, and then using a pattern matching technique to find the candidate detections. In this paper, we propose a phoneme-based approach in which the acoustic frames are first converted into vectors representing the *a posteriori* probabilities for every phoneme. This strategy is specially useful when the language of the task is a priori known. Then, we show how this representation can be used for QbE-STD using both a Segmental Dynamic Time Warping algorithm and a graph-based method. The proposed approach has been evaluated with a QbE-STD task in Spanish, and the results show that it can be an adequate strategy for tackling this kind of problems.

Keywords: Spoken Term Detection, Query-by-Example, Automatic Speech Recognition.

1   Introduction

In the last few years both the amount and the availability of digital data have rapidly and substantially increased. These facts have led to the need of interacting in a multimodal way with a variety of information repositories in order to find useful information in them, opening this way new and important challenges in the field of Language Technologies. The Spoken Term Detection (STD) task is among these challenges. It consists on finding all the occurrences of a *search term*, which ortographic transcription is provided and can be composed of more than one word, in the contents of an audio repository. However, the input may also be an utterance representing the search term. In this case, the problem is known as Query-by-Example Spoken Term Detection (QbE-STD) and both the input query and the collection of documents are acoustic signals. Both of these tasks have been studied lately [1–4], and some examples of their interest and importance are the evaluation campaigns carried out in this line, such as the one organized by NIST in 2006 [5] and the MediaEval evaluations [6]. In this paper, we will focus on the Query-by-Example Spoken Term Detection task.

Most of the methods that have been proposed for the QbE-STD task are based on classical pattern matching algorithms. Specifically, the search is performed by

J. Ruiz-Shulcloper and G. Sanniti di Baja (Eds.): CIARP 2013, Part I, LNCS 8258, pp. 504–511, 2013.
© Springer-Verlag Berlin Heidelberg 2013

means of an algorithm that matches the feature vectors corresponding to both
the queries and the documents in the audio repository, looking for occurrences
of the queries in the documents. The feature vectors are usually a standard
parametrization of the acoustic signal, for example based on cepstrals. Also, in
the recent literature one of the most usual algorithms to perform this search is
Segmental Dynamic Time Warping (SDTW) [1–4].

In this work, we perform a step after the parametrization, in which the posterior probabilities of the phonemes given the acoustic frames are calculated. This
implies that the set of phonemes that are going to be used must be *a priori*
known, but it is not a problem if the language of the task is fixed. These phonetic probabilities are computed by means of a process of acoustic clustering and
classification in terms of acoustic classes, as explained in Section 2. Then, the
phonetic probabilities worked out in this step will be the base for two QbE-STD
algorithms. First, Section 3 shows a SDTW algorithm that uses the Kullback-
Leibler divergence and a specific set of transitions. Section 4 shows a method to
build graphs of phonemes from the phonetic probabilities and an algorithm to
perform the QbE-STD task. This algorithm is based on searching common paths
in the graphs corresponding to the document and the query, allowing edit operations to gain flexibility. A description of the experiments we have performed
and a discussion of their results is shown in Section 5, and finally in Section 6
some conclusions are drawn.

2   Computation of the *a Posteriori* Probabilities of the Phonemes

After a standard parametrization of the acoustic signal using cepstrals, we will
carry out a procedure to compute the *a posteriori* probability of every phoneme
u in a pre-defined set of phonetic units U given each acoustic frame x_t, it is,
$p(u|x_t)$. For this computation, a set of acoustic classes A is obtained using a
clustering procedure on the acoustic feature vector space using the unsupervised
version of the Maximum Likelihood Estimation (MLE) algorithm. Assuming
that the acoustic classes can be modelled as Gaussian distributions, the output
of this procedure is a Gaussian Mixture Model (GMM). The use of conditional
probabilities allows us to compute the phonetic-conditional probability density
$p(x_t|u)$ as follows [7]:

$$p(x_t|u) = \sum_{a \in A} p(x_t|a) \cdot p(a|u) \tag{1}$$

for each $u \in U$, where $p(x_t|a)$ is the acoustic class-conditional probability pro-
vided by the GMM, and $p(a|u)$ is the conditional probability that acoustic class
a was manifested when phonetic unit u was uttered.

The conditional probabilities $p(a|u)$ for all $a \in A$ and for all $u \in U$ are
computed by a progressive refinement algorithm for phonetic segmentation [8].
It starts from an initial coarse segmentation and continues until no improvements
on the segmentation are found. As a labeled corpus for phonetic segmentation

is needed to perform this process, we have used the training subcorpus of the Spanish Albayzin database [9].

Thus, the *a posteriori* probability of each phonetic unit u given an acoustic vector x_t, $p(u|x_t)$, can be rewritten as

$$\Pr(u|x_t) = \frac{\sum\limits_{a \in A} p(x_t|a) \cdot p(a|u)}{\sum\limits_{v \in U} \left(\sum\limits_{a \in A} p(x_t|a) \cdot p(a|v) \right)} \tag{2}$$

In the next two sections we will show two different ways of using these phonetic probabilities for a QbE-STD task.

3   Segmental Dynamic Time Warping with *a Posteriori* Phonetic Probabilities

Segmental DTW (SDTW) [10] is a modification of the well-known Dynamic Time Warping algorithm. The goal of SDTW is to find multiple local alignments of two input utterances, represented as a sequence of vectors. The main difference between SDTW and DTW is that, while in DTW there is only one start point for the alignment, SDTW allows the alignment to start at any point along the speech document. This is very convenient for the QbE-STD task, as the goal is to find all the occurrences of the query in each of the documents.

In our case, the vectors corresponding to the utterances will contain the *a posteriori* probabilities for each phoneme, given each frame.

Instead of using the DTW typical transitions, we have used (as in other works like [1]) a different set of transitions, as shown in Equation 3. This set of movements ensures that the paths found will represent alignments where the number of frames taken in the document is between half and twice the length of the query. Therefore, the minimization function at each point is given by:

$$D(i,j) = \begin{cases} 0 & j < 1 \\ \min \begin{pmatrix} D(i-1, j-1) \\ D(i-2, j-1) \\ D(i-1, j-2) \end{pmatrix} + KL(A(i), B(j)) & j \geq 1 \end{cases} \tag{3}$$

where $A(i)$ is the vector of *a posteriori* phonetic probabilities for the frame i of the speech document, $B(j)$ represents the *a posteriori* probabilities of phonemes for the frame j of the query, and KL is the Kullback–Leibler divergence [11].

All the paths in the Dynamic Programming matrix that arrive to the end of the query are considered candidate detections. However, many of these detections are false positives. To filter out these detections, Algorithm 1 is performed. This way, our final set of detections has only at most d elements, and all of them are the ones with best scores. It must be noted that the sorting performed in the first line of Algorithm 1 could be either in ascending or descending order, depending on the objective function of the search procedure.

Algorithm 1. Algorithm to filter a list of detections

Require: A list of candidate detections CD,
   a maximum number of filtered detections d
Ensure: A list of filtered detections FD
1: SCD = sort the hypothesis in CD by their score
2: $FD2$ = empty list
3: **while** SCD is not empty **do**
4:   h = first element of SCD
5:   Move h to $FD2$
6:   Delete from SCD all the detections whose timespan overlaps h
7: **end while**
8: Determine a threshold t considering the score of the elements in $FD2$
9: FD = first d elements of $FD2$ whose score fulfills the threshold t
10: **return** FD

Determining the threshold t for this algorithm is a task that can be addressed in a variety of ways. In our case, we have performed a linear combination of some statistics of the scores, like the mean, the median, the maximum and the standard deviation. The weights assigned to each of these statistics provide us a range of thresholds that can be used to tune the performance of the system. Also we have considered as the input list of candidate detections CD all the detections found in all the documents for a specific query. This means that the pruning made by this algorithm is local to the specific query, considering all the documents in the repository as a whole. In consequence, for each query at most d detections among all the documents are considered as confirmed detections.

4 A Graph-Based Algorithm for QbE-STD

Taking advantage of the sequentiallity of speech, our graphs of phonemes have a left-to-right topology. Nodes act like time marks, and every node has a timestamp. The arcs have associated the phonetic unit uttered between the timestamps kept by origin and destination nodes, and also its phonetic probability.

The construction algorithm has two steps: phoneme detection, and error correction. In the first step, each vector of phonetic probabilities is analyzed in order to find if there is any probability above a detection threshold. If the probability of a phoneme is above this threshold, we consider that it has been uttered, but the time in which its pronunciation started and finished is still undetermined. In order to fix the starting and ending time of the detected phoneme, a new threshold (called extension threshold), less restrictive than the detection threshold, is used. That is, starting from the frame, or frames, where a phoneme was detected, an extension process is performed considering the previous and following frames that overpass the extension threshold for that phoneme. This extension process finishes as soon as the extension threshold for the phoneme is not exceeded. The reason for using this lower threshold is that the initial or final parts of phonemes are less clearly pronounced and detected than its central part. Both thresholds are empirically determined.

The error correcting step consists on detecting and correcting both spurious aparitions and misses of phonemes. This is the case of very short phonemes, or some gaps in a zone where a phoneme was detected with enough probability.

Finally, the graph of phonemes is built according to these corrections. A node is created whenever the detection of any phonetic unit begins or ends. Arcs are built in a way that all go from a node to the following one. Thus, each arc may represent either a complete detection of a phoneme, or a part of it. The weight of each arc is the accumulated log-probability of the detection between the instants represented by the starting and ending nodes.

4.1   Search Algorithm

Once the documents and the queries are represented as graphs of phonemes, we can take them in pairs to perform the QbE-STD task. The basis of this algorithm is to find, for each node i in the graph corresponding to the document, the common path in both graphs that goes through all the query, finishes at i in the document, and has the maximum combined score, defined as the sum of the weights of both paths individually. To find these common paths, edit operations on the arcs are allowed, in order to make this search more flexible and to correct possible errors made while building the graph of phonemes. Insertion and deletion operations have a constant penalization, while the cost of a substitution may depend on the pair of phonemes being considered. For this work, we have only allowed coincidences, as well as substitutions of vowels by their semivowels, consonants by their semiconsonants and vice versa.

The algorithm that searches for these common paths follows a Dynamic Programming (DP) strategy. Let M be a matrix of dimensions $I \times J$, where I and J are the number of nodes of the graphs representing the document and the query, respectively. Thus, $M(i, j)$ will contain the best score for arriving to node i in the document and j in the query, using both the arcs in the graphs and the edit operations allowed. Also, given an arc a, let $\mathrm{ori}(a)$ and $\mathrm{dest}(a)$ be functions that return respectively the position in the graph of the starting and ending nodes of a, $\mathrm{W}(a)$ a function that returns the weight of the arc, and $\mathrm{S}(a)$ a function that provides the symbol (phoneme) attached to the arc. Thus, the algorithm can be stated as follows:

$$M(i,j) = \begin{cases} 0 & \text{if } j = 0 \\ \max\left\{arcSub(i,j), arcIns(i,j), arcDel(i,j)\right\} & \text{otherwise} \end{cases} \quad (4)$$

where:

$$arcSub(i,j) = \max_{\substack{\forall \text{ arcs } a,b: \\ \mathrm{dest}(a)=i \,\wedge\, \mathrm{dest}(b)=j}} \left\{M(\mathrm{ori}(a), \mathrm{ori}(b)) + \mathrm{W}(a) + \mathrm{W}(b) + k_{sub}(\mathrm{S}(a), \mathrm{S}(b))\right\}$$

$$arcIns(i,j) = \max_{\forall \text{ arc } a: \, \mathrm{dest}(a)=i} \left\{M(\mathrm{ori}(a), j) + k_{ins}\right\}$$

$$arcDel(i,j) = \max_{\forall \text{ arc } b: \, \mathrm{dest}(b)=j} \left\{M(i, \mathrm{ori}(b)) + k_{del}\right\}$$

$$k_{sub}(x, y) = \begin{cases} 0 & \text{if } x = y \\ 0 & \text{if } x \text{ is semivowel or semiconsonant of } y \text{ or vice versa} \\ -\infty & \text{otherwise} \end{cases}$$

k_{ins} and k_{del} are constants that must be empirically determined.

Once the DP matrix has been filled, all the cells corresponding to the last node of the query represent candidate detections. Thus, they must be filtered in order to reject as many false positives as possible. In this case, Algorithm 1 is also used for finding the confirmed detections.

5   Experiments and Results

To evaluate these approaches, we have performed several experiments using the MAVIR database [12]. This is the Query-by-Example Spoken Term Detection corpus that was used in the Search on Speech track of the 2012 Albayzin Evaluation. A feature of this task is that the language of both the queries and the collection of documents is Spanish, so it is *a priori* known.

In this task we can distinguish two kinds of files. First, there are 10 files corresponding to recordings of conferences and academic acts carried out in Madrid between 2006 and 2008. The speech in these files is spontaneous and was acquired in a variety of conditions using different microphones. Also different accents of the Spanish language are represented. In addition, these files are very long, with a duration between 19 and 75 minutes. These facts make this task very hard. Second, the other kind of files is the set of queries, which is composed of 120 terms. The whole set of files is divided this way: 60 queries and 7 documents for development and 60 queries and 3 documents for test.

As it is usual in Information Retrieval (IR) tasks, we have considered the standard Precision and Recall, and its combination by means of the F1-Measure. Figures 1 and 2 show the evolution of these measures for the development set using a variety of thresholds, considering as the maximum number of confirmed detections for the filtering algorithm the one that provided the best results in our experiments. In the case of the graph-based approach, a large amount of combinations of insertion and deletion constants have been tried, and Figure 2 shows the evolution for the configuration that achieved the best results.

Figure 1 shows that for the development set the SDTW approach reaches a Precision of more than 30%, while the best Recall is around 14%. However, in some IR applications it is more important to find some detections with a relatively large precision, than finding them all. Another interesting fact is that there is a point where, even varying the threshold, the results do not change. This happens when too many candidate detections surpass the threshold of the filtering algorithm, and the pruning is just done by considering the maximum number of hypotheses specified beforehand. The results shown in Figure 2 are not as good as the obtained with the SDTW algorithm. This is due to the fact that the difficulty of the task and the noisy conditions of the audio recordings make the graph builder algorithm generate many errors that can not be recovered when the graphs of phonemes are processed.

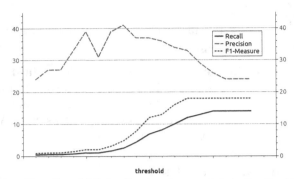

Fig. 1. Precision, Recall and F1 for the development data for the SDTW approach

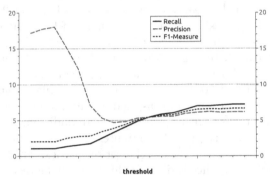

Fig. 2. Precision, Recall and F1 for the development data for the graph-based approach

Table 1 shows the results obtained for the test set using the parameters that optimized the F1-Measure in the development phase.

Table 1. Results obtained for the test set

System	Precision (%)	Recall (%)	F1-Measure (%)
SDTW	31.2	18.3	23.1
Graph-based	9.0	10.2	9.6

In the test set the experiments using Segmental DTW also outperform the experiments with the graphs of phonemes. Thus, the codification of the frames in terms of the posterior probabilities of phonemes seems to be a good representation, and the Segmental DTW algorithm using this representation gives good enough results. However, SDTW has a higher time complexity than the algorithm based on graphs of phonemes, as the number of nodes of the graphs is usually much lower than the number of frames. In consequence, our graph-based approach seems promising, and we will continue working on how to improve it.

6   Conclusions

In this work, we have presented two algorithms for Query-by-Example Spoken Term Detection based on the computation of *a posteriori* phonetic probabilities of the phonemes given the speech signals. One of these algorithms performs a Segmental DTW search, while the other represents the query and the document as graphs of phonemes and searches for common paths in both graphs using edit operations. The experimental results show that our codification of the frames in terms of *a posteriori* probabilities of the phonemes and the proposed algorithms are a good approach to QbE-STD. As future work, we want to improve the performance of the graph-based method presented in this paper, for example trying to make the phoneme detection process more robust.

Acknowledgements. Work partially supported by the Spanish Ministerio de Economía y Competitividad under contract TIN2011-28169-C05-01 and FPU Grant AP2010-4193, and by the Vic. d'Investigació of the UPV (PAID-06-10).

References

1. Anguera, X., Macrae, R., Oliver, N.: Partial sequence matching using an unbounded dynamic time warping algorithm. In: ICASSP, pp. 3582–3585 (2010)
2. Hazen, T., Shen, W., White, C.: Query-by-example spoken term detection using phonetic posteriorgram templates. In: ASRU, pp. 421–426 (2009)
3. Zhang, Y., Glass, J.: Unsupervised spoken keyword spotting via segmental DTW on gaussian posteriorgrams. In: ASRU, pp. 398–403 (2009)
4. Akbacak, M., Vergyri, D., Stolcke, A.: Open-vocabulary spoken term detection using graphone-based hybrid recognition systems. In: ICASSP, pp. 5240–5243 (2008)
5. Fiscus, J.G., Ajot, J., Garofolo, J.S., Doddingtion, G.: Results of the 2006 spoken term detection evaluation. In: Proceedings of ACM SIGIR Workshop on Searching Spontaneous Conversational, pp. 51–55 (2007)
6. Metze, F., Barnard, E., Davel, M., Van Heerden, C., Anguera, X., Gravier, G., Rajput, N., et al.: The spoken web search task. In: Working Notes Proceedings of the MediaEval 2012 Workshop (2012)
7. Gómez, J.A., Castro, M.J.: Automatic segmentation of speech at the phonetic level. In: Caelli, T.M., Amin, A., Duin, R.P.W., Kamel, M.S., de Ridder, D. (eds.) SSPR & SPR 2002. LNCS, vol. 2396, pp. 672–680. Springer, Heidelberg (2002)
8. Gómez, J.A., Sanchis, E., Castro-Bleda, M.J.: Automatic speech segmentation based on acoustical clustering. In: Hancock, E.R., Wilson, R.C., Windeatt, T., Ulusoy, I., Escolano, F. (eds.) SSPR & SPR 2010. LNCS, vol. 6218, pp. 540–548. Springer, Heidelberg (2010)
9. Moreno, A., Poch, D., Bonafonte, A., Lleida, E., Llisterri, J., Marino, J., Nadeu, C.: Albayzin speech database: Design of the phonetic corpus. In: Third European Conference on Speech Communication and Technology (1993)
10. Park, A., Glass, J.: Towards unsupervised pattern discovery in speech. In: ASRU, pp. 53–58 (2005)
11. Kullback, S.: Information theory and statistics. Courier Dover Publications (1997)
12. MAVIR corpus, http://www.lllf.uam.es/ESP/CorpusMavir.html

Method to Correct Artifacts
in Multilead ECG Using Signal Entropy

Beatriz Rodríguez-Alvarez[1], José R. Ledea-Vargas[1], Fernando E. Valdés-Pérez[1],
Renato Peña-Cabrera[2], and José-R. Malleuve-Palancar[3]

[1] Center for Neurosciences Studies, Images and Signals Processing (CENPIS),
Universidad de Oriente, Cuba
{ledeav,bra,fvaldes}@fie.uo.edu.cu
[2] Biomedical Engineering Department, Universidad de Oriente, Cuba
renato.pena@bio.fie.uo.edu
[3] Cardiological Service, S. Lora Hospital, Santiago de Cuba, Cuba
malleuve@medired.scu.sld.cu

Abstract. Artifacts should be corrected previous heart rate variability analysis.
A new method for artifact correction in multilead ECG is proposed in this
paper. The method detects artifacts in the RR series, takes the corresponding
segment of the multilead ECG, uses entropy of the signal for selecting the
"cleanest" ECG channel, and uses the wavelet transform to recalculate positions
of R peaks. The method was evaluated with ECG records of arrhythmia database MIT/BIH, with good results.

Keywords: ECG, artifact correction, entropy, wavelet, multilead ECG.

1   Introduction

The study of the electrocardiogram (ECG) provides great clinical information, not
only for heart disease but others as neuropathy [1], ischemia [2], etc. Each beat is
characterized by the points P, Q, R, S and T, providing information for diagnosis and
prognosis. A topic widely studied is the heart rate variability (HRV) that provides
information about the functioning of the heart and its interaction with the nervous
system, in terms of the balance between sympathetic and vagal systems. HRV is
described by statistical and spectral indexes calculated from time series obtained from
the differences between R peaks (RR series) [3].

The study of HRV in long-term records of ECG obtained by ambulatory
monitoring (usually 24 hours) is most reliable because the patient performs normal
activities. This procedure allows studying the true behavior of the heart in certain
situations. However, artifacts and interference contaminate the information in the
HRV signal, so that many of the monitored patients can be wrongly classified as
healthy subjects [1, 3]. Modern devices allow recording multiple channels, but
sometimes one of them may fail or contain artifacts that are not present in the other.
Therefore researchers have implemented several methods and techniques in order to

J. Ruiz-Shulcloper and G. Sanniti di Baja (Eds.): CIARP 2013, Part I, LNCS 8258, pp. 512–518, 2013.
© Springer-Verlag Berlin Heidelberg 2013

separate or extract useful information from the ECG signals, including the QRS complex detection, artifacts detection and correction, index calculations, etc.

The wavelet transform and entropy analysis have already been successfully used individually or combined in various areas of electrocardiology. In [4] a wavelet entropy (WS) based method is employed to detect QRS complexes in ECG signal from two significant channels. In addition, a method to detect multichannel ECG signals by using combined entropy is proposed in [5].

Methods proposed in [4] and [5] are very effective to detect QRS complexes in presence of artifacts such as baseline drift, and others. These artifacts are not present all the time in the signal, however the calculation based on wavelet and entropy is done for the whole signal. That means a high computing cost. The use of a lower cost computational method for detection of QRS complexes, only using the method based on wavelet and entropy in signal sections with artifacts seems to be a better option.

In this paper we propose a new method for correction of artifacts by combining the entropy for channel selection and the subsequent detection of R peaks with wavelet transform.

2   Entropy and Wavelets

2.1   Entropy

The basic concept of entropy has much to do with the uncertainty that exists in any experiment or random signal. It is also the amount of "noise" or "clutter" that contains or releases a system. Thus, one can speak about the amount of information carried by a signal.

ECG has varying amplitudes, both over time and between patients, or even with the measurement conditions; therefore it is desirable to provide methods for parameters analysis independent of signal amplitude. Entropy measures, which reflect the "order" of the signal, have this feature. The ECG signal has certain monotony from the viewpoint entropy. This can be seen as the appearance of regular and recurring waves (each heartbeat) with variations in the morphology and amplitude. Entropy measures, which quantify this order, look appropriate to detect events associated with muscle movements, noise, interference or artifacts in general [6].

To calculate the entropy is convenient to think about the histogram of the signal. This is done by making discrete the value range of the signal at L intervals. For each interval i there will be a probability of occurrence p_i given by:

$$p_i = \frac{F_i}{\sum_{i=1}^{L} F_i} \tag{1}$$

Where F_i is the amount of signal values that are in the interval i. Shannon entropy E of the signal x is defined by:

$$E(x) = -\sum_{i=1}^{L} p_i \log_2 p_i \tag{2}$$

2.2   Wavelets

A wavelet expansion consists of translations and dilations of one fixed function, the wavelet $\psi \in L^2(R)$, where R denotes the set of real numbers, and $L^2(R)$ denotes the set of measurable, square integrable one-dimensional functions [7]. In the continuous wavelet transform (CWT), the translation and dilation parameters can vary conti-nuously. This means that we use the functions:

$$\psi_{a,b}(t) = \frac{1}{\sqrt{|a|}} \psi(\frac{t-b}{a}) \quad \text{with a,b} \in R \ \ a \neq 0 \tag{3}$$

Where the parameter a is the scale and b is the position parameter. The factor $|a|^{-1/2}$ has been introduced to guarantee energy preservation [8]. Given a continuous signal $f(t) \in L^2(R)$, the CWT of $f(t)$ is:

$$W(a,b) = \int_{-\infty}^{\infty} f(t) \psi^*_{a,b}(t) dt \tag{4}$$

Where $\psi^*_{a,b}(t)$ is the complex conjugate of $\psi_{a,b}(t)$. ECG signals are highly non sta-tioneries, so the CWT is able to locate events in time and frequency. This analysis includes a windows technique with log time intervals for low frequency information, and short time intervals for high frequency information.

3   Artifact Correction Algorithm

The presented algorithm uses ECG signals in n channels, using the redundancy of information being given. The first step is to create the series of positions of the QRS complexes (R series) in any one of ECG channels. These QRS complexes are detected using a method based on the threshold of the derivative [9]. From R series, RR series are constructed in 300 beats segments, as recommended in [3] for short time RR series. The mean RR value of the series is calculated for each segment. The mean value is an artifact robust parameter of the series. Those points of the RR series that deviate more than 20% from the mean RR value are considered artifacts. This threshold has been evaluated empirically by the authors with good results. For each artifact, it is located in the ECG the heartbeat which originates the artifact, and sets the interval to be analyzed. To do this, choose a multi-channel ECG segment between the four seconds before the beat for the artifact detected and four seconds later. In the selected ECG interval the channel of smaller entropy is chosen, calculated according to (2) in the whole 8-second window. The R peaks are detected in this channel using the method based on the wavelet transform, reported in [10, 11], with the Gaussian Wavelet Daubechies function of fourth order and decomposition in 8 levels. The db4 contains good resemblance with the basic QRS shape of the ECG signal. This prominent feature of db4 insisted us to use it as the mother wavelet. The use of 8th level Daubechies wavelets neutralizes the baseline drift.

Then R series is updated with these new values, the RR series is recalculated and the process is repeated until no artifact is present or if the number of iterations is greater than 20-25. This maximal number of iterations is a reasonable limit to the number of artifacts in a short time RR series. Figure 1 shows the steps of the algorithm.

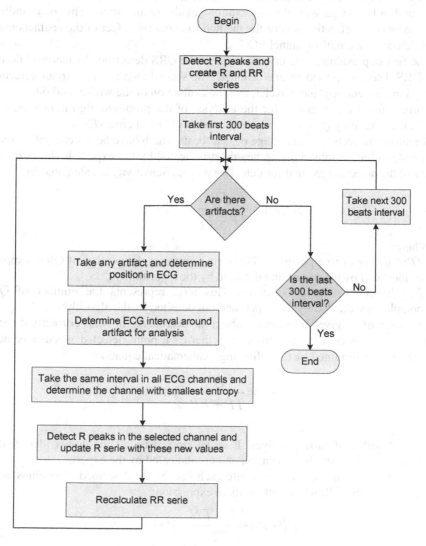

Fig. 1. Algorithm proposed for artifact correction

4   Results and Discussion

The effectiveness of the proposed method was tested using ECG signals of arrhythmia database MIT/BIH. These ECG signals are 30 minutes registers in a range of 0-10 mV, sampled at 360 Hz. The resolution of each sample is 11 bits. The 48 records of this database have a variety of ECG morphologies, including heart disease, which makes them optimal for a qualitative and quantitative assessment of the algorithms described.

109270 beats (almost all of the base) were used, and the effectiveness of the proposed method to detect QRS complexes was proved. The results of this method were compared in two steps with the observations made by an expert. This is an indirect assessment of the effectiveness of the method to avoid the effect of the artifacts in the QRS detection in a multi-channel ECG.

The first step evaluates the effectiveness of the QRS detections by using 1st derivative QRS detector applied in one channel. The second step makes artifact detection, correction with entropy and wavelet, and the evaluation of the whole method.

Three reference parameters for the analysis of the proposed algorithm were estimated: the sensitivity (Se), positive predictability (P^+) and error (E).

Sensitivity reflects the percentage of heartbeats which have been detected correctly by the algorithm on total existing heartbeat indicated by the expert. It shows the capacity of the detection method for detecting a peak. Sensitivity is calculated by:

$$Se(\%) = \frac{TP}{TP + FN} * 100 \tag{5}$$

Where:

TP: Number of true positives. This term represents the number of QRS complexes indicated by the expert and detected by the algorithm.

FN: Number of false negatives. This term represents the number of QRS complexes indicated by the expert and not detected by the algorithm.

The value of P^+ gives information about the percentage of beats correctly detected on total beats detected, ie, the probability that each point detected whether or not a peak R and is determined by the following mathematical equation:

$$P^+(\%) = \frac{TP}{TP + FP} * 100 \tag{6}$$

Where:

FP: Number of false positives. It is determined by all the points identified as QRS complexes by the algorithm, and not indicated by the expert.

Another important aspect to evaluate each one of the described algorithms is the error, given by the following mathematical expression:

$$E(\%) = \frac{FP + FN}{TL} * 100 \tag{6}$$

Where TL is the total number of analyzed beats ($TP + FP$).

Tables 1 and 2 show the results of applying the steps of the method to the MIT-BIH database. Table 1 indicates large number of FN and FP when the 1st derivative QRS detector is applied. Table 2 shows how the number of FN and FP strongly decrease when the artifacts are detected and corrected by the entropy and wavelet method.

Table 1. The results of the first step

TL	TP	FN	FP	*Se* (%)	P^+ (%)	E (%)
109270	101458	7812	1723	92.85	98.33	8.73

Table 2. The results of the proposed algorithm

TL	TP	FN	FP	*Se* (%)	P^+ (%)	E (%)
109270	108717	553	120	99.49	99.89	0.67

Table 2 illustrates that the proposed method achieves an average sensitivity of 99.49%, the positive prediction of 99.89% and the failed detection of 0.67%. These results show high values of sensibility and positive prediction, besides a very low error rate. Then it is possible to conclude that the proposed method can be applied with good results in the detection of QRS complexes in multilead ECG with artifacts. This result may be useful in studies of HRV, and in other applications that require high precision and dependability of the results. The method shows difficulties when artifacts appear in all the channels at the same time. This is not very frequent unless it is an artifact of physiologic origin.

5   Conclusions

The method developed shows very good indicators in detecting QRS complexes in multilead ECG with artifacts, based on the use of the entropy for the selection of the channel, together with the detection of devices using the transformed of wavelet.

References

1. García González, M.A.: Estudio de la variabilidad del ritmo cardíaco mediante técnicas estadísticas, espectrales y no lineales. Tesis doctoral para la obtención del título de doctor. Departamento de Ingeniería Electrónica. Universidad Politécnica de Cataluña (1998)
2. Lemire, D., Pharand, C., Rajaonah, J.-C., Dubé, B., LeBlanc, A.-R.: Wavelet Time Entropy, T wave morphology and myocardial ischemia. IEEE Transactions in Biomedical Engineering 47(7), 967–970 (2000)

3. Malik, M., et al.: Heart rate variability. Standards of measurement, physiological interpretation, and clinical use. Task Force of The European Society of Cardiology and The North American Society of Pacing and Electrophysiology. European Heart. Journal 17, 354–381 (1996)

4. Boqiang, H, Yuanyuan, W: Detecting QRS Complexes of Two-channel ECG Signals by Using Combined Wavelet Entropy. In: IEEE 3rd International Conference on Bioinformatics and Biomedical Engineering, ICBBE 2009, June 11-13, pp. 1-4 (2009) E-ISBN: 978-1-4244-2902-8a

5. Mehta, S.S., Lingayat, N.S.: Combined entropy based method for detection of QRS complexes in 12-lead electrocardiogram using SVM. Computers in Biology and Medicine 38, 138–145 (2008)

6. Bermúdez, A.N., Spinelli, E.M., Muravchik, C.M.: Detección de eventos en señales de EEG mediante Entropía Espectral. XVIII Congreso Argentino de Bioingeniería SABI 2011 - VII Jornadas de Ingeniería Clínica, Mar del Plata, 28 al 30 de Septiembre (2011)

7. Chui, C.K.: Wavelets: a tutorial in theory and applications. Academic Press (1992)

8. Mallat, S.: A theory for multiresolution signal decomposition: the wavelet representation. IEEE Pattern Anal. and Machine Intell. 11(7), 674–693 (1989)

9. Köhler, B., Hennig, C., Orglmeister, R.: The Principles of Software QRS Detection. IEEE Engineering in Medicine and Biology, 42–57 (February 2002)

10. Mahmoodabadi, S.Z., Ahmadian, A., Abolhasani, M.D.: ECG feature extraction using daubechies wavelets. In: Proceedings of the Fifth IASTED International Conference Visualization, Imaging and Image Processing, Benidorm, Spain, September 7-9, pp. 343–348 (2005)

11. Vera, O.E., Duque-Cardona, E., Rivera-Piedrahita, J.: Extracción de características de la señal electrocardiográfica mediante software de análisis matemático. Scientia Et Technica, Universidad Tecnológica de Pereira, Colombia, vol. XII(31), pp. 59–64 (Agosto 2006)

Improvements to the HNR Estimation
Based-on Generalized Variogram

Diana Torres-Boza* and Carlos A. Ferrer

Center for Studies on Electronic and Information Technologies, Central University
Marta Abreu of Las Villas, Carretera de Camajuaí Km 5 ½ Santa Clara Villa Clara, Cuba
{dtb,cferrer}@uclv.edu.cu

Abstract. The presence of an unusual high level of turbulent noise in voice signals is related to air leakage in the glottis as a result of incomplete closure of the vocal cords. Harmonics to Noise Ratio (HNR) is an acoustic measure that intends to appraise the amount of that turbulent noise. Several algorithms have been proposed in both time and frequency domain to estimate HNR. The Generalized Variogram (GV) is a time-domain technique proposed for HNR estimation based on a similitude function between two speech windows. The drawbacks of the GV are related to the biased estimation of the amplitude ratio and the final HNR value. The present work deals with these limitations and proposes unbiased estimators. The experimental results show that the described improvements outperform the original GV.

Keywords: harmonics to noise ratio, additive noise, shimmer, variogram.

1   Introduction

Acoustic measures are a widely used tool to help speech pathologists diagnosing and documenting treatment and therapy progress of laryngeal diseases. Several acoustic measures related to vocal cords diseases have been reported through the years.

Healthy vocal cords produce a quasi-periodic vibration pattern but in dysphonic voices a deviation from this cycle-to-cycle periodicity appears [1]. Pitch perturbation (vocal jitter) is defined as the cycle-to-cycle fundamental frequency variations, amplitude perturbation (vocal shimmer) is defined as the cycle-to cycle amplitude variations, and the additive noise is related to the turbulent noise produced at the glottis and is correlated with the degree of dysphonia [2][4]. This paper is specifically aimed for the improvement of an acoustic measure of additive noise.

Harmonics to Noise Ratio (HNR) is an acoustic measure of the amount of additive noise that appears during the vibration of the glottis [1]. This noise is produced by an air leakage through the vocal cords caused by the presence of pathologies such as nodules, polyps and cancer, among others [1]. HNR estimation can be achieved in

---

* Corresponding author.

J. Ruiz-Shulcloper and G. Sanniti di Baja (Eds.): CIARP 2013, Part I, LNCS 8258, pp. 519–526, 2013.
© Springer-Verlag Berlin Heidelberg 2013

both time and frequency domains. Frequency domain algorithms require the estimation of the harmonic structure, usually by means of Fourier Transform, and it has been criticized for the impossibility to separate measurements of different types of perturbations [5]. Time domain methods have been criticized [3][6][7][8][9] for depending on the correct determination of individual pulse boundaries, among many other method-specific factors. In spite of the latter criticism, this work is specifically centered in time domain HNR estimation, due to the advantage over frequency domain based methods to separate different perturbations.

Reference [9] proposes an HRN estimation technique, based on generalized variogram (GV), that takes into account the non-stationary nature of voice signals and the limitations of boundaries estimation while facing pathological voices. One of the advantages of this method is its ability to estimate the HNR values independently from the temporal or spectral structures of voice signals. The principal limitations are the biased estimation of the gain factor and the influence of the noise component in the harmonic part in the HNR estimator. Based on this, the main goal of this work is to correct these limitations and to evaluate its performance compare not only to the original estimator but to other well-known algorithm proposed in the literature [11].

1.1 HNR Based on Generalized Variogram

For stationary time series the variogram is directly related to the auto covariance function [10]. In [9] the GV is proposed taking into account the properties of the speech signal.

Let $x(n)$ denote a pseudo-periodic signal for some T_0:

$$x(n) = a_k x(n - kT_0), \quad k = 0, 1, 2, \ldots \tag{1}$$

Where a_k is the weighting coefficient and it is related with amplitude changes in the speech signal, T_0 is the length of the glottal cycle and represents the fundamental period.

The formulation of HNR for a voice segment $x(n)$ in dB is given by the expression:

$$HNR_x(dB) = 10 \log \left[\frac{\sum_{n=0}^{N-1} \tilde{x}(n)^2}{\sum_{n=0}^{N-1} e(n)^2} \right] \tag{2}$$

Where the numerator represents the energy of the harmonic component and the denominator is related with the energy of the additive noise component in $x(n)$.

To estimate the energy of the amount of noise (denominator in (2)) the following expression was proposed in [9]:

$$Den = \min_T \left[\sum_{n=1}^{N-1} (x(n) - ax(n-T))^2 \right], \quad -T_{max} < T < -T_{min} \text{ and } T_{min} < T < T_{max} \tag{3}$$

The expression for GV is within the brackets in (3). N is the frame length in samples (chosen as 2.5 ms) and T is related to the glottal pulse length. Since GV is computed in forward and backward directions, T lies within the intervals shown in (3). T_{min} and T_{max} represent the shortest and longest suitable glottal cycle length in samples respectively. These values were fitted to 2.5 ms and 20 ms [2].

The maximum similarity between $x(n)$ and the lagged frame $x(n-T)$ is achieved when expression (3) reaches the minimum value.

The expression for a is defined as:

$$a = \sqrt{\frac{E_{x(n)}}{E_{x(n-T)}}} \tag{4}$$

Where $E_{x(n)}$ and $E_{x(n-T)}$ are the energies at the current and lagged frames respectively.

Having the value of T (T_{opt}) which minimizes the sum of squared errors (3) and the value of a, the noise component in the denominator of HNR_x expression is:

$$e(n) = x(n) - ax(n-T_{opt}), \quad 0 \le n \le N-1 \tag{5}$$

Therefore the expression for the clean signal can be defined as:

$$\tilde{x}(n) = x(n) - e(n) \tag{6}$$

An analysis of the limitations of equations (1), (4), (5) and (6) follows.
The model in (1) does not hold for stationary noise since (1) means that:

$$\tilde{x}(n) + e_k(n) = a_k\left(\tilde{x}(n-kT_0) + e_k(n-kT_0)\right), \quad k = 1, 2, 3, 4, \dots$$
$$= a_k\,\tilde{x}(n-kT_0) + a_k e_k(n-kT_0) \tag{7}$$

Where a proportional term a_k between lagged noise samples $e_k(n-kT_0)$ appear. A more realistic model for the speech signal is given in [12], using the harmonic and noise component terms, as:

$$x(n) = \tilde{x}(n) + e_k(n),$$
$$\tilde{x}(n) = a\,\tilde{x}(n-kT_0), \quad k = 1, 2, 3, 4, \dots \tag{8}$$

From (8) it is possible to obtain an expression for the harmonic component of the shifted frame $\tilde{x}(n-T)$ as:

$$\tilde{x}(n-T) = \frac{\tilde{x}(n)}{a} \tag{9}$$

Substituting (8) and (9) in (4) the following expression is obtained:

$$a^2 = \frac{\sum (\tilde{x}(n) + e_1(n))^2}{\sum (\frac{x(n)}{a} + e_2(n))^2} = \frac{\sum (\tilde{x}(n)^2 + e_1(n)^2)}{\sum (\frac{\tilde{x}(n)^2}{a^2} + e_2(n)^2)} = a^2 \left[\frac{\sum (\tilde{x}(n)^2 + e_1(n)^2)}{\sum (\tilde{x}(n)^2 + a^2 e_2(n)^2)} \right] \tag{10}$$

As can be observed from (10) the original expression to estimate the gain factor a is biased by the factor within the brackets.

Analyzing the numerator of (2) it is possible to substitute it by (5) and (6) as:

$$Num = \sum_{n=1}^{N} \tilde{x}(n)^2 = \sum_{n=1}^{N} (a\, x(n-T))^2 = \sum_{n=1}^{N} (\tilde{x}(n)^2 + a^2 e(n)^2) \tag{11}$$

As can be seen in (11) the numerator of the HNR expression overestimate the real value of HNR as it has a noise term within the numerator. Therefore the original overestimated HNR expression without the log operation can be expressed as:

$$HNR_x = \frac{\sum_{n=0}^{N-1} (\tilde{x}(n)^2 + a^2 e(n)^2)}{\sum_{n=0}^{N-1} e(n)^2} \tag{12}$$

2   Proposed Modifications

The derivation of factor a is a minimization problem. The a value is optimum when the GV expression (3) reaches its minimum value, so the similarity between the two current periods is maximum.

Substituting (8) in the term within the brackets in (3), it is possible to obtain the following expression for the GV:

$$GV = \sum_{n=1}^{N-1} (x(n) - ax(n-T))^2 = \sum_{n=1}^{N-1} (e_1^2(n) + a^2 e_2^2(n)) = (1+a^2)\sum_{n=1}^{N-1} e^2(n) \tag{13}$$

To obtain a, the derivative of (13) respect to a is taken and equated to 0.

$$\frac{dGV}{da} = \left[\frac{GV}{(1+a^2)} \right]' = \left[\frac{\sum_{n=1}^{N-1} (x(n) - ax(n-T))^2}{1+a^2} \right]' = 0 \tag{14}$$

Developing expression (14) the optimal gain factor a is obtained as:

$$a = R + \sqrt{1 + R^2}, \quad \text{where } R = \frac{x^2(n) + x^2(n-T)}{2x(n)x(n-T)} \tag{15}$$

This obtained value of a is similar the one in [12]. Therefore from (13) the corrected noisy component in (2) is obtained as:

$$e_c^2(n) = \min(Den) = \left(\frac{x(n) - ax(n - T_{opt})}{1 + a^2}\right)^2, \quad 0 \le n \le N - 1 \tag{16}$$

Where the gain factor a can be estimated according to (14).

Having expressions to estimate both the gain factor a and the energy of the noise component $e(n)$ by a corrected variogram, an enhanced expression for HNR can be obtained.

Developing equation (12) we can obtain the following expression to estimate HNR as:

$$10\log(HNR_x - a^2) = 10\log\left[\frac{\sum_{n=0}^{N-1} \tilde{x}(n)^2}{\sum_{n=0}^{N-1} e(n)^2}\right] \tag{17}$$

It will be demonstrated that this expression solves the overestimation of the actual values of HNR.

2.1   Experiments

Synthetic signals were generated according to the procedure in [13] and [14] where an all-pole filter with formant frequencies corresponding to a vowel "a" is excited by a train of impulses. As the proposed corrections are related to the amplitude factor a, seven levels of both Gaussian noise and shimmer were introduced to meet a desired signal to noise ratio (SNR) and shimmer in the simulated signals. The added values of shimmer and noise used are shown in Table 1.

Table 1. Levels of actual HNR and Shimmer used for the experiments

Level	1	2	3	4	5	6	7
HNR (dB)	22	18	15	12	8	5	2
Shimm (%)	47.6	40.8	34	27.2	20.4	13.6	6.8

The length of the synthesized signals is 2 s, with sampling frequency Fs = 22050 Hz and mean F_0 = 150 Hz, giving an average of 300 pulses per signal.

The proposed HNR estimation corrections (GVC) were evaluated by comparing them with the original method (GV) proposed in [8] and with a well-known HNR algorithm based on cesptrum estimation (denoted as "Murp") proposed in [11]. Estimated HNR values were also compared with reference values (denoted as "Ref") listed in Table 1 which were added during synthesis of simulation signals.

3   Results

Figure 1 shows estimated HNR values for the synthetic vowel contaminated with only amplitude perturbations (shimmer). The x-axis represents the different levels of synthetized shimmer where 6.8 % denotes the lowest level of perturbation and 47.6% the highest level of contamination. The y-axis represents the estimated values of HNR. In the case of signals synthesized only with shimmer, 30dB of HNR was added to avoid infinite HNR values. The reference values of HNR can be observed in Fig. 1 as an x-dashed line, and the rest of the estimates analyzed as solid lines.

Fig.1 demonstrates the superiority of the GVC over the original GV and the cepstrum-based variants. A biased estimation of the gain factor produces an overestimation of the HNR values facing the shimmered signals. In addition, the inferior performance of GV respect to GVC is related to the introduction of the error term in the HNR equation (2). Cepstrum based algorithm shows the worst performance of the three analyzed estimators. As the shimmer cannot be separated from the additive noise in the frequency domain this estimator doesn't produces values related to additive noise alone but to dysperiodicity in a general sense.

The performance of the algorithms using synthesized signals with only additive noise is shown in Fig.2. Unlike the previous figure, the x-axis corresponds to the HNR (in dB) actual values and are ordered from the noisiest signals (2 dB) to the cleanest one (22dB). It can be observed from the figure that GVC and "Murp" approaches follow more precisely the dashed line which represents reference values of HNR. Therefore there is superiority in the performance of GVC and "Murp" over the original variogram. The GVC approach removes the influence of the noise term in the HNR formula (2).

Results for signals contaminated with both shimmer and additive noise are shown in Fig.3. It can be seen that also the GVC superiority respect to both "Murp" and original variogram methods.

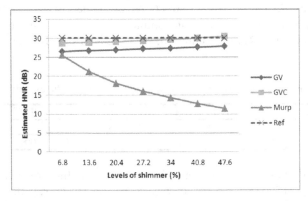

Fig. 1. Results for estimated HNR values for signals contaminated with only shimmer. The dashed line represents the reference values of HNR (30 dB) for each level of shimmer.

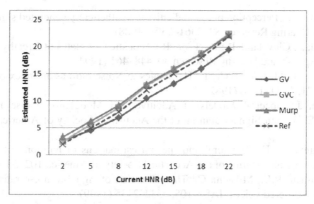

Fig. 2. Results for signals contaminated with only additive noise. The dashed line represents the reference values of HNR for each synthesized level.

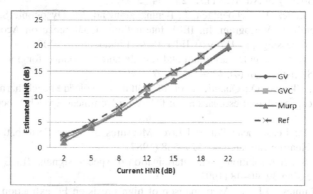

Fig. 3. Results for signals contaminated with both shimmer and additive noise. The dashed line represents the reference values of HNR for each level of perturbations.

4   Conclusions

This work is focused on improving the estimation of the Harmonics to Noise Ratio based on the generalized variogram. The experiments results have demonstrated that the original algorithm proposed in [9] overestimates real values of HNR and the gain factor estimator is biased. As expected the best results corresponds to the proposed method, which removes the influence of the noise from the harmonic part of the HNR estimation formula.

References

1. Hillenbrand, J.A.: Methothological Study of Perturbations and Additive Noise in Synthetically Generated Voice Signals. Journal of Speech and Hearing Research 30, 448–461 (1987)

2. Hillenbrand, J.A.: Perception of aperiodicities in synthetically generated signals. Journal of Speech and Hearing Research 83, 2361–2371 (1988)
3. Hillenbrand, J., Cleveland, R., Erickson, R.: Acoustic Correlates of Breathy Vocal Quality. Journal of Speech and Hearing Research 30, 448–461 (1994)
4. Yumoto, E., Gould, J.W., Baer, T.: Harmonics to Noise ratio as an index of the degree of hoarseness 71, 1544–1550 (1982)
5. Schoengten, J.: Spectral Models of Additive and Modulation Noise in Speech and Phonatory Excitation Signals. Journal of the Acoustical Society of America 113, 553–562 (2003)
6. Qi, Y., Hillman, R.E.: Temporal and spectral estimations of harmonics-to-noise ratio in human voice signals. Journal of the Acoustical Society of America 102, 537–543 (1997)
7. Qi, Y., Hillman, R.E., Milstein, C.: The estimation of signal-to-noise ratio in continuous speech for disordered voices. JASA 105, 2532–2535 (1999)
8. Bettens, F., Grenez, F., Schoengten, J.: Estimation of vocal dysperiodicities in disordered speech by means of distant-sample bidirectional linear predictive analysis. Journal of the Acoustical Society of America 117, 328–334 (2005)
9. Kacha, A., Grenez, F., Schoentgen, J., Benmahammend, K.: Dysphonic Speech Analysis Using Generalized Variogram. In: IEEE International Conference on Acoustics, Speech, and Signal Processing, pp. 917–920. IEEE Press, Philadelphia (2005)
10. Haslett, J.: On the sample variogram and sample autocovariance for non-stationary time series. The Statistician 46(4), 475–485 (1997)
11. Murphy, P., Akande, O.: Quantification of glottal and voiced speech harmonics to noise ratio using cepstral-based estimation. In: ITRW on Nonlinear Speech Processing, pp. 19–22 (2005)
12. Mienkovic, P.: Least mean Squared Error Measures of Voice Perturbations. Journal of Speech and Hearing Research 30, 529–538 (1987)
13. Medan, Y.: Super resolution pitch determination of speech signals. IEEE Transaction on Signal Processing 39, 40–48 (1991)
14. Parsa, V., Jamieson, D.G.: A comparison of high precision F0 extraction algorithms for sustained vowels. Journal of Speech, Language and Hearing Research 42, 112–126 (1999)

Using Three Reassigned Spectrogram Patches and Log-Gabor Filter for Audio Surveillance Application

Sameh Souli[1], Zied Lachiri[2], and Alexander Kuznietsov[3]

[1] École Nationale des Ingénieurs de Tunis
Unité de Recherche Signal, Image et Reconnaissance de Formes
BP. 37 Le Belvédère, 1002 Tunis, Tunisie
soulisameh@yahoo.fr
[2] Institut National des Sciences Appliquées et de Technologie
Département Instrumentation et Mesures
INSAT BP. 676 Centre urbain cedex, Tunis, Tunisie
ziedlachiri@enit.rnu.tn
[3] University of applied Sciences Mittelhessen, Wilhelm-Leuschner-Straße, 13
61169 Friedberg, Germany
alexanderkuznietsov@iem.thm.de

Abstract. In this paper, we propose a robust environmental sound spectrogram classification approach; its purpose is surveillance and security applications based on the reassignment method and log-Gabor filters. Besides, the reassignment method is applied to the spectrogram to improve the readability of the time-frequency representation, and to assure a better localization of the signal components. In this approach the reassigned spectrogram is passed through a bank of 12 log-Gabor filter concatenation applied to three spectrogram patches, and the outputs are averaged and underwent an optimal feature selection procedure based on a mutual information criterion. The proposed method is tested on a large database consists of 1000 environmental sounds belonging to ten classes. The averaged recognition accuracy is of order 90.87% which obtained using the multiclass support vector machines (SVM's).

Keywords: Environmental sounds, Log-Gabor-Filter, Mutual Information, Reassignment Method, SVM Multiclass.

1 Introduction

The environmental sounds domain is vast; it includes the sounds generated in domestic, business, and outdoor environments and can offer many services, for instance surveillance and security applications. Recently, some efforts have been interested in detecting and classifying environmental sounds [1], [2]. In the literature, the majority of studies present approaches for classifying sounds using such as acoustic, cepstral, or spectral descriptors. These descriptors can be used as a combination of some, or even all, of these 1-D audio features together [1]. Recently, some efforts emerge in the new research direction, which demonstrate that image

J. Ruiz-Shulcloper and G. Sanniti di Baja (Eds.): CIARP 2013, Part I, LNCS 8258, pp. 527–534, 2013.

processing techniques can be applied in musical [3], and environmental sounds [4]. In our previous work [4], we have showed that spectrograms can be used as texture images. In order to enhance this work, this paper develops method, based on spectrogram reassignment and spectro-temporal components. However, the spectrogram reassignment is an approach for refocusing the spectrogram by mapping the data to time-frequency coordinates that are nearer to the true region of the analyzed signal support [5].Besides, the reassignment method is applied to the spectrogram to improve the readability of the time-frequency representation, and to assure a better localization of the signal components. Indeed, many studies [6] and [7] show that spectro-temporal modulations play an important role in automatic speech recognition (ASR), in particular log-Gabor filters. Our method begins by spectrogram reassignment of environmental sounds, which then was passed through an averaged 12 log-Gabor filters concatenation applied to three spectrogram patches, and finally passed through an optimal feature procedure based on mutual information. In classification step, we use the SVM's with multiclass approach: One-Against-One. This paper is organized as follows. Section 2 describes environmental sound classification system. Classification results are given in Section 3. Finally conclusions are presented in Section 4.

2   Environmental Sound Classification Based on Reassignment Method and Log-Gabor Filters

2.1   Feature Extraction Method

The method consists in using the reassigned spectrogram patch. The aim is to find the suitable part of spectrogram, where the efficient structure concentrates, which gives a better result. We tested our method using log-Gabor filter for three spectrogram patches. We tested for patch number $N_p = 2,3,4,5$, we remark that the satisfactory result is obtained for $N_p = 3$. The idea is to extract three patches from each reassigned spectrogram. The first patch included frequencies from 0.01Hz to 128Hz, the second patch, from 128Hz to 256Hz, and the third patch, from 256Hz to 512Hz. Indeed, each patch goes through 12 log-Gabor filters $\{G_{11}, G_{12}, ..., G_{16}, G_{21}, ..., G_{25}, G_{26}\}$, followed

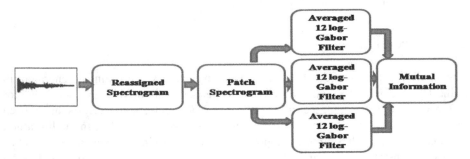

Fig. 1. Feature extraction using 3 spectrogram patches with 12 log-Gabor filters

by an average operation and then, MI feature selection algorithm is used, which constitutes the parameter vector for the classification (Fig.1.).

2.2   Reassignment Method

The spectrogram is the square modulus of the Short Time Fourier Transform $STFT_h(x; t, \omega)$

$$S_h(x; t, \omega) = |STFT_h(x; t, \omega)|^2 \tag{1}$$

$$STFT_h(x; t, \omega) = \int_{-\infty}^{+\infty} x(u)h^*(t - u)e^{-j\omega u}du \tag{2}$$

The disadvantage is manifested by its unseparable kernel allowing the spreads of the time and frequency smoothings bound, and even opposed [8], which leads to the spectrogram a loss of resolution and contrast [9].Hence, the reassignment is going to re-focus the energy spread by the smoothing [10].However, the reassignment application in time–frequency representation provides to run counter to its poor time-frequency concentration.

The reassigned spectrogram obtained by the Short Time Fourier transform (STFT) enhances the concentration of the components in comparison to the spectrogram, and it does not contain any cross terms. The values of the new position of energy contributions $(\hat{t}(x; t, \omega), \hat{\omega}(x; t, \omega))$ are given by the center of gravity of the signal energy located in a bounded domain centered on (t, ω). These coordinates are defined by the smoothing kernel $\phi_{TF}(u, \Omega)$ and computed by means of short-time Fourier transforms in the following way [8]:

$$\hat{t}(x; t, \omega) == t - \mathcal{R} \left\{ \frac{STFT_{Th}(x; t, \omega). STFT^*_h(x; t, \omega)}{|STFT_h(x; t, \omega)|^2} \right\} \tag{3}$$

$$\hat{\omega}(x; t, \omega) == \omega + Im \left\{ \frac{STFT_{Th}(x; t, \omega). STFT^*_h(x; t, \omega)}{|STFT_h(x; t, \omega)|^2} \right\} \tag{4}$$

For more explication, you can see Appendix of [8]. The corresponding equation to the reassignment operators is writing in the following way:

$$MS_h = \iint S_h (x; t, \omega)\delta(t' - \hat{t}(x; t, \omega)). \delta(\omega' - \hat{\omega}(x; t, \omega))dt\frac{d\omega}{2\pi} \tag{5}$$

where $\delta(t)$ is the Dirac impulse

We adopted in this work the reassignment method in order to obtain a clear and easily interpreted spectrogram, whose purpose is to improve the classification system performance realized in previous work [11].

2.3   Log-Gabor Filters

Gabor filters have many useful and important properties, in particular the capacity to decompose an image into its underlying dominant spectro-temporal components [6]. The log-Gabor function in the frequency domain can be described by the transfer function $G(r, \theta)$ with polar coordinates [7]:

$$G(r,\theta) = G_{radial}(r). G_{angular}(r) \tag{6}$$

Where $G_{radial}(r) = e^{-\log(r/f_0)^2/2\sigma_r^2}$, is the frequency response of the radial component and $G_{angular}(r) = exp\left(-(\theta/\theta_0)^2/2\sigma_\theta^2\right)$, represents the frequency response of the angular filter component. We note that (r, θ) are the polar coordinates, f_0 represents the central filter frequency, θ_0 is the orientation angle, σ_r and σ_θ represent the scale bandwidth and angular bandwidth respectively. The log-Gabor feature representation $|S(x,y)|_{m,n}$ of a magnitude spectrogram $s(x,y)$ was calculated as a convolution operation performed separately for the real and imaginary part of the log-Gabor filters:

$$Re(S(x,y))_{m,n} = s(x,y) * Re\big(G(r_m, \theta_n)\big) \tag{7}$$
$$Im(S(x,y))_{m,n} = s(x,y) * Im\big(G(r_m, \theta_n)\big) \tag{8}$$

(x, y) represents the time and frequency coordinates of a spectrogram, and $m = 1, ..., N_r = 2$ and $n = 1, ..., N_\theta = 6$ where N_r devotes the scale number and N_θ the orientation number. This was followed by the magnitude calculation for the filter bank outputs:

$$|S(x,y)| = \sqrt{\left(Re\big(S(x,y)\big)_{m,n}\right)^2 + Im(S(x,y))_{m,n}} \tag{9}$$

2.4   Averaging Log-Gabor Filters

The averaged operation was calculated for each 12 log-Gabor filter appropriate for each three reassigned spectrogram patches. The purpose being to obtain a single output array [7]:

$$|\hat{S}(x,y)| = \frac{1}{N_r N_\theta} \sum_{\substack{m=1 \\ n=1}}^{N_r, N_\theta} |S(x,y)|_{m,n} \tag{10}$$

2.5   Mutual Information

The feature vectors were reduced using the mutual information feature selection algorithm. The information found commonly in two random variables is defined as the mutual information between two variables X and Y, and it is given as [12]:

$$I(X;Y) = \sum_{x \in X}\sum_{y \in Y} p(x,y) log \frac{p(x,y)}{p(x)p(y)} \qquad (11)$$

Where $p(x) = Pr(X = x)$ is the marginal probability density function and $p(x) = Pr(X = x)$, and $p(x,y) = Pr(X = x, Y = y)$ is the joint probability density function.

2.6 SVM Classification

The SVM's is a tool for creating practical algorithms for estimating multidimensional functions [13]. In the nonlinear case, the idea is to use a kernel function $K(x_i, x_j)$, where $K(x_i, x_j)$ satisfies the Mercer conditions [14]. Here, we used a Gaussian RBF kernel whose formula is:

$$k(x, x') = exp\left[\frac{-\|x - x'\|^2}{2\sigma^2}\right]. \qquad (12)$$

Where $\|.\|$ indicates the Euclidean norm in $\Re^d$. We hence adopted one approach of multiclass classification: One-against-One [15]. For classification with SVM we suggest the cross-validation procedure for kernel parameter γ and the constant of regularization C. Indeed, according to [16], this method consists in setting up a grid-search for γ and C. For the implementation of this grid, it is necessary to proceed iteratively, by creating a couple of values γ and C. In this work, we use the following couples C, γ :C=[$2^{(-5)}$, $2^{(-4)}$,..., $2^{(15)}$] et γ=[$2^{(-15)}$, $2^{(-14)}$, ..., $2^{(3)}$].

3   Classification Results and Discussion

Our corpus of sounds comes from commercial CDs [17]. We used 10 classes of environmental sounds as shown in Table 1. All signals have a resolution of 16 bits and a sampling frequency of 44100 Hz that is characterized by a good temporal resolution and a wide frequency band.

Most of the signals are impulsive. We took 2/3 for the training and 1/3 for the test. Reassigned Spectrograms are extracted through Short Time Fourier Transform with the number of frequency points equal to 512, the smoothing Hanning window is used, which divides the signal into segments of length equal to 256 with 192-point overlap. Indeed, the idea consists in application of reassignment method to 3 spectrogram patches, then passed through a log-Gabor filters concatenation, after that an averaged operation is applied, followed by the mutual information criteria for optimization. Results of our approach are shown in Table 2. Besides, we obtained in this approach an averaged accuracy rate of the order 90.87%. This method leads to an increase approximately 4% of averaged recognition compared to the result obtained when we applied the same method but without using reassignment method which we obtained a

Table 1. Classes of Sounds and Number of Samples in the Database Used for Performance Evaluation

Classes	Train	Test	Total
Door slams (Ds)	208	104	312
Explosions (Ep)	38	18	56
Glass breaking (Gb)	38	18	56
Dog barks (Db)	32	16	48
Phone rings (Pr)	32	16	48
Children voices (Cv)	54	26	80
Gunshots (Gs)	150	74	224
Human screams (Hs)	48	24	72
Machines (Mc)	38	18	56
Cymbals (Cy)	32	16	48
Total	670	330	1000

Table 2. Recognition Rates for averaged outputs of 3 Reassigned Spectrogram Patches With 12 log-Gabor filters applied to one-against-one SVM's based classifier with Gaussian RBF kernel

	3 Reassigned Spectrogram Patches with 12 log-Gabor filters concatenation	
Classes	Parameters Kernel (c, γ)	Classif. Rate (%)
Ds	$(2^{(-5)}, 2^{(-6)})$	94.87
Ep	$(2^{(-4)}, 2^{(-6)})$	88.75
Cb	$(2^{(-5)}, 2^{(2)})$	78.57
Db	$(2^{(1)}, 2^{(3)})$	89.58
Pr	$(2^{(15)}, 2^{(1)})$	93.75
Cv	$(2^{(-1)}, 2^{(-6)})$	85.71
Gs	$(2^{(-4)}, 2^{(2)})$	95.83
Hs	$(2^{(-3)}, 2^{(-4)})$	95.58
Mc	$(2^{(-4)}, 2^{(-6)})$	92.85
Cy	$(2^{(-3)}, 2^{(-7)})$	93.30

classification rate of the order 86.78 % [11]. The studies of Chu et al. [1] proposed an approach based on combination of matching pursuit (MP) and MFCCs features. This combination gives the average classification rate of 83.9 % in discriminating fourteen classes with GMM classifier. When comparing this result with our system classification rate, we remark that our system has more significant and better results. We notice that our individual features are significantly better in spite of a limited number of features.

To conclude, we compared also our obtained results with the results attained by Rabaoui et al. [2], who used a combination between energy, Log energy and MFCCs features. This research gives an average classification rate of (90.23%) in the environmental sounds classes. It is slightly lower than our proposed method result (90.87%). Moreover, applying the reassignment method on the environmental sound spectrogram enhances the performance of used system. The experimental results reported in this work show that the reassignment method provides a higher improvement in the environmental sounds classification. Therefore, with the reassignment method we can easily interpret the spectrogram signature. In addition, the important point of the reassignment method is the proper choice of smoothing kernel in order to produce   simultaneously a high concentration of the signal components   [8].The purpose of reassignment method is to build a readable time-frequency representation process.   Previous studies [10], [18] show that using reassignment method can improve the detection, the additive sound modeling, and the classification   performance.   Nevertheless,   features   extracted   from   reassigned spectrogram improve the classification results as shown in Table II. SVMs have proven to be robust in high dimensions. Also SVMs are well founded mathematically to reach good generalization while keeping high classification accuracy. The performance of the proposed classification system has been evaluated and compared with our previous work by using a set of synthetic test signals.   However, the proposed method maintains overall good performance. The experiments results are satisfactory, which encourages us to investigate better in the reassignment method.

4   Conclusion

In this paper, we propose a robust method for environmental sound classification, based on reassignment method and log-Gabor filters. We show how this method is efficient to classify the environmental sounds. Besides, our method uses an averaged 12 log-Gabor filters concatenation applied to 3 reassigned spectrogram patches. Our classification system obtains good averaged classification result of the order 90.87%.

Furthermore, reassignment method improves classification results. It used as the key element of obtaining an optimal classification compared to our previous methods [11]. In addition, this paper deals with robust features used with   one-against-one SVM-based classifier in order to have a system that quietly works, independent of recording conditions. Future research directions will include other methods extracted from image processing to apply in environmental sounds classification and will can be improved while digging deeply into reassignment methods.

References

1. Chu, S., Narayanan, S., Kuo, C.C.J.: Environmental Sound Recognition with Time-Frequency Audio Features. IEEE Trans. on Speech, Audio, and Language Processing 17(6), 1142–1158 (2009)
2. Rabaoui, A., Davy, M., Rossignol, S., Ellouze, N.: Using One-Class SVMs and Wavelets for Audio Surveillance. IEEE Transactions on Information Forensics and Security 3(4), 763–775 (2008)
3. Yu, G., Slotine, J.J.: Fast Wavelet-based Visual Classification. In: Proc. IEEE International Conference on Pattern Recognition, ICPR, Tampa, pp. 1–5 (2008)

4. Souli, S., Lachiri, Z.: Environmental Sounds Classification Based on Visual Features. In: San Martin, C., Kim, S.-W. (eds.) CIARP 2011. LNCS, vol. 7042, pp. 459–466. Springer, Heidelberg (2011)
5. Kelly Fitz, R., Sean Fulop, A.: A unified theory of time-frequency reassignment. Computing Research Repository-CORR, abs/0903.3 (2009)
6. Kleinschmidt, M.: Methods for capturing spectro-temporal modulations in automatic speech recognition. Electrical and Electronic Engineering Acoustics, Speech and Signal Processing Papers, Acta Acustica 88, 416–422 (2002)
7. He, L., Lech, M., Maddage, N., Allen, N.: Stress and Emotion Recognition Using Log-Gabor Filter. In: 3rd International Conference on Affective Computing and Intelligent Interaction and Workshops, ACII, Amsterdam, pp. 1–6 (2009)
8. Auger, F., Flandrin, P.: Improving the Readability of Time-Frequency and Time-Scale Representations by the Reassignment Method. IEEE Trans. Signal Proc. 40, 1068–1089 (1995)
9. Chassande-Mottin, E.: Méthodes de réallocation dans le plan temps-fréquence pour l'analyse et le traitement de signaux non stationnaires. PhD thesis, Cergy-Pontoise University (1998)
10. Millioz, F., Martin, N.: Réallocation du spectrogramme pour la détection de frontières de motifs temps-fréquence. In: Colloque GRETSI, pp. 11–14 (2007)
11. Souli, S., Lachiri, Z.: Multiclass Support Vector Machines for Environmental Sounds Classification in visual domain based on Log-Gabor Filters. International Journal of Speech Technology (IJST) 16(2), 203–213 (2013)
12. Kwak, N., Choi, C.: Input Feature Selection for Classification Problems. IEEE Trans. on Neural Networks 13, 143–159 (2002)
13. Vladimir, V., Vapnik, N.: An Overview of Statistical Learning Theory. IEEE Transactions on Neural Networks 10, 988–999 (1999)
14. Vapnik, V., Chapelle, O.: Bounds on Error Expectation for Support Vector Machines. Journal Neural Computation 12, 2013–2036 (2000)
15. Hsu, C.-W., Lin, C.-J.: A comparison of methods for multi-class support vector machines. J. IEEE Transactions on Neural Networks 13, 415–425 (2002)
16. Hsu, C.-W., Chang, C.-C., Lin, C.-J.: A practical Guide to Support Vector Classification. Department of Computer Science and Information Engineering National Taiwan University, Taipei, Taiwan (2009)
17. The Leonardo Software website, Santa Monica, CA 90401, http://www.leonardosoft.com
18. Fitz, K., Haken, L.: On the Use of Time-Frequency Reassignment in Additive Sound Modeling. J. Audio Eng. Soc. (AES) 50, 879–893 (2002)

Dominant Set Approach to ECG Biometrics

André Lourenço[1,2], Samuel Rota Bulò[3], Carlos Carreiras[2], Hugo Silva[2],
Ana L.N. Fred[2], and Marcello Pelillo[4]

[1] Instituto Superior de Engenharia de Lisboa, Lisbon, Portugal
[2] Instituto de Telecomunicações, Instituto Superior Técnico, Lisbon, Portugal
[3] FBK-irst, via Sommarive, 18, I-38123, Trento, Italy
[4] DAIS, Università Ca' Foscari Venezia, Venice, Italy

Abstract. Electrocardiographic (ECG) signals are emerging as a recent
trend in the field of biometrics. In this paper, we propose a novel ECG
biometric system that combines clustering and classification methodologies. Our approach is based on dominant-set clustering, and provides a
framework for outlier removal and template selection. It enhances the
typical workflows, by making them better suited to new ECG acquisition paradigms that use fingers or hand palms, which lead to signals with
lower signal to noise ratio, and more prone to noise artifacts. Preliminary
results show the potential of the approach, helping to further validate
the highly usable setups and ECG signals as a complementary biometric
modality.

Keywords: Biometrics, ECG, Clustering, Dominant Set, Outlier Detection, Template Selection.

1 Introduction

The ECG is a graphical record of the bioelectrical signal generated by the heart
during each cardiac cycle. Typically, it exhibits both persistent features (such
as the average P-QRS-T morphology, and the short-term average heart rate or
average RR interval), and nonstationary features (such as the individual RR and
QT intervals, and long-term heart rate trends) [1].

A recent application for the ECG is its use for biometric recognition [2–6].
In this paradigm, the development of highly usable setups that use the fingers,
or hand palms, as the signal source, is one of the recent trends, leading to new
challenges [6]. With these atypical setups, the acquired signal has lower signal
to noise ratio, and is more prone to noise artifacts. Figure 1 illustrates an ECG
time series, its main complexes, and examples of two noise types of artifacts
(powerline noise and motion artifacts), which need to be detected and removed,
so that the recognition performance is not deteriorated.

An ECG biometric system prepared to process such signals requires the implementation of new blocks, namely an outlier removal step to distinguish noisy
segments from normal heartbeats. In this paper we present a novel approach
based on *dominant set clustering* [7]. Our approach enables the simultaneous
removal of outlier segments, and the extraction of representative templates.

J. Ruiz-Shulcloper and G. Sanniti di Baja (Eds.): CIARP 2013, Part I, LNCS 8258, pp. 535–542, 2013.
© Springer-Verlag Berlin Heidelberg 2013

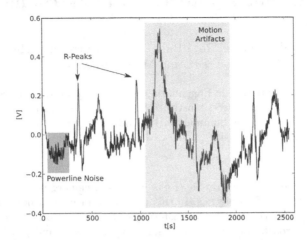

Fig. 1. Example of ECG signals acquired at the fingers with heartbeat waveforms with several R-peak complexes annotated, and corrupting noise (motion artifacts and powerline noise)

The remainder of the paper is organized as follows. In Section 2 we present an overview of ECG biometrics and a summary of our system. In Section 3 we review the dominant set clustering paradigm, and show how it can be used for outlier detection and template extraction. Finally, in Sections 4, 5 and 6 we present the experimental setup, a summary of the results, and outline the main conclusions.

2   ECG Biometric Systems

ECG-based biometric methods can be classified as fiducial, non-fiducial or partially fiducial. Fiducial methods use anchor points (called fiducia) as references [3, 5], where the R-peak of the ECG is typically the main reference, since it is the easiest to distinguish [2, 8]. Non-fiducial methods extract information from the ECG signals without having any reference point [4, 5]. Partially fiducial approaches use fiducial information only for ECG segmentation [3, 6]. We follow a partially fiducial approach, and Figure 2 depicts the block diagram of our biometric system: it starts with the acquisition of raw data, using a custom one-lead sensor with virtual ground and dry Ag/AgCl electrodes [6]; the acquired signal is then converted from analog to digital, and submitted to a data preprocessing block which performs a digital filtering step (band-pass FIR filter order 300, and cutoff frequencies 5-20Hz), and the QRS complex detection [6]; finally, the signal is segmented into individual heartbeats.

Let x_i be an individual heartbeat obtained after segmenting the ECG signal. Each heartbeat is described by a vector of features $x_i = (x_{1i}, \ldots, x_{mi})^\top \in \mathbb{R}^m$,

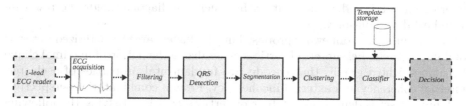

Fig. 2. Block diagram of our ECG biometric recognition approach

whose values, in this paper, are the amplitudes of the ECG heartbeat wave form. Also, consider $X = [\boldsymbol{x}_1, \dots, \boldsymbol{x}_n]$ as the m × n matrix formed by n individual heartbeats. The clustering block assigns each of the instances of X to a cluster. Previous work in the context of ECG biometrics has already approached the topic of outlier detection, evaluating two algorithms [9]: 1) distance-based detection (DMEAN); and 2) clustering with integrated outlier detection criterion, using DBSCAN. The approach presented in this paper is more integrated, and also enables the generation of representative templates on a cluster basis.

For classification, we compare an instance-based learning template-matching approach, through a k-Nearest Neighbor (k-NN) classifier, and with a Support Vector Machine (SVM) classifier, which have been found in the literature to perform adequately [10].

3   Robust Template Selection Using Dominant Sets

In order to select a set of ECG signal templates for a given person in a way to be robust to outliers, we make use of a graph-based clustering approach introduced in [7], known as *dominant set clustering*.

First of all, we cast the ECG clustering task for a given individual into a graph clustering problem. To this end, let $G = (V, \omega)$ be a complete, edge-weighted graph without self-loops, where $V = \{1, \dots, n\}$ is the set of vertices, each vertex $i \in V$ being related to an individual heartbeat $\boldsymbol{x}_i$ as defined in Section 2, and $\omega : V \times V \to \mathbb{R}_+$ being a similarity function providing each edge in $(i, j) \in V \times V$ with a nonnegative weight $\omega_{ij} = \omega(i, j) \geq 0$. The weight function is defined to measure the similarity between two ECG heartbeats, assuming $\omega_{ii} = 0$ for all $i \in V$. In this work, we employ the following similarity measures:

- *Euclidean (Eucl):* $\omega_{ij} = e^{-d_{ij}^2/\sigma^2}$, $d_{ij} = \|\boldsymbol{x}_i - \boldsymbol{x}_j\|$,
- *Cosine (Cos):* $\omega_{ij} = \boldsymbol{x}_i^\top \boldsymbol{x}_j \big/ (\|\boldsymbol{x}_i\|\|\boldsymbol{x}_j\|)$,
- *Discrete Fourier Transform (DFT):* $\omega_{ij} = e^{-d_{ij}^2/\sigma^2}$, $d_{ij} = \|\mathsf{S}^{-1}[\mathcal{F}(\boldsymbol{x}_i) - \mathcal{F}(\boldsymbol{x}_i)]\|$,

where $\sigma > 0$ is a parameter of the Euclidean and DFT similarity measures that we set to the median of the distances among all pairs of ECG signals, *i.e.* $\sigma = \mathrm{median}(\{d_{ij} : i, j \in V\})$. Moreover, $\mathcal{F}$ is the discrete Fourier transform operator and S is a diagonal matrix, in which the diagonal holds the row-wise standard deviations of X.

In the clustering framework proposed in [7], clusters are characterized in terms of dominant sets, *i.e.* subsets of vertices generalizing the notion of maximal clique to edge-weighted graphs that encode two fundamental properties of a cluster: internal coherency and external incoherency. From a combinatorial perspective, a dominant set is defined as a subset of vertices $D \subseteq V$ satisfying the following conditions:

$$w_D(i) > 0, \quad \forall i \in D,$$
$$w_D(i) < 0, \quad \forall i \in V \setminus D.$$

Here, $w_D(i)$ is a recursive characterization of a weight assigned to each element $i \in V$ with respect to the set $D \subseteq V$ (we refer to the original paper [7] for more details). Another characterization of dominant sets is in terms of strict local maximizers of the following simplex-constrained quadratic optimization problem:

$$\max_{\alpha \in \Delta} \alpha^\top W \alpha \tag{1}$$

where W is a matrix defined as $W = [\omega_{ij}]$ and Δ is the *standard simplex*, which is given by $\Delta = \{\alpha \in \mathbb{R}_+^n : \sum_{i \in V} \alpha_i = 1\}$. It is indeed proven [7] that there exists a one-to-one correspondence between dominant sets of G and strict local maximizers of (1). Additionally, there exists also an interesting game-theoretic characterization of dominant sets in terms of evolutionary stable equilibria of two-person non-cooperative strategic games called *clustering games* [11, 12].

In order to extract a dominant set, we make use of the so-called *Infection and Immunization Dynamics* (InImDyn) [13]. This dynamics modifies over time an initial probability distribution (prior distribution) defined over V. At convergence, the distribution is a local solution of (1) and the elements in V having non-zero probability form a dominant set. This procedure allows to extract one dominant set at a time, and one crucial problem to solve is how to enumerate multiple dominant sets in order to detect multiple objects. A commonly used method consists in a *peeling-off strategy*, *i.e.*, one iteratively removes from the graph the elements belonging to newly extracted dominant sets. Another solution, which turns out to be effective, is the one proposed in [14, Sec. 3.4] (we refer to the paper for the details).

3.1   Extraction of the ECG Signal Templates

The problem of template extraction may be posed as follows [15]: given a set of n heartbeats, acquired during one session, extract k templates that "best" represent the variability, as well as the typically observed patterns. There are two main approaches: a) selection of k heartbeats; and b) generation of k representative heartbeats. This problem has already been tackled in other modalities (e.g. signature and fingerprint) [15, 16], and is mainly based on selection.

Our approach is based on template generation using the dominant sets. As a result of the dominant set extraction procedure mentioned in the previous section, we obtain a set of probability distributions over the set of heartbeats $\Gamma = \{\boldsymbol{\alpha}^{(1)}, \ldots, \boldsymbol{\alpha}^{(k)}\}$. Each vector $\boldsymbol{\alpha}^{(i)} \in \Gamma \subset \Delta$ corresponds to a dominant set, and each component of $\boldsymbol{\alpha}^{(i)}$ intuitively represents the probability of being a good representative for the ith extracted cluster [7]. Based on this fact, we compute a template $\boldsymbol{t}^{(i)}$ from the ith cluster as the expected ECG heartbeat under the distribution $\boldsymbol{\alpha}^{(i)}$, $i.e.$

$$\boldsymbol{t}^{(i)} = X\boldsymbol{\alpha}^{(i)}. \tag{2}$$

By repeating this operation for each dominant set extracted from the graph G of ECG signals, we obtain a set of k templates $T = \{\boldsymbol{t}^{(1)}, \ldots, \boldsymbol{t}^{(k)}\}$. Note that a dominant set represents a compact cluster and it is very robust to outliers. Indeed, outliers appear in the vector $\boldsymbol{\alpha}^{(i)}$ as zero components, thus being intrinsically not detrimental to the template computation.

In Figure 3 a) we show the single heartbeats of one of the acquisitions, together with the generated templates. In this case, 3 templates were generated, completely removing the outlier segments. In Figure 3 b) we show the α weights used for this generation (the x-axis represents the partition, and the y-axis represents the weight associated to each partition). Each of the generated templates is based on a portion of the partitions, with several partitions having a zero weight.

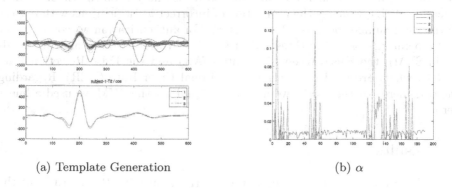

(a) Template Generation   (b) α

Fig. 3. In a) illustration of the single heartbeat waveforms for one of the acquisition sessions and the generated templates; b) α weights used for the generation of these templates

3.2   Exploitation of ECG Signal Templates for Classification

Our classification methodology follows the approach found in [10], where k-NN and SVM classifiers were tested in the context of ECG recognition. Let $X^{(u)}$ denote the matrix of heartbeat waveforms of the uth individual, $u \in \{1, \ldots, q\}$ and let $T^{(u)}$ be the set of ECG signal templates extracted according to the methodology presented in the previous section from $X^{(u)}$. In general, different subjects can have a different number of templates. We construct a training set from the collected templates as

$$\mathbb{D}_{training} = \bigcup_{u \in \{1,\dots,q\}} \left\{ (t, u) : t \in T^{(u)} \right\}, \tag{3}$$

and we train a k-NN or SVM classifier based on it.

4   Experimental Setup

For the evaluation of the proposed approach, we used a dataset consisting of the ECG data from 63 subjects (49 males and 14 females) with an average age of 20.68 ± 2.83 years. The subjects were asked to sit for 2 minutes in a resting position with two fingers, one from the left and another from the right hand, placed in each of the dry electrodes (more details in [6]). The signals were acquired using a bioPLUX research acquisition unit (12-bit resolution and 1kHz sampling frequency). The data consists of two independent acquisition sessions separated by a 3-month interval, entitled "T1" and "T2" [17].

The evaluation of our system is based on: a) analysis of the generated templates; b) a quantitative analysis on the recognition performance. We compare against the performance obtained by the DMEAN algorithm [9], when using as templates, means of 5 heartbeats.

Recognition performance was assessed for both the identification and authentication scenarios. For identification, we based the analysis on the Error of Identification (EID), which is the proportion of incorrect identifications with respect to the total number of tests (Rank-1 error). For authentication we compute, for each operating point (the threshold in k-NN, or the fraction of agreeing models in SVM), the False Acceptance Rate (FAR) and the False Rejection Rate (FRR), which are used to determine the Equal Error Rate (EER). Regarding the classifiers, for the k-NN, we used $k = 1$, and for the SVM we used a linear kernel.

5   Results

Table 1 shows the biometric recognition performance (EER and EID) of the proposed approaches (dominant sets with *Cos*, *DFT* and *Eucl*), against baseline (*DMEAN*), within-session T1 (T1-T1), and across-sessions (training in T1, and testing in T2; T1-T2). For the T1-T1 analysis, we employed cross-validation using 30% of T1 as training data and the rest as testing data, over 30 runs.

We can observe that across-sessions results are much worse than within-session results, which was expected given the fact that, in the within-session case, the training and testing data belong to the same acquisition session and, therefore, the extracted ECG segments exhibit greater similarity, especially in regard to the heart rate. In the across-sessions case, the use of the template generation method produces recognition rates with worse performance, but in the same order of magnitude, when compared with what is obtained with the DMEAN method, which only performs outlier removal. This may be a consequence of having fewer templates than DMEAN approach. The same is not true for the within-session case. In particular, the *Eucl* metric using the SVM classifier outputs the global best results. Concerning the three adopted metrics (*Cos, DFT* and *Eucl*), the results are similar (within each of the train and test conditions), with a preference for the *Eucl* metric. Finally, regarding the classification method, the SVM classifier performs better in all studied cases.

These results suggest that, although the template generation method does not improve the recognition performance for the across-sessions case (the more realistic one), we can still gain from its use in the sense that it reduces the number of templates that are required to train the classifiers, thus achieving better computational efficiency (i.e. the mean number of templates used for training in the *Eucl* is 6.9 templates per subject). Additionally, a fine-tuning of the parameters may lead to better performance.

Table 1. Equal Error Rates (EER) and Identification Errors (EID) in %; proposed proposed approach (DS) vs. DMEAN, baseline presented in [9], without template generation; values in bold represent the best score for each column

Train Method		1-NN				SVM		
		T1-T1		T1-T2		T1-T1		T1-T2
		EER	EID	EER	EID	EER	EID	EER	EID
DMEAN		2.53	**1.01**	**11.90**	**41.57**	1.00	1.22	**9.47**	**38.30**
DS	Cos	2.66	1.90	13.91	47.67	1.26	1.61	11.76	46.45
	DFT	**2.48**	1.28	12.46	44.07	0.99	1.21	11.10	40.63
	Eucl	2.51	1.43	12.31	42.57	**0.75**	**0.86**	10.86	39.91

6 Conclusion

Research on Electrocardiographic (ECG) signals has advanced a long way from its clinical roots, to novel application domains in areas so diverse as biometric recognition. The development of highly usable setups based on fingers or hand palms leads to signals with lower signal to noise ratio, and more artifacts (e.g. motion induced).

The biometric recognition sytems adapted to this new paradigm require the inclusion of outlier detection blocks; furthermore, given that heartbeat waveforms show high intra-subject morphological similarity, template generation can also be a nice add-on to ECG-based biometric systems. In this paper we presented a novel approach based on dominant set clustering. The described system enables the simultaneous generation of templates and removal of outliers. Experimental results have shown that our approach enables high recognition rates comparable to other approaches that also integrate outlier detection, but no template extraction step. Therefore, the main advantage the proposed approach is the improvement of the computational efficiency of the biometric recognition system, given that the number of templates that have to be stored per subject is much smaller, significantly reducing the number of comparisons that have to be made.

Acknowledgments. This work was partially financed by FCT under grants SFRH /PROTEC/49512/2009, PTDC/EEI-SII/2312/2012 (LearningS project) and PEst-OE/EEI/LA0008/2011, and by the ADEETC-ISEL whose support the authors gratefully acknowledge.

References

1. Clifford, G.D.: ECG Statistics, Noise, Artifacts, and Missing Data. In: Clifford, G.D., Azuaje, F., Mcsharry, P. (eds.) Advanced Methods and Tools for ECG Data Analysis. Artech House Publishers (2006)
2. Biel, L., Petterson, O., Phillipson, L., Wide, P.: ECG analysis: A new approach in human identification. IEEE Trans. Inst. and Measurement 50(3), 808–812 (2001)
3. Wang, Y., Agrafioti, F., Hatzinakos, D., Plataniotis, K.N.: Analysis of human electrocardiogram for biometric recognition. EURASIP J. Adv. S. Processing (2008)
4. Chan, A.D.C., Hamdy, M.M., Badre, A., Badee, V.: Wavelet distance measure for person identification using electrocardiograms. IEEE Trans. on Instrumentation and Measurement 57(2), 248–253 (2008)
5. Odinaka, I., Lai, P.H., Kaplan, A., O'Sullivan, J., Sirevaag, E., Rohrbaugh, J.: ECG biometric recognition: A comparative analysis. IEEE Trans. on Information Forensics and Security 7(6), 1812–1824 (2012)
6. Silva, H., Lourenço, A., Canento, F., Fred, A., Raposo, N.: ECG biometrics: Principles and applications. In: Proc. of the 6th Int'l Conf. on Bio-Inspired Systems and Signal Processing, BIOSIGNALS (2013)
7. Pavan, M., Pelillo, M.: Dominant sets and pairwise clustering. IEEE Trans. Pattern Analysis and Machine Intelligence 29(1), 167–172 (2007)
8. Silva, H., Gamboa, H., Fred, A.: One lead ECG based personal identification with feature subspace ensembles. In: Perner, P. (ed.) MLDM 2007. LNCS (LNAI), vol. 4571, pp. 770–783. Springer, Heidelberg (2007)
9. Lourenço, A., Silva, H., Carreiras, C., Fred, A.: Outlier detection in non-intrusive ECG biometric system. In: Kamel, M., Campilho, A. (eds.) ICIAR 2013. LNCS, vol. 7950, pp. 43–52. Springer, Heidelberg (2013)
10. Lourenço, A., Silva, H., Fred, A.L.N.: ECG-based biometrics: A real time classification approach. In: IEEE Int'l W. Machine Learning for Signal Proc. (2012)
11. Torsello, A., Rota Bulò, S., Pelillo, M.: Grouping with asymmetric affinities: A game-theoretic perspective. In: IEEE Conf. Computer Vision and Patt. Recogn., pp. 292–299 (2006)
12. Rota Bulò, S., Pelillo, M.: A game-theoretic approach to hypergraph clustering. IEEE Trans. Patt. Analysis Machine Intell. 35(6), 1312–1327 (2013)
13. Rota Bulò, S., Pelillo, M., Bomze, I.M.: Graph-based quadratic optimization: A fast evolutionary approach. Comp. Vis. and Image Understanding 115, 984–995 (2011)
14. Kontschieder, P., Rota Bulò, S., Donoser, M., Pelillo, M., Bischof, H.: Evolutionary hough games for coherent object detection. Comp. Vis. and Image Understanding 116, 1149–1158 (2012)
15. Uludag, U., Ross, A., Jain, A.: Biometric template selection and update: a case study in fingerprints. Pattern Recognition 37(7), 1533–1542 (2004)
16. Liu, N., Wang, Y.: Template selection for on-line signature verification. In: Proc. of the 19th Int. Conf. on Pattern Recognition (ICPR), pp. 1–4 (December 2008)
17. Silva, H., Lourenço, A., Fred, A.L.N.: Finger ECG signal for user authentication: Usability and performance. In: IEEE BTAS (September 2013)

Onset and Peak Pattern Recognition on Photoplethysmographic Signals Using Neural Networks

Alvaro D. Orjuela-Cañón[1], Denis Delisle-Rodríguez[2], Alberto López-Delis[2],
Ramón Fernandez de la Vara-Prieto[2], and Manuel B. Cuadra-Sanz[3]

[1] GIBIO - Electronic and Biomedical Faculty, Universidad Antonio Nariño,
Bogotá D.C., Colombia
alvorjuela@uan.edu.co
[2] Center of Medical Biophysics, Universidad de Oriente,
Santiago de Cuba, Cuba
{denis.delisle,ramon.fernandez,alberto.lopez}@cbiomed.cu
[3] CIDEI (Research and Technologic Development Center for the Electro-Electronics
and Informatics Industry),
Bogotá D.C., Colombia
mqadra2013@yahoo.es

Abstract. Traditional methodologies use electrocardiographic (ECG) signals to develop automatic methods for onset and peak detection on the arterial pulse wave. In the present work a Multilayer Perceptron (MLP) neural network is used for classifying fiducial points on photoplethysmographic (PPG) signals. System was trained with a dataset of temporal segments from signals located based on information about onset and peak points. Different segments sizes and units in the neural network were used for the classification, and optimal values were searched. Results of the classification reach 98.1% in worse of cases. This proposal takes advantages from MLP neural networks for pattern classification. Additionally, the use of ECG signal was avoided in the presented methodology, making the system robust, less expensive and portable in front of this problem.

Keywords: Arterial Pulse Wave, Artificial Neural Networks, Multilayer Perceptron, Onset Classification, Peak Classification.

1 Introduction

The photoplethysmography (PPG) signal has been used as a simple and low-cost optical technique, which is used for measuring blood volume changes through of the light intensity during the emission and reception on the skin surface. Peripheral body sites such as fingers, ears, toes and forehead are used to obtain these kind of signals, approaching blood volume and perfusion changes due to the dissemination or absorption of the incident light, providing the dynamical part of the signal [1,2].

J. Ruiz-Shulcloper and G. Sanniti di Baja (Eds.): CIARP 2013, Part I, LNCS 8258, pp. 543–550, 2013.
© Springer-Verlag Berlin Heidelberg 2013

Applications of PPG signal treatment can be seen in commercial medical equipment, where measures of oxygen saturation, blood pressure or heart rate monitoring assess autonomic functions and contributes to peripheral vascular diseases diagnosis. In this way, fiducial points detection on PPG signals is used to obtain relevant information such as pulse transit time (PTT) and pulse wave velocity (PWV), which evaluate vascular effects of aging, hypertension, stiffness and atherosclerosis [3,4].

Onset and peak pulses detection is not a trivial task, due to natural conditions as sensor positioning, skin features, breathing, baseline drift, perfusion phenomena, visco-elastic and viscosity property of arteries, arterial stiffness and reflected waves from peripheral sites, which can be easily involved in noise and artifacts. As PPG signal typically has small amplitude, its incident and reflected waveform can be affected for these kind of conditions [5].

Different methods have been developed for this detection task varying its complexity. These can include adaptive threshold, computer-based filtering, feature extraction, and derivative calculation [6,7]. Most of them are assisted by the electrocardiographic (ECG) signal, which provides a cost increment of medical equipment and difficult its clinical applications in the Health Primary System. In [7], morphological similarity of adjacent pulse is used to enhance signal quality and increase the accuracy of the onset pulses detection. A disadvantage of the method is the inclusion of measures from time interval between R to R peak of ECG signal. Additionally, it is applied principal components analysis over adjacent peaks to enhance the onset detection. Information about diastolic point, second derivative and tangent intersection, shows an enhanced accuracy and precision [8]. The use of ECG signal problem, again represents a disadvantage when is not possible obtain this kind of signals. Recently, in [9] a new method is presented, based on filed collected photoplethysmograms. This method does not use ECG signal and works through PPG signal filtering in different ways, but digital filters introduce delays in the temporal signal, which can give wrong information about onset localization in signal. Other function of that algorithm is the detection of peak pulses in the PPG signal.

Neural networks has been used in cardiovascular problems detection, such as QRS detection [10,11], clustering [12,13] and applications with PPG signals [14,15]. Despite its advantages for pattern recognition, few studies have been reported as alternative method for onset and peak pulses detection. An example of this can be found in [16], where Self Organizing Maps (SOM) were employed for the onset and peak detection and classification.

In this paper, it is presented a proposal based on pattern recognition, which uses a Multilayer Perceptron (MLP) to learn the temporal information around onset and peak pulses. Supervised training is implemented, where PPG signals marked by expert observers are used. Onset and peak are designated into a temporal windows used to train the neural network. For validation of the models, the Leave One Out cross validation method is implemented, which is used when the database is the limited size.

2   Materials and Methods

Database is composed by signals from seven volunteers, who participated in the experimental protocol and provide informed consent in accordance with institutional policy. Each subject remains in rest during five minutes in the supine position. Previously to the test, personal and clinical data were collected of each volunteer. Table 1 shows the age and vital signs of the subjects.

Table 1. Characteristics of Volunteers

Subject	Sex	Age(years)	HR(bpm)	SBP(mmHg)	DBP(mmHg)	Breath/min
1	M	19	72	102	68	20
2	M	20	60	98	60	16
3	M	22	80	125	80	17
4	M	20	84	112	72	18
5	F	18	80	110	64	16
6	F	18	88	108	58	22
7	F	18	72	108	68	19
Mean $\pm$ SD		19.3 ± 1.50	76.57 ± 9.36	109 ± 8.54	67.14 ± 7.47	18.28 ± 2.21

HR: Heart rate
SBP: Systolic blood pressure
DBP: Diastolic blood pressure
SD: Standard deviation

Acquisition was performed by an experimental station, which collected physiological signals of each person. This station simultaneously acquires electrocardiography (ECG) and photoplethysmographic (PPG) signals through an ECG channel with bandwidth between 0.15 to 150 Hz and two PPG channels with bandwidth from 0.5 to 16 Hz. Simultaneous ECG and PPG signals were sampled with 1000 Hz and manually marked by trained observers from Center of Medical Biophysics. This task was developed using functions in Matlab software (Mathworks Inc., Natick, MA), which provide additional capabilities such as, add, move and remove the fiducial points of ECG and PPG signals (Fig. 1). These points correspond to peaks values of QRS complex and, onsets and peaks of PPG signal. This information is useful for testing the proposed method.

2.1   Neural Networks Training

Neural networks have the ability of learning complex nonlinear patterns, based on input-output relationships, adjusting a set of free parameters known as synaptic weights. The most common type of networks employed in classification tasks are the Multilayer Perceptrons (MLPs), which have only feed forward connections and are trained in a supervised way [17].

In the present work, MLPs are employed to learn patterns in temporal segments around onset and peak fiducial points on PPG signal. This work is based on the annotations of the expert observers, which marked the onset and peak

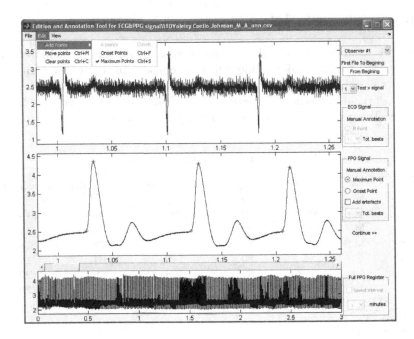

Fig. 1. PPG signal acquisition and annotation system

points. These fiducial points are located in the middle of segment, and then is extracted the temporal segment (Figure 2). The segment size is a topic of study in the present study, then windows with values of 21, 41, 61, 81 and 101 milliseconds were used and observed its relation with the behaviour of the network.

Smaller sizes were not considered because are shorter windows to pattern representation and can be confused with noise segments. In PPG signals, distance between onset and peak is less than 100 milliseconds, due to its nature [18,19]. For this reason, an upper period of time was not considered. Windows with the same size of the onset and peak pattern were extracted to create a third class called noise, these segments were taken from samples before and after of the onset and peak windows. This makes that the noise represents segments of signal without activity involved in other classes.

MLP architecture consists of an input, a hidden layer and a output layer. Number of nodes in the input is given by the segment size; number of units in the hidden layer was heuristically studied, trying 5, 10, 15 and 20 units. In the output layer were used three units, each one identifies each pattern. More layers are not used because two layers are enough for a typical problem of classification [17].

Each segment is normalized before being presented to the network, maintaining its values in the interval from 0 to 1. This contributes to avoid the saturation of the values in the synaptic weights, which are initialized in a random manner. Hyperbolic tangent functions are used in each unit as activation functions. In this way, the units in the output have the value of one when the input belongs to this class, and -1 when does not belong. Training for MLP is developed in a supervised manner, where patterns and its labels are necessary. The resilient backpropagation algorithm was used for the training of the network, due to its fast and stable convergence [20]. Training set must represent the statistics of the data, and its construction is important for a good training, because the network must generalize its performance to new inputs.

In the present study, the database has a limited size, making difficult the division of the data for training and validation. Alternatives as bootstrapping and cross validation methods can be useful in these cases. An example of this kind of methods is the Leave One Out (LOO) method, where the performance of pattern classification models can be evaluated based on LOO error. The applied method consists in training the network with all data, leaving only an observation out. In the present case, six of seven signals were used in the training, each of them with 345 onset and 345 peak points. When training was finished, the validation is calculated using just with the signal not included in the training, also with 345 onset and peak points. Finally, there is many models as observations of database. For this reason the method is employed with databases with limited observations.

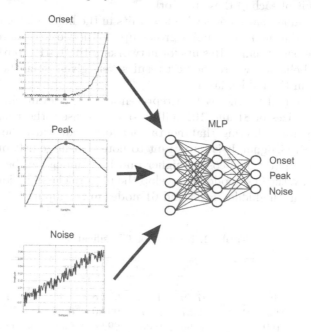

Fig. 2. Onset, peak and noise patterns and MLP Neural Network

The LOO error is a statistical estimator of the behaviour when a learning algorithm is used, and it is very useful for model selection because is slightly biased, despite its empirical error. Also, when the algorithm is stable, LOO error is low [21,22]. The LOO error can be calculated by using:

$$E_{LOO}(f_D) = \frac{1}{m} \sum_{i=1}^{m} \ell(f^i, z_i) \tag{1}$$

where m is the number of samples in the D set, composed by the z_i elements, and it is built the learning algorithm, f^i is the function obtained after training.

These methods have been used in applications where models of regression or structures in time series are required. Also, there have been in areas such as digital signal processing, obtaining good results [23,24].

3   Results and Discussion

As mentioned, windows with 21, 41, 61, 81 and 101 milliseconds were used to represent the patterns of the fiducial points and networks with 5, 10, 15 and 20 units in the hidden layer were trained. The results are presented in the Table 2, where the error was calculated based on expression (1). The results represent the performance of the MLP method for classification, obtaining seven networks due to the validation methodology, where for each window size and number of units was trained one network. Average performance of the technique was computed using the result of each of these networks.

The results show that models with few units in the hidden layer are preferred, because when the number of units grows up the network is more specialized, decreasing the performance. Results for networks with 21, 41 and 61 milliseconds manifest this behavior, where the best results were given when the network just has five units in the hidden layer.

Window size used for the pattern representation is relevant for the obtained models. When sizes of 81 and 101 milliseconds are used, the results reach the maximum possible, showing that neural networks can learn the patterns extracted from PPG signal. It is important to note that large networks are avoid, because the computational cost is higher and its training can be more specialized. In this way, the best model to develop the pattern classification is a network with five units in the hidden layer and 61 nodes in the input.

Table 2. Results for Classification

Window	Units in the hidden layer			
size (ms)	5	10	15	20
21	98.10 ± 1.31	97.79 ± 1.41	97.78 ± 1.46	97.94 ± 1.45
41	99.92 ± 0.14	99.87 ± 0.27	99.90 ± 0.15	99.89 ± 0.19
61	100 ± 0	99.96 ± 0.06	99.96 ± 0.06	99.96 ± 0.06
81	100 ± 0	100 ± 0	100 ± 0	100 ± 0
101	100 ± 0	100 ± 0	100 ± 0	100 ± 0

These results compared with the used method in [16], where a Self Organizing Map (SOM) was implemented to do the classification, are quite close in terms of accuracy. There, accuracy values reach 97.93% using a map of 36 x 10 units in lattice, a Gaussian function as neighborhood function and 2000 iterations. The noise class for the SOM case was not defined, detecting just onset and peak segments. Those results can be compared with accuracy of 100% in this work, but validation for the SOM case was developed in a *hold out* manner.

In addition, it is important to say that the present study does not use the ECG signal for detection, which is a considerable difference due to the smaller amount of information that contains just the PPG signal. This is taken as advantage when the resources are restricted to develop a detection.

4   Conclusions

A proposal for onset and peak pattern classification has been presented, based on MLP networks. Capabilities of this kind of neural networks are exploited to learn onset and peak patterns on PPG signals, using a temporal window as input.

Parameters as the number of units in the hidden layer and the segment size used in the network input were studied. Results show that the best performance can be reach using 61 milliseconds in the temporal window and a neural network with five units in the hidden layer, when the accuracy is 100%.

The results show that the MLP neural network can be used to develop a detector using a sliding temporal window on PPG signals, taking advantage of capabilities from MLP as pattern classifier. The presented work can be complemented in this way, avoiding the use of ECG signal for the detection. Some additional studies can improve the method and obtain better results.

Acknowledgments. This work was supported under grant: PI/UAN-2013-566GB from Universidad Antonio Nariño, Colombia. Also, authors want to thank to Universidad de Oriente for the support in this work.

References

1. Allen, J.: Photoplethysmography and its application in clinical physiological measurement. Physiol. Meas. 28, 1–39 (2007)
2. Challoner, A.V.J.: Photoelectric plethysmography for estimating cutaneous blood flow. In: Rolfe, P. (ed.) Non-Invasive Physiological Measurements, vol. 1, pp. 125–130. Academic, London (1979)
3. Willum-Hansen, T., Staessen, J.A., Torp-Pedersen, C., Rasmussen, S., Thijs, L., Ibsen, H., Jeppesen, J.: Prognostic value of aortic pulse wave velocity as index of arterial stiffness in the general population. Circulation 113, 664–670 (2006)
4. Bistra, N., Ivo, I.: An automated algorithm for fast pulse wave detection. Bioautomation 14(3), 203–216 (2010)
5. Lyengar, N., Peng, C.K., Morin, R., Goldberger, A.L., Lipsitz, L.A.: Age-related alterations in the fractal scaling of cardiac interbeat interval dynamics. American Journal of Physiology (Regulation, Integration and Comparative Physiology) 271, R1078–R1084 (1996)
6. Egidijus, K.R.G., Arunas, V.: Mathematical methods for determining the foot point of the arterial pulse wave and evaluation of proposed methods. Inform. Technol. and Control 3, 29–36 (2005)

7. Xu, P., Bergsneider, M., Hu, X.: Pulse onset detection using neighbor pulse-based signal enhancement. Medical Engineering and Physics 31, 337–345 (2009)
8. Hang, S., Chungkeun, L., Myoungho, L.: Adaptive threshold method for the peak detection of photoplethysmographic waveform. Computer in Biology and Medicine 39, 1145–1152 (2009)
9. Liangyou, C., Andrew, T., Jaques, R.: Automated beat onset and peak detection algorithm for field-collected photoplethysmograms. In: IEEE EMBS, pp. 5689–5692 (2009)
10. Markowska-Kacsmar, U., Kordas, B.: Mining of Electrocardiogram. In: XXI Autumn Meeting of Polish Information Processing Society, Conference Procedings, pp. 169–175 (2005)
11. Acquaticci, F.: Detección de Complejos QRS mediante Redes Neuronales, Buenos Aires Argentina
12. Lagerholm, M., Peterson, C., Braccini, G., Edenbrandt, L., Sörnmo, L.: Clustering ECG Complexes, Using Hermite Functions and Self-Organized Maps. IEEE Transaction on Biomedical Engineering 47(7) (July 2000)
13. Wenyu, Y., Gang, L., Ling, L., Qilian, Y.: ECG Analysis Based on PCA and SOM. In: IEEE Int. Conf. Neural Networks and Signal Processing, Nanjing, China, December 14-17 (2003)
14. Johansson, A.: Neural network for photoplethysmographic respiratory rate monitoring. Medical and Biological Engineering and Computing 41(3), 242–248 (2003)
15. Soltane, M., Ismail, M., Rashid, Z.A.A.: Artificial Neural Networks (ANN) Approach to PPG Signal Classification. International Journal of Computing and Information Sciencies 2(1) (April 2004)
16. Orjuela-Cañón, A., Posada-Quintero, H., Delisle-Rodrıguez, D., Cuadra-Sanz, M., Fernández de la Vara-Prieto, R., López-Delis, A.: Onset and Peak Detection over Pulse Wave Using Supervised SOM Network. International Journal of Bioscience, Biochemistry and Bioinformatics 3(2), 133–137 (2013)
17. Haykin, S.: Neural Networks: A Comprehensive Foundation, 3rd edn. Prentice Hall (1998)
18. Camacho, F.: Statistical Analysis of Central Aortic Blood Pressure Parameters Derived From the Peripheral Pulse, PhD dissertation, University of New South Wales, Sydney (November 2005)
19. Latham, R.D., Westerhof, N., Sipkema, P., Rubal, B.J., Reuderink, P., Murgo, J.P.: Regional wave travel and reflections along the human aorta: A study with six simultaneous micromanometric pressures. Circulation 6, 1257–1269 (1985)
20. Riedmiller, M.: Rprop: Description and Implementation Details. Technical report, University of Karlsruhe (1994)
21. Elisseeff, A.: Leave-one-out error and stability of learning algorithms with applications. Nato Science Series Sub Series III Computer and Systems Sciences 190, 111–130 (2003)
22. Kohavi, R.: A study of cross-validation and bootstrap for accuracy estimation and model selection. In: Proceedings of the 14th International Joint Conference on Artificial Intelligence, pp. 1137–1143 (February 1995)
23. Zoubir, A., Boashash, B.: The Bootstrap and its Application in Signal Processing. IEEE Signal Processing (January 1998)
24. Zoubir, A., Iskander, R.: Bootstrap Techniques for Signal Processing, 1st edn. Cambridge University Press, Cambridge (2004)

Gaussian Segmentation and Tokenization for Low Cost Language Identification

Ana Montalvo, José Ramón Calvo de Lara, and Gabriel Hernández-Sierra

Advanced Technologies Application Center (CENATAV),
7th Street #21416 between 214 and 216, Playa, Havana, Cuba
{amontalvo,jcalvo,gsierra}@cenatav.co.cu
http://www.cenatav.co.cu/

Abstract. Most common approaches to phonotactic language recognition deal with phone decoders as tokenizers. However, units that are not linked to phonetic definitions can be more universals, and therefore conceptually easier to adopt. It is assumed that the overall sound characteristics of all spoken languages can be covered by a broad collection of acoustic units, which can be characterized by acoustic segments. In this paper, such acoustic units, highly desirables for a more general language characterization, are delimited and clustered using Gaussian Mixture Model. A new segmentation method on acoustic units of the speech is proposed for later Gaussian modelling, looking for substitute the phonetic recognizer. This tokenizer is trained over untranscribed data, and it precedes the statistical language modeling phase.

Keywords: Spoken language recognition, Gaussian tokenization, acoustic segment modeling.

1 Introduction

Speech is the acoustic manifestation of the language, and probably the main comunication way between humans. The development of telecommunications and information's digital processing has demanded efforts to understand the mechanisms of communication by speech. Among the numerous applications included in the field of speech signal analysis, is the process of detecting the presence of a given spoken language in a segment of speech by an unknown speaker, commonly referred to as spoken language recognition (LRE)[1].

It is known that humans recognize languages through a perceptual process that is inherent to the auditory system [2]. The perceptual cues that human listeners use, are an important source of inspiration for automatic spoken language recognition.

Many sources of information are imprinted on the speech signal, however those related with LRE task can be grouped in two broad classes, based on prelexical information and based on lexical semantic knowledge [3]. There are experiments which have proved that both, prelexical and lexical semantic knowledge contribute to the human perceptual process for spoken LRE.

J. Ruiz-Shulcloper and G. Sanniti di Baja (Eds.): CIARP 2013, Part I, LNCS 8258, pp. 551–558, 2013.

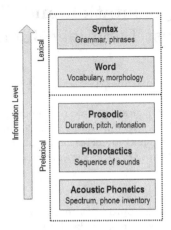

Fig. 1. Levels of perceptual cues used for language recognition

Many representations of those desired cues, that distinctively characterize the diferent spoken languages, have been explored in the past few decades. Articulatory parameters[1], acoustic features [4], prosody [5] and phonotactic citeZissman96 are some of the features explored.

Although higher levels, like lexical and grammatical, contain much more language information than the other levels (see Fig.1) and tend to be more robusts to the effects of channel distortion, they have the disadvantage of being more difficult to generalize (speech recognizers are required for each language to identify it, which requires transcribed audio so difficult to obtain) and can be computationally expensive. This makes the systems based on these standards rarely used in practice [2].

By contrast, the lower levels like the acoustic and prosodic ones, have the advantage of being easy to apply to any number of languages to a relatively low computational cost, but suffer from a lower precision and less robustness to channel variations and noise. On the other hand the intermediates levels like the phonotactic, maintains a balance between robustness, generalization and computational cost. While the acoustic information covers the physical sound patterns, the phonotactic refers to the constraints that determine possible syllables structures in a language.

Nowadays it is possible to distinguish two main groups of techniques for automatic LRE: acoustic level techniques and phonotactic level techniques. The phonotactic information combined with the acoustic information, are the most used features in LRE [7], being the ones based on phonotactics, those who provide the best compromise between the level of prior information needed for training the system and recognition accuracy. Nevertheless, currently, are merged both paradigms in most of comercial systems.

1.1 Problem Description

The phonotactic based systems use observed phono sequences to construct a statistical language model (LM) for each language of interest. This approach have two major drawbacks. Firstly, most of this systems use phonemes, a knowledge-based linguistic concept that is language dependent and in many cases difficult to deal with in speech processing. This systems require one or more phoneme recognizers, and each recognizer requires labeled data that are not always available (especially for rarely observed languages).

Secondly, the decoding phase of all these phonotactic approaches is computationally expensive, particulary when several recognizers in different languages run in parallel as in Parallel Phone recognition followed by LM (PPRLM) [6]. A model of acoustic units, language independent, can solve some of the just mentioned problems.

In this paper we propose to model certain acoustic segments of the speech signal, and to use them for later statistical modelling of each language. In other words, we will substitute the phoneme recognizer of a PRLM system, by a Gaussian tokenizer, trained with acoustic units, obtained trough a data-driven acoustic unit recognizer. This way we eliminate the need of phonetically transcribed data for training, which allows that the tokenizer could be trained on the same acoustic data as that used for the LRE task, thus minimizing any session mismatch. With this method it is easier to increase the number of tokenizers since phonetically transcribed data are not required.

This investigation is focused on the main part of acoustic segmentation techniques, directed towards the LRE. In particular, this represents an incipient attempt to find an alternative representation to phonemes, which is a faintly studied topic today.

There are many other related issues, like channel normalization, channel adaptation, robustness under noisy conditions, but these issues are not investigated this time, they remain for future works.

This paper is organized as follows: Section 2 describes our main contribution which is the segmentation technique of the speech signal. In Section 3 and 4 is explained how the representation chosen was obtained. Then we described in Section 5 the results of the proposed approach, ending in Section 6 with conclusions and futures works.

2 Speech Segmentation

As we said, many sources of information besides the linguistic message are carried on the speech signal. For the particular task of LRE a question that arises is whether phonemes, or other similar linguistically defined units are really needed. The underlying concept of words formed by phonemes may not be necessary. Over this ideas new approaches for LRE started to emerge.

In [9] Torres-Carrasquillo uses a sequence of Gaussian index to model the language information. Adami in [5] uses temporal trajectories of fundamental frequency and short-term energy to segment and label the speech signal into a small set of discrete units to caracterize language. More recently Spada in [10] tried to approximate a phonetic segmentation using the variations in the spectrogram of the speech signal.

Our research contribute on this direction, trying to develop a technique for conditioning the Gaussian Mixture Model (GMM) tokenizer input. The idea was to eliminate the noisy token sequences and give prominence to longer duration events. We used information in the cepstral domain to segment the speech signal, supported by the GMM probability distribution of the feature vectors.

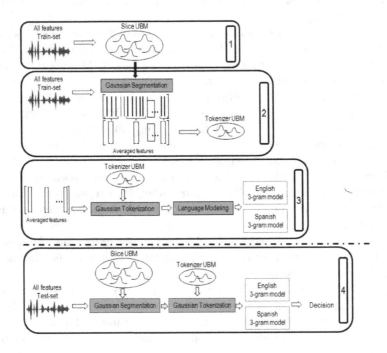

Fig. 2. Proposed Methodology: three first steps from training phase and the 4th from the test phase

2.1 Proposed Methodology

The features vectors can be seen as points in an N-dimensional feature space, where N is the dimension of feature vectors. Together with the influence of the variability sesion effects, these feature vectors represent also the state of our articulation organs. As the movements of our articulation organs are slow, it could be assumed that consecutive features in time domain, will be near in cepstral domain too. In other words, acoustically stable sounds intervals, correspond to consecutive features in cepstral domain.

These ideas motivated us to think that a good way to define acoustic units could be by grouping together nearby features in the cepstral domain. Spada in [10] obtained acoustic segments using a spectral variation function based on the euclidean distance between the static MFCC to the left and the right of the current frame. Our proposal incorporates the dynamic of the features, adding the delta and double-delta information to the analisys. Not only looking for spectrally stable segments, but a more comprehensive pattern.

The first step is the creation of a Universal Background Model (UBM)[12] as is shown in Fig. 2. This model will be called the "slicer" UBM, because once obtained it will indicate the boundaries of the segments. We grant the quality of universal to this model, because it is independent of language and seeks to represent as much as possible acoustic phones, which is why you train it with all the languages that will be involved in the task.

One of the attractive attributes of the GMM is its ability to closely approximate any arbitrarily shaped data distributions, and its ability to model the underlying data classes by the individual Gaussian components. Here this GMM is used to approximate the overall acoustic-phonetic distributions of the languages over the model was trained on.

The trainset is clustered with this model, and the two most likely Gaussians for each frame are analyzed. Two frames will stay together if they share one of their two most probable Gaussians, otherwise they'll be separated, and be part of different acoustic units. If there is a frame whose most probable Gaussians have no relationship with their neighbors, then that frame is removed. For the features corresponding to a same acoustic unit, we compute the average, in this way the whole segment in represented by an average single vector.

With this, we expect to reduce the cost of the systems in terms of resources and computational complexity, without compromising its discriminative power.

3   GMM for Voice Tokenization

After the segmentation is done, another Gaussian cluster is trained, but this time with much less classes. This model will be called the tokenizer UBM, and its function is to represent those acoustic units previously segmented and represented by an average vector, with the index of the most likely Gaussian of the tokenizer just like Torres-Carrasquillo did in [9]. With this approach, the vocabulary or number of tokens in the alphabet, is the same as the number of Gaussians in the UBM tokenizer. For our experiments we use 128 Gaussians clusters.

This aspect will be studied looking for an optimization in future works, because we are tempted to think that exist a relation between the number of clusters and the number of common phones of the languages that participate in the model creation.

4   Language Modeling

The purpose of the LM is to provide a syntax that defines possible tokens sequences and enables the computation of the probability $(P(W|L))$ of the token string $W = (w_1, w_2, ..., w_Q)$ given the LM L.

The statistical LM is created using the training text set, which was generated by means of the previously trained cluster (UBM tokenizer). Making use of the Carnegie Melon University Statistical Language Modeling toolkit [13] we obtained trigram models for each target language. At the testing phase, to estimate the probabilities of an index triplet (3-gram) we compute this quantity as:

$$P(w_i|w_{i-1}, w_{i-2}) = \frac{C(w_{i-2}, w_{i-1}, w_i)}{C(w_{i-2}, w_{i-1})} \tag{1}$$

where $C(w_{i-2}, w_{i-1}, w_i)$ and $C(w_{i-2}, w_{i-1})$ are the frequency count of the triplet (w_{i-2}, w_{i-1}, w_i) and the index duplet $(w_{i-2}, wi - 1)$ respectively, that occurred in the training set.

Thus for every string of Gaussian indexes, the probability of it is calculated as:

$$\log P(W|L) = \sum_{i=1}^{Q} log P_L(w_i|w_{i-1}, w_{i-2}) \tag{2}$$

The language corresponding to the LM that maximizes $P(W|L)$ is selected as the language sought.

5   Experimental Results

The speech signal is divided into overlapping frames, 25 ms length with 10 ms frame shift, where it is supposed to be stationary. Mel Frequency Cepstral Coefficients (MFCC)[11], deltas (Δ) and double-deltas ($\Delta\Delta$) are used to describe each frame.

The experiments were conducted using a part of the Oregon Graduate Institute Multi-Language Telephone Speech (OGI) corpus [14].

A silences detector process took place before the Gausian segmentation step. We use a trigram model to describe each language and the slicer UBM is estimated from the training selected part of the OGI corpus.

The selected target languages were english and spanish, and the training and test sets where defined as follows:

Table 1. Experiment Corpus

Training set			Test set (30s each signal)	
Language	Time	Number of signals	Language	Number of signals
English	1h 23min	102	English	109
Spanish	1h 23min	109	Spanish	45

It is worth noting the small volume of training samples (less than 3 hours) and the fact that we haven't made use of any phonetically transcribed data for the experiments.

The performance measure used for this task is the equal error rate (EER). It represents the system performance when the false acceptance probability (detecting the wrong language for a given test segment) is equal to the missed detection probability (rejecting the correct language).

Table 2. Performance comparison between our Gaussian segmentation based criterion and the Euclidean distance based criterion [10]

Language	EER Gaussian	EER Euclidean
English	22.01%	36.69%
Spanish	24.44%	36.66%

The results are compared using the 30-second test segments.

6   Conclusions

It's been presented a method for segmenting the speech signal into a number of acoustic units, seeking to find a more compact and language-independent representation. Of course the goal was to do this without a significant damage to the performance of the system, and the experimental results have shown promising values of EER for this approach.

For 30s test segments, results were around 23% of EER, which although still far from the results using phonetic recognition is a significant improvement to the proposed made in [10], much more appealing with the small amount of training data which is a limitation very commonly found in real world applications.

Futures studies will be conducted over the idea of increasing the number of tokenizers, looking for analogies with PPRLM, and the selection of more optimal features for the particular task. Also are objectives to incorporate more samples and more languages to the experiments. The aspect of the number of Gaussians clusters used in the GMM tokenizer is also pending of further insights, because as we said there is probably a relation between the number of clusters and the number of common phones of the languages that participate in the model creation.

References

1. Siniscalchi, S., Reed, J., Svendsen, T., Lee, C.: Universal attribute characterization of spoken languages for automatic spoken language recognition. J. Computer Speech & Language 27, 209–227 (2013)
2. Li, H., Ma, B., Lee, K.: Spoken Language Recognition: From Fundamentals to Practice. J. Proceedings of the IEEE 101, 1136–1159 (2013)

3. Zhao, J., Shu, H., Zhang, L., Wang, X., Gong, Q., Li, P.: Cortical competition during language discrimination. J. NeuroImage 43, 624–633 (2008)
4. Sugiyama, M.: Automatic language recognition using acoustic features. In: Proc. ICASSP, pp. 813–816 (1991)
5. Adami, A., Hermansky, H.: Segmentation of speech for speaker and language recognition. In: INTERSPEECH 2003 (2003)
6. Zissman, M.: Comparison of Four Approaches to Automatic Language Identification of Telephone Speech. IEEE Transactions on Speech and Audio Processing Journal 4(1), 31–44 (1996)
7. Kempton, T.: Machine-assisted Phonemic Analysis. University of Sheffield (2012)
8. Muthusamy, Y., Jain, N., Cole, R.: Perceptual Benchmarks for Automatic Language Identification. In: International Conference on Speech and Signal Processing, pp. 333–336 (1994)
9. Torres-Carrasquillo, P., Reynolds, D., Deller, J.: Language identification using Gaussian mixture model tokenization. In: ICASSP, pp. 757–760 (2002)
10. Spada, D., López, I., Toledano, D., González, J.: Acoustic Event Recognition for Low Cost Language Identification. In: V Jornadas en Tecnologías del Habla, pp. 25–28. UAM (2007)
11. Davis, S., Mermelstein, P.: Comparison of parametric representation for monosyllabic word recognition in continuously spoken sentences. IEEE Transactions on Acoustic, Speech and Signal Processing 28, 357–366 (1980)
12. Montalvo, A., Calvo, J.: Métodos para reducir la variabilidad de sesión en el reconocimiento del locutor. Technical report, CENATAV (2012)
13. Rosenfeld, R.: The CMU Statistical Language Modeling Toolkit and its use in the 1994 ARPA CSR Evaluation. ARPA SLT 95 (1995)
14. Muthusamy, Y., Cole, R., Oshika, B.: The Ogi Multi-Language Telephone Speech Corpus. In: ICSLP, pp. 895–898 (1992)

Author Index